HIJAB

WORD OF GOD OR WORD OF MAN?

John Andrew Morrow

With a Foreword by Riffat Hassan

HIJAB

WORD OF GOD OR WORD OF MAN?

John Andrew Morrow

With a Foreword by Riffat Hassan

Academica Press
Washington~London

Library of Congress Cataloging-in-Publication Data

Names: Morrow, John Andrew (author)
Title: Hijab : word of god or word of man | John Andrew Morrow
Description: Washington : Academica Press, 2024. | Includes references.
Identifiers: LCCN 2023949539 | ISBN 9781680535372 (hardcover) |
9781680535389 (e-book)

L'habit ne fait pas le moine.

Contents

Praise for the Book

"Dr. John Andrew Morrow's work on *hijab* is deeply thoughtful and very reasonable. He simply suggests that Muslim women be allowed to learn (or perhaps even insist on learning) the full range of religious opinions on the subject of the Islamic veil and then choose whether to wear *hijab* or not for themselves. He argues for the importance of education, tolerance, free choice, and freedom for women -- all post-Enlightenment values. Morrow is a religious Muslim (he converted when he was sixteen), an academic scholar, and a scholar of Islam. Morrow is an important voice for those who believe that reformation or modernization of Islam must come from within." **Dr. Phyllis Chesler,** Emerita Professor of Psychology at City University of New York, best-selling author, legendary feminist leader, and retired psychotherapist

"Adopting a holistic and multidisciplinary approach, Dr. Morrow explores a wide range of sources to provide valuable insights into diverse opinions concerning *hijab* in Islamic discourses from past and present. The result is an interesting and committed account of one of the most visible and contested symbols of Islam in our time, a battleground for identity politics and struggles over women's rights." **Dr. Ziba Mir-Hosseini,** author of *Journeys Toward Gender Equality in Islam*, Founding member of Musawah, Professorial Research Associate, Centre for Islamic and Middle Eastern Studies, SOAS

"In this well-researched book, Dr. John Andrew Morrow clearly argues that obligatory *hijab* has no foundation in the Qur'an and was fostered by patriarchal traditions, misogyny, suppression of dissent, and political Islam. His conclusions counter the contemporary dominance of the *hijab*, promoted as an iconic symbol by Islamist movements, and endorsed by Islamic feminists and the left. Morrow defends Muslim women's freedom to choose their attire and supports reformers who contest the *hijab.*" **Dr. Ida Lichter,** author of *Muslim Women Reformers: Inspiring Voices against Oppression*

"In this book, John Andrew Morrow explores the so-called *hijab*, a major social and political issue in many so-called 'Islamic' countries, and presents a comprehensive academic discussion of it. The author has done an outstanding job of informing readers about the subject.

Covering women from head to toe is a preoccupation of the Sunni and Shiite clergy and their followers. They are fixated on their beards, turbans, and bathroom rituals, but they are even more obsessed with women's hair and clothing. The Qur'an does not instruct women to cover their hair; nevertheless, the clergy pervert the meaning of a few words and imply such an order. Neither does the Qur'an instruct women to cover their faces; on the contrary, it talks about the beauty of monotheist women. However, the clergy bury women alive in black sacks, erasing their identity in society. Neither does the Qur'an instruct men to enforce a dress code on women, nor on any woman; nevertheless, the clergy insult, berate, and even beat women who do not adhere to their man-made religious rules.

For centuries, the professional religious class has enforced explicit dress codes on women, but the Qur'an never issues such penalties. Despite hundreds of verses that narrate the debates and dialogues of more than two dozen prophets and messengers on a variety of topics including monotheism, freedom, reasoning, critical thinking, honesty, human rights, women's rights, social and economic justice, equality, rule of law, peace, forgiveness, the environment, unity, righteousness and charity, the Qur'an does not provide a single discussion or debate about women's dress code. Yet, the clergymen's major mission is to cover and silence women.

The word *hijab* refers to a wall or partition and has come to refer to the religious prison created for women by men inflicted with numerous psychological and theological diseases, including ignorance, arrogance, and polytheism. This book explores the relationship between women's dress codes and other social and political issues in 'Islamic' societies and argues that reform of women's dress codes is an essential step towards improving the status of women and quality of life in these societies." **Edip Yüksel**, J.D., Qur'anic translator and commentator

"Islam came to free women from the brutal abuses of men. However, after the death of the Prophet Muhammad, and up until now, Muslims and their religious institutions have worked strenuously to control and manipulate women and keep them out of the mainstream using falsehoods and fabrications like the *hijab* and the *niqab*. As John Andrew Morrow's book masterfully demonstrates, the veil is a big lie that has no foundation whatsoever in the Qur'an." **Amin Refaat,** *Executive Vice President, International Qur'anic Center*

Acknowledgments

I wish to acknowledge all the courageous women and men who have assisted me over the years, both overtly and covertly. For a man like me, who lives in the United States of America, the land of the free and the home of the brave, defending the rights of women is an act of defiance. It is a very manly thing to do in my mind. I am not afraid of macho, misogynistic, men. In contrast, to defend the rights of women in most of the Muslim world, in places like Morocco, Algeria, Tunisia, Egypt, Sudan, Yemen, Iraq, Iran, Indonesia, Malaysia, Pakistan, and Afghanistan, among other nations, is a much more serious matter. These brave and intrepid women and men place their safety, freedom, and lives in peril. Some are disowned by their families. They are arrested, imprisoned, beaten, lashed, tortured, raped, and executed for saying things that I take for granted and say without a second thought. A fortunate few flee their countries. They find refugee status in the Western world or enter as immigrants. Still, some are afraid to speak up and speak out due to family and community pressure, not to mention the presence of radical Islamists and violent misogynists in liberal democracies. They may no longer fear the government, as they did in their countries of origin, but they still fear some of the immigrant Muslim men in their midst and their radicalized offspring. Where they can only timidly raise their voices in defense of women's rights, purring like kittens, my male privilege permits me to roar like a lion. But beware, female lion cubs grow into lionesses. They make even more ferocious hunters than alpha males. Most importantly, their power is found in a pack. In sum, Muslim men and women must stand united against misogyny and inequality.

Words of Thanks

I wish to thank Dr. Paul du Quenoy and everyone at Academica Press for supporting my socially engaged scholarship. I wish to express my gratitude to Kristin Morse for the magnificent art that she provided for this work. The series of drawings that I commissioned perfectly capture the vast spectrum of religious opinion as to what constitutes *hijab* or covering in Islam.

Disclaimer

For the sake of concision and style, titles, honorifics, and pious invocations are avoided. No offense is intended by their exclusion. The Prophet Muhammad and the Imams, as portrayed in Islamic narratives, are treated like literary figures, as opposed to historical ones. Whenever it is written that the Prophet said, or such-and-such Imam said, it should be implicitly preceded by "it is reported that," "it is alleged that," "it is related that," "it is claimed that" or "it is purported that." Most of the *hadith* literature consists of myths, legends, and lore collected centuries and even a thousand years after the passing of the Prophet Muhammad and the twelve Imams. Some of it is scandalous, slanderous, and scurrilous. I refuse to attribute evil, obscenity, and immorality to God, the Prophet, and the Imams. I reject any and all traditions that contradict the Qur'an, reason, and common sense. The responsibility for the attribution falls upon the narrators in the chain and the compiler of the collection. Far am I from attributing falsehood to God, the Prophet Muhammad, and the twelve Imams. This is not a work of Islamophobia but of Islamophilia and theophilia. It is a labor of faith and love.

Sources

Most of the sources cited in this work are academic. Some are religious, and a small number are popular. Virtually all of them are Muslim. They include Sunnis, Shiites, Sufis, Mutazilis, Ahmadis, and Qur'anists. Some are clerics and '*ulama*' who were traditionally trained in Islamic universities and seminaries. They feature sheikhs, *mujtahids*, muftis, and "ayatollahs," as well as "grand ayatollahs," sources of emulation, and religious authorities. Others are Western-trained intellectuals. And some are both religious scholars and academics.

Among the authors cited, one finds progressive, secular, and reformist Muslims. The work features the views of both Islamic feminists and secular Muslim feminists. A few writers and activists are women who originate from the Muslim world but who have since left Islam. Since they are women impacted by interpretations of Islam, their voices are equally valid. A Moroccan woman is a Moroccan woman whether she is a Jew, a Christian, a Muslim, or an atheist. The same goes for any other nationality.

The fields of expertise of the authors consulted are varied. To understand veiling, one must draw from various disciplines: history, fashion, sociology, social work, psychology, anthropology, philosophy, religion, law, and jurisprudence, as well as gender studies, women's studies, political sciences, literary studies, Islamic studies, *hadith* studies, and Qur'anic sciences, among others.

The credentials of the authors are diverse. Their political ideologies vary considerably. The weight of their opinions vary. They include respected authorities and a few controversial figures who are not necessarily well regarded. Simply because I cite someone should not be viewed as an endorsement. With the exception of my views, the opinions of the writers quoted in this work are their own. My role is to share them, explain them, expound upon them, question them, and critique them. The overarching objective of this study is to present, as much as possible, the full spectrum of opinion on the subject of the veil in Islam; in other words, the other side of the story, namely, the opinions that are smothered, suppressed, and silenced by hegemonic pro-*hijab* Islam. Let us give women a voice, and let us give them a choice.

Foreword

By Dr. Riffat Hassan,
Professor Emerita, University of Louisville

Dr. John Andrew Morrow is one of the most learned Muslim scholars of our times. Like his other writings, *Hijab: Word of God or Word of Man?* is based on exhaustive and meticulous research. The work is a veritable encyclopedia of information about significant aspects of an issue which is, in my judgment, the most divisive in Islamic societies and communities, having had a serious impact on the lives of Muslim women through the ages.

Dr. Morrow's vast range of knowledge, which subsumes multi-disciplinary perspectives on the issue of Muslim women's attire and conduct in public, and his ability to represent, faithfully and insightfully, a large number of diverse and divergent viewpoints on this subject, is unmatched.

While I have the greatest admiration and respect for Dr. Morrow's scholarly work, what resonates the most deeply with my heart, mind, and spirit, is his profound understanding of the true meaning and essence of Islam as an embodiment of God's highest attributes: Mercy, Compassion, and Justice.

As a lifelong advocate for the Qur'anic rights of Muslim women, I can relate to Dr. Morrow's anger toward "primitive patriarchal misogynists, theological thugs, lascivious lowlifes, and intellectual Lilliputians," guilty of making a travesty of the Will of God who made man and woman equal, by setting up hierarchical systems in which women are always inferior and subordinate to men.

Kudos to Dr. John Andrew Morrow for his reformist vision and courage of conviction in undertaking the *jihad* or sacred scholarly and spiritual struggle to reclaim the soul of Islam.

Preface

As we seek to realign Islam with the Qur'an, since the former has outrun the latter, we must re-examine and re-assess the rationality, morality, and Qur'anicity of all aspects of Islam, questioning our creed and judging our jurisprudence. Tradition is not always traditional, and our practices may not be perfect. Distance provides a panoramic perspective. Rather than bring us closer to the text, interpretation can lead us increasingly away from its meaning. Errors can be compounded over the centuries. Rather than enrich and enhance, layers of exegesis can accumulate like sediments, smothering the living and vibrant sense of the scripture. The rules of the *hijab*, as historically understood and applied, can and must be re-evaluated. This is precisely what is accomplished in this work, which examines the *hijab* in traditional and contemporary contexts.

The first chapter examines women's dress in the Qur'an and *hadith*. It examines the conservative view that has become dominant and hegemonic due to its imposition by Islamic powers past and nation-states present. It explores what the Qur'an really says about matters of modesty and dress. It exposes the treacherous and treasonous translations of the Qur'an that have been made by misogynists. It also delves into the dubious sayings attributed to the Prophet Muhammad and the twelve Imams.

The second chapter asks whether women are indeed vulvas as they are claimed to be in a tradition attributed to the Messenger of God. It demonstrates that women have been reduced from the sum of their parts to a single sexual organ. It traces back the origin of such a sexist belief, not to the Torah, but to the Talmud. Like a gynecologist, it examines the pudenda in Islamic jurisprudence. It lays bare the cultural subjectivity of the sources and extremist modalities. It closes with an exploration of the Christian influence on the dress code of Muslim women.

The third chapter showcases the semantic stretching in which Muslim jurists have engaged, expanding the range of women's covering from their privates parts and bosoms to their entire bodies, hair, and even faces, in an act of exegetical rape. It contextualizes the Qur'anic verse regarding the covering of the bosoms by providing a history of toplessness. It examines the symbolism of the verse in question and how its meaning went from symbolically covering the hearts of women to burying them from head to toe, shutting them up, locking them up, and smacking them up. While the Qur'an only required women to cover their genitals, and recommended that they conceal their breasts, Muslim jurists soon covered them completely in cloaks. If most Muslim scholars viewed women as sources of temptation and equated their beauty with evil, some Sufi scholars took the opposite stance on the subject, and viewed the beauty of women as a reflection of divine beauty. As this chapter demonstrates, an inversion of Qur'anic ethics has taken place in Islam and the religion has been turned upside down.

The fourth chapter discusses the dress of enslaved women and contrasts it with that of free women. It reconsiders the rulings on women's dress issued over the ages and judges the jurists. The fifth chapter provides a history of Muslim women's dress. It provides revealing historical insights into the dress worn by Muslim women over the past fourteen-hundred years. It distinguishes between traditional Islamic dress and the radical Islamist uniform that started to replace it in the 1980s and that has now virtually supplanted it. It addresses the evolution of dress and demonstrates how the veil, a pre-Islamic custom, eventually became a so-called Islamic obligation, essentially turning women into walking vulvas and vaginas.

The sixth chapter examines the reemergence of reformist, rationalist, secularist, Qur'anist, progressive, and revivalist voices. It deals with the role of reason in reviving the Islamic religion. It defines public decency. It calls out the colorphobic fanatics. It cries for freedom and liberty. It compares competing notions of *hijab* in Iran. Finally, it provides an overview of Qur'anist views on the veil.

The seventh chapter provides the perspectives of male, Muslim scholars, intellectuals, writers, and leaders, on the so-called Islamic veil. It amplifies the views and voices of a vast array of authorities. Chapter eight does the same, this time, however, focusing on the views of mostly Muslim females. Like the men in question, some of whom were arrested, and condemned to death, or forced into exile, these women intellectuals, academics, scholars, and activists should be commended for their courage and commitment. Their views deserve to be disseminated far and wide.

Chapter nine demonstrates that no matter how far Muslim women have come, they have a long, long, way to go to achieve the inalienable rights to which they are entitled. It studies how Muslim women feel about *hijab*. It reminds readers of its pre-Islamic pagan origin, rooted in patriarchy, misogyny, and male supremacy. It closes with the contentious yet compelling question: is the *hijab haram*?

The work ends with a series of general conclusions, a timeline that summarizes major events in the history of the *hijab*, a list of rulings on *hijab*, and provides fifteen Islamic options for Muslim women in matters of minimum dress mandated by the Qur'an. To date, this is the most interesting topic that I have researched and potentially the most impactful. Merely proposing that *hijab* is not mandatory is a crime in Iran as is encouraging women to remove it if they so desire. If that is the case, then let the women of Iran, and all Muslim women, cast off their veils in solidarity and hold their *hijabs* up high! Freedom comes first.

Chapter 1

Women's Dress in the Qur'an and *Hadith*

1.1 Introduction

According to Muslim authorities throughout the ages, *hijab* is a religious obligation. For them, Muslim women who fail to observe the *hijab* commit a major sin that merits punishment in hell and even eternal damnation. Since the rise of Islamist movements in the twentieth century, some Muslim jurists have gone as far as to mandate fines, imprisonment, physical punishment, and even death for young girls and women who wear so-called "bad *hijab*" or fail to cover themselves completely. In some parts of the world, one's choice of clothing can kill.

Regarding women's dress, what is the mainstream position according to the Qur'an? What does the Islamic scripture say about the subject? And what about the *hadith* literature, the sayings attributed to the Prophet Muhammad and, for the Shiites, the Imams from his progeny? How are women portrayed in this polemical material? What sources may have influenced the image of women? How did Muslim women dress throughout history? What impact did culture have on the process? Did patriarchy and misogyny play a part? If so, what were the consequences of these interpretations and misinterpretations? Were they universally accepted? If not, what do the other reports express? Finally, in light of the Qur'an, what moral and ethical conclusions can we draw regarding the rules governing women's clothing? These are the questions that are answered in this study.

1.2 The Dominant View

According to the views of many Islamic scholars from the surviving schools of jurisprudence, both major and minor, Muslim women must cover themselves from head to toe, exposing only their faces, hands, and feet, in the presence of all teenage boys and men who are not close family members. Their beauty can only be displayed to their husbands, their fathers, their husband's fathers, their sons, their husband's sons, their brothers or their brother's sons or their sister's son, women servants, male servants free of physical needs, or small children (24:31). Some jurists, however, insist that the feet must also be covered. Since there is a risk that hands and faces might arouse lust in men, these must also be covered, according to some scholars. Hence, for a minority of jurists, women must also veil their faces, partially or entirely, exposing two eyes, just one, or none at all, in the presence of all marriageable men. In short, they must enclose themselves in a *chador* or *burqa*. These are the only options. They are presented as facts as if the matter were written in stone and sent down from heaven by God Himself. Those with such views are convinced they are correct and willing to kill for them. The issue, however, is not as definite as they claim. In fact, the subject of *sitr* or covering is far more nuanced than we have been led to believe. The spectrum of opinion is far more vast, tolerant, and permissive than most have imagined in their wildest dreams.

1.3 What Sayeth the Qur'an?

Considering the inordinate importance attached to the *hijab* by certain Muslims, it is surprising that the Qur'an -- a work of spirituality and morality, as opposed to a book of laws -- has remarkably little to say regarding matters of dress. The *hijab* -- as a veil, symbol of sexual segregation, subordination, and marker of male domination -- is nowhere to be found in its verses. Why? Because it is a work of ethical edification. When dealing with mundane matters of dress, the sacred scripture of Islam calls upon human beings to cover their pudenda, their private parts, namely, their external genitals. As the Qur'an proclaims:

> O you Children of Adam! We have bestowed on you a raiment to cover your shame [*saw'at*] as well as to be an adornment to you. But the raiment of righteousness, that is the best. (7:26)

The Qur'an calls for humans to cover their *saw'at*, or pudendum, a concept that is crucial to Islamic laws regarding the dress of women and which appears in the following verse as well:

> O ye Children of Adam! Let not Satan seduce you in the same manner as he got your parents out of the Garden, stripping them of their raiment, to expose their shame [*saw'at*]. (7:27)

The Qur'an opposes indecency and immorality and encourages believers to avoid lewdness:

> When they do aught that is shameful, they say: "We found our fathers doing so;" and "God commanded us thus." Say: "Nay, God never commands what is shameful: Do ye say of God what ye know not?" (7:28)

It warns that "those people who desired to spread indecency and obscenity among the Believers have a grievous torment in store for them in this world and the Hereafter" (24:19).

The Qur'an encourages women to be decent and cover their beauty and ornaments, except for what must normally appear. It does not define beauty and ornaments or specify the parts that women can ordinarily and typically show. As we read in the Qur'an:

> And say to the believing women that they should lower their gaze and guard their modesty [*furujahunna*]; that they should not display their beauty and ornaments [*zinatahunna*] except what must ordinarily appear thereof [*ma zahara minha*]; that they should draw their coverings [*khumur*] over their bosoms [*juyub*] and not display their beauty [*zinah*] except to their husbands, their fathers, their husbands' fathers, their sons, their husbands' sons, their brothers, or their brothers' sons or their sisters' sons, or their women or the servants whom their right hands possess, or male servants free of physical needs, or small children who have no sense of the shame of sex, and that they should not strike their feet in order to draw attention to their hidden ornaments [*tabarruj*]. And O you Believers! Turn you all together towards God, that you may attain bliss. (24:31).

While some take "guard their modesty" as a command to wear *hijab*, the expression means to guard one's *furuj*, genitals, or private parts. Hence, it is more accurately conveyed as to "guard their chastity." The word *farj*, the plural of which is *furuj*, is derived from the root *f / r / j*. The verb *faraja* means to open, part, separate, split, or breach. The word *farj* means "vagina" and "vulva." The verse tells believing women to protect their vaginas and vulvas. In other words, to remain chaste. It by no means commands women to wear the *hijab*, *burqa*, *chador*, or *niqab*, and to cover themselves from head to toe. As Abdullah Yahya has noted, "to say that the meaning of … *furujahunna* is 'modesty' does an injustice to the Qur'an and spreads confusion among innocent Muslims who mistakenly think that they can trust the accuracy of all translations." After all, "covering one's hair doesn't automatically make someone modest." The fact of the matter is that "there are numerous passages of the Qur'an that are misrepresented or worse still, mistranslated, to give an extremely 'male-centric' view" (Islam 2011).

When commenting upon Qur'an 24:30-31, Ja'far al-Sadiq (702-765), the sixth Imam, stated that God prohibited people from seeing the *furuj* or genitals of another person (Kulayni). He said, "everything in the Qur'an, related to protecting the private parts [*furuj*] relates to fornication [*zinah*], except for this verse, which deals with looking" (Kulayni). If that is so, then the passage from the Qur'an does not mandate the *khimar* or *jilbab*: it calls upon people to avert their eyes from the intimate parts of others. However, it is clear from the verb that it deals with covering the private parts, lowering the gaze, and avoiding fornication.

The consensus of Muslim scholars and jurists across the ages has been that "what normally appears" is "everything that is not part of a woman's *'awrah*" or "shame" that is mentioned in 7:26. The word *'awrah* is Arabic for "pudendum." It comes from the root *'a-w-r* which means "vagina" or "vulva" but is translated euphemistically as "nakedness." It refers to the genitalia, the outer private parts, or shameful parts. Muslim scholars expanded it to mean "that which should be covered." Most translators, like Muhammad Asad, Mustafa Khattab, Safi Kaskas, Wahiuddin Khan, the Study Qur'an, M. Farook Malik, Munir Munshey, Abdel Haleem, Ahmed Ali, 'Ali Quli Qara'i, Musharraf Hussain, Hasan al-Fatih Qaribullah, Sher Ali, Amatul Rahman Omar, George Sale, John Medows Rodwell, and Munir Mezyed, have rendered it as "nakedness." Others, like M.M. Pickthall, Yusuf 'Ali, Shakir, Muhammad Taqi Usmani, Abdul Majid Daryabadi, Hamid S. Aziz, Ali Bakhtiari Nejad, Bilal Muhammad, Maududi, Muhammad Ali, Faridul Haque, Henry Palmer, Linda Barto, and Mir Aneesuddin, have conveyed it as "shame."

Some, like Tala A. Itani, Shabbir Ahmed, and Rashad Khalifa, claim that *saw'at* means "bodies." Laleh Bakhtiar, however, has more accurately translated *saw'at* as "intimate parts," as has T.B. Irving, Abdul Hey, Muhammad Sarwar, Umm Muhammad, and Mohammad Tahir-ul-Qadri, who speak of "private parts" and Muhammad Mahmoud Ghali, Ahmed Raza Khan, and Bijan Moenian who provide "shameful parts." In their first translation, the Monotheist Group claimed that *saw'at* means "wickedness;" however, in their 2013 edition, they replaced that word with "bodies." In the case of Mohammad Shafi, *saw'at* is translated as "carnal desires." Muhammad Ahmed and Samira, however, translate it as "shameful genital parts." Ahmed Hulusi provides an allegorical meaning of the verse, which reads: "We have indeed disclosed for you clothing (knowledge of reality) to cover your corporeality and as adornment" (7:26). A.J. Droge is the most accurate of all when he states that *saw'ah* or "shameful parts" signifies genitalia (92). Euphemisms aside, *saw'ah* literally means "genitals" and "private parts." This is all the Qur'an requires human beings to cover in public as well as in private when in the presence of people who are not closely related.

The expression "guarding one's *furuj*" refers first and foremost to guarding one's chastity and secondly to maintaining modesty. The Qur'an calls upon women to avoid fornication, adultery, and flaunting their "hidden beauty." According to the *Lisan al-'Arab*, an early Arabic dictionary, *zinah* includes "all that which beautifies." The word *zinah* can signify both natural beauty and artificial ornaments. It means embellishment, adornment, decoration, clothes, attire, finery, and toilette. *Zinah al-wajh* means makeup. It is derived from the verb *zana* which means to decorate, adorn, embellish, ornament, dress up, and make oneself up. At least, this is how it was defined in the thirteenth century. The cultures and laws of the time colored these definitions. They do not necessarily reflect the word's meaning in the seventh-century Qur'an.

The term *zinah* has been translated variously. Itani, Hye, Omar, Sarwar, Bakhtiari Nejad, Hussein, Barto, and the Monotheist Group translate it as "beauty." For Munshey and Shafi, it is "beauty and charm." But for Ahamed, it is "beauty and jewels." In the case of Amatul Rahman Omar, it is "(natural and makeup) beauty." As far as Muhammad Ahmed and Samira are concerned, it is "decoration/beauty." However, Sher Ali translates it as "beauty or embellishment." Asad, Irving, Abdel Haleem, Kaskas, Ünal, Ahmed Ali, Hegab, and Qara'i translate it as "charms." Pickthall, Shakir, Bakhtiar, Shaikh, Ghali, Usmani, Umm Muhammad, Daryabadi, Bewley, Bilal Muhammad, Maududi, Khan, Qaribullah, Muhammad Ali, Moeinian, Haque, Tahir-ul-Qadri, Khan / Hilali, the Study Qur'an, and Arberry, Dawood, Hulusi, Sadr-Ameli, Soliman, and Mezyed render it as "adornment." For Sale, Palmer, and Rodwell, the word means "ornaments." Yusuf 'Ali, Malik, and Ahmed translate it as "beauty and ornaments." For Khattab, it refers to "hidden adornments." Yüksel and company translate it as "attraction." For Aziz, the word means "ornaments." However, Khalifa translates *zinah* as "any part of their bodies."

Since the verse speaks specifically about guarding one's *furuj*, an argument could be made to restrict the meaning of *zinah* to one's intimate parts. However, since the term "beauty" is so vague and broad, it could be expanded to cover the entirety of the female form. Ironically, men are not required to cover their beauty, except their genitals, in the most liberal interpretation, and their bodies from the navel to the knee, in the most conservative one. If physical beauty needs to be covered, it should apply equally to men as to women. Some jurists argued that men were not required to cover because they must work. They also relaxed the dress code for enslaved women, both Muslim and non-Muslim, for the same reason. It was only so-called free women, who were confined to their homes, and did not need to work, who were required to cover themselves entirely in public. If that is the case, free women required to work should also be exempted from the so-called Islamic dress code.

According to the Qur'an, a Muslim woman must not display her beauty except for "that which must ordinarily appear thereof" [*ma zahara minha*], or "that which is apparent." For most Muslim jurists, the parts of the *zinah,* exempted from the above injunction, include: 1) the face, the hands, and the feet; and 2) whatever appears of a woman's body owing to uncontrollable factors such as the blowing of the wind, or out of necessity. For a minority of jurists, it includes the face, except for the two eyes; the face, except for one eye; or the face and both eyes. Another group of jurists, albeit a minority, argued that "what normally appears thereof" was everything but the external parts of the female genitalia. For Paola García, this is a very sensible regulation: "it takes into account that from period to period, and from culture to culture, there are great differences in the view of what, aside from her genitals and breasts, is erotic about a woman." This is indeed correct.

The erogenous zones of women vary and shift. They can move to and from various body parts: the feet, ankles, knees, lower legs, upper legs, bosom, midriff, neckline, back, and buttock. In ancient Crete, the focal point of women was their breasts. A variety of necklines was seen among women. The low-cut dress reappeared in the Middle Ages, highlighting the bosom and the back. The corset lifted the breast during the Renaissance, while dresses were cut low. Since the twentieth century, "clothes leave every increasing portions of the body bare" (Kybalova, Herbenova, and Lamararova 15). As Richard Martin (1947-1999) and Harold Koda (b. 1950), two leading fashion historians, summarize:

> Women's arms were liberated in the teens; legs were progressively exposed in the 1920s; some décolletage appeared in the 1930s; fiber and fabrics allowed the body beneath to come out in the 1930s and 1940s; two-piece suits and maillots with apertures bared midriff and sides in the 1940s and 1950s; the navel was exposed in the late 1960s and 1970s; high cuts revealed hips in the 1970s and radical gestures even revealed breasts and buttocks. Anatomy was not destiny, but a map of social desire. (43)

If Western women have liberated their hair, arms, legs, cleavage, bellies, and buttocks, some Muslim women are still struggling to liberate their eyeballs, faces, ears, throat, hair, and elbows. Many of them cannot show their "heads and shoulders, knees and toes."

Everything on a woman can be eroticized: eyes, mouths, lips, ears, hair, eyelashes, eyebrows… For misogynists, who fear and hate the power of female sexuality and seek to suppress, subjugate, and control it, the solution is to seclude women, cover them in potato sacks, or bury them. If God is Beautiful and loves beauty, why can't we? The only men who wish to cover, conceal, and confine women are those who are jealous, sexually insecure, domineering, and controlling. They share the same psychological and spiritual profile as physical and sexual abusers. It is entirely about power and control that is achieved through coercion, threats, intimidation, economic and emotional abuse, male privilege, family, community, social pressure, blame, and isolation. The *hijab* is merely a mark of male authority. Women who wear it are like branded slaves. They are property without independence and agency. The *hijab* is a symbol of subordination to male authority and dominance. Muhammad Farid Vajidi (1875/78-1954), the Egyptian scholar of Islam, put it plainly when he said that the *hijab* is symbolic proof that for a woman "there is only slavery," and that "she cannot be emancipated from this bondage" (Barlas 60). If that is what the veil symbolizes, it is reason enough to tear it off in protest.

The term *khumur* is the plural of the Arabic word *khimar*, meaning a headcover or headscarf. It is derived from the verb *khamara* which means to cover, hide, and conceal. It is related to the word *khamr*, which means wine, literally "something which covers or flogs the mind or the head." For some scholars, the word's root suggests that a *khimar* must cover the head and, consequently, the hair. However, their interpretation of the Qur'an, and their contempt and disdain for women, influenced their understanding of the word. *Khimar* is a derivative of *kh-m-r*. It refers to any covering or cloth, even rugs and carpets used to cover the floor. In practice, women used to wear their *khumur* on their shoulders as much as over their heads. It was a shawl, not a strict, tight, opaque, and often dark material. Most of these shawls were sheer or transparent when the verse was revealed. They were light and breathable. They were beauty accessories with functional purposes. They used them to shield themselves from the sun. They also used them to carry bread and other items, like a purse or a bag.

The term *juyub* is the plural of the Arabic word *jayb*, a derivative of the word *jawb* or cutting, and refers to the slit of the dress. For most Muslim scholars, the headcover must be drawn over the neck and hang over the bosom. Before the revelation of this verse, some Muslim women reportedly tied their headscarves at the back, thus exposing their ears and necks. According to prevailing interpretations of Islam, this verse forbade them from doing so. This argument is hardly convincing. Even if we were to entertain it, the recommendation would be implicit, one that implied that a shawl covered the hair but that it should also hang over the neckline, cleavage, and bosoms.

The Islamic law that requires women to cover their hair has the most feeble foundation. As Edip Yüksel (b. 1957), the Turkish American jurist, author, professor, and Qur'anist, notes, "God advises female Muslims to maintain their chastity and put their covers on their chests, not their heads" (451). What is more, the very ritual of ablution requires women to publicly expose their faces, hair, arms, and feet as an act of worship (5:6) which is not limited to a segregated setting (17:110) (Yüksel 451). As he points out:

> If a man stares at a woman who is taking ablution and is sexually aroused, it is not her fault, but it is either a symptom of his psychological problems or an indication of the deep-rooted problems in that society. By requiring women to cover any of these parts of their bodies, religious scholars have turned a religious ritual into a matter of sexual expression. It is up to women to cover themselves for their own protection. It is not up to men or moral police to mandate or impose this divine instruction on women, since the instruction is personal and specific to women… The language of the instruction is … designed to accommodate different cultures, norms, conditions, and individual comfort level. A divine recommendation to protect women from the harassment of unrighteous men should not be abused to justify the harassment and oppression of self-righteous misogynistic men. (451)

"O wives of the Prophet!" reveals God in the Qur'an, "Ye are not like any of the (other) women: if ye do fear (God), be not too complacent of speech, lest one in whose heart is a disease should be moved with desire: but speak ye a speech (that is) just" (33:32). Muslim scholars used this verse to claim that the voices of women are part of their private parts [*'awrah*]. God further asked the wives of the Prophet Muhammad to "stay quietly in your houses, and make not a dazzling display, like that of the former Times of Ignorance" (33:33). Although this verse was revealed explicitly regarding the spouses of the Prophet, its meaning was generalized and applied to all women to justify cloistering and strict gender segregation in all aspects of life. The term employed is *tabarruj*, interpreted as a woman's wanton display of her beauty in public. In other words, it warns women against vanity. What is more, when correctly vocalized in Arabic, it reads, "behave with dignity in your homes."

The verse in question instructs the wives of the Prophet, and not women as a whole, that they should not *tabarrajna tabarruja al-jahiliyyah al-'ula*, namely, that they should not display their charms, or strut about, as women did in the Days of Ignorance. This has been translated as "do not display yourselves," "bedizen not yourselves," and "do not display your fineries." This could easily be interpreted as discouraging women from being ostentatious, extravagant, flamboyant, garish, gaudy, flashy, or glitzy. It could be calling for humility: not showing off one's wealth. It could also counsel the women in question against flaunting their beauty and bodies with the sinful intent to seduce men.

In his mind-opening and enlightening exegesis of the Qur'an, Cyrille Moreno al-'Ajami has shown that the verb *tabarraja* originally signified "to appear like a tower," namely, "to show off with pride." (2020: 238). Muslim women were supposed to shun the unbridled morals of pre-Islamic times. Exegetes and jurists engaged in semantic stretching to such a point that the verb acquired the sense of "exhibitionism" (2020: 238). The term became pejorative and was used to shame and blame women for not wearing veils or for simply going out of their homes (2020: 239). It reached such a point that the Taliban of the twenty-first century claim that the only way to ensure the *hijab* is observed and enforced is to prohibit women from leaving their homes. For the most extreme of Islamic fundamentalists, women should be under a state of permanent house arrest.

While the verse calls on women to show some decorum to protect themselves from men, it does stress that the men who are provoked are morally and spiritually sick. Jurists, however, ignored this admonishment against men, blamed women for the actions of men, and placed all the burdens upon them. As Ibrahim Bijli Syed (b. 1939), the Indian American physician, Imam, and author, notes:

> Muslim scholars seem to be working under a very different set of assumptions. They seem to be under the mistaken impression that the Qur'an aims to eliminate all sources of temptations and enticement in society, and that women should bear the brunt of the burden in this

> process… Hence, the vast majority of Muslim men want that women should be covered from head to toe except perhaps for one roaming eye, and men may happily swagger around undisturbed by scrumptious female parts. Worst of all, this fundamentally male-indulgent view is presented as God's unquestionable truth.

The Qur'an also advises the wives and daughters of the Prophet, as well as all believing women, to cover themselves when they go out in public, to be recognized, and to avoid harassment:

> O Prophet! Tell your wives and your daughters and the women of the believers to draw their cloaks [*jalabib*] close round them [when they go abroad]. That will be better, so that they may be recognized and not annoyed. God is ever Forgiving, Merciful. (33:59)

Jalabib is the plural of the Arabic word *jilbab*, which means garment, mantle, or cloak. It is derived from the verb *tajalbaba* which means to clothe. Most Arabic dictionaries, like the *Lisan al-'Arab* and others define the *jilbab* as a loose outer garment. It is defined as a "shirt or wide dress" in *al-Munjid* and as "a wide dress, wider than the scarf, and shorter than a robe, that a woman puts upon her head and lets down on her bosom" in *Majma'u al-Bahrayn.*

It should be noted that all Arabic dictionaries were produced during the Islamic period. *Kitab al-'Ayn* dates from the eighth century. *Kitab al-Jim* from the eighth to ninth century. Others date from the tenth and eleventh centuries. The *Lisan al-'Arab* dates from the thirteenth century. And yet others were produced over the centuries until modern times. In other words, the definitions of some words do not necessarily reflect the meanings they had in the seventh century. Some words and key concepts were made to align with the dominant interpretations of the day. They made the words mean what they wanted them to mean. See, for example, the varying translations of *wa yadribna bi-khumurihinna 'ala juyubihinna* (24:31):

> Let them draw their head-coverings over their bosoms. (Asad, Bakhtiar)
> Let them draw their veils over their chests. (Khattab)
> Let them drape [a portion of] their head coverings over their breasts. (Kaskas)
> They should draw their veils over their bosoms. (Yusuf 'Ali, Malik)
> They should fold their shawls over their bosoms. (Khan, Irving)
> Let them wear their head-coverings over their bosoms. (Shakir)
> Let them draw their veils over their hearts. (Hye)
> Let them draw their kerchiefs over their breasts. (Study Qur'an)
> Draw their coverings over their breasts. (Itani)
> Extend their head-coverings over their bosoms (to hide their prominence) (Omar)
> Let them fix (literally: strike) closely their veils over their bosoms. (Ghali)

Let them cover their breasts with their veils. (Sarwar)
Wrap their bosoms with their shawls. (Usmani)
Let them cover their bosoms with their sash (dupatta). (Ahmed)
Ask them to pull their veil-cloths down across their bosom. (Munshey)
They should draw cover over their bodies and bosoms. (Ahamed)
Wrap [a portion of] their headcovers over their chests. (Muhammad)
Let them cast their shawls over their cleavage. (The Monotheist Group)
Let them put forth their shawls over their cleavage. (The Monotheist Groups 2013)
They should let their headscarves fall to cover their necklines. (Abdel Haleem)
They shall draw their scarves over their bosoms. (Daryabadi)
Draw their head-coverings across their breasts. (Bewley)
They should… draw their veils over their bosoms. (Ünal)
Let them draw their scarfs [sic] over their bosoms. (Qara'i)
Let them pull their veils over their bosoms. (Aziz)
They should draw their garments over their bosom. (Bilal Muhammad)
They should pull their scarves over their breasts. (Bakhtiari Nejad)
Cover their bosoms with headscarves. (Hussain)
Draw their veils over their bosoms. (Maududi)
Let them wear their head-coverings over their bosoms/cleavage. (Shafi)
They shall cover their chests. (Khalifa)
Let them draw their veils over their neck (Qaribullah)
Let them wear their head-coverings over their bosoms. (Muhammad Ali)
They should cover their chests with their veils. (Moeinian)
Keep the cover wrapped over their bosoms. (Haque)
They must keep their veils (and head-coverings) drawn over their chests. (Tahir-ul-Qadri)
Cast their veils over their bosoms. (Arberry)
Throw their veils over their bosoms. (Sale, Rodwell)
Let them pull their kerchiefs over their bosoms. (Palmer)
Draw their veils over their bosoms. (Dawood)
Fold their headscarves over their bosoms. (Irving and Hegab)
Let them hang their shawls over their chests (to cover their breasts). (Hulusi)
Draw their veils over *Juyubihinna* (i.e. their bodies, faces, necks, and bosoms, etc.) (Khan and Hilali)
Lengthen upon themselves their outer garments. (Yüksel)
Cast their clothes over their cleavage. (Yüksel)
Let them draw their head coverings over their breasts. (Droge)
Let them drape their breasts with their veils. (Ghabal)

As for *wala yub'dina zinatahunna*, it is translated variously as "charms," "adornment," "beauty," "hidden adornments," "beauty and charm," "beauty and jewels," "finery," "ornaments and beauty," "decoration / beauty," and "embellishment." Muslim scholars have focused on the vague term *zinah*, treating it as a synecdoche for women as a whole. A.J. Droge, however, is correct when he suggests that "charms" or "ornaments" is a euphemism for breasts (229).

As for *yud'nina 'alayhinna min jalabihinna* (33:59), it is rendered variously as:

> Draw their cloaks close round them (when they go abroad). (Pickthall)
> Draw over themselves some of their outer garments [when in public] (Asad)
> They should cast their outer garments over their persons (when abroad). (Yusuf Ali)
> Draw their cloaks over their bodies. (Khattab)
> Brind down over themselves [part] of their outer garments. (Kaskas)
> Draw over themselves some of their outer garments [when in public] Khan)
> Let down upon them their over-garments. (Shakir)
> Draw closer their outer garments over themselves. (Bakhtiar)
> Draw their cloaks close around themselves. (Irving)
> Draw their veils over them. (Hye)
> Draw their cloaks over themselves. (The Study Qur'an)
> They should draw close to them their *Jalabib* (this is a plural of *Jilbab*. It could be an additional outer-garment like a shawl, a cloak, a gown, or an apron). (Omar)
> Draw their outer garments over their persons. (Malik)
> Lengthen their garments. (Itani)
> Draw their outer garments closer to them. (Ghali)
> Cover their bosoms and breasts. (Sarwar)
> They should draw down their shawls over them. (Usmani)
> They should draw their outer garments over their person (when in public). (Ahmed)
> Wrap a loose outer garment completely around their bodies (leaving the face and the figure unobservable). (Munshey)
> Bring down over themselves [part] of their outer garments. (Sahih International)
> They should lengthen upon themselves their outer garments. (The Monotheist Group)
> They should let down upon them their wrapping-garments. (Daryabadi)
> Draw their wraps a little over them. (Ahmed Ali)
> Draw their garments closely round themselves. (Bewley)
> Draw over themselves some of their outer garments (when outside their homes and when before men whom they are not forbidden to marry because

of blood relation). (Ünal)
Draw closely over themselves their *chadors* [when going out]. (Qara'i)
Let down upon them their over-garments (cloaks). (Aziz)
Draw their outer garments over themselves. (Bakhtiari Nejad)
They should draw their outer wear over themselves. (Bilal Muhammad)
Draw their overcoats close around. (Hussain)
Draw a part of their outer coverings around them. (Maududi)
Lengthen upon themselves their outer garments. (Monotheist Group 2013)
Keep putting a part of their wrapping covers over their faces. (Ahmed Raza Khan)
They shall lengthen their garments. (Khalifa)
Draw their veils close to them. (Qaribullah)
Let down upon them their outer garments. (Muhammad Ali)
Draw their veils close to them. (Arberry)
Cast their outer garments over them (Sale)
Let down over them their outer wrappers. (Palmer)
Let their veils fall low. (Rodwell)
Draw their veils close to them. (Mezyed)
They should cover their face with their outer garment [say a scarf] until their front [a Muslim woman's "uniform" completely covers her body, without showing the curvatures of the body. Only the palm of her hands and feet and the face from the front to chin may be visible]. (Moeinian)
They should pull down upon them of their outer cloaks from their heads over their faces. (Sher Ali)
They should draw lower upon them the portions of their (loose) outer coverings from over their heads on to their bosoms (so as to veil therewith the arms, the neck, the hair, and ornaments worn over them). (Amatul Rahman Omar)
Draw their cloaks (veils) all over their bodies (i.e. screen themselves completely except the eyes or one eye to see the way). (Hilali and Khan)
Draw some of their outer clothes over themselves. (Droge)

In a tribal society, where those unprotected were in danger of robbery, rape, abduction, enslavement, and murder, group identification was important. Tribes and nationalities, as well as ethnic and religious groups, adopted distinct attire and identifiable features to signal their origin and affiliation. That way, one could distinguish between friend and foe. Some Imazighen and Arabs tattooed the faces of their women. The men knew they could not sexually assault or slaughter the women of their allies. Women with markers from enemy tribes were treated as fair game. This was precisely the process at work during the time of the Prophet Muhammad. He wanted Muslim men to wear their hair, beards, turbans, and clothing in a certain way. He wanted Muslim women to stand out as members of the *ummah*. The verse was completely contextual. There is no indication that it was meant to have universal applications. As Paola García, the Mexican American Sufi author, dancer, and jurist, observes,

> The universality of Islam invalidates the claim that veiling of any kind is mandatory for all Muslim women and … negates the notion of particular clothing requirements… The Qur'an states… "We have created you from male and female and made you into nations and tribes that you may know one another" (49:13). The Qur'an recognizes … and accepts cultural differences… Clothing is among the most salient manifestations of culture. (Had God intended uniformity of dress upon embracing Islam, the Qur'an would have indicated so, but it most definitely does not)… The Qur'an, instructing modesty as a principle, illustrated it with the practices that were common at the time … The Qur'an's mandate is the general principle of modesty, rather than veiling and seclusion, which are cultural manifestations that pertain to a specific context. Otherwise, how could it be true that Islam is universal and timeless, all humans and cultures equal under it, none superior to another, yet simultaneously true that all women, irrespective of the time and place they exist in, who accept Islam as their faith, should proceed to adopt the dress mores of seventh century Arabia? This is entirely absurd and not Islamic but rather cultural…
>
> The way modesty was expressed before and during the lifetime of the Prophet is quite different from how it is manifested in other societies. Because Islam is a religion for all times, it logically does not follow that despite the religion's universality and timelessness, Muslim women all over the world must continue to show their modesty and piety in 1400-year-old Arab standards. Moreover, "Allah intends for [us] ease and does not intend for [us] hardship" (2:185)… There is no dispute about the importance of modesty or about the fact that modesty is required and central to Islam for both men and women. But claiming that modesty demands… that a Muslim woman living in New York City in 2014 wear garb that originated, was useful in, and symbolized modesty and dignity in the desert of Arabia 1400 years ago is completely ridiculous.

In any event, the Qur'an notes that the dress code in question could be relaxed around relatives. To be precise:

> The women may relax around their fathers, their sons, their brothers, the sons of their brothers, the sons of their sisters, the other women, and their servants. They shall reverence God. God witnesses all things. (33:55)

The Qur'an also extends this dispensation to older women:

> The elderly women who do not expect to get married commit nothing

> wrong by relaxing their dress code, provided they do not reveal too much of their bodies. To maintain modesty is better for them. God is Hearer, Knower. (24:60)

Finally, the Qur'an encourages Muslims to wear lovely clothing: "O children of Adam! Wear your beautiful apparel at every time and place of prayer" (7:31). If believers should always be in a position to pray, they should always be attractive. This is all that the scripture of Islam has to offer concerning women's dress.

Despite its overemphasis by Muslim scholars and jurists, the attire worn by women is not a primary or central concern in the Qur'an. Considering that it contains 6,236 or 6,666 verses, depending on how one counts them, only half a dozen of them dealing with clothing, including the *khimar*, *jilbab*, and *saw'at*, less than 0.0009% of the Qur'an addresses women's attire. Of all the issues discussed in the Qur'an, women's dress was the least of its concerns. Its overemphasis comes at the expense of the major themes of the Qur'an, the very ones upon which any pious and believing Muslim should focus upon first and foremost. The order of importance is the one established by God. A concordance of words, verbs, and themes found in the Qur'an shows that the *hijab*, the modern obsession and infatuation of the Islamists, among their other false idols, is devoid of basis.

1.4 Treacherous Translations

As any serious and rigorous research reveals, the rules regarding *hijab*, developed by both Sunni and Shiite jurists, do not rely on clear Qur'anic evidence. They are not even reading between the lines. More than interpretation and extrapolation, it is a case of interpolation. They are making the verses express visibly absent meaning. The farfetched claims of the *fuqaha'* strain credulity. Take, for example, the dishonest translation of 24:31 produced by Muhammad Taqi-ud-Din Hilali (1893-1987), the Moroccan Salafi, and Muhammad Muhsin Khan (1927-2021), the Afghan Salafi:

> And tell the believing women to lower their gaze (from looking at forbidden things), and protect their private parts (from illegal sexual acts, etc.) and not to show off their adornment except only that which is apparent (like palms of hands or one eye or both eyes for necessity to see the way, or outer dress like veil, gloves, head-cover, apron, etc.), and to draw their veils all over *Juyubihinna* (i.e. their bodies, faces, necks and bosoms, etc.) and not to reveal their adornment except to their husbands, their fathers, their husband's fathers, their sons, their husband's sons, their brothers or their brother's sons, or their sister's sons, or their (Muslim) women (i.e. their sisters in Islam), or the (female) slaves whom their right hands possess, or old male servants who lack vigor, or small children who have no sense of the shame of

> sex. And let them not stamp their feet, so as to reveal what they hide of their adornment. And all of you beg God to forgive you all, O believers, that you may be successful. (24:31)

This is not a translation. It is a repulsive fabrication. Fanatics have produced misleading and incorrect translations based on fabricated prophetic traditions. The problem is that most Muslims do not speak, read, or understand classical Arabic, and even most Arab dialect speakers do not comprehend it despite claims to the contrary. They are *told* by scholars what the Qur'an means. Those who read these translations genuinely believe they accurately represent the meaning: they do not. Muslims are force-fed misogynistic material as if it were the Word of God. It is not. Nowhere does the verse state that women must "show only… one eye or both eyes." What is more, *juyub* does not mean "bodies," "faces," or "necks" in the Arabic language. This is a lie. Nor does the text say "(Muslim) women" and "(female) slaves." These so-called scholars are not trying to derive meaning from the Qur'an: they are trying to impose juristic rulings, theological concepts, and social norms upon it. They engage in hermeneutic rape. The same sort of exegetical sexual assault can be seen in the Hilali / Khan translation of 33:59, which reads:

> O Prophet! Tell your wives and your daughters and the women of the believers to draw their cloaks (veils) all over their bodies (i.e. screen themselves completely except the eyes or one eye to see the way). That will be better, that they should be known (as free respectable women) so as not to be annoyed. And God is Ever Oft-Forgiving, Most Merciful. (33:59)

In standard translations of the Qur'an, such as the one completed by Nessim Joseph Dawood (1927-2014), an Iraqi Jew, for example, the opening chapter of the Qur'an reads:

> Guide us to the straight path, the path of those whom you have favored, not of those who have incurred your wrath, nor of those who have gone astray.

In the Wahhabi translation completed by Hilali / Khan, it reads:

> Guide us to the Straight Way. The Way of those on whom You have bestowed Your Grace, not (the way) of those who have earned Your Anger (such as the Jews), nor of those who went astray (such as the Christians).

These interpolations, printed in parentheses, are absent in the Arabic. If 3:113-114 says that:

> There are among the People of the Book some upright men who all night long recite the revelations of God and worship Him, who believe

> in God and the Last Day, who enjoin justice and forbid evil.

Hilali and Khan transform this into:

> a party of the people of the Scripture stand for the right, they recite the Verses of God during the hours of the night, prostrating themselves in prayer. They believe in God and the Last Day; they enjoin *al-ma'ruf* (Islamic Monotheism and following Prophet Muhammad SAW) and forbid *al-munkar* (polytheism, disbelief and opposing Prophet Muhammad SAW); and they hasten in (all) good works; and they are among the righteous.

They take these pluralistic verses that prove that there are believers among the People of the Book and rewrite them, turning the Jews and Christians into Muslims. When God says that:

> Truly those who believe, and those who are Jews, and the Sabeans, and the Christians -- whosoever believes in God and the Last day and works righteousness, no fear shall come upon them, nor shall they grieve. (5:69)

Hilali and Khan make this conditional on believing in the Islamic understanding of divine unity and the prophethood of Muhammad:

> Surely, those who believe (in the Oneness of God, in His messenger Muhammad SAW and all that was revealed to him from God), those who are the Jews and the Sabians and the Christians, -- whosoever believed in God and the Last Day, and worked righteousness, on them shall be no fear, nor shall they grieve. (5:69)

Almighty God is intransigent when it comes to selling the signs of God for a vile price: those who hide the true meaning of Scripture (3:187). God warns that:

> Woe to those who write the Book with their own hands, and then say: "This is from God," to traffic with it for miserable price! Woe to them for what their hands do write, and for the gain they make thereby. (2:79)

The Qur'an condemns those who "changed it for a saying other than that which had been spoken to them" (2:59). The Qur'an denounces the fact that "a party from among them indeed used to hear the Word of God, then altered it after they had understood it, and they know (this)" (2:75-77).

The Qur'an speaks of "a party amongst those who distort the Book with their tongue that you may consider it to be (a part) of the Book, and they say, 'It is from God,' while it is not from God, and they tell a lie against God whilst they know" (3:77-79). It reminds readers of those who "altered the words from their places" (4:46, 5:13 and 5:41). It admonishes those who "concealed that which Muhammad had made clear" (5:15). Some Jews and Christians may have manipulated the meaning of their scriptures; however, the same can be said of some Muslims.

Extremists, both Sunni and Shiite, quickly label Muslims as apostates, heretics, or infidels, and call for them to be killed. However, the real unbelievers, those who corrupt the Qur'an, are the ones more richly deserving to be metaphorically burnt at the stake and to roast in hell. If the translations are terrible, the interpretations are even worse. Many translators, extremist as they may be, try to remain faithful to the Qur'an out of reverence for the text. They only show their dark and deviant side when they interpret the Qur'an or derive rulings from it. The Wahhabis are so callous that they desecrate the Qur'an directly. Just as they impose their ideology upon the Qur'an, they also insert their misogyny and extremist ideology. As Naëm Bestandji (b. 1971), the French scholar, researcher, and activist of Tunisian parentage, has noted, these fallacious translations play a central role in Islamist proselytization (2021: 93). Not only have they flooded the world with their adulterated translations of the Qur'an, but they have discredited and suppressed translations that are true to the original Arabic or whose commentaries are "too liberal" for their taste (2021: 93).

Despite the desires of Hilali and Khan, and their Saudi Salafi sponsors, to impose the *burqa* on Muslim women, when it should really have been imposed on them as misogynistic men, 33:59 simply asks women to draw their robes, tunics, or cloaks, around themselves or to lower their garments, depending on one's interpretation. It does not speak about covering their entire bodies, and it certainly does not say they should leave only an eye or two. The item of clothing in question, of which we have images in art and statues, literary descriptions, and even physical examples from the period, had short sleeves or no sleeves at all. The *jilbab* was like a poncho. Some were sewn down the side. Others were not. Its décolletage featured a plunging neckline that reached below the sternum or beyond. Some had knitted buttons on the chest. However, others did not. As the writer from Qur'an Islam notes:

> The command to "lower their garment" also proves that the woman is not commanded to be covered from head to toe. For if that was the case and women must be covered down to their toes, there would be no meaning to "lower their garments." How can a woman lower a garment that is already down to the ground?

Hilali and Khan's claim that the *burqa* is the dress of "free respectable women" is value ridden in the worst of ways. To insert such words into the Qur'an, words that are not present, is deceitful, dishonest, scandalous, and blasphemous. Consider Maududi's (1903-1979) misrepresentation of the very same verse:

> O Prophet! Enjoin your wives and daughters and the women of the believers that they should let down over their faces a part of their outer

> garments; it is expected that they will thus be recognized and not molested. God is Forgiving and Merciful. (33:59)

Maududi, the Islamist ideologue, believed that Muslim women were required to veil their faces. Rather than follow the Qur'an, he forced his views upon it. Who called him out? And who called out Hilali and Khan? However, when Leila Mehree Bakhtiar (1938-2020), the Iranian American Islamic scholar, author, translator, and psychologist, translated *idribuhunna*, traditionally translated as "beat them" or "strike them," as "go away from them," which is one of dictionary definitions of the Arabic verb *daraba*, she was accused of changing the Qur'an and was condemned to death by so-called Muslim scholars.

However, when extremists and misogynists attribute falsehood to God, inserting in the text of the Qur'an what is not there, namely, that it is a divine decree that women veil their faces, they are not held accountable for their actions, which, according to Islamic standards are tantamount to blasphemy, heresy, apostasy, and infidelity. What can be more wicked than presenting one's own personal views as those of God? Such men have god-complexes. Not only do they have the audacity to speak in God's name, but they adulterate the Qur'an, insert inexistent content, and present the Word of Man as the Word of God.

For Christoph Luxenberg, the author of *The Syro-Aramaic Reading of the Koran*, the *khimar* verse is literally non-sensical in Arabic. As he explains,

> There is a passage in Sura 24, verse 31, which in Arabic reads, "That they should beat their *khumurs* against their bags." It is an incomprehensible phrase, for which the following interpretation has been sought: "That they should extend their kerchiefs from their heads to their breasts." But if this passage is read in the light of Syro-Aramaic, it simply means: "They should fasten their belts around their waists." (Magister)

While this might evoke a chastity belt, for some, that is not exactly the case. As Luxenberg expounds, "The belt is associated with chastity: Mary is depicted with a belt fastened around her waist... Christ also ties an apron around his waist before washing the Apostles' feet. There are clearly many parallels with the Christian faith" (Magister). He is indeed correct. "Fasten the belt of truth around your waist," notes the Bible, "and put on the breastplate of righteousness" (Ephesians 6:14). Viewed from the Aramaic Gospel tradition, Qur'an 24:31 does not impose a dress code on women: it calls upon them to be chaste. A verse that was metaphorical in origin was taken literally by later Muslim exegetes who severed it from its Biblical context. Following the same approach as Luxenberg, but taking it even further, Gabriel Sawma (b. 1945), a recognized authority on Islam, reexamined the following Qur'anic verse:

> And say to the believing women that they should lower their gaze and

> guard their modesty; that they should not display their beauty and ornaments except what must ordinarily appear thereof; that they should draw their coverings over their bosoms. (24:31)

Sawma argues that the word *furuj* was misinterpreted as "private parts" when it comes from the Syriac *frag* which means "to adorn" (363). Consequently, the verse that call upon women to "guard their private parts," "be modest," or "guard their modesty" (24:31), namely *wa yahfadna furujahunna* means the exact opposite. Instead of commanding women to conceal and cover themselves up completely, it counsels them to adorn and beautify themselves. Understood this way, verse 24:31 would complement 7:31 which tells believers to wear beautiful clothing and apparel and to adorn themselves at every time and place of prayer. Since God should be remembered at all times and places, this would be a universal injunction.

As traditionally understood, verses 24:31 and 7:31, among others, contradict one another. In one place God tells women to cover their *zinah* or beauty while in another He tells them to showcase it. For Sawma, the root of the problem resides in the fact that the term *zinah* has been understood as "artificial beauty, adornment, and ornaments" when, in reality, it comes from the Syriac *zuno / zuna* which means "to resist or guard oneself" (364). Far from meaning "head-coverings" or "veils," the word *khumur* derives from the Aramaic root *k/m/r* and the Syriac *kumro* which mean "to isolate" (365). For Sawma, when the Arabic consonantal skeleton is vocalized in Syriac, Qur'an 4:31 reads as follows:

> And say to the believing women that they should shut their doors and be inaccessible; that they should be diligent of their adornment and not separate themselves (or be alone), except when they clean themselves; that they should not scorch themselves and wear garments to cover their bosoms. (362-365)

As he explains,

> The *hadith* interpretation of the Qur'an has institutionalized the veil in some Muslim countries, and has become traditionally accepted in most of the Islamic world… There are passages in the Qur'an [that call] for women to dress decently… The Arabic word *hijab* can be translated into veil. Other meanings… include: screen, cover, mantle, curtain, drapes, partition, division, divider, etc. The Qur'anic word *hijab* is derived from the Aramaic *hgb* meaning conceal [and the] Syriac *hugobo*… The Qur'anic verse 24:31 requires women to use their cover, *khimar*, being a dress, a shirt, a shawl, a blouse, etc. to cover their private parts… (365-366)

As for 33:59, which is construed to call upon women to wear *jalabib*, so-called loose outer coverings or cloaks, its meaning is entirely different in Syriac and

Aramaic. According to Sawma, the word *jalabib* signifies "appearance." When read in Arabic, 33:59 can be translated as follows:

> O Prophet! Tell they wives and daughters and the believing women, that they should cast their outer garments over their persons, when abroad: that is most convenient, that they should be known, as such, and not molested. (Yusuf Ali)

When read in Syriac and Aramaic, the same verse can mean:

> O Prophet! Tell thy wives and thy daughters and the women of the believers who adhere to the doctrine from the appearance of their eyes. They are recognized for their adherence, so they are safe. (401)

For Sawma, the verse has absolutely nothing to do with *hijab* or so-called Islamic modest dress. As odd as this interpretation and translation might seem to some, it is no stranger than those made by some Muslims in which the meaning is transmogrified. While I do not subscribe to the thesis that the language of the Qur'an is Aramaic or Syriac, I recognize that, in some cases, these languages, and others, represent a substrata. What is more, I am convinced that the Qur'an, which is written in some sort of archaic merchant and trader Arabic, has been misinterpreted, mistranslated, and misread by Muslims throughout the ages to varying degrees.

1.5 What Sayeth the *Hadith*?

Authoritarian interpretations of Islamic dress may have been imposed on Muslim women as if they were absolute and unquestionable facts, decreed upon high by the Most High and mandated by His messenger, Muhammad (570-632), the son of 'Abd Allah and Aminah, however, they are merely that: the opinions of fallible medieval men that have been maintained by the mindless and the mendacious even though they are devoid of any solid basis in the sole primary source of Islam. If the Qur'an provides no clear and unequivocal commands regarding the obligation of *hijab*, as conceived, and instituted by the jurists, perhaps we can find some clarity in the sayings attributed to the Prophet Muhammad and, for the Shiites, the Imams from his household.

Curiously, when it comes to women's dress, and the head-covering or headscarf in particular, the *hadith* literature has remarkably little to offer as well. Much of the Islamic jurisprudence of dress relies on a central tradition that describes an encounter between the Prophet Muhammad and his sister-in-law, Asma' (d. 692), the daughter of his companion, Abu Bakr (d. 634) and the sister of 'A'ishah (d. 678), who was one of his wives. One day, it is reported, Asma' visited the Messenger of God wearing transparent clothing. When he saw what she was wearing, the Prophet told her, "After a woman reaches the age of menstruation, it is not fit that anything be seen of her except this and this" (Abu Dawud). Which parts? We do not know. The traditionists who recorded this saying typically mention that he specified the body parts gesturally (Amer 33). As far as Abu Dawud (817-889), the collector of prophetic sayings, assumed, the Prophet Muhammad pointed to his face and hands (Amer 33).

Although it was the basis upon which many jurists ruled that Muslim women were required to cover everything but their faces and hands in the presence non-*mahram* men, traditionists have categorized this *hadith* as being *mursal*; a technical term that means that it is not cited on the authority of a companion of the Prophet but the follower of one. In other words, there is a break in the chain. The person quoting the Prophet Muhammad could not have heard him make such a statement as he was not present or living at that time. Some traditionists do not view this omission as a problem as they trust that the second generation of Muslims, the followers of the companions, reliably transmitted the sayings of the Prophet Muhammad that were quoted by the first, namely, the companions of the Prophet. That is hardly reassuring for historians and scholars. To make matters worse, some of the narrators in the chain are viewed as *munkar*, rejected, or denounced as untrustworthy, and *da'if* or weak. For Abdelaziz Kacem (b. 1933), the Tunisian academic, and author of *Le voile est-il islamique?* [*Is the Veil Islamic?*], the collection of traditions in which it is found is among the least creditable (Winter 25). As far as Cyrille Moreno al-'Ajami is concerned, "this saying was falsely attributed to the Prophet and merely reflects the opinions of later exegetes and jurists" (2020: 135).

"Even though this *hadith* exhibits all the traits of a report that ought to have been discarded immediately for being unreliable and rejected," notes Sahar Amer, an Egyptian academic who specializes in French and Arab studies, "it has actually become a central one in the Islamic justification of veiling" (33). As she explains:

> Lynda Clark has pointed out this report's questionable reliability despite its inclusion in Abu Dawud's canonical late ninth-century *hadith* collection... It is cited only in his collection and is not attested anywhere else... This report is cited by Abu Dawud… two hundred years after the Prophet's death and is not supported by an unbroken chain of reporters going all the way back to the Prophet or to one of his companions to guarantee its authenticity… It is the only *hadith* cited in Abu Dawud's chapter "That of a woman's adornment that may [be allowed to] appear," as though he was desperately trying to find a report to support his interpretation of Q. 24:31, or perhaps, his own views on women's proper attire. (48; see Clark 270)

What Amer fails to mention, however, is that for many Muslim jurists, relying on a weak tradition was better than relying on reason and the opinions of men. As we will see, however, such traditions were the opinions of men attributed to the Prophet Muhammad to give them legislative weight. Be that as it may, the tradition does not stand up to scholarly scrutiny. As Usama Hasan, a British academic of Indian ancestry, and a former jihadist, expounds:

> the scholars of *hadith*, including Abu Dawud… agree that this narration is not authentic, since the narrator from 'A'ishah, Khalid b. Durayk, never actually met her... It is argued that Asma,' sister-in-law of the Prophet, wife of the … companion al-Zubayr b. al-'Awwam, and mother of … 'Abd Allah … and 'Urwah b. al-Zubayr, was … a woman of great piety: it is unthinkable that she would have appeared in public wearing revealing or transparent clothing… The jurists who argue that covering the face is obligatory are adamant that this *hadith* is inadmissible in legal discussions of the topic. Since the *hadith* of Asma' is not authentic and given the diversity of views of the jurists on the topic… the Prophet … did not specify exactly which parts of her body every woman should cover or display … but taught general values and guidelines that would adapt according to time, place, context, and culture. This is a holistic reading of the texts that is characteristic of the approach to Islamic law in terms of its higher objectives, the *maqasid al-shari'ah*, and is especially relevant to Muslims living as minority faith communities yet full citizens in relatively new contexts such as the modern Western world. (7-8)

In a derivative tradition, Bayhaqi (994-1066), a collector of prophetic sayings, quotes 'A'ishah as saying that her sister Asma' once visited her while wearing a dress from Syria that was made of material that was *shafaqah*, sheer, see-through, transparent, or translucent. When the Prophet saw her, he said, "These are the kinds of clothes which have been prohibited in *Surah al-Nur*." He then asked her to change into something else. While Bayhaqi's work is not included among the six canonical books of traditions of the Sunnis, suggesting this tradition is weak, its content is illuminating. It specifies that the clothing that was prohibited by *Surah al-Nur* was sheer, transparent, see-through clothing. Based on this commentary of the verse, attributed to the Prophet Muhammad, the verse was not dictating the strict so-called Islamic dress code as we understand it but basic modesty.

Usama Hassan may find it difficult to believe that Asma' would wear see-through clothing. His problem is that he is looking at this tradition from modern Muslim lenses. His preconceptions cloud his glasses. He operates from a premise that a pious woman could not possibly wear translucent clothing and that early Muslim women dressed similarly to the ones he has seen during his lifetime, particularly in so-called Islamic lands. However, Asma's attire was precisely what women in the region wore in the seventh century. In fact, women continued to wear sheer fabrics and colorful clothing for generations to come.

The favored material had breathability, moisture-wicking properties, and helped regulate body temperature, keeping women dry and comfortable in hot weather. Whoever composed this tradition, generations, and centuries after the Prophet Muhammad, wanted to condemn and prohibit a fashion trend that was functional and well-suited to the climate in the region and replace it with suffocating black veils and cloaks. Although the jurists used this tradition to claim that women must cover everything but their faces and hands after puberty, they ignored its other implication; namely, that girls who have not menstruated can wear sheer, see-through clothing. If one premise is false, then so is the other.

Abu Dawud cites other traditions to support his view on the veil, the attire of women, and their place in society. 'A'ishah, for example, said, "When *Surah al-Nur* came down, they [the women of Ansar] took curtains, tore them, and made coverings [*khumur*] with them." This tradition, however, is classified as *da'if* or weak in its chain of oral narrators. According to another tradition compiled by Abu Dawud, and a similar one recorded by Ibn Majah (d. c. 886), 'A'ishah noted that "riders would pass us when we accompanied the Messenger of God while we were in the sacred state (wearing *ihram*)" and that "when they came by us, one of us would let down her outer garment [*jilbab*] from her head over her face, and when they had passed on, we would uncover our faces." This tradition, circulated to promote the obligation of wearing the face-veil, is also graded as *da'if* or feeble.

If the wives of the Prophet Muhammad veiled their faces -- and there is no reliable and acceptable evidence that they did -- it was not because it was compulsory but rather to dissimulate their identities, much like wealthy, famous, and important figures do for reasons of privacy and security. Those riders could have been raiders. Dignitaries ride in the back of tinted vehicles. They do not ride public transportation. Celebrities often disguise themselves in public. They do not want to draw undue attention for matters of safety.

In another tradition recorded by Abu Dawud, Umm Salamah states that "when the verse 'that they should cast their outer garments over their persons' was revealed, the women of Ansar came out as if they had crows over their heads by wearing outer garments." This tradition is treated as authentic by some Sunni scholars. The same can be said of the tradition that states that "God does not accept the prayer of an adult woman unless she wears a covering [*khimar*]" (Abu Dawud, Tirmidhi, Ibn Majah). At most, this tradition might be construed as an obligation to veil one's head during prayer. Covering the head in prayer was common in many faith traditions at the time, including Judaism and Christianity. It symbolized humility before God. In another tradition, Umm Salamah (d. c. 680) asked her husband, the Messenger of God: "Can a woman pray in a shirt and veil without wearing a lower garment?" He replied: "If the shirt is ample and covers the surface of her feet" (Malik, Muslim, Abu Dawud, and Nasa'i). If genuine, these instructions apply to the clothing worn during ritual prayers, not necessarily to everyday dress.

In another tradition, Umm Atiyyah told the Messenger of God that one of her friends wanted to attend the 'Id celebrations, but she did not have an outer garment. The Prophet told her: "Let her sister cover her with her outer garment" (Muslim). In other words, let her borrow some clothing. Once again, at most, this applies to clothing to be worn during ritual prayers. The question must also be asked: if this woman did not have an outer garment, what did she wear when going out of the home, to the market, or to visit family and friends? Or are we to assume she lived in complete seclusion and never left her home?

According to another tradition, collected by Malik (711-795), Hafsah bint 'Abd al-Rahman, the granddaughter of Abu Bakr, visited her aunt, 'A'ishah, while wearing a transparent head covering. Unlike her husband, the Prophet Muhammad, who had gently encouraged Asma' not to wear a nude dress, 'A'isha tore the sheer shawl from her niece Hafsah's head and replaced it with an opaque one. This tradition was likely concocted by a person who believed that there was compulsion in religion, that people could act as vigilantes, and that a morality police should always be on patrol to compel people to abide by so-called religious rules, regulations, and laws. This and other traditions transmitted by Malik were largely excluded from the authentic canon of the Sunnis since their chains of transmission are incomplete or abridged. Other traditions used to support the laws of *hijab* include a tradition in which Dihyah ibn Khalifah al-Kalbi, a companion of the Messenger of God, explains that:

> When the Prophet was brought some pieces of fine Egyptian linen, he gave me one and said: "Divide it into two; cut one of the pieces into a shirt and give the other to your wife for a veil [*khimar*]." Then, when he turned away, he said, "And order your wife to wear a garment below it and not show her figure." (Ahmad, Bayhaqi, Abu Dawud, Bazzar)

Even if it were authentic, which it is not, as it is classified as *da'if* or weak, this tradition hardly supports the obligation of the headscarf. Rather, it discourages women from wearing transparent clothing. Moreover, the call to wear the translucent material on top of the opaque one applied to her figure, namely, the part covering her body, and not the *khimar*, which would be worn around her shoulders, neck, or hair, depending on the weather. In another tradition, some women from Syria came to 'A'ishah. She asked them if they came from a place where women go to bathhouses to bathe. When they said they did, she stated that the Prophet said: "If a woman takes off her clothes in a place other than her house, she tears the veil between her and God, the Exalted" (Abu Dawud). Once again, this tradition discourages nudity, even in public same-sex settings. It supports the view held by some jurists that Muslim women were obliged to cover themselves even in the presence of non-Muslim women as the latter might describe their beauty to disbelieving men.

In another fanciful tradition, it is reported that the Prophet Muhammad foretold that the day would come when "Some women are clothed but naked, inclining to evil and seducing with it. They will not enter Paradise, nor smell its fragrance, even though it can be found from a distance of five hundred years of travel" (Malik). Once again, this does not impose the so-called Islamic *hijab* as conceived by most Muslim jurists. It discourages women from wearing see-through or skintight clothing to sexually provoke and seduce men. Intent and context matter. It is a question of *makan wa zaman*, time, and place.

In another fraudulent tradition, recorded by Bayhaqi, the Prophet Muhammad states that "The worst of your women unveil their beauty, take pride in their appearance, and they are hypocrites. None of them will enter Paradise except as rarely as you see a red-beaked crow." The noun used is *mutabar'rijat,* those who engage in *tabarruj*, namely, flaunting their beauty, and *mutakhayalat*, namely, "those who strut about." Hence, the Arabic expression is much stronger than merely "unveiling their beauty" and "taking pride." It describes women who intentionally show off their beauty and bodies for the purpose of sin. Once again, this tradition is a general appeal to modesty, not the imposition of the *chador* or *burqa*. Irrespective of its chain of narration, which happens to be unreliable, the content of this tradition, which accuses women who "unveil their beauty" with hypocrisy and threatens them with hellfire, is inadmissible in content.

The Arabic term used in several prophetic traditions is *tabarruj*. Some authorities believe that it describes the failure to abide by the rules of *hijab*, however slight. For others, the term is much stronger than that. It refers to showing off one's beauty, a wanton, excessive, and shameless display of sensuality and sexuality, adopting an enticing gate, and strutting oneself in front of male strangers. It involves showing, exhibiting, or displaying what excites the lust of men. How much that involves depends on the perspective of men. For some, showing the neck is *tabarruj*. For others, even showing the face is *tabarruj*. And yet for others, even exposing ornaments like earrings, rings, necklaces, and bracelets is an act of *tabarruj*. Some even prohibit women from plucking their eyebrows or removing facial hair. Such was the view of Ibn Hazm (994-1064), a leading figure in the Zahiri school of jurisprudence. Ultimately, the term means "to flaunt" and cannot be limited to a woman's person, form, countenance, clothing, or demeanor. It is also a term that applies to men. Neither of the two sexes should engage in flaunting in any form.

For many Muslim men, and the women they have convinced, dupped, deceived, intimidated, or threatened, *tabarruj*, which they define as not observing *hijab* as prescribed by male jurists, is disobedience to God and His Messenger, and a grave destructive sin that incurs the curse of God and expulsion from His Mercy. According to them, the failure to abide by the rules of *hijab* is an act of hypocrisy, a disgrace, a lack of chastity, and a shameful action. For them, not wearing *hijab* is the way of the Jews, the filth from pre-Islamic times, an animal act, a door to widespread evil, and a sign of decadence and decline. What is more, it is darkness on the Day of Resurrection and an attribute of the people of hell. How charming, not to mention sexist, racist, anti-Jewish, and anti-Christian.

Take, for example, the reasons for wearing *hijab* listed on the website supervised by the Salafist Sa'd ibn 'Abdullah al-Humayyid. Women who wear *hijab* are described as dignified, noble, liberated, purified, protected, respected, confident, obedient, and guarded pearls. How beautiful! However, women who do not wear *hijab* are described as dishonored, degraded, subjugated, sullied, slaves, exposed, laughed at, insecure, sinners, and prostitutes (Alukah). The adjectives used to describe *hijabis* are beautiful. However, their antonyms are applied to non-*hijabis*.

There are scores of believing and chaste women who do not drape themselves from head to toe, who show their hair, arms, legs, and even more. The ambiguity and subjectivity of "beauty" or "ornaments" leaves women at the mercy of lascivious men. It all revolves around the definition of the words *zinah* and *'awrah*. If "unveiling one's beauty" is a metaphor for "exposing one's genitals," "fornicating," or "committing adultery," then the meaning of the tradition is sound. From a Judeo-Christian-Islamic perspective, sex outside of marriage is a mortal sin. Claiming that such women deserve punishment in the hereafter unless they repent is consistent with the moral message of these faith traditions. To claim, however, that a Muslim woman who shows her face, hair, hands, feet, forearms, or legs is a hypocrite who will be damned to hell is disturbingly misogynistic. Are there not vain men? Are there not men who show off their beauty and bodies to seduce women? Where are the traditions threatening them with eternal torment?

Few people from the Judeo-Christian-Islamic tradition would argue that a woman who shows her vagina in public or offers it in fornication or adultery has not committed a sin for which a serious consequence is in order. The prohibition, it appears, applies to literally and metaphorically "exposing one's intimate parts." Showing one's hair is different from showing one's pubic hair. The Church fathers, however, believed that the hair on women's heads evoked pubic hair. It was, therefore, indecent and had to be covered or shaven (Bestandji 2021: 262). According to the ancient Hebrews, fallen angels lusted over the hair of human women. As such, married orthodox Jewish women are required to cover their hair or shave it off. Pre-Christian theologians adopted these bizarre, irrational, and absurd beliefs. As Rose Weitz (b. 1952), the sociologist, explains:

> [They] believed that Eve, and all women after her, were inherently more susceptible than men to the passions of the flesh and the Devil's seduction. As a result, women posed constant dangers to men's souls, having the power to tempt men, as Eve had tempted Adam. (Sherrow xxii)

If God is so concerned about protecting righteous men and perverted men from wicked women, why did he give them hair? In his infinite wisdom, why did He not create them bald?

The Jewish, Christian, and Muslim attitudes toward women's hair are rooted in an ancient hair taboo. Some early cultures invested hair with magical powers. Since hair could arouse and seduce men, it was viewed as dangerous. Since women could make men's private parts move from a distance, surely it was a matter of sorcery, magic, and witchcraft. Should Muslim women have to wear *hijab* to not arouse the jinn, the demons of the pre-Islamic Arabs? God forbid women would tempt fairy folk, leprechauns, pixies, elves, gnomes, brownies, sprites, boggarts, and hobs. Yes, indeed, twenty-first-century Muslim women scholars, engineers, medical doctors, scientists, and astrophysicists, should be concerned about not sexually provoking magical beings. What some men present as the Word of God is nothing but ignorant pagan superstition.

Just like showing one's hair is not like showing one's vulva, wearing lipstick is not the same as sexual penetration. It defies reason and divine justice. If a woman who shows her hair, beautifies herself, wears pants, a miniskirt, or even a bikini is a fornicator, an adulteress, and a hypocrite who will burn in hell, she might as well just reject man-made religion and its misogynistic male deity, become a sexually liberated woman, worship the Goddess, or become an atheist. "For some women," states Patricia Monaghan, "finding room for feminine divinity means leaving monotheistic religion entirely. Some become secularists, but other search for new religious affiliations" (55). Alternatively, they could steer clear from all extremes and reinfuse their religion with the Sacred Feminine.

In any event, strict rules of *hijab* lead to obsessive-compulsive behavior in women who fear hellfire for showing a single strand of hair or invalidating their ritual prayers. Throughout Islamic history, many Muslim women covered their heads; however, like Jewish women, they showed their ears, throats, and varying degrees of hair. They did not wear suffocating stranglehold *hijabs*. The vast majority of them were moderate regarding coverings and dresses. What is more, many did not wear headscarves. They wore different kinds of hats, turbans, and wraps.

The fanatical, infantile, black-and-white thinking, devoid of degrees and shades of gray, which is exhibited by many male Muslim authorities is the product of slow-witted, narcissistic, minds. In psychology, it is referred to as "splitting" or all-or-nothing thinking. It is found in people who cannot reconcile positives and negatives into a cohesive, realistic, whole. These unintelligent, low IQ extremists, for whom there is no middle ground, cannot acknowledge nuances. This type of extremist thinking is typical of Islamic thought where intolerant verses abrogate tolerant ones and the most radical traditions prevail over the most moderate ones. From a psychological perspective, much Islamic thought is the product of primitive, unrefined, extreme, infantile, and emotional minds, incapable of critical thought, logic, reasoning, and subtlety.

In his Qur'anic commentary, Qurtubi (1214-1273), the exegete and *hadith* specialist, claims that the Prophet saw a bride wearing a sheer dress and said:

"She is not a woman who believes in *Surah al-Nur* who wears this." He also alleges that a group of women from the tribe of Tamim visited 'A'ishah while wearing thin clothing. Upon seeing them, the Messenger of God said, "If you are believers, then these are not the clothes of believers. But, if you are not believers, do as you please." Devoid of chains of narrations, these late, isolated traditions, are devoid of any aura of authenticity. Even if they were genuine, they discourage wearing transparent clothing as was the fashion at the time. The phrase, "do as you please," however, could have had far-reaching ramifications had it been adopted as a legal adage. It would clarify that "there is no coercion in religion" also means "there is no coercion in dress." If the tradition from Qurtubi is treated as inauthentic, a similar tradition, recorded by Bukhari and Muslim, the most authentic books of prophetic sayings according to the Sunnis, says the same thing: "If you have no shame, do what you please." If this is the case, what authority do Islamic fundamentalists have to impose *hijab* on Muslim and non-Muslim women? As the Prophet Muhammad said himself, they should be free to dress as they please.

The Twelver Shiites have their own traditions that male jurists use to impose their understanding of *hijab* on women. These collections by Kulayni (864-941), Saduq (d. 991), and Tusi (995-1067), not to mention Majlisi (1627-1699), were compiled at a much later date than the Sunni ones. An estimated 98% or more are sayings, not of the Prophet Muhammad, but of various Shiite Imams, approximately 80% of which are attributed to Ja'far al-Sadiq (702-765). For most Muslims, who happen to be Sunnis, the opinions of these personalities, while generally respected, have no doctrinal or jurisprudential authority. And unlike Sunni traditions, which are supposed to trace back to the Prophet Muhammad, or, at the very least, to his companions, Shiite traditions almost exclusively trace back to one of the twelve Imams, meaning they are all broken or disconnected. However, it is interesting to note that the same scarcity of traditions supporting *hijab* found in Sunni sources also applies to Shiite ones. The sayings are very rare. They are like needles in haystacks.

In one tradition, transmitted by Majlisi in *Hayat al-qulub*, Ja'far al-Sadiq claims that 'Abd Allah ibn Sallam (550-663), a Jewish rabbi, and convert to Islam, asked the Prophet Muhammad if Eve was made from all of Adam or just one part of him. The Messenger of God responded, "From the internal. If she were created from an external part, she would have been allowed, like men, to go out without *hijab* (veil). Therefore it is necessary that men should have their women covered in *hijab*." This tradition is an obvious forgery. The belief that Eve was created from Adam's rib was borrowed by Muslims from Christianity and Judaism. It is entirely devoid of a Qur'anic basis. The tradition claims that women must wear *hijab* because they were made from an internal part of Adam. If they were not made from an inner part of Adam, they would not need to wear *hijab*. Since Eve was not made from an inner part of Adam, or any part of him at all, the logical conclusion is that women are under no requirement to observe so-called Islamic dress.

In another dubious tradition, the Prophet states that "Whichever woman discards her veil (*khimar*) in a house other than her husband's has indeed disgraced her veil (*hijab*)" (Nu'man, vol 2: 198). In yet another, he warns women against bedecking themselves with gold and silk (Nu'man, vol. 2: 200). However, none of these are prohibited to women according to Islamic jurisprudence. He even banned women from braiding their hair and letting their bangs hang loose (Hubeali *Hijab*: 6-7). The Messenger of God said: "It is not appropriate for a woman who is menstruating to have locks of hair in front, or [to display] the luxuriance of her hair" (Nu'man, vol. 2: 148). It is also reported that 'Ali "prohibited women from having locks of hair hanging in front or on their sides, and from using henna to make ornamental designs [on their hands]" (Nu'man, vol. 2: 148).

In another fraudulent tradition, 'Ali (d. 661) reports that the Prophet prohibited the ornamentation of women for someone other than her husband, saying, "If she does so, it is the right of God, Almighty and Glorious, to burn her in Hell" (Saduq). He also said that any husband who allows his wife to attend marriage feasts, to participate in mourning sessions, or to visit the sick, will be hurled headlong into the Fire" (Nu'man, vol. 2: 201). In short, a woman should not leave the house for social or religious functions. He also warned people, and this would seem to apply to women, not to perform their ritual prayers while wearing see-through clothing (Hubeali: *Hijab* 19).

According to one bogus tradition, Zayn al-'Abidin (659-713) said that "Hair is one of two beauties" ('Amili). Such a statement cannot be cited as an injunction that requires women to cover their hair. What is more, what is the other beauty that he does not mention? Their vaginas? Their breasts? Their legs? If the hair is one of two beauties that need be covered, then what is the only other one? This feeble tradition, which was collected in *Wasa'il al-shi'ah*, dates from the seventeenth century, and cannot be cited as evidence to support a jurisprudential ruling. However, it does appear to be based on a saying of the Prophet Muhammad: "Whenever anyone desires to marry a woman, he should inquire about her hair, as he does about her countenance, for verily, hair, is one of the two signs of beauty" (Nu'man, vol. 2: 180). This weak tradition emerged from a culture of arranged marriages in which women covered their faces. Otherwise, why inquire about a woman's face? It cannot trace back to the seventh century. As is virtually always the case, Nu'man (d. 974) does not provide chains of narration.

In one tradition, Muhammad al-Baqir (676-743) encouraged women to be immodest with their husbands but modest among other men ('Amili). This hardly mandates strict restrictions on dress. In another tradition, Ja'far al-Sadiq states that the *zinah* or beauty that women must not display is found under the *khimar* (headscarf) up to the wrists (Kulayni, 'Amili). He advised women to perform their prayers wearing three garments: a loincloth [*izar*], a *dira*‘, a type of *kaftan*, with short to medium sleeves, and a *khimar* (Hubeali *Hijab*: 18). In the event she lacked three garments, she could wear two if they provided sufficient coverage. Unless the *khimar* was extremely long, the arms of the woman would have been exposed.

In yet another tradition, the sixth Imam explained that only women too old to marry could show their heads and arms (Hubeali *Hijab*: 9). He is also reported to have said that it was improper for a Muslim woman to uncover herself in front of Jewish or Christian women as they could describe their beauty to their husbands (Hubeali *Hijab* 6). A tradition attributed to Musa al-Kazim (745-799) states that women may only show their faces, hands, and wrists in the presence of unrelated men (‘Arusi). In yet another, ‘Ali al-Rida (765- 818) asserts that "A woman does not have to cover her head in the presence of a boy who has not yet reached puberty" (‘Amili, Saduq). Finally, in response to some inquiries, he wrote that "looking at the hair of married and unmarried women is prohibited" (‘Amili).

There are a few more Sunni and Shiite traditions on the *hijab*; however, this overview provides the gist. The six major books of Sunni traditions were collected over two hundred years after the passing of the Prophet, while the four major Shiite ones were collected over three hundred years after. Majlisi's *Bihar al-anwar* and ‘Amili's (1624-1693) *Wasa'il al-shi*‘*ah* were compiled over a thousand years after Muhammad's death. These works contain a microscopic number of traditions supporting the *hijab*. They also include a slightly larger body of traditions that generally emphasize modesty. There are traditions in which the Prophet Muhammad and the Imams stress the importance of covering one's ‘*awrah* and not exposing it to others. They apply to concealing one's pudendum and not engaging in illicit sex.

Not surprisingly, the jurists ignore the traditions that stress that women should beautify and adorn themselves in public, and when going to the mosque, insisting they apply henna, wear earrings, bracelets, and necklaces, and should apply light perfume. In one tradition, the Prophet says that women should use perfume with a light fragrance (Abu Dawud, Nas'ai). However, there are plenty of traditions that state that women should not wear perfume to the mosque; otherwise, their prayers will not be accepted (Malik, Muslim, Ibn Majah). Others claim that women who wear perfume and pass through a group of men are promiscuous (Abu Dawud, Tirmidhi). Some state that women who do so are adulteresses (Nasa'i, Ibn Khuzaymah, Ibn Hibban, Hakim). Some assert that angels curse them until they go home (Majlisi). Others say that such women are deprived of blessings until they return to their houses (Tabarani, Majlisi).

There are plenty of traditions, however, where the opposite is true, and the Prophet Muhammad encourages, and even demands, women to groom themselves, dye their hair, and apply henna to their hands. According to Ja‘far al-Sadiq, the Prophet "commanded women never to be without jewelry"

(Nu'man, vol. 2: 144). For 'Ali, "it does not behoove a woman to divest herself of all ornaments; she should at least wear something as minimal as a necklace around her neck" (Nu'man, vol. 2: 144). He also stated that "it is not proper for a woman to pray without dyeing herself with henna; and if she has not been able to do so, she should at least apply an aromatic paste [*khaluq*]" (Nu'man, vol. 2: 148). The beauty product in question, made with saffron, was used as blush. Hence, we have traditions where applying henna is commanded and others where it is prohibited. In another tradition, Ja'far al-Sadiq states that "women should not give up adornment, be it only with a necklace" and that "she should not have untinged hands, be it with a little henna" (Majlisi). He even states that elderly women should not give up adornment" (Majlisi). In the time of the Prophet, women used lipstick, blush, eyeliner, and painted their hands and nails with henna. They also used to dye their hair. After all, women should be attractive, presentable well-groomed, and classy. It shows that they have self-respect and earn the respect of others. Muslim women should be cultured and self-confident.

There are, however, traditions in which the Prophet commands men to "prohibit your women from coming to the mosque while adorned" (Ibn Majah). Why would the Prophet and the Imams tell women to wear jewelry if they were to be covered under their clothing? Why apply henna if one cannot show any skin? So, the Prophet Muhammad and the Imams were not opposed to women showing their *zinah*, beauty, or ornaments. They distinguished between decency and indecency, and between beautification and provocation. This nuance was lost on the jurists. They had Manicheistic minds. This is not surprising. Many were former dualists or descendants of dualists. In fact, some were certainly secret Jews, Christians, Gnostics, Sabeans, Manicheans, and Zoroastrians who feigned to be Muslims. That being said, the most significant number of traditions used to impose and enforce strict *hijab* evince a frightening fear and hatred of women and the power posed by their sexuality which must be restrained at all costs and by all means.

Commonly quoted prophetic traditions that promise infernal damnation and punishment to purportedly immodest women include the following ones:

> In later generations of my *ummah*, there will be women who will be dressed but naked, who would be inclined to evil and make their husbands inclined towards it. On top of their heads [what looks like] camel humps. Curse them, for they are truly cursed. They will not enter Paradise or [even] get a smell of it. (Muslim, Tabarani)

> Two are the types amongst the denizens of Hell ... people having flogs like the tails of the ox with them and they will be beating people, and the women who would be dressed but would appear naked, who are seduced and seduce others. Their heads would be like the humps of the *bukht* camel inclined to one side. They will not enter Paradise and they

> will not smell its fragrance whereas it can be perceived from a great distance. (Muslim)
>
> In the next world I saw a group of men whose bodies were being cut into slices with pairs of scissors. I inquired to Gabriel: "Who are these people?" Gabriel replied: "These are the very same people who used to embellish their persons." Then I saw a well. This well emitted a foul smell and painful cries were coming out of it. I asked Gabriel: "Who are these people?" Gabriel replied: "These are the women who used to embellish their bodies and performed unlawful deeds." (Suyuti)

These women did not merely polish themselves up real nice. They did so with the intent and purpose of committing fornication and adultery. There is a difference between a woman who embellishes herself to go to a fine restaurant with her husband, and another who slips on a little red dress and goes to a discotheque to cheat on her husband. Rather than blindly believe such traditions, they must be examined critically. Does a woman who does not cover her hair merit eternal malediction and torture in hell? Has she committed a mortal or capital sin? One must wonder.

In another tradition, 'Ali and Fatimah visited the Prophet Muhammad only to find him in tears. They asked for the reason for his sadness, and he replied:

> O 'Alī, on the night of my ascension [*mi'raj*] I saw women of my *ummah* who were being so severely punished that I became concerned for them and started crying. I saw a woman who had been hung by her breasts. Then I saw a second woman who was eating her own flesh and fire raged below her. A third woman was hanging by her tongue, and boiling water was being poured down her throat. A fourth was bent over, her hands and feet were tied together, and snakes and scorpions were crawling all over her. A fifth was deaf, dumb, and blind, enclosed in a cage of fire, her brains oozing out of holes in her skull. Her body was falling apart due to leprosy. Another was hung by her feet, inside and over. Yet another woman's body was being shredded to pieces by scissors made of fire. One woman had the head of a pig and a body of a donkey and was being given several kinds of punishments. Another had the face of a dog; fire was entering her body from her posterior and coming out of her mouth and the angels were giving her a beating with iron rods.

Fatimah then inquired of her father: "Please, tell me, what did those women do [to deserve such punishment]?" The Messenger of God replied:

> Listen, my dear: the one who was hanging from her breasts used to deny her husband his rightful pleasure; the one hanging by her feet used to go out of her house without her husband's permission; the one eating her own flesh used to beautify herself and show her body to men

> other than her husband; the one whose hands and feet were tied together, and who was covered with snakes and scorpions never used to care about impurity and was not careful about *ghusl* [after menses, intercourse, etc.], thus taking her prayers lightly. The deaf, dumb, and blind used to bear children through adultery but claim the children belonged to her husband. The one whose body was being cut by scissors made of fire never observed *hijab* in front of non-*mahram* men. The one whose body was being burned and who was eating her own intestines used to provide other women to men for sex. The one with the face of a pig and a body of a donkey was a back biter and a liar. And the one with the face of a dog and who had fire entering her behind and coming out of her face was a jealous woman. (Kulayni)

These traditions, worthy of the worst horror films, depict a sadistic God who relishes in torturing and tormenting women. The *Mi'raj* or heavenly ascent of the Prophet Muhammad inspired many Muslim litterateurs and produced a rich body of creative religious works. The earliest account of this mystical journey, vision, or dream, the nature of which was disputed by the family and companions of the Prophet, was viewed as inauthentic by early Muslim authorities like Ibn Ishaq (704-767). The descriptions of what supposedly happened grew exponentially in the *hadith* literature, prophetic biographies, and Qur'anic commentaries over the centuries, reaching epic proportions. It was like a blank canvas or a white page that invited people to let their imaginations run wild. In short, these traditions are patently false. They fall into the category of legends and fairy tales. They are literary hate crimes against women.

The traditions in question say nothing about Muhammad and his view of women. They say mountains about the men who invented them. Like psychotic serial killers and women slashers, they reveled in their fantasies of women being tortured and dismembered for such sins as going out of their homes, making themselves pretty to go out in public, failing to bathe after sex, and for missing some prayers. Sure, we could argue that a woman who commits adultery merits a reasonable punishment, including one who carries the children of other men and attributes them to her husband. Sure, a female pimp merits severe punishment. And yes, a backbiter, a liar, or a jealous woman should face the consequences of her deeds. However, do they deserve the punishments described in this perfidious tradition collected by Kulayni?

Does a woman who fails to wear a *hijab* in front of men deserve to be sliced and diced by scissors of fire? Does she deserve to hang from her hair in hell, so her brain boils, as depicted in a lengthy tradition transmitted by Majlisi? Does the punishment fit the crime? Is this a depiction of a just, merciful, compassionate, and loving God? The men and women who assert that a woman will spend fifty thousand to seventy thousand years in hell for showing a single strand of hair should compose themselves and consider a crucial question: "What is the punishment promised for those who lie in the name of God?"

Early advocates of *hijab* equated it with seclusion. Women were property and men had to be protected from them. As one can only imagine, Muslim modernists viewed the veil and *purdah* as signs and symbols of backwardness, ignorance, and illiteracy, as they most certainly are. According to traditions attributed to the Prophet and the Imams, women should be kept ignorant, and not taught how to read and write. Misogynists were making them mirror their views. With the rise of Islamism in the sixties and seventies, apologists and Islamists rebranded *hijab* as liberation and protection. Protection from what? Protection from whom? Protection from men? This reminds one of mafia protection payments. It was not "you pay us, and we will protect you from others" but "you pay us to protect you from us."

If the Qur'an suggests that distinctive, modest, clothing, that identifies a woman as a Muslim, could provide protection, signaling that she had the security of a collective, the traditions do not present the *hijab* as protecting women. They are concerned about protecting men from supposedly wicked and sexually insatiable women. The traditions do not condemn men who ogle women, catcall them, harass them, and sexually assault them. No, not at all. Women are the target of their wrath. Why must women wear *hijabs*? The answer, from the traditions attributed to the Prophet Muhammad and the twelve Imams, is telling.

According to the *hadith* literature, women are evil, women are wicked, women are temptresses, women are seductresses, women are sexually insatiable, women are unfaithful, women are corrupt, women are corruptors, women are crooked by nature, created from a bent rib, if you try to straighten them out, you will break them, women are worldly, women who leave their homes without the permission of their husbands are adulteresses, women who wear perfume in public are adulteresses, women who adorn themselves in public are adulteresses, women who do not observe sexual segregation are adulteresses, women who do not wear *hijab* are hypocrites who will burn in hell; women are vaginas, women consist of ten private parts, since women are vaginas, they should be feared, and their bodies locked up in their homes, the ambition of women is to find men for sex, women are sex toys, women are for rent and for hire, the best women are horny ones, women are like sex dolls, and women are play-things to be sodomized. And it continues.

The worst women are those who resist sex like recalcitrant animals, a woman is like a donkey or a black dog: she breaks the prayers of men if she passes in front of them, even if a woman licks the puss from her husband's sores, she has not fulfilled her dues, an old mat is better than a barren woman, women are inferior to men, women are defective in intellect and religion, there is no piety in women, the evidence of two women equals that of one man, God made women stupid, menstruation and pregnancy are punishments to prevent them from fornicating and committing adultery constantly, women should be made to go hungry, women should be deprived of sufficient clothing to prevent them from leaving their homes, since God left women backward, they must be left backward, and if women knew the rights that their husbands had upon them, they would wipe the dust from their husbands feet with their faces. And not only that.

Women should not be consulted, anyone who follows a woman will go astray, men should not obey women, husbands should do the opposite of what their wives say, no nation will succeed if they select a woman as their leader, people who entrust themselves to women will never be saved, it is a disgrace to obey women, men who obey women will be ruined, prosperity lies in opposing women, whoever obeys his wife, God will cast him into hell face first, were it not for women, God would have been truly worshipped, were it not for Eve, no woman would have cheated on her husband, women are like sheep, women are bad omens, women are devils, women are the snares of Satan, women are the soldiers of Iblis, ninety-nine percent of women are destined to hell-fire, and were it not for women, all men would go to Paradise. And not only that.

Women are slaves of their spouses, husbands should hang their whips where their wives can see them, women can be beaten by their husbands for just causes, if a woman refuses to have sexual intercourse with her husband, he can lock her in a room, tie her to a bed, beat her, and take her by force, women who do not satisfy their husbands sexually will burn in hell, women should prostrate themselves before their husbands, women are only properly covered when they are dead and buried, and the majority of the inhabitants of hell are women. And the list of these traditions attributed to the Prophet, and parroted by the companions, and the Imams goes on and on and on. As Ismail Kurban Husein Poonawala (b. 1937), an Indian professor of Arabic, points out, these traditions have "grave theological, moral, and social consequences" as "they contribute to the denigration of the moral status of women" (Nu'man, vol. 2: 200).

Some of the women-hating traditions in question, found in Sunni and Shiite books of *ahadith*, are categorized as weak, others as good, and yet others are viewed as authentic, genuine, and agreed upon. If even one of them is historically accurate, then the whole house of cards upon which Islam is built crumbles to the ground. No man of God, prophet of God, messenger of God, and decent human being would slander women in the collective in such a hateful fashion. Although some traditions start with "the worst of women," and thereby avoid unacceptable overgeneralizations, many simply start with "women..." They place all women in the same category, denying them their individuality, and agency. They promote sexist, women-hating, stereotypes and prejudices.

Even the most despicable of misogynistic gangster rappers, who rap that "a bitch is a bitch," have the decency of acknowledging that "not all women are bitches." When the Prophet or 'Ali say that "Women are deficient in intelligence and religion," it applies to all women. If they were inspired by God, surely, they should have known better. Otherwise, they were just ordinary men, products of their time and place. For believers, the sole option that remains is to treat such sayings as slanderous and defamatory forgeries. It is imperative to expose the hatred at the heart of the religion of the fanatics and refute the fake traditions they attribute to the Prophet Muhammad. It is a duty to expose the false faith of the fanatics, their animosity toward Jews and Christians, their opposition to art, music, and sculpture, and their deep-rooted hatred of women.

All the despicable, woman-hating, sayings attributed to the Prophet Muhammad and the Imams are alive and well today. They are repeated verbatim by Islamists and conservative Muslims all the time. As part of their campaign to impose *hijab*, the Iranians came up with slogans of all kinds. They stressed that veiling was a divine duty, that a woman's virtue, dignity, and chastity was tied to her *hijab*, that the veil provided safety, and that it prevents corruption. They accused women who wear "bad *hijab*" of being the toys of Satan and having mental disorders. Their husbands were devoid of honor. They accused improperly veiled women of being a stain on the "Islamic" Republic of Iran that had to be eliminated immediately. Others called for "death to the improperly veiled woman" (Shirazi 106-108) "While Reza Shah's order to unveil did not entail any major reforms for women," observes Faegheh Shirazi (b. 1952), a professor of Middle Eastern Studies, "Khomeini's fixation on the proper *hijab* also did not improve the lot of the Iranian woman" (106). Not at all. The first thing he did after he attained power was to "put women in their place" by mandating *hijab*, lowering the age of marriage of girls to nine, and systematically dismantling their rights. It suffices to say that men who view women as soldiers of Satan will interpret Islam differently from those who view them as gorgeous, life-giving, goddesses.

Although some Muslims construct their own fantasy Islam that is empowering to women, by being highly selective, lacking knowledge, or willful ignorance, the Islamic tradition, as it has been transmitted over the past millennium and a half is not one that is remotely woman friendly. Mind you, some women had it worse in other religions and cultures. While some minority currents in Islam might be more woman-loving, the main body of the tradition has always been woman-hating. That is not to say that God is sexist or that the Qur'an, the Prophet, and the Imams were misogynists. What it does say is that most Muslim scholars throughout the ages have been, and are, sexists and misogynists. Claims of scholarly consensus across the ages are completely and utterly meaningless as agreeing upon a wrong does not make it right. As Bestandji's work amply exposes, "there is no consensus regarding the veil among Muslims" ("2018: part four). It is only the consensus of Islamist "scholars" (2018: part four). Be that as it may, the Qur'an is clear that majority opinion does not matter and a minority opinion can be correct (6:116, 7:102, 7:187). The most convincing argument is the one that counts.

1.6 Conclusions

As a close reading of the Qur'an demonstrates, there is no definitive proof that Muslim women are required to cover themselves completely, except for an eye or two. There is no conclusive evidence that Muslim women are required to cover themselves entirely apart from the face and hands. There is no absolute confirmation that Muslim women are required to cover themselves totally except for the face, hands, and feet.

When it comes to the minimum that Muslim women must cover in the presence of unmarriageable males, the only unambiguous, indisputable, incontrovertible, indubitable, undeniable, and explicit proof found in the Qur'an regards the requirement to cover their external genital organs, along with a recommendation to cover their breasts, bosoms, and chests.

The sayings of the Prophet Muhammad and the Shiite Imams cited to support the rules of *hijab*, as conceived by some clerics, contradict the clear sense of the Qur'an, were compiled centuries after the Messenger of God and the Imams from his Household, and are inauthentic, anachronistic, and ahistorical. A sound study of the sources suggests that God, the Prophet, and the Imams opposed public nudity, required public decency, and encouraged modesty and humility in both dress and demeanor. Such general guidelines, grounded in flexibility, are in keeping with Islam's universality.

Chapter 2

Are Women Vulvas?

2.1 Introduction

As we have seen in chapter one, the dominant Islamic laws regarding women's dress find no inarguable, undebatable, incontestable, and irrefutable basis in the Qur'an. They are not evidence-based. If and when God gives commands and decrees laws, He is unambiguous. He does not employ figurative language. When God prohibits something or mandates something, He uses clear imperatives. The Ten Commandments, authentic or not, divine or not, are completely comprehensible. And even though Jesus taught in parables, the few laws he gave were lucid. When drawing laws from the Qur'an, we should hold it to the same reasonable standard of clarity. After all, as God states in the Qur'an, "We did not leave anything out of this book" (6:38). So, let us compare what the Qur'an says when it comes to matters of dress with what the jurists claim that it says, wanted it to say, or forced it to say.

2.1 Reductionism Exposed

Ask Muslim scholars today about the meaning of the word '*awrah* alluded in 7:26 -- or most of them for the past millennium, for that matter -- and they will invariably insist that it involves the entire female body with the possible exception of the face and hands. Some will stress that the feet must also be covered; however ugly, calloused, wart-covered, fungus-infested, and foul-smelling they may be. It is reassuring to know that God, in His infinite wisdom, cares about men with foot fetishes and does not want them to be led astray by some toes. Others will emphasize that the face must also be veiled, however hideous it may be. In fact, some Muslim scholars argued that the face-veil was a mercy upon men that protected them from seeing ugly female faces. And they will argue, in all absurdity, that ulotrichous hair must be covered, and that even bald women must cover their heads. Yes, cover that hair, or shave it off as married Orthodox Jewish women do. It should not be seen. This is presented as absolute truth and a divine decree.

Although the Prophet said that "God is beautiful and loves beauty" (Muslim, Tabarani, and Ibn 'Arabi), for most jurists, Muslim women are destined to be drab, dull, and dour. This stands in sharp contrast with the Qur'an, in which God asks, "Who has forbidden the adornment [*zinah*] of God which He has produced for His servants?" (7:32). What is more, if women's hair is such a source of seduction, that it must be concealed in public at all cost, why did God create it? The real issue is not hair. After all, Muslim jurists have ruled that even bald women are required to cover their heads. The real issue is power, control, surrender, and submission.

The Qur'an claims God sent prophets and messengers to all tribes and nations. Were all those women required to veil their hair? Were they committing a mortal sin by not covering it? There is a clear continuum in monotheistic belief throughout human history. However, there is no evidence believing women were required to cover their hair. Christian, Jewish, and other monotheistic traditions do not bear this out. Moreover, the vast majority of Muslim women, from the dawn of Islam until current times, did not veil themselves according to the criteria created by the most conservative clerics. In fact, the clerics disagreed on how much a woman was required to cover, ranging from as little as a thong bikini or G-string to everything, including the eyes. If God and the Prophet had issued a clear command, such divergence of opinion would not have been possible.

If controlling what women wear were not enough, the most extreme of Muslim misogynists will even decree that women, as a whole, are '*awrat*, namely, they are *de facto* private parts. In short, women are walking vulvas. If women are vaginas because they have vaginas, these scholars should be asked, does that make men penises because they have penises? In some cases, perhaps it does. Muslim men, women, and children are taught that women are private parts on the authority of the Prophet Muhammad. Imagine the psychological, spiritual, and sociological consequences of embracing and absorbing this pseudo-religious teaching, the sexism it creates in males, and the sense of inferiority and sexual objectification it produces in females. As Naëm Bestandji notes, "The heads of women have become the equivalent of their pubis, a genital organ" (2021: 95). This explains why Muslim women today claim they feel "naked" without their veils (2021: 95).

To make matters worse, some Muslim scholars even claim that the voices of women form part of their '*awrah*. This ruling was borrowed from the Talmud. Orthodox rabbis also insist that women's voices are a part of their '*ervah*. At least, the rabbis limit this to the singing voices of women. Some Muslim jurists believe that it even applies to the speaking voices of women, which should not be heard by unmarriageable males, unless there is a need or necessity. Others treat it as '*awrah* if it is suggestive or alluring. If men should not listen to the voices of women, as they might become aroused, then the same should apply to women listening to the voices of men.

"[The whole of] a woman is '*awrah*," stated the Prophet, "so if she goes out, the devil makes her the source of seduction" (Mubarakfuri qtd. Abou El

Fadl 2013: 236, Tirmidhi, Ibn Hibban, Abu Dawud). If a woman, in her entirety, is a vulva, then, it is, without question, an obligation for her to be completely enveloped. This tradition, invented by men who believe in the *burqa*, made a mistake. If a woman is *'awrah*, then so are her hands and so are her eyes. The exemption, allowing a woman to expose her eyes, or a single eye, so that she can see where she is going, would have no basis. That eye is a vagina. It must be covered.

In another dishonest tradition, the Prophet Muhammad says that "women… are *'ayy* [weak] and *'awrah* [exposed genitals]" (Nu'man, vol. 2: 197). "A woman has ten *'awrahs*," the Messenger of God said, "her husband covers one of her *'awrahs*, and when she dies, the grave covers the rest" (Ghazali qtd. Abou El Fadl 2013: 236). As Khaled Abou El Fadl (b. 1963), the Egyptian Kuwaiti American jurist, notes, "the logical conclusion to be drawn from this tradition is that for a woman to be thoroughly modest, she ought to be dead and buried" (2013: 236). In fact, it is a common saying among Islamist misogynists that a woman should only leave her house for her marriage and her funeral. A life of imprisonment is all that the Islam of the women-hating fanatics has to offer. It is a form of femicide.

For these lascivious and lust-crazed men, who would most certainly fail Anatomy 101, a woman's hair and vulva are the same, an ear is like a clitoris, and a big toe is the same as a breast. Some jurists went as far as prohibiting men from looking at a woman's cut hair or nail clippings. And these perverts who get sexually aroused by elbows, fingers, noses, cut hair, and nail clippings dare attack Western culture for objectifying and exploiting women when they, the Muslim misogynists, treat women as private parts? In fact, they seek to convince little girls that they are sources of seduction responsible for men's sins, compel them to cover their hair and bodies, and confine them in their homes. They reduce women to being sexual objects. This is the most misogynistic message imaginable. They take lust and immorality and present them as piety. As Ayaan Hirsi Ali (b. 1969), the Somali Dutch American activist, expresses in *The Caged Virgin*:

> Girls have to cover themselves, make themselves invisible… For this reason, they feel constantly guilty and ashamed, became it is impossible to live a normal life and be invisible to men. Girls constantly think they are doing something wrong. Not only is their external freedom to choose where to go or where not to go inhibited, but so is their inner freedom. (2006: 22)

She may be the spokesperson for Islamophobia in the West; however, she is right on this specific subject. Referring to women as *'awrat*, vaginas, or female genitalia, as is done in Arabic, Persian, and languages from the Indian subcontinent, is as sexist, misogynistic, and derogatory as calling them cunts in English. In the Indian subcontinent, some conscious women have called on men and women to cease referring to women as *'awrat* in Hindi, Urdu, and other languages, asking them to use respectful Sanskrit words for women (TNI News). Imagine, rejecting a sexist Islamic term of Arabic origin in favor of Hindu terminology.

As can be appreciated, the sexist sayings attributed to the Prophet Muhammad have spread far and wide and have negatively impacted women's rights and freedom. He is claimed to have said "(The whole of) a woman is a private part (*'awrah*), and so if she goes out, the devil makes her a source of seduction;" "I have not left in my people a *fitnah* [source of sedition and temptation] more harmful to men than women," and that "women are the snares of the devil" (223). "Surely," notes Leena El-Ali, "no one who has read the Qur'an can possibly believe that the messenger whom God chose to bring it to us could possibly have said such things" (223). The heretics, deviants, and disbelievers are not those who reject such sayings. They are those who accept them as authentic, thereby insulting God and the Prophet.

Another popular term used by Arab Islamists and misogynists to refer to women is *hurmah*, which means "prohibited," "forbidden," "outlawed," "banned," "restricted," and "taboo," but which is often used in the sense of "broad," "bitch," "whore," and "slut." By addressing women as such, these men make it clear that these women have no right to be in the public sphere. They should be completely covered, accompanied by a male relative, or better yet, they should remain in their homes where they belong. While *hijab* may be viewed as liberating by some Muslim women, particularly Western converts, who view it as an expression of opposition to sexual objectification and promiscuity, for many Muslim women, it remains an instrument of oppression, coercion, control, and terror. In fact, in the Maghrib, any woman who fails to abide by the strictest interpretation of the veil is viewed by misogynists as being *aryanah* or naked. As Bestandji concludes, the veil sexually objectifies women far more than sexist advertising does (2021: 216). In fact, notes Jane Kramer (b. 1938), an American journalist, "many feminists would argue that the Islamist obsession with covering up women's bodies is a deeper form of pornography than an obsession with uncovering them." For the intellectuals from *Révolution Féministe*, the veil perpetually hypersexualizes women (Samint).

Since men cannot control their lust, argue misogynistic Muslim men and the females they have indoctrinated, women should be placed under house arrest and, if they appear in public, they must only do so with their portable *purdah*, accompanied by a male relative, and observe strict gender segregation. And if, God forbid, a female should be sexually assaulted, then, by God, if was her fault, she provoked it, and she should be punished for it unless four men witnessed the act. Hence, the convenient rape laws in countries like Pakistan, where women are punished for fornication or adultery if they cannot produce four male witnesses to prove they were sexually assaulted. After all, the word of a woman has no worth. The same goes for little Muslim girls who have the courage to point the finger at the father, older brother, or uncle who has been sexually abusing them. Without witnesses, she had no rights according to many jurists. After all, the accused man has rights as well, rights designed by men to protect their fellow men.

Muslim jurists may argue that Muslim girls and women must cover their hair around non-related males as it provokes sexual excitement in men and leads to corruption. In Saduq's *'Illal al-shara'i,* 'Ali al-Rida says that "looking at the hair of veiled women is prohibited, whether they are married or not, due to what is there from the excitement of men, and what the excitement invites to, to the corruption and the entering into what is not permissible" (vol. 2, part 9: 6). This tradition is narrated on the authority of Muhammad al-Sinan, who is weak, untrustworthy, and known for his extremist views and associations (Muslim). It is also found in a book by Saduq, who was criticized for gathering traditions without considering their authenticity. Not only is the chain of authority of this tradition questionable, but so is its content. The headscarf is mandatory because the hair of women arouses men. Logically, if women's hair does not sexually excite men, then there should be no need to cover it. While hair can be a sexual fetish, so can shoes. Where does one draw the line? And why are women those who must change their behavior on account of men who have little to no self-control or self-respect? If women's hair is so tantalizing, men should lower their gaze. To top it all off, this work by Saduq is saturated with preposterous explanations for Islamic laws.

Ja'far al-Sadiq made exceptions for nomadic women, slave women, and non-Muslim women, such as blacks, who are *ahl al-dhimmah*, "because even if they were prevented [from showing their hair], they would still end up doing it" (Saduq). According to the Qur'an, however, "no bearer of a burden shall bear the burden of another" (39:7). As Ibrahim B. Syed (b. 1939), an advocate of an Islamic Renaissance, notes, "the weakness of men cannot be the source of hardship and suffering for women, and any approach that does not acknowledge this fact, in my view, is not true to the spirit or letter of the Qur'an." The Qur'an, notes Bestandji, places equal emphasis on the chastity of women *and* men (2021: 91). Nowadays, he notes, the verses concerning men have magically disappeared from the rhetoric of the Islamists who place the burden of family "honor" entirely upon women: or to be precise, between the legs of women (2021: 91).

'Ali Motahhari (b. 1958), the son of Morteza Motahhari (1919-1979), the Iranian scholar and philosopher, went so far as to claim that not wearing *hijab* was an "animal right" and that he wanted to live in a society where men got sexually aroused at the sight of a woman's hand, as opposed to the West where, he claims, white men have become so desensitized to the allures of women that they have become impotent, forcing white women to have sex with black immigrant men. In his sexist and racist words:

> Not wearing *hijab* for women isn't freedom. It is like an animal

> instinct. Men in Iran are aroused by unveiled women. Western men aren't aroused because they're sick. That's why Western women choose African men… If somebody is not aroused on the beach, then he is sick. God wants us to get aroused. Men must be aroused. It is good that a young man is aroused by seeing the hand of a woman. (My Stealthy Freedom, Iran Wire)

A proponent of state-imposed and police-enforced obligatory *hijab*, 'Ali Motahhari is convinced that voluntary *hijab* "will lead to nudity" (Iran International).

Men, not women, are responsible for their gaze. A man who would lose sexual control over himself and succumb to sin at the sight of a woman's hand or hair is no man at all. Such a person has zero control over his *nafs* or animal impulses. For people who are sane of mind and pure of heart, exposing hair is not like exposing one's vagina. In the words of Usama Hasan:

> A rationalist reading would argue that uncovered female hair does not generally cause sexual temptation in modern Western societies (and others), and that, therefore, the requirement to cover the hair should no longer apply. This has been the view of modernist reformers such as … Ahmad Khan of British India and the late … Zaki Badawi, former Imam and Khatib of the Regent's Park Mosque and founder of the Muslim College, both in London… The veil … mentioned in this *ayah* is a means, not an end: the purpose is to cover the chest area, not the head…. Women in Arabia would cover their heads to protect them from the heat of the sun, but sometimes leave their breasts exposed, as found in some Islamic descriptions of the *Jahiliyyah* period and in some Byzantine-era depictions from Syria… The commandment in this *ayah* comprises a very practical method for covering the bosom, i.e. with an existing and available piece of clothing… (14)

Although absolutism and authoritarianism eventually prevailed, and Islam's heartbeat flatlined, there was a wide fluctuation in scholarly opinion during the early development of the Muslim faith. Some early scholars of Islam were far more open-minded than those of today. Diversity of opinion was valued to a greater degree. Moreover, while many agreed to disagree, they generally did not excommunicate one another due to differences of opinion, call each other apostates and infidels, and place hits on one another like underworld drug lords. This is not to say that such things did not happen. This is to say that the situation has deteriorated significantly. During its best and brightest periods, classical Islamic civilization generally provided scholars and intellectuals with greater freedom to think than many have today in the Muslim world, particularly under so-called Islamic rule.

Early Muslim scholars discussed and debated the meaning and extent of the word '*awrah*. They explained that linguistically and etymologically, the word *'awrah* signifies something shameful that should be hidden from public view. It was embarrassing or repulsive. It is the semantic equivalent of the Latin *pudenda* or shameful parts. As Ibn Manzur (1232-1311), the lexicographer, defined, "the *'awrah* of the man and the woman consists of their two private parts." He stated that "the *'awrah* is everything that causes embarrassment if exposed." He explains that "The *'awar* has only one eye," not referring to the *niqab*, but the fact that a private part is an orifice, an opening, or a hole. He also notes that the Qur'an figuratively describes homes as *'awrah* (33:13). As we read in the Qur'an:

> And when a faction of them said, "O people of Yathrib, there is no stability for you [here], so return [home]." And a party of them asked permission of the Prophet, saying, "Indeed, our houses are unprotected [*'awrah*] while they were not exposed." They did not intend except to flee.

The Arabic word *'awrah* implies protection, safety, vulnerability, security, and privacy concerning a home. It allegedly derives from the root *'a-w-r*, which means "to lose an eye." It signifies nudity and nakedness. It means something that should be protected for reasons of safety and vulnerability.

The literal meaning of the word *'awrah* is lucid in Arabic. It means an "opening." It is something that should not be exposed or revealed for reasons of security, protection, shame, or privacy. It is used to allegorically describe "the opening in the defenses of the enemy." In other words, it is a hole or a point of entry. So, more than cleavage, *'awrah* also refers to orifices. And it is not referring to one's mouth, ears, or nostrils. It was well understood by jurists who spoke of the *'awratayn*, namely, the two external private parts: the reproductive organs -- the penis, testicles, and vagina -- as well as the anus. And they agreed the gluteus maximus covers the anus; and hence, is naturally concealed.

Anyone who claims that the *'awrah* involves anything more than the genitals is being linguistically and etymologically unfaithful. It is as absurd in Arabic as in English to claim that a woman's hair and vagina are the same or that a nose is the same as a nipple. Although they knew what *'awrah* meant, some jurists, influenced by factors outside the Qur'an, including spurious secondary sources, cultural influences, pre-Islamic pagan impulses, and social-engineering agendas, sought to expand its semantic range to dominate and subjugate the female gender.

According to the *Sirah* of Ibn Ishaq, some Jews reportedly tied up the garment of a Muslim woman, which caused her *'awrah* to be exposed. She called for help, and some Muslims rescued her and killed one of the culprits. It is reported that this group of Jews then ganged up on the Muslim and murdered him. If we accept this narration as authentic, we must ask ourselves some simple questions. Did these Jews merely expose the hair of the Muslim woman? Her nose? Her arms? Her little toe? Or her legs? No. They exposed her genitals.

They lifted her dress or skirt. In short, she was on the verge of being sexually assaulted by a group of men. As can be appreciated, the *'awrah* is nothing more than the *furuj*, namely, the private parts. Would the companions of the Prophet have killed men for merely removing a Muslim woman's headscarf? Is such an act grounds for death in Islam? If this account is correct, the men were killed because they were tearing off a Muslim woman's clothing to gang-rape her. In short, they were killed in the act of committing a crime.

2.3 Talmudic Influences on Islamic Jurisprudence

To better understand the Arabic word *'awrah*, we can turn to the Bible and the Hebrew language. Originally, as we read in Genesis 2:25, both Adam and Eve walked around nude, lacking both garments and "shame" (Silverman 1). Nudity was a pure and natural state prior to sin. It was God's original law. The concept of modesty did not exist. In Hebrew, this "shame" or "nudity" is called *'arummim*, and God had them conceal it with leaves and then loincloths: a simple article of clothing covering the genitals. If they were married, and the only people around, why did they need to cover their private parts?

In any event, the meaning of *'ervah*, the Hebrew equivalent of the Arabic *'awrah*, is evident: it concerns the private parts, not the entire body. In the Bible, it describes the pudenda. In fact, it does so over fifty times. It figuratively describes disgrace, shame, indecency, and uncleanliness less than a handful of times. If God wanted women to cover themselves completely, He would not have told them to cover their *'awrah* or genitals. He would have commanded them to cover their bodies.

As rabbis David Booth, Ashira Konigsburg, and Baruch Frydman-Kohl admit in *Modesty Inside Out: A Contemporary Guide to Tzniut*, a work approved by the Committee on Jewish Law and Standards, which represents the *halakhic* positions of the conservative movement:

> Although rabbinic sources describe many actions as exposing *'ervah*, the minimum requirement of modesty is to cover genitalia and anus. This limit depends on … Deuteronomy 23:13-15 and Leviticus 18-20. The Torah prohibits the uncovering of nakedness, or *'ervah*… Reading the two sources together suggests that *'ervah* means specifically the genitals. The punishment in Leviticus is for one who exposes their reproductive organs. Similarly, the organs for urination and defecation must remain covered… Brown, Driver, Briggs in their biblical lexicon define *'ervah* as "pudenda," meaning genitalia. (7-8)

Rather than rely solely on the Torah, the written law, namely, the five books of Moses from the Old Testament, which never overtly speak about modest clothing, Jewish jurists also drew upon the oral law, the Mishnah, which, in written form, is included in the Talmud, which consists of rabbinic legal discussions. "But while the Torah generally construed 'nakeness' as genital," explains Silverman:

> the Talmud rephrased the concept as any exposure of female skin in excess... of a handbreadth... To be sure, the rabbis repeatedly counseled men... to disregard a woman's voice, hair, legs, "even... her small finger." But the real solution in rabbinic culture to the male libido was not for men to police their own behavior. It was for women... to cover their bodies with ample clothing. Women were thus made accountable for their own conduct, as well as the behavior of men who might cave at the merest sight of female flesh. (38-39, see also 87)

For some Jewish rabbis, seeing a woman's little finger was the same as gazing at her private parts (Silverman 87). Not only are they prohibited from praying within sight of female "nakedness," ultra-Orthodox Jews are not even allowed to be within earshot of women's voices (Silverman 87). As Silverman notes:

> In the rabbinic worldview... men are possessed by innate and uncontrollable desires dangerously unleashed by the merest sight and sound of a woman. But the rabbis did not seek to constrain men by censoring the masculine gaze -- a gaze that essentially transforms, as per the Talmud, the entirety of womanhood into pudenda. Rather, the rabbis overdressed women. A "partially revealed shoulder," wrote rabbi Falk recently in his 600-page compendium on female etiquette: "presents a stumbling block to a man who happens to see the woman or girl. It is essential that women and girls realize that it is their responsibility to ensure that men do not transgress... even inadvertently..." Men's failings are thus made women's burden. The solution to male sexuality is for women to conceal their bodies. (87)

Although there is no command for women to cover their hair in the Torah, Jewish rabbis determined that women's hair becomes part of their private parts or "nakedness" upon marriage (Silverman 6, 90). How a woman's hair can magically go from modest to lewd, from pure to impure, from innocent to sexually arousing, and from sinless to sinful, from one moment to the next, namely immediately after the recitation of a marriage formula, is not explained by the rabbis. It must be some mysterious form of transubstantiation. "Hair itself was not the issue," argues Silverman (90). Rather, "hair and clothing symbolized the rabbis' efforts to govern female agency, fertility, and sexuality" (90). In the words of Silverman,

> *tzniut* appears as a form of religious fanaticism -- worse, an ideological effort to dress patriarchy in a pleasing rhetorical coat. Wigs, long hems, below-the-elbow sleeves, and high collars, like Muslim headscarves and *burkinis*, constitute an anti-fashion that rightly belongs, if anywhere today, at the margins of normal citizenship. (111)

The Old Testament, which dates from 500 BC, its commentary, the Jerusalem Talmud, which dates from 400 CE, and the Babylonian Talmud, which dates from 500 CE, can dictate women's dress as much as they want. Physical evidence, however, including the reliefs of the capture of Lachish by Sennacherib (705 to 680 BCE), does not support the claim that Jewish women covered themselves according to the rules found in the Torah and the Talmud. On the contrary, "they went bare headed with a ribbon in their hair and their faces uncovered" (Boucher 57). It was only in the third century that we have evidence from Tertullian that Jewish women veiled themselves outdoors. As such, he recommended that the Christian women of Carthage do the same (Boucher 58). However, this was not the strict Islamist style veil. They covered part of their hair with hats, headdresses, and shawls. They showed their ears and earrings. They exposed their forearms. They showed their feet. The V-neck of their dresses extended to the middle of their chest: their cleavage was only partially covered by jewelry (Braun 566).

Muslim jurists did not invent misogyny. On the contrary, they faithfully followed in the footsteps of Jewish jurists. They chased them right down the rabbit hole. They did the same with Christian scholars and, in some cases, with Zoroastrian priests. When it came to the interpretation of the Qur'an, Muslim exegetes drew upon *Isra'iliyyat* or Jewish lore. When it came to developing laws, Muslim jurists drew from Jewish law. Not only were Muslim scholars profoundly influenced by Judaism, but some were converts from Judaism. In contrast, others were Cryptic Jews, namely, Jewish men who converted to Islam out of convenience and who feigned to be Muslims while continuing to practice Judaism in private. The Jewish influence on Islam is so strong that one could suggest that rabbis-turned-shaykhs set out to Judaize Islam. If you cannot beat them, join them, and make them like you. Many sayings and teachings of the Prophet Muhammad appear to have been drawn from the Talmud. Likewise, some legal principles and rulings made by Muslim jurists were drawn from Jewish law. Lynda Clark wonders whether Jewish and Muslim jurists developed these laws together (285: note 151). Considering that Islam is a continuation of Judaism and Christianity, and a repository of apocrypha, parallels between the three faiths are not surprising.

As Silverman has noted, many Orthodox Jewish women view *tzniut*, the Jewish equivalent of the *hijab*, "as a radical, liberating alternative to the sexualized and sexist objectification of female bodies that pervades contemporary culture" (87). For them, "religious modesty highlights inner beauty and moral substance, not superficial appearances" (87). As Silverman points out, these are the same arguments that Muslims make to support the veiling of women in Islam (87). However, as Silverman stresses, "this modern interpretation finds little support from traditional sources" (87). In fact, "from this angle, *tzniut* amounts to little more than male power dressed as female honor" (87). Sadly, the same can also be said of the *hijab* in Islam. In response to the sex-crazed culture of the modern secular world, some women turn to Islam and the *hijab* in the belief that it is liberating when, in reality, some of its injunctions can be seen as degrading and humiliating. In fact, for some Muslim women, the *hijab* is an instrument of oppression that symbolizes total sexual segregation from society (Chesler 2005: 155).

Some modern-day Muslims may claim that the *hijab* is about modesty, symbolizes respect for women, and represents chastity. However, these are not the reasons that Muslim exegetes and jurists invoked when imposing "Islamic" dress upon women. It was not about protecting women: it was about protecting men from women. It was not about respecting women but disrespecting them. It was not about honoring women but about dishonoring them. It was not about empowering women but disempowering them. Moreover, it was not about freeing them, as some modern-day apologists and propagandists may deceptively claim. It was about restraining, controlling, and confining them. For Jewish and Muslim jurists, women were made responsible, not only for male behavior but for the entire community's ethical standing (Silverman 89). All societal problems were blamed on the sins of women. As Silverman notes, the purpose of veiling women was "to symbolically enclose them within male authority" (7).

While orthodox Jews focus on literally following the laws of the Talmud, conservative Jews have a more nuanced understanding of *tzniut*. *Modesty Inside and Out*, by rabbis Booth, Konigsburg, and Frydman-Kohl (b. 1951) provides a more balanced understanding of the subject that is neither ultra-orthodox nor ultra-liberal. They recognize that modesty is a central Jewish value connected to humility (1-2). They criticize the focus on specific forms of dress as contradictory to the *halakhah* (2). As rabbi Norman Lamm (1927-2020), an orthodox scholar, admits, "it would be a pity to limit our understanding of *tzniut* to that which can be measured by a ruler" (2). For rabbi Dov Linzer (b. 1966), the focus should be "on modesty in all ways for men and women" (3). As Booth, Konigsburg, and Frydman-Kohl stress, modesty is contextual (8). "Depending on who is making the determination," they write, "it can encompass pubic hair, a woman's breasts, a married woman's uncovered hair, a man's thighs, shoulders, and even a woman's voice" (8). And while Silverman seems to put all rabbinical authorities in the same sexist basket, some recognized that modesty was determined by context and culture. In the words of Booth, Konigsburg, and Frydman-Kohl:

> Cultural norms have *halakhic* significance for determining appropriate dress. In a context where it is normal to go swimming in a bathing suit... such behavior is permissible. A man wearing a bathing suit in a business environment is problematic because it is so different to the typical office attire and so will draw the eye. Flapper dresses in the 1920s were initially quite shocking; as society became accustomed to

> the style, the dresses began to be seen as appropriate. Shorts or sleeveless tops for men or women may be inappropriate, depending on the context, because they raise similar issues of context and modesty... A tank top might be appropriate at the beach but not in *shul*, in part, because it surprises. The change in people's expectations affects their perception of modesty and appropriate attire... A person has a responsibility to others and should choose clothing suitable to the context. One might assume that as women's breasts in our culture are often hyper-sexualized, they must certainly constitute '*ervah*. But this assumption is mistaken. For example, because of the commonplace occurrence of breast-feeding, rabbi Yosef Hayyim of Baghdad (known as Ben Ish Hai, 1835-1909) considered the exposed breasts of a nursing mother as any other normally exposed body part... (9-10)

As rabbis Booth, Konigsburg, and Frydman-Kohl admit, "rabbinic literature expands the minimal Torah-based modesty rules into broader expectations of dress" (10). As rabbi Marc D. Angel (b. 1945) recognizes, "the Torah does not enumerate rules relating to modesty in thought, dress, and speech... Rather these rules are inferred." As he notes:

> the early rabbinic opinions... emerged from a context where women... were deemed to be subservient to men... Classic rabbinic literature assumes that women are ... a source of sexual temptation to men, and... should ... dress ... so as not to arouse men's passions.

As we have seen, some rabbis went so far as stating that "anyone who gazes even at a woman's little finger is as if he gazes at her private parts" (10). A woman's leg became '*ervah*. Her hair became '*ervah*. And even her voice became '*ervah*. The rabbis prohibited women from wearing perfume and colored clothing lest it arouse men (12-13). They outlawed "any social interaction between men and women" (13). Eventually, the definition of '*ervah* was expanded to such an extent that women were viewed entirely as private parts that were prohibited from sight (13). They were expected to remain secluded in their homes, sheltered from the masculine gaze.

Some rabbis, however, like Joseph Ben Moses Joselein (1423-1490) and Mordecai Yoffe (1530-1612) did not "conceive of modesty as a fixed practice determined by Talmudic precedent" (15). They "understood modesty as dependent on social context" (15). For them, "the practices described by the Talmud are socially determined examples that may be obviated by a new reality" (16).

For modern conservative rabbis, *tzniut* is not merely a matter of dress but of thought and action. It has outer and inner dimensions. They recognize that "in our egalitarian and open society, much personal behavior and display of parts of the body that were considered by earlier generations of rabbis to constitute erotic stimulation are no longer applicable to us and should no longer be viewed as problematic" (18). They define '*ervah* as "explicitly erotic zones" (18), a view that is more consistent with the Torah than the Talmud. And while they praise those who choose to dress modestly, they warn that "*tzniut* is misused when the onlooker's gaze and gossip is devoted to what others are wearing" (19). In other words, it is "better to focus on our own dress and thoughts" (19).

As can be appreciated, the Muslim notion of '*awrah* derives directly from the Talmudic understanding of '*ervah*. Jewish and Muslim jurists have passionately debated the subject of female modesty for over a millennium. Despite minor technical differences, the parallels between their arguments are revealing. While both the Torah and the Qur'an specify that men and women must cover their genitals, the male, patriarchal, and misogynistic jurists of both religious traditions distorted and perverted the supposed divine dictate found in their respective scriptures to control and confine women, objectifying them to the extreme. Although such distortion was denounced in Qur'an (2:75, 2:79, 5:13, 6:78, 6:91), it did not prevent Muslim jurists from engaging in it and adulterating its teachings.

Although the Torah limited the '*ervah* to the external genitalia, Jewish rabbis, relying on the Talmud, expanded its meaning to cover most of the female form. For orthodox Jews, any female older than three or seven years old must cover her collar bone, her arms to the bottom of the elbow, and her legs to the bottom of her knees, when both standing and sitting. It is preferable if the sleeves extend to the wrists and the dress to the ankles. If the woman is married, she must cover her hair with a *mitpahat* or *tichel*, namely, a headscarf, *shpitzel*, snood, hat, beret, or even with a sheitel or wig, typically on top of a shaved head. Some Hasidic rabbis encourage the wig, a practice that traces back to ancient Egyptian times (Sabbahy 69). Others, especially Sephardic ones, prohibit it. The Jewish practice of wig-wearing, however, dates back to Talmudic times and was a feminine aid to beauty (Rubens 8). So, the covering of the hair was not so much about concealing beauty as reminding the woman that she was married, something that could be accomplished by means of a wig. As for those who wore a headscarf, it usually exposed their necks, throats, ears, and parts of their hair. Unmarried girls and women were not required to cover their hair at all.

In the Mishnah, notes Alfred Rubens (1903-1998), "the custom for Jewish married women to have their head covered… is described as a 'Jewish ordinance' but its Biblical origin based on Numbers 5:18 is questionable" (8). Be that as it may, the rabbis expected married Jewish women to cover their hair. Any woman who went outside with her hair uncovered was assumed to be a virgin (8). The function of the head covering among the Jews was not the same as among the Muslims. For the former, it distinguished between single girls who were virgins and married women who were not. For the latter, the distinction was between the pre-pubescent and the pubescent, between girls and women. As it did not apply to enslaved women, it also distinguished between slave-girls and free women.

Although the Qur'an limited the '*awrah* to the external genitalia, Muslim jurists, relying on the *hadith* genre, expanded its meaning to cover most of the female form. For most Muslim jurists, females past puberty must cover everything but their faces, hands, and feet, although some argue that the feet and the face must also be covered. Some go as far as requiring the hands to be covered as well. Unlike Jewish women, who adopt the head-covering upon marriage, all Muslim girls, past puberty, or nine years old and over, according to some Shiites jurists, must cover their hair, ears, throats, and necks. If announcing that one was married, as Jewish women did by covering their hair, could be viewed as a source of pride, adopting a headscarf, as a public signal that a Muslim girl has had her period, can be a source of embarrassment. Where does privacy come into play?

If Judaism is divided into sects, the same can be said of Islam. Orthodox Jewish women follow the laws of *tzniut* strictly. Jewish women who follow Reformed Judaism do not follow them and have no mandatory dress code. Followers of Conservative Judaism attempt to avoid both extremes. They may wear regular attire, without any apparent religious or ethnic affiliation, while attempting to remain modest. Most women do not cover their hair publicly, although some do during religious services.

In the Muslim community, differences in dress are not so much a matter of sectarian affiliation but of cultural influence, ideology, and conservatism. There are Sunni and Shiite women who wear the *burqa*, the *chador*, the *litham*, and other face-veils, completely covering themselves in black. There are conservative Sunni and Shiite women, more moderate ones, and very liberal ones as well. Sufi women, in general, tend to be more lax in matters of *hijab*, as Sufi scholars avoid literalism and stress the spiritual sense of the Qur'an. The same can be said of the Ahmadiyyah and the follower of Warith Deen Mohammed (1933-2008). The women who wear *hijab* the least, or not at all, tend to be followers of Qur'anic, modernist, progressive, feminist, or reformist movements. Otherwise, they are conservative or liberal secularists on the right or left of the political spectrum.

2.4 The Pudenda in Islamic Jurisprudence

When addressing the subject of '*awrah*, Muslim jurists typically divided their discussion between free and enslaved men, as well as free and enslaved women. Regarding free and enslaved men, some jurists ruled that they only needed to cover their genitals. In other words, a simple loincloth sufficed. Others, however, felt that both the groin and the posterior needed to be concealed (Abou El Fadl 257: note 107). They did not consider men's thighs part of their '*awrah* (Abou El Fadl 257: note 107). Many jurists, however, ruled that free men were required to cover themselves between the waist and knees (Abou El Fadl 257: note 107).

When praying behind men, early Sunni traditions relate that the Prophet warned his female companions not to look up while in prostration as they could inadvertently sneak a peek at men's private parts in the rows in front of them. The women claimed that this was a distraction. This prompted the Prophet to extend the '*awrah* of men from the waist to the knees. Some scholars stressed that this was only obligatory in the presence of women and that, among men, only the genitals had to be covered. Reportedly, this was the position of Ja'far al-Sadiq, who stated: "Private parts are two: the front and the back. The back is covered by the rump. If you cover the penis and the testicles, you have covered your private parts" (Kulayni). In fact, he stated that it was enough to cover one's genitals with one's hand when among men in a Turkish bath (Kulayni). He also said that lime paste, a hair remover, was sufficient covering in a bathhouse (Kulayni). As for seeing the private parts of non-Muslims, he stated that "Looking at the private parts of non-Muslims is like looking at the private parts of donkeys" (Kulayni). He also permitted reading the Qur'an and having sex in a bathhouse (Kulayni).

As Usama Hasan explains, the Qur'anic revelations regarding clothing must be examined in their historical and socio-cultural context:

> Many of the Prophet's companions had very little clothing, and often only one garment or piece of cloth that was insufficient to cover the whole body: recorded examples are those of Amr b. Salamah, Mus'ab b. 'Umayr and the Prophet's daughter, Fatimah. Even whole rows of men were in this position whilst praying, with short garments tied above their shoulders such that their private parts were barely covered, and their legs were bare: the women in the rows behind were commanded not to raise their heads from prostration until the men were sitting with folded legs... Underwear was virtually unknown… When the Prophet was asked whether it was acceptable to pray in one garment, he replied, "Does each of you have two garments?" In similar vein, Bukhari sets out a chapter heading: "In How Many Garments May a Woman Pray?" and begins with the statement of Ikrimah, "If she covers her body with a single garment, it is sufficient." (15-16)

Generally speaking, jurists believed that what must be covered during ritual prayers should also be covered in public spaces (Abou El Fadl 257: note 107). However, there were differences on this issue as well. 'Abd al-Rahman al-Awza'i (707-774), the leading representative of an early but no longer extant school of jurisprudence, believed that the thigh was part of a man's '*awrah* in the mosque, but not in the bathhouse (Haddad). In the bath, it was limited to his genitals. So, some jurists evidently distinguished between the public and private spheres. In other words, what one has to cover in prayer is not necessarily what one has to cover outside of it.

Many Hanafi jurists ruled that a man's prayer was valid if three-quarters of his body was covered (Abou El Fadl 257: note 107). In contrast, some Maliki and Imami jurists ruled that men did not need to cover their '*awrah* during prayers (Abou El Fadl 257: note 107). They treated it as recommended instead of compulsory (Abou El Fadl 257: note 107). In fact, many jurists ruled that the five ritual prayers were obligatory even without clothing (Abou El Fadl 257: note 107). If one had ritually impure clothing, some Imami jurists ruled that it was best to pray in the nude. Friday prayer remained obligatory for some Sunni jurists even if the congregation had no clothing (Abou El Fadl 257: note 107). Consequently, people could pray naked, so long as they formed a single row (Abou El Fadl 257: note 107).

While the notion of nude congregational prayers would scandalize most Muslims today, and even proposing such a possibility could get someone killed, works of Islamic jurisprudence, as well as historical accounts, reveal that there was a time when some Muslim women prayed in the nude or in as little attire as women wear on the seashore in places like South Beach, Florida, Aruba, Australia, Venezuela, Brazil, Spain, and southern France. This is evidence enough that Muslims have not become more tolerant over time. On the contrary, it is proof positive they have grown increasingly intolerant and ultra-conservative over the past thousand years.

When it came to what slave women were required to cover, classical Muslim jurists were generally lax in their rulings. In other words, they issued edicts of convenience to serve the *status quo* and the predatory commercial interests of the time. Some ruled that the '*awrah* of a slave girl was limited to her vagina. Others ruled that it consisted of the area between the navel and the knees (Abou El Fadl 257: note 107). In other words, it was the same as that of free men. These jurists did not view the breasts of female slaves as part of their shameful parts. In fact, Anas ibn Malik (612-709) reports that "The slave-girls of 'Umar used to serve us with uncovered hair and their breasts shaking" (Bayhaqi).

Some jurists held that the '*awrah* of female slaves extended from the chest to the knees and from the arms down to the elbows (Abou El Fadl 257: note 107). Most ruled that female slaves did not have to cover their hair in prayer (Abou El Fadl 257: note 107, 259: note 123 and 127). In fact, Ja'far al-Sadiq explicitly stated that female slaves were not to wear headscarves during prayers (Kulayni). He is also quoted as saying that free Muslim women could show their hair and legs in the presence of their male slaves and that there was no objection to free women holding fast to their black male slaves while riding camels and horses (Kulayni).

Some Hanafi scholars stated that female slaves only had to cover their breasts during prayer but not outside of it (Abou El Fadl 259: note 123). A minority ruled that they should cover their breasts in public (Abou El Fadl 257: note 107). However, the consensus was that slave women could not publicly cover their hair (Abou El Fadl 241, 257: note 107). The aim of this prohibition was to distinguish free women from those that were property. In fact, both 'Umar ibn al-Khattab (c. 586-644) and Muhammad al-Baqir beat female slaves for having the audacity to cover their hair in public, as if they were free women (Ibn Shaybah, Nu'man). This was violently coerced classism. And only a handful of late jurists argued that slave girls should cover their breasts or hair in cases where it could cause *fitnah* or public disorder (Abou El Fadl 259: note 123).

As scandalous as it may seem to many Muslims in our day and age, it was customary for female slaves and servants to appear in public topless in many parts of the Islamic world. They did so in pre-Islamic times (Jebara 109). They did so during the time of the Prophet Muhammad and the four caliphs. In fact, they did so, in some parts, until the end of the Ottoman Empire in the early twentieth century. The proof can be found in plenty of artwork and even photographs. Moreover, as shocking as it may sound, some Muslim women publicly expose their breasts, particularly in parts of black Africa. In fact, the Iranian government has paid black African women to cover their breasts in public to promote greater Islamization in West Africa. As most Iranians would agree, this is a wise way to spend their hard-earned tax money (Taheri 121). Islamists in other parts of the world, particularly in Egypt, have also been paying prominent women, singers, and actresses, to don the *hijab* and end their careers. Still, there is no shortage of Muslim women who wear one-piece bathing suits, bikinis, thongs, and go topless on beaches around the world.

As for free women, the extent of their '*awrah* was subject to dispute. Some scholars claimed that the only thing that free women were required to cover was their vaginas. Others included the breasts in this definition. In fact, they argued that there was nothing inherently shameful in a woman's body. Another group of early scholars ruled that women were not required to cover their hair or calves (Abou El Fadl 257: note 107). In other words, a woman was free to show her hair in public. Moreover, she could wear a skirt or dress that reached her knees.

Some jurists believed women were required to cover their hair, but only in prayer and not in public spaces (Abou El Fadl 257: note 107). Furthermore, while they concluded that women should cover their hair and most of their bodies, some jurists specifically excluded the forearm or the entire arm from the '*awrah* (Abou El Fadl 257: note 107). In other words, women could wear short sleeves or even go sleeveless. Usama Hasan provides a variety of views on the subject. As he explains:

> Jassas reports the following views from different authorities: that a man may look at the hair of his mother, sister, maternal aunt, and paternal aunt, but that it is disliked to look at their legs below the knees (Ibrahim

> al-Nakha'i); it is not allowed for a woman to remove her headcover in front of her brother (Hasan Basri); it is disliked for a man to look or stare at the hair of his daughter or sister (Tawus and Sha'bi). Jassas then provides the rather far-fetched interpretation that these narrations refer to situations where a man may be afflicted with incestuous temptation…
>
> Mahalli and Suyuti state in their commentary on the Qur'an that a woman only needs to cover her body between the navel and knees in front of her father, brothers, and everyone else mentioned in the *ayah* of the headcover, and that therefore she may appear topless in front of them.
>
> Tabari also quotes from Ibn Mas'ud that the "believing women" to whom this *ayah* is addressed refers only to free women and not slaves. This interpretation led some jurists to the view that female slaves were only required to cover their bodies between the navel and knees in public and could therefore walk around topless. The Hanafi jurist al-Jassas says that female slaves are not required to cover their faces or hair and that even men who are strangers may look at their hair, arms, legs below the knees, chests, and breasts.
>
> Most, if not all, of the primary narrations … from early authorities are of disputed authenticity, which partly explains why the jurisprudence based on them is not mainstream… Assuming that at least some of them are authentic, they would appear to illustrate that early understanding of these *ayat* was strongly conditioned by culture and context: for example, the insistence by some jurists that a woman must cover her head in front of her father and brothers. (9-10)

The legal discussions on the extent of the *'awrah* were not theoretical. They reflected lived realities. Considering that, in the minds of the jurists, *hijab* was only required of free women, "the question arises as to why the presence of unveiled slave women and women from other religions in Islamic society, whose numbers have by no means been small, did not rob society of its decency in any way?" (Soroush). Were Muslim men more civilized than they are today? Did they have greater self-control? Was it that breasts were not sexualized? Was it that the pagan Arab *laissez-faire* attitude regarding nudity persisted into early Islam? Or was it that the early Arab Muslims relieved the sexual tension and frustration caused by nude and semi-nude women in the public sphere with their numerous sex slaves? Were they more decent or less decent?

2.5 An Historical Insight into the Dress of Muslim Women

The sculptures and frescoes found in Umayyad palaces, commissioned by early Muslim rulers, depict clad, semi-clad, and unclad women (Stillman 37). Some are naked above the waist, wearing only an *izar*, a wrapping that covers them from the navel to the knees, while others also wear a *sirwal* or undergarment

(Stillman 37). Others wear tight, sleeveless, full-length dresses (37). And yet others wear extremely sheer, see-through blouses (37). Many also wear head veils (37).

The case of Qusayr Amra, in current-day Jordan, is revealing. Built between 723 and 745, by Walid ibn Yazid, who would become the Umayyad caliph Walid II (706-744), a detailed examination of the extensive frescoes that richly decorate the walls of the desert castle, fortress, garrison, and residence palace, provides a vivid representation of the period approximately one hundred years after the passing of the Prophet Muhammad. The audience hall contains a large painting of a woman bathing while admired by a group of men and women. Her hair is uncovered. She is topless and wears a see-through miniskirt (Universes).

To the right of the bathing woman, one finds a group of male athletes wearing the equivalent of bikini briefs (Universes). On the southern arch of the western aisle, one finds the image of a dancing girl. She wears a sheer miniskirt that exposes her calves and parts of her thighs. While covering her breasts, her vest exposes her upper chest and her midriff. She is essentially wearing belly-dancing attire (Universes). On the northern wall of the western aisle, one finds a large painting of a swimming woman. Except for bracelets, she is entirely nude, with her posterior prominently above water, along with her back, arms, legs, and one breast (Universes). To the lower right, one finds the painting of another woman. Her hair is uncovered. Except for her jewelry, she is basically nude, with her breasts and legs prominently displayed (Universes).

The eastern wall of the apodyterium features a nude woman in contemplation. Although her pubis is concealed, the medium breasts are on prominent display (Universes). In the southern tympanum tepidarium, one finds three nude women: one is facing away, holding a child, providing a full view of her legs, buttocks, and back. On the left is a seated woman with long, flowing hair. Only her upper body has survived; however, her left breast is evident. On the right, one finds a woman carrying a bucket, providing full frontal nudity (Universes). The eastern tympanum tepidarium depicts another nude woman holding a baby (Universes). The western tympanum also represents a bathing scene with more full-frontal nudity (Universes).

The case of Khirbat al-Mafjar, another fortified palace complex, located in the Palestinian city of Jericho in the West Bank, which is considered to have been constructed during the reign of Hisham ibn ‘Abd al-Malik (r. 724-743), or perhaps as a residence for his nephew, Walid II, is equally enthralling. As Betsy Williams notes, “The most striking interior decoration at the site is undoubtedly the stucco sculptures of partially nude women. These figures are depicted wearing skirts with twisted belts and with elaborate hairstyles.” One such statue features a topless woman with thick, styled, hair, earrings, and dark eyes surrounded by eyeliner and eye shadow. She wears a miniskirt that goes from below her belly button to above her knees. In another one of his desert retreats, Qasar al-Mshatta, in modern-day Jordan, was found the remains of another statue; in this case, a female torso depicting a woman in bikini briefs and a sheer throw-over. Amazingly, she is dressed in the same attire that women wear around pools, beaches, and resorts around the world today. What did early Muslim women wear to swim at pools and beaches in the seventh and eighth centuries? It most certainly was not the *burqini*. It was very much the bikini.

Although these artistic renditions date from several generations after the rise of Islam, and some decorate a hammam or bath complex, they demonstrate that women used to expose their hair and bodies in the presence of unrelated males and that some women even wore headscarves while exposing their breasts. Consequently, there was no correlation between the *khimar* and modesty, as understood by later Muslims. It was merely a fashion accessory, among others. The claim that these images depict a den of debauchery, a type of Playboy mansion, that they were produced by non-Muslims following Byzantine motifs and are therefore not representative of the "Islamic" clothing of the period, is inadmissible. On the contrary, they provide snapshots of the past and an accurate depiction of the dress that prevailed in several social settings.

We are not dealing with an isolated case. In fact, "nudes and semi-nudes were rather common in Umayyad caliphal art" (Ettinghausen 597). The semi-nude portraits of the Virgin Mary, painted by Frithjof Schuon (1907-1998), have caused much controversy in some circles, and were viewed as deviating from Islam. However, when viewed in the context of the history of Islamic art, and art in general, they form part of a continuum. In fact, they follow the traditional depiction of the Goddess. There is indeed nudity in Islamic art, even in religious Islamic art. In early Fatimid amulets, Fatimah al-Zahra was represented with a prominent vagina, and bulging breasts, in the same fashion as previous goddesses had been (Pérez Rivera). Sacrifices were made in her name.

The adulation of the Goddess was transferred to the Virgin Mary. Likewise, the adulation of the Goddess and the Virgin Mary was transferred to Fatimah, who was given the very same titles of *al-Batul*, the Virgin, the Blessed One, the Resplendent, the Queen of Heaven, and the Creatress. It is called religious syncretism. For some, the fact that Muhammad described Fatimah as *umm abiha*, the mother of her father, and that her name derives from *fatir* or creator, suggests that she was the manifestation of the Sacred Feminine that was the source of his wisdom (Azal). In actual fact, *umm abiha* was a common epithet that fathers gave affectionately to their daughters. That did not stop extremists from exalting her status beyond the acceptable. Some Shiite and Sufi sources claim that Fatimah, along with Muhammad, 'Ali, and the rest of the twelve Imams, existed prior to creation, and everything that exists was made out of their light. Others claim that they control the universe. While some Shiites and Sufis pray to Fatimah, and ask her intercession, others went so far as to deify her outright.

There was no prohibition against figurative and nude art in early Islam. "After all," notes Amr El-Abyad, "slave-girls walked around topless."

Consequently, nudity was treated as a reflection of reality. When the ‘Abbasids came to power, as was the case of other puritans, every attempt was made to eradicate all traces of previous, “un-Islamic” rule, and practices. Figurative art was destroyed or painted over. Manuscripts were burned. It was a veritable iconoclastic purge. While rare, examples of nudity in Islamic art have survived throughout the centuries, particularly in illuminated manuscripts, and erotic manuals. As much as images of Muhammad infuriate ignorant, intolerant, Islamists, there are many surviving portrayals of Muhammad, and other sacred figures, all made by Muslim artists, that have survived, showing that it was not viewed as a problematic issue in the past (see Grabar, Gruber, Rahim, and others).

Even though the dress code eventually became increasingly stricter, so much so that many women were entirely wrapped and veiled by the end of ‘Abbasid rule, the situation was more relaxed outside of the Middle East. Ibn Battutah (1304-1369), who narrated what he observed during his travels throughout the fourteenth-century Islamic world, came across many nude, topless, or scantily clad Muslim women. Speaking of the Muslim women of the Maldives, he observed that:

> Most of them wear only one apron from the navel to the ground, the rest of their bodies being uncovered. It is thus that they walk abroad in the bazaars and elsewhere. When I was a *qadi* there, I tried to put an end to this practice and ordered them to wear clothes, but I met with no success. No woman was admitted to my presence in a lawsuit unless her body was covered, but apart from that I was unable to affect anything. Some of them wear shirts in addition to the waistcloth, their shirts having short and wide sleeves.... They wear anklets also and necklaces of gold on their chests. (Ibn Battutah 234)

When he traveled to the Land of the Blacks in Africa, he noted that the women of the Masuffah of Iwalatan “have no shame before men and do not veil themselves, yet they are punctilious about their prayers” (Ibn Battutah 284). Although they did not cover their hair, he never questioned the validity of their ritual prayers.

Speaking of the Muslims of Mali, he observed that they avoided injustice, provided safety in their country, were punctual in their prayers, and paid great attention to memorizing the Qur’an (Ibn Battutah 289-290). On the negative side, he noted that:

> Among their bad practices are that the women servants, slave girls, and young daughters appear naked before people, exposing their genitals. Women who come before the sultan are naked and unveiled, and so are his daughters. On the night of the twenty-seventh of Ramadan, I saw about a hundred naked slave girls come out of his palace with food; with them were two daughters of the sultan with full breasts, and they too had no veil. (Ibn Battutah 290)

So, evidently, it was not just slave girls but free Muslim girls and women who exposed their breasts and their genitals. Ibn Battutah, who came from a more conservative culture, disapproved of such customs. Imagine hundreds of topless teenage girls attending the celebration of Laylat al-Qadr at the spiritual peak of Ramadan. At the same time, however, he never doubted that these skin-showing people were believing and devout Muslims. He demonstrated a level of tolerance that would be difficult to find among most Muslims in our day and age. Moreover, he was a Sunni Muslim cleric from the Maliki school of jurisprudence. Why, then, must the Middle Eastern *burka*, *niqab*, or *hijab* be the model of Islamic dress for women? Why not the traditional attire of the Muslim women from India, Indonesia, Africa, and the Maldives? Why the cultural and religious imperialism and imposition? Why homogeneity as opposed to sartorial diversity and plurality?

2.6 Cultural Subjectivity and Extremist Modalities

Although there was great latitude regarding matters of clothing across cultures and geography, most Muslim jurists, namely, those whose opinions prevailed since they found state sponsorship, concluded that the '*awrah* of women consisted of their entire body, excluding the face and hands. The Imamis eventually extended this to the feet. And some Sunni jurists, who were implacably intolerant, insisted upon covering the face as well, a position adopted by a minority of Shiite jurists. In so doing, they did not rely on explicit or implicit evidence from the Qur'an or sayings of the Prophet. On the contrary, they adopted and mandated the pre-Islamic custom of female face-veiling. We know from Strabo (d. 23) that some Persian women veiled their faces in the first century. We also know from Tertullian (d. c. 220), a prolific early Christian author, that some pagan Arab women veiled their entire faces, except for the eyes, in the third century. They did not veil out of modesty. They did so to emphasize their most erotic features: their eyes.

Influenced by their pre-Islamic cultural practices and inspired by the face-veiling of some elite Byzantine women, Arab and Persian jurists took the word '*awrah*, which merely means private parts, shameful parts, and genitals, and stretched it to encompass the entirety of the female form. She could not be seen. She could not be smelled. She could not be heard. Her mere presence in the public sphere was intolerable. The mistakes that male jurists made were many. The consequences of their rulings have been catastrophic for women's rights in the Muslim world, producing socio-economic, spiritual, and psychological damage.

When interpreting 7:26, Muslim jurists focused on the segment that says, "cover your shame [*sa'wat*]," and applied it to Muslim women. However, in the verse in question, the Qur'an addresses all of humanity: "O you Children of Adam!" (7:26). Consequently, the dress code it invokes applies to human beings collectively, not Muslim men and women specifically. It is a universal minimum requirement. It distinguishes the civilized from the savage. It separates human beings from apes and animals. As Toby Fischer-Mirkin notes in her study on the psychology of dress, public sexuality is unthinkable in any civilized society: "propriety dictates that the body be at least partially covered at all times" (65). In fact, "revealing a little is, and always has been, much more tantalizing than baring everything" (58).

As for the Qur'anic verse in question, it is the parallel of Genesis 3:21 in which God states that He made garments for Adam and Eve and clothed them. Moreover, when the Qur'an speaks of "the garment of God-consciousness that is the best," it is an echo of Isaiah 61:10 in which the biblical prophet praises God for "clothing me with the garments of salvation" and covering him in "the robe of righteousness." For Muslim mystics, with a deep as opposed to superficial understanding of the Qur'an, these *hijab* verses are not literal. They are metaphorical. Consider, for example, the commentary, exegesis, and unveiling of the verses provided by Kashani (1252-1261-1329-1334):

> "[Then Satan whispered to them] that he might manifest to them that which was hidden to them of their shameful parts," (7:20) in other words, that he might make manifest upon them, by making them incline to [physical] nature, what had been veiled from them upon their disengagement from physical affairs, corporeal pleasures, despicable traits of character, animal acts and predatorial and bestial acts which man is ashamed to manifest and is averse to revealing, and which manliness impels him to conceal, since these constitutes shameful parts from the point of view of the intellect which disdains them and deems them vile. (262)
>
> "[O Children of Adam! We have sent down on you] a garment to conceal your shameful parts," (7:26) that is to say, a divine law that covers up the vile aspects of your descriptions and the lewdness of your acts, and feathers, that is, beauty that will distance you from any likeness to neglected cattle and that will adorn you with virtuous character traits and beautiful acts, and the garment of God-fearing, that is, the attribute of abstinence and caution against the attribute of the soul, that is better, than the sum total of the pillars of the law, since it is the fundament and the basis of religion. (263)

As Sachiko Murata notes,

> The Koran addresses the children of Adam, telling them what conclusions they should draw from the story. God has sent down a "garment" to cover those "shameful parts" that were exposed when Adam and Eve ate of the fruit. The shameful parts are the ugly character traits that grow up in the rational soul when it becomes attached to the world. The garment is the revealed law, the Sharia,

> which rectifies character traits and brins the soul into harmony with the intellect. (276)

For some Sufi exegetes, the *hijab* / *khimar* / *jilbab* / *saw'ah* verses do not mandate a code of modest dress. They provide a plan for character development and spiritual perfection.

While Qur'anic and Biblical verses call for some modicum of modesty, their focus is more on morality than attire. When the Qur'an asks women to cover their bosoms with their shawls, it signifies that they should clothe their hearts in modesty, humility, and piety. Like Jesus in the Gospel, who criticized those who circumcised themselves physically but did not circumcise their hearts spiritually, the Qur'an implicitly criticizes technical codes of modest dress that do not correspond with the ethical condition and state of the soul. Abdolkarim Souroush (b. 1945), the Iranian reformist intellectual, is not the first to note that the jurists have reduced *hijab* to an article of clothing while ignoring its mythical element.

The story of Adam and Eve, in the Bible and the Qur'an, is precisely that, a story, a story of origins. In contrast, the people of the Andes believe that their ancestors entered this world "fully clothed, wearing the dress which identified the sex and ethnic origin of the wearer" (Barnes and Eicher 2). As Ruth Barnes (b. 1947) and Joanne Bubolz Eicher (b. 1930), specialists in fashion, explain, dress is a cultural phenomenon. It is a question of identity. It links people geographically and historically to a particular community. It includes and excludes. It conveys social and economic status. It categorizes people in terms of age and gender. It can be connected to political or spiritual power (1-2). Not only is it an indicator of gender, but it is also a producer of gender (7). Dress operates according to the same parameters in Judaism, Christianity, Islam, and other religions and cultures. Religion is only one of many factors at play.

What is feminine, what is masculine, what is appropriate, and what is inappropriate varies tremendously depending on time and place. It is entirely relative. Take the symbolism of hair, for example:

> Long loose hair in women once indicated youth and virginity, while braided or bound hair could symbolize either a married woman or, conversely, a courtesan. In Christian art, the redeemed and sanctified St. Mary of Magdalene is often shown with very long, loose hair as a symbol of her chastity, love, and humility. (154)

In some cultures, a woman who exposes her hair is a harlot. In others, it is precisely the opposite: a woman who wears a veil is a whore. For some, it symbolizes piety, peace, and emancipation. For others, it is a symbol of patriarchal submission, extremism, and terrorism. As Mark O'Connell and Raje Airey note, "the symbolism of the veil has varied in different times and places according to social, religious, and political conditions" (64). In Iran, during the anti-Shah movement, "black veils became revolutionary symbols" (64). However, "upon establishing an Islamic republic, the veil once again became a part of the state's definition of women" (64). "Modern Islamic feminists," however, "are now trying to differentiate between patriarchal traditions and the values of Islam, with the veil now a complex symbol, often meaning different things to different people, affected by religion, culture, or gender" (64).

In Iran, the veil has shifted from a symbol of freedom to one of suppression. Islamic feminism, however, is an oxymoron. A feminist puts women first. An Islamist puts Islam first. An "Islamic feminist" wishes to put a veneer of feminism on Islam. Rather than fight for women, Bestandji notes, they defend their patriarchal oppression and servitude (2021: 239). It is part of women's inhumanity toward women. As Mahnaz Afkhami (b. 1941), an Iranian Muslim and liberal feminist, elucidates,

> Our difference with Islamic feminists is that we don't try to fit feminism in the Qur'an. We say that women have certain inalienable rights. The epistemology of Islam is contrary to women's right… I call myself a Muslim and a feminist. I am not an Islamic feminist -- that's a contradiction in terms. (Khan 2018)

Hair has meaning; however, its symbolism varies throughout time and place and from gender to gender. As Paola García notes:

> No person, male or female, living in a modern society, let's say, contemporary America, Europe, or Asia (and even many parts of North Africa and the Middle East), would consider a woman showing her hair to be immodest. Neither are men these days particularly provoked by the sight of a woman's hair. Among today's morally questionable fashions and cultural practices, a woman's uncovered hair is hardly a temptation or a show of moral laxity. But let's imagine that it were in fact a "temptation." Let's pretend present-day men were somehow so weak as to be provoked by glancing a woman's hair, still, the solution is within themselves. Modesty is also required of, and was first mandated to, men: they are ordered to lower their gaze, purify their thoughts and dress modestly too. The answer is not for women to make it their central preoccupation to ensure by all means that they do not cause men any impure thoughts. This is, again, absurd: Islam teaches that in the eyes of God, each person is responsible for his or her own actions.

As for the interpretation of 7:26, the early commentaries of the Qur'an are intriguing. Tabari (839-923), the historian, jurist, and exegete of the Qur'an, cites a long list of opinions. Some scholars held that the verse was revealed regarding the nude circumambulation of the Ka'bah. The pagan Arabs believed that no clothing was worthy of the gods, and hence, they appeared before them in the nude, in their birthday suits. Some commentators mentioned that the

Quraysh only allowed clothing made in Mecca to be worn in the precinct of the Ka'bah. In other words, local merchants and traders had cornered the market to profit even more from the pilgrimage. In response, some people preferred to perform their religious rituals while naked rather than get bamboozled. Some sources claim that male pilgrims would circumambulate nude during the day while female pilgrims would circumambulate nude during the night. And yet others, cited by Tabari, explained that "There were people among the Arabs who used to go around naked in their homes." According to this interpretation, the revelation was directed at Arabs, regardless of religion. It was only in the year 630 that the Prophet Muhammad sent Abu Hurayrah and 'Ali to Mecca to declare that after that year "no naked person will be allowed to circumambulate the Ka'bah" (Bukhari). The goal of God, the Qur'an, and the Prophet was not to shroud human beings and conceal all human skin. They did not aspire to eradicate semi-nudity. The objective was far less ambitious. It was to prohibit public nudity.

There is no doubt, however, that some of the Arabs of the seventh century used to appear naked in both their homes and in public. As Yedida Kalfon Stillman (1946-1998), a Sephardic scholar from Morocco, who specialized in Islamic and Jewish culture, points out, Jahili society had an "easygoing attitude to nudity" (11). Far from commanding the *khimar*, the *hijab*, the *jilbab*, the *chador*, the *niqab*, and the *burqa*, 7:26 was discouraging nudity and calling for public and private decency. And even so, the Qur'an stresses that piety and righteousness are superior to clothing. As we say in French, *ce n'est pas l'habit qui fait the moine*, namely, the clothing does not make the monk. In fact, medieval Arabic dictionaries define *libas* or "clothing" as "that which conceals or covers the pudenda" (Stillman 11). In other words, if your genitals are covered, you are considered clothed.

While Muslim jurists insist on the requirement to "cover your shame" (7:26), imposing identical dress upon women, typically black, that destroys their individuality and denies their femininity, they ignore that the purpose of clothing was not only to maintain a minimum amount of decency but also to protect from the elements as well as to adorn. Hence, the claim that all beauty must be covered is incorrect and unsubstantiated. The same applies to the opposition to colors and the imposition of a black patriarchal prison uniform. Consequently, as far as the Qur'an is concerned, women may dress as they please, and beautify themselves as they wish, so long as they cover the minimum that decency requires to be covered.

As part of their androcrentic analysis, Muslim jurists invariably ignore the overriding element of the verse in question, namely, that the focus is not on physical covering but on the covering and protection that is provided by genuine modesty and chastity, namely, "the raiment of righteousness, that is the best" (7:26), an echo of the prophet Isaiah who clothed ancient loins in righteousness (11:5). Unlike Muslim jurists, who overemphasized the outer, the Qur'an emphasizes the inner. As Amina Wadud (b. 1952), the African American Muslim theologian, explains in *Inside the Gender Jihad: Women's Reform in Islam*:

> The *hijab* of coercion and the *hijab* of choice look the same. The *hijab* of oppression and the *hijab* of liberation look the same. The *hijab* of deception and the *hijab* of integrity look the same. You can no more tell the extent of a Muslim woman's sense of personal bodily integrity or piety from 45 inches of cloth than you can spot a fly on a wall at two thousand feet. (219-220)

Many Muslims have mocked the alleged hypocrisy of women who wear black outfits that cover them from head to toe, even covering their faces, only to remove them on flights out of Saudi Arabia and Iran and replace them with skimpy and sexy dresses. As Mustafa Akyol (b. 1972), the Turkish journalist and author, has noted, they are not choosing hypocrisy: "rather, it was imposed on them… rigid religious laws" were "forcing them to do something they did not want to do" (2).

For many Muslims, *hijab* has become the sixth pillar of Islam, or even the first for that matter, even though classical theologians never placed it among the foundations of faith or the branches of religion. Even Mehran Kamrava (b. 1964), the Iranian American Professor of Government, claims that "*hijab* goes to the core of women's place and position in Islam" (220). Many Muslims judge a woman's Islamicity most superficially. It is religious reductionism. If she wears *hijab*, she is a good Muslim. If she does not wear *hijab*, then she is a bad Muslim. However, some harlots and hypocrites wear *hijab* and pious and righteous women do not. Some supermodels remain chaste until marriage. Some virgins wear bikinis. The *hijab* means nothing. The heart means everything. We are supposed to judge people based on their character, not their clothing. We do not judge books by their covers. After all, the Qur'an teaches us: "the best dress is the dress of *taqwa*" (7:26). The Prophet himself asserted that "God does not look at your appearance… but rather, He looks at your hearts and actions" (Muslim). It is dishonest to claim that the headscarf is mandatory according to the Qur'an, thereby driving scores of women away from Islam. By and large, the people who are obsessed with imposing the *hijab* do not show the same zeal when it comes to religious commandments that are vital to Muslims.

Without righteousness, wearing a *hijab* is worthless. And what is better than *hijab* is piety. Modesty without piety is not meritorious. Ideally, piety will increase physical modesty. The combination of both is the best. The focus should not be on dress first. It should be on faith and righteousness. The turban does not make the scholar. Dressing like a doctor does not make one a doctor. Putting on a costume of a firefighter does not make one a firefighter. Likewise, wearing a headscarf, an *abayah*, a *chador*, or a *niqab* does not signify that a woman is good and God-fearing. As Nimat Hafez Barazangi (b. 1943), the Syrian American who specializes in Islam and gender, has understood:

> A woman who self-identifies with the Qur'anic worldview realizes that Islamic teachings regarding modesty are neither rigid nor intended to make her feel guilty of tempting the males, and neither is following these guidelines a function of control, submission, segregation, or restriction of action, as usually perceived, and practiced. These guidelines are for individual chastity and social protocol, with the aim of respecting privacy and lineage. If these teachings are not internalized as such, they can also not be fully realized in practice, even if the individual's behavior suggests otherwise. A woman who practices wearing the cloak and a head covering without understanding the above modesty principle, for instance, is not practicing Islam, but a social custom. On the contrary, a woman who internalizes Islamic principles of morality and justice demands the observation of the modesty principle not in terms of its prohibitive, rigid law for females, as is rationalized by some male interpreters, but in terms of the guiding principles of the Qur'an on morality for both males and females. (2006: 65-66)

As Barazangi points out, '*awrah* is not about a particular part of the body or its entirety: it is about modesty and chastity. To impose the *khimar*, a customary practice of men and women in the desert environment, only on women, and to extend its meaning to *hijab*, a curtain or divider, to separate females from males "results in injustice for the female and for the Qur'an" (2006: 66). There is no *purdah* or sexual segregation in Qur'anic Islam. It is neither traditional nor moderate. It is a negative foreign adoption and a detrimental innovation plain and simple. It is a step backwards from the advances introduced by the Qur'an and which were supposed to continue.

The very concept of cloistering women is profoundly pagan. In ancient Mesopotamia, among the Sumerians, Babylonians, and Assyrians, a priestess, or sacred prostitute, was consecrated to the temple. At the same time, their female followers, the wives of men, were cloistered in their homes. A wife was not valued for her beauty or femininity, but for her faithfulness and fertility (Stol 404). A good and respectable wife stayed in her home while a whore walked the streets, particularly at night (Stol 403-404). In Sumer and Babylonia, Stol notes, "the woman on the street would easily be taken for a prostitute" (399). Any woman who walked around in public by herself, and stood on the street, was one who was devoid of family ties and protection. It should be recalled that the so-called *hijab* verses were revealed in relation to married Muslim women going out at night and being taken for prostitutes. As such, they were instructed to "cover their breasts and the jewels on their breasts" as a signal that they were not selling their bodies. This surely says something about the level of culture in

Medina and Arabia at the time. It also indicates that Medina, under the rule of Muhammad, was not some Islamic utopia, filled with virtuous men and women, unless one considers lascivious men who solicited the wives of the Prophet for sex to be pious and righteous.

For ultra-misogynist Muslims, women belong in a harem or *harim*, a place prohibited to all men but the husband. A woman is a *hurmah*. She is property prohibited to other men to the exclusion of her spouse. These words are all derived from the same root as *haram* or forbidden. They all convey the idea of social isolation of women (Stol 399). These words, however, trace back to the Akkadian *harimtu*, which means, "a woman set apart," but which signified a whore, a *qadishtu* or sacred slut from which we get the Biblical Hebrew, *qadesha*, as a "devoted woman."

By confining, covering, and controlling women, Muslims are replicating the social and religious practices of Middle Eastern pagans. These customs predated the Prophet Muhammad by thousands of years. They survived during his lifetime. Despite his attempts to reform or eradicate them, they were embraced, Islamicized, and emphasized by early Muslims, both laity, and scholars, and continue to be practiced, perpetuated, and promoted in our times. The pagan and polytheistic practices of the ancient Mesopotamians, Sumerians, Babylonians, and Assyrians were rebranded as Islamic, including, patriarchy, sexual segregation, the hyper-sexualization of women, veils, and all.

Although it prevailed in certain cultures prior to the spread of Islam, and was integrated into the religion, in other parts, the custom of secluding women only spread gradually among Muslims. Hence, it was not a generalized practice. In early eighteenth-century Egypt, for example, only 2.5% of homes had separate entrances and quarters for women. By the middle of that century, it rose to 40%. However, by its end, 84% of the homes were sexually segregated (El Guindi 2000: 151).

As for the time of the Prophet Muhammad, the evidence points to integration rather than segregation (Abou-Taleb 194-196). The Messenger of God asked a woman to ride with him on his mule; he stroked the neck of a woman with a lump; he mingled with women; he placed a necklace around a woman's neck; he placed a garment on a woman; he used to visit women and sleep in their homes; he rested his head on a woman's lap while she applied kohl to his eyes and inspected his hair (Abou-Taleb 195). As Amira Abou-Taleb, the theologian, observes, "it is difficult to reconcile the above anecdotes with the myriad mentions… that the Prophet refused to shake hands with women" (195). As the author recognizes, sexual segregation entered Islam through foreign Persian influence (Abou-Taleb 198).

One of the most misinterpreted verses of all, when it comes to Muslim women's dress, is 24:31. Muslim jurists claim that this verse commands women to cover themselves, from head to toe, concealing their entire bodies, with the exception of their hands and feet. However, according to some, even these parts are supposed to be covered. Nevertheless, others include the mandatory covering of the face. The text, however, does not support any of these fanciful and forced interpretations. The scholars in question seek to squeeze water from a stone. As Bahram Eftekhari recognizes, the verse merely "describes chaste attire; decent without drawing attention, as implied in 'normally displayed'" (224). It does not specify a restrictive dress code. As Nikki Keddie (b. 1930), the American scholar of Eastern, Iranian, and women's history, explains:

> This verse was later interpreted as meaning covering the whole body, including hair, and most of the face. This interpretation is illogical. If the whole body and face were meant, there would be no reason to tell women to veil their bosoms specifically, while the later interpretation of "adornment" to mean everything but the hands, feet and (possibly) the face is a forced one. (22)

Some of the female companions of the Prophet used to raise their skirts when nursing warriors in battle, exposing their ankles and calves (Bukhari). Women, like 'A'ishah, used to ride horses, donkeys, and camels. Considering they wore dresses and not pants, they could not ride without exposing parts of their legs and possibly their thighs. The Prophet, however, never prohibited women from mounting animals. As Tabari (839- 923), Abu Yusuf (738-798), and Sarakhsi (1009-1090) noted, some early authorities did not include the arms or forearms in the '*awrah* of women. As Ibn 'Abidin (1784-1836) noted, "a minority opinion ... states that her arms are not prohibited" (Amin 2000: 38). For example, it was understood that women who worked in bakeries could roll up their sleeves. Other accommodations were made for women who worked in other fields. And, as Ibn 'Ashur (1879-1973) noted, a minority of early jurists ruled that women could expose their heads and hair in public (Hasan 12). In his words:

> the practices mentioned in the *hadith* were, according to the Arabic traditions of the time, indications of a woman's lack of chastity... The prohibition of these practices was actually aimed at preventing promiscuity or the violation of the woman's honor when people associate her with such traits. Similarly, we read the following verse in the Qur'an: "O Prophet! Tell your wives and your daughters, as well as [other] believing women, that they should draw over themselves some of their outer garments [when in public]: this will be more conducive to their being recognized [as decent women] and not annoyed" (33:59). This is a legislation that took into consideration an Arab tradition, and therefore it does not necessarily apply to people whose women do not wear this dress style. (139-140)

When interpreting 24:31, jurists have focused on the requirement of women "not to display their beauty and ornaments." For them, this applies to the near entirety or entirety of the female form, including, for some, their very voices.

Women are not to be seen, and they are not to be heard. They are *fitnah*: sources of sedition, temptation, and corruption in society. They are "omnisexual" as Fatima Mernissi (1940- 2015), the Moroccan sociologist expressed (Badran 170-171). However, what exactly constitutes the "beauty" of a woman?

> Is it her eyes, her cheeks, her hair, her nose…? It has turned out to be an obsession of many Muslim men to demand that a Muslim woman must cover her hair… The tragedy is heightened by the Qur'anic fact that idol worship is the absolute worst sin; worse than murder…, adultery, and corruption. Nowhere in the Qur'an do we find the requirement that a woman must cover her hair. The Qur'an orders Muslim men and women to dress modestly and subdue their eyes and tells the Muslim women … to lengthen their dresses and cover their chests (24:31 & 33:59). Many of these men … distort the Arabic word *khimar*, which … means "cover:" any kind of cover, over anything… They … insist that it is a cover that must come from above, after covering the woman's hair. They even dig up some Arabic dictionaries, written by equally oppressive men, that advocate the same absurdity… Since it is God's law that those with doubt in their hearts will always dwell on the multi-meaning verses, we have to thank God for exposing them… (Masjid Tuscon: "The Woman's Hair")

To claim that the word *zinah*, which means finery, applies to the entirety of women, save an eye, is extreme semantic stretching. It is a coerced interpretation. If God wanted women to cover their hair and specific parts of their bodies, He could have said so directly. In fact, He was clear about the need for them to cover their private parts, namely, their pudenda, in 7:26. Similar verses, which ask women not to show their ornaments, are found in the Bible. However, these are not applied to the female form. They discourage women from flaunting their wealth and jewels. They discourage the ostentatious display of wealth. They encourage modesty: "I want women to be modest in their appearance" (1 Timothy 2:9). Hair, however, was not required to be covered as it was a covering: "If a woman has long hair, it is a glory to her: for [her] hair is given to her for a covering" (1 Corinthians 11:15).

2.7 Christian Influences on Islamic Dress

The *Didascalia Apostolorum*, namely, *The Teachings of the Apostles*, directly addresses the veil. This apocryphal work, attributed to the Twelve Apostles, which belongs to the genre of Church Orders, is believed to have been written by a bishop from northern Syria in the third century. The work, which appears to have been in circulation in Arabia before the emergence of Islam, finds echoes in the Qur'an.

"Let the woman be submissive to her husband," states the *Didascalia*, "because the head of the woman is the man" (Gibson 8), an order which is also translated as "And let a woman also be subject to her husband, because the head of the woman is the man" (Connolly). This order finds its parallel in the Qur'an's "Men are the protectors and maintainers of women because God has made one of them to excel the other" (4:34). Addressing matters of modesty, the *Didascalia* orders women as follows:

> If thou wishest to be faithful [*mhmnt*'], please thy husband only [*l-b'lky*], and when thou walkest in the marketplace, cover thy head with thy garment, that by thy veil the greatness of thy beauty be covered; do not adorn the face of thine eyes, but look down and walk veiled... (DA III, 26, 5-11, Gibson 9-10)

R. Hugh Connolly (1873-1948), a monk and scholar, who specialized in Syriac studies, translates the same portion as such:

> If thou wouldst be a faithful woman, please thy husband only. And when thou walkest in the street, cover thy head with thy robe, that by reason of thy veil thy great beauty may be hidden. And adorn not thy natural face; but walk with downcast looks, being veiled.

The segment in question shares striking parallels with the following Qur'anic verses:

> And say to the believing women [*mu'minat*] that they should lower their gaze and guard their modesty; that they should not display their beauty and ornaments except what must ordinarily appear thereof; that they should draw their coverings over their bosoms and not display their beauty except to their husbands [*li-bu'ulatihinna*]... and that they should not strike their feet in order to draw attention to their hidden ornaments. (24:31)

As David Stephan Powers (b.1951), the American scholar of Near Eastern Studies, duly notes:

> Besides the clear thematic parallels between the two texts, one also finds clear linguistic parallels, such as *mhmnt*' and *mu'minat* as well as *l-b'lky* and *li-bu'ulatihinna*. Once again, these thematic and linguistic parallels prove the existence of a common legal environment which suggests that the audience of the Qur'an was familiar with the Syriac *Didascalia*. In the same way that it does with the Talmud, the Qur'an modifies certain rules of the Syriac *Didascalia* in order to adapt them to an Arab context. (636; cf. Zellentin 38-39)

Furthermore, although Powers mentions them not, the following Qur'anic verses also resonate with the teachings of the *Didascalia*:

> O Prophet! Tell your wives and your daughters and the women of the believers to draw their cloaks close round them [when they go abroad].

> That will be better, so that they may be recognized and not annoyed. God is ever Forgiving, Merciful. (33:59)
>
> O you Children of Adam! We have bestowed on you a raiment to cover your shame as well as to be an adornment to you. But the raiment of righteousness, that is the best. Such are among the Signs of God, that they may receive admonition. (7:26)
>
> O Consorts of the Prophet! Ye are not like any of the [other] women: If ye do fear [God], be not too complaisant of speech, lest one in whose heart is a disease should be moved with desire: but speak ye a speech that is just. And be dignified in your houses, and make not a dazzling display, like that of the former Times of Ignorance. (33:32-33)

Compare these Qur'anic verses to the following orders from the *Didascalia*:

> O chaste woman! Do not adorn thyself so as to please other men, and do not plait the plaits of harlotry, nor wear the garments of lasciviousness, nor put on golden shoes, that thou mayest be like those that are such, that thou attract not to thyself those that are captivated by such things. Even if thou sinnest not by this act of abomination, nevertheless in this thou sinnest, that thou obliges and makest him to lust after thee. (Gibson 9)

If the *Didascalia* states that believing women should cover their heads from all men other than their husbands, the Qur'an speaks of believing women covering their beauty and their bosoms from non-related males. The *Didascalia* is clear about covering the hair with a veil. The Qur'an is not. It is clear about covering the bosom. As Jesus taught, the spirit of the law prevails over its letter. If the *Didascalia* only allows women to show their beauty to their husbands, the Qur'an allows them to show their beauty to:

> their husbands, their fathers, their husbands' fathers, their sons, their husbands' sons, their brothers, or their brothers' sons or their sisters' sons, or their women or the servants whom their right hands possess, or male servants free of physical needs, or small children who have no sense of the shame of sex. (24:31)

Moreover, while the *Didascalia* is stricter in the sense of only allowing women to show their beauty to their husbands, it is more flexible than Islamic law in that it allows women to wash themselves in mixed gender public baths when women-only facilities are unavailable on the condition they do so "with chastity and modesty and bashfulness and moderation" (Gibson 10).

Although the Qur'an endorses the veiling of women, notes theologian Holger Michael Zellentin (b. 1976), it altered its application shifting the veil from the head to the bosom (36), expanding the obligation from married women to unmarried women, broadening the category of exempted males from husbands to close male family members, and requiring both men and women to cast down their looks (40). "While the *Didascalia* emphasizes the veiling of the head," writes Zellentin, "the Qur'an emphasizes that of the bosom (even if later Muslim tradition understood it in line with the *Didascalia*)" (40). The veil, however, is conspicuously absent from the *Constitutiones Apostolorum* or *Apostolic Constitutions*, where the emphasis is placed on lowering the gaze, the covering of women, and the need to conceal one's beauty (40).

Considering that the Qur'an was manifestly conversing with scores of canonical and apocryphal Jewish and Christian sources, its additions and omissions are significant. It de-emphasizes or ignores certain aspects while it emphasizes others. In some cases, the Qur'an modifies or corrects Jewish and Christian accounts to serve its purpose. The Qur'an assumes its audience is familiar with a rich literary, legal, and religious universe. Unless one is familiar with the Qur'an's sub-text, one can hardly hope to have a clear, consistent, and accurate understanding of the text. Muslims look at the plant of the Qur'an while entirely ignoring the existence of its roots. What is more, they fail to understand that it belongs to a species that belongs to a genus, a family, an order, a class, a phylum, a kingdom, a domain, and a life form. Muslim scholars are boxed in. Their interpretations are introverted. They are fixated with a few fields produced at a particular period of time. They know little to nothing of what came after, and even less of what came before. They operate in isolation and echo chambers. They do not have the slightest notion that ideas have genealogies and ancestries. The ignore influences. They are oblivious to origins.

If the Qur'an was alluding to the *Didascalia* when it comes to matters of modest, feminine attire, its author, divine or human, depending on one's perspective, deliberately decided to downplay the covering of the hair with a headscarf. The *Didascalia* calls upon women to cover their heads and hair with their garments or robes. The Qur'an, however, calls upon women to cover their cleavage or bosoms with their *khumur* or shawls, which were worn on the shoulders. Moreover, when the Qur'an does speak of *jalabib* (33:59), it tells women to cover themselves with them or to draw them around themselves, namely, to wrap themselves up. Once again, there is no explicit call to cover the hair, much less the face. One does not legislate through inference, conjecture, or speculation. "If all the trees on the earth were pens and the ocean, with seven more oceans, were ink, they would not suffice to record all the Words of God" (31:27). God does not lack words. His words cannot be exhausted. When God commands, He does not whisper. He does not hint or insinuate. He is precise.

For the conclusion to be true, namely, that the head-covering is obligatory, its initial argument must also be true. However, if the Qur'an does not call for the covering of the hair, then the conclusion that it is obligatory does not follow logically. The jurists claim that "*hijab* is obligatory." They support this argument by arguing that "the Qur'an says that *hijab* is obligatory." Not only is the contention incorrect, but so is the premise used to support it. The argument lacks logical validity. While the Qur'an does not command the veil, early

Muslim scholars absorbed Christian teachings. St. Paul, for example, claimed that "a woman… brings shame on her head if she prays… bare headed" (1 Corinthians 11: 5). This command to veil one's hair was taken from Jewish practice; however, it only applied during prayer. It was not required to be worn permanently. As Ruth Peles Rubinstein (d. 2019), a sociologist of fashion, notes in *Dress Codes*:

> Between AD 100 and 500, the church fathers defined the fundamental characteristics of seductive attire as ornamentation, varied colors of clothing, and styles of dress that exposed body parts. Clement of Alexandria (ca AD 150-220) argued that to prevent male transgression, women should cover their bodies from head to toe… "Their dresses should not be overtly soft and clinging and should be hemmed below the ankles rather than above the knees… For that style of dress is grave and protects her from being gazed at." "And," he added, "she will not fall who puts before her eyes modesty and her shawl; nor will she invite another to fall into sin by uncovering her face."
>
> Clement required that women wear veils but forbade them to circumvent the purpose by wearing purple ones because colors attract attention, and "inflame lusts." As Enoch … argued, "If God wanted dresses made of purple and scarlet wool, he would have created purple and scarlet sheep…" Clement complained that certain ornaments used by women served as symbols of adultery… Tertullian attributed to Enoch the observation that women learned about cosmetics from the fallen angels.
>
> The objection to ornament and the injunction against adornment was clearly expressed by Cyprian in … *The Clothing of a Virgin*: " Let your countenance remain in you incorrupt, your neck unadorned… let not rings be made in your ears, nor precious chains of bracelets and necklaces encircle your arms or your neck; let your feet be free from golden bands, your hair stained from no dye, and your eyes worthy of beholding God…" In the first Epistle to Timothy, women are advised to "adorn themselves modestly and sensibly in seemly apparel not with braided hair or gold or pearls or costly attire but with good deeds, as befits women who profess religion."
>
> The church's desire to dampen women's sexual allure by requiring that they keep their heads and bodies covered has had several unintended consequences. First, the woman's body has become like a chalkboard upon which she can write or erase sexual intentions… The second … consequence is because body parts that have been covered can be uncovered, all parts of the female body have been sexualized… A third consequence is that proscribed attire became the category of dress identified as likely to arouse sexual desire; it was cataloged, recognized, and used deliberately for that purpose. (104-105)

The Quakers, the Mennonites, and the Amish, among other groups, revived these early church practices. For Quaker women and men, covering one's head was an act of dissent against people who perceived themselves as socially and financially superior. Since they insisted that all human beings were equal, they refused to remove their head covering. Quaker men only did so for God. The Quakers, like the Mennonites, the Amish, and related groups, take 1 Corinthians 11:1-17 literally. Although Paul only advised women to cover their heads in prayer, following Jewish practice, these groups took it further and insisted that women should always be ready to pray outdoors and indoors. Hence, they always wear the kappe, head covering, or prayer cap, taking it off only to wash and comb their hair. The men, in contrast, are required to remove their hats while in prayer.

The head covering worn by these Christian women is precisely that, a covering of the head, and not of all the hair. Their hairlines can be seen. So can their necks and throats. In many Amish communities, girls must start covering their heads at the age of four, inspired by Jewish practice. They partially cover their heads out of respect for God. It symbolizes submission to God. For single women, it signifies submission to their fathers. For married women, it is a sign of submission to their husbands. It also marks marital status. Single women wear black bonnets, while married ones wear white ones. Like Jewish and Muslim women, these Christian women view the failure to cover their heads as a sin that could lead to hell. According to most of their ordinances, these Christian women must wear long, modest dresses. They can be full-length or half-calf. Some communities require women to wear long sleeves. Others permit them to wear short sleeves, but they are not permitted to be sleeveless.

It could be claimed that the Qur'anic verses that call for covering and criticize ornamentation are echoes of early Christian writings. The Qur'an, however, lacks the precision that is found in these sources. Its exhortations are deliberately vague or diluted. Any explicit parallels are found in the *hadith* literature, jurisprudential treaties, theological works, and Qur'anic commentaries. It is beyond doubt that early Muslim writings were drawing water from the well of Christianity, Judaism, and other traditions, while rarely ever acknowledging the sources they were paraphrasing, citing, plagiarizing, and appropriating. There is truly nothing new under the sun.

Although many people view jewelry, body art, and clothing as benign, it is because they are artistically and aesthetically illiterate and oblivious to the sense and meaning of their symbolism. Ornamentation is invested with meaning. Even after people embraced monotheistic faiths, like Judaism, Christianity, and Islam, pagan symbolism persisted. When the Qur'an counsels that women should not to expose their *zinah*, which can mean both beauty and jewels, it might be referring to pagan practices.

The bracelets, armlets, necklaces, earrings, and nose-rings worn by women at the time of the Prophet Muhammad evoked pagan gods, beliefs, practices, and superstitions. They were embedded with magical meaning. They featured symbols representing the Goddess, be it Ishtar, Venus, Aphrodite, al-Lat, Manat, al-'Uzza, or others. They evoked the Goddess of fertility and prostitution. They wore shells, representing female genitals, and models of penises, sending the message that "I am available to anyone" (Stol 405). The Qur'an, however, wanted believing women to send the message that "I am a married woman, and I am untouchable" by calling upon them cover their hearts and private parts.

Unbeknownst to most of them, Muslim women continue to adorn their persons and homes with goddess symbols. The most conspicuous of them include the veil which was worn by al-Lat, al-'Uzza, Manat, Ishtar, Brigid, Hestia, Cailleach, and numerous other goddesses throughout the world. The veil symbolized sacred marriage and union between a worshipper and a goddess. Veiling was a bond between the Goddess and the pagan. Believers covered their hair in honor of their Goddess. The same symbolism entered into Christianity where the veils of nuns symbolized their marriage to Christ. The *khamsah*, or so-called Hand of Fatimah, is one of the most ancient symbols of the Goddess. It was associated with Tanit, Mullissu, Innana, Ishtar, Venus, Aphrodite, and Isis. Pagan women today continue to cover their hair to pay homage to their polytheistic beliefs. Plenty of pagan resources promote the practice. For many women, the veil is indeed a divine command, not merely a cultural custom. Why would the One God or One Goddess want monotheistic women to emulate the polytheistic women who surrounded them?

Since ancient times, there was a nexus between jewels, bosoms, and genitals. It was not so much about covering hair, breasts, and jewelry, but rather, a question of symbolic communication. A woman who showed her breasts but covered her hair signaled that she was married and off limits. A woman who showed her breasts and uncovered her hair conveyed that she was sexually available. A woman who covered her hair, and exposed her breasts, was not fair game for men. However, a woman who did not cover her hair, exposed her breasts, and adorned them with necklaces representing fertility, or any other ornaments that invoked the Goddess, signaled that she was open to intimacy.

Ultimately, who cares what Paul of Tarsus, Tertullian or the Church Fathers said regarding women's dress? Their views did not have divine authority. Christians should be concerned about what Christ said, and Christ said nothing regarding the obligation of women to veil themselves. Surely, the traditionalist theologian, Rama P. Coomaraswamy (1929-2006), would object. In the views of this Sedevacantist, "the veiling of a woman is an Apostolic command (I Cor, XI: 4-16), and hence the attitude of a faithful Catholic is one which accepts Apostolic injunctions without question." Far from traditionalist, this is the position of fundamentalists and extremists of all faiths: obey and do not ask questions. However, even angels ask questions. And so do prophets and messengers of God. The faithful should do the same.

The arguments used by Coomaraswamy to support women's veiling are based on the statements of Paul. The first reason is that "the head of every man is Christ; and the head of every woman is the man." The second is "because of angels." The first is patriarchal gender subordination and subjugation which Coomaraswamy presents as "higher realities of which men and women are reflections." The second is out of respect for angels. He admits that Justin, Clement, and Tertullian believed that women had to cover their hair lest they provoke "angels" to lust. However, he rejects that view in favor of the one held by Thomas, and Anselm, who took the term to mean good and holy men, like priests and bishops, "who might be provoked to lust by the beauty of women with uncovered heads." Such men would hardly be godly. Coomaraswamy cites many Church fathers to support the veiling of women, during prayer, and even in public, but not among family and close friends. He fails to mention that some, like Clement of Alexandria, believed that women should be confined to private quarters and not seen in public (Hopwood-Phillips).

Clement (d. c 215) wrote that women should be overwhelmed with shame at being women. Tertullian (d. 220) believed women were "the devil's gateway" and they were "a temple built over a sewer." John Chrysostom (d. 407) believed that women were "weak and fickle" and that men were superior to them. Not only did Augustine (d. 430) view women as having little intelligence, but he also viewed them as temptresses like Eve. He also believed that women were not made in the image of God. Bernard (d. 1153) stated that women were the organs of the devil. Bonaventure (d. 1274) claimed that women were instruments of the devil. And Ambrose (d. 397) insisted that women were inferior to men. The misogynistic statements of the Church Fathers can and do fill volumes. Do these misogynistic views invalidate all their works and thoughts? Certainly not. However, their views on all matters relating to women must be dismissed and discarded.

2.8 Conclusions

Rather than blindly obey religious leaders, the Qur'an urges believers to ask: "bring your proof, if you are truthful" (2:111, 21:24, 27:64). The Qur'an also warns that, if a sinful, immoral, troublemaking, ungodly, evil, disobedient, wicked, or perverted person makes a claim, believers must investigate it, verify its correctness, and carefully ascertain the evidence, lest they hurt or wrong a people unwittingly or out of ignorance, and then become remorseful and repentant for doing so (49:6). In other words, check yourself before you wreck yourself.

Who cares if the four Sunni schools of thought, and the three Shiite ones, decreed that women needed to cover their hair? Muslims are supposed to follow Muhammad, but even more so, to follow God, and God never decreed the *hijab* in the Qur'an. Did God create the heavens and the earth so we could follow jurists? Even the sixth Imam insisted that any sayings attributed to him, the other Imams, or the Prophet Muhammad, that contradicted the Qur'an should be thrown against a wall. Any views, be they *ahadith* or *fatawa*, that find no basis in the Qur'an have no weight of authority.

Taqlid or the blind following of jurists provides no protection in the hereafter and does not excuse one from error and accountability. Some Imams lead to heaven, but others lead to hellfire (17:71; 40: 47-48). The Qur'an describes the people of hell blaming their predecessors for misleading them and asking God to give them a double punishment. God, however, responds by doubling the punishment of both the leaders and the followers (7:38-39; 33:66-68). Human beings have hearts, souls, and minds. They also have a transcendent and innate ability to distinguish between good and evil. Muslims should not believe in God because they follow Muhammad. They should follow Muhammad because they believe in God. Moreover, a Muslim must believe in God and obey God. What is more, a Muslim, as a human being, is the *khalifah* of God on earth, and the *khalifah* of God in human beings is their intellect. We are not duty-bound to follow the views of people who lived over a thousand years ago. If God is closer to us than our jugular veins (50:16), we need only peer inside ourselves. The path to God is not only exterior: it is interior. Do not be a dog on a leash. Run with the wolves.

Chapter 3

Boobs, Bosoms and Beyond

3.1 Introduction

For most Muslim jurists, Qur'anic verse 24:31 makes the headscarf and complete body covering religiously mandatory. However, the Qur'an says that women "should guard their modesty," which literally means their genitals or *furuj* and that "they should draw their coverings over their bosoms [*walyadribna bi khumurihinna 'ala juyubihinna*]." The verb *daraba*, in this context, means "to draw," "to wrap," "to cast," "to throw," or "to cover." The word *khimar* means "covering." It is misleading to interpret or translate it as a "veil," "headscarf," or "head-covering."

3.2 Semantic Stretching: From Bosoms to Hair to Faces

Translators and commentators with preconceived notions regarding Islam wish to imply that the women addressed in the verse were already wearing headscarves, while exposing their breasts, and were asked to draw them over their bosoms. For Muslim jurists, the covering of the hair is implied. This is a false inference and a forced interpretation. Rather than say that women "should draw their head-coverings over their breasts," the verse actually says that "they should draw their coverings over their breasts." As Mehdi Azaiez (b. 1974), the professor of Islamic theology, stresses, referencing Qur'an translators Régis Blachère (1900-1973) (*Coran* 379), and Richard Bell (1876-1952) (*Commentary*, vol. 1: 599), "The command to draw (*walyadribna*) their 'veils' applies only to the chest (*juyubihinna*) and not to faces" (878).

One of the most blatant and egregious misrepresentations of the Qur'an, however, is the claim that 33:53 mandates the face veil. "When you ask [his] womenfolk for something," it reads, "do ask them from behind a curtain [*hijab*]" (33:53). As Jan M.F. Van Reeth (b. 1960), the Flemish Qur'an scholar, and professor of Eastern Christianity, notes, "It clearly means a curtain or another screen and not a veil that hides the face; the verse therefore has no relation with the obligation of Muslim women to wear the veil as some have pretended" (II: 1139).

Those who wish to impose the *burqa* and the *niqab* upon women claim that Qur'an 33:59, which speaks of the *jilbab*, was revealed before 24:31, which speaks of the *khimar*. It seems illogical to believe that a woman wearing a *jilbab*, as imagined by the jurists, would somehow be exposing her breasts. The logical progression would be: 1) cover your genitals, 2) cover your breasts; and 3) cover your body as needed, and as required, at times and places where there is a lack of law and order and where one's safety might be compromised. This dress code was revealed during a state of siege and might also apply to similar dangerous situations. Just like the war verses were not meant to be applied in perpetuity, and Muslims were not supposed to be in a constant state of military conflict with non-Muslims, the verses calling for Muslim women to distinguish themselves by their dress were not meant to be applied in times of peace, safety, and security.

Both the commentaries of the Qur'an regarding the revelation of the so-called *hijab* and the traditions forged to support them are filled with logical fallacies. In no place in the Qur'an does God command women to cover their hair or wear *hijab* -- much less the *burqa* and the *niqab*. When God speaks, He speaks clearly. When He commands, He commands clearly. Prohibited matters are not obscure in the Qur'an. The language used is not vague, cryptic, equivocal, and ambiguous. Whether one accepts them as divinely revealed or reformulations of Hammurabi's Code, there is no ambiguity in the Ten Commandments.

For many feminists, however, part of the problem resides precisely in the fact that it is He who speaks in the Bible and the Qur'an. Were She to speak, the outcome would have been different. When women and men worshipped or at least revered the Sacred Feminine or Mother Goddess, femininity was often celebrated; not shamed and suppressed. It could be argued that the animosity towards women found in Judaism, Christianity, and Islam, manifested in patriarchy and misogyny, was part of a gender war in which the followers of God the Father wanted to suppress any signs of God the Mother.

The breasts of women, sacred symbols of life and maternity, went from being proudly displayed to being covered. If the right hand symbolizes the Sacred Masculine, and the left hand symbolizes the Sacred Feminine, is it any surprise that traditionists claimed that the Prophet Muhammad commanded his followers to use their left hands to wash their anuses of feces after defecation? While this custom is found in many eastern cultures, others were ambidextrous when it came to cleaning impurities. Is it any surprise that a man like Shafi'i (767-820) would rule that touching a woman, intentionally or not, and with sexual desire or not, breaks the ritual ablution of men?

Women, for some Muslim jurists, were viewed as ritually impure. They were placed in the same category as dogs, pigs, urine, sperm, and fecal matter. Not only did they break ritual ablution through touch but, in the views of some, like Abu Hurayrah (602-678), they broke the ritual prayers of men by merely passing in front of men, a view that outraged 'A'ishah, the wife of the Prophet (Muslim). Abu Hurayrah (d. c. 681) claimed that the Prophet said, "Prayer is interrupted by a woman, a donkey, and a dog" (Muslim). However, 'A'ishah scolded him for lying about the Messenger of God, saying, "You have likened us to donkeys and dogs!?" (Bukhari).

While it is true that some Arab women -- pagan, Jewish, and Christian -- used to cover their hair, they did not always do so for religious reasons. The primary reason was to protect themselves, their eyes and skin, from the scorching sun, the wind, and the blowing sand (Ross 35, 37, 46). Dark, but transparent veils essentially acted as sunglasses for women (Ross 46). Men also used their turbans for the same purpose. The traditional clothing of Bedouin Arab women was comfortable and practical (Ross 37). It suited their environment. The secondary reason that they wore scarves was a social custom. They wore veils to beautify themselves. Some used it to enhance sexual appeal. In fact, in the Bible, Tamar wore a face-veil to disguise herself as a prostitute (38:14-15). It was only in 208, two centuries after Christ, that "Tertullian wrote that Christian women should cover their heads before entering a place of worship," and it was only in the fourth century that "the church embraced the veil as a sign of religious devotion" (Scott 56-57). Among Arab women, veils and headgear were identifiers. They varied from village to village, tribe to tribe, and clan to clan. Like men, who could be identified based on their headdress and attire, women were also identified based on the style of their head coverings (Ross 46-51).

Some Muslim jurists claim that God wanted Muslim women to distinguish themselves from Jewish and Christian women -- who tied their scarves around their necks, and who exposed their throats, and potentially some cleavage -- by allowing their scarves to cover their necks; however, there is no textual evidence to support this view. It is the product of speculation. What is more, some Jewish and Christian women used to wear headscarves that were identical to those of Muslim women; namely, that covered their hair, ears, necks, and bosoms. In fact, early Umayyad art depicts women with scarves that hang down their backs. In other words, even generations after the revelation of the Qur'an, Muslim women still wore their scarves in the so-called pagan, Jewish, and Christian fashion.

Just like Qur'anic verse 7:26 was addressed to the "Children of Adam," namely, humanity, 24:31 was directed to all "believing women" which includes but is not limited to Muslim women as the noun "believer" and the verb "to believe" were also applied to Jews and Christians in the Qur'an and the *Constitution of Medina*. In other words, it appears that this verse was aimed at the entire community in Medina: Muslims, Jews, and Christians. Covering or uncovering the hair was not the primary concern. The reason for the revelation was to encourage women to cover "their bosoms," literally and figuratively. The Arabic word in question is *juyub* which is the plural of *jayb*. The word means "cleavage," "bosoms," and "breasts." It can also refer to the heart and the chest.

As Muhammad Asad (1900-1992), the Austro-Hungarian born Jew, Muslim convert, Qur'an translator and commentator, explains:

> The noun *khimar* … denotes the head-covering customarily used by Arabian women as an ornament (not as *hijab* to cover their head) before and after the advent of Islam. According to most … classical commentators, it was worn in pre-Islamic times … as an ornament and was let down loosely over the wearer's back; and since, in accordance with the fashion prevalent at the time, the upper part of a woman's tunic had a wide opening in the front, her chest was left bare…. The injunction to cover the bosom by means of a *khimar* … does not necessarily relate to the use of a *khimar* as such but is … meant to make it clear that a woman's chest is not included in the concept of "what may decently be apparent" of her body and should not … be displayed. Covering the head… is not a requirement. In the matter of *hijab*, the conscience of an honest, sincere believer alone can be the true judge, as has been said by the noble Prophet: "Ask for the verdict of your conscience and discard what pricks it."
>
> My interpolation … of the word "decently" reflects the interpretation of the phrase *illa ma zahara minha* by several of the earliest Islamic scholars, and particularly by al-Qiffal [904-976] (quoted by Razi), as "that which a human being may openly show in accordance with prevailing custom (*al-'adah al-jariyyah*)." Although the traditional exponents of Islamic law have for centuries been inclined to restrict the definition of "what may (decently) be apparent" to a woman's face, hands, and feet -- and sometimes even less than that -- we may safely assume that the meaning of *illa ma zahara minha* is much wider, and that the deliberate vagueness of this phrase is meant to allow for all the time-bound changes that are necessary for man's moral and social growth. The pivotal clause in the above injunction is the demand, addressed in identical terms to men as well as to women, to "lower their gaze and be mindful of their chastity:" and this determines the extent of what, at any given time, may legitimately -- i.e., in consonance with the Qur'anic principles of social morality -- be considered "decent" or "indecent" in a person's outward appearance.

As can be appreciated, some Qur'anic commentators concluded that God was commanding Muslim women to cover their cleavage in 24:31. Others, however, like Maturidi (853- 944) and Qurtubi (1214-1273), claim that God was commanding them to cover their breasts (Nasr 875, note 31). "Most exegetes," writes Muhammad Shahrur (1938-2019), the Syrian philosopher and author, "even go so far as to say that only her breasts are really covered by the term *al-juyub*" (311). As Khaled Abou El Fadl notes:

> Women, Muslim, and non-Muslim, in Medina, normally would wear long head-covers -- the cloth usually would be thrown behind the ears

> and shoulders. They would also wear vests open in the front, leaving their chests exposed... The practice of exposing the breasts was common until late in Islam. Several early authorities state that the Qur'anic verse primarily sought to have women cover their chests up to the beginning of the cleavage area. (241)

In fact, the women from the tribes of northern Arabia, along with the Arabs from the marshlands of Iraq, used to expose their breasts like the Nabateans (Nasr 875, note 31). This type of dress, where the breasts were exposed, was once common throughout the ancient Near East (Nasr 875, note 31). As Ibn Kathir (c. 1300-1373), the Arab historian, exegete, and scholar, noted, the verse "draw their veils over their *juyub*,"

> means that they should wear the outer garment in such a way as to cover their chests and ribs, so they will be different from the women of the *jahiliyyah*, who did not do that but would pass in front of men with their chests completely uncovered, and with their necks, forelocks, hair, and earrings uncovered.

He also explained that it was revealed in response to the fact women were going out without lower garments, exposing their chests, forelocks, and anklets. Since women in seventh century Arabia "wore an ornamental piece of cloth that trailed down the back of the head, and their tunics opened widely at the chest, showing their bare breasts," Sumbul Ali-Karamali (b. 1964), the South Asian American jurist, explains that "this verse instructed women to cover their breasts with what they were already wearing" (159).

Since the word *jayb* is derived from *j-y-b*, which means an opening, a cleft, a crack, or a slip that opens up between two sides, namely "cleavage," Muhammad Shahrur believed that the interpretation of early commentators and jurists, who limited the word *juyub* to "breasts," was inexcusably reductionist (311). In his view, "the *juyub* parts of a woman are her genitals, buttocks, breasts, and armpits" (311). Similarly, Ralph Ghadban translates *furuj* as "the folds on one's body," referring specifically to "the armpits, the area between the thighs and buttocks, and … the cleavage" (Prenner 122)

As Muhammad Sadiq, the Qur'anist, stresses, "The Arabic word for chest (*jayb*) is in the verse 24:31, but the Arabic words for head (*ra'as*) or hair (*sha'r*) are not in the verse. The commandment in the verse is clear: cover your chest." As he notes, "most of the translators, obviously influenced by fabricated *hadith* translate the word as 'veil' and thus mislead people into believing that this verse is advocating the covering of the head and face."

While a *khimar*, headscarf, or shawl is not long enough to cover anything but the head, the neck, and the upper chest, a *jilbab* could potentially extend from the shoulders down to the posterior. In most cases, it would not be long enough to cover the legs. Another garment, such as a wrap, would be required. This is precisely what Ibn 'Abbas (619-687) and Ibn Mas'ud (594-c. 652/653) said. According to them, a *jilbab* was no more than a *rida*, namely, a shawl or a wrapper that covered the upper body. Only a minority of scholars felt it referred to a headcover, face-veil, or mask. So, "how did we go from the Qur'anic vision of beautiful clothing covering intimate parts… to no less than a dress code for women… covering not only the hair but all flesh?" (El-Ali 243). After all, there is nothing beautiful about a *burka*. It is a hideous and heretical monstrosity, an offense to the senses, a spiritual sacrilege, and an insult to the intellect. As Leena El-Ali, the Lebanese-British-American businesswoman and author, summarizes, jurists from the ninth century onwards:

> Gradually expanded the meaning of a woman's (natural) adornment over and beyond the breasts (24:31); converted the "cloak" verse from a security-via-identification measure into a divine command for all Muslim women at all times (33:59); and to varying degrees extended and ordained "elite" practice of separating the Prophet's wives from most men to all Muslim women (33:53). (243)

3.3 A Short History of Toplessness

Nudity forms part of the history of humanity. In fact, human beings were naked for more than a million years. Anatomically modern ones went around in the nude for approximately one hundred thousand years. It was only as they expanded into colder climates that they felt the need to cover. After the loincloth, thong, and mini skirt were produced by ancient human beings, female toplessness was normative throughout warm parts of the world for nearly two hundred thousand years. In tropical climates, women continued to go bare breasted into the middle of the twentieth century, a practice that survives in isolated regions.

Are we to assume that all these nude and semi-nude human beings were cast into hell for committing mortal sins? If God was so concerned about modest dress, why, one must wonder, did he allow human beings to wander around naked for a million years and semi-nude for nearly two hundred thousand years? Critics may claim that the rules of *tzniut* or *hijab* did not apply to pre-Adamites and early homo sapiens. Could God not have taught them how to clothe themselves modestly? Why has God, particularly in the Islamic imagination, become so increasingly prudish with age? Could it be that God is merely the projection of man?

Female toplessness is not a new phenomenon found on beaches worldwide as an act of comfort, liberation, feminism, seduction, provocation, hedonism, a belief in nudism, or a desire to absorb vitamin D or avoid tan lines. It goes back to ancient times when exposing breasts was natural, practical, functional, and fashionable. In some cases, baring one's breasts was supremely spiritual, an affirmation of womanhood, and a celebration of the Sacred Feminine.

In some cultures, it was only when the Sacred Feminine was suppressed and the Sacred Masculine prevailed, that women were forced to cover up. The sexuality of women, which had been the subject of praise, became the subject of censure. Their bodies were viewed as a threat to the New Male Order. Their femininity had to be restrained and contained. Otherwise, it had to be exploited and degraded to defile it. Anything and everything that recalled God, the Mother, was viewed as a danger by the believers in God, the Father. If, in some cultures, the Sacred Feminine reigned supreme, and in others, it coexisted with the Sacred Masculine, the new spiritual male supremacists wished to erase every sign of the Goddess. They have waged a war against women that has never abated.

The followers of the Goddess, however, resisted. In fact, her symbols are pervasive throughout the Muslim world in literature, art, and architecture. Ironically and paradoxically, they were embraced as symbols of Islam itself. Although some Muslims have been inadvertently revering the Goddess, others have worshipped her more openly. In fact, traces of paganism have persisted in much of the Arab and Berber world under the thin veil of Islam. For example, the cult of Aisha Qandisha in Morocco is that of Kadesh, the sacred harlot. Many of the ancient goddesses were downgraded to genies and saints. Among Shiites, at least, Fatimah absorbed many of the attributes of the Goddess.

As much as God the Father deserves criticism, so does the Goddess Mother and Her quench for human sacrifice, including, the ritual killing of first-born children and baby girls who were placed in urns and smothered in sand. When the Qur'an refers to "the girl-child that was buried alive," it was not simply speaking of infanticide. It was referring to the ritual sacrifice of baby girls. The Bedouins of the Sinai used to sacrifice children to the Venus-star (Gray 170; Frayne and Stuckey: s.v. 'Attar). The lambs sacrificed at the Ka'bah have replaced the babies that were slaughtered by Arab polytheists.

Despite the claims of myth-mongering white feminists, many of the polytheistic cultures that worshipped goddesses were patriarchal, sexist, discriminatory, and misogynistic. Embracing them is far from empowering. Adoring goddesses does not correspond to an improvement in the social status of women. After all, many of these cultures permitted wife-beating. The pagan Arabs worshipped a triad of goddesses. Were pre-Islamic women well-treated? Most importantly, it was the Goddess that imposed the veil upon women to symbolize that they were sacred prostitutes. The fact of the matter is that both God and the Goddess are human concoctions. Neither Father God nor Mother Goddess speak for themselves. Human beings, virtually always men, serve as their spokespersons. Hence, humans are to blame for their own actions.

As far as Islamic theology is concerned, the Creator is genderless and balances "masculine" and "feminine" attributes. When Muslim scholars speak of the Sacred Feminine and the Sacred Masculine it is within the monotheistic conception. God the Father and God the Mother are two sides of the same

Divine Reality. Horrors were committed in both their names. Human sacrifices were also made to God the Father, be it Yahweh, Allah or His other names. Simply because human beings corrupted the monotheistic creed, and committed crimes in the name of God and Goddess, such as 'El and Asherah, does not deny the Divine Duality of Divine Unity. Both Yahweh and Allah denounced and prohibited human sacrifice and infanticide in the Bible and the Qur'an.

For Patricia Monaghan, "Judaism, Christianity, and Islam… are all based on a single, male god" (51). Jewish, Christian, and Muslim theologians would dispute this point. God, in all these traditions, is genderless. As she attests, "no other world religions have so thoroughly denied the possibility of goddesses" (51). How could they not? They are monotheistic. They reject, not only goddesses, but gods. Monaghan also claims that "Islam is the most rigorous in excluding the feminine divine" (55). Such a claim is preposterous. An entire encyclopedia could be written about Islam and the Sacred Feminine.

However suppressed it may be by some Muslims, the divine feminine is pervasive in many expressions of Islam. Monaghan should read the *Tao of Islam* by Sachiko Murata and Sufi sources. Most unfortunately, she claims that "no parallel religion based on a single goddess, exclusive of a male divine figure, has been found" (51). In other words, for Monaghan, there is no monotheist Goddess religion. This claim, which is widely disseminated, places women at a false fork on the spiritual path: follow the feminine goddess religions that are polytheistic or follow the masculine God the Father religions that are monotheistic. Jewish, Christian, and Muslim women may seek the Sacred Feminine, but they are not willing to do so at the expense of monotheism. They are not prepared to become polytheists or pantheists.

The fact of the matter, however, is that there does indeed exist a primordial monotheistic Goddess religion, that of the Kogi people from the Sierra Nevada in Colombia, the heirs of a lost civilization that has preserved its primordial pre-contact faith. They are monotheists and God is Woman. They worship Aluna alone, the Goddess, and the Great Mother who represents oneness. She is an all-pervasive force of love that permeates all of creation. The purpose of existence is to submit to Aluna in mystical union (Morrow 2010: 215-216, 233-237). The Kogi or Kagaba Indians are not the only monotheistic indigenous people who are matriarchal and believe in a Sole Female Deity. So were the Yaruros, who worshipped Kuma, the Great Mother. They were an ascetic and mystical people with a rich spiritual worldview (Morrow 2010: 216, 218, 219, 220, 221, 223, 238). Although the Americas were dominated by polytheists, there were monotheistic First Nations. However, many of those believed that the Creator, known as Wakan Tanka, or Gichi Manitou, was genderless.

Allah may be genderless according to Islamic theology; however, He is perceived as masculine and referred to as such. Nothing, however, prevents Muslims from viewing Allah / Allat as both God and Goddess who can be invoked as He or She. After all, the name Allah has a feminine ending: a *ta marbutah* whose dots were consumed by patriarchs. The pantheons of the ancient Semites featured divine couples: El and Asherah, El and Elat, Yahweh and Asherah, Allah and Allat. With the rise of monotheism, the Masculine Deity essentially absorbed the Feminine Deity. Monotheistic theology is a projection of patriarchy.

As can be appreciated, scholarly rigor requires religion to be contextualized historically, sociologically, and psychologically. Jewish, Christian, and Muslim rules regarding modesty must be viewed from a panoramic perspective. Why, when, and how were they introduced? What reality were they responding to? Why did they wish to distinguish themselves from disbelievers? A survey of nudity and toplessness is revealing.

"Since the climate of Egypt was very warn," writes Douglas Gorsline (1913-1985), the American painter and writer, "nakedness was common; and modesty, in our present cultural sense of the word, did not exist" (4). Ancient Egyptian women, both lower and upper class, used to wear tight-fitting sheaths and short dresses that completely exposed one or two breasts (Watson 24, 25, plate 2, plate 4, plate 6, Payne 39-40, Sposito 22-23, Racinet 25, Leventon 15, Yarwood 139, Giafferri plate 1, plate 3, plate 5, Boucher 94-95, Gorsline 5-6, Peacock 9-10, Houston plate 1, 76, 77-85, Kybalova, Herbenova, and Lamarova 42-43). "Egyptian women did not consider it necessary to cover their breasts," point out Kybalova, Herbenova, and Lamarova (39). As Blanche Payne (1894-1972), the American costume historian, describes:

> Women working in the fields wore short skirts... Their upper bodies were bare... The basic garment for women of all classes was a tubular dress that extended from just below the breasts to the lower calf... Sheath gowns could have one, two, or no tapered straps over the shoulders. Statues show that the straps, if present, covered the breasts, but concealment did not seem to be a concern. (39)

Ancient Egyptian women exposed their arms and, in some cases, their legs, even wearing the equivalent of tank-tops and miniskirts (Giafferri plate 4). Even their longer dresses were see-through (Groseline 5, Laver 9). Some wore bead net dresses (Sanchez, DK 16). Servants wore even less. In fact, they were usually nude (Groseline 5). As James Laver (1899-1975), the English author, critic, art historian, and museum curator, points out, "many of the lower classes, and the slaves in the palaces, went about almost, if not completely, naked" (16). In ancient Egypt, "the wearing of clothes was a kind of class distinction" (16). The upper classes wore more clothing. The lower classes wore less. Some slave girls wore dresses that extended from below their breasts down to their knees (Bruhn 3). Others wore only micro bikini bottoms and decorative collars, sometimes with a cape (Bruhn 3). As for headdresses, they were generally reserved for the rulers (Kybalova, Hervenova, and Lamarova 39)

As for Assyrian women, some showed considerable cleavage (Giafferri plate 12), while others exposed one of their breasts (Giafferri 15). Sumerian women showed their entire torso (Tortora and Marcketti 48). They wore skirts held in place by a padded belt tied at the waist or mid-torso, just below the breasts (Houston 109). Their upper bodies were entirely exposed (Houston 109-110).

In the late twentieth and early twentieth century, celebrities like Rose McGowan (b. 1973), Rihanna (b. 1988), and Bleona Qereti (b. 1979) have worn barely-there mesh dresses to music awards, designs inspired by ancient Egyptian fashion. Since they covered their nipples with pasties, and wore thong panties, they were considerably more modest than their ancient Egyptian counterparts. The sheer and nude dresses worn by other stars, including Bella Hadid (b. 1996), Kendall Jenner (b. 1995), Jennifer Lopez (b. 1969), Imaan Hammam (b. 1996), Kim Kardashian (b. 1980), Taylor Swift (b. 1989), Megan Fox (b. 1986), Beyoncé (b. 1981), and others, which, in some cases, allow the breasts to be seen, are more in keeping with ancient Egyptian fashion (see Escalante, Wahi, and others). Few, however, have gone so far as to allow their intimate parts to be exposed through the mesh or sheer fabric, as would have been normal during the days of the Pharaohs.

If Asiyyah ever existed, and she was the wife of a Pharoah, perhaps Ramses II (d. 1213 BCE), then this is the precisely the type of clothing she would have historically worn. Whether she was Nefertiti (d. c. 1255 BCE), or another royal consort, she is depicted as exposing her cleavage, arms, bellybutton, legs, and her entire breasts (Laver 19, Boucher 99). In some sculptures, she appears completely nude. If Asiyyah were a royal, she would have dressed in long dresses that exposed her bosom (Bruhn 3). She would have worn garments that were so fine that they were transparent to show the body's divinity (DK 18).

Although she looked and dressed like Kim Kardashian in a nude dress, and was married to a wicked, disbelieving man, Asiyyah is revered by Muslims as one of the four greatest women of all times, along with the Virgin Mary, Khadijah, and Fatimah. Patently, wearing "revealing clothing" does not preclude sanctity. She dressed as attractively as a modern actress, singer, celebrity, or star attending an awards ceremony. The fact remains that there is no definitive historical, literary, or archeological proof of the existence of Asiyyah and Moses. For some scholars, the account of Asiyyah shows every indication of being derived from the legend of St. Catherine of Alexandria or Asia Aikaterina, the Pure Catherine (d. 305) (Walker 45-48).

In ancient Sumer, the earliest known civilization of Mesopotamia (6000-5000 BCE), women wore a wrap over their basic skirt (Basye 16). "If the fabric was long," notes Ali Basye, a fashion historian, "the ends were slipped up and under a belt and over one shoulder, creating what we know as a Roman toga; otherwise, the gals went topless" (18).

As for Cretan women, they dressed in open bodices, which uplifted their exposed, naked breasts, while wearing tight, short, miniskirts (Payne 61, 63, Yarwood 288-289, Boucher 79-84, 87, Cosgrave 33-34, Gorsline 8, Peacock 12, Garland 1013, Laver 21-22, Basye 22, DK 20-21, Bruhn 9, Kybalova, Herbenova, and Lamarova 50-53). They wore "smoothly fitted bodices, laced or otherwise, fastened beneath the breasts, leaving the breasts exposed" (Tortora and Marcketti 55). At times, they went entirely topless, wearing only long dresses, without breast-lifting bodices (Bruhn 9). The culture of these Neolithic Minoans (2600-1450 BCE) from Crete "distinguished itself as a peaceful, non-warring society that worshipped females: in fact, its rulers were quite likely women" (Basye 23). It was "a society dominated by the female" (Kybalova, Herbenova, and Lamarova 51)

Like their sisters on Crete, Mynecean women also exposed their breasts (Payne 66). And this also applied to some Greek women (Racinet 57, Cosgrave 44, Gorsline 12, Peacock 15). In fact, "the upper torsos of women were originally bared," notes Gorseline, "later… the exposure of the breasts in a calculated bodice frame was adopted" (9). Some Greek women wore gowns of Assyrian inspiration that exposed one breast along with the entire leg, from the hip down, on the opposite side (Giafferri plate 21). In fact, it was common for women to wear such tunics outdoors (Giafferri plate 22, plate 23, plate 24, plate 35). Some even wore outfits that exposed both breasts (Giafferri plate 22). What is more, some Greek women exposed not only their breasts but their midriffs as well, wearing gowns so low on their hips that their pubic area was visible (Giafferri plate 25). "In Greek and Roman costume," notes Gorseline, "the influence of pagan ethics and a bland climate is still apparent; thus there was considerable nakedness" (9). "Clothes," he points out, "were strikingly loose and free; perhaps at no other time in history have such practical and graceful garments been popular" (9).

Among the Romans, some women publicly exposed one or two breasts, and some dancers wore transparent costumes (Giafferri plate 31, plate 33, Gorseline 12). The bikini was not invented by Louis Réard (1896- 1984), the French fashion designer, on July 5, 1946: it was worn by Roman women as early as the third-fourth century CE (Boucher 122, Tortora and Marcketti 90, Casgrave 77, Peacock 20, Garland 29, Laver 40). Writing about "The Bikini in Sicily, 400 AD," Madge Garland (1898-1990), the fashion academic, remarked:

> In 1951 excavations near Piazza Armerina in Sicily brought to light the ruins of a luxurious villa and revealed a mosaic pavement in a remarkable state of preservation. On it were seen an astonishing series of pictures of girl gymnasts. The world was amazed to find that on the beaches of the Mediterranean fifteen hundred years ago the girls were dressed in exactly the same bikinis as they wear today. For the two-piece bathing suit was thought to be a new and rather vulgar modern

> fashion when it was launched several years before these fascinating mosaics were rediscovered. The Sicilian girls are shown with their hair curled but flying in the wind, their bodies almost naked, but their eyes carefully made up… the brief loincloth and still briefer brassière are identical to those we are accustomed to call bikinis. (29)

Since this groundbreaking discovery, "shaped leather Roman underwear from the same period has been found" (DK 35). This suggests that Roman women also wore bikini bottoms when exercising or swimming. We know for certain that some Roman women would wear a drapery that was fastened by one shoulder, and on the hips, which would expose half of their bodies, from their neck down to their mid-thighs, showcasing one of their breasts, their bellybuttons, hips, and upper thighs, and a tease of the pubic area (Giafferri plate 35). Moreover, female Roman slaves would drape dresses around their naked torsos (Giafferri plate 35).

These same women, Egyptian, Assyrian, Greek, and Roman, who were often scantily clad, would also wear outfits featuring head coverings and veils for beautification. However common the headscarf may have been in late Sassanid times, it tended to hang loosely at the back and did not cover the neckline (Houston 183). In others cases, they wore a bandeau with ribbons at the back (183). What is more, it was obviously a fashion accessory meant to highlight beauty, and not conceal it. In fact, some women would wear a long, loose, skirt covering the feet, while wearing nothing above the waist. One depiction shows a topless woman swinging her long headscarf over her head (183). Germanic women were no different. They wore long garments that left a breast exposed (Bruhn 22).

Women appeared topless in many parts of the world in the seventh century and beyond. This style of dress or undress was found among the Imazighen, black Africans, Indians, Indonesians, and Polynesians, among many other populations. Most surprising is the fact that Muslim women were wearing bikinis in the Mediterranean region in the early eighth century when bathing, in mixed, public gatherings, going, quite often, entirely topless. The bikini beach and pool culture had extended into Umayyad times. In fact, the female bather depicted at Qusayr Amra "wears the skimpiest of bikini bottoms" (Ali 230). As Muhammad Shahrur points out:

> In seventh-century Arabia, Arab Bedouin women dressed themselves in public by basically covering their breasts with a long shawl; while inside their private homes they wore clothes that did not cover that area of their body… Only a woman's breasts could be revealed when she walked in public. Hence, they were seen as the private parts she must cover. (311)

As Sahar Amer admits in *What is Veiling?* "Women from the pre-Islamic period … traditionally wore a *jilbab*, which was a type of vest or shirt open in the front that left the chest entirely exposed" (43). As she explains:

> In a society where poverty was prevalent and clothing scarce, the Qur'anic verses mandating women to cover their bosoms with their *khimars* (Q. 24:31) and to draw their *jalabib* closer to their bodies (Q. 33:59) did not mean … that women were expected to cover completely. Rather … these Qur'anic verses are best interpreted as general guidelines about modesty and morality, as a recommendation to Muslim women to cover their chests with the same pieces of cloth they were already wearing… *Hijab* in Islam is much less about clothing, much less about an injunction to wear specific attire, than it is about adopting a modest demeanor, remaining humble, and avoiding pride and conceit. (43)

In such a social and cultural context, where women exposed their chests in public and private, covering one's hair would have been considered a trivial matter. More important issues needed to be tackled. And this is precisely what the Qur'an addressed, namely, the desire for women to draw their shawls over their *juyub*, their upper private parts. As Shahrur explains:

> A woman's body is divided into two parts: a) an exposed (visible) part: the verse says, "except what (must ordinarily) appear thereof" (*illa ma zahara minha*); these outer parts are what can be seen of a female body: the head, back, shoulders, arms, legs, and such, constituting her physical appearance (in public); b) an unexposed (invisible) part: parts of her body that God has not exposed to the eyes; a woman's unexposed part is called *juyub*. (309)

What distinguished believing women from disbelieving women was not whether they covered their hair or not, it was whether they covered their private parts and breasts. In fact, some of the women who covered their hair used to expose their breasts. And the significance of covering the heart and the breasts was not simply an outward sign of physical modesty, it was a symbol of inner modesty as the chest, the bosom, and the breasts stood for faith in the Divinity, spirituality, piety, chastity, marital fidelity, maternity, lactation, and legitimacy of progeny. In other words, "the rainment of righteousness, that is the best" (7:26). Clearly, one can only comprehend the Qur'anic call for women to cover their '*awrah* and their *juyub* if one understands the history of costume.

Not only was the revelation responding to existing modes of dress but to the entire history of fashion from ancient to medieval times and, for believers, into the future. The Qur'an's understanding of costume transcends time and place. It seems to be directly dealing with women in ancient Egypt, Crete, Assyria, Arabia, India, and beyond, with their bodices that showed the entire breasts, and their mesh, sheer, and nude dresses that exposed everything, legs, thighs, buttock, back, midriff, and chest. When understood in the context of the history of women's clothing, the Qur'anic verses regarding covering the genitals and the breasts take on an entirely new meaning. Far from being conservative, these injunctions call for basic, simple, public decency, and allow women an enormous amount of leeway in matters of dress. Such rules allow fashion to flourish. The Qur'anic dress code is not conservative. If anything, it is ultra-liberal, liberating, and emancipating. All it calls for is the covering of one's genitals.

Islamic fundamentalists hate all things beautiful, the foremost of which are women, the finest blessings in this world. They denigrate their divinely decreed status. They disseminate fabricated sayings of the Prophet Muhammad in which women are slandered, degraded, and debased. They ignore the qualities and virtues of women as they are found in the Qur'an. Scholars who are faithful to the spirit of the Qur'an debunk allegations that women are prohibited from adorning themselves. They demonstrate that God encourages them to wear "fine apparel" (7:26, 7:31). They show how the Qur'an describes in glorious detail the purity, beauty, fine grooming, and elegant clothing of the people of paradise. It describes its female inhabitants as "closely guarded pearls" (22:23), "adorned ... with bracelets made of gold and... green garments made of the finest silk and rich brocade" (18:31), "gold bracelets and pearls" (22:23), as well as "green velvet, satin, and silver ornaments" (76:21). The Qur'an calls upon Muslims to wear fine, spotlessly clean clothing and beautiful accessories when they meet together. They are supposed to be adorned and appealing. If we take the people of Paradise as our example, nothing prevents Muslims from being righteous and attractive.

In sharp contrast to the Islam of the extremists, fanatics, and misogynists, who went as far as making adornments and accessories unlawful to women, "the Qur'an attaches the greatest value to women," and condemns those who wish to forbid beauty and ornamentation (7:32). As the Qur'an states quite clearly, "We have sent down clothing to you to conceal your private parts, as well as an ornament to you" (7:26). God, however, has no desire to shut women away and cover their bodies up. Relying on fabricated *hadiths*, Islamist fanatics and extremists insist that makeup, grooming, cleanliness, and looking attractive are unlawful. It is no surprise that Muslim fundamentalists are renowned for looking filthy, dirty, untidy, unkept, careless, and crude.

The Qur'an calls upon believers to be beautiful, however, many fanatics are ugly and filthy, uncouth and unkept. Likewise, they wish to make Muslim women repulsive, unattractive, unappealing, ill-groomed, and second-class citizens. Some go as far as to ban women from plucking their eyebrows, removing facial hair, wearing wigs, nice clothing, and beautifying themselves with tattoos, striving to make them ugly instead of attractive. They prevent them from wearing perfume. Some even ban deodorant as a prohibited innovation. Far from prohibited, makeup is a means of beautification. Since God loves beauty, it is only fitting for human beings to be beautiful. Women, like flowers, trees, butterflies, and birds, have been created to be attractive. They are an adornment of this world. Some women are most certainly the most beautiful beings in creation. Such beauty emerges through grooming.

There may be material from the Qur'an and the *hadith* that can be used to issue rulings that prohibit women from wearing beautiful clothing, makeup, jewelry, henna, and perfume in public. However, there is material from the Qur'an and the *hadith* that can be used to permit, encourage, and even mandate women to beautify themselves, to clad themselves in clothing of the finest fabrics, to apply makeup, henna, and perfume, and to wear jewelry. It all depends on the sources that one accepts or rejects, strengthens, or weakens, authenticates, or repudiates, amplifies, or silences.

The centrality of beauty in Islam is not lost on Leena El-Ali. She notes that God, in verse 7:31, "articulates His desire to see us looking beautiful" (206), and asks a pertinent question: "why is all the emphasis in our societies placed on pious clothing but absolutely none on *beautiful* clothing?" (206). As far as she is concerned, the Qur'anic philosophy of dress is simple and straightforward, beautiful, and comfortable, as opposed to drab, constricting, and uncomfortable, not to mention claustrophobic:

> Clothing is intended to cover one's private parts (7:26), which 24:30-31 … show to mean the groin area; clothing/attire is meant to be beautiful. (7:26, 7:31); no amount or type of covering can rival the clothing of reverence (7:26); and beautiful clothing/attire is a gift from God that no one can forbid. (7:32, 7:33). (209)

Keeping this crystal-clear Qur'anic foundation in mind, Leena El-Ali notes that both men and women are required to guard their private parts, namely, the groin area or their chastity (24:30-31, 34:58-60, 70:29-30), "while restricting women to exposing their natural ornaments i.e. their breasts, only to relatives, household members, and children" (210). As she explains:

> For shocking as it seems to use today, it was customary for women in Medina at that time to wear tunics or vests with wide openings in the front that left the breasts exposed… 24:31… put an end to this fashion among the followers of the Prophet at least in front of "strangers," as the verse clearly appears to accept the custom's continuation in front of all sorts of relatives and household occupants of both sexes. The verse instructs believing women to draw their *khimar*, a pre-Qur'anic ornamental shawl that women used to drape loosely over their heads and necks/shoulders, over their *exposed* breasts to cover them, in effect making it clear that a woman's breasts are no longer to "ordinarily appear" before anyone outside of a still surprisingly long list of related and unrelated men and women the verse makes an exception for. This is an extraordinary accommodation by the Qur'an, despite its declared disapproval of breast-baring, to prevailing customs, and what was then

> considered by society as acceptable flesh to show in broad public. (210-211)

For El-Ali, verses 24:58 and 24:59, "proceed to address men and women *together* with regard to not exposing their full *nakedness* at home to the rest of the household" (211). Finally, verse 24:32 takes "an even more lenient position on baring the breasts by elderly women who are past their sexual phase, although the Qur'an adds that it is nonetheless better for them to keep their breasts covered even then" (211). As El-Ali, observes:

> Most interpretations render "adornment" (*zeena*) in these verses of chapter 24 to mean much more than a woman's breasts or even groin area despite no less than three instances in 24:31 that literally identify the topic as "breasts," "private parts," and "intimate parts…" Such interpretations extend "adornment" to a woman's very shape and/or almost all of her skin and hair and/or even any ornamental jewelry she may be wearing, rather than simply the natural adornment of a woman's breasts, despite: 1) The explicit reference her to drawing the shawl *over their breasts* and only showing otherwise what skin would ordinarily appear in the course of daily life; 2) The explicit reference to both men and women guarding their *private parts*; 3) The explicit reference to children who have no consciousness yet of *women's private parts*; 4) The reports about *the chest-bearing women's fashion* of the time that continued late into the Prophet's mission; 5) And the very *definition of clothing/attire* (which includes jewelry per 35:12) in the Qur'an as something intended by God to be beautify, to be encouraged, and never forbidden, and therefore necessarily visible. (211-212)

In light of the above, there is evidently a deep divide between what is Qur'anic and what has come to be considered "Islamic." The situation has degenerated so far that "women's clothing is today discussed by many jurists as if it were a public safety measure" (223). As El-Ali concludes:

> When the above five verse of chapter 24 are looked at together, both the meaning of "private or intimate parts" and the Qur'an equal expectation of what men and women's' clothing must cover becomes crystal clear: both men and women are expected to cover their private/intimate parts, i.e. groin areas, and women would ideally also cover their breasts in broad public. (212)

The Usuli Twelver Shiites go so far as to claim that unless one is a jurist, it is obligatory to follow one. In their view, all acts are invalid unless they are in accordance with the rulings of a *mujtahid*. Nothing, then, should prevent a Muslim from following the views and rulings of qualified jurists, even those who hold that women are only mandated to cover their '*awratayn* or two private parts. However, when jurists issue rulings that displease paleoconservative clerics, they are treated as deviants, heretics, apostates, and infidels. As Ismail Kurban Husein Poonawala (b. 1937) notes, this oppressive climate of intimidation and terror prevails throughout the Muslim world (Nu‘man, vol. 2: 238). The Akhbari Twelver Shiites reject *ijtihad* and curse jurists. They believe in following the *ahadith* that were transmitted by the twelve Imams. Once again, one's views, laws, and regulations will depend on which traditions one treats as genuine. The same applies to the Sunnis, the Sufis, and other sects.

For good or for worse, people have the power to shape Islam as they please. The Religion of God is in the hands of Man. So, where are the views and voices of women when it comes to defining *ma zahara minha* or "what appears thereof" (24:31)? And why must it be fixed and not contextual? Why can it not vary? What normally appears of a woman at work, in a court of law, in a bakery, in a factory, in a place of prayer, in a park, at a gym, in ballet, in sports, at a wedding, at a fine restaurant, at a concert, at the pool, or at the beach can and should vary. As Sumbul Ali Karamali notes:

> What normally appears is not an objective measure but a subjective one. What "ordinarily" appears in one culture might be incident in another: in traditional Indian culture, short blouses baring midriffs "ordinarily appeared," but miniskirts would have been shocking; in twentieth-century American street dress, bare legs more "ordinarily appeared" than bare midriffs. Circumstance also dictates modesty: someone who might wear a bikini at the beach would probably not wear one to a funeral. And norms fluctuate over time too: in Turkey and Indonesia, the latter of which has the largest population of Muslims in the world, many women didn't start wearing headscarves until thirty years ago. (157-158)

Although the expression "except that which is necessary" (24:31) may sound vague, for the Qur'an-only community it is "because they have not understood the mercy of God" (Submission). For Leena El-Ali,

> The Qur'an… give an extraordinary example of what might "customarily" appear… it makes allowance for not covering the breasts, of all things -- since it was customary practice among many at the time -- while limiting its acceptability henceforth in front of only family members, domestic servants, and slaves even if they are male (also 24:31)…. The vast majority of early jurists were tolerant of all sorts of exposure by women that was deemed customary or practical, though this leniency was extended only to Muslim women who were servants or slaves and so worked for a living, but not to freewomen (ironically). (342)

If jurists generally decreed that enslaved Muslim women could expose their torsos, breasts, backs, bellies, arms, and legs in public, and were prohibited from covering their hair, even in prayer, what do we make of such rulings in our day and age? For Ibn Hazm (994-1064), the polymath, historian, traditionist, jurist, philosopher, and theologian, the rules of free Muslim women should apply to enslaved Muslim women. All should cover. An argument could also be made that the freedom that was accorded to enslaved women can and should be accorded to all free Muslim women.

As Ali Basye asks in her delightful *The Long [and Short] of It: The Madcap History of the Skirt*, how did we go from a society ruled by power babes, like Crete, where women's costume consisted of "billowing, tiered skirts, corsets, and elaborate embroidery, jewelry, color, and decoration… a sexy forerunner of high-court fashion of the Renaissance" to thousands of years of Dowdy Debbies? (24). Her answer is witty as ever:

> Maybe the 2,000 years of zero-tolerance patriarchal rule that followed the footloose, fashionable spirit of the Minoans had something to do with it. Take away a woman's self-esteem and she becomes… frumpy. In fact, the men of the Middle Ages were the real fashion plates, while women suffered their repression in those dang dirndls. Perhaps men understand that with a little fashion freedom, women might get assertive enough to do something daring like, you know, try to vote, or get an education. (25)

3.4 From Veiling Women's Hearts to Cover Them Up, Shut Them Up, and Lock them Up

The covering of one's breasts conveyed a modest monotheistic worldview. Muslim jurists, it seems, obsessed with expanding the semantic range of "beauty" and "ornaments," missed the main spiritual and ethical message by a hundred leagues. The same can be said when they interpreted "be not too complaisant of speech" (33:32) to mean that the voices of women were private parts when, according to Tabari and Qurtubi, the verse merely advised against flirtatious talk that could arouse sexual desire (Nasr 1028, note 32). In practice, however, scholars have cited the verse to justify the prohibition of the female voice in the public sphere.

"And stay quietly in your houses," the verse continues, "and make not a dazzling display, like that of the former Times of Ignorance" (33:32). The first part of this verse is used to confine women in their homes. As noted by Razi (1150-1210), Tabari, and Zamakhshari (1075-1144), the verb, however, derives from either *qarna* or *qarara*; the former "conveys the sense of dignity and sobriety" while the latter "indicates that one should remain in one's residence" which "has led to strident puritanical interpretations that severely limit the freedom of women" (Nasr 1028: note 33). In reality, the verse should read "Abide in your homes with dignity" (33:32). And while the verse was directed to the wives of the Prophet, who were asked to avoid flaunting their finery in public, it has typically been treated as a rule that applies to all Muslim women, namely, "cover them up and lock them up."

And while it is used to justify the mandatory complete covering of women, the second segment of the verse, "Bedizen not yourself with the bedizenment of the Time of Ignorance" (33:33) or "flaunt not your charms" (33:33), was revealed, according to Ibn al-Jawzi (c. 1116-1201), Ibn Kathir (c. 1300-1373), and Tabari, to discourage free Muslim women from exposing their beauty and walking seductively to sexually arouse men (Nasr 1028: note 33). It was not merely about clothing. It was about deliberately provocative demeanor and sinful and seductive ill-intention. However, it was the consensus of many Sunni and Shiite scholars that it was not a sin for Muslim men to look at the hair and bodies of non-Muslim women. It was only prohibited if it led to sin. As Sahar Amer points out, however, "this passage explicitly singles out the wives of the Prophet… Only they were expected to behave in a particular way, in contrast to Muslim women in general" (45). What is more:

> The counsel not to "flaunt their finery" is close to that of 1 Timothy 2:9, "Similarly, women are to wear suitable clothes and to be dressed quietly and modestly, without braided hair or gold and jewelry or expensive clothes." (Reynolds 644)

If we read 33:33 in the light of its Biblical reflexes, the verse is counseling the wives of the Prophet to dress humbly and modestly. For Ibn Rushd (1126-1198), the Andalusian polymath and jurist, the dress code mentioned in the Qur'an does not mandate the face veil. It simply encourages modesty (Akyol 2022: 123). Edip Yüksel, the Turkish American activist and Qur'anist, goes as far as calling the face veil "a satanic innovation designed to turn women into the slaves of men who claim to be lords and masters" (452).

3.5 Cover Them in Cloaks

Another oft-invoked verse that Muslim jurists use to cover women in cloth and bury them in *burqas* is 33:59. Along with 7:26 and 24:31, they claim that 33:59 is a call for women to be completely covered and concealed. "O Prophet!" commands God, "Tell your wives and your daughters and the women of the believers to draw their cloaks [*jalabib*] close round them [when they go abroad]. That will be better, so that they may be recognized and not annoyed. God is ever Forgiving, Merciful" (33:59).

For most Muslim commentators, like Ibn Kathir, Qurtubi, and Tha'labi (d. 1035), this verse commands free Muslim women to cover their hair, ears, throats, and chests (Nasr 875: note 31). Others insist it commands the body to be covered, save the face, hands, and perhaps the feet. And yet others claim that it commands that the face be covered, as well. Incapable of disassociating himself from the ultra-conservative Iranian cultural context, and perhaps in an attempt to please the radical Islamists in power, Ali Quli Qara'i (b. 1947), the Indian American translator of the Qur'an, goes as far as to turn *jalabib* into *chadors*. The text, however, does not support these interpretations. The women of Medina who lived during the time of the Prophet never wore *chadors*. The translator is projecting Iranian dress upon seventh-century Arabs. What is more, the ancient *chador* was a two-piece, often colorful, garment, not the black Islamist *chador* imposed by Khomeini and company. It was not the "stupid, medieval rag" that Oriana Fallaci (1929-2006) tore off in the presence of the "supreme leader" (Timsit).

In the Qur'an, God asks the Prophet to tell his wives, daughters, and the women of the believers, which would include Muslims, Christians, and Jews, to "draw their *jalabib* close round them." The word *jalabib* is the plural of *jilbab*. A *jilbab* is not necessarily a cloak. In fact, *jilbab* is sometimes a synonym for *khimar*. As Khaled Abou El Fadl notes, "*Jilbab* refers to a garment that is larger than a *khimar* and generally covers a woman's head and chest area but may also cover their entire body" (256, note 106). As Jan M.F. Van Reeth clarifies, referencing Arthur Jeffery (d. 1959) (102), "the word *jalabib* is of Ethiopian origin and means a *cloak*; hence, it has nothing to do with a veil" (114). In fact, historians of costume believe that "all clothing probably originated with the loincloth; the next development was the tunic" (Gorseline 3). The Qur'an appears to echo this primordial call to modesty: cover the genitals with a loincloth and cover the upper body with a tunic.

Although 33:59 could be construed as a call for women to cover their entire bodies, it would appear, in light of 24:31, that it is primarily a call for women to cover their breasts as well as the private parts they were asked to conceal in 7:26. Moreover, while not every imperative used in the Qur'an translates into a religious obligation, in this verse in question, God states that covering oneself in a *jilbab* "will be better." In other words, "it will be better" is not an order. It is not an obligation. It is a recommendation or an exhortation. It is encouraged.

Since the purpose of wearing the *jilbab* is qualified as opposed to unconditional, "that they may be recognized and not annoyed," it cannot be construed as universal. Furthermore, since God immediately stresses His forgiveness and mercy, it seems difficult to argue that failing to wear a *jilbab* is punishable in this world or the next. If that were the case, namely, that women who show their hair will hang from it in hell, God should have been more explicit regarding the severity of this so-called sin. There is a tradition to this effect, and it has been depicted artistically in pictorial accounts of the Prophet's Night Journey; however, its authenticity is questioned. As Ali Dashti (1897-1982), the Iranian rationalist, who was tortured to death under Khomeini's regime, pointed out, "Islamic portrayals of the night journey turn it into fables" (7).

If 24:31 told women they should not display their bosoms to avoid drawing attention to themselves, 33:59 asks them to cover themselves "so that they may be recognized and not annoyed." The covering in question was an identity marker. It was meant to distinguish believing women from disbelieving women, unavailable women from available women, protected women from unprotected women (Ahmed 15, 26). In the Near East of the time, along with other ancient societies, women who appeared in public were treated as prostitutes (Barlas 2019: 59). Unless they were identified as being under the protection of men, they were considered fair targets for harassment and sexual assault (Barlas 2019: 59).

The case of Zunayrah or Zinnirah al-Rumiyyah, who was freed by Abu Bakr, is telling and tragic. This Greek Christian woman was a public concubine who was collectively owned by the Banu Makhzum tribe. As Mansour Fahmy (1886-1959), the Egyptian sociologist and feminist, noted in his 1913 thesis, in seventh-century Arabia, not all slave girls were allocated to individual owners. Some belonged to the whole tribe, and the whole tribe could have their way with them (Chebel 65). It is possible that this inhumanity triggered the revelation of the *jilbab* verse (33:59). It called upon free women to distinguish themselves from "public women" who were tribally owned sex slaves. As Mohamed Talbi (1921-2017), the Tunisian historian and Islamologist, has pointed out, at the time of the Prophet Muhammad, and even during his rule, slavery was common in Mecca and Medina, as it was along all trade routes (Bestandji 2021: 86; 2018: Part Two). In such a dangerous environment, it was sound for free Muslim women to seek to distinguish themselves from women who were forced into prostitution.

To protect believing women from being accosted by non-Muslim men, and harassed by degenerate Muslim men, particularly at night, God told the Prophet that believing women should cover their bosoms so they would stand out and avoid being accosted by perverted predators. Since antiquity, notes Bestandji, veiled women were viewed as virtuous, while unveiled women were viewed as "sluts" or "unchaste" (2018: Part Two). The situation in Arabia was very much like the one in the Roman Empire where dress marked social status. If a man violated a young girl, he committed a lesser offense. If he violated a woman who was not dressed as a respectable woman, it was a much lesser offense. If he violated a married woman who was not wearing the clothing of a matron, he was not liable. Abducting and sexually assaulting women were not crimes but civil delicts (Phang 97). They were "insults" or "outrages." Respectable young virgin girls and married women could sue for damages; however, prostitutes could not (Phang 96-97). In Rome, a married woman was distinguished by her long *palla*. Enslaved women were not thus cloaked. They wore shorter shawls or capes. Prostitutes, however, covered neither their hair nor their bodies. In short, the more a woman covered, the higher her status. The more she showed, the lower her status (Phang 103).

In medieval Europe, "rape was situational: a woman's marital status, virginity, religious vows, or property ownership shaped whether she could bring a charge of rape" (22). Most cases of sexual assault were met with indifference. When a woman was married, however, the situation was taken more seriously as rape constituted a violation of a husband's property rights. In theory, the punishment for rape could be severe, including the removal of eyes and testicles (Tuten 21). In practice, most punishments or settlements were negotiated between families (Tuten 22). In the Middle Ages, in England, like elsewhere, it was basically impossible for a prostitute who was sexually assaulted to seek justice "as her consent was already implicit in her profession" (Edwards 151). Women of status could sue for sexual assault, however, "bondwomen, maidservants, and other low-status women… had little legal recourse" (Edwards 157-158).

The social and legal situation in Arabia was essentially the same as it was in most of the region. Unprotected girls and women were viewed as fair game for sexual harassment, abduction, and rape. Women of status and wealth, who were identifiable as wives by their clothing, had some semblance of protection. If the Qur'an counseled the women of the believers to cover their bosoms in public, particularly at night, it could have been directed to those that were married. Perhaps it applied to all believing women. If so, then the Prophet was shifting the protection of women from their husbands to the entire community. The women in question were supposed to be protected, not because they were wives, but because they were members of the Muslim community. This is in keeping with the Prophet's attempt to shift loyalty from family, tribe, and clan, to that of religion or Islam. Was the Prophet only concerned about protecting free Muslim women, particularly those who were married, or was he attempting to protect all women? The Qur'an suggests that the purpose of the *khimar* was to differentiate free Muslim women from other women. Were enslaved women, Muslim and non-Muslim, left defenseless? Were free, non-Muslim women, left at the mercy of sexual predators? If one thing is clear it is that the call to cast a *khimar* over one's bosoms was a response to sickening social circumstances.

Does the Qur'an perpetually impose this sexist and classist dress code, and the social system that produced it, upon Muslim women, thereby making them guilty of provoking men and responsible for any sexual harassment and assault if they fail to abide by it? When a disease has been cured, there is no need to continue taking medicine. Otherwise, it produces harm. What is more, the sartorial medicine was merely treating a symptom, and not the underlying cause of the social illness. The *khimar* was viewed as a temporary solution to a problem. One should not seek to recreate, institute or perpetuate it.

If the purpose of these dress codes for free and married women was to protect them from harassment, sexual assault, and kidnapping, they did not function. Even honorable women could not pursue men in courts of law unless there were male witnesses to the crime. In Europe, as in Arabia, the victims were often punished more than the rapists, getting fined for having sex outside of marriage. If they got pregnant as a result of the rape, it was viewed as evidence that they had consented to the sex, as it was believed that a woman would only "release her seed" if she was free and willing. These dress codes, which were found among Christians as much as Muslims, only protected "honorable" women: free and married ones. It was wardrobe that signaled whether a woman was decent or not or whether she had rights or not. For civilized human beings, all girls and women have inalienable rights, including the right to not be accosted, intimidated, groped, manhandled, and raped.

As Bestandji asks, does the Qur'an impose a dress code on women to excuse men from immoral behavior if they see a strand of hair or a forearm? "The answer is no," he responds, "Islam does not excuse, nor does it authorize men to sexually harass or aggress a woman who is uncovered" (2018: Part Two). However, as Khaled Abou El Fadl points out:

> Other sources report that the purpose was precisely the opposite: Muslim women would cover with the *jilbab* so that scoundrels could not tell the difference between a slave and a free woman, and so they would be unable to harass either. It is clear by the very language of the verse that the purpose of this injunction is to protect women from harm, and in my view, it is also clear that the narrative sought to support equity between classes and the equal treatment of women of divergent social status. (2016)

The fact of the matter, however, is that we do not know for certain why the *'awrah, khimar* and *jilbab* verses were revealed. The historical reasons allude us. Why? Because the *asbab al-nuzul* literature, namely, the works on the reasons for revelation, are suspicious. They were composed centuries after the fact, are filled with contradictions, and often provide details that are useless when it comes to understanding the moral and ethical message of the Qur'anic verses and how they apply to us in our day and age. Moreover, there appears to have been collusion between commentators, traditionists, and jurists to come to certain conclusions regarding the dress code for Muslim women (Amer 34).

As Irfan Ahmad Khan (1931-2018), the Indian American Qur'anic commentator, expressed, "Neither considerations of occasions of revelations nor commentaries of earlier people will be permitted to block the further growth of Qur'anic understanding" (2019: 38). As Tanveer Azmat, the scholar of religion, has acknowledged, canonical *tafsir* is not helpful when approaching the issues of our age: freedom of expression and conscience, the emancipation of women, racial issues, and matters of war" (2016: 179). Hence, we need a new hermeneutic in which "the humanistic and ethical aspects of the Qur'an take a center stage" (2016: 181).

As Asma Barlas (b. 1950), the Pakistani American academic who specializes in Islam and women's studies, explains, 33:59 and 24:30 were revealed in a slave-owning society. The purpose of mandating the *jilbab* was to signal the sexual non-availability of Muslim women to non-Muslim men who were willing to grant it such a meaning (Barlas 2019: 59, Ahmed 14-15, 26). The *jilbab* was not meant to hide Muslim women from men; it was meant to render them visible for the sake of their protection (Barlas 2019: 59). It was a form of recognition/protection (Barlas 2019: 59). In fact, Ibn 'Arabi warned that excessive covering prevented recognition of women and therefore defeated the purpose of 33:59. In his view, the verse in question did not obligate excessive covering. It was revealed to distinguish free Muslim women from slave women who "walk bare-headed, or with a facemask only," namely, wearing a veil without a headcover or a wrapper around their bodies (Barlas 2019: 59). As for the reference to the *jilbab* in 33:59, it is entirely at the discretion of women. When and where women feel safe in democratic and civilized societies, they may feel no need to cover up entirely. Whether they cover or uncover, women should not be harassed because of the way they dress.

3.6 Sufi Insights on the Beauty of Women

Since, in his view, there is nothing but God, Ibn 'Arabi (1165-1240), the Arab Andalusian scholar, jurist, mystic, poet, and philosopher, viewed women as reflections of God. As he explains in *The Bezels of Wisdom*:

> When man contemplates Beauty in woman he beholds [Him]… the Apostle loved women by reason of [the possibility] of perfect contemplation of the Reality in them. Contemplation of the Reality without formal support is not possible, since God in His essence, is far beyond all need of the cosmos. Since, therefore, some form of support is necessary, the best and most perfect kind is the contemplation of God in women. The greatest union is that between man and woman, corresponding as it does to the turning of God toward the one He has created in His own image, to make him His vicegerent, so that He might behold Himself in him. (275)

As R.W.J. Austin (b. 1938), the British specialist in Islamic mysticism, comments:

> the attracting beauty of woman, far from being a snare to delude man, should rather become for him that perfect reflection, as formal beauty, of his own spiritual path, being, as she is, that quintessential sign or clue from which he might best learn to know his own true self, which is, in turn, to know his Lord. (270)

Although most mainstream Sunni and Shiite scholars equated beauty with temptation and evil, Sufi sages, like Fakhruddin 'Iraqi (1213-1289), viewed it very differently. "For them," writes Seyyed Hossein Nasr (b. 1933), the Iranian American philosopher, "beauty is not the cause of seduction, but the occasion for recollection of the spiritual archetypes" (1982: xii). Rather than hate women for being beautiful and attractive, Sufis view them as theophanies of God and mirrors of *al-Jamil*, the Beautiful. After all, "God is Beautiful and He loves beauty," said the Messenger of God (Muslim). And while the Sufis were not entirely immune from sexism, it was not as accentuated among them as it was among the Sunnis and Shiites. As Rumi (d. 1273) wrote: "Woman is a ray of God. She is not just the earthly beloved. She is creative, not created" (90). In reality, neither God nor Islam are opposed to beauty. In fact, as Khaled Abou El-Fadl perceives:

> All Qur'anic legal injunctions represent trajectories in the course of an entire moral and ethical project, and this project… is best represented in the well-known prophetic teaching that God is beautiful and loves beauty, and that God wants human beings to promote beauty in everything they say and do. (El-Ali xi-xii)

Beauty is not bad. It is not to be concealed and cloistered. It is to be celebrated. If "God is Beautiful and love beauty" (Muslim, Tabarani, and Ibn 'Arabi), why do Islamic fundamentalists hate beauty? And, if they hate beauty, does not that not automatically imply they hate God, who is Beautiful? After all, they hate everything that is beautiful. They ban the beauty of women in the public sphere. They prohibit music, sculpture, the depiction of animate objects in art, and even photography. They are ugly and love ugliness.

Why do women want to be beautiful? An entire field is devoted to this subject. The desire to be beautiful is instilled in women. It is biological, evolutionary, psychological, and spiritual. Beauty impresses people. It is associated with skills and professionalism. It makes women feel good. It attracts people. It supports relationships. It creates harmony. It plays a central role in mate selection and retention. It is vital: a matter of life. Men are drawn to beautiful women. They subconsciously seek fertile women to pass on their genes. The more attractive the woman, the more likely she will find a high-quality mate. Plants need light for the purpose of photosynthesis. Women also need to let their beauty shine to ensure they thrive. To prevent women from being beautiful is to deprive them of oxygen. As Nick Meyer reports,

> A 2007 review published in the *New England Journal of Medicine* found that 30 to 50 percent of adults and kids who covered up were vitamin D deficient, even in sunny areas of Australia, Lebanon, Saudi Arabia, India, and other nations. Another study published in the journal *Endocrine Practice* found that Arab American women wearing the *hijab* had half the levels of vitamin D as those who didn't adhere as closely to the dress code… The more conservatively each woman dressed, the lower her level of vitamin D was recorded. Those who wore *hijab* but also ate vitamin D-rich foods such as oily fish or fortified milk had higher levels (though not as high as those who did not wear *hijabs*. [see Hobbs and Lite]

A large body of scientific studies conducted in Canada, Bangladesh, Iran, Turkey, Jordan, Saudi Arabia, Turkey, Lebanon, Morocco, England, Finland, the Netherlands, and France, have all demonstrated that *hijab*-wearing women who wear concealing clothing suffer from vitamin D deficiency, a condition that leads to musculoskeletal issues (Ojah and Welch).

As Benjamin Plackett reports, "studies have consistently shown that more than 70% of Arab women are vitamin D deficient." A 2010 study of women in the United Arab Emirates found that 75% of them were severely deficient in vitamin C (Plackett). A study conducted in Jordan in 2011 found that the dress style of women was related to vitamin D deficiency. Women who wore *hijab* had a lower vitamin D status than those who wore western style clothing. The deficiency was even greater in those that wore *niqab* (Batieha). A study conducted by Khitam Mohammad in 2016 found that 76% of new mothers in Jordan were deficient in vitamin D (Plackett). Studies conducted in Saudi Arabia found that 76% to 85% of women there suffered from inadequate vitamin D levels (Mohammed). A study carried out in the Sudan found that "the correlation between vitamin D level and residence outside Khartoum, sun-exposed face and hands, and face and limbs in comparison with being completely covered were found to be statistically significant." A staggering 82.6% of women who were completely covered suffered from vitamin D insufficient despite access to tropical sunshine (Husain). The *hijab* was conspicuously the cause.

A study in Australia found that 68.1% of Muslim women suffered from severe vitamin D deficiency (Diamond). According to Dame Sally Davies, the chief medical officer for England, the rise of rickets in the United Kingdom is related to the use of religious garments (National Post). In the UK, "health official are so alarmed by increasing cases of rickets among the Asian population… that children and mothers will be offered vitamin supplements" (Jenkins). According to experts, "the wearing of *hijab*" reduces sunlight absorption (BBC News). As Craig Oates, director of development and engagement, noted, "We need vitamin D to prevent rickets and because of cultural issues primarily people are not getting enough sunlight. If you are covering up most of your skin and you're not exposed to sunlight then you're going to have a vitamin D deficiency" (BBC News)."

According to WebMD, vitamin D lowers blood pressure. It reduces the risk of diabetes, heart attack, arthritis, multiple sclerosis, and many other preventable diseases (Meyer). According to Bashir Khan, "vitamin D deficiency is directly proportional to major clinical conditions such as cardiovascular diseases, diabetes, malignancy, and multiple sclerosis." Lack of vitamin D is associated with osteoporosis in women and rickets in their children, as their milk does not contain high enough levels of this essential vitamin. Lack of vitamin D causes fatigue and contributes to depression. It can also cause muscle and hair lost. Even more disconcerting is the association between vitamin D deficiency and miscarriages. Since an alarming number of Muslim women who cover their skin suffer from vitamin D deficiency, including muscle and bone loss, doctors warn women in *hijab* need sunlight to treat and prevent illness. While diet and supplements might help, there is not evidence that they will prevent any future diseases caused by vitamin D deficiency. The only proven and effective treatment for vitamin D deficiency is absorbing sunlight through exposed skin. How much sunshine do human beings need. Let science speak:

> Those with inadequate sun exposure -- including disabled people, infants, the elderly, dark-skinned people, and those who live at northern latitudes during the winter -- are at risk of low vitamin D3 production, which can lead to a loss of bone density and an increased risk of fractures. Disabled people… are often less likely to go outdoors, and people over the age of 70 don't produce vitamin D3 from their skin as effectively. As for people with darker skin, they have more melanin, so less UV light gets absorbed to create vitamin D3. They need more sun exposure to produce vitamin D3 than those with lighter skin… We have to look at all the variables that affect vitamin D3 production: … skin pigmentation, … general age, … latitude, … time of day … and the season of the year.
>
> A study done in Valencia, Spain, measured the amount of sunlight necessary to produce a sufficient amount of vitamin D in those with lighter skin… The researchers took into account the amount of clothing and the season of the year. In spring and summer, 25 percent of the body (the hands, face, neck and arms) is exposed to the sun, and in these seasons, about 8 to 10 minutes of sun exposure at noon produces the recommended amount of vitamin D. In the winter, only 10 percent of the body is exposed, and nearly 2 hours of sun exposure at noon is needed to produce a sufficient amount of vitamin D.
>
> Another study compared the geographic extremes of Miami and Boston. Researchers studied people who tanned well, but who still burned when exposed to sun. In the summer in Miami -- with 25 percent of the body exposed to the sun -- a person would need only 3 minutes of sun exposure to make a sufficient amount of vitamin D. That same person -- when placed in Boston in the winter -- would need 23 minutes at noon to produce enough vitamin D. Then again, Boston in the winter is really cold, so you would probably have only 5 percent or less of your body exposed to the sun. Thus, 23 minutes in the sun in Boston would need to be stretched to more than 2 hours in order to ensure sufficient sun exposure. In addition, if you have darker skin pigment, the time needed to produce sufficient vitamin D would be even longer. (Ashley)

Islamic apologists and misogynists are quick to claim that the *hijab* and the *burka* do not cause vitamin D deficiency. However, since when do they care about the health and welfare of women? They believe in following blind dogmas and worshipping their ideological idols. Despite the health dangers posed by the *hijab*, many Muslim women who were informed of these findings, which can fill an entire volume, insisted that they would continue to cover themselves completely. Human beings require substantial sunlight, ideally on a daily basis. Vitamin D is absorbed through the hair and exposed sin. In fact, it is absorbed the most in the torso area. Hence, the more that is revealed, the better. The darker the skin, the greater the need for unveiling hair and skin. It is impossible for Muslim women who cover completely or almost totally to absorb enough vitamin D. The situation is all the more severe when they settle in the northern and southern hemispheres, in places such as Canada, the United States, Europe, Argentina, and Australia.

If *hijabis* and *niqabis* require supplements to prevent vitamin D deficiency, Islam is not universal and Allah is not omniscient. Vitamins were only discovered in the early twentieth century. They only became commercially available in the late 1930s and 1940s. It was only in the 1950s that they became reasonably popular and their use only increased exponentially in the final decades of the twentieth century and the early twenty-first century. Was it the will of God that all *hijabis* and *niqabis* who lived before our times suffer from health issues since they did not have access to supplements? So much for the claim that the Qur'an is compatible with science. The *hijab* does not fit. It is time to take it off. Skin and hair need sunlight. Presumably, God knows this but misogynistic men did not. Some *purdah* promoters counter that women can wear tan-through *burkinis*. However, such a product is a twenty-first century development. Did God condemn all Muslim women to ill health prior to its invention?

The issue, however, is not merely a lack of vitamin D. Women who wear *hijab*, and particularly those who wear *burkas* and face-veils, suffer from disproportionately higher rates of obesity and cardiovascular problems (Economist, Middle East Online, Emirates 24/7). The *hijab* encourages inactivity as exercise in the public sphere is viewed as an act of immodesty. Since their peripheral vision is blocked, *burka*-wearing women are victims of more traffic accidents. Those who wear such attire throughout their lives may also suffer from eye damage. As Stephanie Dubitsky details,

> The mandatory act of wearing *burqas*… causes health risks. They are so heavy and enveloping that they restrict women's activities by making it difficult for them to move. The simple act of walking outside becomes hazardous because the mesh opening severely restricts women's field of vision and they are unable to see their path clearly. In addition, *burqas* are linked to hearing loss, skin problems, headaches, cardiac disorder, asthma, and also can contribute to mental health problems. PHR revealed that the Afghan women who participated in its

> study demonstrated alarmingly high levels of mental illness: 97% displayed symptoms of major depression, and 86% reported signs of anxiety.

For some Muslim women, blindly following the absurd, however harmful it may be, is more comforting than logic, reason, and critical thinking. These are the same women who insist on fasting while pregnant although such a practice has been associated with negative outcomes in children. These are the same women who marry their first cousins although such incestuous marriages double the risk of birth defects in children. Ah, but of course, God and His Messenger know best! They patently ignore prophetic traditions that strongly discourage or even prohibit the practice.

According to Sunni and Shiite traditionists, the Prophet Muhammad warned, "Do not marry within the family, as that leads to children that are thin and weak;" "Do not marry within the family, since the child will be born thin and weak;" "Marry outside the family, lest the offspring be thin and weak;" and "Do not marry close relatives because the offspring of such marriage will be weak. Defects of such marriages will not be rectified until three generations of marriages with non-relatives" (Ibn Hajar, Ibn Mulaqqin, Subki, Tabataba'i). Caliph 'Umar also warned that "You all have become thin and weak, so marry outside the family" (Iraqi). Many Muslim scholars insist that these traditions are forgeries and thereby prefer to promote incest. Believers with brains view them as authentic since they agree with science and genetics.

As is apparent to any rational and reasonable human being, regardless of their religion or lack thereof, the so-called Islamic rules of modest dress are profoundly damaging to the health and welfare of humanity. The *hijab* is detrimental physically, psychologically, spiritually, and socially. It produces unhealthy and imbalanced individuals and societies. It is entirely unnatural. If modest dress is a health hazard to women and children, why would an omniscient deity mandate it? He most certainly would not. If this doctrine is not divine, and not prophetic, then it is product of malevolent men who falsely claimed to speak for God and His Prophet.

3.7 The Qur'an and Reality: An Inversion of Ethics

When it comes to Qur'anic verses 33:59, 7:26 and 24:31, Asma Barlas concluded they are not premised on "a view of the human body… as corrupt and corrupting" (2019: 59). In her view, the focus of these verses was not on the bodies of women but the sexual misconduct of men (2019: 59). Unlike conservative exegesis, the intent was to protect women, not to make them disappear from public view (2019: 60). In other words, misogynistic Muslim scholars inverted the meaning of the verses. As Ziauddin Sardar (b. 1951), the British-Pakistani scholar, writer, and public intellectual, notes:

> Modesty cannot become the rainment of righteousness of an entire society when it is the burden and obligation of only one half of the population. Traditional interpretation in fact performs an inversion of Qur'anic principles by making women responsible for the lack of moral probity and modesty, not to say the sexual obsession of men. Reading verses 24:30 and 31 together make it abundantly clear how perverse this habit is. In fact, it is not so much perverse as potentially perverted, a license for lechery, which is exactly what the Qur'an's balanced approach seeks to end. (334)
>
> I can see no Qur'anic warrant for *burqas*, *chadors*, *abayas*, and *niqab*. There is no legal requirement, sanctioned by the Qur'an of the Prophet that compels Muslim women to wear specific dress, to hide their faces in public, or to shroud themselves from top to bottom. Had this been the case, the injunction of the Qur'an for men and women to "lower their gaze" would hardly make any sense. And I find the whole notion that certain men, in the guise of moral police, should go around telling women to cover themselves totally reprehensible. And there are just as many women prepared to serve as harridan scourges ready to tell other women that not even a strand of hair should be allowed on public view. (334)

And while Barlas recognizes that a *jahili* pagan ethos persists in Western societies, there are laws in place to protect women from sexual harassment, which, she admits, have yet to be enacted in most Muslim nations (2019: 60-61). What she fails to admit is the fact that this heathen ethos is alive and well. In fact, it is particularly prevalent in many so-called Muslim-majority nations, where the rate of sexual harassment is far greater than in the Western world. As Mona Eltahawy (b. 1967), the Egyptian American journalist and feminist commentator, points out:

> Almost 100% of Egyptian girls and women report being sexually harassed... Before leaving home, every woman I know braces herself for the obstacle course of offensive words, groping hands, and worse that await her in the streets she takes to school, university, and work... 96.5% of Egyptian woman have experienced unwelcome physical contact, while 95.5 % have been subjected to verbal harassment on the streets... In Yemen... 90% of ... women have experienced harassment, specifically pinching... nearly all women in Yemen are covered from head to toe... The extraordinarily high incidence of harassment in Yemen gives the lie to the conservatives who claim women bring harassment upon themselves by dressing "immodestly." (77)

Rather than reduce sexual harassment, the mandatory *hijab* in Iran has made it worse. Women describe it as relentless (The Guardian). In one study conducted in Mazandaran Province, nearly 90% of women reported they had been sexually harassed verbally and nearly 95% reported being physically groped (Higgs).

As Phyllis Chesler (b. 1940), the distinguished American writer, psychotherapist, and professor, points out, “being fully covered does not save a Muslim woman from being harassed, stalked, raped, and battered in public places, or raped or beaten at home by her husband” (2017: 256). As Ayaan Hirsi Ali puts it:

> Whether she is a virgin, married, divorced, or widowed, if she works outside the house, if she moves freely in public without a chaperone, if she ignores the modesty dress code, she is deemed immodest. A woman who has no male relatives to protect her is, by default, also considered immodest. They can be leered at, harassed, groped, or sexually assaulted because the perpetrators have no consequences to fear, whether because there is no one to retaliate on her behalf or because the woman is simply thought to be “asking for it.” (2021: 150-151)

Speaking of some Lebanese-Australian men who were convicted of a series of gang-rapes in Sydney, Taj Aldin al-Hilali, a so-called Islamic scholar, showed unparalleled empathy, not for the victims, but for the rapists:

> If you take out uncovered meat and place it outside in the street… without a cover, and the cats come and eat it… whose fault is it, the cats, or the uncovered meat? The uncovered meat is the problem… If she [the victim] was in her room, in her home, in her *hijab*, no problem would have occurred. (Ali, 2021: 174, Winter 27, Fatah 287)

This was the Salafi “religious authority” to whom the Arab-Australian “inventor” of the *burkini* turned to certify her product (Samint). For feminists, she profits from the oppression of women. Feiz Muhammad, another “shaykh” from the same country, stated that sexual assault victims deserved to be raped: “She has no one to blame but herself for she has displayed her beauty to the whole world. Strapless, backless, sleeveless -- they are nothing but satanical.” Likewise, a Danish Muslim leader asserted that “Women who don’t wear headscarves are in many ways themselves to blame if they are raped” (Ali, 2021: 174).

When asked whether raped women deserved to be punished in Islam, a panel headed by Yusuf al-Qaradawi responded that “for her to be absolved of guilt, a raped woman must have shown good conduct” (Syla and Henry). In other words, if she failed to respect *hijab*, she was guilty of provoking the sexual assault. The reality, however, is that Muslim women are sexually assaulted by Muslim men even if they are in full *hijab*. In fact, sexual assault is so rampant in some Muslim societies that it commonly takes place during the pilgrimage to Mecca, even in the precinct of the Ka‘bah, a fact that has been brought to light by many women (Ali, 2021: 153).

If this is how many Muslim men view and treat Muslim women, one can only imagine how they view and treat non-Muslim women. Writing during the crusades, historian Imad al-Din (1125-1201) described Western women as immodest whores who, "glowed with ardor for carnal intercourse... offering themselves for sin... They were all licentious harlots... appearing proudly in public, ardent and inflamed, tinted, and painted, desirable and appetizing... blued-eyed and gray-eyed, broken-down little fools... abandoning all decency and shame" (Ali, 2021: 151-152). In other words, these "infidel" women provocateurs "wanted it" and "were asking for it." When we compare such words and attitudes to those of Muslim grooming gangs, pimps, and human traffickers, we see a culture that has not evolved ethically and humanely, is stagnant in its sexism, and marred by its misogyny.

If over a thousand years of imposed *hijab*, in one form or another, has failed to prevent Muslim men from sexually harassing Muslim women, then it is as effective for personal protection as a water pistol, a toy gun, or a talisman. Moreover, by linking morality to dress, warns Barlas, "conservatives are legitimizing pathologies that lead men to murder unveiled women in the name of Islam" (2019: 61). Islamists believe in *hijab*. They do not believe in women. It is not about defending the *hijab*. It is about defending the dignity and humanity of women, protecting them from men who see them as sexual objects and respecting their rights and freedom. As Amina Wadud points out:

> If men respected women as equal human beings and not as objects of their sexual fantasies, then even a naked woman should be safe from male abuse. Furthermore, with regard to the particular items of a Muslim women's dress styles, including the *hijab*, when a Serbian soldier in the rape camps can rip a two-year-old girl's body apart by raping her, it is obviously naïve to assume that any amount of head covering would have made a difference or created any real change in deep-seated male sexual aberrations. (221)

For most classical Muslim scholars, the requirement for modesty applies solely to free Muslim women. In short, it applied in the context of "a slave-owning society in which sexual abuse, especially of slaves, was rampant" (Barlas 59). For Ibn Hazm (994-1064), the Andalusian jurist, such a double standard, which implied that God and the Prophet were not concerned about the harassment of enslaved women, was inconceivable. He refused to believe that there was a different dress code for free women and enslaved ones. He believed their '*awrah* was the same (Abou El Fadl 259: note 123). This was also the stance of early jurists like Dawud ibn 'Ali (d. 883/884), who is regarded as the founder of the Zahiri school of jurisprudence (Abou El Fadl 259: note 126). In fact, Ibn Hazm had some choice words when referring to scholars who held that only free women should cover their breasts:

> We absolve ourselves of this corrupt explanation that is a slip-up of a person of knowledge, a blunder by a respected, intelligent man, or a fabrication by a wicked liar! This is because it says that God has given free rein to the perverted to attack the dignity of Muslim maidservants, and this is an eternal affliction! … No two people of Islam disagree that molestation of, or fornication or adultery with a slave-woman is prohibited as that with a freewoman, as are the subsequent criminal punishments, with no difference between the two cases. For this and other reasons, it is incumbent that we must not accept the saying of anyone after the Messenger of God… unless they attribute it to him. (qtd. Gabriel and Hannan 69)

The reasons invoked by Muslim jurists, both past and present, to justify the obligatory *hijab*, namely, the complete covering of women, from head to toe, in every single society, and for all time to come, are unconvincing. God says that women should cover their bosoms with their scarves or shawls "so that they may be recognized" (33:59). Recognized by whom? Distinguished from whom? According to the reasons for revelation, differentiated from disbelieving women. If the majority of the women in a given society are believers, then where is the need to distinguish them from the disbelievers who have disappeared?

If these free believing Muslim women were required to distinguish themselves from enslaved women, to avoid sexual propositions, as some masters used to send their slave girls out to prostitute themselves, wherein lies the need to do so in a day and age where slavery is prohibited internationally? Why would ordinary women need to distinguish themselves from prostitutes? It is prostitutes who signal they are for sale through attire, location, demeanor, and body language. In a healthy society, women do not need to prove that they are not harlots. It is assumed they are not hookers and call-girls unless they explicitly suggest otherwise. The exception does not make the norm. The majority does not have to prove that it is not the minority.

In the Qur'an, God says that women should cover their bosoms with shawls, cloaks, or robes to prevent them from being "annoyed" or harassed (33:59). Annoyed by whom? According to the reasons for revelation, harassed, accosted, and potentially sexually assaulted by non-Muslim men. According to the Qur'anic commentary of 'Ali ibn Ibrahim al-Qummi (d. 919), the women were being harassed by young men, who would hit on them, when they went out for the evening, night, and dawn prayers. If so, these young men were complete and total degenerates. Should a woman from New York wear the *burqa* because men, mostly African Americans and Latinos, catcall her constantly? (Bliss). After all, 'Ali is reported to have said that men's first look was forgiven; however, their second look at women was a sin. Once again, the onus is on men to act like gentlemen. Abla Hasan, the Syrian American professor of Arabic, rejects the claim that 33:59 refers to sexual harassment, insisting that it refers only to "minor harm" (Hubeali *Hijab*: 110). The verse, however, poses questions that beg to be answered. As Syed Osman Sher (b. 1935), the Indian Canadian author, asks in *Religion, God, and Islam*:

> Can the women now be protected from molestation simply by wearing an outer garment, or by being recognized as Muslims? . . . Are the Muslims living in the dark streets of Makkah and Medina of those days that they need protection through such contrivances? If a veil is prescribed for the streets, is it applicable also when a woman is inside a building among the family members, close relatives, and friends? Does it become obligatory for a woman to cover herself from head to foot, sometimes only to bare the eyes? (Fatah 294)

If most men in a given society are believing Muslims, who are obliged to lower their gazes and guard their genitals or *furuj* (24:30-31), and cover themselves in God-consciousness (7:26), wherein lies the need for believing Muslim women to completely conceal themselves beneath cloaks? They should be safe around real Muslim men. The fact of the matter, however, is that:

> The Islamist hatred of women burns brightly across the region -- now more than ever... The obsession with controlling women and our bodies stems from the suspicion that, without restraints, women are just a few degrees short of sexual insatiability... Yet while the clerics busy themselves suppressing female desire, it is the men who cannot control themselves... Men grope and sexually assault us, and yet we are blamed for it because we were in the wrong place at the wrong time, wearing the wrong thing. (Eltahawy 11)

If men are the weaker sex, and cannot control themselves, perhaps they are the ones who should be veiled, confined, or perhaps caged like animals. If girls should have their sexuality severed through female genital mutilation to prevent them from sinning, perhaps the jurists who made these rulings should be subjected to castration for the same reason. It is reported that the Prophet Muhammad instructed Umm Habibah and/or Umm ‘Atiyyah, a “female circumciser,” or, better yet, a female genital mutilator, how to correctly complete the procedure, insisting that it was permitted, and not prohibited (Kulayni and Majlisi). The tradition is narrated on the authority of Muhammad ibn Muslim, a notorious liar, and extremist, who attributed lies to the Imams. In this case, he claimed that Ja‘far al-Sadiq had quoted the Prophet as saying so. Although it is defended by some Shiite scholars, the tradition is a patent forgery. The chain is disconnected for six generations, and it contains narrators who were infamous for their dishonesty.

Why is the burden placed on women when it comes to chastity, purity, and honor? Why are they held responsible for the lust of men? Why are they blamed, and why are their freedoms restricted due to the vices and sins of men? This is the predator blaming the prey. Since these sorts of men harass all women, regardless of whether they wear *hijab* or not, what is the point of wearing *hijab* in the first place? The pandemic of sexual harassment in the Muslim world is a testament to the epic and monumental failure of *hijab*. As Mark Walia, the American religious historian, summarizes:

> An Islamic perspective on sexual harassment… flows from the basic perception that determines Muslim societies' response to rape… Women should expect unwanted advances because they have entered into the public space and thus whipped up male passion to the boiling point, even if veiled. Women shopping in the market, walking on the streets, working as street vendors, or just standing next to men onboard crowded public transport can expect to be propositioned, even pinched around the genitals and buttocks by excited young men…
>
> Identical scenes take place every day in Syria, Egypt, Nigeria, Pakistan, and all points in between. The molesters and harassers are never held accountable for their deeds because it is simply assumed that men cannot restrain themselves around females. As an example of Muslims' tendency to blame women for their own sexual harassment, we need only turn to an incident that occurred in Egypt during October 2016.
>
> On the evening of *Eid-al-Fitr*, a crowd of frustrated young men in downtown Cairo went on "what can only be described as a sexual frenzy. They ran around grabbing every girl in sight, whether a *niqabi* … or *hijabi*, or uncovered… even pregnant ones. They grabbed them, molested them… [it] lasted for five hours from 7:30 pm to 12:30 am."
>
> When terrified females approached Cairo police officers for aid, they refused to intervene, making light of the men's conduct by saying "what do you want us to do? It is Eid. Happy Eid to you too!" This one situation typified the "boys will be boys" attitude towards sexual harassment, a conviction that women appearing in public should blame themselves for a man's lascivious conduct.

One of the most horrific manifestations of hatred of women by sexually frustrated religious fanatics consists of acid attacks. They involve throwing acid or corrosive substances on women to disfigure, maim, torture, or kill them. They are motivated by sexual frustration, lust, jealousy, and rejection of marriage proposals. Many attacks are religiously inspired and target girls and women who are accused of not wearing strict *hijab* or who attend school. While not an exclusively Muslim crime, as men of all religions and ethnicities have committed acid attacks, it is a tactic popular among radical Islamists in Afghanistan, Nigeria, Bangladesh, Iran, the Levant, and Pakistan. Over one thousand such incidents are estimated to occur every year throughout the world. They are committed by men of all religions, and no religion, including Jews.

In the United States, some militant Jews strive to impose so-called modest dress codes in their communities. Take, for example, the campaign by the

Tznius Poster Committee in Crown Heights, Brooklyn, that posted the following modesty sign throughout the community:

> Crown Heights is the neighborhood of the Lubavitcher Rebbe. Out of respect to the Rebbe and his community, we request that all women and girls, whether living here or visiting, adhere at all times to laws of modesty, including: CLOSED NECKLINE IN BACK, SIDE AND FRONT (COLLAR BONE SHOULD REMAIN COVERED). ELBOWS COVERED IN ALL POSITIONS. KNEES COVERED BY DRESS/SKIRT IN ALL POSITIONS. PROPER COVERING OF THE ENTIRE LEG AND FOOT. NO SLITS. IN ADDITION, THE LUBAVITCHER REBBE HAS MADE HEARFELT REQUEST THAT MARRIED WOMEN WEAR ONLY … FULL WIGS IN PUBLIC (NOT A TICHEL OR HAT) … Modesty in all places and at all times makes Hashem [God] dwell amongst us and protect us. (Silverman 97)

"In this conservative worldview," notes Silverman, "a Hasidic woman wears her fate -- and that of her community -- on her sleeves" (97). There are Jewish-owned stores in the United States that refuse entry to anyone, Jewish or non-Jewish, who does not abide by the rules of *tzniut*. Others take a far more violent approach to enforcement of women's attire (97). As Silverman notes:

> In Israel, ultra-Orthodox men burned "clothes of impurity" in streets, set afire fashionable boutiques, and sprayed bleach on improperly attired women. A "modesty squad" horrifyingly burned a fourteen-year-old girl with acid. "She cried all the way to the hospital." (98)

The time has long come to turn the tables. If men would like women to be chaste, they should be examples of chastity. As the Prophet admonished men: "Be chaste yourselves, and your women will be chaste as well" (Considine 2020: 93, Tabarani, Hakim, Daylami). Rather than force women to cover themselves in potato sacks, mobile tents, and Glad garbage bags, why not force bad Muslim men to cover their eyes or stare at the ground? Perhaps we can have female religious police in stiletto heels and skimpy leather outfits whipping men who stare at women and harass them. Alternatively, these men might take the advice of Jesus and rip out their sinful, adulterous eyes. As he said: "If your eye causes you to sin, gouge it out" (Mark 9:47). Unless, of course, one believes the preposterous and hyperbolic claim that Fatimah, the daughter of Muhammad, was required to veil herself in the presence of a blind man (Nu'man, vol. 2: 198).

Rather than arrest, incarcerate, whip, beat, rape, and even kill Muslim women for the claim of being immodest, why not arrest, incarcerate, and whip the sinful Muslim men who sexually harass them? Why the undue emphasis on the modesty of Muslim women and the *laissez-faire* attitude applied to Muslim men? Since there are societies, particularly non-Muslim ones, where women are generally not sexually harassed, and where laws are in place to protect them from such perverts, degenerates, and predators, wherein lies the requirement for them to cover themselves completely? Why Iranian *hijab* patrols that harass women? Why not anti-harassment patrols aimed at men?

If the purpose of the revelations in question was for Muslim women *not to be harassed*, wherein lies the requirement for them to visibly identify themselves as Muslims in societies where that might place them at increased risk for Islamophobic harassment, intimidation, and violence? It defeats the purpose of the verses in question. Research reveals that girls and women in *hijab* can trigger negative and aggressive attitudes (Pogontseva). Irrespective of whether they wear makeup, "more men evaluate girls wearing *hijab* as hostile" (Pogontseva).

If the purpose of *hijab* is modesty, modesty does not require an explicit religious identification. Modesty, after all, is humility, and there is sagacity in subtlety. It is not necessary or advisable to wear one's faith or ethnicity on one's sleeve or one's forehead, like a target. People are entitled to privacy. They do not feel the need to distinguish themselves from others constantly. Many times, they merely wish to belong to the community or move around incognito.

If the purpose of the pertinent verses was to establish class-status, in a society where Muslims wanted to assert themselves as the new elite, wherein lies the wisdom in so doing when they are already dominant in the Muslim world? And what benefit would this have in societies where such a religious and racialized identity marker places the wearer in a precarious and potentially perilous second-class position? According to Khaled Abou El Fadl:

> it is an error for a Muslim woman to continue wearing the headscarf, or the *hijab*, if doing so brings such a person undue attention, or puts her at risk of harm, of any sort, or even stands as an obstacle to her ability to testify on behalf of God and to educate non-Muslims as to the truth of the Islamic message. (2016)

As Asma Barlas explains, the two verses in question, 33:59 and 24:30, "are addressed only to the Prophet; that is, they are not a universal mandate for all Muslim men to force women to comply with them" (2019: 58). Since God prohibits compulsion in religion (2:256), she concludes that "no one can force a moral praxis upon another person" (2019: 58).

If, however, we accept that these verses apply, by extension, to all Muslim women, they are a moral exhortation and not a mandatory legal decree that can be imposed by force and enforced by corporal punishment, incarceration, and potential execution on grounds of "spreading corruption on earth" (5:33), the ever-invoked excuse of the Islamists that is applied to all those who oppose their hypocrisy, oppression, injustice, cruelty, absolutism, and totalitarianism. It is basically at catch-all phrase used by the regime to describe any form of opposition.

After re-examining the evidence, some self-described progressive Muslim academics have concluded that 33:59 was revealed in the context of the civil war in Medina (Amer 44). In short:

> wearing a *jilbab* was a response to a specific historical situation, a practical solution to a whole web of military conflicts and social tensions. It was not an injunction to dress in a particular way, valid for all women at all times and in all places, regardless of the safety of their environs. (44-45)

While 33:55 also addresses the issue of dress, the verse in question is often sidelined by Muslim scholars. It stresses the permissibility of the Prophet's wives to relax the dress code around relatives, women, and servants. Some scholars stress that these servants must be female; however, this is inferred and not explicitly indicated. Consequently, the claim of some jurists that Muslim women must also cover themselves from non-Muslim women, in the same way they cover themselves from men, is not supported by this Qur'anic verse, neither is the view that they must completely cover themselves in the presence of familiar males who may not be related. It merely means that one can be more at ease in one's home than in public.

The fact that Muslim women of a certain age "commit nothing wrong by relaxing their dress code, provided they do not reveal too much of their bodies" since "to maintain modesty is better for them" is also stressed in 24:60. Women who no longer anticipate marriage may "lay aside their garments." The word used is *thiyab*, which, for Razi (d. 1209), the polymath, means garments (Nasr 886: note 60). For Ibn Kathir, Muqatil (d. 767), Maturidi (d. 944), Qurtubi (d. 1273), and Tha'labi (d. 1036), it refers to the *jilbab*. For Razi and Tabari (d. 923), it refers to the *khimar* (Nasr 886: note 60). For Muqatil, Tabari, and Zamakhshari (d. 1074), it also includes the *rida'* or *milhafah*, namely, the wrap (Nasr 886: note 60). While these rules were only supposed to apply to women of menstruating age, they have been extended to prepubescent girls by claiming that nine-year-old girls are women, and equally applied to women past the child-bearing age, another example of oppressive overreach.

Finally, the Qur'an advises Muslims to wear beautiful clothing when they pray at home or in mosques: "O Children of Adam! Wear your beautiful apparel at every time and place of prayer" (7:31) or "Put on your adornment at every place of prayer" (7:31). The word that is translated as "beautiful apparel" or "adornment" is *zinah*, literally, "beauty." If 24:31 told women "not to display their beauty and ornaments," namely their *zinah*, "except what must ordinarily appear thereof," 7:31 orders women (and men) to show their beauty "at every time and place of prayer." Consequently, the claim that Muslim women must conceal their natural beauty and ornaments in public is contradictory. If Muslims are encouraged to remember God at all times, they should do their best to be beautiful at all times.

As Bronwyn Winter, the scholar of Transnational Studies, notes, "the proviso 'except what emerges' is sufficiently vague and suggestive to be open to a fascinating range of interpretations, from the most restrictive to the most liberal" (25). According to the Qur'an, clothing serves two purposes: 1) to cover the private parts / genitalia, which, if exposed, is a source of shame or embarrassment (7:26); and 2) as an adornment, namely, to beautify oneself (7:31). Finally, the Qur'an states that the best of clothing is that of righteousness (7:26); namely, what matters most is not what one wears but how one behaves.

As can be appreciated, 24:31 "doesn't literally, nor based on context, require women to cover their hair" (Yahya). Rather than speak of the female form, as exegetes concluded, it is possible that the Qur'an was condemning materialism. In other words, 24:31 would be similar to Isaiah 3:16-23 in which a previous prophet berated excessive ornamentation:

> The Lord says, "The women of Zion are haughty, walking along with outstretched necks, flirting with their eyes, strutting along with swaying hips, with ornaments jingling on their ankles.... The Lord will bring sores on the heads of the women of Zion; the Lord will make their scalps bald." In that day, the Lord will snatch away their finery: the bangles and headbands and crescent necklaces, the earrings and bracelets and veils, the headdresses and anklets and sashes, the perfume bottles and charms, the signet rings and nose rings, the fine robes and the capes and cloaks, the purses and mirrors, and the linen garments and tiaras and shawls.

If a woman covers her entire body and face, what remains of the beauty that "must ordinarily appear?" A black body bag? In the case of prayer, the beauty that should usually show is undoubtedly the face. In fact, the Prophet Muhammad pointed out that women should not veil their faces during the pilgrimage. As Barlas notes, "the Qur'an uses the words *jilbab* (cloak) and *khumur* (shawl), both of which, in ordinary usage, cover the bosom (*juyub*) and neck, not the face, head, hands, or feet" (2019: 58-59). Therefore, there is no basis for the face veil, *niqab*, *litham*, or *burqa* in Islam. Likewise, the case for compulsory head covering or *khimar* has little foundation. As Latifa, an Afghan woman, expressed:

> I climb out of my *burqa* feeling humiliated and furious. My face belongs to me. The Koran says that a woman can be veiled, but that she must remain recognizable. The Taliban want to steal my face, forbid us all faces. (Bailey and Tawadros 132)

"Many people say that they support a woman's right to choose to wear the *niqab* because it is her natural right," writes Mona Eltahawy, "but what their doing is supporting an ideology that does not believe in a woman's right to do anything *except* cover her face" (61). "To claim that the wearing of *niqab* is a feminist issue," she asserts, "is to turn feminism on its head" (62). As Phyllis Chesler notes:

> the *burqa* is not religiously mandated. In the past, many Muslim countries either banned the *burqa* or allowed women and their families to choose how women would dress. From a human rights point of view, the *burqa* demoralizes the wearer and all women who see her: hobbled, hidden, invisible, unable, or forbidden to join the social conversation. (2013: 198)

The issue is not the right to wear a headscarf. The issue is the right not to wear a headscarf, a *chador*, or a *burqa* and to not be pressured or forced to do so. The coercion is not limited to government policy as in Iran, Afghanistan, and Saudi Arabia, it includes social pressure and intimidation in Muslim-majority nations and even the Western world. As Olivier Guitta (b. 1970), a foreign affairs and counter-terrorism consultant, reports:

> A survey conducted in France in May 2033 found that 77% of girls wearing the *hijab* said they did so because of threats from Islamist groups. A series in the newspaper *Libération* in 2003 documented how Muslim women and girls in France who refuse to wear the *hijab* are insulted, rejected, and often threatened by Muslim males. One of the teenage girls interviewed said, "Every day, bearded men come to me and advise me strongly on wearing the veil. It is a war. For now, there are no dead, but there are looks and words that do kill." Muslim women who try to rebel are considered "whores" and treated as outcasts. Some of them want to move to areas "with no Muslims" to escape.

Jane Kramer (b. 1938), the American journalist, has well described the spread of Islamist networks in France. If, decades ago, the few women who wore headscarves did so out of culture or piety, the considerable number of those who do so are "expressing subservience to (or fear of) the radical indoctrination of young French-born Muslim men… Islamist provocateurs, protection racketeers, and preachers." Many women who wear *hijab*, out of conviction or fear, have little to no knowledge of Islam. "I see these girls in veils," stated Dalil Boubaker (b. 1940), the rector of the Grand Mosque of Paris, and "I ask them: 'What do you know of Islam? Nothing? Not even the Islamic dates?' I say to them, 'Learn something about all this. Learn your religion before you go out and make a spectacle of yourselves in the streets'" (Kramer).

In the ghettos of France, veritable incubators of terrorism, which Islamist vigilantes patrol, often providing more law and order than the absent police, the *hijab* has become the equivalent of gang signs and colors. As Kramer notes, girls who do not conform are "excoriated, or chased, or beaten by fanatical young men meting out 'Islamic justice.' Sometimes, the girls were gangraped." In 2002, an unveiled Muslim girl … was burned alive." Writing in 2011, Ida Lichter (b. 1947), a psychologist and author, reported that "gang rapes have been increasing by 15 to 20 percent each year in the *banlieues* and there have been a series of shocking murders of young women" (121).

Most of these rapists and gang-gang rapist rapists walk free. They terrorize the members of the community. They threaten witnesses with retaliatory rape against their womenfolk, the burning of their homes, and murder. The few that are arrested are never charged with rape. Their cases are downgraded to lighter offenses. Some get fines. Others receive suspended sentences. And yet others receive paltry prison sentences of one year in cushy French prisons that are more like resorts than penitentiaries. After all, these "vacation destinations" are already at capacity in France and the State has shown nothing but indifference toward the plight of women, mostly Arab, Amazigh, and Muslim, but also French, who live in the slums of the Republic. They suffer from five thousand to seven thousand gang-rapes per year. Those are just the ones that are reported.

When girls are gang-raped by twenty-five to fifty teenagers and men at a time, in an atmosphere of complete indifference, where the victims are shamed, shunned, and blamed by their families and communities, and where the perpetrators are defended by the very same, there is little to no hope for justice. And since the French government refuses to keep race-based statistics, their media and government are willfully blind to the cultural, religious, ethnic, and racial identity of the assailants. The victims are mostly girls of North African ancestry, along with some French girls, while their torturers are almost exclusively North African Arabs, Imazighen, and black Africans, virtually all of whom identify as Muslims. Whether they are observant or not, most Muslims have been marinated in the same religiously and culturally rooted misogyny. They share the same view of women as black American gangster rappers, pimps, and drug dealers. The problem is not just religion. It is not just culture. It is a toxic, reactive, and corrosive combination of the worst elements from both. It is time to call a spade a spade. To address any problem, you must first identify it, not pretend it does not exist based on political correctness.

For many Westerners and moderate Muslims, the spread of Islamist attire should cause as much concern as the massive adoption of Nazi uniforms. While some Islamists engage in a dual discourse, many are explicit about their intentions. They are at war against the West and the infidels. They wish to conquer our lands and impose *shari'ah* law upon all. They have long put their thoughts into action and have committed countless acts of terrorism. For critics, patriots, and nationalists, the members of these Islamist movements are not citizens: they are enemy combatants who have pledged allegiance to a foreign ideology and sworn loyalty to foreign leaders. They are enemies within our midst and fall into the same category as gangs, crime syndicates, and cartels.

Commenting on the *hijab* controversy in France, Iqbal al-Gharbi, the Tunisian anthropologist, explained that:

> The veil is just the tip of the iceberg. Behind the veil, there is the regressive interpretation of the *shari'ah*. There are the three essential inequalities which define this interpretation: inequality between man and women, Muslim, and non-Muslim, between free man and slave. (Guitta)

As Bestandji warns, the Islamists exploit secularism and inclusion to promote religious sexism (2021: 266-268). However, the extremist manifestations of Islam should not prevail over civil and human rights (2021: 268). Regrettably, "intersectionalist feminists prefer Islamist sexism to the universality of feminism" (2021: 277). When women are brutalized in the name of Islam, they maintain a pathetic silence (Chesler 2018: 416-418). Richard Martineau (b. 1961), the French-Canadian commentator, hits the nail on the head:

> Hatred of the West is blinding the left. Feminists should with one voice condemn Islamist misogyny. Instead, they spend time and energy justifying the unjustifiable, claiming that Eastern misogyny (which is "cultural") is more acceptable than Western misogyny (which is "political").

Since God did not define "what must ordinarily appear thereof," in the text, the extent of what is uncovered is determined by time and context. As Zaki Badawi (d. 2006), the Egyptian scholar of Islam, said, "it is left to custom" (Goodwin 30). It is what appears in customary practice. It is an issue of propriety. It is a question of functionality. One does not wear loose-fitting clothing while riding ski lifts or rides in amusement parks due to the danger of strangulation. When working on a factory line, one does not wear flowing garments that can get caught in the machinery. One does not go swimming in cloaks, socks, and shoes. One does not run while wearing long robes upon which one can trip. One does not wear a suit and tie in a Turkish bath. One does not wear a bikini in a business office. One covers oneself adequately according to the circumstances. As Zaki Badawi (1922-2006), the Egyptian Islamic scholar, explained:

> There has never been an Islamic obligation for women to cover at any time. In fact, veiling the face is an innovation that has no foundation whatsoever in Islam… The *hijab* veil (which covers all of a Muslim woman's hair) is also not obligatory. (Goodwin 30)

As for what can be exposed in the presence of non-marriable family members, namely, the "beauty" women can show in front of "their husbands, their fathers, their husbands' fathers, their sons, their husbands' sons, their brothers, or their brothers' sons or their sisters' sons, or their women or the servants whom their right hands possess, or male servants free of physical needs, or small children who have no sense of the shame of sex" (24:31), it is described as that which is not normally shown in public.

For example, a woman may expose her private parts to her husband. She could wear much less at home than she would normally do in public. In cramped quarters, she might have to undress or even bathe in the presence of close family members while maintaining as much modesty and decorum as possible. What would be a sin or unseemly in public is not necessarily so in private. In fact, many of the homes in seventh-century Arabia consisted of a single room where all activities occurred. Many homes were devoid of doors. Bathing was often in public baths where women, and their children, might use the same room. As Muhammad Shahrur, the Syrian intellectual, explains:

> Some may think that our interpretation of *zinah* allows a woman to appear half-naked in front of anyone listed in verse 31 (with only her genitals covered). This may indeed happen but only by accident, through absent-mindedness, or by force, while the *zawj* husband is the only person who is legally entitled to see her lower private parts… As for a woman's upper private parts (breasts and armpits), a woman will not be prosecuted if she reveals them in front of the six types of men mentioned in the list. If it happens, it is not regarded as *halal* or *haram*, but she should be criticized as being immodest (even though it is sanctioned by *the Book*). (2009: 312)

As for the call for women "not to strike their feet in order to draw attention to their hidden ornaments," (24:31), it is both literal and allegorical. The Arab women of the time used to wear anklets, bracelets, and hip belts that would cling. Some had bells. The traditional clothing of belly-dancers traces back to the pre-Islamic period. Unchaste women, who fornicated freely or prostituted themselves for profit and / or pleasure, indicated their sexual availability by shaking their bracelets, anklets, and hip belts. It was a non-verbal "come and get it." The sound signified that she was sexually available or for sale.

Chaste, believing, women would not expose these ornaments in public. They could, however, show these coins and bells in private, among close family members. Even if they dangled, they could not be construed as an invitation to sexual infidelity. The Qur'an was not commanding women to cover their bodies completely. It prohibited them from fornicating, committing adultery, and prostituting themselves. The prohibition is not the presence of the female body in public. The prohibition is against selling the human body on street corners and other settings.

The word *zinah*, however, has both positive and negative connotations. While it means "beauty," it can also be used in the sense of "worldly sources of beauty and status" (11:15, 16:8, 18:28, 46), which can be sources of pride, temptation, and worldliness (Nasr 417: note 31). The word *zinah* can also apply to clothing (Nasr 417: note 31). As Almighty God warns, "O Children of Adam!

Let not Satan tempt you, as he caused your parents to go forth from the Garden, stripping them of their rainment to show them their nakedness" (7:28). In other words, Satan removed their *zinah* or beauty to show their '*awrah* or private parts.

3.8 Conclusions

Considering that it was customary for pagan Arabs to circumambulate the Ka'bah in the nude, as reported by Tabari and Zamakhshari (Nasr 416: note 28, Dashti 55), among others, the call for Muslim women to "show their beauty" when they pray might not be a call for strict *hijab*, as jurists would like us to believe, but rather a call for Muslim women to maintain their dignity by avoiding public nudity. Placed in their socio-cultural and historical context, the so-called *hijab* verses are not so much about *hijab* as they are about encouraging Muslim women to abstain from nakedness and conceal their "hidden ornaments," namely, their genitals and their breasts. In so doing, God gives women vast freedom.

The beauty that Satan removed from Adam and Eve was not their literal clothing; the sense of modesty that covered them. In fact, it was only after their beauty was removed that they felt the need to cover their shameful parts. Rather than bring out one's inner beauty, the imposition of so-called Islamic dress can have the opposite effect and bring out a person's inner ugliness. It can also have adverse outcomes. In Iran, for example, the imposition of mandatory *hijab* laws correlates with an alarming increase in the suicide rate among little girls. It snuffs the life out of them. It has also increased anti-religious sentiment and contempt for clerics. The mandatory *hijab* laws repel many women from religion. Even pious people view the *hijab* laws as a hassle and a burden. Whether they live in Iran or the Western world, Muslim girls suffer under the veil, the detrimental impact of which has been documented by Bestandji (2021: 187-188). Some claim that the *hijab* makes them flower. For others, it devastates their self-esteem and makes them wither away. Some Muslim women get so frustrated, exasperated, and depressed about the constant bad hair days caused by the *hijab* that they shave their heads. "What does it matter?" they assert, "Nobody is going to see it anyway." Rather than help their spiritual and social development, it hinders it.

When God speaks of "the raiment of reverence that is best" (7:27), it refers, as Razi, Tabari, and Zamakhshari believe, to faith, modesty, righteous deeds, beautiful behavior, and fear of God (Nasr 415: note 26). "For this reason," notes *The Study Qur'an*, "al-Razi maintains that the private parts (or 'shame') of believers are always covered, while those of the profligate are always 'uncovered,' even when they are clothed" (Nasr 415: note 26). This was made clear by Ja'far al-Sadiq in *The Lantern of the Path*. When commenting upon covering one's *saw'at* or genitals, as called upon in 7:27, the sixth Imam stated that "the best adornment of the believer's garment is precaution, and the most blessed garment is belief" (17). He stated that "you should clothe your inward part as you clothe your outward part with your garment. Let your inward truth be veiled in awe of God, and let your outward truth be veiled in obedience" (17). Once again, it is not ultimately about clothing and covering; it is about piety, reverence, and righteousness. It is not just about one's attire. It is about one's comportment. In closing, women may have vulvas, but they are not vulvas.

For Ahmed Subhy Mansour (b. 1949), the Egyptian American activist and Qur'anist, it is scandalous to consider women as "'*awrat*, the intimate parts of the body, which is to say, flawed erring vessels that lack religious piety and reasoning minds and that should be covered away from prying eyes!" (Women's Right). Such a view deprives women of their dignity. Women are manifestations of the Sacred Feminine worthy of respect, honor, and reverence, in the same way that men are manifestations of the Sacred Masculine and are worthy of the same. The Qur'an does not impose cult or army-like uniformity to destroy individuality. It celebrates beauty and human diversity.

Chapter 4

Foundations of Falsehood Built on Shifting Sands

4.1 Introduction

So far, this study has shown that the rulings regarding mandatory *hijab* are inconsistent with the Qur'anic message of inner and outer modesty. When it comes to men, jurists concluded they must cover their reproductive organs, namely, their genitals. Some included their buttocks. Others called for covering everything from the navel to the knee. Men, it would seem, were granted enormous freedom, latitude, and leeway when it came to dress. While many Muslim men wore long robes, and some jurists ruled that it was recommended for men to cover their thighs, chests, and arms, they were certainly not required to do so. In fact, some only wore loincloths. Nobody policed their dress and punished them for showing too much skin. In most cases, however, the same type of freedom was not afforded to women, particularly free women who were subjected to severe restrictions and limitations. This chapter compares the dress of enslaved women to that of free women, reconsiders the rulings issued by Muslim jurists over the past thousand years and more, and examines how their views of women influenced their restrictive edicts.

4.2 The Dress of Enslaved Women

When it came to enslaved females, Islamic judicial opinions ranged from the requirement to cover their vaginas and anuses, the requirement to cover their bodies from the navel to the knee while remaining topless, or the obligation to cover their torsos down to their knees and arms down to their elbows (Abou El Fadl 2013: 257). How, then, can modern-day scholars and Islamists claim that the *hijab* is about modesty when classical jurists allowed slave girls to go around topless in public and private and even prohibited them from covering up like free Muslim women? As Khaled Abou El Fadl asks rightly and intelligently: "What is the basis for this distinction? Is the hair, arms, or chest of a slave-girl less capable of inducing seduction than that of a free woman?" (2006: 196). As terrible as it may be to force a woman to uncover, it is even worse to prevent a woman from freely covering within reason. Decidedly, the jurists in question considered dress a marker of social class instead of personal modesty. Some argued that it was a concession or accommodation made to women who were not free as part of Islam's mercy and tolerance. How about extending that mercy and tolerance to free women? Since when do enslaved women get more rights and freedoms than free women? If that is the case, then some Muslim women would prefer to change their status from wives to slaves or, better yet, extending the same freedoms to all women.

If the Muslim men of the past could control themselves in the presence of topless teenage girls and adult women, is it too much to demand modern Muslim men to tolerate the presence of a woman's hair? What kind of men or animals have these Islamic laws created? Men who get turned on by shoes with any type of heel. Men who are aroused by colored headscarves. Men who get erections from hearing the sound of women's shoes. Men who get sexually excited by the warmth that a woman leaves behind on a chair. Men who cannot tolerate the sight, smell, or sound of a woman without running the risk of masturbating themselves or sexually assaulting the woman in question.

Islamic laws have not produced the society of the righteous and pious they promised. They have created societies of perverts and moral degenerates: men who have no respect for women and are incapable of controlling themselves. It would seem that Muslim men, rather than Muslim women, are the perma-adolescents who never mature. Many Muslim men, namely, those who constantly harass and grope women, have the maturity or immaturity of thirteen-year-old boys. They view women as female dogs in heat when they are horny goats.

4.3 The Dress of Free Women

When it came to free women, however, the variety of opinions was even more remarkable. The '*awrah* of a free woman was as little as her vagina to her entire body, head, face, and voice. Some required the breasts to be covered. Some included the torso and arms to the elbows (Abou El Fadl 2013: 257). Some allowed the forearm or entire arms to be shown (Abou El Fadl 2013: 257). Others allowed women to show their calves (Abou El Fadl 2013: 257, Nasr 875: note 31). And yet others required them to cover their hair during prayers but not outside of them (Abou El Fadl 2013: 257). What women were required to cover was not black and white. There was a whole spectrum of opinions from the highly liberal and liberated to the ultra-conservative and restrictive. Some rulings wanted complete control over women's dress. Others granted women greater freedom to dress as they desired. Still, why should men be making rules regarding the dress of women like control freaks? Why should women be denied agency?

Most importantly, why are the jurists' rulings out of harmony with the Qur'anic text? Rather than interpret the Qur'an by the Qur'an as the Qur'an teaches, and rely upon reason as it equally instructs, the jurists in question were influenced by external factors, not the least of which was the fraudulent *hadith* literature. While there is a paltry number of sayings on the subject of *hijab* that are attributed to the Prophet Muhammad and the twelve Imams, they were recorded centuries to a thousand years after the fact, are dubious in authenticity, pose serious contextual and historical issues, contradict the plain sense meaning of the Qur'an, and appear to have been introduced as legal maxims to justify the repressive rulings of jurists.

4.4 Reconsidering the Rulings

As Khaled About El Fadl has found, "there are no reliably dispositive *hadith* traditions on the subject of *hijab*" (2016). Refuting them requires little effort; however, that would require a study of its own, and this scholarly work concentrates primarily on the Qur'an. Although they can be refuted based on their chains of narration, their objectionable and unconscionable content is enough to condemn them as women-hating forgeries. After all, notes Juan Cole (b. 1952), the American historian, "many of these sayings are essentially folk literature or dubious, and some are transparent forgeries" (204). In light of the fact that the rulings of classical jurists focused on the social status of women, we are therefore forced "to focus on and give weight to the Qur'anic discourse above all else" (Abou El Fadl 2016).

According to the history of Qur'anic revelations, the so-called *hijab* verses were revealed in the third, fifth, or seventh year of the *hijrah* to address the sexual harassment of Muslim women. If we accept this claim, it establishes that there was no so-called *hijab* for the first twelve years of Islam in Mecca and the first three, five, or seven years in Mecca: a total of fifteen, seventeen, or nineteen years in which a dress code did not constrain women. That would also imply that women were not required to cover their hair or other body parts, except for their private parts, during prayer or in public. And if the sources are correct, there are reports that Umm Habibah, a wife of the Prophet, did not wear the *khimar* or headscarf (Abou El Fadl 2013: 256-257, note 106). What is more:

> the great descendant of the Prophet, Sakinah bint al-Husayn bin 'Ali (also known as Fatimah al-Kubra) is reported to have invented a hairdo or style known as *al-turrah al-sukayniyyah* (Sukaynah-style curls) that she wore in public. She refused to cover her hair and is reported to have been imitated by the noble women of the *Hijaz*. (Abou El Fadl 2016)

Sukaynah, as she was known, was a proud *barzah*, an unveiled woman who did not lower her head in the presence of men, who received visitors at home, and was sharp of intelligence (Mernissi 191-192). The trauma of witnessing the slaughter of her father Husayn, and her family members, at Karbala, explains her revolt against the "Islamic" *status quo*, including the *hijab*. As Mernissi notes:

> Sukaynah … was celebrated for her beauty… an explosive mixture of physical attractiveness, critical intelligence, and caustic wit. The most powerful men debated with her; caliphs and princes proposed marriage to her, which she disdained for political reasons… She ended up marrying five, some say, six, husbands. She quarreled with some of them, made passionate declarations of love to others, brought one to court for infidelity, and never pledged… obedience… to any of them… She stipulated that she would not obey her husband, but would do as she pleased, and that she did not acknowledge that her husband had the right to practice polygyny… All her life Sukaynah harbored feelings of contempt … for the Umayyad dynasty and its bloody methods. She attacked the dynasty in the mosques and insulted its governors and representatives every time she had the opportunity, even arranging occasions for this purpose. She made one of her husbands sign a marriage contract that officially specified her right to *nushuz*, that rebellion against marital control that so tormented the *fuqaha*. She claimed the right to be a *nashiz*, and paraded it, like her beauty and her talent, to assert the importance and vitality of women in the Arab tradition. (192-192)

No wonder Twelver Shiite scholars wrote her out of existence, claiming she died at Karbala or shortly thereafter.

While most of the jurisprudential opinions that have survived trace back to centuries after the passing of the Prophet, one primitive edict survives, that of Sa'id ibn Jubayr (655-714), who is considered one the earliest legal authorities in Islam. A leading member of the followers of the companions, this man of Abyssinian origin was reportedly a companion of 'Ali and one of the first five companions of Zayn al-'Abidin. Unlike later jurists, he did not believe Muslim women needed to cover their hair. He considered it recommended and felt that the failure to cover the hair was reprehensible (Nasr 875: note 31, Abou El Fadl 2016: 240). It was not, however, a sin for women's hair to go uncovered. And if it was reproachable for a woman to uncover her hair, it was due to the customs and cultures of the time, not a universal divine decree applicable in all circumstances.

On what grounds did Sa'id ibn Jubayr issue this revealing ruling? Based on the fact that hair is not explicitly mentioned in 24:31 (Nasr 875: note 31). If God required women to cover their hair, and it is a major sin not to do so, one that merits punishment in this life and hell in the hereafter, the least He could have done was tell them so in no uncertain terms. Otherwise, it is simply not fair. And it certainly is not just. Commands must be clear and unambiguous. As far as believing Muslims are concerned, the Qur'an is clear and unquestionable in its commands. They are convinced that it was protected and preserved by the grace of God. The same cannot be said of the *hadith* literature, the commentaries of the Qur'an, and the edicts of jurists. Authentic traditions can be used to understand the Qur'an; however, they cannot contradict it. A person cannot be punished for placing the Qur'an before the *sunnah* and using the Qur'an as the criteria for authenticating the *sunnah*. According to Islam, God revealed but one book. Muslims, however, turned to other books, compilations of sayings attributed to the Prophet, the companions, and the Imams, placing them on par, or even above the Qur'an. The Word of Man thereby prevailed over the Word of God.

Despite the fact that they were compiled centuries after the passing of the Prophet Muhammad, and were transmitted by fallible human beings, Muslim jurists relied extensively on the *hadith* literature, and many believed that the Qur'an's need for the *sunnah* was greater than the *sunnah*'s need for the Qur'an. In other words, many of them accorded greater weight to the *hadith* literature than they did to the Qur'an. They used the *hadith* to expand upon the meaning of the Qur'an instead of using the Qur'an to determine the authenticity of the *hadith*. The result is a misreading of the only primary source in Islam: the Qur'an.

The very names of Muslim sects show how they have placed the buggy before the horse. They are the *ahl al-sunnah*, the people who follow the *sunnah*. They are the *ahl al-bayt*, the people who follow the descendants of the Prophet Muhammad. They are the *usulis*, namely, the people who follow the sources of traditions. They are the *akhbaris*, namely, the people who follow the narrations of the Imams. They are the *ahl al-tasawwuf*, the people of mysticism. Where are the *ahl Allah*, the people of God? Where are the *ahl al-Qur'an*, the people of the Qur'an, the Qur'anists, those who follow the Qur'an first and foremost? After all, as Gamal al-Banna (1920-2013), the prominent Egyptian intellectual, asserted, only the Qur'an merits "immortalization" (Hasan 12). And where are the *ahl al-'adl wa al-tawhid*, the people of justice and monotheism? Where are those who rely on justice and reason? Where are the *ahl al-'aql*, the people of reason? Where are the rationalist monotheists?

4.5 Judging the Jurists

When it came to issuing jurisprudential rulings, Muslim scholars relied on the Qur'an and the *hadith*. Some included the sayings of the companions and Imams. Some relied on reason. Others rejected reason, logic, and analogy. Some considered consensus as an interpretive tool. And yet others rejected it. The same can be said for local customs, the greater good, and other sources of *ijtihad* or derivation of rulings.

What these scholars did not consider, however, was history, society, and culture. They did not consider the question of subjectivity. They graded traditions based on chains of narration and, occasionally, based on their content. They judged narrators on the basis of how much they confirmed their views. If a tradition agreed with their views, they strengthened it. If it disagreed with their views, they weakened it. They never considered factors that could have influenced them, such as patriarchy, sexism, and misogyny. They never considered the culture of the narrators, commentators, and jurists that preceded them. They never considered personal history, ancestry, or former religious affiliation. Except for certain sectarian or theological inclinations, they never screened their sources for potential bias.

Who were these authors? Where did they live? What was their race or ethnicity? What was their religion of origin or the religion of their immediate ancestors? Were they pagans? Were they Jewish? Were they Christians? Were they Zoroastrians? Were they Sabeans? Were they Hindus? Did they strive to be objective? In what ways could they have been subjective? Why did they engage in scholarly work? Who were their patrons? Why did they patronize them? What were their motivations? What did they have to gain? Who commissioned the works they wrote? Who disseminated them? Who stood to benefit? Moreover, since the focus is on the *hijab*, how did they view women? Were they married? Did they own sex slaves? Did they buy and sell human beings? How did they treat women? Were they sexist? Were they misogynistic? Did they marry pre-pubescent girls? Did they believe in female genital mutilation? Did they beat their wives? What could have colored their interpretations? These questions barely scratch the surface.

It is not enough to read what these scholars had to say about the so-called *hijab* verses in question. We need to ask why they said so and question the reasons, the rationale, the motivations, and biases, conscious and subconscious, behind their interpretations. When these background checks are completed, the psycho-social profiles of the scholars in question help us understand their interpretations. They were products of their time and should not be placed on pedestals. The findings force us to reflect upon the interpretive foundations of Islam and reconsider its results. This is a matter of basic oversight and transparency that exposes subjectivity.

If one acts with due diligence, and completes the required background checks, one invariably finds that the scholars who demanded that women be covered from head to toe were the same scholars who insisted that women should be confined in their homes. They were the same scholars who believed that girls should be sexually mutilated, for their own good, namely, to prevent them from becoming insatiable: so-called imposed chastity by means of female genital mutilation which is a crime against humanity and divinity.

The scholars who demanded that women be covered from head to toe were the same scholars who insisted that husbands had the right to beat their wives, tie them to their beds, and rape them. They were the same scholars who ruled that married women did not have rights over their bodies and that their husbands had unfettered access to their oral, vaginal, and, according to some Shiite jurists, anal orifices, without the need for consent. Married or unmarried, free or slaves, women were property.

The scholars who demanded that women be covered from head to toe were the same scholars who insisted that wives had to service their husbands upon demand. In contrast, they ruled that husbands only had to sleep with their wives once every four months. They ruled that all property belonged to the husband and that wives did not even own the clothing on their backs. They denied women the right to marry and divorce freely. Ibn Rush, however, dissented (Akyol 2022: 123).

The scholars in question enshrined inequitable inheritance and custody rights. They denied women parity in testimony. They discouraged the education of women, insisting they should remain illiterate. They were those who deprived women of every imaginable right that was granted to them by God and His Prophet. We cannot expect gender justice from men like Ibn Kathir, who insisted that "men are better than women" (Hasan 51). The situation in modern times is still the same. As Riffat Hassan (b. 1943), the Pakistani American theologian and Islamic feminist, writes:

> That men and women have been created equal by God, having the same rights and responsibilities as representatives on earth is a fundamental Qur'anic teaching. Not only is this not the perspective of the present-day, but it also is not the view of the majority of Muslims in the world. (2021)

The scholars who demanded that women be covered from head to toe were those who viewed women as inferior, second-class beings in a state of permanent adolescence and who never matured. They were the same scholars who believed that were it not for men, women would never have been created. They were the same scholars who claimed that menstruation was a curse of God upon women to prevent them from fornicating and committing adultery all month long. They were the same scholars who believed women were private parts, sources of sedition, snakes, scorpions, and devils. They were the same scholars who were convinced that women were haunted by Satan and were the ropes of Iblis.

The scholars who demanded that women be covered from head to toe were the same scholars who taught that there was no piety in women and that men should never obey them in any matter. They were the same scholars who said women had beauty, but only men had brains. They were the same scholars who believed all women were lust-crazed and unfaithful by nature and had to be locked up in their homes for their good and the safety of society. They were the same scholars who ruled that if a dog, a donkey, or a woman passed in front of a man while praying, his prayer was invalidated. They were those who viewed the urine of baby boys as ritually clean but that of baby girls as impure.

One of the sickest books I have ever read is *Women Who Deserve to Go to Hell* by the Egyptian author Mansur 'Abdul-Hakim (b. 1955), a work that is proudly displayed on the windows and shelves of Islamist bookstores in the West. Misogynistic Muslim men devour this popular work of hate propaganda. It confirms their belief that "women... will be a majority in hell" and that women are deficient in intelligence and religion (15). Women who grumble will go to hell. Women who adorn themselves will go to hell. Women who pluck their eyebrows will go to hell. Women who cut their hair short will go to hell. Women who cry in distress will go to hell. Women who are arrogant will go to hell. Women who are quarrelsome will go to hell. Women who are disobedient will go to hell. The first half focuses on why women deserve to go to hell. The second offers a gruesome description of the sadistic tortures they will receive from Almighty Allah, the Most Compassionate, the Most Merciful. Although misogynists find such works emboldening and empowering, they are works that psychologically and spiritually abuse women. They inflict real violence upon women. In the words of Riffat Hassan:

> Male-centered and male-dominated Muslim societies have continued to assert, glibly and tirelessly, that Islam has given women more rights than any other religion, while keeping women in physical, mental, and emotional confinement and depriving them of the opportunity to actualize their human potential. (1999: 250)

As much as they claim that "Islam respects women" and "Islam gives women the dignity they deserve," it is clear that far too many Muslim men hate, despise, and loathe women with a passion. At the same time, there are many others who love, respect, and revere women. It should be remembered that there are sexists in all faith traditions, and they regurgitate the same arguments *ad infinitum* and *ad nauseam*. Islam, after all, is what Muslims do with it. In theory, revelation may be the work of God, but religion is the creation of man. In practice, however, it appears that many so-called revelations were altered by men or created out of the blue by them.

Either way, when you get to know the interpreters, regardless of their professed faith tradition, you get to understand the reasons for their interpretations. After one has done so, one must ask oneself: from where did they get these ideas? For indeed, they are not rooted in the Qur'an in the case of Muslims. Consequently, they must come from some external sources. In many cases, these misogynistic notions are found in the *hadith* literature. However, since the Prophet was the Qur'an walking and Qur'an talking, the sayings and actions of the Messenger of God cannot contradict the revelation of God. The same can be said of the sayings of the twelve Imams. If they held some of the views attributed to them, which are treated as authentic by some traditionists and jurists, then they were neither infallible nor guided by God. They were ordinary human beings, the product of their time, who, along with their sexism, suffered from delusions of grandeur. For most faithful and thinking Muslims, this is unacceptable. The negative sayings attributed to them are incompatible with the positive ones. They cannot be reconciled. Truth trumps falsehood. Good prevails over evil.

The sole solution that reconciles faith and reason is to treat the traditions in question as women-hating forgeries. Since he or she who seeks finds, research divulges that these misogynistic notions were drawn directly from the heathen Arabs, the pagan Greeks, the Jews, the Christians, and the Zoroastrians. They were introduced into the Islamic canon to ensure the continuity of the *status quo* and the protection of vested social and gender interests. The prophetic mission was subverted, and Islam was inverted. The Sacred Feminine was suppressed, and male supremacy was enshrined and given the blessing of God, the Prophet, and the twelve Imams. As Abla Hasan explains:

> Convoluted contradictions between the Qur'anic text and the *hadith* made any possible reconciliation a difficult task that caused many to make choices that were not necessarily faithful to the Qur'anic text... Prioritizing *hadith* over the Qur'anic text sometimes went beyond the mere desire to explain the Qur'an, and became an active effort to falsify Islamic history... (11)

Some scholars did so knowingly. Others did so naively, honestly believing that their inherited sources were genuine. Others may have acted faithfully but failed to recognize, address, and check their subjectivity. Some, however, came close to conveying the original meaning of the Qur'an. Others seem to have succeeded in doing so despite the odds that were against them. It is not the entire canon of interpretation that needs to be rejected, nor every reading and ruling of every scholar.

Interpretations must never be accepted uncritically. Edicts must never be followed blindly without examining the evidence. As Abla Hasan affirms, "we cannot claim that early scholars were more capable of understanding these verses than scholars are today" (19). Consequently, "scholars should not be denied the right to authenticate, refine, and even rethink the authenticity of canonical *hadith* collections" (Hasan 12). Every opinion must be freshly examined in light of the Qur'an as a whole. As Abla Hasan explains:

> We can easily understand the fear of change and the resistance to any attempt to rethink the Qur'an. However, this fear doesn't have any solid ground since confusing the project of rethinking the Qur'an and the fear of changing the Qur'an depends only on the myth that by rethinking the Qur'an modern scholars are changing the unchanged meaning of the text. While what they do in fact is nothing but changing a meaning that has already been changed. (19)

What is called for is critical thinking. "Theological schools," however, "did not encourage critical thinking the way they encouraged the reassertion and glorification of already existing theological arguments" (Hasan 15). What is more, "an overwhelming cultural-based patriarchal reading of the Qur'anic text dominated almost all available pre-modern commentaries and schools of jurisprudence" (Hasan 16). As Gamal al-Banna (1920-2013), the Egyptian author and Muslim reformer, put it, "they [forged] the Qur'an and projected their concepts on it" (Hasan 16).

4.6 Conclusions

As we have seen, some scholars have strayed from the core meaning of the Qur'an when it comes to matters of female modesty, not to mention everything else related to women. The Qur'an discouraged nudity and encouraged women to cover their private parts. This was the position of some early authorities. This view was mentioned in passing by Tabari and it was espoused by Ibn 'Arabi. In the words of this great mystic and jurist:

> Some people say that all of a woman's body, with the exception of her face and hands, constitutes her '*awrah*. Another group excludes her feet from being '*awrah*, while a third considers all of her body without exception to constitute the '*awrah*... In our opinion, the only parts of her body that are '*awrah* are her genitals. God, the Exalted says: "When they tasted of the tree, their shameful parts became manifest to them, and they began to sew together the leaves of the Garden over their bodies." God put Adam and Eve on equal footing regarding the covering of their shameful parts, which are their genitals. If women are still ordered to cover their bodies, it is for the sake of modesty, and not because their bodies are shameful. (qtd. Shaykh 124)

Scholars like Marnia Lazreg (b. 1941), a Tunisian American sociologist, also share this position. "Since the text mentions bosoms and pudenda," she reasons, "dressing in a way that does not reveal these would satisfy the requirements of appropriate dress for women" (Hasan 107).

The call for women to cover their private parts was expanded to the region between the navel and the knees. It stretched to include the torso. It expanded to cover the arms. The coverage continued to grow and came to include the calves. It eventually encompassed the hair, not only during prayers but in all public spheres. All that was left were the hands and the feet. Even this was too much for some salacious and depraved men, and the feet were included in what needed to be covered. Finally, even the hands and the face succumbed, thanks to the rulings of certain jurists (Barlas 2019: 58), and women were swallowed alive by the *hijab*, the *chador*, the *niqab*, and the *purdah*: the pre-Islamic pagan custom of completely covering and confining women which came to be viewed as recommended by some Muslim jurists and obligatory to others. They literally ended up being buried alive in walking tents and sensory deprivation chambers.

Chapter 5

The Imposition of "Islamic" Dress Upon Women

5.1 Introduction

As a comprehensive and exhaustive study of history, dress, costume, and thought illustrates, the imposition of strict so-called Islamic dress upon women did not occur sequentially. It was chaotic. Partisans of all positions coexisted during the same periods. Over time, however, there was a general trend from the more permissive to the more restrictive. Eventually, the most extreme interpretations prevailed thanks to the support they received from political and economic powers. As we have seen, the dress code for women was extremely relaxed under Umayyad rule in the Middle East and Muslim Spain. Although head coverings were common, as fashion accessories and social markers, they were not typically tied around the front. They would hang behind the shoulders or loosely over the bosom. The material was often sheer or see-through. Some women did not cover their hair at all. And not only that. Some covered their hair while exposing their arms, torsos, backs, bosoms, and all. How is that for *hijab*?

5.2 A History of Muslim Women's Dress

Many Muslim scholars tend to live in echo chambers. They spend their time studying a narrow body of antiquated and obsolete books. Their outlook is myopic and introverted. As a result, they give Muslims the mistaken notion that the *hijab*, as they conceive it, has always been the norm in the Islamic world. This is a position that many scholars parrot. A simple survey of art, literature, and dress over the past fourteen hundred years shows that this is not the case. While some critics might claim that Islamic art does not reflect reality, many historians have concluded that "Arab painting… woodcarving, and metal inlays are, on the whole, accurate mirrors of their times" (Stillman 4). This applies to period pieces. They reflect the time in which they were produced. This is not the case with later works of art that depict the life and times of the Prophet Muhammad. The figures represented in such works are full of anachronistic clothing and accoutrement. Such artwork does not represent seventh-century

Arabian attire. So, how did Muslim women dress? It varied according to time and place.

Muslim women in Moghul India used to wear sheer headscarves that would hang to the sides and back instead of being tied below the neck. Their throats were customarily exposed, as were their forearms. They did not cover their feet (Racinet 192-193, 195, 196, Leventon 203). Not only did some expose their midriffs with their saris, but it was also a custom among certain women to show their breasts (188). Muslim women throughout Asia used to go around with their hair partially or entirely uncovered (Racinet 218-219). In parts of India, it was customary for lower-class women to uncover their breasts and for higher-class women to cover them. The Islamic fundamentalist neo-*hijab* innovation only started to appear in India and Pakistan in the late twentieth century.

While headcovers, turbans, or hats were normal, most Persian, Afghan, Pashtun, Indian, Turkoman, Arab, and Kurdish women did not completely cover their hair (Racinet 223-225, Scarce 168, 174). They used to show their feet, and some would show their stomachs (Racinet 224-227). Some women did wear the ancient equivalent of the *niqab* and *chador*; however, this was limited to the urban upper class (Racinet 224-225).

While married Persian women covered their hair with hats and shawls, this was not the case for unmarried girls (Vecellio 143). They often wore hats and turbans, some with shawls dangling from the back; however, their ears, throats, and necks, were visible (Vecellio 143). Sure, some women covered themselves completely, face, and all, but these were wealthy matrons (Vecellio 142). This was not the attire of ordinary women.

In his two-volume work published in 1720, Sir John Chardin (1643-1713), the French jeweler and traveler, provided illustrations of Safavid fashion. The women all wore headdresses. One matron wore a light-colored *burka*. The others wore crowns, hats, turbans, or wraps. Out of four, the throat of only one was concealed. The rest exposed their throats and ears. In fact, all four of them showed long strands of hair flowing down to their mid-backs or even beyond their waists (Ridgeon figure 2). Similarly, some Afghan women used to expose their long hair (Bruhn 177). *Pars Times* provides numerous photo galleries depicting historical and period costumes in Iran, Iranian traditional costume, and fashion in pre-revolutionary Iran, which lend perspective to Islamic dress. The *Encyclopedia Iranica* also provides an excellent historical overview of clothing in Iran.

In North Africa, Amazigh women usually exposed their forearms, upper arms, calves, and, in some cases, half of their thighs (Racinet 242-243). Since agricultural workers wore short dresses and miniskirts, they had no qualms about showing their feet, legs, and thighs. Although they typically wore head coverings, they were more like turbans and hats than headscarves. They exposed their ears, necks, throats, and upper chest and showed cleavage in some cases (Racinet 242-243). Moorish women used to wear crowns and scarves on their heads (Racinet 248). Their long headscarves were thrown behind their backs, exposing their neck and upper chest (Racinet 248). Some just wrapped the back of their hair, showing their bangs, ears, throats, and necks (Vecellio 132-133). The women of Algeria also wore scarves and hats; however, they would hang behind their backs. They would show their necks and, in some cases, their upper chest (Racinet 251). The women of Tlemcen did not even wear headscarves, veils, or shawls over their heads (Vecellio 427). They would tie up their hair, decorate it, and show their ears, necks, throats, and necklines (Vecellio 134).

The Kabyle and Arab women of Algeria and Tunisia would show their calves, knees, and half of their upper thighs (Racinet 354; Leventon 260-261). Most wore a headdress, none of which resembled the modern version of *hijab* (Racinet 254). While some women covered their faces, it did not prevent them from showing some hair (Racinet 160). As for the nomadic and sedentary women of the Sahara, small scarves were common; however, most of their hair was exposed (Racinet 259). Some wore sheer sleeves, and some showed their lower legs (Racinet 259). As Bestandji observes, for Islamists "to present the *hijab*, the *jilbab,* and the *niqab* to North Africans as traditional clothing, when they are not, is a master stroke" (2021 207-208).

Turkish women were relatively modest; however, their dress style did not meet the stringent so-called *shari'ah* standards of modern Islamists. They wore hats, turbans, and scarves but showed their necks and some of their hair (Racinet 267, Scarce 61, 62, 66-67, 91, Vecellio 118). Some cloaked themselves completely in *chadors* (Racinet 267). Others showed varying degrees of hair (Racinet 275). Many showed most of their hair (Bruhn 90, 170-171). The necklines of their dresses could be very low cut (Braun 627). Any headwear was a fashion accessory, not a religious obligation (Braun 1017). While head coverings were common among Kurdish women, they normally showed some hair (Racinet 278-282, Leventon 217, Bruhn 173-174). The same applied to Muslim women in the European Ottoman Empire (Racinet 695, 697). For example, Albanian women displayed their necks, bangs, and long tresses of hair (Bruhn 135). The clothing worn by Muslims was very similar to that worn by Christians. Women were not required to cover their hair. They all wore beautiful and attractive clothing.

The imposition of strict "Islamic" dress was invariably associated with extremists and misogynists: the 'Abbasids and the Almohads (Stillman 96, 146). When 'Abd al-Rahman I (731-788) and other Umayyad refugees set up power in al-Andalus, they attempted "to replicate as much as possible the society of the Syrian caliphate under which veiling may not as yet have been as strict and universal as it became under the 'Abbasids who supplanted them" (Stillman 146). Consequently, a more relaxed attitude toward women's dress persisted in al-Andalus (Stillman 146). As Norman Roth, the American historian, writes:

> In Muslim Spain, eighth-twelfth centuries, Jews, and Muslims were

> virtually indistinguishable in their clothing, which in southern al-Andalus at least consisted of loose linen or silk gowns; also, the *jubba*, a flowing robe with large sleeves and of various colors, such as green, orange or rose worn by both men and women. Women also wore the *qami*, a fine tunic of transparent gauze. Women, Muslim or Jewish, generally, did not wear veils, and in the early period they were usually worn by men (2018: 40-41)

The *qamisa*, which was often white or pale in color, was made of sheer silk or very lightly woven linen. This breathable material was designed to wick perspiration. The transparent, see-through, or translucent blouses worn by Muslim women in al-Andalus resembled the nude dresses popularized in the twenty-first century and which are made of organza, lace, muslin, voile, tulle, and gauze, as well as natural silk, cotton, or synthetic fibers like rayon or nylon. The neckline of the *qamisa* would sit at the woman's clavicle where it was tied in a bow. The slit of the dress plunged just below the breast to facilitate the feeding of babies.

When the Arabs conquered the Iberian Peninsula in 711, they introduced Islamic courtly attire which consisted of the crossover coat, the *jubba*, the *qamisa*, the *sarwal* or pants, *tiraz* bands, *tavlasans* or shawls, veils with a filet tied around the crown, the *ghifara,* a green or red wool cap, *babuj* or slippers, as well as the *shirka*, a thong like sandal With the exception of the *qamisa, tavlasan*, and veil, costume was unisex in al-Andalus (Stillman 86; Siege of Seville). The *tavlasan* was two to three yards long, made of heavy silk or wool, and could wrap around the entire body (Siege of Seville). Some were opaque; however, others were sheer (Siege of Seville). When worn, it rarely covered the throats of women. In fact, "In every other Islamic caliphate women were governed by *Hadiths* (laws), that prohibited them from being unveiled in public, in al-Andalus the *Hadiths* were not strictly enforced, and women were often seen bare headed in public" (Siege of Sevilla). The fact that the *khimar* and *hijab* never got a foothold in al-Andalus confirms the claim that it was the product of the counterfeit *hadith* literature and specious *shari'ah.* The early Muslims in al-Andalus followed the Qur'an and the traditional Islam that had been transmitted to them by the first generations of the faith. As we read in *Medieval Jewish Civilization*:

> Veils were not common for women and, in fact, in the early Muslim period were worn more by men. This is incidentally confirmed by Ibn 'Ezra [1089/1092-1167], who wrote that the veil is a long, thin piece of cloth covering the head and is worn by women only in a few places; "for in the land of Ishmael [Arabia], Spain, Africa, Egypt, Babylon, and Baghdad it is worn on the head by distinguished men and not by women" (commentary on Ex 29.36). (Roth 2003:173)

Strikingly, the veil, in the Maghrib and al-Andalus was worn by men. This supports the claim that there was no mandatory veil in early Islam. It was only adopted, centuries later by women as a result of Middle Eastern influence, namely, the 'Abbasid project to invent and impose an "orthodox" or intolerant Islam that was characterized by *hijab*, gender segregation, polygyny, harems, and sexual slavery. In al-Andalus, which reflected and retained traces of early, tolerant, Islam, the situation changed with the rise of the Almoravids in the second part of the twelfth century. They imposed a dress code aimed at distinguishing Jews and Christians from Muslims (Roth 2018: 41). The Almohads took matters to an even greater extreme through radical religious reforms that severely restricted the rights and social participation of Jews and Christians along with women of all religions.

In the Middle East, the imposition of so-called "strict *hijab*" took place at an earlier time. In fact, "by the 'Abbasid period, veiling is clearly taken for granted" (Stillman 142). Moreover, by the High Middle Ages, "the *niqab* seems to have become a basic part of the feminine wardrobe and one of the most common face veils in the Levant" (Stillman 143). In the words of Yedida Kalfon Stillman (d. 1998), the Moroccan American ethnologist:

> Although we cannot identify any precise or specific time when *hijab* became universal, strict veiling practices probably evolved as the norms for middle- and upper-class Muslim women over the first two centuries of the Islamic era in the cities and towns of the caliphate, especially as following the Prophet's *sunnah* became increasingly important and the traditionalists began collecting and producing an ever-expanding body of *hadith*. (140)

We know for a fact that "veiling and even covering of the hair were contested in Islamic jurisprudential discourse until at least two or three centuries after Muhammad" (Ali-Karamali 158). What was required to cover and what was required to conceal were the subject of centuries of debate. Even those who believed that women could show their hands, faces, and feet, disagreed on their definitions:

> Did "hands" mean hands up to the wrist or the elbow? If "feet" could be visible, did that mean feet to the ankle? To the calf? Or even to the knees? Did the face include the neck? Where did the covering for the chest begin -- at the base of the neck or the cleavage? Did the hair have to be covered or only hair from the crown? Some early jurists, despite viewing uncovered hair with disfavor, maintained that the Qur'an did not explicitly require the covering of hair. The Prophet never forced a woman to cover her hair. In fact, Muslim women as late as the ninth century -- two centuries after the Prophet -- even prayed with their heads uncovered... This couldn't have transpired if the Qur'an had been clear about head covering. (Ali-Karamali 158)

While extreme expressions of *hijab*, *niqab*, and *purdah* came to prevail in certain urban centers in the Middle East, village women continued to appear unveiled both in and out of doors (Stillman 144). The stranglehold of the jurists was incomplete, and clothing in much of the Muslim world remained practical and functional. It reflected the culture, class, and occupation of the woman. It was not one-size-fits-all. While some might claim that this study favors the *hijab* of ethnicity over the *hijab* of Islamicity, the real question that must be asked is whether the so-called Islamic *hijab* is actually Islamic. The answer comes from specialists in the history of costume, dress, and attire.

Although "*hijab* has become a sort of pan-Islamic uniform… the contemporary Islamist outfit is similar in all Muslim countries" (Stillman 158-159). It has deprived the Islamic world of its rich and varied fashion history. The Islamists wish to turn Muslim women into a single monolithic mass through the visibility of the veil (Bestandji 2021: 257). As Bestandji argues, "the purpose of the veil is to mark women as inferior, to hierarchize humanity, and to stigmatize and discriminate against its feminine half" (2021: 258). The Islamist uniform they wish to impose on women is both racist and sexist (Bestandji 2021: 261).

In the Muslim regions of Europe, North Africa, the Middle East, and parts of Asia, women wore a wide variety of head-coverings, few of which covered their hair, ears, necks, and throats completely. By the beginning of the twentieth century, "unveiling was now steadily becoming the norm" (Ahmed 2011: 43). By the 1950s and 1960s, however, few, if any, Muslim women covered their hair in the large cities of the Arab and Persian world. The women in Casablanca, Algiers, Tunis, Cairo, Baghdad, and Tehran dressed like those from Paris, London, Los Angeles, and New York. These women never unveiled. They had never veiled before. And the women who did cover their hair, partially, or even completely, did so in the traditional manner of their regions. "Islam sans veil," notes Leila Ahmed, "was essentially to us 'true' Islam -- Islam stripped … of centuries' worth of false and backward cultural accretions" (2011: 43). The fact that Muslim women did not veil did not mean they were secular or irreligious (2011: 43). The veil, which had been worn by women of all faiths in the past, was more of a cultural norm than a religious imperative (2011: 36, 47).

It was only in the 1970s, with the rise of radical movements, like the Muslim Brotherhood, that the Islamist *hijab* surfaced (49). As Leila Ahmed notes, "the coverings of the women of the Muslim Brotherhood… were not like any traditional veils" (2011: 49). They signaled they were not like other Muslim women, who were traditional or westernized, and they were opposed to them (2011: 49). For the Muslim Brotherhood, the veil was "a foundational Islamic requirement" (2011: 49). Consequently,

> the veil of the Brotherhood women was a visual emblem of the Brotherhood's commitment to a form of Islam requiring *hijab*, and at the same time, it signaled their opposition to the dominant classes and the direction in which they were taking society. (2011: 49)

Within a matter or decades, due to Islamist proselytization, supported by billions of dollars from the House of Saud, and the propaganda from the "Islamic" Republic of Iran, *hijab*-wearing women went from minorities to majorities. Traditional and modern dress, which was varied, colorful, and more relaxed, was replaced by dark, rigid attire, and tight headscarves. Diversity, freedom, and flexibility had given way to uniformity. Traditional costume disappeared and was replaced by Islamist attire from the Middle East (Bestandji 2021: 208). Moreover, "as numerous observers have rightly pointed out, this kind of *hijab* and the general phenomenon of *al-zayy al-islami* [Islamic dress] are new fashions, not traditional, but neo-traditionalist, incorporating only certain elements of older styles" (Stillman 159-160). "Even in the most conservative parts of India, Pakistan, and Bangladesh," notes Tarek Fatah (1949-2023), the Pakistani Canadian author, "the obsession of tucking every little piece of hair under an elastic sort of wrap was unheard of before the 1970s oil boom" (290).

Before the plague of Islamism spread from Saudi Arabia and Iran, Muslim women and men were more moderate in matters of dress in East and West, North and South. Well into the 1960s and 1970s, Muslim women in the West only covered their hair with kerchiefs while in prayer (Howell 250). In African American mosques in the United States, they wore "short sleeves, three-quarter sleeves, skirts worn just below the knees, and hair swept up in fashionable hats" (Howell 251). "Ironically," notes Howell, "it was several older men who made a point of consistently covering their heads to mark themselves as Muslim, always wearing Kufi caps or modified fezzes" (250). The new, radical, concept of *hijab* was introduced by immigrant Muslims, or Western Muslims who were educated by and under the direction of foreign Muslims. At the time, many black American Muslim men associated the *hijab* with foreign men who oppressed their women by insisting they be covered to the extreme (Howell 251). They viewed "their own practices of gender differentiation as sufficiently modest, while also appropriately respectful of women and culturally familiar" (251).

Prior to the spread of radical Islam in the West, men and women prayed in the same room. They sat and ate at the same tables. There was no mandatory *hijab* in the mosques. There was no strict requirements regarding the type of head covering worn by women during worship. Women showed their arms and lower legs during prayer (Howell 249-257). Suddenly, however, "these styles of dress were no longer acceptable; in fact, they were denounced as sinful" (Howell 251-252). In a short span of time, gender segregation was introduced, women were relegated to praying in backrooms, attics, and basements, and, in some cases discouraged, and even prohibited from attending the mosque. While many Muslims resisted, most succumbed to the new "Islamic revival." Eventually, "the most conservative voice, and the loudest," was able to dictate the norms of the Muslim community (Howell 254-255).

As anyone who surveys the history of costume will acknowledge, the way that many Muslim women dress today -- with tight headscarves that cover the head, throat, and chin and with black *abayahs*, *chadors*, and *niqabs* -- is not the way that Muslim women have traditionally dressed over the past fourteen hundred years. The traditional clothing of Muslim women was relatively modest. However, it did not necessarily cover the entirety of the arms and legs. What is more, it was beautiful, not bland, and it came in a myriad of colors. The headscarves were not tight. They were light. In some cases, they were loose and white. In others, they were stylish and lavishly adorned. Muslim women looked like flowers. Their clothing was a celebration of life, creation, and Creator. Now they look like ninjas.

For most of Islamic history, the appearance of Arabian women combined dress, ornamentation, hairdressing, and beauty culture (Ross 14). The women of southern Arabia wore headdresses; however, they showed their ears, earrings, and throats (Vecellio 149). The women of northern Arabia did not even wear shawls or scarves over their hair. They used to wear decorative hats. While they tied up their hair, they did not hide it entirely. And though their Roman-style togas were long, they had short sleeves, and their entire arms were exposed and decorated with bracelets and upper armlets (Vecellio 149). Some married women veiled their faces. Others did not, showing their long shiny black hair (Braun 950).

Arab women wore richly colored clothing, which was ultra-feminine, yet modest. Their traditional dresses were "enthralling -- exhibiting great visual appeal" (Ross 14). The harmonious color hues were exotic (14). Today, however, "clothing and hairstyles... are almost identical throughout the Peninsula" (14). Until recent times, the attire of Arab women had been a kaleidoscope of beautiful and bright colors that contrasted with their monochromatic environment (Ross 13). It was common for them to expose their hair, necklines, and a degree of *décolleté* (Ross contents page, 10, 12-13, 20-21, 55, 56, 57, 64-65, 70, 72, 74, 75, 76, 79, 80, 82, 85, 87, 89, 91, 95, 104, 110, 113, 115, 117, 130, 141, Braun 707). Some even wore hats instead of scarves on their heads (Ross 95) or in addition to them (96-97, 101).

The situation was similar in other Arab lands, like Lebanon and Syria, where women wore an assortment of hats, commonly showing their long, flowing hair, and their necklines (Braun 944, 885). And the same applied to Egypt (950) and Central Asia (1030). For example, the traditional dress of Chechnyan women, and other females from the Caucasus, included hats, sheer or see-through veils, and long dresses. Their hair, necklines, and ears were exposed. They looked like elegant angels. The Islamist attire imposed by Ramzan Kadyrov (b. 1976) since 2007 is an affront to Chechen culture, a religious innovation, a foreign imposition, and a break from time-honored custom and tradition.

Before the rise of Islamism in the 1970s, Palestinian women often showed their arms, throats, and ears in public. Many, but not all, wore headdresses; however, they were not tight-fitting and exposed some of their hair. They wore beautiful, colorful, and richly ornamented clothing (Weir). They were not "bad Muslims." They were not ignorant. They were traditional Muslim women who wore traditional Islamic clothing, not some monochromatic modern Islamist invention designed by people devoid of taste. And, for most of Islamic history, it was unbefitting for a man to uncover his head in public. Men used to wear headdresses as well. According to some schools of Islamic jurisprudence, it was virtually inconceivable for a man to pray with his head uncovered.

For most of Islamic history, Muslim women from India and Pakistan wore sheer scarves, show some hair, or wear no scarves at all. It was normal for them to show their arms. For most of history, Muslim women from the Arab and Amazigh world used to wear ornate headdresses decorated with coins, which only partially covered their heads but allowed their long hair and locks to flow down their faces and backs. They covered part of their heads but exposed their necks and upper chests. In some cases, they showed cleavage. Their breasts were not a source of shame.

For most of Islamic history, Muslim women from Bosnia did not completely cover their hair, and they almost always exposed their throats and necklines (Scarce 102-103). For most of history, Muslim women from Somalia did not cover their hair. In fact, they normally exposed their full arms along with one or two shoulders.

For most of history, Muslim women from Malaysia and Indonesia did not wear headscarves. Many women would go around bare-breasted due to the heat and humidity. This custom gradually disappeared through contact with conservative forms of Islam and Christianity. Among the Dayak women of Indonesia, two thirds of whom are Christian and a third of whom are Muslim, only large-breasted or married women with sagging breasts covered their bosoms. They only did so because they interfered with their work and needed to support their weight. In places like Bali, there was nothing immodest about girls and women showing their breasts. However, showing one's thighs was perceived as provocative. In fact, in the land of the sarong, which includes parts of southeast Asia, Indonesia, and Polynesia, it was more important for women to cover their thighs than their breasts. In fact, in both the North and South Pacific, including Pacific Asia, the standard costume consisted of a lower body covering for both sexes.

Prior to Western contact, Polynesian and Hawaiian women wore only dresses that extended from below their bellybuttons to above or below their knees. The missionaries obliged them to cover their bellybuttons, as it was viewed as indecent. They also forced them to conceal their breasts; hence, the appearance of coconut shell bras and other tops. Westerners hyper sexualized Hawaiian and Polynesian women. The dances they performed during religious ceremonies were transformed into sensual spectacles to entertain predominantly white Western Christian men. The women of these islands have revolted in many ways. One of the first acts of rebellion was to lower their dresses to expose their bellybuttons as a sign of defiance against the assault waged by Christian missionaries against indigenous culture. Throughout the Pacific, there has been a resurgence of traditional practices, including tattoos, celebrations, and ceremonies.

In the second millennium, television channels in Indonesia blur out the legs and cleavage of beauty contestants wearing the traditional kebaya, an article of clothing that dates from colonial times, claiming that they wish to respect "eastern values." Which "eastern values?" Middle Eastern values? Islamic fundamentalist values? They are certainly not upholding traditional Indonesian and Islamic ones. Prior to colonial contact, the women in the archipelago were accustomed to going around bare breasted in daily life. There was no difference between the chest of a woman and that of a man.

When Dea Basuri, a young woman, uploaded an album of historical photos titled "The Culture of Real Indonesian Women," her page was suspended for "nudity" and "explicit content." Facebook insisted that it was responding to the reality that we live in a "globalized world" and that it did not want to offend anyone. Offend whom? Islamic fundamentalists? By posting black and white historical photos, Dea Basuri wanted to show how Indonesian women dressed in the recent past.

While there are some exceptions, the spread of Christianity and Islam has been detrimental to the rights and freedoms of women in many parts of the world. Many of them had greater rights prior to Christian and Islamic contact and colonialism. Their cultures tended to be matriarchal or egalitarian. They had healthier notions of modesty, decency, and sexuality. Cultural imperialism devasted indigenous cultures in the Middle East, North Africa, Sub-Saharan Africa, Asia, the Pacific, and the Americas. In places like Hawaii and Polynesia, innocence was replaced with corruption and paradise was turned into hell.

If we survey the history of costume in the Muslim world, we see that some women used to cover the crown of their hair. However, they left their long hair exposed. What is more, some of them used to expose their ears, adorning them with earrings. They also showed their necklines and covered them with necklaces. If they were Islamically required to cover everything except their faces and hands, few Muslim women would have fulfilled these requirements over the past fourteen hundred centuries.

As much as some Islamists like to denounce *bid'ah* or innovation, they encourage deviation by promoting a dress style that is not traditionally Islamic. They might claim that it is Qur'anic; however, that presumes that the way Muslims dressed from the seventh century until the twentieth century was not Qur'anic. In reality, it is the Islamist interpretation of *hijab* that is not Islamic, much less Qur'anic, and totally anachronistic.

Some would argue that Muslim women of the past did not respect Islamic law in matters of dress. After all, it was common for them to expose their hair, necks, upper chests, arms, feet, and even parts of their legs, knees, and thighs, in public and in prayer. If the extremist jurists and Islamists are correct, and their radical interpretation of *hijab* is a requirement for the five daily prayers, then the prayers of millions of Muslim women over fourteen centuries have been invalid. In the United States, 40% of Muslim women never wear *hijab*; 36% wear it all the time, and 24% wear it some of the time (Lewis 49). Are the deeds of the 64% worthless? Will they hang from their hair in hell while their brains boil?

5.3 Islamic Dress or Islamist Dress?

In reality, so-called Islamic attire, as currently understood, is a dress code promoted and popularized by Islamists in the final decades of the twentieth century. Instead of an act of piety, points out Tarek Fatah, the Pakistani Canadian journalist, "the *hijab* has become more of a political statement" (290). As Mona Eltahawy (b. 1967), the Egyptian American feminist, notes:

> In the countries where Islamists have pushed for veiling, the types of veils they promote are new. Unlike traditional forms of dress, which often had a much looser, more flowing aspect, the veils that the Islamists promote are worn tightly around the head, often accompanied, in more conservative circles, with buttoned-down coats and cloaks in black and dark blue. (45)

Not only did the Islamist *hijab* spread throughout much of the Muslim world in the 1970s and the decades that followed, by the 1990s it was widely adopted by Muslim women in the Western world, particularly Europe, Canada, and the United States. As Leila Ahmed notes:

> The definitions of Islamists as to what "true" Islam was and what forms of dress and practices were "mandated" by Islam began to gain power in the Middle East in the 1970s and in America too by the 1990s... Today it is above all Islamists and Islamist-grounded institutions who are the authorities defining and determining the beliefs and practices of Islam in this country. So powerful and effective have Islamist definitions of Islam become today in America and the West (and elsewhere), that even Muslims who grew up thinking they were believing Muslims and for whom Islam was above all a spiritual and ethical resource might well come to doubt their own sense and understanding of Islam. Finding themselves alienated by and feeling no empathy with the views and practices of this now dominant form of Islam -- from its obligatory *hijab* to its activist social and political agenda -- they perhaps begin to wonder if they are in fact Muslims after all: if *this* is Islam. (2011: 299)

With virtually all mosques under the direct or indirect influence of Muslim fundamentalists, Islamists, sexists, and misogynists, the new doctrine of the *hijab* was imposed upon women in the mosque and madrasas. Muslim men and women were expected to enforce it inside and outside the mosque. Indoctrination and peer pressure served their purpose perfectly well. Entire generations of Muslims were convinced that the new Islamist *hijab* was a central pillar of Islam. The Islamists, both Sunni and Shiite, have hijacked Islam. They have convinced both Muslims and non-Muslims that "this Islamist form of Islam" is "Islam *tout court*" (Ahmed 2011: 299). By failing to curtail political Islam, Muslim communities and societies were metamorphosed:

> The signs of European modernity were obliterated while Islamic signs (adapted to an Americanized urban landscape) were restored; the most obvious of these signs, and the most polemic, is the wearing of veils by women. With a few rare exceptions, even the most Westernized women conformed to this return to Islamic norm; the elegant ones created headgear to fit the circumstance, which fit tightly around their hair and kept it hidden. (Meddeb 109)

Thanks to billions in petro-dollars, planetary-wide propaganda, clever publication relations campaigns, the control of Islamic publishing and mosques, and the censoring and suppression of alternate voices, the Islamists co-opted and hijacked Islam. They even enlisted their allies, the leftists, liberals, and woke mob, to denounce all those who oppose Islamic extremism, the foremost of whom are moderate, traditional, spiritual, and civilizational Muslims, of being "Islamophobic." Their antipathy is towards Islamism: not Islam.

Despite identifying the role of radical Islamism in the spread of the *hijab*, and acknowledging its steady ascendency, it is disconcerting that Leila Ahmed's findings provide her with "grounds for optimism" (305). So what if Islamic conferences host women speakers? So what if they elect women leaders? So what if they address women's issues? So what if they present themselves as Islamic feminists? If anything, they are Islamist feminists. Leila Ahmed seems to have succumbed to the propaganda of the radical Islamists. She believes that the spread of *hijab* and the rise of Muslim feminists in the United States represents a new stage in the history of struggle for women's rights in Islam (2011: 306). It marks a new chapter in the history of Islam in America and the West (2011: 306). She seems have abandoned the struggle for the soul of Islam. She appears to have thrown in the towel, resigning herself to the New Islamist Order.

Leila Ahmed, the woman who inspired and encouraged Muslims to challenge the patriarchy and misogyny of the veil, describes developments in the Islamist movement in the United States in positive terms. It is all window-dressing. From "interfaith dialogue," "social justice," and "women's rights," it is all part of a public relations campaign. Some of the most moderate Muslim leaders in the Western world are high-ranking members of radical Islamist movements. They are foreign operatives engaged in deep cover operations. They are members of sleeper cells. They are hiding in plain sight. They say one thing in public and the opposite in private. They promote peace with Jews and Christians while longing to slaughter them. They pretend to care about blacks and indigenous peoples when they are vile racists. They speak of women's rights when they are the most misogynistic of men on earth. So what if women-hating women are playing larger roles in Muslim affairs? So what if Islamist women preach their women-hating Islam from the podium? A female fascist leader is still a fascist. So what if women have become leaders of Islamist and terrorist movements, urging their male comrades to rape Sunni, Shiite, Christian, and Yezidi women, training women to commit suicide bombings, and committing such horrific acts themselves?

The dominant form of Islam that is propagated today is radical, political Islam, in its Sunni or Shiite variety. It is the Islam of the Islamists. It is not traditional Islam. It is not classical, civilizational, Islam. It is not spiritual Islam. It is not modernist, progressive, moderate, or reformist Islam. It is not Qur'anic or rational Islam. It is not humanistic Islam. While it is true that all religions change and evolve over the ages, most of them have progressed in a positive direction. The same cannot be said of Islam in its radical and regressive tendency. As cultural critic Abdulwahab Meddeb (1946-2014) described:

> We are witnessing a curious inversion in the politics and economics of the human body. Islam proposes a prudish city, whose inhabitants are sick with nihilism and resentment. Meanwhile, the Western body has freed itself from inherited constraints. This is an extravagant inversion of which Islamic devotees are not aware, since they are proud enough of their state to propose their virtuous society as a counterexample to the Western society, which is supposed to be one of vice. Don't they oppose their modest society to the immodest foreign society? Don't they sing the praises of discretion and dissimulation, and belittle the exhibitionism of the West? Don't they celebrate the veiled, or reclusive, feminine body by lambasting Western nudity and promiscuity? They never realize that they are being proud of the very signs of their illness. (120)

If Muslims are not presented with options, Islamist Islam, even Islamist "Feminist" Islam will completely take over the faith. Rather than opt for a different version of Islam, moral, mature, and rational Muslims will have no choice but to reject the only option. They will conclude that Islam is the problem, not just the dominant version of it. They will realize that it cannot be reformed. Their rage will be directed, not only at political Islam, and the Islamic movement, but at Islam itself in all of its expressions. For Azam Kamguian (b. 1958), the Iranian writer and women's rights activist, "the movement for secularism and atheism, for modern ideas and culture, for individual freedom, for women's liberation, and civil liberties has been widespread and deep"

(Lichter 168-169). She believes "any change in Iran… will have a significant impact on the region and worldwide" (169). She is convinced that,

> The people of the world must rise up and support our struggle to eradicate their right wing… genocidal, and murderous Islamic movement, and support our battle for the Enlightenment in the Middle East. I call … all atheists, secularists, and freethinkers to join our camp and strengthen the movement to free ourselves and Iranian society from political Islam, to get rid of Islam, and to abolish it from the state, education, and public life. (170)

If such secular radicals get their way, the mullahs will be hanging by their turbans from trees, *hijabs* will be torn from women's heads, religious seminaries will be incinerated, shrines will be desecrated, and no symbol of Islam will be safe. If they wish to survive, the Islamists in power must not retrench themselves and become increasingly and desperately radicalized, resorting to greater repression, brutality, and murder. The only avenue left for them is radical reform, de-escalation, moderation, secularization, and genuine democratization.

Iranian Islamists at the service of Khamenei and the Revolutionary Guards approached a Western Muslim scholar asking him to help them confront the epidemic of atheism that was spreading in Iran. He thought to himself, "how ironic, the disease is asking for the cure." They are the very reason that Iranians are rejecting Islam and religion. They also asked him to help them "fight Western feminism." He told them: "that should be the role of Muslim women, not men." They rolled their eyes, smirked, and shook their heads, responding: "You know very well that we don't have any women who are willing and able to do so." That was his point precisely. Nearly half a century of "Islamic" rule and the Iranian Islamists cannot produce a single female intellectual or scholar to combat "the scourge of feminism."

Iranian state-controlled media even asked the Western Muslim scholar to help find a Muslim woman convert who insisted on her right to wear the *hijab*. Obviously, they wanted a white one: blacks are not appealing to them, but they will do when there are no others. And surely, they intended to exploit her as part of their state propaganda. Once again, they did not understand the irony of their request. A white American convert, sick of being sexualized, may choose to wear the *hijab*, which marks her, in the eyes of Muslims, as a complete sexual object. In the United States, however, she has the right to wear what she wishes. She can wear a headscarf if she so desires. But she can also cast it off, and slip into a little black dress with high heels. How could such a woman be a spokesperson for Iran's mandatory *hijab* policy, which is enforced with brutal force? In most of the world, she has a choice. In Iran, she simply does not. Islamists may speak about "rights," "freedom," and "respect," but they do not even understand such basic concepts. The only freedom that Iranian women have is the "freedom not to have a choice." The Islamist ideologues engage in coercive persuasion. They practice doublespeak. They deliberately obscure, distort, disguise, or reverse the meaning of words to brainwash people.

For their own sanity and spirituality, Muslim men and women need to know that the "Islamic" dress being imposed upon them by Islamists through rhetoric and force is a modern radical innovation that is devoid of any Qur'anic roots. Extremist modalities should not bind Muslims. They have every right to adopt a more moderate, practical, and relaxed attitude toward appropriate dress that is suitable in different circumstances. As Bestandji duly notes:

> The veil (*hijab*, *jilbab*, *niqab*, depending on the degree of zeal), in its current forms, was invented at the beginning of the twentieth century in the Middle East by the Wahhabis, the Muslim Brotherhood (the Afghan *burqa* and the Iranian *chador* have a different history and are not as widespread in the world). It was imposed only thirty or so years in the Maghreb by violence (in Algeria), and the relentless social, political, and mediatic proselytism of the Islamists... Evolution calls for the removal of the veil as many women did in the 1960s and 1970s. (2018: Part Four)

As Ida Lichter notes, Elham Man'ea (b. 1966), the Yemeni-Swiss academic, stresses that "the spread of *hijab* as mandatory Islamic dress was made possible through colossal petrodollar funding for relentless Wahhabi propaganda" (369).

For Tarek Fatah, one of the most disturbing aspects of the *hijab* is how ultra-conservative women have taken the lead in promoting it as an Islamic obligation. In his words:

> The most troubling aspect of the *hijab* controversy is that it is not only men but also ultra-conservative Muslim women who have taken the lead in promoting the head cover or the face mask as a mandatory obligation of Islam. The defense of the *hijab* has become the defense of Islam, as if Islam and the *hijab* are one and the same. However, the defenders cannot explain why the only legitimate covering of the head has to be one that originates from among the Muslim Brotherhood followers in Egypt and Palestine, and not the head covers worn in Bangladesh or Somalia. Perhaps these young women know that what they wear on their heads is a political symbol, not a religious one, that says, "I am hereby rejecting what the West stands for, and in doing so, I will also reject my own heritage, my mother's, and my grandmother's, and mimic an adopted identity of an Islamist activist working for the Muslim Brotherhood." (294-295)

As fervent as some Muslim women may be about the *hijab*, studies reveal that most of them of them cannot provide any scriptural evidence for it (Fatah 295). They claim that "I know it is in the Qur'an, but I don't know where" (Meshal 89; Fatah 295). When pressed for references, they point to "the verses that everyone talks about" (Meshal 89; Fatah 295). When pressed for a specific verse, they tell people to "ask a Muslim scholar" (Meshal 89, Fatah 295).

Rather than obey God, the Qur'an, or the Prophet, some women are pressured or shamed into wearing it by mosques, Muslim organizations, clerics, family, and individuals in their religious communities (Fatah 295-296). Its spread is the product of propaganda and pressure. They have a "shallow familiarity with Islamic texts" and their "religious knowledge is primarily acquired as a result of oral transmission and... through family and mosque" (Meshal 89). As Leena El-Ali notes, "many Muslims do not actually read the Qur'an, and local or imported trends fill the vacuum" (59). As she explains:

> Much of the Muslim world is illiterate... Some of the more populous or strategic countries... have very high rates of illiteracy, including Afghanistan (61.8%), Mali (61.9%), Pakistan (41.3%), Bangladesh (38.5%), Yemen (29.9%), Morocco (19.8%), and Tunisia (18.2%). Elsewhere, populous countries with significant Muslim populations where the illiteracy rate is also high, include Nigeria (40.4%) and India (27.9%)... Some reports have suggested that close to 40% of the Muslim world is illiterate. (60)

Even when Muslims read the Qur'an, notes El-Ali, they do so technically, but not reflectively (60). What is more, "many Muslims... read translations of the Qur'an that are either heavily influenced by an agenda, or predominantly influenced by accepted cultural norms" (61). What is more, many of these translations contain blatant and blasphemous lies against God, not the least of which is claiming that the Qur'an tells women to wear the *chador* and the *niqab*.

5.4 The Evolution of Dress

As François Boucher (1885-1966), the French art historian, museum curator, and writer, explains, "clothing has to do with covering one's body and depends primarily on climate, health, and textile" (9). Costume, however, "reflects social factors, such as religious beliefs, magic, aesthetics, personal status, the wish to be distinguished from or to emulate one's fellows" (9). For the Greeks and the Chinese, early humans covered their bodies to protect themselves from the elements (9). According to the Bible and the Qur'an, it was a matter of modesty and beautification (9). For ethnologists and psychologists it was due to taboo, magical influence, and the desire to please (9). Although some religious groups introduce modesty taboos, Boucher points out that "modesty in itself does not automatically lead to wearing clothes" (10). As Kybalova, Hervenova, and Lamarova note:

> To clothe the naked body with a garment may be regarded as symbolizing chastity and modesty. But such an interpretation seems almost too narrow and limited. After all, even the amulet was once a form of clothing: it serves as a barrier or bridge between the exposed

> vulnerable human body and the good or evil spirits of the surrounding world. (17)

The earliest attire human beings wore included necklaces, bracelets, and anklets (Boucher 28). Later, the loincloth developed. If Adam and Eve ever existed, and everything indicates they are merely archetypes of the ancients, the only thing they would have worn would have been loincloths that covered their genitals. If climate were a factor in colder regions, in warmer ones the covering of the genitals "would have been in response to a religious idea of taboo rather than because of a physical need to protect" (Boucher 22). Initially made from hides, these loincloths would later be made of cloth (22). As Ali Basye points out, nearly thirty thousand years ago:

> Ice Age babes were trekking the tundra in rather stylish, low-slung, frayed skirts, some of which featured detailed fringe, twisted strings, and curiously tapered, tailcoat-like backsides. Sewn with delicate woven cloth, the skirts were paired with strapless bandeaux (essentially cupless bras), belts, multiple bracelets, and jaunty haberdashery. (15)

If anything, their attire was very Madonna, circa "Like a Virgin" (15). Ancient women invented fashion. With their leather loincloths, bikini tops, and fur boots, they had style, sex appeal, and strength (17).

Be that as it may, Greek women were among the first to sew the front and the back of the loincloth to turn it into a miniskirt. These types of skirts were worn by men and women for thousands of years and continue to be worn to this day (Basye: 6-7). In fact, for much of human history, and across societies, clothing was unisex (Basye 18). Both men and women wore skirts. Their length, however, had more to do with social class and wealth than modesty: "servants and soldiers wore shorter lengths; royalty and deities flaunted their wealth by wearing them longer" (Basye 18).

Eventually, the skirts of wealthier women got longer until they reached the ankles. The skirts of men got higher until, during the Middle Ages, they disappeared, leaving men only wearing stockings, which latter evolved into pants (Basye 27-30). Viewed as masculine attire in Europe, harem pants also developed in the Muslim Middle East, where they were viewed as women's attire. The miniskirt, which evolved from the loincloth, has been worn by human beings since prehistoric times (Boucher 20). Far from being immodest, it was the very embodiment of modesty. If anything, it is an iconic article of clothing. So, rather than forcing women to wear long skirts, as fundamentalists desire, Ali Basye proposes that such men embrace the skirt themselves (31).

As costume evolved over the ages, it was used to communicate group membership, attract attention, and specify age group, tribal classification, social status, and marital status, such as bachelor, married, or widower (Boucher 22). There are no constants when it comes to clothing, style, fashion, makeup, ornamentation, and body decoration (see Reynolds). They are in a constant state of flux. Skirts, which are associated with women, used to be worn by both genders. Length of hair among men and women was often the same. Hairstyles and headdresses have continually changed. High heels, now associated with women, were worn by Persian horsemen. The style was imitated by French royalty and was then adopted by upper-class women. If girls tend to dress like boys when they are young in the West, boys used to dress as girls in past centuries.

Attempting to impose a permanent and universal dress code is irrational, untraditional, and impossible. The traditions attributed to the Prophet Muhammad, in which he curses men who look like women and women who look like men, cannot be correct. Why? Because Arab men and women wore the same clothing. They all wore the same dresses. The garments reportedly worn by the Prophet Muhammad, Fatimah al-Zahra, Husayn, and Abu Hanifah, found in the Chamber of Relics at Topkapi Museum in Istanbul, Turkey, are virtually identical in design.

A simple study of costume history reveals that fashion has fluctuated among Muslim women as in other cultures. Like all aspects of clothing, accessories have evolved over the ages. Women's headwear is ever evolving, like neckwear, footwear, and hairstyles (Leventon 314-319). In the western world, its history is well-documented. In ancient Greece, the "kerchief was the more usual form of head covering" (Sichel 7). In ancient Rome, the most common head covering was the veil (Sichel 8). In ancient Roman Britain, "headwear consisted of the cloak or cape being pulled over the head" (Sichel 10).

Among the Saxons and Normans, "veils... were worn indoors, as well as outdoors... completely covering the hair" (Sichel 11). In medieval times, the wimple became popular (Sichel 14). In the sixteenth century, undercaps came into vogue (Sichel 20). In the seventeenth century, "head coverings were generally worn less and less" (Sichel 27). In the eighteenth century, caps were all the craze (Sichel 38). In the nineteenth century, "caps became less popular" and were replaced by turbans, toques, and bonnets (Sichel 54). In the twentieth century, "bonnets were replaced by hats or toques" (Sichel 66).

As much as some Muslim apologists claim that the *hijab* has been worn throughout history, and that women used to cover their hair, that is not the case. All one has to do is peruse pictorial histories of costume to see that such claims are patently false. Christian women have not veiled their hair for the past two thousand years. Some did so during mass; however, not on a daily basis. Quite often, the scarf's purpose was to adorn, as opposed to conceal, the bosom. In some cases, women wore sheer veils on their heads along with dresses with such low necklines that one or two breasts were fully exposed (Kybalova, Herbenova, and Lamarova 370).

From the fourth century, the white veil became a symbol of purity worn by Christian brides (370). The black veil became a sign of mourning (370). By the tenth and eleventh centuries, Christian women wore veils that reached their shoulders (370). In the late Middle Ages, "the veil once more came to Europe from the Orient as a hat decoration" (370). In the fourteenth and fifteen centuries, "a veil cult prevailed at the court of Burgundy" (370). Both men and women wore them. In the sixteenth century, the veil disappeared (370). It was rarely found during the Baroque and Rococo period (370). It reappeared in the early Victorian period, where it was used to decorate the top hats of women (370). Tulle veils appeared in the nineteenth century (370). Veils also became popular at the end of the nineteenth century and early twentieth century.

The headdresses worn by Western Christian women over the past two thousand years were not uniform. They varied in style. Fashions changed. And some women did not cover their hair at all. They were not the Christian equivalent of the post-1970s Islamist *hijab*. In response to the *hijab* protests that started to rock Iran since 2017, Iranian Islamists have claimed anachronistically that even pre-Islamic women from Persepolis "observed *hijab*." Some claim they wore *chador*. Manifesting his ignorance of costume history, 'Ali Khamenei, asserted that "*Hijab* Have [sic] Roots in All Cultures." He alleged that,

> Even in Europe until two or three hundred years ago, aristocratic women used to wear *hijab* on their faces. Perhaps you have noticed this in some historical movies. They used to wear a kind of *hijab* on their faces so as to stop others from seeing them. This is an honor for women. In ancient Persia, the wives of aristocrats and senior officials used to wear *hijab*. But the wives of ordinary people did not all wear *hijab*, and there was no obligation to do so. Then Islam stepped in and abolished all these discriminations and said that women must wear *hijab*. It meant that the right to wear *hijab* was for all women.

European women never wore *hijab* in the sense that Khamenei understands it. According to his tortured logic, by making *hijab* mandatory, Islam ensured it was a right for all women. A right is not compulsory. People are not punished for failing to exercise a right. Apparently, there is no limit to the dishonesty of religious dinosaurs, not to mention their revisionism. For example, they invoke the Virgin Mary to impose their interpretation of *hijab*. They claim that the mother of Jesus is always depicted as wearing a veil. This is false. She also appears wearing a crown and, in some instances, wearing a bodice, with her firm bulging breasts completely uncovered (Kybalova, Herbenova, and Lamarova 461).

If the Virgin Mary can be exploited to promote the *hijab*, she can also be deployed to promote the lace-up bodice. Since she is also depicted as being semi-nude, or even nude, she could be a poster girl for toplessness and nudism. It would be no less shameless than the Islamist efforts to appropriate the Virgin

Mary to support the sexist, misogynistic, and patriarchal prison uniform they wish to impose on girls and women.

"If the Virgin Mary can show her breasts," women could argue, "why can't we?" "If a loincloth was good enough for Eve," they could claim, "a miniskirt suffices plenty." "If a leaf was good enough for Eve," some would assert, "a bikini bottom should be enough for us." If Muslim women in the twenty-first century must veil, because some women did so in medieval times, it should also be remembered that men used to wear gowns, skirts, and kilts, basically dresses, as well. If it is traditional for women to wear *hijab*, then it is traditional for men to wear dresses, as well.

When it comes to the veil or headscarf, we are not dealing with a universal divinely decreed dress code. The same women who covered their hair could uncover much of their bodies. Furthermore, women did not constantly conceal their hair in most cultures throughout the ages. Christian women did not veil their hair in their homes, even in the presence of unrelated male guests. They did so in church. And they did so in public to mark the fact that they were married. And even so, they did not completely cover their hair. The point was to cover part of the head: the crown. In some cases, the covering was out of cultural and religious norms of modesty. However, in many cases, it was a means of beautification.

As Madge Garland's (d. 1990) work, *The Changing Face of Beauty*, manifests, standards of beauty have shifted over the past 3,500 years, with emphasis shifting, and detail varying widely. Although hats and headdresses have certainly played an important part in a lady's wardrobe, as Georgine de Courtais has shown, they formed part of changing fashions. The covering of women's hair has not been a historical constant. It was rarely complete, always evolving, and was motivated by fashion as opposed to religion. Its primary purpose was beautification and embellishment: not concealment.

The headwear in the Muslim world has also evolved over the ages. The *hijab* that is worn by Muslim women today is a modern creation. It is not the same sort of head covering that Muslim women wore in the past, and it certainly is not the *khimar* or covering mentioned in the Qur'an. There is nothing sacred about it. When it comes to clothing, the fashion cycle should be kept in mind:

> A dress seems immodest ten years before its time. Shameless five years before its time. Daring one year before its time, then fashionable. Unfashionable one year after its time. Hideous ten years after its time. Ridiculous twenty years after its time. Curious thirty years after its time. Amusing fifty years after its time. Enchanting seventy years after its time. Romantic one hundred years after its time. Exceedingly beautiful one hundred and fifty years after its time. (Sichet 6)

Religions and cultures can be conservative. Some foolishly seek to freeze fashion and stop the natural course of its evolution. The traditional clothing of some indigenous people in Spanish America is stuck in colonial times. Amish clothing did not evolve much beyond the nineteenth century. Orthodox Jewish dress is derived from nineteenth-century European clothing. And while clothing also evolved in the Muslim world, the rise of Islamism in the twentieth and twenty-first centuries has tried to force fashion back to an imaginary period.

God, one would presume, cares more about what is in a person's heart than what is on one's head. God never told Moses to command women to cover their hair in the Torah. The requirement for married women to cover their hair surfaces in certain rabbinic currents (Zellentin 36, note 46). God never told Jesus to command women to cover their hair in the New Testament. It was, however, introduced by early Christians as a requirement for women in worship (Zellentin 37, note 46). In the Epistles, Paul (d. 64/67) said "every woman who prays or prophesies with her head uncovered dishonors her head" (1 Corinthians 11:6). However, a little later, he states that "long hair is given to her as a covering" (1 Corinthians 11:15). As Zellentin notes, "the practice was later extended as a permanent garment to consecrated virgins and widows" (37, note 46). Likewise, God never told the Prophet Muhammad to command women to cover their hair in the Qur'an, the so-called Final Testament. In the case of Judaism, Christianity, and Islam, the practice of head covering derives from the oral as opposed to written tradition. This practice was bound to ancient cultures.

The veil is an article of clothing. It is not a divine duty, a dogma, or a doctrine. Over the ages, it has been associated with "elegance, modesty, humility, subservience, marriage, and death" (Yarwood 425). "In the East," notes Doreen Yarwood (1919-1999), the English historian of clothing, "the veil has traditionally represented humility and subservience" (427). While humility is a virtue, subservience is not. The rules regarding *hijab* were made by men, not by the Prophet Muhammad, and much less by God. At the same time, one must not forget that the Prophet was himself a man who, for reasons of pragmatism, adapted the teachings of Islam to Arab culture and Jewish tradition to attract converts. As Yarwood points out:

> Instructions in the Koran on the subject of women's behavior and attire in public is not dogmatic and provides guidance rather than rigid rules. Women are enjoined to look away from temptation and to preserve their chastity; they are not instructed to veil their faces so that they may not be seen. Because of this, each society has interpreted this guidance according to its age and former traditions.... Societies with a history of rigid male domination interpreted the Koran to mean a strict veiling of their women in public, others were more tolerant in their understanding... (73)

5.5 The Veil: From Pre-Islamic Custom to Islamic Obligation

Although it is widely believed that Muslim women must cover their hair in public, prominent Shiite scholars like Muhammad Hasan al-Najafi (1785- 1849), who was a source of emulation, did not believe that it was obligatory (Takim 2022: 43). As he explained, this edict was based on precaution as opposed to a clear and explicit requirement (Takim 2022: 43). Likewise, Ahmad Ghabal (1954-2012), the Iranian *mujtahid*, also concluded that "there was no scholarly agreement that mandated the covering of the hair in public" (Takim 2022: 44).

Qasim Amin (1863-1908), the Egyptian jurist and Islamic modernist, who is known as "the father of feminism" and "the liberator of women" was correct when he claimed that "the veil is not a custom particular to us. Muslims did not invent it. It was a prevalent custom in many nations and its disappearance was the result of the societal changes which accompanied the change and progress of civilization" (37). As he noted:

> The *shari'ah* does not stipulate the use of the veil... This custom is a product of the interaction among nations. Muslims were attracted to the veil, approved it, exaggerated its use, and dressed it up in religious raiment, just as other harmful customs have become firmly established in the name of religion, but of which religion is innocent.... The ... face-cover and the veil are not part of the *shari'ah*, in terms either of piety or morality. They have been handed down to us from ancient civilizations that preceded Islam and have continued to survive... (Amin 2000: 37, 43)

Mansour Fahmy (1886-1959), another pioneer in the field of so-called Islamic feminism, concluded that the headscarf was the product of culture, traditions, and customs, and had no foundation in Islam (Mahmoud). In her impactful *al-Sufur wa al-hijab* [*Unveiling and Veiling*], published in 1928, Nazira Zin al-Din [Zeineddine] (1908-1976), a Druze intellectual who was well-versed in Islamic studies, concluded that a clear conscience was better than the veil, that the *hijab* was not obligatory for women, and that the opinions of male jurists were wrong (37).

The so-called obligation of *hijab*, which has no basis in the Qur'an and the authentic *sunnah*, has been exaggerated to the point that it has become the very emblem of Islam. As Usama Hasan, a senior researcher in Islamic studies, observes:

> The issue of women's dress is blown out of all proportion to the far more fundamental and essential Qur'anic themes of faith, prayer, charity, spiritual purification and progress, and the constant remembrance of God. The noble Qur'anic term of *hijab*, which in its highest sense refers to the veil between humanity and God that is lifted in the Hereafter for those who purify their souls sufficiently, has been reduced and incorrectly applied in modern discourse to a mere piece of clothing on a woman's head.
>
> Traditionalist readings of the Qur'an tend to insist that women

> cover up in public, possibly including the face, hands, and feet. These readings can be seen to be strongly influenced by culture and context, with many traditional views on the subject of veiling being problematic for even modern traditionalists, ranging from the extremely harsh to the extremely permissive.
>
> A holistic reading of the relevant Qur'anic texts, balancing tradition with reason and law with spirit, would simply suggest the following: believing men and women are to dress and behave modestly in public; people should be careful when looking at the opposite sex, avoid lustful glances, lewd or lascivious behavior, and guard their chastity; sexualization of the public space is to be avoided; women, like men, have every right to participate in the public space in matters such as politics, education, commerce, healthcare, agriculture, leisure and worship. (17)

Early Islam was characterized by a vast diversity of interpretations. These were colored by class, society, and culture. As Leila Ahmed notes,

> the uniformity of interpretation and the generally minimal differences characterizing the versions of Islam that survived reflect not unanimity of understanding but rather the triumph of the religious and social vision of the 'Abbasid state at this formative moment in history. (1992: 99)

Orthodoxy is the product of power. *Victori sunt spolia.* To the victor belongs the spoils. This so-called orthodox party viewed groups whose women did not veil, whose men and women practiced monogamy, and whose men and women socialized together, as being debauched and obscene (Ahmed 1992: 99).

The critics in question, however, came from societies where it was customary for men to keep dozens of wives and sex-slaves (Ahmed 1992: 99). They placed an Islamic stamp on patriarchy, polygyny, slavery, concubinage, sexual segregation, sexual inequality, and domestic violence. The heretics in their eyes were the groups that practiced monogamy, opposed slavery and concubinage, did not veil their women, did not segregate women, and were more egalitarian. In retrospect, these so-called deviants and heretics were right while the orthodox party was wrong. The rocket of Islam was knocked off course. Some would argue that it is high time to correct it before it crashes and burns. Others would argue that it already has and that we have to pick up the pieces and start again from scratch with a new Islamic genesis. From the ashes we will grow roses. Others prefer to wait and place hope in the reformation and restoration of Islam that will come from the promised Messiah and the Mahdi. Others hold that they must lay the path and set the stage for them. And yet others believe that such beliefs prevent people from taking action themselves. In other words, the onus of change is on us.

5.6 Turning Women into Twats

In "*Hijab* and Women in Islam," posted on FaithFreedom.org is a photograph of a Muslim woman who is completely enveloped in a *burqa* with her entire face covered. In contrast to the bodiless floating faces of Muslims who wear *hijabs* and *abayahs*, this woman, like those who wear *burqas*, is reduced to a faceless, bodiless, black blob. As Mouna Naim, noted, such attire reduces women "to formless, uniform, shadows" (Fatah 298). They are transformed into specters. The text below the thought-provoking image states that "this woman thinks she is 100% vagina." It asks:

> What is the subliminal message this woman is sending? The subliminal message is that every square inch of my body is [a] private part, every square inch of it can make you horny. Therefore my entire body is an '*awrat*, (lit. pudendum, genital) and I am a sex object from head to toe. People cover their private parts. This woman thinks her entire body is [a] private part. Does this in any way arouse respect? Only one who thinks with her genitals may think so.

Below appears the photograph of some Muslim women who are mostly covered in more mainstream Islamic dress, namely, covering everything but their faces. The text describes them in the following terms:

> These women have determined that all their bodies, except their faces, are extensions of their genitals, including their heads. Thinking with their genitals they can't distinguish the difference between their hair and their pubic hair. To them both are embarrassing and should be covered. Thinking with their genitals these ambulant vaginas are fighting for the right to be humiliated, beaten, and treated as sex objects.

The website in question is unquestionably Islamophobic. In fact, it expresses the frustrations of many ex-Muslims. It is just the other side of the coin in the black-white dichotomy. As much as the website contains objectionable and inaccurate information, this article in question is entirely on-target regarding so-called Islamic modest dress.

Another poignant piece was produced by the cartoonist Malcolm Paul Evans (b. 1945) in which he contrasts a woman in a black *abayah* and scarf with only her eyes exposed and a blonde, bikini-clad woman, with high-heeled beach sandals and sunglasses. The covered woman thinks to herself: "Nothing covered but her eyes, what a cruel male-dominated culture!" The uncovered woman thinks to herself: "Everything covered but her eyes, what a cruel male-dominated culture!"

While one might presume that the woman to the right is an eastern Muslim while the woman to the left is a Western non-Muslim -- and perhaps this is part of the contrast that the cartoonist intended -- the bikini-clad beauty could also be a Muslim, one who holds that the only parts that a woman has to conceal in public are her private parts, and perhaps her breasts, as per the Qur'an (7:26-27; 24:31). After all, when asked from whom we should conceal our private parts, the Prophet replied, "Conceal your private parts except from your wife and from whom your right hands possess" (Abu Dawud and Tirmidhi). He was then asked about covering the private parts while in public. The Messenger of God answered, "If it is in your power that no one looks at it, then no one should look at it" (Abu Dawud and Tirmidhi). The tradition in question demonstrates that nudity should be avoided if possible and if within one's ability. It does provide some flexibility and leniency. It does not hold people responsible for the gaze of others.

As the Prophet said, "If you are able to not let anyone see it, then do not let them see it." He was referring to protecting the *'awrah*, namely, the genitalia. If one exposed ones private parts inadvertently, in a public bath, for example, and another person looked at them, one could not be held responsible. Following this principle, no woman who covers her private parts should be blamed if anyone looks at them, or anything else that normally appears. The principle that "if it arouses a man, it is prohibited" has reached absurd and oppressive proportions. "If high heels might arouse a man, they are prohibited;" "If shoes that squeak might arouse a man, they are prohibited;" "If colored headscarves might arouse a man, they are prohibited;" "If colored eye lenses might arouse a man, they are prohibited." When does such madness end? It is the dictatorship of the pervert. What is a woman with naturally blue or green eyes to do? Cover them with sunglasses as her colored eyes might turn on a creep?

Why don't we reverse the roles and address what women find attractive. Women are overwhelmingly attracted to men with facial hair, favoring a light beard or heavy stubble. For women, facial hair symbolizes virility, maturity, and masculinity. Paradoxically, it is recommended or mandatory for Muslim men to grow beards. Perhaps they should not or should wear a *niqab* to cover it. After all, if it can arouse someone, then it is prohibited. Women are mostly attracted to the eyes, smiles, teeth, and muscles of men. They are aroused by narrow waists, V-shaped torsos, and broad shoulders. They are turned on by the smell of men, strong arms, sculpted chests, muscular thighs, firm buttocks, and masculine voices. Should a man's voice be treated as part of his *'awrah*? Women are also attracted to the way men walk, the way they dress, and the wealth they display. They are drawn to men who wear red. Women are as physically attracted to men as men are to women. What is more, they have the same sex drive. The laws of *hijab* should apply to both genders or none of them.

This conflict at the heart of Islam is conveyed in the sociological artwork of Malcolm Paul Evans. There have been Muslim scholars, from the dawn of Islam to its dusk, who believed that the *'awrah* of women consisted of the outer parts of the female genitalia. Some included the breasts in this category, but others did not. Hence, in the Islamic context, a woman in a *burqa* and *niqab* versus a topless woman in a thong would provide a better juxtaposition.

The cartoon, however, presents a straw-man argument as these are not the only two options available. The dichotomies presented are false. Yes, both of the women are being dominated and manipulated. However, there are critical differences. The American woman may dress that way on a beach. She does not dress that way in daily life. The Muslim woman has no choice. Either she is forced by her husband, family, community, or the law of the land, or she is coerced through divine and religious terror. In the Western world, many Muslim women are not forced by family members to wear the *hijab*. At times, they do so despite their opposition. If they adopt it, it is because they are manipulated into doing so by misogynistic Muslim preachers and authors who pass off patriarchy as piety. Others self-radicalize for various reasons.

The first woman in the cartoon has a choice. The second does not. The bikini babe may be subjected to the influence of beauty norms, fashion, and societal pressure; however, she is in no way oppressed in the same way as the *burqa*-wearing woman from Iran, Afghanistan, Saudi Arabia, Yemen, or elsewhere. Nobody is beating up the blonde so that she can wear skimpy swimming attire. She has freedom and agency. It is sad to say that some Muslim girls and women are beaten into wearing the *hijab*.

When looking at the cartoon, some observers will conclude that the skin-showing woman is a slut and that the cloaked woman is chaste. This is the classic case of judging a book by its cover. The woman in the bikini could be a virgin or a chaste wife, while the one in the *burqa* could be a whore. In fact, in parts of the Muslim world, prostitutes cover themselves more than regular women, out of shame, to conceal their identity, or to identify themselves as sex workers. The ordinary women in Iran, for example, tend to show more hair and wear more fashionable clothing.

While it escapes many viewers, another fact emerges: the woman in the bikini is properly attired to go tanning or swimming. The same cannot be said of the other woman who would die of a heat stroke or drown in the ocean. The blonde's high heels could be bad for her back, and too much sun might lead to cancer; however, the Muslim woman surely suffers from vitamin D deficiency which could becoming life-threatening. The bikini-wearing woman surely attracts the male gaze; however, so does the one wearing a *burqa*. They are both extremes. And they are both valued by men for their bodies. The first one for recreational sex. The second one for procreative sex. They are still sex objects. Again, the main difference resides in the fact that the white woman owns her own body while the foreign woman's body is owned by her husband.

The cartoon conveys the all-or-nothing mentality of Muslim jurists. Clothing options form a continuum. Many women, both Muslim and non-Muslim, dress somewhere between these two extremes. While the bikini wearing woman can wear denim shorts on top of her bikini bottom, a halter top, or even opt for a full-size swimsuit, the Muslim woman does not have such flexibility or freedom. The western woman will not be persecuted for her choices. The Muslim one will. What is more, a woman who wears a string bikini to a beach does not view herself as oppressed. On the contrary, she feels liberated and emancipated.

Democratic, secular, nations liberate women. Religious nations control, subjugate, and cover them. As for women who call on the West to "bring your democracy, not your bikinis," Mimunt Hamido Yahia reminds them that it was only after the end of the National Catholicism of Francisco Franco (1892-1975), the fascist dictator, that it became possible for them to wear bikinis in Spain (2021). Before that, they were subjected to a strict Catholic dress code. Legally, they could not even shake hands with unrelated men unless they wore gloves (2021). "Ladies," stresses Yahia, "without bikinis, there is no democracy" (2021).

Ironically, it was a Roman Catholic priest, Rodrigo Bocanegra, who convinced Franco to permit foreign women to wear bikinis on beaches in Spain, as it would stimulate the economy (Burgos). The fascist dictator legalized the two-piece bathing suit with a smile in 1953. That being said, priests in other parts of the world, including Chile, refused to give communion to women who wore bikinis. Some even threatened to excommunicate them (Andrés Serrano, Riedemann). What Muslim women are experiencing in places like Iran, Saudi Arabia, and Afghanistan, was also experienced by Christian women in Europe and the Americas.

5.7 Christian Dress Codes

Since the time of the early Church, Christian women have covered their hair in prayer and at mass. Wearing of head-coverings was mandated by the *Code of Canon Law of 1917*; however, it was abrogated by the *Code of Canon Law of 1983*. Pope Pius XI (r. 1922-1939) was so strict about modest dress that he declared that "women who wear immodest dress shall be denied Holy Communion" (Joselit). According to his standard of modest dress,

> A dress cannot be called decent which is cut deeper than two fingers breadth under the pit of the throat; which does not cover the arms at least to the elbows; and scarcely reaches a bit beyond the knees. Furthermore, dresses of transparent materials are improper.

Traditionalist Catholics have maintained these standards and even expanded upon them. For example, Cardinal Giuseppe Siri (1906-1989) stated in 1960 that it was not proper for women to wear pants. Some traditionalist and conservative Muslims hold the same view. They ignore the fact that both men and women have worn pants and trousers since antiquity and that they were the typical attire of Muslim women in many parts of the world. As for the Roman Catholic Church, it eventually updated its dress code to changing times and circumstances. According to the *Catechism*,

> 2521 Purity requires modesty, an integral part of temperance. Modesty protects the intimate center of the person. It means refusing to unveil what should remain hidden. It is ordered to chastity to whose sensitivity it bears witness. It guides how one looks at others and behaves toward them in conformity with the dignity of persons and their solidarity.
>
> 2522 Modesty protects the mystery of persons and their love. It encourages patience and moderation in loving relationships; it requires that the conditions for the definitive giving and commitment of man and woman to one another be fulfilled. Modesty is decency. It inspires one's choice of clothing. It keeps silence or reserve where there is evident risk of unhealthy curiosity. It is discreet.
>
> 2523 There is a modesty of the feelings as well as of the body. It protests, for example, against the voyeuristic explorations of the human body in certain advertisements, or against the solicitations of certain media that go too far in the exhibition of intimate things. Modesty inspires a way of life which makes it possible to resist the allurements of fashion and the pressures of prevailing ideologies.
>
> 2524 The forms taken by modesty vary from one culture to another. Everywhere, however, modesty exists as an intuition of the spiritual dignity proper to man. It is born with the awakening consciousness of being a subject. Teaching modesty to children and adolescents means awakening in them respect for the human person.

This guidance follows the spirit, not only of the Bible, but of the Qur'an, as well. Muslims have much to learn from Christian and Jewish authorities.

Although Catholic standards of decent dress have evolved, some Protestant denominations maintain stricter standards. According to *The Discipline of the Evangelical Wesleyan Church*, "we require our women to appear in public with dresses of modest length, sleeves of modest length, modest necklines and modest hose; the wearing of split skirts, slacks, jeans… is forbidden" (41, 57-58). The Pentecostals promote modest clothing and oppose adornment, jewelry and makeup. Some of their denominations continue to ordain women's head-covering.

Although they are not viewed as Christians by orthodox believers, groups like the Church of Jesus Christ of Latter-Day Saints discourage "short shorts and short skirts, shirts that do not cover the stomach, and clothing that does not cover the shoulders or is low-cut in the front or the back" and expect women to wear skirts or dresses that reach the knee during services (Ingram). Likewise, the Witnesses require their women to wear modest dresses and shirts. Pants are prohibited.

5.8 *Hijab* and Mental Health

As for the *niqab*, *litham*, *burqa*, *chador*, and even the simple headscarf, studies suggest that they can cause psychological problems in Muslim girls and women, leading some to self-loathing and suicide. Women who veil themselves can suffer from stigma, paranoia, exhaustion, social anxiety, and other health issues. They can feel oppressed. While the *hijab* can have negative psychological consequences, some studies suggest that it can have positive ones as well. All of these studies, however, rely on small population samples, are myopic in focus, fail to account for variables, come to opposite conclusions, and have limited validity, if any at all. Consequently, their findings cannot be generalized. When it comes to comprehending the *hijab* and its consequences, a multi-disciplinary approach is in order.

There is no doubt that some girls and women struggle with living up to impossible ideals of beauty and bodies in our globalized world. Some starve themselves to death trying to become thin. However, nobody will imprison, lash, or kill them for their fashion choices. It is only the Muslim woman who risks being stoned to death. Ultimately, women should not dress for women, nor should they dress for men. They should dress for themselves. Although "tyrannical Arab traditions have given a false impression that a woman must be covered from head to toe; such is not a Qur'anic or Islamic dress." There is no "Muslim uniform" for women (Masjid Tuscon: "Dress Code for Women Based on the Qur'an").

5.9 Conclusions

As can be appreciated, from a plethora of points of view on a myriad of issues, produced by the proliferation of schools of jurisprudence during the first few centuries of Islam, diversity of thought was radically reduced. From approximately one hundred and fifty schools of jurisprudence, a little over half a dozen came to survive: the Maliki, the Hanafi, the Shafi'i, the Hanbali, the Zaydi, the Ismaili, the Imami, and the 'Ibadi. The minority positions, which were often more positive toward women, were suppressed and silenced, the jurists who issued them were excoriated, marginalized, cancelled, and even exterminated, and the schools that expressed them disappeared. The Muslim world went from a lush biodiversity of opinion that included positions favorable to women to a monolithic monoculture of misogyny producing a single species of patriarchal plants. Thanks to the overgrazing of oppressors, the pasture of plural opinion was deliberately and irremediably degraded leading to erosion and desertification. Increasingly, more and more Muslim scholars have committed themselves to restoring fertility to the ideological environment of Islam to make it one that is welcoming and nurturing to women. This process involves retrieving the rulings of lost schools of jurisprudence, and issuing new ones, to provide diverse opinions and options.

Chapter 6

The Reemergence of Reformist, Rationalist, Secularist, Qur'anist, Progressive, and Revivalist Voices

6.1 Introduction

In the past few decades, in particular, critical scholars, who follow Islam's rich and diverse intellectual tradition, as opposed to blind and uncritical emulation, have started to rediscover, and revive the lost legacy of Islamic jurisprudence. This plurality of voices, which was snuffed out over the centuries by proponents of patriarchy and sexual segregation, challenges the unreasonable, unethical, intransigent, and authoritarian interpretations that are patently incompatible with the Qur'an's universal moral and ethical message and its lofty principles. Islam, these minority scholars have shown, was far more tolerant during its first centuries than it has been for its last thousand years.

6.2 The Role of Reason in Islamic Revival

As far as many committed Muslims are concerned, the Islamic tradition must be purged and purified from inadmissible social and cultural accretions. This is not a return to the "pious predecessors" of the Salafis but a return to the Qur'an, God, and reason. While there is a place in Islam for diverse opinions, there is no place for immoral, unethical, and unjust opinions that contradict the Qur'an and the rational and moral compass that God inculcated in human beings. There is no racism in Islam, and there is no sexism in Islam. Like a patient who desperately needs a life-saving blood transfusion, Islam must be reinfused with a wide variety of tolerant interpretations to survive and thrive. Overall, these moderate, lenient, accommodating, and liberal rulings have been excluded from the dominant narrative. Those that do simply survive as sidenotes.

If Islam is a universal religion, it must apply at all times and places. As it currently exists, Islam is only suitable for specific sexist and patriarchal populations. By and large, Muslims struggle to integrate into other societies and adapt to modernity. If the full spectrum of Islamic positions were presented to Muslim women and recognized as valid and legitimate, including rulings rooted in informed interpretations of the Qur'an, what is rigid and inflexible would appear dynamic and flexible, and what is archaic and reactionary would suddenly seem vibrant, adaptive, progressive, and forward-thinking. As Muhammad Mujtahid-Shabistari (b. 1936), the Iranian philosopher and theologian, elucidates, "the *shari'ah* is not a solid edifice" (Ridgeon 2). It can be reinterpreted be free-thinking individuals (2). Far from monolithic, the *shari'ah* can be "liberal, progressive, and broad-minded" (2).

Had Muslims continued to promote logic, reason, and freedom of thought, and women had been granted the rights and liberties that God and the Prophet granted them, one can only imagine what the Muslim world would look like today. The explosion of scientific thought and progress in all fields could have continued unabated. The Muslim Golden Age could still be flourishing. In fact, we could be in the Muslim Platinum Age or the Muslim Silicon Age. Since women's rights are linked to the material progress of any civilization, the stifling and suppression of women played a significant part in the downfall of Islamic culture and power in the world. The resurrection of global Islamic civilization depends directly on the rights of women.

6.3 Public Decency

If Islam is revived and breaks from its brittle medieval mold, it could, by the grace of God, realign itself with the religion of truth, the religion of the primordial form. The eternal and immutable law is one of decency, covering one's external genitals in public. The failure to do so is an act of obscenity that can be punished. As for modesty, the meaning and application of which changes with time and place and is necessarily temporary, it should be encouraged. The Qur'an establishes limits: the minimum and the maximum. As Rachel Woodlock, an Islamic scholar, and self-described Muslim feminist convert who wears *hijab*, summarizes, "Both a naked woman and a totally covered woman have brought themselves outside the bounds of Qur'anic respectability, according to Shahrur." As Abdul Mustaqim, the Indonesian Islamic scholar, further explains:

> In the case of woman's attire … Shahrur considers the minimum limit of woman's attire to … covering the chest (breasts) and genitals so as not to be naked. Its maximum limit is the covering of the whole body excluding the palms of one's hand and one's face… The woman who does not wear *hijab* has in fact fulfilled God's stipulation…. Women who cover their whole body including the face are considered to have gone beyond … God's limits… Women who cover their face and their whole body are "not Islamic."

The minimum a woman must cover is her private parts in the literal sense. Covering the reproductive organ would be mandatory, while covering the bosom would be recommended. It is what distinguishes between indecency and decency. It is decency that is required by law. A woman who wears a bikini may not be particularly modest. However, she is not guilty of public indecency. She has not committed a crime. And she has not sinned unless she intentionally set out to sexually excite men to seduce them. In contrast, the maximum a woman must cover is her entire body, except her face, hands, and feet. According to context, everything between the minimum and the maximum is tolerable, but not necessarily commendable. Edip Yüksel, for example, does not believe that the bikini is modest; however, he feels that it meets the minimum Qur'anic standard of public decency (Girl Praying in Bikini).

The followers of fables, legends, myth, and lore may have equated the *hijab* with Islam. In reality, however, the Qur'an only encourages women to "draw their coverings over their breasts" (24:31). Verse 24:31 says nothing about covering the hair; only covering the chest, namely, the *juyub*, the bosom. The passage contains no reference to a "head-covering" nor "drawing down." The reference to "hidden ornaments" indicates the sexual organs and breasts. Consequently, God has granted women freedom of dress within perspicuously defined limits. As much as it may shock the sensibilities of some Muslims, the claim that the bikini is the *hijab* of Islam is in line with the views of Islamic jurists who ruled that the *'awrah* was limited to the external genitalia. In short, it meets the minimum requirement of covering the private parts. As Richard Martin and Harold Koda noted, "the bathing suit is, in every period, the decisive limit of civilized clothing" (52).

Few rational and reasonable people would disagree that the appropriate dress on a beach or a pool differs from what is appropriate in a gym, a factory, a business, a school, or a court of law. Consideration must be given to context: geography, climate, education, employment, culture, age, gender, and class. Consideration must be given to body type, taste, style, and fashion. When it comes to Islamic modest dress, the claim that "one-size-fits-all" is fallacious. It deprives Islam of its universality, flexibility, and adaptability. It is not an issue of promoting debauchery. It is about setting limits, the minimum, and the maximum, while encouraging, as opposed to imposing, a dress code through laws, corporal punishment, lengthy prison sentences, torture, rape, and murder. Most importantly, it is about freedom, human dignity, and tolerance. By depriving women of their free will, notes Leena El-Ali, men are not protecting anyone: "they are obstructing God's plan" (87).

6.4 Colorphobic Fanatics

Muslim jurists and Islamists should open their minds and open some books. They should study the history of dress, costume, and fashion. In so doing, minds are opened and views are modified. To their surprise, they might learn that clothing has continually evolved. They might discover that, throughout history, Muslim women have never worn the style of clothing that jurists and Islamists wished to impose upon them. In response to the imposition of "Islamic" dress by the Taliban in 2021, consisting of black, all-enveloping *burqas*, *niqabs*, and gowns, Afghan American historian Bahar Jalali rightly stated, "No woman has ever dressed like this in the history of Afghanistan. This is utterly foreign and alien to Afghan culture" (Siddiqui). Islamists, it is evident, have an aversion to color and beauty. The clothing of their choice is the color of their souls. Afghan women are proud of their traditional outfits. The attire imposed upon them by the Islamists is neither Afghan nor Islamic. For Jalali, fashion is a form of resistance. Hence, the #donotouchmyclothes campaign.

The claim that women cannot wear colorful clothing because it might sexually excite men has no Qur'anic basis, despite appearing in an extensive list of edicts down to our days. The Islamic edicts prohibiting colors are the same ones issued by Orthodox Jewish rabbis against eye-catching colors such as red and pink. As hard as it is to fathom for orthodox Jews and Muslims, women's sartorial choices should not be dictated by men who get sexually aroused by colors. Some peer-reviewed studies indicate that certain colors, particularly red, are associated with arousal (Buechner and Maier). One study found that men gave higher tips to waitresses who wore red instead of white (Gueguen and Jacob). Another showed that "women wearing red were perceived by men as more sexually receptive, and it is precisely this receptivity that men found attractive" (Pazda and Elliot, see also Fischer-Mirkin 28-30). While some might argue that the rulings against ladies in red are evidence-based, the orthodox rabbis and Shiite jurists missed the mark for women are more sexually aroused by men who wear red or who are pictured against a red background (Elliot 399-417). If red turns men on, it also turns women on. So why not prohibit men from wearing red? And why not ban red paint while they are at it? As Valerie Steele (b. 1955), the American fashion historian, explains,

> Red is a powerful and provocative color. Brides wear red in China and India because it is the color of happiness... But the symbolism of red is ambiguous, with both positive and negative connotations. Red is strongly associated with sexuality, especially female sexuality... The Scarlet Woman of the Bible was a sexually "evil" female, an adulteress or prostitute... Throughout much of recorded history, the high cost of producing red dyes meant that red clothing was worn only by those with power and status.

The color of rooms was also found to increase the frequency of sex in another study. People who had purple rooms had the most sex, followed by those with red, sky blue, pink, and black (Fellizar). Another found that the most arousing colors were green-yellow, blue-green, and green, whereas the least arousing were purple-blue and yellow-red (Valdez and Mehrabian). As anthropologist Stephen Juan (1949-2018) cautions:

> There is much behavioral science research showing the most popular skin color, eye color, or hair color in terms of sexual attractiveness. But there is little on what is the most sexually attractive color… It is impossible to determine the most sexually attractive color due to the many confounding variables involved. Different cultures have different attitudes and preferences in the attribution of qualities of color and behavior… "Black" is associated with death in European countries. But "white" is associated with death in China and "purple" is associated with death in Brazil.
>
> As for sexual attractiveness, there is an enormous cultural component in this as well. Gender is another confounding variable. What might be perceived as a highly sexually attractive color on a woman may not be perceived as such on a man. And what might be a highly sexually attractive color to a woman may not be so to a man. Individuals associate particular colors with particular things in their lives. Thus, any color could be "the most sexually attractive" to a particular individual. There are other confounding variables too… Red, black, and copper/bronze would seem to head the list of the most sexually attractive colors. (Juan)

Orthodox Jews, ultra-conservative Muslims, and radical Islamists may insist on wearing black; however, this color is one of the most sexually attractive to men. Some Shiite jurists, including Sa'id al-Hakim (1936-2021), have also ruled that women cannot wear colored contact lenses lest they sexually arouse men. What of women with natural blue, green, and purple eyes? What of women with grey and black eyes? Should their eyes be gouged out or covered up because some pervert might get aroused by them?

Some Christian monks and nuns wear black clothing. However, there are no prohibited colors among the Amish. Girls wear brighter colors like yellows, pinks, and shades of red. Married women normally wear darker clothing: purple, blue, wine, brown, grey, and black. Although rules vary from one church district to another, and there was a time when some communities shied away from red, younger Amish women do indeed wear red. Some only permit solid colors, while others allow patterns. There is nothing sexually provocative about a young Amish woman in a red dress. As beautiful as she may be, she remains modest. She will not get sexually propositioned, but she might get a sincere marriage proposal. Despite misconceptions to the contrary, there is a slight degree of fashion evolution among the Amish, often young girls who introduce new fabrics or colors based on what materials are available.

Taste differs from men to women and from culture to culture. Not only are colors associated with sexual attraction, but they also determine shopping habits. Red-orange and black and royal blue appeal to impulse buyers. Budget shoppers respond best to pink, teal, light blue, and navy. More traditional buyers are influenced by pastels, including pink, rose, and sky blue. Should rabbis and shaykhs pass edicts prohibiting a wide array of colors since they encourage spending instead of thriftiness? When does this madness end? Why don't we eradicate all sinful colors from nature while we are at it? Oddly, God Himself presents colors as a wonder in the Qur'an. He states that "the diversity of… your colors" is a sign of God (30:22). Similarly, the Qur'an asks: "who is better than God at coloring?" (2:138). God has no qualms mentioning colors in the Qur'an, including yellow, white, black, green, blue, red, pink, and dark green. They carry symbolic and aesthetic connotations (see Al-Shawi). As Hadas Hirsch, the specialist in Middle East history, notes,

> The Koran refers to colors … nine times (30:22, 35:28, 39:21, 2:69, 35:27, 16:69) as a divine grace for human beings of a multicolored world, as evident from surah 16:1: "And that which He multiplied for you in the earth of diverse hues." Some verses even mention by name the colors red, yellow, green, black, white, and blue.

As Hirsch has noted, in Islam, "as with many other colors, red has ambivalent meanings: it is the color of ripe fruit and of love, both of which are positive, but at the same time, it is the color of fire, which is both positive and negative (warming and burning), and the color of war and blood." Among some nomadic tribes, red is associated with fertility. According to one tradition, the Prophet prohibited men from wearing a certain shade of red, without providing any reason. However, other hues of red were permitted, and he himself wore red clothing. Although women were not mentioned in this discussion, "we can assume that they were permitted to wear red clothing in its various hues" (Hirsch). Prohibiting Muslims from wearing a certain shade of red, or even yellow, as another tradition indicates, since the latter was the color associated with concubines, exotic dancers, and transexuals, is bound by culture, time, and context. Prohibiting Muslim women from wearing bright colors is as retrograde as requiring Jews to wear yellow, Christians to wear blue, or Samaritans to wear red, as some Muslim rulers commanded.

As Hirsch summarizes, Muslim jurists categorized colors as permitted, preferred, and prohibited, "based on their symbolic interpretations and perceptions of adornment and aesthetics." They used colors "to establish and reinforce gendered differentiation [that] reflects the patriarchal and hierarchal nature of Muslim societies." Finally, colors were used to "create a religious-political differentiation between the Muslim ruling elite and two different subject populations, namely, their non-Muslim tributaries and rebels against the regime."

Despite the views of totalitarian Muslim jurists, who yearned to control every aspect of life, beauty, colors, and fashion are not evil and sinful. They serve a myriad of purposes, not the least of which include inspiring attraction, courtship, falling in love, marriage, procreation, and the creation of families. It is unnatural and unsound to suppress fashion, colors, and clothing, and impose a homogeneous depersonalizing, demoralizing, and dehumanizing dress code. Such practices are associated with the army, religious cults, and totalitarian societies. Homogenous dress codes are used to break down people to refashion them as required by authorities. It destroys their individuality, turning them into a mindless, brainwashed, collective mass. They become like black ants in a colony or a flock of black crows. It destroys human diversity. It is an assault against beauty.

Fashion is a powerful force. Clothing is a form of non-verbal communication. It is a complex code, filled with meaning, which serves scores of social functions. It provides visual clues about a person's community. It marks age, gender, class, status, profession, vocation, religion, and geographical origin. Compelling women to wear black *burqas* is like imposing illiteracy. To deprive a woman of her right to dress, as she pleases, for different occasions and purposes, and send signals, is to deny her the right to speak, to suppress her voice and her choice, and to silence her. Such sensory deprivation is unnatural and unhealthy for individuals and societies.

While the *hijab* highlights the face of the woman, not all women have pretty faces. Hence, if they wish to find a mate and a life partner, women need to highlight their assets and attributes: beautiful hair, silky skin, lovely hands, manicured nails, full lips, gorgeous eyes, a long neck, a sinuous back, a tight curvy backside, well-shaped cleavage, long legs, or a narrow waist (Fischer-Mirkin 58). "Any outfit that displays the body too much obviously loses its allure," cautions Fischer-Mirkin, "because when the mystery is lost, so is the interest" (58).

Not all women who dress provocatively are promiscuous. They are not all seeking sexual attention. Some are expressing their sensuality. Others are expressing a desire for power and equality. And yet others are proclaiming their female potency (Fischer-Mirkin 56). At the same time, there are promiscuous women who dress modestly. In fact, as Arabic literature like the *One Hundred and One Nights* unveils, the veil was often used to facilitate discretion for sexual indiscretion. The so-called Islamic dress code does not cut down on corruption. Men who wish to meet up with women to commit fornication or adultery merely wear *chadors* to gain unfettered access to their homes in complete confidentiality.

If the role of *hijab* is to reduce fornication and adultery, it simply does not work. The obsession with intact hymens merely produces an increase in oral and anal sex, along with hymenoplasty before marriage (Yahia 32). While some Muslim women make it to marriage as virgins, virtually no Muslim men do, showcasing the patriarchal double standard. They are free to fornicate, commit adultery, and frequent prostitutes. Some Muslim men in the UK may fornicate less; however, some rape more (Gannon; Morrow 2020: 120-126). And if they do not rape there, then they join Islamist terrorist groups abroad so they can violate as many sex slaves as possible. After all, the Islamists believe in slavery and concubinage (Morrow, *Islam & Slavery*, 2023). For them, it is an article of faith, and anyone who opposes such practices is an apostate, a heretic, a deviant, a hypocrite, and a disbeliever who deserves to die. The Salafi-Wahhabis insist that "logic is prohibited in Islam." One cannot reason with people who cannot reason and who do not believe in reason. The only language they understand is that of violence. This is not to suggest that they are all beyond salvation. Many moderate, peaceful, spiritual, progressive, tolerant, and loving Muslims are former Islamist radicals. Some people have the potential to repent, atone, and make amends. It is a question of contrition.

The absence of female beauty in the public sphere, and social interaction between both sexes, increases same-sex attraction and sexual activity. In places where strict *hijab* and gender segregation prevail, there is a crisis of masculinity. In the absence of women, some men direct their desires towards other males who have adopted feminine traits and assume passive, feminine, receptive roles, in homosexual encounters. They are heterosexual men who engage in homosexuality to satisfy basic human sexual urges. Muslim men, in nations with mandatory *hijab*, behave like incarcerated men. They redirect their sexual frustrations. Some turn to men. Many turn to boys. There are also traditional homosexuals in the Middle East. Despite the dangers inherent in such illegal activities, which can result in execution in places like Saudi Arabia and Iran, homosexuality flourishes. In Saudi Arabia, it is an open secret. For some, it is a "gay heaven" (Fanack). As far as some scholars are concerned, the misogyny of the Islamic extremists leads to pederasty and child sexual abuse (Morrow, *Islam & Slavery*, 2023: 128, 132, 226).

By removing female beauty from the public sphere, in an attempt to suppress heterosexual desire, the fanatics redirected male lust toward men. The same phenomenon takes place among incarcerated men. Without women, some men turn to homosexuality to satisfy their sexual desires. The same happens to women when men are absent, be it in penitentiaries, or in harems. Muslim jurists essentially turned their societies into prisons for men and women.

Since women were erased from existence, prepubescent boys became objects of male lust. Classical works of Islamic jurisprudence describe "beardless boys" as seductive and a source of sin. They claim that each boy is surrounded by satanic entities. Some state that boys are more dangerous than women (Morrow, *Islam & Slavery* 2023: 131-132). And yet others insisted that they were so irresistible that they should be required to wear *hijab*. Had such a view taken hold, it is possible that Muslim boys would have been required to veil themselves until they reached puberty and grew beards. In fact, Ibn 'Abidin (1784-1836), ruled that boys who reached puberty, but were devoid of facial hair, were to be treated as women; that is, their entire bodies, from top to bottom, were considered a private part or '*awrah* (Morrow 132). The analysis of a renowned psychologist might be in order, that of Phyllis Chesler. As she explains,

> Wherever women are forced to wear *chadors*, *burqas*, *niqab*, you can be sure that children are also being abused. For men… who are brought up apart from -- and taught to fear and despise women -- their major erotic and social drives will be male-centric, not female-centric. Homosexual pederasty accompanies extreme gender apartheid in an extreme way. (2017: 217)

Likewise, since they could not channel their attraction toward women, some men focused it on pre-pubescent girls who, unlike teenagers and women, were not required to veil themselves. Hence, the disturbing body of Islamic jurisprudence that permits men to marry prepubescent girls, even newborn babies, and pleasure themselves with them (Morrow, *Controversies in Islam*, 2023: 66-127).

In addition to increased homoeroticism, lack of exposure to women in the public sphere produces increased impotence rates in men. The nations where strict *hijab* and gender segregation prevail are among the largest consumers of pornography and erectile disfunction drugs. In fact, "the Middle East has the highest per capita share of Viagra users in the world, with Saudi Arabia, the United Arab Emirates, and Egypt topping the list" (Quillen). What is more, they have some of the highest rates of prostitution on the planet. In Dubai alone, it is estimated that "45,000 women are trapped in prostitution networks" not to mention teenage boys (Rosenblum). For journalist Amalia Rosenblum, "visiting Dubai is like standing on the sidelines of a gang rape."

As much as Islamists despise colors and insist that women wear black and dark blue clothing, Muslim women worldwide wore bright and colorful clothing for most of history. The clothing and scarves worn by Muslim women in early times were more "modern and liberal" than those worn in later times. It is only relatively recently that these black outfits, which are highly incongruent with history, culture, and place (El-Ali 223), have spread like the plague, gangrene, and the black death. Prior to the rise of Islamic fundamentalism and political Islam, particularly the spread of the Muslim Brotherhood, and the 1979 revolution in Iran, Muslim women wore colorful and fashionable clothing. Even the more conservative ones, like the womenfolk from Mohammad Kazem Shariatmadari's (1906-1986) family, wore bright, colorful, *chadors*. Nowadays, women are banned from entering the holy shrines of the Shiites in Iran and Iraq unless they cloak themselves in black *chadors*. The contrast between Iran before the 1979 revolution and after is stark. Women's clothing went from beautiful, modern, and colorful, to ugly, medieval, black, and bleak. The same can be said for Muslim countries that are not under Islamist rule. In the 1960s, 1970s, and early 1980s, the beaches in Morocco, Algeria, and Tunisia were filled with bikini-clad beauties. Those same beaches now feature demonstrations by Islamist women in black *burqas*, an entirely foreign attire that was imported from the Middle East by Muslim fundamentalists.

6.5 A Matter of Freedom and Liberty

Although Abla Hasan believes that the headscarf is an Islamic duty, she insists that it must be a free choice (117) and that "it is not compulsory" (122, note 42). She also recognizes that women who do not wear the headscarf are not necessarily less virtuous, serious, and devout than veiled women (110) and that there are other ways of being modest (116). Some flirtatious women wear *hijab*. Likewise, there are sexy women who set firm boundaries. There are *hijabis* who are easy, and non-*hijabis* who are as inaccessible as Kilimanjaro. There is a reason that the word "hoejabi" has entered the urban vernacular in the English-speaking Western world. It refers to women who wear a headscarf with extremely tight clothing and who exhibit the characteristics of a whore. There are even chador-wearing wives who commit adultery and have affairs. Any self-respecting nun would cast off her habit, and renounce her vows, prior to being promiscuous. If the *hijab* is a religious symbol, like a crucifix, open sinners should not insist on wearing it. Like corrupt and oppressive politicians who wear turbans and clerical garb, they damage the image of the Islamic faith.

As Qur'anists, so-called Islamic feminists, Muslim academics, and some traditional scholars of Islam have concluded over the past decades, relying on the rulings of previously marginalized religious authorities, *hijab*, as understood by the ultra-conservatives and Islamists, is most certainly not obligatory. This view has been shared by scholars like Leila Ahmed, Amina Wadud, Aysha A. Hidayatullah, Khaled Abou El Fadl, Ayesha S. Chaudhry, Asma Barlas, Nimat Hafez Barazangi, Asma Lamrabet, and Muhammad Shahrur, among many others.

For Shahrur, the only thing that God requests that women cover is cleavage, namely, their genitals, buttocks, breasts, and armpits (311). In his view, Muslim women who wear shorts and t-shirts in public abide by the lower legal limit of the Islamic dress code (328, note 74). For Shahrur:

> Women are required to cover their upper private parts (breasts and armpits) in addition to their lower private parts, her thick *'awrah* (this constitutes the lower limit for all women). This definition, however, does not cover dresses for special occasions (parties, opera, concerts, etc.). As for the concept of "from the navel to the knee," we conclude that *fiqh* jurists unashamedly invented this. (326)

While many scholars are against the imposition of *hijab* on women, Asma Lamrabet (b. 1961), the Moroccan Islamic feminist, holds that the *khimar* or headscarf "can neither be imposed nor forbidden since in both cases this would reflect a totalitarian logic, it is up to women and women alone to choose whether to wear it or not, and not to anyone else" (2018: 163). For others, however, the ultra-conservative pseudo-Islamic dress that prevails among certain Arabs, Iranians, and Afghans, adopted as the Islamist uniform worldwide, has no place in Europe, the Americas, or elsewhere. Consequently, they oppose its imposition (Ahmed 1992: 179-181).

Increasingly, even Muslim scholars who hold that the *hijab* is religiously obligatory are opposed to its imposition on the part of state actors, morality policy, and religious vigilantes. Such was the view of the late Mahmoud Taleghani (1911-1979), a Twelver Shiite religious authority with whom Khomeini publicly agreed (1902-1989), acknowledging that "*hijab* is not compulsory" (Pars Time). Khomeini, however, soon recanted his public statements, and imposed strict Islamic dress on all women in public settings. This was consistent with his view that women who did not observe *hijab* were whores. In fact, notes found in Morteza Motahhari's pocketbook, which included topics he planned to discuss with Khomeini, included one that called for "delaying the question of *hijab* until the establishment of Islamic rule" (Iran Wire). It would seem that Khomeini's promises of moderation were a ploy to appease the people's concerns. He had always planned to impose *hijab* and other Islamic rules by force. If Khomeini was reactionary, there was a reason. As noted in *Pars Times*, "the excesses of the Pahlavi dynasty were mainly responsible for the imposition of *hijab* on Iranian women after the revolution."

In a radio and television interview in March of 1979, Taleghani argued that nobody should force women to wear the *hijab*. He complained that certain elements were trying separate a great faction of the revolution -- women -- from the revolution. He stressed that nobody had the right to insult women. When asked whether it was even obligatory for women to wear the *hijab*, Taleghani responded:

> While this [*hijab*] is not obligatory for [Muslims], how can we say that the religious minorities of Christians, Zoroastrians, and Jews should wear *hijab* -- most of whom, especially the Jews and Zoroastrians that I have encountered, observe the old Iranian tradition [of *hijab*]? It is not even obligatory for them. (Kayhan)

If her father were alive today, asserts Taleghani's daughter, he would have thrown his turban on the ground to protest the "Islamic" Republic's oppression of women (Iran International). Although claims that Taleghani was assassinated on orders of Khomeini or his partisans have been dismissed in the past (Morrow 2012: 188-189), new information and revelations can cause scholars to reconsider their previous positions. Khomeini and Taleghani did not see eye-to-eye on many matters. Taleghani rivalled or surpassed Khomeini in popularity. In fact, he could bring people out to march at the snap of his fingers. On March 8, 1979, thousands of women, many of them Taleghani supporters, protested the idea of imposing *hijab*, calling for "freedom of choice in clothes" (Maranlou).

While Taleghani was insisting that *hijab* was not obligatory and could not be coerced, and Khomeini publicly agreed to appease the masses, the former was secretly planning to make it legally mandatory as soon as he had consolidated enough power. How could he not? He stated in a *fatwa* that it was a major and mortal sin not to wear *hijab* (Ridgeon 231). In other words, he held that it led to hell like murder, adultery, and rape. Curiously, pointed out Mohsen Kadivar, there is no mention of *hijab* in Khomeini's list of forty-five major sins (Ridgeon 231).

We also know that many Khomeini loyalists believed that anyone who opposed mandatory *hijab* was an apostate at war with Islam who deserved to die. Taleghani, it is now clear, was viewed as a rival and a threat by Khomeini and the people in his entourage. In light of the extrajudicial executions in which Khomeini and his partisans were involved, and which the repressive Khamenei regime has perpetuated, using the state apparatus and clandestine means, some scholars would not be surprised to learn that a hit was placed on Taleghani.

Taleghani died under highly suspicious circumstances on September 10, 1979 (Morrow 2012: 188-189). The convenient death of the popular, charismatic, and beloved leader paved the way for Khomeini's consolidation of power, and the imposition of obligatory *hijab*, which was achieved in April of 1983. Rather than be enforced by thugs and vigilantes, who used threats, intimidation, and violence, to coerce women to cover, not to mention throwing acid at them to permanently deface them, the police and courts of law would now enforce *hijab*, with women being unleashed upon women.

Since 1983, few Iranians dared oppose the mandatory *hijab*, out of fear of imprisonment, torture, and execution, on the grounds of "spreading corruption on earth," "waging war against God," and accusations of apostasy. They had even more significant battles to wage, and the issue was sidelined. Fear was also a major factor. After all, in 1991 the Prosecutor-General of Iran, declared that "anyone who rejects the principle of *hijab* is an apostate and the punishment for an apostate under Islamic law is death" (Lichter 158). For its victims, the veil is an anagram for evil.

Despite the dangers posed by freedom of thought and expression, over the years, more Iranians, scholars, and laypeople, have garnered the courage to express their opposition to obligatory *hijab*, some paying the ultimate price for doing so. Interestingly, most of the leading reformists in Iran are the children, grandchildren, and great grandchildren of the leaders of the Islamic revolution. Even Hasan Khomeini (b. 1972), the grandson of Khomeini, believes that *hijab* should not be imposed by force upon women. This view is shared by Muhammad Kazem Mousavi Bojnourdi (b. 1942). It is also the dominant one emanating from the Shiite seminary in Najaf. As Muhammad Ishaq al-Fayyad (b. 1930), one of the most senior sources of emulation in Iraq, stated: "using force and intimidation in promoting the *hijab* is not effective" (Rasanah 9).

Cunning and clever, the radical Islamists may have seized upon the concept of "choice" to defend and propagate the veil. However, as Bestandji warns, "this 'free choice' only goes in one direction" (2021: 303). The only "free choice" they promote is the "free choice" to not have one (2021: 290). Rather than take the defensive, the Islamists take the offensive: "What right do you have to tell women how or how not to dress?" The Muslim fundamentalists, however, engage in a double discourse. They claim that the *hijab* is a religious obligation in Islam and that there is no coercion in religion. "After years of indoctrination," asks Bestandji, "which woman would make the 'free choice' to burn in hell for eternity?" (2021: 298).

> If a Muslim woman wants to follow her religion, she has to veil herself. She does not have a choice. If she wants to please God, she must veil herself. She does not have a choice. If she wants to be respected as a woman, she must veil herself... The free choice presented ... by Islamist marketing is actually a decision consistent with what is expected by those who prescribe veiling (again, the Qur'an does not prescribe it.) (2021: 298)

As Bestandji points out, "for the veil to be a choice, it cannot be an 'obligation'" (2021: 298). Some extremists concede this fact willingly. They state quite clearly that "the *hijab* is not a choice. It is an obligation that requires submission." Muslim women cannot make an informed and enlightened choice when they are only presented with one point of view, and different interpretations are demonized (2021: 298).

The choice presented to Muslim women is biased, between right and wrong, heaven or hell, as well as belief and disbelief. No woman can make a "free choice" under such psychologically and spiritually abusive conditions. A choice is only free when both alternatives have a moral equivalence (2021: 297). In reality, Muslim women have but three choices. They can wear *hijab* and hope to go to heaven. If they believe in *hijab*, and fail to wear it, they are sinners who deserve to go to hell. Perhaps God will be merciful to them, forgive them, or release them from the fire. If, however, they do not believe in the *hijab*, they are viewed as disbelievers, and eternal damnation will be their lot. If the only options include being a believing, submissive, Muslim, being a sinner, or being a hypocrite and an infidel, one cannot speak of a "free choice."

The goal of the Islamists, however, is to conquer public spaces and show their symbols on the farthest horizons. They wish to impose the *hijab* progressively (2021: 306). Their propaganda is supported by Western, so-called, feminists (2021: 314). For the Islamists, the *hijab* is the banner of conquest of Islam, and women are their advance troops. This is not to say that every woman who wears a headscarf is a radical Islamist, a jihadist, or a terrorist. Some have simply been convinced by male, and sometimes female, Islamists, that it is obligatory to wear it. They mistakenly believe that this extremist interpretation is Islam (2021: 335). Whether they wear the *hijab* for radical, cultural, or religious reasons, the women who do so share one common denominator: they all accept to surrender to male authority (2021: 335). After all, "the most effective system of oppression is the one that succeeds in convincing the oppressed of the validity of their oppression" (Samint). As Bestandji qualifies:

> If Muslim women are convinced that the word of the Islamists is more credible, if they refuse, as many do, to compare the different analyzes of the Qur'anic texts because they prefer to remain faithful to the *shari'ah*, if they wish to bathe in obscurantism and opt for voluntary servitude, they have the right to do so… It should be specified that their "choice" is not dictated by the Qur'an but by their interpretation (or at least the interpretation of their "scholars")... The most concealing veil is not placed on their head. It is posed on their critical spirit, of which physical veiling is also the symbol (2021: 104)

Ultimately, the *hijab* is not a matter of free choice. As Bestandji asserts, "If no man prescribed the veil, no woman would wear it" (2021: 319, 2022). So-called solidarity on the part of Western allies, feminist, woke, or otherwise, is damaging to Muslim women who struggle against the sexism of the coerced *hijab*. For Mona Eltahawy, "Western women who wear the veil contribute to the subjugation of women in other parts of the world" (Bestandji 2021: 319). Sexism should not be supported or celebrated.

6.6 Competing Notions of *Hijab* in Iran

As Ziba Mir-Hosseini, the Iranian-born legal anthropologist, who specializes in Islamic law and gender, has shown, Morteza Mottahari (d. 1979) promoted *hijab* as a form of "protection" (2011: 198) whereas 'Ali Shari'ati (1933-1977) viewed it as a symbol of protest (2011: 199-200). However much he promoted the *hijab* as a revolutionary gesture, one that came in response to the Shah's brutal ban on attire he viewed as backwards, Shari'ati's wife and daughters did not veil themselves. They dressed liberally and fashionably and even wore bathing suits to European beaches, something that most Shiite Muslim clerics and conservatives would have viewed as scandalous. Had he survived, and not died of a heart attack two years before the 1979 revolution, he would have ended up exiled, imprisoned, or executed by radical elements for being intellectually Westernized. After the death of Shari'ati, and the assassination of Motahhari, Iranian Islamist hardliners, Khomeini included, decided to impose the *hijab* by force (200-202), while persecuting, imprisoning, and silencing more pragmatic Muslim scholars and leaders who espoused a more moderate and tolerant approach.

While a minority of radicals and conservatives continue to believe that the failure to wear *hijab* should be a punishable offense, most Iranians, men and women, view *hijab* as a matter of personal choice. "Having lost the public debate over *hijab* as imposition," notes Mir-Hosseini, "the hardliners in the "Islamic" Republic have returned to using the arms of the state by which they imposed it in the 1980s" (2011: 203). Although the enemies of Iran may wish to weaponize the anti-*hijab* movement, pretending they care about women, when they only care about their economic and political interests, the dissent and discontent in Iran are real, and the *hijab* is simply a symbol and a synecdoche. The protests in Iran are the product of decades of pent-up anger. The clash between the government, schoolgirls, women, and their supporters pits two competing and arguably incompatible worldviews.

In 2022, Mohamad Ali Ayazi, an Iranian cleric, voiced his strong opposition to compulsory *hijab*. Citing Morteza Motahhari, Mohammed Beheshti, (b. 1928-1981) and Mahmoud Taleghani, he stated that "forcing women to wear *hijab* is not a religious practice and is against the Islamic code, the *shari'ah*" (Radio Farda). According to his son, Alireza, Mohammad Behesthi opposed obligatory *hijab* and allowed women to visit his office without wearing it (Radio Farda).

6.7 Qur'anist Views on the *Hijab*

Far from a recent *fitnah* or sedition, the Qur'anists, *ahl al-Qur'an* or *qur'aniyyun* are as old as the Qur'an itself. After all, before the compilation of sayings supposedly stated by the Prophet Muhammad, something that happened centuries after his physical passing, the only book that Muslims followed was the Qur'an. Curiously, these canonical sources of *hadith* contain traditions in which the Prophet Muhammad himself prohibited the writing of his sayings while others have him insisting upon it (Musa 25-29, Abu Rayyah, Azami 27-29).

Not only are there accounts of Abu Bakr destroying his compilations of sayings of the Prophet Muhammad, but there are also accounts that 'Umar prohibited the practice of recording *hadith* and destroyed existing collections during his rule as the second caliph (Musa 25-29). When he appointed a governor to Kufah, he warned him about the spread of *hadith* and told him to call the people back to the Qur'an. "Do not distract them with the *hadiths*," he said, "bare the Qur'an and spare the *hadith* from God's messenger" (Musa 25-29). By the time 'Abd al-Malik ibn Marwan (r. 685-705) came to power, he received complaints that people had:

> abandoned the judgment of their Lord and took *hadiths* for their religion; and they claim that they have obtained knowledge other than from the Koran . . . They believed in a book which was not from God, written by the hands of men; they then attributed it to the Messenger of God. (Musa 37-38)

Throughout the centuries, groups like the *ahl al-kalam*, the *mu'tazilah*, and other Qur'an-centric scholars argued that the *sunnah* of the Prophet Muhammad was to be found in the Qur'an alone (Brown 15-16). While some Qur'anists accepted *ahadith* if they agreed with the Qur'an, and others rejected them entirely, they all agreed that most of the material was filled with falsehood and innovations.

Mahmud Abu Rayyah (d. 1970), and numerous other scholars, have produced devastating critiques of the *hadith* literature. "I believe only in the Qur'an," professed Mohamed Talbi, "not in the *shar'iah*. I only treat a *hadith* as true if it agrees with the Qur'an" (Zouari). As far as Bestandji is concerned:

> It is impossible for a saying that was uttered… in 630…to be exactly the same in 840 after having been transmitted orally by tens, if not hundreds of people. *Hadiths*, by definition, cannot be credible, regardless of the degree of their alleged reliability. (2021: 80)

The Qur'anists are also fiercely critical of the clerical class, lambasting them for corrupting Islam beyond recognition. Many reject Sunni, Shiite, and Sufi Islam, asserting that "Islam is the Qur'an only." In response, as one would expect, Sunni and Shiite clerics have labelled them as "apostates," "heretics," "animals," "infidels," "*fitnah*-mongers," "Mu'tazilis," persecuted them in courts of law, expelled them from their teaching positions at seminaries and universities, forcibly divorced some of them from their spouses, condemned them to death, and, in some cases, have had them executed by the apparatus of the state or murdered extra-judicially by terrorists at their service. The response of some Qur'anists has been to treat all other so-called Muslims in the same fashion, accusing them of being "polytheists," "idol-worshippers," and "disbelievers."

Some Qur'anists can be very moderate and tolerant. Others can be quite extreme, having adopted the worse qualities of the Salafis and Jihadis they despise, namely, an obsession with "innovation" as well as indiscriminate accusations of apostasy. While it is one thing to accuse radical, violent, Islamists and Takfiris, like ISIS, of being outside the fold of Islam, it is another thing entirely to label all mainstream Sunnis, Sufis, and Shiites as being so as well.

Far from forming a united front or school of thought and law, the Qur'anist movement, in the twentieth and twenty-first centuries, has shown a tendency to fragment and split into smaller groups, primarily due to differing methodologies. Some scholars, who issue rulings directly from the Qur'an, without relying on the *sunnah*, do not identify as Qur'anists. In some cases, they seem sincere. In others, they do so to reduce the risk of imprisonment and execution. Irrespective of how one labels oneself, anyone who does not toe the party line of the nation-state, be it Sunnism, Salafism, Wahhabism, or Political Twelver Shiism, runs the risk of being accused of "apostasy" or "waging war against God." Such is the intolerance that prevails in much of the so-called Muslim world.

Although they agree upon the primacy of the Qur'an, Qur'anist scholars have expressed differing opinions regarding the *hijab*. Some, like Abdulaziz Bayindir (b. 1951), the Turkish Islamic jurist, are very conservative, and argue that women must cover their hair and bodies except their faces, hands, and feet (Women Swimming; Why do Muslim Women Cover their Hair and Body?). With the noted exception of Bayindir, virtually all other Qur'anist scholars do not believe that Islam imposes a specific dress code on women, except for covering their private parts and lowering the gaze, literally or symbolically. What is more, Qur'anist women, like many if not most Sufi women, for that matter, generally do not wear *hijab*.

6.8 Conclusions

Muslims with an emotional and defensive connection to Islam, as opposed to an intellectual and spiritual one, will surely take offense to the arguments and evidence presented in this book. They will claim that the advocates of dynamic or alternative jurisprudence are deviants who encourage women to cast off the *hijab* and parade themselves like pole dancers. Intellectuals are accustomed to the insults of the mentally and spiritually immature. They might offend some Muslims; however, others find them ingratiating and treat them as compliments. After all, they used to cast refuse on the Prophet Muhammad when he prayed at the Ka'bah. To criticize imposed "Islamic" dress is not to promote immodesty and immorality. As Phyllis Chesler notes:

> I do not believe that the antidote to Western semi-nudity is to force women into ambulatory body bags. I favor modesty for both men and women, and I am aware that the Qur'an does, too, however, the *burqa* is not merely modest… it is a sensory deprivation chamber, a moving prison-shroud that renders women socially invisible. Are Muslim men immodest because they do not wear *burqas*? (2013: 14). Pointing out that women are treated as sex objects in the West does not mean that putting women in body bags proves that they are more respected or better protected. Those who make this argument fail to understand how thoroughly women are sexualized and also sexually abused in the Muslim world. (2017: 185)

The same goes for questioning the dominant definition of '*awrah*, the extent of religiously mandated covering, and the headscarf requirement, especially when they are based on sources of questionable credibility and biased interpretations. Sumbul Ali-Karamali errs when she claims that "early Islamic scholars' discussion about head covering for women took place in the context of social norms, hardship, class status, history, and women's safety, not oppression or patriarchy" (160). Their interpretations were profoundly colored by their sexism and patriarchy. Their rulings were grounded in woman-hating *ahadith*. Take, for example, Ghazzali's view of the opposite sex:

> The race of women consists of ten species, and the character of each (of these) corresponds and is related to the distinctive quality of one of the animals. One (species) resembles the pig, another the ape, another the goat, another the snake, another the mule, another the scorpion, another the mouse, another the pigeon, another the fox, and another the sheep.

The question begs to be asked. How can men who believe in such nonsense respect their wives and women? And what is more, how can men who hold such views issue just and equitable edicts regarding women?

As Bestandji reminds us, the Qur'an cannot be interpreted literally since the Arabic language of the seventh century is not the same as the dialects that are spoken today (2022). He is indeed correct. There are not, nor have there been for over a thousand years, native speakers of classical Arabic. In fact, even the Arabs at the time of the Prophet had difficulty understanding the words and meanings of the Qur'an. It was already archaic when it was revealed. It baffled and bedazzled the Prophet's contemporaries who viewed it as "ancient tales." If the Qur'an were so clear, notes Bestandji, thousands of volumes would never have been produced trying to explain it (2022). The Qur'an is laconic and the words it uses have numerous different meanings (2022). If one really respects the Qur'an, one should not follow it literally, but focus on its spirit (2022).

Chapter 7

The Views of Men on the *Hijab*

7.1 Introduction

"Men are in charge of women" (4:34), observed the Qur'an in the seventh century, an observation treated as a prescription due to a myopic, atomistic, interpretation that has dominated Islam to this day. In reality, it states that "men should stand up for women," namely, defend and protect them (Sawma 215). As Cyrille Moreno al-'Ajami argues, the verse should be translated as follows, "Men have responsibilities towards women" (2020: 50). According to most interpretations, the Qur'an states that "men have a degree over [women]" (4:34). However, it affirms that "God has made a distinction between them," namely, they consist of two genders (Sawma 216). More mindful men realize that Islam espouses equality. Men and women are "light upon light" (24:35) and garments for one another (1:187). They should compliment each other in complete harmony. Since Muslim men turned Allah into God, the woman-hating Father, and strove to annihilate any trace of the Goddess Mother, it is no surprise that Islamic law, with a few obsolete exceptions, is not gender egalitarian and subjects women to discrimination and injustice. In fact, ninety-nine percent of man-made Islamic laws regarding women support their oppression, suppression, and repression. They clearly contradict the spirit of the Qur'an.

While many men are to blame, "no bearer of burdens will bear the burden of another" (35:18). After all, "they are not all the same" (3:113). Hence, there is no room for misandry; however reasonable it may be for women to hold such views in light of thousands of years of mistreatment by men. As this study has shown, many Muslim men have always loved, respected, and revered women as sacred and strove to defend their rights and dignity. Throughout the ages, the conservative, patriarchal, sexist, macho, and misogynistic extremists and fanatics have spared no effort when it came to suppressing and silencing the voices and views of the philogynists: the lovers of women. Condemned to obscurity, incarceration, and execution, they are men who put their principles before their interests. Their views on the veil are valid and merit validation, dissemination, consideration, and acclamation.

7.1 Tahar Haddad

Tahar Haddad (1899-1935), the Tunisian author, scholar, and reformer, published the seminal *Notre Femme dans la charia et la societé* [*Our Women in the Shari'ah and Society*] in 1930, becoming a towering figure of feminism, particularly in Tunisia, Morocco, and France. On the subject of *hijab*, he noted that veiling, as defined by the self-identified guardians of religion, was not rooted in the Qur'an or part of women's traditional dress, be it in Tunisia or Syria. He noted that "there is a strong similarity between veils women place over their faces to prevent immorality, and the muzzle that is placed on the snouts of dogs to prevent them from biting passers-by" (Azmeh). The veil, in his view, was not the product of female immorality. Rather, it was the product of male immorality: fornication, pederasty, polygamy, forced marriage, untrammeled divorce, and poverty (Azmeh). Due to his feminist views, Sunni scholars declared him a heretic and an apostate. His degree was revoked. He was shunned by the legal, theological, clerical, and intellectual establishment, and was even prohibited from getting married. He died in poverty and isolation, remaining loyal and faithful to God and the Qur'an alone.

7.2 King Hassan II

In 1989, the so-called "Islamic veil crisis" erupted in France. As Fatima Houda-Pepin relates,

> A father of Moroccan origin attended a Salafist mosque there. Overnight, he decided to defy the law on secularism and ordered his two young daughters (aged 10 and 13) to go to school wearing headscarves. An unprecedented crisis shook France. Islamists soon went to the front in a monster demonstration. Their banner… said: "The veil is our identity…" The King of Morocco, Hassan II [1929-1999], also the Commander of the Believers, had sent a clear message to the father of the little girls via his embassy in Paris. He said… 1) there is no such thing as an "Islamic" headscarf; 2) Between the veil and education, choose education; 3) the law of the land is the law. Respect French law. (2020)

7.3 Amir Hossein Torkashvand

Although the leading Shiite scholars and their supporters seem incapable of compromise, as they are more ideological than theological, and are primarily concerned with entrenching gender hierarchies, some have re-examined the issue of the veil and have come to conclusions "that are totally different from the mainstream jurisprudence of *hijab* in Shia Islam" (Jalaeipour 2016: 108). As Zahra Jalaeipour, the Iranian researcher, relates:

> According to Torkashvand, there are three different views on the

> meaning of the word *'awrah* in Shia *fiqh*. The first view is the most popular and dominant and is approved by the majority of the *'ulama'*. In this view, *'awrah* in men is the part between their knees and navel, and for women, it refers to all parts of the body except for the face and hands. A number of *marjas* believe the foot can also be shown. The second view, which Torkashvand called the "original view," is in his opinion the correct view about the limits of *'awrah* for both men and women. In this view, *'awrah* for men refers only to the middle part (the genitals), and for women it refers to the part of the body between the shoulders and the knees. According to this view, covering the rest of the body -- the head, neck, arms, and knee to foot -- is not compulsory. The third view that Torkashvand mentioned is that *'awrah* for both men and women is the same and refers only to the genitals. This view is not very well known, and there is very little evidence for it. (2016: 108)

The first view, which Torkashvand (b. 1964) shares, is the predominant view in Shiism as well as Sunnism. It is a view that finds no clear and direct support in the Qur'an. It is an interpretation that relies entirely on a small number of tremendously tardy traditions attributed to the Prophet Muhammad and some of the twelve Imams, predominantly Ja'far al-Sadiq. They date from centuries after their respective demises, were recorded in urban centers, like Baghdad, Kufah, Ray, and Qum, in Iraq and Persia. These accounts are distant in both time and location from the places of residence of the Prophet and the sixth Imam. If anything, they reflect the views of the communities that created them to justify their jurisprudence.

The second view, shared by Torkashvand, is supposedly the original and authentic one. It is more moderate and flexible than the first view. The definition of the *'awrah* for men is the standard Sunni and Shiite one. The claim that women must cover all, minus the head, neck, arms, and knees to feet, does find support from some early scholars of Islam and some *ahadith*; however, it finds no explicit endorsement from the Qur'an itself.

As for the third view, namely, that the *'awrah* of men and women is the same, and consists of their genitals, Torkshvand claims that it is not well known and alleges that there is scant evidence to support it. While it is true that it is not well known to most Muslims -- and even some scholars, for that matter, who show little familiarity with early Islamic sources, particularly those that other sects and schools of thought produced -- the view that the *'awrah* of men and women are one and the same, was mentioned, but not endorsed by Tabari. However, it was upheld by Ibn 'Arabi (d. 1240) and other religious authorities, including Abu 'Ali Muhammad ibn Ahmad ibn al-Junayd al-Iskafi (c. 902/903-991), a pioneering Twelver Shiite jurist who engaged in theoretical analysis and deployed reason in deducing rational laws. He ruled that,

> What is obligatory to cover of the body is the genitals -- the front and

> the back -- for the man and the woman and this proves that both men and women are equal in this regard, that what is obligatory to cover is the genitals -- front and back -- and nothing else. (Kadivar, Hilli).

Hijab enforcers claim that Ibn Junayd was talking about the minimum clothing required for ritual prayer. However, the consensus of jurists from all schools was that the coverage required during *salat* was the same that was mandated in public and in the presence of those who are non-*mahram*.

Imagine how different the Muslim world would be today had this egalitarian ruling become the dominant one regarding the dress of men and women. Ibn Junayd was not the first to hold it. It is not a late view or some sort of minority report. In fact, it is the oldest view on the matter. During the early days of Islam, Muslim women wore skimpy bikinis to go swimming. They were not "bad Muslims." They were not ignorant. They were following the religion as they understood it, as it had been taught to them, and as it had been transmitted up to that point, prior to the development of Islamic jurisprudence and the invention of the *hadith* literature. They followed the living *sunnah*, as opposed to the book-based *sunnah*, that was disconnected from reality and was devoid of cultural, historical, and religious continuity.

As Ahmad Ghabal noted, the expression "nothing else" or "except for these" that appears in 24:31 "is clear about the lack of necessity for covering the rest of the woman's body (except the necessity of covering the two '*awrat*)" (Ridgeon 187). The views of Ibn Junayd have been cited by Twelver Shiite jurists throughout the ages, including Shahid al-'Awwal, Majlisi, Muhaqqiq Tabataba'i, Muhaqqiq Naraqi, and others. It is unrealistic to claim they were falsely attributed to him. What is more, notes Ghabal, anyone who follows the view of Ibn Junayd regarding the issue of covering remains within the bounds of the Muhammadan *shari'ah* (Ridgeon 187). This point cannot be overstated. The view that the '*awrah* of women is limited to their vaginas and anuses is ancient. It was a view that was respected even by scholars who believed that women should cover everything but their faces and hands. They may have believed that the restrictive definition of *hijab* was "the most correct;" however, some of them recognized that the more permissive rulings were also valid. They never accused Ibn Junayd of being an apostate, a heretic, or an infidel for holding such views. They never arrested, charged, defrocked, fined, lashed, imprisoned, or executed him as would be his fate in Islamist Iran.

If we place the Qur'an on a pedestal and treat it as the primary source of Islamic law, the view that the '*awrah* of men and women consists solely of their genitals is the only interpretation that is lucidly, literally, and indisputably supported by the Qur'an. There is no clear, direct command in the Qur'an that says that women must cover their hair, heads, ears, and throats. No where does it command women to cover all their bodies. No such words appear in the '*awrah*, *khimar*, and *jilbab* verses. All it says is that women must cover their two private parts, and they are encouraged to cover their *juyub* or bosoms.

As Amir Torkashvand notes in his study, "all the '*ulama*' and *marjas* think that the *shari'ah* law is based on what Prophet Mohammad did in his time, and that the Islamic laws of our time are the same as those of the Prophet's time" (108). However, his research implies that Islamic law, as we understand it, at least in relation to the rights of women and their code of dress, is not consistent with the historical record. If he did not say so directly, it was out of fear for his safety. As Jalaeipour points out, "publicly taking such a stance in Iran could turn out to be very costly for him, as it did in the case of Eshkevari and Ghabel (who were both sentenced to prison and banned from wearing the official dress of Shia clerics in public)" (2016: 109). In the case of Torkashvand, the Iranian government refused him permission to publish *Hijab-i Shari'i dar Asr-i Payghambar* [*Legal Hijab in the Age of the Prophet*], his thousand-page plus book (Ridgeon 214). The work, however, has circulated online and has drawn considerable attention from clerics and secular academics (Ridgeon 214). It deserves to be translated into Arabic and English and printed in book format by a major publisher.

7.4 Hassan Eshkevari

The first scholar in question, Hassan Yousefi Eshkevari (b. 1950), is a prominent reformist Iranian cleric, intellectual, and *mujtahid.* Jalaeipour summarizes his findings as follows:

> First, … we should determine whether *hijab* is justified on … the Qur'an. After scrutinizing all words in the Qur'an that relate to *hijab* and evaluating their meaning at the time, he found that … *hijab* in Shia *fiqh* was not based on Qur'anic evidence. Eshkevari believes that we cannot attest that covering the head is *vajeb* (compulsory) based on the Qur'an.
>
> Secondly, even if … we were to assume that the common interpretation of *hijab* is based on the Qur'an, it would … not be a fixed and unchangeable law…. Islamic law has two different types of laws… "devotional laws," like daily prayers, fasting and pilgrimage… [and] "social laws," … about inheritance, slavery, marriage, war, [and] *hijab* … Social laws have changed in different times and are not fixed in the … way that devotional laws are…. *Hijab* law is a "social law" and not a "devotional law…" it can change from period to period and place to place, regardless of how it was described in the Qur'an.
>
> Thirdly, even were *hijab* both based on Qur'an and a devotional or unchangeable Islamic law, there is … no Islamic basis to believe that one has the right to compel others to observe the law by force, as the current Iranian government does. Eshkevari … is committed to the principles of Islam, and … believes that many Islamic laws like *hijab*

are changeable. He mentions six reasons in his human rights article (Eshkevari, 2010) to argue that the social laws of Islam can change.

> Eshkevari emphasized that we should justify *hijab* rationally... There are at least two important reasons for *hijab*: … modesty, and … identity…. The issue of identity falls outside the realm of religion, and modesty does not necessarily require covering the head and neck. It can be achieved differently in contemporary societies -- especially in places like Europe, where the headscarf is not common... Unlike many jurists, he believes that a woman can be modest and, at the same time, not cover her hair…. Eshkevari engages with the issue not simply in jurisprudential terms but also in more rational terms. The issue of the veil in and by itself does not seem to signify anything integral to a woman's religious practice or faith here. (2016: 116-117)

As for Eshkevari's first point, it is correct and factual. The rulings regarding *hijab* have no clear Qur'anic foundation. Even if we accepted that the rules had an implicit basis, and God legislates via inference, Eshkevari believes such rules were contextual and, therefore, subject to change as part of cultural and societal evolution. This second point put him in hot water with those jurists who believe that *shar'iah* law is immutable. They seem to forget that jurists like themselves derived those "divine" laws in the first place, as if they sat upon the Throne of the Almighty and were His spokespersons. Like their predecessors, their rulings are merely educated opinions and interpretations. They are not absolute. They are not binding upon others. His third point, namely, that there is absolutely no basis for compelling women to wear *hijab*, and to punish those who fail to wear it, by fines, incarceration, corporal punishment, or execution, is completely Qur'anic: there is no compulsion or coercion in faith and religious practice (2:256). As Abdulwahab Meddeb (1946-2014), the scholar of comparative literature, elaborates, relying on al-Razi:

> God did not construct the question of faith on force … and violence… but based it on the possibility of persuasion… and free choice. God made clear and obvious the path that leads to faith… Recourse to constraint is unacceptable… violence annuls the testing… "May he who wants, believe, and may he who wants, remain unbelieving;" "If your Lord had wanted, all those who people the Earth would believe. It is not up to you to force people to believe…" It is this aspect of the Qur'an … which the fanatics of Islam, sick with their suicidal fever full of hatred, should be reminded. (191-192)

The radicals, who ascribe to an autocratic and totalitarian ideology, may claim they are "promoting good and forbidding evil" (3:104). Did the Prophet Muhammad physically force women to veil themselves? Did he force them to pay fines? Did he punish them physically for failing to cover their hair? Did he accuse those who opposed *hijab* of being apostates? Did he execute them? Did the Imams from the Household of the Prophet ever do such things? Did the caliphs and sultans coerce women to cover? Where is the precedent for compulsory *hijab* and criminalizing its non-adherence? Where is the precedent for forcing non-Muslim women to cover their hair? On the contrary, under some intolerant Islamic dynasties, they were prohibited from doing so. The mandatory *hijab* policies of the "Islamic" Republic of Iran are a negative, detrimental, and damaging innovation in Islamic law.

As Eshkevari and others understand, the *hijab* is not the be-all and end-all of Islam as many have made it out to be. Religion concerns faith, worship, God-consciousness, piety, charity, and righteousness. For some Muslim women, the *hijab* is a proud profession of their faith. If it is a free, conscious, and informed choice, then all the power is to them. It is not proper, however, to dismiss the faith and piety of Muslim women who make a free, conscious, and informed choice not to wear it.

While Eshkevari's arguments are entirely reasonable and appropriate, and any academic should be entitled to express his views without endangering his freedom and safety, he was targeted for expressing them at a conference in Berlin in 2000. Upon return to Iran, he was arrested on August 6, charged with apostasy, and "waging war on God," among other charges that resulted in a death sentence (Ridgeon 23, 144). The authorities claimed he was an apostate due to denying the alleged immutability of Islamic laws and his opposition to obligatory veiling (Ridgeon 144-145). As Ridgeon reports, "his arrest resulted in a number of respected religious authorities rushing to his defense, including Ayatollah ʻAli Akbar Muhtashami, Ayatollah ʻAli Garami, and Mehdi Karubi (the speaker of the parliament)" (145).

ʻAli Akbar Mohtashamipur (1947-2021), like many other Iranian reformists, had a long history as a hardliner. A close associate of Khomeini, he spent time with him in Najaf and accompanied him to France. A radical to the core, he received military training in a Fatah camp in Lebanon, and co-founded an armed group with the son of Hossein ʻAli Montazeri in Lebanon. An active participant in the Iranian Revolution of 1979, he rose to become interior minister, during which time he played a pivotal role in creating the Lebanese Hezbollah. He was reportedly involved in organizing terrorist attacks and suicide bombings, including the downing of Pan Am Flight 103, which resulted in the deaths of two hundred and seventy innocent human beings.

Despite his animosity towards the West and Israel, he became a supporter and advisor to Mohammad Khatami (r. 1997-2005), the reformist Iranian president. This radical-turned-reformist became a strong supporter of freedom of expression. He denounced the indictment of Eshkevari as a "politically motivated act" and warned that "a pious Muslim cannot be easily accused of such crimes" (CNN). Hardliners had gone so far as to compare Eshkevari to Salman Rushdie (b. 1947) (CNN), the novelist condemned to death for blasphemy by Khomeini, who never even read *The Satanic Verses*, not even translated passages.

Besides Mohtashamipur, who had revolutionary credentials, Mohammad Ali Gerami Qomi (b. 1938), a "grand ayatollah," namely, a *marja* or source of emulation, came to his defense, bringing traditional clerical credentials. Eshkevari was also supported by Mehdi Karoubi (b. 1937, a *mujtahid* who had studied under Montazeri (d. 2009) and Khomeini (d. 1989) and who was endorsed by "grand ayatollah" Sane'i (d. 2020). Had he not had powerful friends, he surely would have been executed as others before and after him. Fortunately, after Eshkevari appealed the decision, the court "withheld the death penalty, "disrobed" him, and sentenced him to five years in prison" (Radio Farda). For his own safety, he was forced to seek refuge in Europe (Ridgeon 23).

7.5 Ahmad Ghabal

The second scholar mentioned by Jalaeipour in her study on *hijab* is Ahmad Ghabal (1954-2012), which is also transliterated as Ghabel, Qabel or Qabil. As she notes:

> apart from Ahmad Ghabel, all other *mujtahids* and *marjas* in Shia Islam believe that women should cover all parts of their body except their hands and face. Ghabel, who lived in Qom, was the first contemporary *mujtahid* to announce that covering one's head and neck is only *mustahab* (recommended) and not *vajeb* (compulsory). He supported his view using evidence from within traditional *fiqh* to demonstrate that women are permitted to show their neck and hair but are still obliged to cover the rest of their bodies. (Jalaeipour 2016: 106)

Ghabal's views on the veil are collected in *Ahkam-e Banovan dar Shariat-e Mohammadi (Ordinances Regarding Women in Muhammad's Shari'ah)*, which includes his *fatwa* on "The Desirability of Covering for the Head and the Neck," a twenty-four-page section "On the *Hijab*," and two short sections of answers on the subject. Since the *fatwa* is the distillation of his detailed juristic analysis, it is the sole writing that needs to be reproduced. The edict is as follows:

> 1. The principle of covering the '*awrat* for male and female Muslims is necessary.
>
> 2. Jurists have different opinions about what is included in the '*awrat* (especially in relation to women).
>
> 3. The majority of jurists have considered covering the head necessary for free (non-slave) Muslim women, and they hold the head and neck too among parts included in the '*awrat*.
>
> 4. Ibn Junayd Iskafi, who is one of the famous Shi'i jurists and who lived in the same generation as the masters of Shaykh Mufid,

considered the parts comprising the '*awrat* in men and women as the same and equal.

5. All the Shi'i jurists (indeed, all the Islamic jurists) considered covering the head and the neck unnecessary for Muslim women who were slaves; rather, much like … Saduq and a group of clerics from Qum (in the time of … Saduq), they considered it illegal… for slave women to cover the head; whereas covering the '*awrat* was necessary from them.

6. Sahib-i Javahir considered covering parts of the body (with the exception of the face, hands, and feet as far as the ankle, the neck, and head hair) as consensual (*ijma'i*). In other words, regarding those exceptions, the opinions of the jurists varied, and no agreement existed.

7. He cites the words of … Tabataba'i, the master of Sahib-i Javahir and Sahib-i Madarik [and] says that covering the "head and neck" is unnecessary in their opinion, and he writes, "Judge Ibn Baraj had attributed to some Shi'i clerics [the belief] that covering the head and neck is unnecessary."

8. Sahib-i Javahir has expressed his opinion in this manner: "Covering head hair is based upon [observing] caution." Indeed, [he gave] a stronger… [opinion for caution]; therefore, he has not issued a clear *fatwa* for the need [to cover] it; rather based on caution and probability, firstly he has [expressed] caution and… preferred covering it.

9. From all of these studies it is clear that the issue is controversial, and the consensus of Muslims on this act (covering the head and neck) has not been reached.

10. Some [Qur'anic] verses and reliable narrations appear [to support] its non-compulsory nature (like 33:59…) although there are also some verses and reliable narrations that mention the necessity to cover the head…. The requirement to harmonize (*jam'i 'urfi*) necessary proofs and non-necessary proofs depends on the contexts. If [the harmonization] is practiced according to this rule, the conclusion of the verses and narrations support the non-necessity of covering the head and neck, and only affirm preference (*isthihab*).

Regarding the aforementioned topic, I consider it necessary to cover the body based on scientific proofs, but covering the head and neck is legally desirable (*mustahabb-i shar'i*). (Ridgeon 182-183)

Minoo Mirshahvalad provides the following commentary on Qabil's *fatwa*:

In the Koran there was no… evidence … that women were bound to cover their heads and necks… Covering the '*awrah* … was the obligation of both men and women; however, the sense of '*awrah* was not clear because there was not an *ijma'* … among jurists on whether women were completely '*awrah* and if not which parts of their bodies could be left exposed to non-*mahrams*.

One piece of evidence of this lack of consensus about the limits of covering... was that not all Muslim women were treated equally by Shi'a jurists. Muslim *kanizes* (slave women) were not supposed to wear headcovers since they were not deemed worthy of respect. If concerns of social disorder had stood on the basis of the definition of women's attire and the presence of unveiled women had been considered a cause of sexual disturbance, the *kanizes* would have been bound to wear the veil as they were both Muslim and women. Qabel here made a comparison with Sasanian Iran when restrictive seclusion was performed against noble women to stress the un-Islamic roots of *hijab*.

He reported different *fatwas* of ... Shi'a jurists from the Middle Ages up to ... contemporary time. The Iraqi scholar of the fourth century [*hijri*], Ibn Junayd al-Iskafi, whose field of expertise... included *fiqh*, *kalam*, Arabic literature, and lexicology, was the one who emanated the most controversial *fatwa* in the Shi'a history about attire. The '*awrah*, in Iskafi's view, in both sexes, consisted of the same organs; hence, the only covering demanded, regardless of sex, included genital organs.

Muhammad Muhaqiq Damad (d. 1968) and the Lebanese Muhammad Mehdi Shams al-Din (d. 2001) declared that veiling in the Koran was only recommended, and no necessity could be applied to it. Apart from the Koran... there was no acknowledged *hadith* that entailed the necessity of covering of women's hair and necks.... Even an Akhbari scholar like Muhammad Baqir Majlesi (d. 1699) ... confirmed that among most Shi'a jurists there was no mention of the necessity of head covers for women...

Qabel's concern was to demonstrate that, differently from the usual jurists' claims, there was no consensus about the necessity of the covering of head and neck. If jurists had reached consensus over a certain issue... historical studies on its roots and the motives behind that ordinance would have become impossible. This is why Qabel put great emphasis on the lack of a general consensus on this issue. He ... maintained that even though some kind of *ijma*' had occurred among jurists it was a *madraki ijma*' [a consensus based on uncertain evidence], which is devoid of any value. Two examples of jurists ... who rejected the essentiality of the women's head cover, are Muhaqiq Ardabili (d. 1585) and Aqa Ridha Hamedani Najafi (d. 1904)...

Qabel noticed a controversial issue in the works of some contemporary jurists wherein the women's head cover had been called the "flag of Islam" even though such a sacralized attire could be an extremely tight outfit. It meant... that if a woman wore a skin-tight overall whose texture did not display her skin color but revealed the form of all parts of her body, while she had covered her hair, [she]

> could appear in street and on the Iranian television without any problem! …
>
> Qabel declared that the absence of a scholarly consensus had left the question open… He invited jurists to adopt dynamic *ijtihad* regarding this issue… Qabel as a *mujtahid* emanated his own *fatwa*: covering hair and neck for women was only *mustahab* (recommended) and not *wajib* (necessary). (90-93)\

Unlike other jurists who held that what a woman covers during prayers is the same that she must cover before an onlooker, Ghabel "believed in the desirability and lack of necessity for covering" (Ridgeon 232, note 60).

For Ghabal, the notion that free women were obliged to cover their hair, yet enslaved women were obliged to show it, was illogical:

> What difference exists between slave women and non-slaves in terms of incitement [to corruption]…? At the time of the Imams some of the female slaves were from Iran and Europe, and they were more beautiful and attractive due to the variety in hair color than many of the Arab women in Mecca, Medina, and Yemen; [so] it is necessary to find a suitable response to defend the rationality of the Muhammadan *shari'ah* in today's world, just as in the past. Since the source of beauty in the head and neck lies in the beauty of the "eyes, eyebrow, nose, teeth, chin, and their arrangement," and Islam has considered it unnecessary to cover these, what particular attraction is there in a woman's hair and neck that the necessity of covering them has made this kind of topic so prominent among Muslims? (Ridgeon 200)

Ghabal was also keen to point out the hypocrisy and double standard of the Iranian government, which insists that women cover every strand of hair while allowing them to wear tight leggings and blouses which show their shapes (Ridgeon 181, 199-200). He could not comprehend the obsession about women's hair. As he explained in his last interview,

> The issue of *hijab* is [about] covering the body, not covering the head and neck. I don't understand all this sensitivity about a single strand of hair? Where have they got it from? In fact, these discussions reflect demagoguery more than a scientific discussion. What does it mean when according to a jurist a single strand of hair causes God's throne to tremble, and then the very same jurist says that it is not necessary to cover the shape of a woman's body. (Ridgeon 181)

Since the Qur'an does not command women to cover their hair and heads directly and definitively, it is disingenuous to claim that the headscarf is obligatory, that it can be coerced, and that women who fail to wear it can be subjected to punishment in this life and the hereafter. The competent commentator and the cautious law-abiding jurist can only conclude that it is *mustahab* if he relies on the *hadith* literature. However, as any serious scholar on the subject should realize, the few traditions cited to support the obligatory *hijab* are specious. They are simply not sound. Scholars, however, adopted the adage that even a weak *hadith* is superior to reason and logic. In other words, in the absence of a legislative verse of the Qur'an or a genuine prophetic tradition, a weak one, a *hadith* of questionable authenticity, could be used to establish a ruling and a law. Such an approach is foolish and fraught with peril when it comes to matters as serious as religion, and so far-reaching and consequential issues such as the *hijab* and the seclusion of women.

A follower of Hossein Ali Montazeri (1922-2009), a former close associate of Khomeini and designated successor who became an outspoken critic of the Islamist regime, Ahmad Ghabal was arrested and served various prison sentences between 2001 and 2012. He was transferred to a hospital for a "brain tumor," eventually "fell into a coma," and died while under "hospital arrest." As this is the fate of many of Iran's political prisoners, his death is viewed by many as suspicious.

7.6 Abul-Ghasem Fanaei

As for the third scholar studied by Jalaeipour, Abul-Ghasem Fanaei (b. 1959), he happens to be "a prominent and influential Iranian Muslim intellectual who is both a Qom educated *mujtahid* and a moral philosopher" (2016: 18). Jalaeipour summarizes his views as follows:

> One cannot conclude that *hijab* meant covering the whole body except for the hands and face in all places and times on the basis of two verses in the Qur'an.... The *hijab* verses in the Qur'an have two connotations. Firstly, they ask practicing Muslim believers not to show off (*tabarroj*) to attract the sexual attention of men other than their *mahrams*. Secondly, they articulate that *hijab*'s main function is to protect women from men's harassment and to keep them safe when they go outside. Both connotations lead to the conclusion that *hijab* cannot mean the same thing in different times and places. For example, if you are in Spain, wearing a bikini by the sea might not be seen as showing off or be a danger to women's safety. In other places, not wearing a scarf could make women stand out and also make them unsafe. Therefore, unlike most Shia jurists, ... *hijab* does not have a fixed and inflexible limitation, and that people who live in different parts of the world can have different ways of practicing *hijab*... We cannot label *hijab* as one predefined mode of covering. (2016: 110-111)

Rather than treat the Qur'an as a timeless book of laws, Fanaei focuses on its higher objectives; namely, he asks the question: why? Moreover, he attempts to derive moral principles from its verses. He is an advocate of "jurisprudence within the boundaries of morality" as opposed to "morality within the boundaries of jurisprudence" practiced by the jurists. After all, the Prophet Muhammad said, "I came to perfect morality" and not "I came to perfect jurisprudence." When it comes to *hijab*, Fanaei is at a loss to find Qur'anic evidence to support it. One does not make laws and limit the freedom of women based on two vague verses.

If one thing is clear, the verses in question discourage showing off and deliberately trying to arouse others sexually. That is the principle. As for the purpose, that is equally evident: to prevent women from being sexually harassed and keep them safe. Obviously, there are other ways besides cloaking them in *chadors*, burying them in *burqas*, or keeping them under lock and key like domestic prisoners.

As the Prophet Muhammad said so himself, "By He in whose hands is my soul, verily, God will not bring this matter [Islam] into completion until women travel from Hirah and circumambulate the Ka'bah without being accompanied by anyone" (Ahmad). He also told one of his companions, "If you live a long life, you will surely see women traveling from Hirah until they circumambulate the Ka'bah, fearing no one except God" (Bukhari).

Hirah was an ancient city in Mesopotamia. It is located south of Kufah in modern-day Iraq. The Prophet promised that Islam, if truly applied, would provide women with international safety, namely, they could take journeys over one thousand miles without needing an armed male guardian for personal protection. Unfortunately, Muslims never delivered on the promise of the Prophet. Moreover, even when social safety was provided, they refused to grant women freedom of movement.

Considering that *hijab*-wearing women are routinely sexually harassed throughout the Arab world and much of the Muslim world; considering that Islamists have sexually assaulted *hijab*-wearing women around the planet, and that *burqa*-wearing women have been gang-raped in places like Syria, Iraq, and Afghanistan, it is evident that "Islamic" modest dress means nothing to such sub-human men and that it fails to protect women. In fact, bikini-clad women are much safer in the non-Muslim world than *hijab*-wearing women are in most of the Muslim world. Go figure. It is not girls and women who should be covered and confined for their safety. The men who harass them are the ones who need to be shunned and shamed, policed, and punished.

7.7 Mohsen Kadivar

As for Mohsen Kadivar (b. 1959), the fourth scholar studied by Jalaeipour, he is a slightly more conservative reformist jurist. Like many jurists, he once held the old ideas regarding the *hijab*. However, with further study and consideration, his views evolved gradually, culminating in his current ones. As Jalaeipour explains:

> Kadivar believes that the minimum boundaries of *hijab* remain the

> same. Women must cover from the neck to the knees. Depending on context, the rest of the body should also be covered to the degree necessary to remain protected and modest. It is not always necessary to cover one's head… He mentioned that it might not be necessary for Muslim women who live in Western countries to cover their heads, because wearing a scarf is not common. The argument revolved around the point of making women stand out in a society whose norms are different. (2016: 115)

Rather than requiring women to cover their entire bodies, Kadivar limited the '*awrah* to everything between the neck and the knees. Hence, calves need not be covered. While he believed in the headscarf, he also felt that it could be cast aside depending on if the circumstances warrant it.

In *Ta'moli Dar Massa'leye Hijab* [*Reflections on the Question of Hijab*,' Mohsen Kadivar makes some critical observations. As Minoo Mirshahvalad summarizes:

> Regarding Shi'a narratives, Kadivar has noticed that there is a quantitative difference in the accounts of central Imams (Muhammad al-Baqir, Ja'far al-Sadiq, Musa al-Kazim and 'Ali ibn Musa al-Rida) on this issue compared to those of the Prophet and 'Ali… Most reports that have come down to us from the Shi'a Imams on this topic can be traced back to the period that goes from 94 to 203 of the Islamic calendar. Even though the quantity of the *hadiths* of these central Imams derives from the fact that they enjoyed more freedom… the quality of their narratives with regard to the veil testifies to a change in the women's social status. Kadivar presupposes that women's clothing only in the second Islamic century gained its current restrictive form and in the first century followed the Koranic guidelines. In the Koran … there is not any hint to the necessity of covering face, neck, forearms, and legs. In addition, if we take into consideration the type of questions that the followers of the four aforementioned Imams asked them regarding gender relations, it becomes clear that in the second Islamic century the norms of covering were not yet established, however, subsequently we have restrictive *hadiths*. (98-99)

After studying the views of fifty-four Shiite jurists from the fourth century until the present, Kadivar showed how the limits of covering continued to expand over the centuries (Mirshahvalad 99). He also revealed a revolutionary *fatwa* by Muhaqqiq Ardabili (d. 1585) regarding the verse "except what [ordinarily] appears thereof" (24:31). As Ardabili explains in *Zubdat al-bayan fi ayat al-ahkam*, the interpretation of this verse depends on habits and customs (Mirshahvalad 100). In other words, it is not set in stone and varies depending on the time period and the culture.

Fortunately, for those who do not speak Persian, Kadivar's *Reflections on the Question of Hijab* has been translated into English by Lloyd Ridgeon in *Hijab: Three Modern Iranian Seminarian Perspectives*. The full study is required reading for anyone who wishes to understand the history and evolution of the *hijab* (236-263). As it is far too lengthy to reproduce here, all that can be offered is an overview.

In "Understanding the Revelation of the Verses on the *Hijab*," Kadivar provides much needed historical context: 1) The Arabs of the *Hijaz* were poor and uncivilized; 2) They wore a single long piece of cloth with an opening for the head and neck or merely a loin cloth. The head, neck, and parts of the chest, arms, and legs were exposed. Since the cloth was not sown, and the sides moved, other parts of the bodies of men and women were also customarily exposed; 3) The Arabs of the time did not view nudity negatively. Men and women circumambulated the Ka'bah completely in the nude. What is more, "they did not make a great effort to conceal their gaze at other people's sexual organs;" 4) The elite may have lived in stone or mud homes; however, most people lived in habitations made of date-straw or in tents. They did not have many rooms, or any rooms at all, and lacked doors and curtains. It was normal for people to peer into the living places of other people; 5) They had no private toilets. People used to respond to the call of nature in public and used to talk and tease each other. Both men and women socialized in such settings; 6) Bathing was limited due to water scarcity and would take place in public, in rivers, ponds, and pools. There was no such thing as sexually segregated bathing. It was normal for men and women to bathe in public while completely naked; 7) Sexual relations were unfettered, including promiscuity, prostitution, spouse-swapping, and other practices (Ridgeon 237).

In "Fundamental Qur'anic Questions about the *Hijab*," Kadivar notes that the Qur'an was concerned with women covering their private parts and their bodies except for the arms below the elbows and the legs below the knees. The parts that remained uncovered were 1) the chest; 2) the head and the neck; and 3) the forearms, shins, and calves to the feet (Ridgeon 238-239). Kadivar then proceeds to examine the Qur'anic verses related to covering. He finds two points of importance in 33:59: firstly, that women should draw their cloaks around themselves; and secondly, the reason for this command, namely, their being pestered (Ridgeon 239). He notes that the term *jilbab* is ambiguous as it has three meanings: 1) a sheet that covers the body; 2) a wimple and scarf, and 3), a shirt and baggy clothes (Ridgeon 239-240). The verse does not describe or explain the *jilbab*; it emphasizes how it is used, namely, drawing it around, which in turn has two meanings, to bring close or to lower (Ridgeon 240). Considering the type of clothing worn at the time, which had slits along the sides, it is clear to Kadivar that the verse was not introducing a new form of clothing but encouraging women to cover the exposed parts of their attire (Ridgeon 240). "The new message of the verse," he notes, "is this: cover the body properly with clothes" (Ridgeon 240). "Whether prohibiting or permitting," he stresses, "the verse has nothing to do with covering the head and hair" (Ridgeon 240).

In "The Reason for Covering," Kadivar provides two possible reasons: 1) to be recognized as pure, chaste, and noble; and 2) to be recognized as free women as opposed to slaves since, supposedly, immoral men would not harass free women who wore this distinct attire (Ridgeon 240). This second interpretation, which is very prevalent, poses problems. As Kadivar observes, "the result of [this] corruption is that innocent slaves remain defenseless before immoral people" (Ridgeon 240). Such a possibility "opposes Qur'anic righteousness and Islamic standards" (Ridgeon 240). The verse, notes Kadivar, does not explicitly address the covering of the hair. As such, to fulfil the explicit reason, "it is sufficient for a believing woman to guard her body" (Ridgeon 241).

For Kadivar, 24:31 is the most important Qur'anic verse dealing with covering. It requires believers to lower their gaze and to cover their private parts (Ridgeon 241). Women, in particular, have the added responsibility to avoid displaying their finery and to cover their chests, breasts, and necks with the *khimar* (Ridgeon 241). As Kadivar notes, the Qur'an distinguishes between two types of finery, their hidden beauty, namely, their private parts, and their outer beauty (Ridgeon 242). It is only the hidden beauty that must be concealed in the public sphere. The parts of a woman's body that were visible at the time of revelation, including the forearms, lower legs, face, neck, and hair, fall into the category of "that which is visible" (Ridgeon 242). "The principal message of the verse," concludes Kadivar, "is the prohibition of nakedness. Taking off clothes in front of those who are not *mahram* is not allowed" (Ridgeon 242).

In "Covering the *Juyub* with the *Khimar*," Kadivar notes that the term *khimar* has three meanings: 1) a head covering, 2) a cloak, and 3) a shawl (Ridgeon 242). Whatever it is, the article of clothing was intended to cover the *juyub*, which can refer to 1) the parting in two sides of a garment; 2) the cleavage of a woman's chest; and 3) a woman's private parts (Ridgeon 242). When the Qur'an asks women to "draw their *khumur* over their *juyub*," it refers to covering the cleavage of the breasts, the private parts, and even any other opening or closing that causes arousal (Ridgeon 243). For Kadivar, the verse requires women to cover from the neck to the knees and upper arms (Ridgeon 243). It does not, however, "indicate the necessity of covering the hair and head" (Ridgeon 243). As for the verse "except that which is visible," Kadivar notes that there is no Qur'anic basis for the *fatwas* that limit this to the face, hands, and feet (Ridgeon 244).

In "The *Hijab* in Shi'i Narrations," Kadivar examines premises, covers discussions, and makes many findings, namely: 1) not one command about *hijab* is attributed to the Prophet; 2) not one command on the principle questions of the *hijab* is attributed to 'Ali; 3) there is not a single *hadith* about *hijab* on the authority of Fatimah; 4) nearly all the commands related to *hijab* appear two centuries after the Prophet and are attributed to Muhammad al-Baqir, Ja'far al-Sadiq, Musa al-Kazim, and 'Ali al-Rida; 5) there is not a single narration by multiple reporters about the commands of *hijab*; 6) most commands on *hijab* lack corroboration and few feature sound chains of transmission; 7) there are contradictory traditions regarding the requirement to cover the hair during ritual prayers; 8) the extent of covering in front of relatives is less than the usual limit; 9) the claim that the outer beauty is limited to the face and hands is based on a single tradition from Imam Sadiq; however, in other traditions it includes what is under the *khimar*, and above the wrists, and includes the forearms; 10) the meaning and extent of *jilbab* and *khimar* are inconsistent in the traditions; 11) some men living at the end of the second century of the *hijra*, during the time of 'Ali al-Rida, had never heard that it was prohibited to see the hair of women and they were required to cover it; 12) traditions attributed to Ja'far al-Sadiq state that a man can look at a woman's hair at the time of a marriage proposal; 13) it is permissible to look at the hair of non-Muslim women and any other part they normally uncover; 14) it is permissible to look at the hair of women who refuse to cover it; 15) it is related that Musa al-Kazim and 'Ali al-Rida required pubescent girls to cover their hair in front of non-*mahrams*; 16) Imam Rida is reported to have distinguished between looking at women in a manner that was chaste and looking at them lewdly and with lust; 17) a tradition claims that Fatima stated that men should not see women while another unreliable one claims they even had to cover in front of blind men; and, finally, 18) a tradition on the authority of Ja'far al-Sadiq claims that the Prophet stated that "Women are '*awrat*. Cover '*awrat* in the house" (Ridgeon 261-263). Kadivar concludes that the principal commands regarding *hijab* appeared nearly two and a half centuries after the Prophet, based on traditions attributed to Ja'far al-Sadiq (Ridgeon 263). The *fatwas* mandating *hijab* are all based on these traditions (Ridgeon 263). The conclusion is so self-evident that Kadivar sees no need to mention it.

For Kadivar, it is not only the rulings regarding the *hijab* and women that need to be revised, but all rulings. In his view, all rulings should be tested against four criteria: reasonability, justice, ethics, and effectiveness (2023a). Although Muslims should preserve principles and standards, any rulings must address today's needs, contexts, and standards (2023a). He also believes that human dignity must be considered when deriving rulings (2023b). Finally, he stresses that for anything to be Islamic, it must first be reasonable, just, moral, and functional (2023c). For Kadivar, these principles must inform any reform of women's attire.

Like many like-minded scholar, he was persecuted by the Iranian regime. Kadivar "was arrested in 1999 and spent 18 months in prison before he was able to leave Iran" where he found work as a university professor (Ridgeon 23). Unlike Iran, and much of the Muslim world, where academic freedom is limited or non-existent, the liberty that is fostered in the United States has allowed him to express his thoughts without fear and to derive jurisprudential rulings in a conducive environment.

7.8 Moslem Khalafi

Other scholars overlooked by Jalaeipour include Moslem Khalafi (b. 1969), an Iranian researcher who published an article titled "Baz Negareshi Daroon Dini Be Hijab" or "A Religious Revision of *Hijab*" in 2007. As Minoo Mirshahvalad summarizes, Khalafi:

> provides a list of extremely permissive and extremely restrictive narratives about *hijab*. Khalafi observes that some Shi'a accounts are so limitative that they clearly legitimize the imprisonment of women... Some reports, with authentic origins, are so permissive that they allow women to pray without any headcover and men to look at their beautiful faces even with sexual intention.... He asks a very important question... Considering the existing contradictions in the Shi'a reports on modesty and women's attire, he asked, "Why have only those narratives that necessitate the veil gained visibility in Iran?" (92-93)

These moderate positions on women's dress in Islam might seem more palatable to many Muslims; however, the conservatives in places like Iran refuse to consider them. In fact, opposing Iran's *hijab* policy can land one in jail; however, questioning the Islamic and Qur'anic legitimacy of *hijab* itself can result in execution on the grounds of alleged apostasy. The Islamists have turned an article of clothing into an article of faith. That would lead some to ask: who are the real heretics and apostates?

7.9 Mohammad Hashim Kamali

In 2011, Mohammad Hashim Kamali, an Islamic scholar of Afghan origin and law professor at the International Islamic University of Malaysia, who was described by one writer as "the most widely read living author on Islamic law in the English language," published an article titled "Islamic Family Law Reform: Problems and Perspectives." The most remarkable segment of the study revolves around the veil. In his words,

> There is no mandate on veiling (*hijab*) and face cover (*niqab*) in the Qur'an and *Sunnah*. The ... evidence in these sources shows that during the Prophet's time women participated in public life and most of the women companions did not practice the *hijab*, except for the wives of the Prophet, who began to practice it after the revelation of the Qur'anic verse (33:59) concerning them. Even after this event, other female companions did not practice the *hijab*, as they knew that the Qur'anic directive was addressed to the Prophet's wives only. Women's participation in the life of the community during this time

> was dignified and social encounters took place at the initiative of men and women as and when the occasion arose. Women were also allowed to take part in congregational prayers and attend the mosques without restrictions. (49)

It is true that the Qur'an does not mandate veiling in any form or fashion. It is correct that there is no *bona fide* basis for this practice in any genuine prophetic traditions. The claim that the *hijab* only applied to the wives of the Prophet is not accurate. Some of his wives did not cover their hair even after the revelation of the verses in question. The claim that many female companions of the Prophet did not wear *hijab* is veracious.

> The Qur'an advocates modesty and decorum and cautions against provocative behavior ... (cf., 7:26, 7:31, 24:30, 24:60, and 33:53). This is the basic message but the text does not specify exactly how modesty is achieved. Modesty is important for the upkeep of moral standards in society, and the Qur'an has addressed it without any quantitative specifications of the kind that subsequently preoccupied the jurists and cultural trend setters in different times and places. The Qur'an reminds the believers, men and women alike, to lower their gaze and avoid "temptatious" behavior. Covering the body parts during worship and social encounters is treated in the *fiqh* writings on *'awrah*, on which the leading schools have also recorded differential rulings and interpretations over details. Yet suitable coverage of body parts for purposes of worship and mosque attendance is generally accepted by all the *fiqh* schools. (49)

These arguments are correct and coherent. The jurists from the various school of law differed on the definition of *'awrah* and the extent of its coverage; however, they all agreed that it should be suitably covered in prayer and in public. Readjusting the extent of the *'awrah* is not a rejection of *hijab*. The difference is in the definition and the degree. As many scholars before him have done, Kamil notes that,

> Notwithstanding variable customary practices on the uses of *hijab* and *niqab*, these were apparently in use in Iran's Sassanid society prior to the advent of Islam, and segregation of the sexes was in evidence in the Christian Middle East and Mediterranean regions at the time of the rise of Islam. During the Prophet's lifetime... his wives were the only Muslim women required to veil. After his demise and following the Muslim conquests of the adjoining territories, where upper-class women veiled, the veil became a commonplace item of clothing among upper-class Muslim women "by a process of assimilation that no one has yet ascertained in much detail." 'Abd al-Halim Abu Shaqqah's encyclopedic six-volume work remains the most exhaustive and acclaimed work on this subject to date. The author entitles his

> monumental work by the self-explanatory title, *Tahrir al-mar'ah fi 'asr al-risalah* (*Liberation of Women during the Prophet's Era*). He has noted that women's participation in public life is established by no less than 300 *hadiths*, and it becomes, as such, an approved *sunnah* of the Prophet. (49-50)

The veil, in any of its forms, as well as the sexual segregation that it symbolizes, are products of a process of cultural assimilation. They are not the *sunnah* of God and the Prophet Muhammad. God, the Prophet, the Qur'an, and Islam-Original liberated and emancipated women. To reject the veil is not to reject Islam, but to revindicate and reclaim it. In contrast, to impose the veil is to subvert the Qur'an.

7.10 Mohamed al-Talbi

Mohamed al-Talbi (1921-2017), the Tunisian historian and Islamologist, published a work titled *L'islam n'est pas voile, il est culture: rénovation de la pensée musulmane [Islam is not the Veil, it is a Religion: Renovation of Muslim Thought]*. As a testimony to its influence and impact, both of its printings have sold out. "What does the Qur'an say about the veil?" asks Talbi. "Nothing. Absolutely nothing," he responds. "Nowhere does it address a woman's head" (Talbi 2008, Bestandji 2021: 112). As he states, "God did not reveal the Qur'an to teach women how to fix their hair" (Bestandji 2021: 112). Commenting on 24:31, the *khimar* verse, Talbi pointed out that:

> Anything that hides something, including a crowd, a grove, or the secrets of human hearts, is a *khimar*. The question that arises is the following: in common everyday usage, did the *khimar* designate a "headscarf" that women wore obligatorily, and always on their heads? As a historian, I say no. (Bestandji 2021: 91-92)

As for the *jayb* that this *khimar* was supposed to cover, Talbi provides some linguistic, cultural, and historical context:

> In the generic sense, the term designates, in a garment, a more or less wide cutout, at the level of the collar, to let the head pass, and more or less, uncovers the chest.... Naturally, the cutout at the level of the collar can vary *ad infinitum*, let us say, or almost, down to the navel in any case, and then allows the gaze to plunge into the infernal abyss of perdition, as the prostitutes did, and what the Qur'an reproaches, if only to avoid misunderstandings, which were surely frequent in countries where prostitution was the most lucrative job. (Bestandji 2021: 92)

For Talbi, the *hijab* is a fraud that was perpetrated by the *shari'ah*, which was created by conservative men who inherited the pre-Islamic hostility toward women (Bestandji 2021: 86). For them, women were good for one thing only, pleasuring them behind tightly closed doors, or as a source of profit through prostitution (2021: 86). Commenting upon 33:59, the so-called *jilbab* verse, Talbi makes the following pertinent points:

> Allah does not use the term "cover," which in Arabic is *satara*, *akhfa*, or *ghatta*. He uses the verda *adna,* which means "to bring closer." And this verb is used with the particle *min*, which means "a part of." Allah does not require Muslim women to cover themselves from head to toe. They are only asked to bring their *jalabib* (cloaks) closer, not entirely, but only a part, without indicating in what proportion -- the choice is left to them -- on themselves, without indication on which part of the body. The choice is also left to them. To turn *jalabib* -- outer garments that one throws over the shoulders, and which it is recommended to tighten the slits when going out -- into a veil that transforms women into crows, is frankly to falsify the meaning of the Qur'an. (Bestandji 2021: 85)

Due to his strict adherence to the Qur'an and reason, his defense of women's rights, his devastating critiques of the *hadith* literature, and his fierce opposition to Islamists and fundamentalists, he was condemned to death by three Islamist movements.

7.11 Joseph A. Islam

Joseph A. Islam argues that, based on a close linguistic analysis of the relevant verses, "there is no specific reference to covering of the hair." What is more, "the Arabic word *hijab* has never been used to signify or insinuate this" (Hijaab). Although the verse, in his view, should be rendered as "draw their coverings over their chests" (24:31), he cautions that the hair could, in some cases, fall into the category of the broad term *zinah*, which should also be covered in the presence of the people not listed in the verse (Khimar). Based on 24:58, which mentions that elderly women may "lay aside their [outer] garments [*thiyab*]," Joseph A. Islam feels that "there is a clear expectation from the Qur'an that women will have their arms and legs covered by wearing a suitable garment" since the thobe provided such coverage (Hijaab). So, for him, it would seem, a woman must cover everything but her hair, hands, and feet. However, in some cases, women might be required to cover their hair (Khimaar). These views are incorrect. *Zinah* is a metaphor for private parts: not hair. It is in keeping with politeness. If anything is clear, it is that there is no clear expectation that women cover their limbs.

For another Qur'anist, who operates the True Islam website, Muslim women are required to abide by four rules: 1) wear the best garments (Qur'an 7:26), 2) cover their cleavage (Qur'an 24:31), and 3) not reveal their beauty spots, except their head (face and hair), arms, and lower legs; 4) and lengthen their garments (Qur'an 33:59). According to this writer, the beauty spots of women include their thighs, breasts, and backsides. As the author explains, the '*awrah* of women consists of their "nakedness." It cannot possibly refer to their hair as verse 24:31 says that women shall not show their beauty to "children who are yet to attain awareness of women's '*awrah*." As the writer notes, "the words in 24:31 do not speak of children who are not used to seeing women's hair!"

7.12 Lafif Lakhdar

Lafif Lakhdar (1934-2013), the French-Tunisian writer and journalist, who was a close friend and colleague of Ahmed Ben Bella (1916-2012), the first president of Algeria, viewed the *hijab* with derision:

> [Forbidding the *hijab*] restores esteem to a woman's body. How so? A man's body is partly shameful -- from the navel to the knee. A woman's body is shameful in its entirety, apart from the face and the hands. Muslim women aren't equal to Muslim men even in the value of their bodies! One French psychoanalyst thinks that French Islamists demand [that women] wear the *hijab* because a woman's hair makes them think of hair she has elsewhere, and this inflates their passions. This reduces women to sex. The subconscious meaning of this is that every woman with her hair uncovered is a whore whom any Muslim is entitled to violate. This is why the Islamic jurisprudents forbade Muslim slave girls to wear the *hijab*, and likewise non-Muslim women -- i.e., Muslims have the right to violate them whenever they want. (382)

For many Muslim women, questioning *hijab* is like questioning their faith in God, the Qur'an, and the Prophet. This is because this idea has been inculcated in them. Even when they cast off the veil, after seriously studying the various opinions on the subject, many remain tormented with guilt, fear of judgment, and terror of eternal damnation. This is the natural result of spiritual and psychological abuse. As Lakhdar notes, "A great number of Muslim women have internalized the Islamic jurisprudence, which was written by men and for men. This is what one French sociologist called "symbolic violence," meaning that the victim -- in this case the Muslim woman -- accepts the view of her executioner" (Lichter 382).

7.13 Kassim Ahmad

Kassim Ahmad (1933-2017), a prominent Malaysian thinker and philosopher, also opposed the obligation of the *hijab* at considerable cost. In his words,

> The *tudung* or full-fledged headscarf is not ordained by God. The corrupt religious scholars insists on Muslim women to cover their '*aurat*. '*Aurat* is an Arabic word meaning nakedness. Thus a woman's hair is not her '*aurat* or nakedness. I would put to men's chauvinism to

> conceal the beauty of their women. God knows better and ordains appropriately to conceal their beauty. Seventy years ago women did not wear the *tudung*. My mother never did. Her contemporaries never did. They wore *selendang*, a partial headcover... the complete headcover is a new teaching after the theocratic revolution in Iran in 1979. I am sure the Iranian women themselves will revolt against this unhealthy attire that allows no air to run over her hair… Some people regard this as fashion. However, not all Muslim women agree with this. A fashion that has negative results … is not to be tolerated.

He was detained from 1976 to 1981 on grounds of being a subversive. His work, *Hadith: A Re-Evaluation*, was banned by the Home Ministry in 1986. The "Islamic Inquisition" accused him of being an apostate and a heretic for calling into question the so-called obligatory *hijab*. He knew very well that Malaysian and Indonesian women only started to adopt the *hijab* and *jilbab* in the 1980s. It was an imported and imposed Islamist uniform that was presented as a pillar of faith. For decades now, Indonesian girls have been bullied and traumatized into wearing *hijab* (Lamb). "Every strand of hair you show," they are threatened, "is a step in hellfire."

7.14 Khaled Abou El Fadl

In 2016, Khaled Abou El Fadl (b. 1963), a jurist, and a world authority on Islamic law, published a "Fatwa on Permissibility of Not Wearing *Hijab*." Some of its most salient points are as follows:

> It is an error for a Muslim woman to continue wearing the headscarf, or the *hijab* if doing so brings such a person undue attention or puts her at risk of harm of any sort, or even stands as an obstacle to her ability to testify on behalf of God and to educate non-Muslims as to the truth of the Islamic message… Many scholars have argued that *khimar* by definition is a piece of cloth that covers a woman's entire body and is drawn upon the face, so in effect, enclosing a woman's entire body in a veil. Many others have argued that a *khimar* is a piece of cloth that covers the hair and the entire body except for the face… Both schools of thought -- that which contends that the *khimar* covers the face, and that which contends that the *khimar* covers the hair but not the face -- are ahistorical in presuming the existence of an historical practice that has not been proven.
>
> The evidence that the *khimar* in pre-Islamic *Hijaz* covered the face or covered the hair is simply not there. The only thing that the verse allows us to say conclusively is that Muslim women were called upon to draw a piece of cloth (*khimar*) over the *juyub* (bosoms) -- whether it covered the hair or the face, we don't know. In other words, the Qur'an in this verse calls upon women to cover their bosoms. Anything beyond that would require extensive research into the social practices of *khimar*

dressing at the time of revelation, and the historical evidence is far more diverse and complex than many contemporary scholars assume it to be…

What is considered to be *zinah*, or the ornaments, is a question of applied ethics -- i.e. it differs from one place to another and from one time to another. What is considered to be immodest ornamental displays of beautification in a part of Africa could be entirely different than the same in Mongolia. In essence, the Qur'an is counseling against the immodest flouting of physical appearance. There is no evidence that displaying of the hair is by definition a part of a woman's *zinah*. Depending on the place and context, a woman could be modest while not covering her hair, and the opposite is also true. A woman can cover her hair but still be immodest by displaying her *zinah*. In many ways … it is clear that the Qur'an is repeating and reaffirming a long-established biblical command to lower the gaze, be modest, and avoid displays of flashiness and vain conceit…

It bears emphasis that if one takes both Qur'anic revelations, what seems clear to me is that the Qur'an is placing great emphasis on modesty and humility. The narratives on *khimar* and *jilbab* do not necessarily generate the kind of uniform and determinative headgear and attire known as the *hijab* in our contemporary age…

If the *hijab* causes women to stand out, and brings unwanted attention to them, and poses the risk of bringing harm to women -- and considering that per the social habits and customs of the United States, a woman exposing her hair would not be considered immodest or licentious to any extent -- it is permissible for a woman NOT to wear a head-covering in the United States… It is contrary to the purposes of *shari'ah* for a woman to expose herself to harm of any kind simply for the purposes of covering her hair. Indeed, it is far more consistent with the purposes of *shari'ah* for a woman to place more emphasis on educating her fellow citizens about Islam and Muslims instead of focusing on her physical appearance…

It is … ironic that in the modern age the *hijab* has become symbolic of Islamic identity. Historically and theologically, head-covering is found among certain Christian and Jewish sects and is supported in these traditions with textual injunctions which are far more clear and determinative than in their Islamic counterpart. It is … ironic that modern Muslims, at least since the late 1970s, have chosen to make the head-covering an integral component of identity politics when their own scriptural injunctions are far less dispositive than their Jewish and Christian counterparts. There is nothing uniquely Islamic about the *hijab* except for the fact that Muslim social movements, at least since the late 1970s, have chosen to make it a part of Islamic catechism… Humility, modesty, and personal piety are far more worthy in Allah's eyes than any formal physical attire regardless of its sanctified appearance.

7.15 Ahmed Subhy Mansour

Ahmed Subhy Mansour (b. 1949) and his Qur'anist colleagues from Egypt believe that the *hijab* is an un-Islamic and anti-Islamic innovation. He views the *hijab* and the *niqab* as "invented myths… that have nothing to do at all with the Qur'an" (Awra). He believes that women can show their hair, necks, arms to the elbows, and feet to the ankles, and they are also advised to cover their legs (Women' Clothes). He views the wearing of excessive makeup, miniskirts, monokinis, bikinis, and clothes that reveal the thighs and the cleavage of the breasts, to be minor sins or mishaps (Women's Clothes). Even if she shows her cleavage and bare legs, argues Mansour, "this is not a grave sin" (Fatwas Part Seventy-Three). Even if women wear revealing clothing that exposes their breasts, legs, and thighs, he insists they are not fornicators or adulteresses. They may have committed a minor sin or mistake that God is completely capable of forgiving (4:31) (Women's Clothes). The major sin, in his mind, is attributing false doctrines, practices, and laws to God. As he explains:

> When we compare a woman in *niqab* and another woman in a bikini, the latter is making a small mistake or small sin (i.e., showing her cleavage and upper legs, thus disobeying Qur'anic advice in this respect) that may be forgiven by atoning for it by good deeds and imploring God's pardon, as long as she does not commit the grave sin of fornication, whereas the former is falling into the trap of polytheism, a major sin that makes her deserve Hell if she dies without repenting the sin of ascribing such falsehood (i.e., *niqab*) to Islam. (Women's Clothes n page)

Unlike many Shiite and Sunni scholars, who claim that not abiding by *hijab* is a major sin that merits hell, and that women who fail to cover themselves are whores, downgrading the wearing of the bikini to a minor sin, or no sin at all, is a major development in Islamic legal, moral, and ethical discourse. After all, women who show their hair are blamed for every calamity imaginable, including earthquakes and losing wars. Many Muslims believed that the Arabs lost the 1967 war against Israel due to the bad conduct of their women. "It is women," people asserted, "God is punishing us because women are not wearing headscarves" (Shahrur 511). "How could that be?" thought Muhammad Shahrur, "Israeli women are in bikinis, and they defeated us" (511).

7.16 Tareq Oubrou

Tareq Oubrou (b. 1959), an Imam from Bordeaux, France, was the product of an Islamist upbringing. However, he has also evolved like other Muslim scholars.

As he declared in 2013, "the veil is not a religious obligation… It is false to affirm that there is a verse in the Qur'an that obliges a Muslim woman, regardless of her culture of origin, to cover her head" (Bestandji 2021: 114-115, 2018: part four). As he notes, the *hijab* and *jilbab* of today are not those from the time of the Prophet (Bestandji 2021: 115). "Islam," he explains, "never created a dress code: it simply responded to existing cultures" (Bestandji 2021: 115). For him, women who wear the *hijab* and the *jilbab* today live in a complete fantasy (Bestandji 2018: part four). This former radical now believes that the veil has become an obsession for Muslims that reduces women to a headscarf (Zaman)

7.17 Hannibal Genseric

In an article titled "The Veil is neither Arabic nor Islamic," which was published in 2014, Hannibal Genseric, an Amazigh engineer, journalist, and activist, provided a superb synthesis of the veil's history. He found that:

> When the veil first made its appearance, its purpose was to hide prostitutes from the eyes of the population in order to distinguish them from other women. "Respectable" women were those who were not veiled. In archaic Semitic and Middle Eastern traditions, long before the appearance of Islam, the veil was a symbol of submission of a woman to a man, indicating that she belonged to him, be it, her husband and, if she was not married, her father, his brother, or even his uncle (if the others were deceased). At all times and in all places, fundamentalist sects of all religions have perpetuated this archaic tradition. Today, the veil has a political and sectarian meaning, it has nothing to do with the Muslim religion.

Since he views the *hijab* as the symbol of political Islam, Genseric finds it incredible that "reputedly democratic countries, such as France, authorize the veil (*burqa*, *hijab*, etc.) and prohibit the wearing of the swastika." When it comes to tackling the problem posed by the *hijab*, Genseric invokes the astute approach of Mustapha Kemal Atatürk (c. 1881-1938), the President of Turkey from 1923 to 1938, in which he inverted the decrees of people like Mullah Omar, caliph 'Umar, and the ancient Assyrians. He decreed that, "With immediate effect, all Turkish women have the right to dress as they wish. However, all prostitutes must wear the *burqa*." "The next day," notes Genseric, "there were no longer any *burqas* to be seen in Turkey."

Unfortunately, asserts Genseric, "it is not every day that the Muslim world has a Kemal Atatürk or a Habib Bourguiba." He laments the fact that two of the most socially modern nations in the Muslim world, Turkey, and Tunisia, were now living under Islamist dictatorships. He decries the support that these regimes receive from the West. He finds it despicable to see American and French presidents bow down before Arab kings, who are the worst despots of modern times.

7.18 Salah Horchani

Salah Horchani, the Tunisian academic and university professor, made contributions to the *hijab* debate in a 2016 article. He noted that Islamists like to play the victim card while co-opting human rights to advance their hidden project. They defend the right to wear the *hijab*, the *burkini*, and the *niqab* based on the principles of freedom and tolerance. Not only are these principles in which radical Muslims do not believe but they are principles they actively combat by trying to prevent others from exercising them: notably, by their campaigns to prevent women from wearing bikinis along the beach in places like Morocco, Algeria, and Tunisia. He reminded readers of the statement of John Stuart Mill (1806–1873), the British philosopher, who noted, "The principle of freedom cannot require that he should be free not to be free. It is not freedom to be allowed to alienate his freedom." Horchani pointed out that:

> the wearing of the veil, a custom, initially, urban and pagan, is culturally of non-evangelical Christian origin, and that nowhere in the Qur'an is it mentioned that the wearing of the headscarf (neither the veil nor, *a fortiori*, the *burkini* and the *niqab*) is a prescription for believers any much more than the wearing of beards, skull caps, *qamis* and mustaches is a prescription for believers. (Horchani, Samint)

He also makes an important point that not all women who wear *hijabs* and *burkinis* are Islamists. Their motivations are multiple. As he explains:

> for a Muslim, wearing the headscarf, the veil, the *burkini*, the *niqab*, the beard, the skullcap, the *qamis* and the mustache is, in reality, an individual, partisan, social, cultural choice, …, or an aesthetic one, free or made out of fear, under pressure, constraint, threat, blackmail,… or the sheep effect of Panurge, when individuals follow others without even thinking, or simply to live in peace in a neighborhood, for example, not tolerating being looked down upon by others, but in no case is it a choice motivated by any real religious obligation. (Horchani)

7.19 Edip Yüksel

Edip Yüksel, the Turkish American jurist, scholar, author, activist, philosophy professor, translator, and exegete, addresses the issue of women's dress from a strictly and rigorously Qur'anic perspective, namely, from the point of view of uncorrupted and unadulterated Islam that is not tainted by spurious and scurrilous secondary sources, namely, the toxic trio that consists of fabricated *hadith,* fallacious fatwas, and sexist *shari'ah* laws. As he explains in his commentary of 24: 30-31,

> Righteous men and women should not dress provocatively. An

> affirming woman should wear a dress (33:59) and cover her chest. God uses flexible language to allow culture, time, climate, age, and social dynamics and other factors to play a role in the decision. The underlying reason for this recommendation is the protection of women from potential harassment by males. There is nothing in the Qur'an that instructs the government or the society to force women, in the name of God, to cover themselves. A punishment neither in this world nor in hereafter is issued. While the male clerics and the followers of their misogynistic teachings are sunk up to their eyebrows in the mud of *shirk,* the only unforgivable sin, somehow, they are scrupulously obsessed with imposing dress codes on women. When they attain power, they bury women alive in black sacks. Does sanctifying the dress code of Christian nuns have anything to do with their psychological and sexual problems? The verses recommending that monotheist women cover themselves aim to protect them from the harassment of unrighteous men. Ironically, women are now harassed more by the self-righteous men.
>
> It is up to women, not men, to determine the length of their dresses, and whether they will cover their breasts or not. It is one thing to remind a monotheist woman nicely to be modest for her protection and to maintain social order. But to use this issue to patronize and subjugate women is not what the Qur'an expects from us. Even worse is to impose this recommendation on women who are not affirmers of the Qur'an, since that violates additional Qur'anic principles.
>
> The male clerics who covered their intelligence by their obsessive interference with women's hair and dress, do not even notice the lesson in verse 7:26. Despite the verse informing us that women used to walk in the street with their faces uncovered in front of Muhammad (33:52), they still have the audacity to preach to women to cover their faces with veils. See 33:55. For the Biblical account of women's dress, which is mostly ignored by Christians, see Genesis 24:65; Jeremiah 4:30; Ezekiel 16:10; Zephaniah 1:8; 1Timothy 2:9; 1 Peter 3:3; 1 Corinthians 11:15.

As he points out in his commentary on 7:26, "some translators and commentators render the word *sawa* as "sin" or "ugly parts" or "genitals." He also observes that Qur'an 33:52 treats attraction to women's beauty as entirely natural. Nonetheless, "those who traded the progressive precepts of the Qur'an with the misogynistic culture of the medieval pagan, Jewish, and Christian communities covered women from head to toe while stripping them of their identities." Yüksel's stance of women's dress is summarized by the statement he has shared on social media: "Neither enslaving women by burying them in black sacks, nor exploiting women by turning them into meat packs."

7.20 Shabir Ally

Shabbir Ally, a Canadian of Guyanese origin, who has a doctorate in Islamic studies from the University of Toronto, and hosts the popular *Let the Qur'an Speak* program, which as of 2022, has received nearly thirty million views, devoted several shows to the evolution of *hijab*. He explained that there was no clear mandate for the *hijab* in the Qur'an or the *sunnah* and that there was no evidence that failing to cover one's hair was a sin for a woman. He also expressed his opposition to mandatory *hijab* in Muslim majority nations. Although he was very delicate in his approach, and treated past opinions with tact, religious fanatics, both ignorant and educated, started to question whether he was really a Muslim. Many went as far as to accuse him of being an apostate and an infidel. The man, however, completed his dissertation on Qur'anic exegesis.

7.21 Ghaleb Bencheikh

As Ghaleb Bencheikh (b. 1960), the Franco-Algerian Islamologist, and a president of the *Fondation de l'Islam en France*, has noted, the veil is an act of regression that is both terrible and tragic. He blames its spread on the pseudo-Islamic revolution of Khomeini which spread its influence from Jakarta to Dakar and the suburbs of the Europe (Bestandji 2021: 114, 2018: part four). He denounces the obsession with the veil and defends a reformed Islam (France Fraternités). He believes "the veil is an attack on human dignity" (Ben Rhouma). He views the imposition of the veil on innocent little girls as a means of eroticizing their bodies (Twitter). Not only is such a practice devoid of any canonical injunction, but he also views it as a serious form of child abuse (Twitter).

7.22 Cyrille Moreno al-'Ajami

For Cyrille Moreno al-'Ajami, a French Muslim medical doctor, Arabist, Islamologist, theologian, and specialist in Qur'anic exegesis, the term *khimar*, as used in the Qur'an 24:31, refers to any fabric (Bestandji 201: 92). Rather than command women to cover their hair, the Qur'an merely recommends they cover their cleavage with a fabric or article of clothing of any kind (2018). "When Islam makes it obligatory for every Muslim woman to wear the veil," notes al-'Ajami, "it does so without any Qur'anic basis" (2018). Consequently, "nothing obliges a Muslim women to veil herself" (2018). As a result of his meticulous Qur'anic analysis, the literal meaning of 33:59 comes to light:

> 1. Contextually, this verse has a strictly limited and circumstantial character that cannot be generalized. 2. This verse only concerns the wives of the Prophet and the Muslims of Medina. 3. This verse does not prescribe, in any literal sense, wearing any kind of veil. This logical

> position also applies to 24:31, the so-called "veiling verse." 4. This verse decrees a mode of dress aimed to outplay Muhammad's opponents and was not motivated by a code of modesty. 5. This verse does not indicate that Muslim women are required to distinguish themselves from non-Muslim women by wearing specific attire. 6. This verse does not suggest that Muslim women must conceal their bodies to protect themselves from the appetite of men. 7. In reality, the Qur'an condemns men who harass Muslim women. (2018)

As al-'Ajami explains, the Qur'an calls upon women, like men, to be modest and decent (2018). At the same time, he notes, nothing prevents women from veiling, so long as it is compatible with the morals invoked in other verses (2018). However, "if the veil expresses the lack of liberty and inequality of women, it contravenes the egalitarian recommendations of the verve and others" (2018). At the same time, any attempt to prohibit women from veiling is an unacceptable lack of respect for personal freedom (2018). That being said, al-'Ajami deplores that the original purpose of the *khimar* and the *jilbab* in the Qur'an has been reversed. As he acknowledges, "the *hijab* has become a form of exhibition and exuberance" (Bestandji 2021: 103). "The *hijab* is no longer what hides," he points out (2021: 103). Its purpose is to stand out and to be seen (2021: 103). In other words, there is nothing modest or discrete about it. In much of the world. the women who wear *hijab* draw more attention to themselves than if they wore jeans and a t-shirt. They wish to stand out as opposed to blending it inconspicuously.

7.23 Naëm Bestandji

One of the most devastating critiques of *hijab* to date has been made by Naëm Bestandj (b. 1971) in *Le Linceul du Feminisme* or *The Death Shroud of Feminism*. For this French-born secularist activist of Tunisian parentage, and other feminist, universalist, and secular Muslims, who rely on the Qur'an for evidence, the mandatory *hijab* is a "sexist heresy" (2018: part one). In fact, his entire website is a veritable onslaught against the spread and threat of radical Islamic fundamentalism. He denounces that Islamists, who are fundamentally anti-secular, anti-democratic, and opposed to human rights, exploit secular institutions to advance their totalitarian agenda (2018: part one). He stresses that the veil or headscarf is nowhere to be found in the Qur'an and that it was only later invented by the *shari'ah* (2018: part one) by men who inherited a pre-Islamic animosity toward women (2018: part two). "The Islamists pretend to apply the Qur'an to the letter," he writes. However, "the Qur'an has never used the word *hijab*." As he explains, "this term does not appear in any of its 6,236 verses" (2021: 82). On the contrary, it is the product of Islamic jurisprudence and *shari'ah* law (2021: 82).

Despite devious translations and interpretations disseminated by Islamists, he notes that "there is nothing in the Qur'an that requires women to cover their hair, much less their entire bodies" (2018: part three). The meaning of the term *jalabib*, which is typically translated into French by Islamists as "long veils" to justify the *hijab*, *niqab*, *burqa*, or *chador*, has been the subject of scholarly debate among theologians, jurists, and exegetes, for more than a millennium (2021: 84-85). For Islamists, this verse commands women to veil themselves completely. Not only does the term not mean *hijab* or veil -- it actually means a shawl or a mantel, namely, a sleeveless garment -- but the word "large" does not appear in verse 33:59 (2021: 84). As Bestandji argues, this verse "never prescribed a dress code, and even less a religious injunction, applicable at all times and places, that turns women into sexual objects that need to be concealed" (2021: 88). Fortunately, some French translations are more attuned to the sense of the original Arabic. Ahmed Derrous, for example, translated 24:31 as *voiler leurs poitrines* or "cover their bosom," while Claude Étienne Savary conveyed it as *qu'elles aient le sein couvert*, "let them cover their breasts." According to such literal and faithful translations, the Qur'anic verse in question even permits bikini-style attire.

As for verse 24:31, which Islamists misuse to mandate the *hijab*, it does not deal with covering the hair of women, much less their bodies (2021: 90). As Bestandji notes, "the only anatomical part that is clearly mentioned is the chest" (2021: 90). What is more, there is no indication that this shawl must cover the hair. Despite the claims of the Islamists, the terms *khimar* and *zinah* are vague and undefined (2021: 90). As he asks, "What is meant by 'ornaments'? What is this 'veil'? What are the 'hidden parts' of women that children can see in their innocence? The buttock? The pubis? The elbows? The nose? The hair? A toe?" (2021: 90). What is clear is that this distinction in dress was meant to help identify Muslim women, who were supposed to be more virtuous than others, and to protect them from being insulted or assaulted by men who might otherwise treat them like prostitutes (2021: 88). This "veil," which covered the bosom, was a means, and not an end (2021: 86). It was introduced in a time and place where prostitution was rampant, as it was along the trade routes of Arabia where Mecca and Medina were located (2021: 86). The situation, of course, has long changed. As Bestandji points out:

> The offenders, the troublemakers, and the perverts of today are the fundamentalists. Declaring that the veil is obligatory for Muslim women who "respect themselves," because they would naturally be sexual objects that should be covered to not to excite men, is an offense to all humanity. This objectification of women to the point of making them appetizing pieces of meat that should be wrapped so as not to attract carnivores, ulcerates universalist feminists, including Muslim women, and most of our society. (2021: 88)

If the Qur'an does not specify any precise part of the body that women need to cover, notes Bestandji, and does not provide any punishment for not doing so, the "scholars," along the centuries, and even today, promised them all the tortures of hell if they refused to veil themselves. As he notes, however, "there is nothing spiritual in veiling oneself" (2018: part three). Not only do they impose a veil on their heads, but women who do so impose a veil on their minds, one that was imposed on them by sexually obsessed men (2018: part three). Rationalist Muslims, in his mind, are far more faithful to and respectful of religious texts than Islamists in their feigned literalism (2018: part three).

As Bestandji explains, Islam is found in the soul and heart. It is not found on the heads of women. To insist upon veiling one's hair, thereby opposing the Qur'anic text, is not pious. It is masochism and blasphemy (2018: part two). He cites Soheib Bencheikh (b. 1961), the grand mufti of Marseille, France, who insists that "the *hijab* is not a religious symbol" (2021: 89, part two). Its goal was to protect the dignity of women (2021: 89, 2018: part two). Today, argues the mufti, the *hijab* of women is free, mandatory, secular education (Bestandji 2021: 89, 2018). For Bestandji, "secularism is a fundamental guarantee" for the emancipation of women (2018: part two). The best way to protect women is by providing them with an education and economic independence (2021: 89). "The veil," he argues, "is an impediment" (2018). As Bestandji explains:

> Whatever the interpretation, whether the veil is a religious prescription or not, nothing, absolutely nothing can justify it today. The Qur'an authorizes polygamy by validating a contemporary custom of the first Muslims (even if it leans towards monogamy by imposing the condition of equality between each wife, which is humanly impossible). It authorizes marriage with young girls, mutilation to punish thieves, etc. Do we accept this today? Even if the prescription of the veil had been real, wearing it in the seventh century could be understood. Bringing it to the twenty-first century is an anachronism that makes it sexism. (2018: part four)

For Bestandji, "the veil was created and prescribed by men to control women's bodies" (2018: part three). "From a vague and secondary subject mentioned in the Qur'an," he laments, "it has now become a definitive and primordial injunction" (2018: Part Two). For the proponents of *hijab*, women who fail to abide by it are less pious as Muslims and less respectable as women (2018: Part Two). They judge a woman's degree of religious conviction in square inches of material (2018: part four). He is being far too mild. In fact, many view women who do not wear *hijab*, as they narrowly conceive, as being sinners, sluts, hypocrites, disbelievers, apostates, depraved prostitutes, and whores (Samint).

As the title of Bestandji's book indicates, the veil is the death shroud of feminism (2021: mon livre). Muslim women who fail to wear the veil are accused of lacking shame and morals. Radical Muslims view them as unchaste and impure (2016). Islamists have threatened to slit their throats from jugular to jugular (Fatah 281). Some have been disfigured with acid by religiously deranged sociopaths.

As Bestandji notes, "the veil, an apocryphal invention, is now the sixth pillar of Islam" when, in reality, it is nothing short of "a theological aberration and a blasphemy" (2018: part two). It is a "sexist innovation inspired by patriarchal traditions" (2018: part four). As far as he is concerned, there is nothing religious about the veil (2018: part four). In fact, it is a spiritual step backwards (2018: part four). The spread of the veil is not benign: it marks the growing influence of radical political Islamism in society. As Betandji explains, the Islamists view the veil as a form of proselytization (2021: 343, 2022). The more "inclusive" the environment, the more Islamism makes inroads thanks to the "useful idiots" on the left who accuse anyone who questions the veil of being racist (2021: 343, 338).

Marketed by Islamists as a form of feminism, the veil cannot be compared to miniskirts or high heels, items women can select, based on context, and to which they are not bound (Bestandji 2017). Presented as a form of emancipation, it soon becomes a prison. As he notes, "the veil was not created to mark femininity. It was created to hide it" (2017). For him, "the veil is a racist textile marker created to stigmatize half of humanity" so that sexual apartheid can be established (2017). What is more, unlike the *hijab*, the miniskirt and high heels are not the flag-bearers of a totalitarian ideology (2017). As Bestandji argues, "Islamism advances by covering the bodies of women" ("L'islamisme" 2019). They are conquering new grounds and claiming new territories. Although "the veil is an Islamist, as opposed to Qur'anic prescription," notes Bestandji, corporations have jumped on the "halal," "modest," and "Islamic" fashion bandwagon to profit from the demonization of the female body and to make sexism acceptable ("La diabolisation" 2019). As he warns, "These slow but steady advances by the veil (*hijab*, *jelbab*, *burqini*, etc.) prepare the ground for the retrograde and totalitarian ideas that accompany it: decline in diversity, and the demonization of the smallest square centimeter of women's bodies. ("La diabolisation" 2019).

Tala Raassi (b. 1980), an American-born Iranian who was imprisoned and given forty lashes for wearing a miniskirt in the privacy of a friend's home, fled Iran, and settled in the United States where she became a bikini designer. Despite suffering at the hands of Iranian Islamists, she believes that attempts to ban the *burkini* are a form of religious discrimination and intolerance (Raasi). She is opposed to forcing women to wear such attire; however, she insists upon the right to choose. For her, "fashion is freedom." In her words:

> Everyone should wear bikinis, but because I love fashion, and I believe that fashion is a form of freedom, women all around the world should be able to wear what they desire without the fear of judgment,

> punishment, or coercion… Freedom is not about the amount of clothing you put on or take off, but about having the choice to do so. I saw women who wore *hijabs*, covered from head to toe, walking on the same beaches as women in their European-cut bikinis. Their freedom of choice empowered me. I found a new respect for women who covered by their choice for "their" religious beliefs. I also respected those who fearlessly wore bikinis. There is something very powerful about standing up for your beliefs, even if you're in the minority.

For Bestandji, however, the *burqini* is not a free choice as the women who wear it have been shamed into doing so by sexually obsessed Islamist men (Burqini). He finds it supremely hypocritical that these women are covered completely, preventing them from properly swimming or enjoying the sun, while Muslim men wear shorts, t-shirts, bathing suits, and speedos (Burqini). For Bestandji, "this adaptation of veiling to bathing makes it possible to make municipal swimming pools a new terrain of politico-religious conquest" (Burqini).

Bestandji highlights the hypocrisy of Islamists who present historical photographs of women's swimwear to argue their case for the *burqini*. In so doing, they express their nostalgia for a time when women were encumbered by layers of clothing and had little to no rights in any area (2021: 273). For them, the "good old days" were those when women were kept in their place. They even invoke the habits of nuns to justify the *hijab* and the *jilbab*. The comparison is entirely dishonest. The attire worn by nuns in the past, which is no longer obligatory, is ecclesiastic in nature. Lay women were never required to wear it. It was never imposed on girls in Catholic schools (2021: 266). Moreover, the *hijab* is not like a cross or even a kippa (2021: 259). Nobody is coerced into wearing these discrete religious items.

Comparing the veil to a shawl is also duplicitous. As Bestandji notes, "The shawl and the veil have nothing in common, be it in their shapes, sizes, history, meanings, and the conditions of their wearing" (2021: 270). Byzantine Christian women were indeed encouraged to cover their hair: "just *how* women covered their hair changed over the centuries" (Hopwood-Phillips). Over the centuries, they included padded head rolls, figure-eight turbans, and cylinder head-wraps (Hopwood-Phillips). The headwear also varied according to social class (Hopwood-Phillips). "While it is possible to confirm that covering a woman was a Byzantine ideal," notes Hopwood-Phillips, the historian and archeologist:

> the total coverage of female hair was not a major concern in notions of modesty. Rather, the amount of hair covered varied according to circumstance and social setting. Beyond church contexts, where head coverage was a given, there could be a number of acceptable fractions i.e. the presence of the veil mattered more than its role/position.

What is more, "it was even possible for loose hair to be considered honorable." This same attitude appears to have prevailed for much of Muslim history, where covering the head for women, as it was for men, was considered a symbol of humility before God. Married Christian women covered their hair in late medieval times and the Middle Ages. However, "these standards changed over time and varied in different regions" (Edwards 128). In fact, the veil and the wimple gave way to fashionable hats (Tutten 97). What is more, long, uncovered, loose hair was the model for unmarried girls (Tutten 96). The strict, obsessive-compulsive, rules of Muslim jurists, which prohibit showing a single strand of hair as a sin, were not observed by the vast majority of Muslim women until the rise of radical Islamism, both Sunnite and Shiite, in the 1970s and beyond.

To compare the *hijab* to the shawl of Grace Kelly (1929-1982), the American actress who became Princess of Monaco, as French Islamists do, is a disservice to Muslim women. The same goes for Muslim apologists who claim that "Jennifer Lopez wears a headscarf sometimes, and she is applauded for her style; nobody calls her a raghead" (Ali-Karamali 162). The difference cannot be greater. J-Lo does not have to cover every hair on her head, along with the rest of her body, save her face and hands. She is not threatened with hellfire for showing her hair or the rest of her body. And if she is praised for her style, it most certainly is not by Muslims. The more religious they are the more likely they are to view her as an infidel whore who is destined for hell.

Equating the *hijab* to the mini-skirt and high heels, as Islamists and intersectionalist feminists do, is equally abhorrent and reprehensible. As Bestandji stresses, "miniskirts and stiletto heels are worn for certain occasions; not permanently" (2021: 275-276). Women wear them by choice. Men do not force their womenfolk to wear miniskirts, stiletto heels, and bikinis. They do not threaten to kill women who refuse to wear them. What is more, "only extremist Muslim women wear the *hijab*: no woman would ever wear the *hijab*, the *jilbab*, or the *niqab* for reasons of femininity" (2021: 276). Moreover:

> No country has passed any law to make it compulsory to wear miniskirts and stiletto heels in public spaces. There is no truth or religious police anywhere to ensure that every woman wears just that, as there is for wearing the veil in Saudi Arabia or Iran. Is there a totalitarian ideology that imposes miniskirts and high heels on pain of imprisonment, corporal punishment, or even stoning, as for the veil? Have there been attacks in the name of this same ideology? Have women been murdered for refusing to wear miniskirts like they have for refusing to wear the veil? The mini-skirt and stiletto heels are not the standard-bearers of a totalitarian ideology. (2021: 277)

The *hijab*, *jilbab*, *niqab*, *chador*, and *burqini* are not forms of modest dress and fashion. They are forms of anti-fashion. The purpose of fashion is to beautify. The purpose of the so-called *shari'ah* compliant clothing is to remove all beauty from the public sphere. Such clothing has been marketed as "fashionable" by soulless multinational corporations that wish to profit from the oppression and subjugation of women. Those who clamor for the rights of women to wear the veil in sports or *burqinis* in pools and beaches, and who celebrate sexism, trample upon the bloodied bodies of Muslim girls and women who were slaughtered for opposing it (Bestandji 2021: 333). Take, for example, the case of seventeen-year-old Katia Bengana and twenty-two-year-old Amel Zenoune Zouani, two Algerians who were murdered for refusing to wear the veil. One was shot multiple times. The other had her throat slit (Bestandji 2021: 333). Many more have been killed around the world for refusing to cover their hair. They died for their choice.

For the intellectuals from *Révolution Féministe*, the *burkini* is an act of violence against women that forms part of a woman-hating continuum: "polygyny, female genital mutilation, sexual crimes against children… antisemitism and hatred for the West, among others" (Samint). Islamists can make it colorful or fashionable, argues Bestandji, however, the veil remains the veil, with all the sexist, patriarchal, and political weight it embodies (2021: 278). Islamic scholar Shadi Hamid (b. 1983) can claim all he wants that:

> All four Sunni *madhabs* (schools of law) consider covering the hair to be obligatory by *ijma*' or consensus, regardless of geographic context. We don't have to like this (and perhaps one day there will be more dissenting voices like Khaled Abou El Fadl), but we can't ignore or dismiss it either. Legal debates aside, there are endless millions of Muslim women who believe that covering their hair is religiously mandated, so, for them, it is inextricably tied to Islam and to their own personal relationship to God. To insist otherwise is to deny the agency, autonomy, and choice of these Muslim women.

However, this is circular reasoning. So long as there is an obligation, there can be no choice. What is more, presenting women with four options that are all the same is not a choice either. As is done in this work, presenting women with all opinions allows them to make an informed decision on a personal matter. Even so, such women are still subjected to family and social pressures that prevent them from freely making a choice. For a free choice to be made, all options must be accepted as valid and equal. The fact remains that many Muslim women are denied agency, autonomy, and choice -- not by Western critics of imposed *hijab* -- but by Muslim conservatives, extremists, misogynists, and some so-called Islamic feminists.

Despite her tragic experiences, Raasi does not seem to seize the fact that the proponents of the *hijab* and the *burqini* adhere to an ideology that wishes to deprive women of their freedom to dress as they freely choose; not as slaves of fashion, but as informed consumers whose dollars determine the direction of clothing design. Women are no longer shaped by fashion. As earners with income, they shape fashion.

Women have rights and women have voices. However, as Khaled Abou El Fadl notes, "the male-dominated interpretive tradition of Islam has often frustrated and defeated the Qur'an's affirmative action and made the divine will largely unresponsive and unsympathetic to women's agency and autonomy" (El-Ali xi). Women's voices are simply not heard on matters such as equality and modesty (Ridgeon 6). "There is no doubt," observes Abdulaziz Sachedina (b. 1942), the Khoja Twelver Shiite academic, "that the tone of the rulings is set by the powerful male jurist who, in most cases, ignores the female evaluation of her own social situation" (Ridgeon 6-7).

If, as Muslims believe, "the Qur'an is God's revealed book, and that this revelation is relevant and valid for every place, time, and age," stresses Abou El Fadl, "it must continue to address the ever-changing needs of men and women" (El-Ali x). For Leena El-Ali, "the Qur'anic God was a relentless advocate for women's rights who issued instructions that we would today call 'affirmative action' targeting gender equality" (xvii).

As Abou El Fadl points out, "women made demands upon the Prophet and God, and often obtained results that by the standards of the time can be described as socially equitable and progressive" (El-Ali x). "The problem," he notes, "is what becomes of this dynamic after the Prophet dies, and the path to divine revelation is severed" (El-Ali x). This issue, however, is theological. It is the product of the Sunni belief that the Qur'an is uncreated and eternal. This view was rejected by the Mutazilites and the Shiites for whom the Qur'an was God's Word created in time. As Mahmoud Hussein, (1921-2009), the Egyptian philosopher and author, noted, "God transcends time. His Word is inscribed in time. At no moment in the Qur'an is it permitted to confound God and His Word. At no moment is it permitted to deduce, from the eternity of God, the eternity of His Word" (Bestandji 2021: 81).

Verses that applied to circumstances, events, and individuals in the seventh century were legitimate 1300 years ago (Bestandji: 2021: 102). However, the wives of the Prophet are not the only Muslim women on the planet (2021: 102). The *khimar* and *jilbab* verses were never intended to be atemporal and universal (2021: 102). What is more, they were never described as obligatory in the Qur'an. As Bestandji points out:

> The words "obligatory" or "forbidden" do not appear in any of these verses. Finally, no sanction is provided for in the event of poor adjustment of one's shawl, mantle, or fabric, unlike adultery or theft for example. Moreover, for this, it would have been necessary to precisely define the areas to be hidden in order to avoid unfair subjective condemnation. (2021: 99)

Most importantly, no promise is made to women that wearing a mantle or shawl to cover their cleavage will bring them closer to God (2021: 103). The so-called *hijab* verses have nothing to do with spirituality (2021: 97). They are concerned with the management or mores and social hierarchy (2021: 97). As Bestandji admits in all honesty, they are profoundly sexist (2021: 97). Even so, they do not recommend, or even oblige women to veil themselves from head to toe, or even to hide their hair (2021: 97). They are the product of a period that was steeped in patriarchy (2021: 97). These verses are merely a reflection of the socio-cultural context in which they were revealed (2021: 97). What is more:

> the fact that these are mere recommendations and not divine orders explains why no divine sanction is mentioned: no threat of hell or even banishments or earthly punishments like whipping or stoning. There is nothing… Then it appeared over the centuries, with the evolution of *fiqh* and the establishment of *shari'ah,* which are based on the interpretations of the exegetes of their time. (2021: 103)

To adopt the *hijab*, which was invented by jurists during the development of Islamic jurisprudence and *shari'ah* law, is an act of human regression (Bestandji 2021: 105). As the Qur'an states explicitly, the "raiment of righteousness," or the "attire of piety" (7:26) is not material: it is spiritual (Bestandji 2021: 103). As Bestandji notes, this is a verse that the sexually obsessed advocates of the *hijab* willingly ignore or dismiss (2021: 103). For him, this is further proof that rationalist and progressive Muslim women are more faithful and respectful of religious texts than the Islamic fundamentalists in their so-called literalist approach (2021: 103). The Qur'anic interpretation of the Islamists is not Islamic: it is an extrapolation made by the sexually obsessed (2021: 104).

For Bestandji, the pseudo-religiosity and spirituality that the Islamists give to the veil masks their obsession: "Islamists are haunted by sexuality. From their 'Islamization' until their death, they only think about it from morning till night" (2021: 104). As Bestandji captures, the proponents of *hijab* view men as animals (2021: 179-181) and women as temptations (2021: 182-183). They impose their definition of modesty upon women which has nothing to do with spirituality (2021: 184-187).

They treat women as sexual objects (2021: 188-189). They depict them as candies and lollipops that attract flies, meat that attracts carnivores, and as walking sex toys (2021: 193). Is that not objectification? They claim that the only way women can be respected is by covering themselves completely (2021: 193). They claim to speak for God (2021: 195). They claim that women who do not wear the veil displease God (2021: 196-198) and that non-veiled women are the allies of Satan (2021: 198-199). They claim that the veil leads to heaven while its lack leads to hell (2021: 199). They portray women who refuse to veil as being depraved (2021: 294). They demonize unveiled women to frighten them into accepting the veil as a "free choice" (2021: 199). They place the fear of the Day of Judgment into unveiled women (2021: 200). They insist that women who do not wear the veil will burn in hell (2021: 201-205).

7.24 Conclusions

The views surveyed in this chapter all come from qualified and competent men. They feature Sunni Muslims, Shiite Muslims, and Qur'anist Muslims. Some are the product of Sunni and Shiite seminaries. They include '*ulama,*' clerics, or scholars. Some are *mujtahids* and *muftis*, namely, jurists entitled to issue legal edicts. Others are the products of universities. They include intellectuals, scholars, and professors with expertise in a wide arrays of field. They feature historians, philosophers, jurists, and specialists in Islamic studies. Some are clerics and academics with advanced degrees from seminaries and universities.

In the Court of Islam and Public Opinion, all parties are entitled to express their views and present their evidence. Otherwise, the Court makes a mockery of justice. For much of Islamic history, a single, solitary view has been imposed from upon high as if it represented a divine decree. This has been especially so since the so-called "Islamic revival" and the rise of Islamist movements in the twentieth century. The spread of the invented neo-*hijab* has gone hand in hand with the spread of radical Islamist ideology. Muslim intellectuals, scholars, clerics, academics, jurists, and authorities have been fighting this ideology and its ostentatious symbol -- the *hijab* -- since its inception. Their words need to be heard and their warnings need to be heeded.

Chapter 8

The Views of Women on the *Hijab*

8.1 Introduction

Women represent half of humanity. They should co-exist in symbiosis with men on the grounds of equality. Ideally, half of elected offices should be occupied by men and half by women. Men and women should be equally represented in all fields. The views of women should hold as much weight as those of men, and on matters pertaining to women, even more so. The preceding chapter presented the views of male scholars on the *hijab*. This chapter focuses on the views of women. If the views of the previously mentioned men are unfamiliar to most Muslims, since they have been suppressed by male misogynists, the views of the women who follow have been suffocated all the more so. Out of objectivity, and to counter the asphyxiating subjectivity of the misogynists that suffocates all free debate and discussion, it is imperative to amplify the voices of these men and especially these women. Why? Because religion is manufactured, dominated, and controlled by men and women who toe the line. The women of Islam must wrest control of it and reshape it for their sake, their daughters, and their granddaughters. And for the sakes of their sons and grandsons as well. Hear their voices!

8.2 Wassyla Tamzali

In 2010, Wassyla Tamzali (b. 1941), the Algerian attorney, writer, secular Muslim feminist, and freethinker, published a book titled *Niqab?* Not only does she oppose the *niqab,* but she also rejects the obligatory *hijab*. As she states in an article,

> Accepting the practice, North African or not, Muslim or not, of hiding one's hair, of not being treated by a male doctor, of not shaking hands with men, that is, accepting practices of strict sexist segregation, seems to me to be a bad answer to a real problem. ... How can it not ... be said that the veil is ... the symbol of this enslavement of women and that its scope cannot be altered by its frivolous use or misinterpretation by some?
>
> Girls... in France who... wear the veil... have fallen into a trap.

Some started to wear the veil for play, for provocation, but also for rebellion..., finding there a definition of freedom... You cannot express your freedom by throwing yourself, hands and feet tied, into a culture whose objective is the domination of women... The veil is ... a bulwark against gender-based, symbolic, or expressed violence. There are schools and universities, places in Algeria, where one can no longer be unveiled. In Algerian Arabic it is said that an unveiled woman is naked, which says a lot. It is an illusory rampart... [considering] the escalation of violence in the Arab streets where there are more and more veiled women.

The more you repress sexuality, the more it is present. Men's eyes are becoming increasingly heavy and concupiscent. This repression leads to real pathological deviances that result in the most barbaric acts against women, with the Afghan *burqa* ... representing the most accomplished and theatrical form of these deviances. If women and girls, by veiling themselves, believe that they are safe from men's desires, the opposite is true. The concealment of women's bodies has the effect of increasing sexual crimes and harassment, exacerbating women's fear and men's greed...

At the heart of this madness is the obsession with virginity... and the disproportionate importance given to the preservation of the hymen. Although Muslim men want to get married, and only to virgins, births outside marriage are numerous and lead to a wide range of aberrations, abandonment of children, infanticide, murderous fury of fathers and brothers against pregnant girls and abusive use of sodomy and its clinical traumas.

I will never say that the veil is innocent. Never. It is much more than a religious sign, as is a cross, for example: it is *the* sign of women's oppression. It is a serious matter to trivialize it. I have trouble understanding Quebec women who support the demands of veiled women. They would never think that the *hijab* is without consequence for themselves or their daughters. Why is this more acceptable for a Muslim woman?

I grew up in a Muslim family, in one of the first generations of women to be unveiled in Algeria. There is a tendency to deny this part of history, but in almost all Arab countries, from the 1920s to the 1960s, women said no to the veil. They went out. They went to college. It showed that you can be an Arab and a Muslim and not cover yourself. Religion does not prescribe anything on this subject. "The veil is not Muslim, it is patriarchal," wrote Mohamed Talbi, a leading expert on Islam. It is a political tool to dominate women. In some countries, it starts very early, with four-year-old girls already covered from head to toe.

Wearing the veil cannot be claimed as an act of freedom. Even if,

> in the West, veiled women study, earn a good living, go to the movies, and have a husband who does the dishes. Even if it is a personal choice, you can easily alienate yourself... They reinforce a vision of a woman's place in society that emerged from the old patriarchal model. They take for granted the discourse on women in certain interpretations of the religion. That is what we must deconstruct… The wearing of the veil is spreading in the Maghreb and everywhere else… In some Paris suburbs, girls can no longer go out without their *hijab*. Their brothers are watching them. It was unimaginable fifteen years ago.
>
> The left must understand that wearing the veil is a political act to which we must respond with a political act. How is it possible that a left that claims to be feminist accepts to veil women, denying the whole political struggle on women's rights and on the place of women's oppression that is the body? … The left has not grasped the extent of the problem. The veil is no longer the sign of an anthropological culture but of a political culture… I do not accept a political culture that discriminates against women… To accept prostitution out of pragmatism is to accept the prostitution system, and that is not acceptable; to accept the veil out of pragmatism is to accept the causes of sexist segregation, and that is not acceptable. To refuse practices harmful to women, whether they come from the Islamic tradition or are very clearly prescribed by Koranic texts, is not to be Islamophobic, it is simply to be feminist.

Rejecting the *hijab* is neither racist nor sexist. On the contrary, it is an act of opposition toward racism, sexism, sexual discrimination, and gender segregation. While Tamzali believes that women may do as they please and recognizes they should have the right to cover their hair if they so desire, she also views the adoption of the veil on the part of girls and women as the symptom of a pathology.

8.3 Riffat Hasan

As Riffat Hassan (b. 1943), a leading scholar of the Qur'an, and recipient of the Mary K. Bonsteel Tachau Gender Equity Award, has remarked, conservative Muslims rely on a weak *hadith* "to compel women to cover themselves from head to foot, leaving only the face and hands uncovered" (1999: 275). "Ultraconservatives," however, "have gone even further, requiring that a woman also cover her face" (1999: 275). "Certainly," she writes, "there are no Qur'anic statements which justify the rigid restrictions regarding segregation and veiling which have been imposed on women in the name of Islam" (1999: 275). She also asks a pertinent question: "If, for instance, the Qur'an had intended for women to be completely veiled, why would it have required Muslim men to lower their gaze when looking at them?" (1999: 275). As Yusuf al-Qaradawi (1926-2022) admitted, "had the entire body, including the face, been covered, it would have made no sense to command them to lower their gaze, since there would have been nothing to be seen" (135).

8.4 Hélé Béji

In 2011, Hélé Béji (b. 1948), a prominent Tunisian intellectual and author, published *Islam Pride*, in which she foresaw the return of the veil and examined the motivations of the women who were adopting it. Basically, the promises that came with independence were not honored. Modernism and secularism were imposed through authoritarian rule. Civil society provided all kinds of rights, except the right to criticize those in power. Tunisia, like much of the Muslim world, experienced secularism without democracy and human rights. The Islamists harvested this discontent. They presented political Islam as the only alternative to authoritarian leaders, despots, and military dictators.

While she is against the *hijab*, she does not support banning it. She tried to avoid calling it "barbaric;" however, deep down, this is precisely how she views it. While she is angry at veiled women, she simultaneously pities them. "The veil," in her view, "destroys the universal feminine." The veil divides women. It places them into two categories: the veiled and the unveiled. They have created a "civil war" between women. Béji refuses to surrender to fatalism. She is convinced that "one day, they will unveil themselves, but not by force." In her view, the rise of the veil results from the failure of secularism. As she stresses, secular ideas are ineffective when combating the veil for it was secular notions of "freedom of conscience" that permitted it to spread like wildfire, only to undermine secularism itself.

For Hélé Béji, the veil is not merely a symbol of submission but one of self-affirmation. Were it simply the symptom of ancient domination, it would be easier to combat. For Islamist women, the veil is vindicated. It is an act of rebellion and defiance. It is "the puritanical costume of another form of feminism." It is a religious "coming-out," a type of "Islam pride." The portrait she paints of these "born-again," revolutionary, Muslim *hijabis* produces pity. They are women who are terrified of the world, the pressure to find employment, the brutality of competition, and the disappearance of the traditional family. For Béji, the veil is the product of the failure of progressive ideologies. It is the visible expression of the bankruptcy of the Muslim world, both politically and morally. The women who wear the *hijab* feel powerless in the face of modern states. They suffer from sexual frustration, involuntary celibacy, romantic failure, one-parent families, semi-orphaned children, the destruction of human ties, drug addiction, the cult of productivity, and the stress caused by the rat race of work. They are lashing out at modernity by grasping desperately at an invented Islamist tradition which, is itself, the product of the system they loathe.

As Hélé Béji describes, "the veil is black ash cast on the light of tradition." As she explains, the Islamic tradition must not be equated with obscurantism. It must be distinguished from religion. Communitarianism must be understood as a reaction to excess and individualism. For many young women, the Islam proposed by the Islamists helps to fill a void. To women who are weary of freedom, the Islamists offer submission. They invoke a golden age, which never existed, and pretend that this utopia can be restored by using cynical and inhuman methods. For Hélé Béji, "they transform Tradition into a monster." In fact, "the religious ideology called Salafism or Islamism dehumanizes the Tradition more rapidly than all the transgressions of the modern world." In their search to revive Islam, they destroy it more thoroughly and completely than the so-called enemies of Islam they so despise.

As much as a total ban on the *hijab* is justified as part of the historical struggle for the emancipation of women, Hélé Béji does not believe that it would be effective. As much as she would lose her dignity if forced to put a handkerchief over her head, veiled women would feel the same way if forced to remove it. While she would prefer not to see women in *burqas*, or *burkinis*, as it revolts and offends her, she realizes that the veil is also a reaction. Consequently:

> I am absolutely in favor of the law that prohibits the veil at school, since they are minors, who should be free from the diktats imposed by their families or neighborhoods. To veil a little girl is a violation of the rights of children. The State must protect her by all means. This is beyond question.

8.5 Yasmin Alibhai-Brown

For Yasmin Alibhai-Brown (b. 1949), a British journalist and author, "the *hijab*, *burqa*, and *niqab* are visible signs of… a retreat from progressive values." As she explains,

> Veils for me represent … religious arrogance and subjugation; they … desexualize and fervidly sexualize. Women are … seen as sexual creatures whose hair and bodies incite desire and disorder in the public space. The claim that veils protect women from lasciviousness and disrespect carries an element of self-deception… Little girls are being asked to don *hijabs* and *jilbabs*, turned into sexual beings long before puberty. You can even buy stretchy baby *hijabs* with fake Calvin Klein and Versace logos. Like a half-naked woman, a veiled female to me represents an affront to female dignity, autonomy, and potential. Both are marionettes, and have internalized messages about femaleness.
>
> Do those who choose to veil think of women in Iran, Saudi Arabia, Afghanistan, Pakistan, Iraq, and even the West, who are prosecuted, flogged, tortured, or killed for not complying? This is not a

> freestanding choice -- it cannot be. Although we hear from vocal British *hijabis* and *niqabis*, those who are forced cannot speak out. A fully *burqaed* woman once turned up at my house, a graduate, covered in cuts, burns, bruises, and bites. Do we know how many wounded, veiled women walk around hidden among us? Sexual violence in Saudi Arabia and Iran is appallingly high, as is body dysmorphia.

8.6 Fatima Houda-Pepin

Fatima Houda-Pepin (b. 1951), a Moroccan-born Berber, is a political scientist and Quebec politician who served in the National Assembly of Quebec from 1994 to 2014. She has provided a particularly poignant insight into the context of the so-called *hijab* verse. She holds that "at the origins of the so-called Islamic veil, there is rape and prostitution" (2020). Speaking of Islamic fundamentalists, she notes that,

> The main source on which they still rely today, to make the so-called "Islamic veil" a fundamental right at the same level as freedom of religion, is verse 59 of Sura 33, "The Coalition," revealed in 627, the year the Prophet Muhammad was to fight the coalition that came to besiege him in Medina. They attacked women, raped, and forced them into prostitution (*ta'arrud*). Verse 59 will resolve this dilemma. "O Prophet! Tell your wives and daughters and the women of the believers to bring a piece of their veil close to their faces, as this is more likely to make them recognizable from other women and thus prevent them from being bothered. God is infinitely absolute and merciful." Islamists will refrain from explaining the context...
>
> This verse has only moral significance. It is specifically addressed to the women of Medina's high society to prevent them from being offended by *ta'arrud*. It is suggested that they "bring a piece of their veil close to them" and fold it over their faces. Why is that? To distinguish them from other women. And which other women were they to be distinguished from? Slaves... The so-called "Islamic veil" made a distinction between free women who should not be bothered (because they are veiled) and slaves who can be given over to rape and prostitution because they are not. Those who today allege freedom of religion in defense of the so-called Islamic veil must bear in mind the date 627, the day the veil became a symbol of discrimination against black slaves and their enslavement to rape and prostitution. (2020)

Houda-Pepin's criticism may be generally sound; however, her claim that the Qur'an mentions covering the face shows the extent to which the radicals have convinced people of their claims. The Qur'anic verse in question does not mention the head, the hair, or the face. It merely mentions covering the *juyub*, namely, cleavage and bosom, to avoid being harassed. When? At night? Why? Because the Muslims were in the midst of a civil war. Medina was a dangerous place filled with brothels, hypocrites, harassers, and predators. Some of the tribes had women who, rather than be owned privately, were owned collectively. They would wander the streets in a dazed stupor awaiting to be sexually assaulted by any and all tribesmen who wanted to have their way with them.

Under such perilous social conditions, Muslim women risked being raped, especially when they went out at night. Hence, a visible marker was placed on them, and word was given to the enemies of Islam, the disbelievers, and dual loyalists, that they were under the protection of the Prophet Muhammad and the Muslims. Women at the time would expose their cleavage or breasts, typically bedecked with numerous necklaces. In order to be distinguished from ordinary women, women of ill-repute, and sexually trafficked women, Muslim women were told to cover their bosoms with a shawl. It was a temporary, time and context bound, injunction, and not a universal one. Where there is law and order, safety and security, women may dress as they please and as is appropriate to the setting. That could include modest dress in a mosque and a bikini at the beach. But, then again, it depends on the beach. There are beaches where it is not safe for women to do so. It depends on the country, the city, the town, and the stretch of beach. Much of this is informed by law, culture, education, and class. The fancier the location, the ritzier the resort, and the richer the clientèle, the safer it is, and the less a woman can wear. Women are safe among civilized men. Such is not the case among savages.

Muslim women are not safe among some so-called Muslim men. As Phylis Chesler reports, girls and women who travel from Iraq, Syria, Afghanistan, and Turkey, into Europe "are continually groped and sexually assaulted, even penetrated in every possible orifice, by gangs of male Muslim immigrants" (2017: 459). "If they want to live," she notes, "their husbands and fathers can do nothing" (459). In Europe, Muslim migrants, in gangs of dozens, hundreds, and at times, thousands, have committed scores of sexual assaults. On New Year's Eve, in both Germany and Austria, "attackers… simultaneously stuck their fingers into every female orifice; groped, licked, hit, and terrified every vulnerable woman who was out celebrating the holiday" (Chesler 2017: 445). Mind you, just as many women get sexually assaulted during the Carnival in Rio. So, the issue is not merely race or religion. The problem is patriarchal and misogynistic men.

Nothing, of course, compares to the horrors of Hassi Messaoud, where, in 2001, Amar Taleb, the fundamentalist Imam, incited a mob of three hundred men to hunt down female fornicators which, he defined, as any woman who was not accompanied by a male guardian, as part of a *jihad* against immorality. At least forty women were attacked, brutalized, sexually assaulted, mutilated, and dragged naked in the streets. Several women were murdered. The attackers cut off breasts and genitalia. Some were even buried alive. And what of the case of Lara Logan (b. 1971), the CBC correspondent who was the victim of a thousand-man gang rape in Cairo in 2011? Islam did not protect women in the seventh century any more than it protects them now. Muslim women remain victims of religious, cultural, and gender violence on every continent. As Mona Eltahawy (b. 1967) puts it,

> Name me an Arab country, and I'll recite a litany of abuses against women occurring in that country, abuses fueled by a toxic mix of culture and religion that few seem willing to disentangle lest they blaspheme or offend. When more than 90% of women who have ever married in Egypt have had their genitals cut in the name of "purity," then surely, we must all blaspheme. When Egyptian women are subjected to "virginity tests" merely for speaking out, it's not time for silence. When an article in the Egyptian criminal code says that if a woman is beaten by her husband "with good intentions," no punitive damages can be obtained, then to hell with political correctness. And what, pray tell, are "good intentions?" They are legally deemed to include any beating that is not "severe" or "directed to the face." What all this means is that when it comes to the status of women in the Arab world, it's not better than you think. It's much, much worse. (6)

8.7 Asma Barlas

Asma Barlas (b. 1950), the Pakistani American academic, argues that the Qur'an mandates women and men to be modest and not make a spectacle of themselves (185). According to her reading of the Qur'an,

> The real veil is in the eyes/gaze... First, it requires both men and women to dress modestly... Second, it describes modesty of dress rather sparingly as the covering of private parts... Third... the function of the *khumur* (shawl) is to cover the bosom... Muslim commentators overlook this fact and focus instead on words like "adornment," which the Qur'an does not define but which they define so broadly as to include even the face and hair. This obsession with the female body has spawned forms of veiling the Qur'an does not mandate. (184)

As far as Barlas is concerned, "there is absolutely nothing in these values that supports the conservative Muslim position on the female body... or the practice of veiling and segregating women as a way to make them invisible" (185). Rather than view the *hijab* as the symbol of an Islamic society, Barlas argues that it is the hallmark of a *jahili* society (60). As she explains,

> It is remarkable that women should have to fend off abuse in a society that claims to be Islamic, given that the rule of Islam, by ordaining sexual modesty for men and women, runs counter to the rule of the veil, brought on by *jahili* male promiscuity... Hence, Muslim men who feel they have the right to assault or kill unveiled women in some so-called Islamic societies are living by *jahili* precepts, not by Qur'anic ethics, which enjoin modesty and restraint on both sexes. (60)

8.8 Amina Wadud

Amina Wadud (b. 1952), the African American Muslim theologian, has chosen to wear *hijab* for most of her life. With age and experience, her attitude toward the veil has become more nuanced. In her words,

> I do not consider it a religious obligation, nor do I ascribe to it any religious significance or moral value *per se*. It is certainly not the penultimate denotation of modesty, as mandated by the Qur'an, "the best dress is the dress of *taqwa*" (7:26). While the *hijab* can give some semblance of a woman's affiliation with "Islam," it offers no guarantee of respect or protection. Those who reduce women to their sexuality will continue to do so… (219)

Wadud recognizes that "women observe or ignore the traditional head covering or *hijab* with or without full intention or volition" (2018: 223). She admits that her devotion to the *hijab* is a paradox since she does not consider it obligatory (2018: 223). She finds it troubling that Muslim men, even in prayer, "cannot keep their minds on Allah and away from their lust" (223). As her *hijab* mantra goes, "If you think that the difference between heaven and hell is 45 inches of material, boy will you be surprised" (219).

8.9 Chahla Chafiq

Chahla Chafiq (b. 1954), a secular Muslim and left-wing activist fled the Khomeini regime in 1982. After settling in France, she completed a doctoral degree in sociology, and authored many books on the veil, Islam, and gender. As she explains,

> There are various reasons why a woman may veil herself… This gesture trivializes a sexual sign and symbolizes a femininity that is submissive to men. Women's bodies are thus marked as objects of sexual lust. This goes hand in hand with the demonization of women's liberation, presented in Islamist propaganda as a source of moral depravity and family dislocation. The question is obviously different depending on whether you wear it by choice or by constraint. An Islamist woman is not found behind every veil. But the dialogue must not stop at the question of choice… It must continue by exploring the trajectory of the person concerned, the atmosphere in which she lives, and the social and political evolution of her environment.
>
> Some sociologists and intellectuals believe that free choice closes the subject… The choice of the veil is not equivalent to the choice of a lipstick. Women are forced, in the name of god, to have a sexist relationship with their own bodies. It becomes a place of sin and temptation. In the same movement, men appear to be carriers of

uncontrollable virility… This leads to establishing gender diversity as dangerous and demonizing sexual relations. What are the consequences in terms of gender equality and women's freedom? It is this question that must be answered.

The "chosen" veil, a very common phenomenon nowadays, is a trap. At the origins of Islam, when this religion did not yet exist as the source of laws, the veil did not exist. It arrived later, with *shari'ah* law and its vision of the patriarchal family where the man is the head and protects the woman (inferior in law, she is worth half a man) and the children. For this to happen, women have a duty to serve the family. The veil is proposed to them to embody the gendered division and hierarchization of roles. It symbolically creates a gendered wall, supposed to protect the boundaries of lawful and unlawful by separating the sexes… By marking women with this division, it sexualizes them. It marks their bodies as a place of temptation, disorder, sin, that disrupts the group's chastity.

Many young women who choose the veil say they do so in order not to be considered sexual objects, when it is precisely the sexual dimension of the female body that this choice exacerbates… In some cases, wearing the veil is a choice… What are the consequences of this choice for gender equality and women's freedom? … Why is this choice not offered to men? Some will say: "They have a beard." Yes, but it is still very different: the beard is a way to show off manhood, while the philosophy of the veil is to hide femininity so as not to awaken temptations. (2020)

8.10 Fawzia Zouari

Fawzia Zouari (b. 1955), the Tunisian writer and journalist, laments the fact that the Muslim world is moving backwards. As she sadly attests,

> We are … facing a regression of women's rights. We are faced with a paradoxical situation of women who are veiling themselves while our fight was to unveil ourselves… These centuries of tyranny against women… have shaped my personality and my future. When one has been raised like me by a mother whose neck, throat, leg curvature, or the slightest hair no one could ever see, or when one has had sisters like mine cloistered in the name of a law prohibiting their bodies, one can understand my reaction to the veil, in its suffered and imposed practice, even more in its claimed choice. I forgive my mother who has never been to school and to whom no one has explained the injustice of a tradition in which she wanted to confine us too. But I cannot excuse such behavior on the part of anyone who is educated and aware of the century's issues.
>
> I cannot defend a sign that, in our societies, has always relegated

> women behind walls.... I cannot accept that we voluntarily veil ourselves and pretend that we are not condemned to supporting roles. I cannot accept that we choose to be subjected. Just as I remain cautious before those who honor God to measure our faith by the length of our dresses and the number of locks escaping from our clothes. Would they matter more, these dresses and hair, than the love we carry in our hearts for Him? Would the veil be the only way to ensure our salvation in His eyes -- otherwise we would be worthless? All these questions, I already asked myself when I was a child. And here I am now half a century later asking them again. (2020)

8.11 Elham Man'ea

For Elham Man'ea (b. 1966), the Yemeni-Swiss scholar, the *hijab* is a political issue exploited by Iran, Saudi Arabia, and the Muslim Brotherhood (Lichter 369). She exposes, and systematically debunks, the arguments they use to convince women to wear the veil, as follows:

> The first argument is based on the assumption that the Arab man is a lecherous animal that cannot control its urges, and therefore, one must be on guard against it… This premise is unfair to the Arab man, whom we know as a brother, a father, a husband, and as a human being… He is capable of controlling his urges. This first argument also includes a humiliating premise about women, since it portrays the woman as nothing more than a sex tool -- not as a human being but as [a collection] of private parts.
>
> The second argument is based [on] the premise that there is a connection between wearing the veil and establishing a good society. On the contrary, the forced segregation [of the sexes] has led to homosexual relations… [and] has not prevented some girls from having [sexual] relations out of wedlock…
>
> The third argument rests on the premise that [Islam] has a firm position on the issue of the veil, while the fact is that there are many [different] religious texts on the subject. [When you read them] you will see that not only is there an abundance of texts, but that they also have numerous interpretations… As a matter of fact, the third argument, which claims that it is religion that imposes wearing the veil on women, is the weakest argument, since we never heard of it before the late 1970s, and we didn't see it implemented until the "orthodox" interpretation of Islam became the most prevalent interpretation in the Arab and Muslim world. (Lichter 370)

8.12 Razika Adnani

Razika Adnani, a Franco-Algerian philosopher and Islamologist, is a leading opponent of what she perceives to be "archaic dogmas." She is considered one of the foremost promoters of rational, progressive and reformist Islam in France. Like many scholars of Islam, she stresses that the veil is devoid of divine basis:

> The veil is neither a founding principle of Islam nor a principle of the practice of Islam. The founding principles of Islam are faith in the existence of a single God, the prophecy of Muhammad and the sacredness of the Qur'an. The principles of the practice of Islam are *shahada*, prayer, almsgiving, *hajj* (pilgrimage to Mecca), and fasting… According to Muslim theology, wearing the veil is in no way proof of a person's belonging to Islam and a person can have faith and put it into practice without having to wear the veil. The proof is that many women claiming their Islamicity do not wear the veil. The concealment of the hair of the woman representing the main part of the veil is indeed not mentioned in any Qur'anic verse. (2019)

As Adnani explains, the veil is not simply a religious symbol: "If the veil continues to be imposed today, it is because many men see in it the last emblem of their domination over women, and many women are unable to escape from an inferior image of themselves buried in their being for centuries" (2019). She believes that "the State is the primary guarantor of gender equality; it bears the responsibility of protecting women from any practice aimed at keeping them in a position of inferiority" (2019). Not only is she opposed to radical Islamists, but she is also opposed to Islamic feminists. In her estimation,

> "Islamic feminists" have done much harm to women's rights struggles, especially since the 1970s. By claiming Islam as the source of legitimacy for their struggle and as the framework for its scope, they claim that they only demand what is validated by Islam. However, they have never been able to prove to conservatives that the inequalities that exist in the Koran are not inequalities, as they claim. This explains why Muslim women who call themselves feminists today accept the legal inequalities that discriminate against them…
>
> The veil is a means with which to measure the success of Islamists and fundamentalists, a "veilometer" to assess the reinforcement of the religion as the ancients thought and practiced it, including in the West. Islamic feminists have played an important role in this phenomenon of the return of the veil. They have encouraged many female academics and managers to wear it as a sign of emancipation: to be feminist, but in accordance with the recommendations of the Koran. But the veil is fundamentally discriminatory. It discriminates against women in relation to men and against non-veiled women in relation to veiled women. But it must be emphasized that many women also wear the veil in an act of religious exhibitionism. (2022)

For Adnani, "the morality of a person is not measured by the length of her skirt but by her behavior and her respect for the rules of morality" (2022). As she recalls, human beings appeared nude in the world (2022). They lived on earth a long time before they fabricated clothing (2022). In warm regions, like Africa, she reminds readers, women went around topless in public until very recently, and it did not make them less chaste or virtuous (2022). "The veil," insists Adnani, "is a form of discrimination that is imposing itself in the public sphere" (2022).

Unlike other scholars who seek to distinguish Islam from Islamism, she views them as one and the same (2022). While it pleases Muslims when people claim that "Islam is a religion of peace and love," and that the problems are only caused by a minority of deviant fanatics, such statements do not reflect reality and evade the real issues (2022). For Adnani, it is not enough to reinterpret the texts (2022). Some must be treated as obsolete and abrogated (2022). This approach was done in the past; hence, what prevents Muslims from using it today? (2022) It is not a matter of removing verses from the Qur'an but declaring they are no longer applicable (2022). Not only must the Qur'an be reinterpreted, but all the theories and concepts that relate to it must be reformed (2022). For such a metamorphosis to occur, however, Muslims must free their minds from fundamentalism and embrace free and rational thought (2022). Most of them, however, refuse to recognize that Islam itself is the problem, namely, the ways it has been interpreted (2022). Instead of thinking freely, most Muslims, even modernists, insist upon placing limits upon it (2022).

8.13 Ibtissame Betty Lachgar

For Ibtissame "Betty" Lachgar (b. 1975), a Moroccan clinical psychologist and secular feminist activist, veiling is the product of a fundamentalist interpretation of Islam. More than a garment, she views the veil as a sexist and political symbol (2020). As a clothing injunction, it is diametrically opposed to the principles of feminism (2020). In her view, "Women's veiling is not a freedom or a choice; in a macho culture, it fully contributes to their invisibility" (2020). Although some Muslim women claim Islam can be feminized, Lachgar feels that "Neither reform nor reinterpretation of this religion will lead to women's liberation" (2020). For her, "feminism based on Islam is a sham: no more and no less" (2020). As an avowed atheist, however, her views will fall on deaf ears among many believers.

8.14 Leila Lesbet

Leila Lesbet is an Algerian educator who fled the Islamist insurgency that terrorized her country between 1991-2002. After arriving in Canada, she became a member of the *Fédération des femmes du Québec* (FFQ) [Federation of Women of Quebec]. She was saddened to see the organization openly supports the veiling of women. Not only was she flabbergasted to see that the fundamentalist Islam that she had fled was being preached in mosques in

Quebec, but that so-called secular feminists were supporting its sexist doctrines regarding women. As she expresses, "It is an Islam I don't know, even though I grew up with very religious, very conservative parents" (2020). She views the veil as a message of submission and a political symbol. "The veil," she explains, "is not a matter of modesty and prudishness, but a means of controlling women's bodies" (2020). "In Muslim countries," she recalls, "women are raped because they refuse to wear it" (2020). "This veil and *burqa* that we are defending here," she reminds secularists and feminists, "are stained with the blood of all the teenage girls and women who wanted to say no" (2020). As such, she is a staunch defender of secularism in Quebec and serves as the president of *Pour les droits des femmes du Québec* [For the Rights of Women in Quebec].

8.15 Nadia El-Mabrouk

Nadia El-Mabrouk, a Quebecker of Tunisian origin, a university professor, and member of the *Association Québécoise des Nord-Africains pour la Laïcité* [Quebecker Association of North Africans for Secularism] and *Pour les Droits des Femmes du Québec* [For the Rights of Women in Quebec], strongly opposes the so-called Islamic veil. As she argues,

> The Islamic veil is not just a garment, it conditions children to conform to religious dogmas that are imposed on them. It sends the shocking idea that the little girl's body would be an object of seduction that would have to be hidden from the eyes of boys, while they are not under any constraint. It stigmatizes Muslim girls in the schoolyard and is a barrier to their interaction with other children. It hinders their movements and prevents them from participating fully in physical activities, not to mention the discomfort it causes in often overheated classrooms. How can free choice be advocated for such young children?
>
> The practice of veiling little girls is neither a Koranic prescription nor the legacy of ancestral traditions that should be preserved. In most Arab countries, it has emerged recently with the rise of Islamic fundamentalism. Islamic scholars, including Ghaleb and Soheib Bencheikh, do not hesitate to call it abuse of young girls. Tunisia, a country whose religion is Islam, has even banned the veil in elementary schools in 2015 on the grounds that it goes against children's rights. A poll conducted at the time indicated that 75% of Tunisians were in favor of the ban. (2020)

8.16 Sérénade Chafik

Sérénade Chafik (b. 1965), a French-Egyptian writer, social worker, and secular feminist activist, was saved by her father from female genital mutilation. She suffered through two marriages in Egypt, fled to France, and went on a twenty-nine-day hunger strike to protest her daughter's imminent excision. It took ten years of toil and legal struggle to finally reunite with her daughter, Leïla. She denounces the *hijab* in the following terms,

> The veil is an essential issue for Islamists. It is no coincidence that the first measure of the Islamic State was to force women to wear it. The veil has always been used as an instrument for society's appropriation of women's bodies. These bodies become a collective property. The veil is … the most visible propaganda tool to affirm… Islamization... The veil limits women's movement, the space they can occupy, and the vision they can have of themselves. We refuse to see that the veil has a function, that of controlling girls and women. It induces in education that they are only sexual objects, that they are guilty temptresses, that their body represents sin and that therefore it must be hidden. The girl is no longer a child. She is the object of male desire. (2020)

8.17 Chahdortt Djavann

Chahdortt Djavann was born in Iran in 1967. She was raised by her father on love of books and hatred of mullahs. In June 1980, at the age of thirteen, she was arrested and imprisoned for protesting against the Khomeini regime. Brutally beaten, two of her ribs were broken. She fled Iran in 1991 and settled in France in 1993 where she taught herself French and went to university. She has published numerous books denouncing Islamism and the veil. She asserts that "the veil is a form of a physical and psycho-sexual violence inflicted on girls" (2020). She speaks out of experience, "I wore the veil for ten years. It was the veil or death. I know what I'm talking about" (2020). Her outrage is heartfelt,

> Why do we hide girls, only girls, teenagers of sixteen, fourteen, twelve, ten, nine, seven years old? Why are we hiding their bodies, their hair? What does it really mean to veil girls? What are we trying to instill in them? Because initially they didn't choose to be veiled. They were veiled. And how do you live in a veiled teenage body? After all, why don't we hide Muslim boys? Can't their body, their hair make girls desire them? But girls are not made to have desire, in Islam, only to be the object of men's desire. Don't we hide what we're ashamed of?...
>
> Among Muslims, from birth, a girl is a disgrace to hide since she is not a male child. She is … insufficient, powerless, and inferior. Any attempt at sexual intercourse by a man before marriage is her fault. She is the potential object of rape, sin, incest, and even theft since men can steal her modesty with a simple look… She represents guilt, since she creates desire … in a man. A girl is a permanent threat to Islamic dogmas and morals.
>
> She is the potential object of the crime, having her throat slit by the

father or the brother to wash away the stained honor. Because Muslim men's honor is washed with girls' blood! A girl is considered a shame and a danger... She may violate the men's honor. I would like to know why a man would feel dishonored if the woman violates the rules of modesty. Why is the honor of Muslim men inscribed on the bodies of Muslim women? Let them assume their honor on their own!...

When you veil a girl, you ... teach her that if any part of her skin and hair protrudes from this fabric, any attempt at rape is her responsibility. And we know that this is happening in some countries. Saying "the veil is my choice"' doesn't say what the veil is. Islamists trapped everyone. Everyone is relaying the Islamists' discourse. I am deeply shocked that fashion brands like Marks and Spencer offer integral swimsuits that hide the whole body.

In Muslim societies, women are invisible, buried, because they cannot be exterminated. We need them to procreate, to satisfy men's sexual needs... Since we cannot exterminate them, we bury them in the dark. In the most barbaric systems, women are veiled. Why do we put up with it here? Because they are women and Muslim. In the name of cultural difference? Why not accept stoning and excision in this case? In all Muslim countries, there are marriages of underage girls with aging men. It is a cultural difference, is it not? But here it is considered a crime: pedophilia. What do these intellectuals and Islamologists think about it?

I decided to write when I saw 12-year-old girls starting to wear the veil and when I heard some intellectuals say that sending veiled students out of school would only make their situation worse. These ... people did not think that tolerating veiled girls in school would only increase the pressure on Muslim teenage girls. Some veil advocates explain that this is a way for girls ... to protect themselves from boys.

This is unacceptable. It is tantamount to bowing to violence... It is in countries where women are veiled that there is the most prostitution and pedophilia! I am asking for ... a ban on veil-wearing for minors... In Islam, a veiled girl is considered nubile... She is a girl who is placed on the marriage market and ... the sex market. When you see 9-year-old girls wearing the veil, you're practically in pedophilia! There are laws in France to protect minors from all forms of sexual abuse... The veil is a physical and psycho-sexual violence inflicted on girls. It is equivalent to disposing of their bodies, to defining the teenager as a sexual object intended to satisfy men's desires. This is barbarism!

The veil defines women psychologically, socially, sexually, and legally as sub-men. The veil is the yellow star of the female condition. It marks female bodies as humiliated, guilty, sources of worry, anguish, threatening, dirty, impure, sources of discomfort and sin, these unhealthy objects, coveted, desired and forbidden, hidden and exposed, locked up, abused, circulated around men, like shadows. If… young Jews started wearing the yellow star, claiming "it is my freedom;" if young blacks decided to wear chains around their necks and feet, saying "it is my freedom," wouldn't society react? When you try to nuance it by using the words "headscarf" or "headband," I reply: "Between the *burka* and the colored headscarf, the meaning is the same." Talking about headscarves, about headbands, is just a semantic cowardice; it is a miserable rhetorical trick.

Boys, girls, women, and men can wear a cross or Fatima's hand around their neck, referring to religious figures and the Christian or Muslim faith. It is an ornament, while the veil is reserved for women. On the religious, historical, anthropological, social, and legal level, it has meanings, functions and scope that structure the Islamic society. The veil concretizes and materializes the sexual apartheid and the inferiority of women's rights… It is the symbol of … Islamic ideology, the Islamist banner, and the flag of the *ummah*.

Veiling teenage girls and women was an essential prerequisite for initiating the massive re-Islamization of youth from Muslim immigrant backgrounds, preventing them from being fully integrated by the unholy West… To finally create a Muslim community that would be anti-Western. The method of re-Islamization in the West is identical to the one used in Muslim countries, such as Iran, Algeria, Morocco, Tunisia… because it operates, above all, on Muslim youth. Wearing the headscarf here is a support for the Islamist dictatorships that impose the *burka* there. The veil is the very emblem of Islamist dogma. Islam can quite live without it, but there is no Islamist country without the veil.

8.18 Djemila Benhabib

Born in Ukraine to an Algerian father and a Greek Cypriot mother, Djemila Benhabib (b. 1972) grew up in Algeria. Her family was forced to flee the country after the *Front Islamique du Dhihad Armé* [the Islamic Front for Armed Jihad] sentenced them to death. After living in France as a refugee, she finally settled in Quebec, where her struggle against radical Islam and the veiling of young girls resulted in harassment and intimidation by Islamists in Canada. The author of numerous works, she is known for her staunch secularism and vehement opposition to Islamic fundamentalism. In her words,

> The veil is an obsessive relationship to the body, to the flesh, to sex. The veil is the control of women's sexuality. Let us not be naive enough to believe that the *hijab* would be acceptable, even progressive, while the *burqa* would be retrograde and unacceptable. The difference between the two is only due to the size of the fabric. The meaning remains the same: the archaic manifestation of women's oppression and

> submission. These women claim that they veil themselves so as not to attract the attention of men and awaken their impulses. This conception, which considers women as "unfulfilled temptresses" and men as "perpetual predators," is totally infantile and primary.
>
> I am not ashamed to have been born a woman. I don't have to apologize for that. I don't have to hide from it. Islamists blame women for their sexual desires, miseries, and sexual frustrations. They're sex maniacs. Women's hatred and submission crystallize their ideology. There can be no free and emancipated women -- or men for that matter -- in an Islamic state. Engels was right to say that "the degree of women's emancipation is the measure of the degree of general emancipation." (2020)

Benhabib is particularly incensed and infuriated by "*Hijab* Day." She condemns those who celebrate it in the following terms:

> This veil you are promoting is not universally valid. You exclude yourself and your close ones from it. Deep down, you get the light, and I get the prison. Strange conception. There is racism right there… The veil? Never! Not here, not there, not anywhere else… You make me a "whore." You designate me as a sexual prey. You're calling for my rape. If you have ever walked the streets of Cairo, Casablanca, or Algiers, you must have noticed that at the end of the promenade there is an open-air prison for women. Their bodies are scrutinized, hated, fantasized, scalpel-cut, when they are not soiled by tough hands ready in all lowliness to grab a piece of flesh. With or without veil, from cradle to grave, we are but a mass of desolation. How could it be otherwise when "females" are seen as fortresses to be assaulted, flesh balls to be rubbed against on the subway and buses, battlefields where you unwind after a football game, mats on which you wipe your feet without even thinking about it? If this veil were just another piece of clothing, it would not be so forcefully and rigorously imposed on Iranian and Saudi women, to name but two examples. When it is worn, the woman's body becomes the possession of the man, the imam, the tyrant, and Allah, all sharing the same detestation of women. "Submit, obey, accept your sub-humanity!" (2020)

8.19 Malika Boussouf

Malika Boussouf, an Algerian psychologist, and journalist was the target of a death *fatwa* issued by the *Groupe Armée Islamique* [Armed Islamic Group] which forced her to live in hiding while being tracked by terrorists. The author of *Musulmanes et laïques en révolte* (2014) [*Muslim and Secular Women in Revolt*], Malika Boussouf is an outspoken opponent of Islamic fundamentalists, their banner, the veil, and their war on women (2020).

> I don't know what the term "Islamic veil" means! The other two monotheistic religions are not to be outdone in this respect. All fanaticisms strongly recommend the confinement of women. All demand from them a total and absolute submission. What is a veil, but the physical illustration of this enslavement ordered by all the fundamentalists on earth? … The wearing of the *hijab* is growing everywhere. What started in the 1990s is becoming generalized social behavior. Women, to put an end to the injunctions and reproaches from men, their families, and the group, wear the veil. At the same time, according to a Ministry of Health survey, 59% of women believe that a husband has the right to beat up his wife. Patriarchy… still has a bright future ahead of it. (2020)

When she expresses her anger regarding the status of women, she clarifies that,

> There is nothing specific to Islam, all monotheistic religions are fundamentalists, they oppress men but especially women because every time we want, in a society, to control men, we go through their women, and that suits them well. Women are conditioned to be beaten. Religion was made by men and for men, to allow them to maintain themselves as rulers and keep power. (2020)

8.20 Leïla Babès

Leïla Babès is an Algerian-born French sociologist of religion and specialist in contemporary Islam. She is the author of several books dealing with Islam and gender, among other topics, including *Le voile démystifié* [*The Veil Unveiled*] (2004). Her view on the veil is thoughtful and insightful. As she explains,

> The outcry in the Muslim world over the French law banning religious symbols in public schools has revealed two facts that are totally new in Islamic history. Firstly, the almost hysterical reactions that have been expressed here and there about the veil, which has become a worldwide phenomenon, the emblematic sign of a community, clearly show a fracture in the Muslim consciousness. Never before, neither in the caliphate period nor even since the emergence of the first Islamic ideologues at the beginning of the twentieth century-- who made the veil a fundamental precept by misrepresenting it as the *hijab*, which the Koran reserves exclusively for the Prophet's wives -- had the woman's body been the subject of a debate involving the fate of the entire community. It is as if the social body was merging with the female body. Secondly, what is striking is the recurrence in unison just about everywhere of a discourse that has been circulating in Islamic circles for some years now, according to which the veil is a religious belief and practice. This is a gigantic mystification whose mechanisms are easy to dismantle.

But why so much noise for this piece of fabric? Why don't these Muslims protest to get beautiful mosques instead of those obscure prayer rooms that give such a miserable image of their religion? After all, prayer is one of Islam's cultural foundations along with profession of faith, *zakat*, fasting and pilgrimage. The veil is neither one of the five pillars of observance nor is it an element of Muslim dogma ... along with belief in God, angels, books, prophets, and Judgment Day. There is absolutely no difference in this area of faith, worship, spirituality, and status of the believer between men and women. The Koran and the prophetic tradition are clear on this. If... the veil was a religious obligation... then what are men waiting for to veil themselves? ...

This trickery is the work of men, and it affects the female body. The veil has always been, since its appearance nearly two millennia ago, a means of subjecting women to men's guardianship. This rule of "branding"' women of the clan, wives, virgins, high-ranking women, accompanied by a taboo on hair, will be found almost everywhere in the Mediterranean region. Islamists who believe that the Koran invented the veil are mistaken. The veil has nothing religious about it, it is not even the work of Jewish or Christian believers, it is a custom established by pagan peoples, *jahiliyyah* men, in that Age of Ignorance of "true religion." The Koran does not "prescribe" the veil. It only recommends that women wear it in a decent manner -- which is not described anywhere -- and that they cover their necklines. The ethical principles that the Koran advocates are modesty and a reserved attitude towards attraction between the sexes, principles that apply to both women and men. Everything else is phantasmagoria. Therefore, there is nothing religious about the veil. It has to do with men having an obsessive relationship with the female body...

Women are the main object of such fixation when defending a liberticidal conception. The veil is such an essential symbol for the Islamist order that it makes it possible to mark a strict differentiation of the sexes, assigning women to a particular place. By accentuating the ban on women's bodies, it makes them incapable of discovering themselves, of making themselves visible, of taking over the public space, of gaining access to power; in short: of being equal to men. But it is on another level that the deep springs of this pathos are at play: the sexual level... It is on this terrain that obsession has been unfolding for the past two thousand years. The Koran does not give any other argument in the three verses relating to the "veil," systematically calling men and their sexual motivations into question. By legislating on the veil, the divine text has tried to regulate the libidinal instincts of men, always ready to covet women indiscriminately, starting with the Prophet's own wives. These men were neither Jews, nor Christians, nor polytheists, they were Muslims.

What can we conclude from all this? That fourteen centuries after the foundation of Islam, Muslims, who today wave the veil as the community's banner, have forgotten or pretend to forget the exercise of *jihad*, which the Prophet himself called the greater *jihad* to distinguish it from armed combat; that personal effort of ethical and spiritual perfection designed to control one's own instincts.

By making women's bodies the object of all lust, and the veil a means of ensuring their tranquility, men allow themselves not to make this effort… It is women who pay the price for this childish attitude that allows men to take refuge in the comfort of non-responsibility. Continuing to assert that the veil is an eternal and unspecified prescription instead of accomplishing [the greater] *jihad* is to recognize that Muslim men are uneducated men, unable to control their animal instincts. Is this not acknowledging Islam's failure as a religion of responsibility? How do we explain this divide? How did we get to the point where Islam became the religion of the veil?

After the eradication by the proponents of an exclusively legal conception of Islam of what has made this great civilization great, what is left of encyclopedic knowledge and humanism, philosophy, theology, and mysticism? Preachers who are disciples of a handful of reactionary "theologians," responsible for the civilizational and intellectual impoverishment of a religion that has become a prisoner of a paranoid reading that only holds on to prohibitions and obligations. The veil is truly the epitome of the state of intellectual, cultural, and spiritual decay in which contemporary Islamic thought finds itself.

8.21 Zineb El Rhazoui

Zineb El Rhazoui (b. 1982) is Moroccan-born French journalist with a long history of activism in secular and feminist movements, including, *Ni Putes Ni Soumises* [Neither Sluts Nor Submissive Women]. Her experience with the veil is telling:

> I went to school in Morocco where the teaching of religion was compulsory, but women did not wear the veil, or at least not the one we know today. This one appeared in the 1980s with some young women from university circles in major cities close to emerging Islamist organizations… I was able to observe closely this country's evolution, which is not the worst in its kind, but the fact is that radicalization was gradually increasing. At the time, it was possible to wear a skirt and use public transport, today only women who own a car can dress relatively as they wish.
>
> Some feminists have long since capitulated in this war being waged by Islamists. Thus, in order not to be called Islamophobes, they accept male guardianship over Muslim women, particularly in the form

of the veil. However, this veil in all its forms is far from being a banal fabric synonymous with freedom of expression, the right to dress as one pleases, a symbol of modesty, or spirituality. It is indeed a sexist militant instrument to advance Islamic fascism by domesticating women.

Forcing a woman to wear a garment she did not choose is violence, but rather than punishing the perpetrator, these feminists propose to live with it. This amounts to being silent in front of a woman who has a black eye for fear that she will withdraw into herself and give up all social life.

Accepting the veil and its most rigid variations in the name of freedom to dress as one wishes is the very negation of feminism. How can one accept an outfit, enacted by "heaven," and mandatory in many countries, if the offenders are physically punished in the public place.

What would these pro-veil feminists say to these Saudi women that the Moutawa agents, the "Committee for the Promotion of Virtue and the Prevention of Vice" quibble in the street or shopping malls, with sticks, like cattle that do not walk straight, for a strand of hair that protrudes? That their *niqab* is just a piece of fabric worn in the name of freedom to dress as you wish?

In France, we see how the notion of individual freedom is reclaimed to defend the veil wearers. The veil is by definition the denial of women's freedom, but it does not matter to Islamists: they only praise the "freedom" to be Islamist when in reality it is a consent. In countries where the veil is a mandatory uniform under penalty of corporal punishment, the same Islamists do not defend the individual's freedom to dress as one wishes.

Antiracism is also diverted by them and emptied of all nobility: they will never denounce the Islamic precepts that prohibit interreligious unions as being racist. Islamists who cry out against racism make it meaningless, because for them, it is not a struggle for universalism, to erase the differences between human beings, but rather a struggle to impose their own difference as universal. Islamists denounce the racism of others because they want to have a monopoly on racism.

There is also a part of the feminist movement that accepts the veil as a "freedom" while it serves as a visual marking technique, not for those who wear it, as they claim in France, but for those who do not wear it in countries where it is legally or socially obligatory. Not to wear the veil in a context where it proliferates is to be immediately identified as not adhering to the Islamist ideology. These feminists have accepted another intellectual imposture: Islamic feminism. Since when does Islam have anything to teach us about women's liberation?

I can imagine that those who now wear the veil, full or partial,

> were not forced *manu militari* to do so. If this had been the case, there would have been complaints, because in France, laws allow people to defend themselves. On the other hand, this is far from being a free choice. Algerian feminist Wassyla Tamzali saw hundreds of thousands of women in Algeria during the Black Decade make this "free choice" all at once. It is strange, is it not? …
>
> Wassyla Tamzali explains that the veil is not a choice, but a consent. For me, it will become a piece of clothing like any other on the day that Saudi women can wear a veil on Monday, jeans on Tuesday, and a bikini on Wednesday. On that day, I will say "OK." But as long as there are places where women are covered from head to toe and are whipped by religious police if they don't, don't talk to me about choices.
>
> Those who talk about choice in France are in reality either women who have consented to wear the veil, or Islamic ideology activists who use the dialectical tools of human rights and individual freedoms to impose the denial of human rights and freedom. This is a uniform in Saudi Arabia and other countries.
>
> As a feminist, I can only be fiercely opposed to the veil, whether integral or a simple scarf, because its function remains the same: to cover the woman, to make her ugly to reduce unexpected erections. It is an insult both to the woman, perceived as a sexual object to be covered, and to the man, seen as a rutting primate who cannot help but rape as soon as he sees a tuft of hair. But beware, this aversion to the veil does not mean that I deny human dignity to all women wearing it. Because behind the veil, there is a human being, who has rights. But these women have rights as individuals and citizens, not as ninjas covered from head to toe.

A passionate critic of Islam, she served as the religion expert for *Charlie Hebdo*. Although she survived the 2015 massacre, she has been the subject of death edicts from Daesh and other Islamists. The most protected woman in France, she is forced to live under twenty-four-hour police protection. Considering the hatred, intolerance, and violence that she has faced, she snaps at those who accuse her of disrespecting Islam. As she asks:

> Why the hell should I respect Islam? Does it respect me? The day Islam shows the slightest bit of consideration to women, first of all, and secondly toward free-thinkers, I promise you I will rethink my positions. (2020)

8.22 Yağmur Uygarkızı

Political scientist Yağmur Uygarkızı (b. 1996) is a radical feminist of Turkish origin who views the veil as misogynistic. In her words,

> It is the manifestation of a desire not to see women in the public -- male -- space. The veil aims to erase women. If you dare to leave your home, at least have the decency to cover your dreadful and so arousing female body. Hide the fact that you are a woman. The positive -- superior -- man can move around freely, you negative -- inferior -- woman must be contained. The veil also acts as a leash. The woman cannot exist independently of a master. She has to be owned by a male figure to be honorable, whether this figure is a god or a parent. And the woman can only exist to their eyes of her legitimate proprietor. Vision concretizes existence. If one cannot see women, then one is one step closer to eliminating us. The veil is the punishment for the fault of being born female...
>
> The veil is the epitome of the growing acceptance of sexist practices under the guise of foreign mystique. Among those practices, there is: the refusal of touching women, female genital mutilation, domestic violence, virginity tests, etc. The type of list one wishes was exhaustive. It is not by defending sexism that you bring in more cultural diversity. The veil subordinates women to men, setting a glaring divide between the two. It is not about freedom; it implies many constraints. Self-effacement is not a right... It took less than fifteen years for Atatürk's secular Turkey to be veiled up. But this is not just Turkey. This is Iran, Algeria, Tunisia, Egypt, and more. Women have already experienced these things. The veil is only the tip of a continental iceberg of misogynist violence. It is the beginning of the end. (2020)

"Since veiling was prior to Islam, and has been recuperated by different religions," she reasons "there must be something intrinsic to veiling that renders it appealing to patriarchal institutions" (2021). "The veil," she notes, "is not any type of clothing" (2021):

> Within a wardrobe, it falls under the category of headwear. Someone's head is one of the first things we look at to communicate and it is also metaphoric, often seen as embodying intellect. As such, headwear conveys meaning and is highly codified: suffice to think of crowns or turbans to see how. Headwear can be functional, like beanies in winter, but the veil is certainly not since the thermometer has little effect on it. Moreover, a headscarf goes beyond a simple object placed on a head: it entirely covers the hair of women, another deeply symbolic body part... Sometimes they even cover the face. Lorella Zanardi, talking of plastic surgery, explains that most facial muscles solely serve the purpose of communication by conveying emotions: if that part is erased for one sex only, the symbolism is at its pinnacle.

"Claiming veiling is feminist," warns Uygarkızı, "demonstrates a deep reductionism of feminist principles" (2021). As she elucidates,

> Veiling is a sex-based practice, therefore inevitably sexual… the veil requires external gaze to exist… By hiding, the veil displays. Veiling must necessarily be practiced in a social setting, visible to others to make sense… "Look at me," says the veil… The veil is a portable device of communication between men through women. The woman is effaced under the veil as the veil becomes ostentatious…
>
> The contemporary discourse on veiling pretends that a millennia-old archaic practice is a previously unheard-of revolutionary product that will shield you from male oppression. What it denotes… is a vision of feminism as a safe haven from oppression, not a challenge to it, and of sexualization as women's personal responsibility, not men's… Veiling has posed no tangible threat to consumer culture and femininity. That is because veiling is a practice reserved to women reinforcing stereotypes about how a woman should look and dress like. Less evident is the fact that veiling and modesty do not necessarily go hand in hand… Veiling is a conspicuous sexualizing practice: it must be visible and convey information about the sex and sexuality of women to men. In that sense, the relational and ambivalent nature of veiling is confirmed.

For Uygarkızı, "veiling… is an intrinsically harmful practice" that reduces women to objects (2021). A whole person, she explains, consists of body and mind (2021). When a woman is parceled into legs, breasts, and buttocks, she becomes an object. With veiling, she explains, an external object, a piece of clothing, "becomes so embedded in the construction of the personal self that the woman cannot envision herself without it" (2021). In the process, a new whole is created, in which the object defines the woman and the *hijabi* is born (2021). In fact, they regularly describes themselves, not as women, but as *hijabis* and *niqabis*. As she explains,

> In this process of objectification, the veil swaps places with the woman to her detriment: the veil gains its own subjectivity… As the veil becomes part of a woman, the two engage in a frenetic diabolic dance, where the two are confused. The veil leads the dance…. In this choreography, the veil has engulfed the woman: she can no longer exist independent of it; unveiling would equate to mutilating oneself… What this means is that a patriarchal practice is incorporated into women: just like the veiled woman cannot have an independent existence from the veil. She becomes dependent on men for her self-definition. (2021)

8.23 Fatemeh Sadegui

The daughter of Sadeq Khalkhali (1926-2003), the notorious "hanging judge" who summarily sentenced thousands of Iranians to death, Fatemeh Sadeghi (b. 1971) is a political scientist who specializes in gender studies. Like many hardliners, Khalkhali became a reformist toward the end of his life, and supported the election of President Mohammad Khatami (b. 1943) in 1997. In 2008, Sadegui authored an essay titled "Why We Say No to Forced *Hijab*," which has been widely circulated. The poignant piece paints a traumatic portrait of compulsory *hijab*. In her words,

> Let me tell you about how my painful experience with the *hijab* started. I remember the day when I had to wear a headscarf for the first time in front of the boys in our family who were my playmates and often competitors. I felt humiliated. I felt paralyzed and crushed in their eyes. I could especially read the following message in the eyes of one of them: "See how you were vanquished?" The story was not just about covering my body. It was much more. On many occasions when I was busy playing or preoccupied with myself, I heard chiding voices from various corners: "Sit properly. Straighten your outfit. All your body parts are uncovered. Pull you scarf forward, Your veil is too far back on your head, Your neck is showing, Your hair is showing," etc. I never knew the meaning behind these reprimands and even why I was being addressed in such a manner.
>
> The personal experiences and humiliation which the *hijab* has caused me and many others, cannot be found in any of the precious and often reprinted books of the clergy in Qum... Let me tell you that after those childhood experiences, the most humiliating sentence about the *hijab* which I have heard, has been the following: "For a woman, the *hijab* is like a pearl which covers a jewel." I could tolerate more respectable sentences such as "Sister, your *hijab* is a more powerful weapon than my blood." But I could never tolerate the former sentence.
>
> The former sentence contains an insult which can be understood by any human being. Without having met the creators of that sentence, I can tell that they were experts in the psychology of personality disorders. Can you guess why? This sentence combines praise and humiliation. A woman is praised but only as a being who must be beautiful. Anyway, you know this better than I do. In the latter sentence however, I sense a type of respect. I like its combativeness along with the respect that it has for my femininity, even though it does not understand me and dismisses me as a woman.
>
> As I was growing up, I realized that this story has gained more complex dimensions. Soon I understood that there is a difference between the headscarf and the veil. If the headscarf was to sexually control me --although very unsuccessfully -- or to pull me out of the realm of childhood and force me to become a woman, the veil was something else. I could see that my mother and many other women around me, used the veil in a variety of ways. They did not wear the same veil at all places and they did not cover themselves as tightly in all places. Especially when a grand clergyman was to visit our house or when we were to visit a grand clergyman, they would hold their veils

more tightly. Naturally under these circumstances, I was told, "Watch your *hijab*," meaning, hold it more tightly. Were these men considered more representative of the outsider category than other men? I think so. The higher the class and rank [of a man], the more the [woman's] face was to be covered. The *hijab* had an inextricable relationship with power.

The veil was not just a cover. It allowed for thousands of ways of establishing distance, symbolic gestures, blending in, differentiating oneself, and giving or gaining benefits. I too had to learn how to use the veil in the aristocratic hierarchy of power of the clergy. I had to learn how to use it as an instrument of power and impose it on others. I had to learn how to use the cues to become a prominent person among other prominent people, to become recognized, to become seen, to gain benefits. I proved not talented at this task.

Wearing the headscarf or the overcoat was not enough. Thus, the first time I surreptitiously tried wearing an overcoat and a headscarf, I felt naked. Now I know that more than any feeling of physical nakedness, what made me distressed and confused was the loss of the consequences [of wearing the veil], all the symbols, the benefits and distinction and prominence, the aristocracy. Nevertheless, wearing the overcoat and the headscarf had an adventurous and awesome benefit despite the fear and the dangers. Along with many other consequences, losing the social and political benefits that accompanied the *hijab* and the veil forced me to step in a different direction. By wearing the overcoat and headscarf I became empty and lost my identity. Now I needed to build a new identity.

When I asked a very famous clergyman whether the *hijab* was based on Sharia law, he said something along the lines of the following: "There is no such *hijab* in *shari'ah* law. The question concerns the civil code." Another who was a famous clergyman of his time and taught at the *hawzah* and at a university, revealed that in Sharia law, the *hijab* does not even mean covering one's head. He surprised me by inviting me to reconsider my own manner of covering my body. Nevertheless, neither of these clergymen ever openly expressed his viewpoint in public. Similarly many others do not. We know that the few who have had the courage to express their views have been defrocked and punished in other ways…

The works of Mottahari and his likes cannot answer the above simple questions, even if they are published thousands more times thanks to the large budgets of the Ministry of Culture and the Organization of Islamic Propaganda. Mottahari himself was well aware of the fact that the viewpoint of the reactionary clergy can no longer answer the questions of the new generation. That is why he named his book, *The Question of the Hijab* and tried to adopt a so-called scientific

> attitude toward this momentous subject.
>
> Everyone knows well that there is only one solution to the question of the *hijab*: Covering oneself should be left to women's individual choice. If the institution of the family, society and Islamic government depends on the *hijab*, then the problem is to be found in that institution, the foundation of that family, that society and that government, all of which require bold but necessary revision... This will not happen, at least not in the near future... The attitude of the Islamic regime or at least important parts of it are more confrontational toward women than ever. Such a confrontational attitude toward women is unprecedented among incumbent administrations since the beginning of the revolution. One has to ask what is causing this brutality of which the attitude toward the *hijab* is only one of many dimensions...
>
> As women we have been critiquing and will critique the varieties of the compulsory *hijab* for years. We have done so in implicit and explicit ways, with irony, protest, argumentation, civil resistance and in many other forms. Today, given the confrontational attitude of the Islamic regime, it seems that we need to speak about this issue again. We have to say "no" to it. We have to start a new discourse. They cannot put an end to this matter simply and with an order from this or that commander and the arrests of many women on the streets and private companies, and the firing of women office workers. I believe that a major confrontation is on the way. This is a confrontation that the perpetrators of the "social safety plans" and "the elevation of public decency" have initiated...

Shortly after its publication, Sadegui was suspended from her teaching post at Azad University of Karaj. She has remained undeterred. A staunch supporter of secularism, she continues to be a vocal opponent of the obligatory *hijab*. As she explains,

> Soon after her death, Mahsa [Amini] became a symbol of full-scale humiliation in today's Iran. First, she was a woman; being a woman in Iran means being subject to humiliation and discrimination. Second, she was arrested because of her *hijab*, which is one of the most visible manifestations of the oppression of women. Third, she was brutally tortured and murdered by the police while in custody; her death confirms the Iranian police's brutality. Fourth, she was a citizen of one of the most deprived and repressed Iranian provinces, namely Kurdistan. And finally, after her death, the repression apparatus turned to fabricating scenarios and spreading lies to justify her death. The protests have focused on two main issues: mandatory *hijab* and police brutality. The first is the demand for freedom, the second is the demand for dignity. Both of these have been absent from political life in Iran, yet they have a clear and prominent presence in almost all slogans of

> this movement, especially the slogan "Woman, life, freedom." (Attalah)

Speaking of Iran's theocrats, Fatemeh Sadegui summarized the situation very well,

> The main problem is in the government's approach to society. It has tied its identity to domination and force. The discourse of Iranian officials is full of contempt. They have a commanding tone and words full of contempt for others. Even when they want to talk normally, their tongues only turn to sarcasm, hatred and misdirection. This command-and-control discourse has a strong root in jurisprudence. Generally, jurists' job is to command and they don't have the patience to oppose and criticize. They do not understand the simple fact that with this ruling discourse, they cannot control the new generation, which the jurists and authorities neither know nor understand.

According to all indications, many of the Islamist ideologues in power, and their infinitesimally small legion of cult-like supporters, cannot be reformed. They have long lost the support of the street. As Fatemeh Sadegui has noted, a social revolution has taken place in Iran and it is one that rejects the violent and oppressive rule of the Islamists and their obsession with death and martyrdom. As Sadegui notes, however, "life is sacred." The opponents of the regime, who represent the oppressed majority, believe in "Women, Life, and Freedom." Far from "defending Islam," "many Iranians now think that this government not only endangered life but is also destroying Iranian civilization, history, and identity."

8.24 Mimunt Hamido Yahia

In 2022, Mimunt Hamido Yahia (b. 1961), a Spaniard of Moroccan Berber ancestry, who grew up in Melilla, Spain, in North Africa, published a powerful, thoughtful, and provocative work titled *No nos taparán: Islam, velo, patriarcado* [*They Will Not Cover Us Up: Islam, Veil, Patriarchy*]. The title evokes the anti-fascist slogan from the Spanish Civil War -- *no pasarán*, namely, "they shall not pass." In the Spanish context, it signified that the Catholic fascists would not be allowed to prevail and triumph. In Yahia's case, *no nos taparán* means that we will not allow the Islamo-fascists to veil the hair, the minds, the mouths, and, to use the word she employs for impact, the cunts of women.

More than a book, *No Nos Taparán* [*The Will Not Cover Us Up*] is a movement of women from Muslim backgrounds who are opposed to the expansion of Islamic fundamentalism and its most salient symbol, the veil. They reject the control of religion over their lives. They reject European policies that promote fundamentalism to the detriment of Muslims. The website addresses the veil, mind, mouth, and pardon the term, cunt. The section on "the veil" reads as follows:

> **What does the veil mean** in the Muslim religion? The veil, often called *hijab*... is a garment that is intended to hide the beauty of women so as not to excite men, thereby preventing sexual harassment, assault, or rape... It hides hair and neckline, but it can also be extended to cover the face except for the eyes (known as *niqab*) or the entire face (*burqa*). Islamic theology considers that men are naturally inclined to harass or sexually assault women... To avoid this, women are required to cover their "charms."
>
> In non-Muslim countries, where the vast majority of women do not wear headscarves, the *hijab* is now increasingly used to visually identify Muslim women from non-Muslims. Thus, it has become the identity symbol for a group of people who refuse to mix or be confused with those who do not share their faith. **We reject the veil** for both reasons.
>
> **We do not believe** that men have the natural impulse to sexually assault or rape the women around them. We believe that harassment is a symptom of a serious social disease and that, if it occurs, men should be educated so that they learn to live with women, as opposed to hiding women. By making women responsible for preventing sexual harassment, the veil justifies and legitimizes it.
>
> **We do not want** to display our religion, whichever we have, in public. We do not want to be a uniformed group, identified with a specific ideology. We do not want to be subjected to the visual control of those who claim to represent us. If we are Muslims, it is our business; they will not force us to prove it.
>
> **We want to prevent** women born into Muslim families from feeling compelled to identify themselves as such by wearing the veil. But if in a community -- be it a Muslim country or an immigrant neighborhood in Spain -- the vast majority of women born Muslim wear veils, not doing so becomes a heroic action and exposes whoever does so to continuous pressure, harassment, and insults from family and neighbors: when everyone wears a veil, not doing so turns a girl into a whore as well as a legitimate prey for harassment.
>
> **Wearing a veil** legitimizes harassment, establishes segregation by religion, and exerts pressure on others. That is why we say: "No to the veil."

These positions are sound and reasonable. The section on the mind argues that,

> **Fundamentalist Islam** tries to colonize the minds of all people who are born into Muslim families. It claims to be the main identity of its adherents. Compared to the "West," (a geographical term), they speak of the "Muslim world," as if all its inhabitants were characterized

primarily by religion.

> We refuse to be defined primarily on the basis of religion. We are Moroccan, Spanish, Egyptian or Turkish. Our identity is formed by multiple factors -- nationality, language, culture -- and religion is just one more element. This religion is enormously diverse. The Islam that our grandmothers practiced in the Rif was very different from what they practice today in Qatar. We reject that a certain fundamentalist vision of Islam seeks to eradicate our traditions, our culture, and replace them with a uniform Islamic identity.
>
> We open the debate on the process of formation of the religion called Islam, a process that is still ongoing and that cannot be hidden with the not so rational dogma that Islam, in its current form, was created by divine intervention in one fell swoop fourteen years ago in Arabia, to arrive as it is to our days.

These positions are also palatable. Islam is a rich, diverse, and variegated religious tradition that has developed in hundreds of different directions. It did not appear out of the blue, fully formed. It evolved and continues to do so. To suck the oxygen out of a living faith tradition is to snuff it out. Muslims need room to breathe. As for the section on the mouth, it explains that,

> **Criticizing the centers of power** of fundamentalist Islam is practically a taboo today both in countries that officially declare themselves Islamic, and in Europe, which has coined the term "Islamophobia" to shield fundamentalists against their detractors.
>
> In almost all Islamic countries, regimes use Islam to legitimize their power and stifle any discussion on the role of religion in public life, even when they tolerate political criticism in other respects. Declaring yourself an atheist does not appear as a crime in the legislation of countries such as Morocco, Tunisia, or Egypt, but it is treated as if it were prohibited, just like any other opinion that questions the laws that force the application of Islamic norms in the public sphere. There is no freedom in Islam as long as the police persecute anyone who disputes the faith.
>
> In Europe, the word "Islamophobia" is not only used to describe racist acts directed against Muslims -- which is logically a crime, because racism is a crime -- but it is also applied to any criticism of Islam as a religion, its orthodox commandments or the most severe regulations promulgated in recent years by its theologians. One is allowed to criticize -- and rightly so -- the power of the Christian Church. However, one is prohibited, at all costs, from criticizing the centers of Islamist power.
>
> When we women, who were born under so-called "Islamic" laws, criticize the patriarchal repression justified by these norms, there is never a shortage of Europeans, often people who have never seen an

> Islamic country up close or a ghetto dominated by fundamentalists in Europe, who denounce us as "Islamophobic," and demand that we be silenced to prevent us from attacking "Muslims." The press and television invite the defenders of political Islam, usually imams or women who, through the veil, display their adherence to the fundamentalist current. However, they never invite those who oppose the power of the Mosque.
>
> We will not be silent. We will denounce the influence of religious centers of power. To criticize the norms that they try to promote, expand, and impose, is not to attack Muslims. Rather, it is to defend Muslims, especially Muslim women, against their oppressors.

Once again, there is nothing objectionable about these positions. Islam, like any other religion, is exploited for socio-political reasons. Islam, as both a religion and political movement, is not beyond criticism. Islam and Islamism can and should be subject to critique. Finally, in the section on the cunt, we read that,

> **The repression of women's sexuality** is the main obsession of the three great monotheistic religions, Judaism, Christianity, and Islam. But while Christianity in most of Europe has lost the power to impose this obsession through law, and few people who consider themselves Christian follow religious norms regarding sex, in Muslim communities sexual repression is only advancing.
>
> The obsession of being a virgin at marriage has been common to patriarchal traditions throughout the Mediterranean, regardless of religion, but the advance of fundamentalist Islam in recent decades has put an end to the evolution experienced during the twentieth century in the Maghreb. Under the pretext of being a divine commandment, families control their daughters more and more and put more and more barriers to their experiences with the other sex.
>
> In immigrant communities in Europe, this repression is even greater because the Islamic rule that prohibits women from marrying men who are not of the same faith is also introduced. For this reason, contact between teenage girls and boys of the same age are restricted and prevented, all in order to keep them "pure" for a marriage with a Muslim man. We oppose sexual taboos. The greater the taboo, the greater the ignorance of the body, one's own and that of the other sex, the greater the harassment, abuse, and sexual violence. We ask for more sexual education in schools and we oppose schools segregated by sex. We oppose religious leaders demanding separate spaces or hours for boys and girls in public swimming pools or school sports activities. We denounce the propagation of an ideology that considers "chastity" the greatest value of women and we reaffirm our right to choose at all times with whom to share our bodies, our sexuality. **Because there is no freedom for women without sexual freedom.**

It is indeed correct that Judaism, Christianity, and Islam, suffer from a sexual obsession that is particularly accentuated among the fundamentalists of these faith traditions where it reaches pathological proportions. As a result of secularism, the importance of chastity had diminished or disappeared among many Jews, Christians, and even some Muslims. For Yahia, the solution is a sexual revolution among Muslims. In solving a problem, this would only create scores of others. It is naïve to believe that secular people are less obsessed about sex than religious people. This fact is demonstrated by rates of sexual activity, the consumption of pornography, and the pandemic of prostitution. There is no doubt that gender segregation does not produce healthy societies and that boys, girls, men, and women, should mingle and interact at all stages of development, so they can learn to live together respectfully and harmoniously.

Rather than remove Islam from the equation, it would be wiser to reform it. Secularism is no panacea. Secularists, both left and right wing, have a long history of oppressing women and depriving them of rights. In fact, up to the twentieth century, when women were deprived of rights in the West, including property, inheritance, the vote, and divorce, men and women converted to Islam because it gave them greater rights. There are deeply religious Muslim men who respect women and deeply religious men who are women phobic. Many of the Muslim men who harass and assault women may be religious; however, just as many of them are irreligious. Whether or not their religion remains, their culture is still the same. Macho misogynists and sexists come in many colors and wear many different hats. Honoring and protecting women requires a multi-pronged approach. A religious, cultural, political, economic, and educational metamorphosis is required.

For Mimunt Hamido Yahia, Islam's emphasis on chastity and Muslims' obsession with virginity, is the product of patriarchy. There is no doubt that the obsession with intact hymens is idolatrous and un-Islamic. It was not found among the pre-Islamic Arabs. It was not found among early Muslims. Neither the Prophet, nor his companions, were obsessed with marrying virgins. Only one of his wives was a virgin. The rest were widows and divorcees. The traditions in which the Prophet Muhammad and the Imams insist that men should marry virgins reflect much later mores.

The Qur'an calls all believers to be chaste: both men and women. There is no patriarchy or gender inequality in that. However, among virtually all Muslims, it matters not if a man maintains his virginity until marriage (in fact, in many cultures, he would be the object of mockery); however, a girl's life can depend on the integrity of her hymen. Their view on the matter is utterly demented. The value and worth of a woman is not determined by a thin piece of tissue at the opening of her vagina. The Qur'an is not the problem. It cannot be blamed if Muslims from most cultures have failed to live up to its universal standards of chastity.

If Muslim girls and women are expected to be chaste, but Muslim boys and men are not, Yahia's solution is to ensure that all of them are unchaste. Let them fornicate and commit adultery to the content of their private parts. While many Muslims would empathize with the other demands made by Yahia, this final one, regarding liberating the cunt, will alienate virtually every last one of them. Rather than call for equality through debauchery, a more moral approach would be to call for chastity for all, both men and women, which is consistent with Qur'anic values.

The website of *We Will Not Be Covered Up* was produced to promote the book. It provides a foretaste of what is to come. As one may expect, the cover of Mimunt Hamido Yahia's book is captivating and visually thought-provoking. The sky is blue. The background is the ocean with medium waves. A woman in a black bikini, short hair, and a nice tan is about to enter the water. The picture of health, she is fit, slim, and firm. Behind her are two people sitting on the sand. A presumably middle-aged, broadly built woman is sitting a short distance behind the bikini-clad beauty. She is dressed entirely in what appears to be a black *burka*. She is a black shadow whose forms, besides being plump and out of shape, cannot be distinguished. There is a man to her right, presumably her husband, in similar shape. He is wearing a tight red t-shirt or polo shirt. He seems to be wearing jeans or Bermudas that go down to his knees or past them. His butt crack is exposed. His hairstyle is Western. He appears clear shaven or merely has day old stumble. He is wearing black sunglasses. He might be averting his gaze from the young woman in the two-piece bathing suit but, in all likelihood, he is staring right at her firm ass as it bulges bountifully out of her bikini bottom. His wife appears to be doing the same thing. This photograph truly tells a thousand words or more.

The woman in the black bikini is at the center of the photograph. She is the subject of the book. She could be a secular European, but she could just as easily be North African, Moroccan, Tunisian, or Algerian. Many Muslim women wear bikinis. They are fewer than in the 1960s, 1970s, and 1980s. They were once the majority but have now become the minority in many parts. Why should one presume that a bikini clad woman is not a Muslim? Why have we come to expect a Muslim woman to wear a *burkini* or to swim fully dressed? Either way, the woman's short hair seems to signal that she is a secular woman or a feminist. Perhaps she is a Muslim who rejects the sexist belief that a woman is prohibited from cutting her hair short. Perhaps she rejects the claim that a woman's hair, like the rest of her body, is a private part.

The woman in the black *burka* is to the left. The left has traditionally been associated with the femininity. The man is to the right. The right has traditionally been associated with masculinity. The Muslims at the back represent patriarchy and inequality. They are behind and they are backwards. They live in an imaginary past. The bikini wearing woman in center focus stands for equality and equilibrium. She is slightly blurred. Her image is not sharp, signifying that she is being sidelined and eclipsed by societal forces when she should be front and center. Unlike the woman in the black *burka*, the woman in the black bikini has individuality, personality, and agency. They are both the subject of the book and the object of the look. They are both sexualized. Their intimate parts are covered in black. For the liberated woman, her private parts are limited to her buttocks, vulva, and breasts. She is a goddess who celebrates the Goddess. She is the very symbol of life, love, and fertility. For the suppressed and submissive woman, who bows to the idol of patriarchy and misogyny, her private parts apply to the entirety of her form. The contrast does not end there.

It is as absurd to wear a black *burka* to a beach, in hundred-degree weather, and to swim fully clothed, as it is to wear a bikini to go downhill skiing when it is icy cold. The attire is entirely inappropriate. While the *burka* clad woman is baking in the sun as an amorphous mass, the bikini clad one is active. *Burka* woman is unhealthy and suffers from vitamin D deficiency while bikini woman is healthy and vitaminized. The former is under the guardianship of her husband, while the latter is free and independent. The woman in the black *burka* is concerned about ultra-conservative religious rules of modesty. Her husband, however, with his butt-crack on nauseating display, feels no compulsion to cover himself up or explicitly identify himself as a Muslim. He is free. He can wear a bathing suit and shorts. He can expose his torso in public. He can pass for a Westerner or a non-Muslim on the pretext of avoiding stereotypes and racism. His wife, however, has no such options. She is utterly othered. She is the black banner of Islamic imperialism. If the woman's black *burkini* screams *no nos taparán* or "we will not be covered up" and "we will not be replaced," the black *burka* cries of conquest. It defiantly asserts that "we will not integrate with you infidels."

Unlike the woman in the black *burka*, who is compelled to cover by her own religious, political, and ideological conviction, or coerced into doing so by her household or community, the woman in the black bikini has liberty. She is concerned with practicality, fashion, and functionality, while abiding by public decency laws. She has no qualms about showing her beauty as her secular society and culture provide her with safety. However, in the photograph, she is outnumbered two to one, symbolizing that women, secular, and Muslim, feel like they are under siege by the Islamists who continue to conquer more territories, including pools and beaches. Welcome to your new vacation destination, Taliban Springs! Muhammad ibn 'Abdul-Wahhab Waterpark! Ibn Taymiyyah's Beach Resort!

Beaches, pools, resorts, and waterparks filled with stern-faced, black *burka*-clad women, and bearded Islamist men are not welcoming places for people who are not of their kind. Women and men, even Muslims, who do not share their radical Islamic ideology, feel completely uncomfortable in their intimidating presence. Women are not free to be free around such people. Nobody wants to suntan in a bikini, or swim in a one-piece bathing suit, in the company of Osama Ben Ladin, Abu Bakr al-Baghdadi, and the members of their harems. The fact of the matter, however, is that radical Islamists vacation in Las Vegas, Dubai, and other sites of debauchery, where they drink alcohol, hang out in strip clubs, and frequent prostitutes. They only wish to deny *their* women of freedom.

Ultimately, and most importantly, the question asked by the photograph is clear: which of these women has more rights and liberties? Miss Black Burka? Or Miss Black Bikini? The answer is self-evident to anyone who has a shred of common sense. However, herein lies the problem: only two options are provided. Women have the choice of slipping into black bikinis to proclaim their emancipation or they can suffocate themselves in black *burkas* to showcase their submission. Perhaps the purpose is to be hyperbolic. In reality, the options available to women include everything in between these extremes. Why not wear a tankini? Why not wear a swim-skirt? Why not wear a one-piece swimsuit? Why should the only two options be "uncover yourself almost completely" or "cover yourself up completely?" People on both sides of the argument seek to control women when women should control themselves. They have voices and they have choices.

The reality, however, is that "choice" is an illusion. Unless women live in a complete cultural vacuum and design their clothing without being subjected to influences of any kind, which is impossible, the choices we make, in matters of fashion, are already made. We choose from the choices that are presented to us. The same multi-billion dollar per year industry that pushes the bikini is the same capitalist force that promotes the *hijab*, the *niqab*, and the *burkini*.

As for Mimunt Hamido Yahia's book, it packs a powerful punch. It will make heads spin. It is a veritable wake-up call for women and the men who love and respect them. When she remembers her childhood with nostalgia, and compares the Muslim community today, she realizes to what point we have been colonized by Wahhabism (16). She surveys the history and ideology of the Salafi-Wahhabi movement and stresses that much of this extremism was brought back to Morocco by North Africans from Europe (17). In other words, it did not enter directly from Saudi Arabia or Egypt. It exploited the weaknesses inherent to secular liberal democracies to sow their seeds of Salafism and Wahhabism and converted Muslim immigrants and their children to its cause.

Muslims radicalized in Europe set about to "re-Islamize" their cultures of origin. Their wives and daughters were the first to sport the deliberately distinctive and defiant Islamist *hijab* in Morocco to stress that they were the most Muslim of Muslims. Most Moroccan women, until the 1980s, did not cover their hair or, if they did so, wore Berber scarves tied around the back of their necks. They showed their ears, throats, bangs, and even locks and braids of hair. The new wave of radicalized women, however, covered everything. "Why," Yahia asks, "do women have to cover their hair according to such people?"

> In orthodox Islamic theology… hair is considered an erotic attribute of women that can arouse … men. If a man gets excited, he will try to have sex with that woman. He can harass her, try to touch her, and even try to rape her… The veil serves a sexual function: to avoid arousing men's lust. If a man sees our hair… he cannot control himself and will feel the primitive urge to rape us… Muslim men view themselves as rapists and Muslim women consider their brothers, cousins, fathers, or uncles to be potential rapists: men who cannot control themselves at the sight of the hair of a Muslim woman... This only applies to the hair of a Muslim woman because others can go about as they wish, and nobody will feel like raping them… or perhaps it does not matter what happens to them. It does … matter for us Muslim women: we belong to those male rapists and, unless we go out decently dressed, they believe they have the right to admonish us or directly to rape us. And we will be held responsible for having failed to uphold the norms of essential decorum, which require that we be immediately identifiable as good Muslim at first sight. This theological basis of the *hijab* is not one among many interpretations: it is the official and only one. (17-18)

The paleoconservative interpretation of the *hijab* may be preponderant. The caveman concept of the *hijab* may have imposed itself. It may have become hegemonic. However, as Yahia stresses, "it is not the only interpretation… there are also theologians who insist that the veil is unnecessary and devoid of theological foundation," pointing out the position of Nasr Hamid Abu Zayd, who was a professor at the University of al-Azhar (20). The fact remains that the most radical of Sunnis and Shiites have such a stranglehold on Islamic discourse that they have convinced virtually all Muslims that their interpretation of *hijab* is absolute and unquestionable, an indisputable fact, a pillar of Islam, and a matter of faith and creed. In so doing, they have turned a piece of cloth into an idol and produced inherently imbalanced societies in which women are divided into two classes: the chaste and the unchaste:

> In a normal country, be it European or North African, nobody jumps a woman and tries to rape her because she has shown a lock of hair… As the Salafi-Wahabi ideology has spread, so has the idea that girls are obliged to publicly demonstrate that they are decent and are not going around arousing men. If in the middle of the twentieth century it was normal to go around with hair uncovered in any Moroccan city, that it no longer the case: now, there is no shortage of men who interpret the absence of the veil as a provocation. It is a type of signal: if I do not cover myself, it is because I wish to arouse you because that is how much of a slut that I am. (20-21)

As a public symbol, notes Yahia, the veil is only imposed on women. As she asks, "When was the last time you saw a man wearing a djellaba, baggy trousers, slippers, and turbans, walking around the streets of Spain?" (21) There are some, she notes. However, they are one in a thousand, and they tend to be preachers who are a subject of ridicule to Moroccan immigrants (21). However, these same men, impose *hijab* on "their" women: wives, sisters, daughters, and even their mothers while they go around in jeans and t-shirts (21). To add to the hypocrisy, these men are startled by any suggestion that women could be aroused by men in tight pants (22). Surely, only an indecent woman would ever suggest such a thing. And although the Qur'an commands men to lower their gaze, this is never the topic of any sermon at a mosque (22). The fact that Muslim men harass women and make catcalls is a matter that should be brushed aside. They are only being men, after all. If men harass women, it is something normal and a natural reaction to sexual provocation.

Mimunt Hamido Yahia wishes to make one thing clear. The new Islamist Islam that has spread throughout the world over the past half-century is not the Islam of her parents. It is a new Islam (23). No child was expected to pray or fast the month of Ramadan. No girl was expected to wear the *hijab*. They were children. They were innocent and they were free. According to traditional, classical Islam, prayer, and fasting start at adolescence. Until they have their periods, girls are girls. They can go anywhere they want. They can climb trees, mix with men, even in mosques, and swim while wearing panties. She stresses that even the most orthodox theologians, who view the veil as obligatory, only believe that it is required of women and not pre-pubescent girls (23). "The purpose of modesty," she notes, "is to prevent arousal: a girl cannot arouse anyone" (23). In fact, "only pedophiles would think otherwise" (23). Yahia pinpoints the source of the problem:

> I think that recalcitrant Islamists who recommend that girls wear *hijabs* from birth should be taken to court for promoting pedophilia. Asking a five-year-old to hide her "charms" is to consider her a sexual object. This is the mentality in which the Salafists live. (24)

The fact is that these are precisely the type of people we are dealing with. The sad reality is that Muslims born in the 1970s and after have never known a world without Islamists. Little do they know that their mothers, grandmothers, and great grandmothers did not wear *hijab*. They showed their hair. They wore white, Western-style, wedding dresses. They wore bikinis to the beach. They were not judged. They lived in more tolerant times. In fact, there was a time, in the late sixties, when Moroccan women were wearing bikinis to beaches and pools when it was illegal to do so in Spain (27). Now, if a girl does not wear *hijab*, the neighbors think she is indecent. If she take her *hijab* off at school, another Islamist girl will rat on her, tell her brothers, and shame the family. While it was normal for people from the same neighborhood to watch out for one another, the arrival and presence of Salafi preachers, and their supporters, has created a culture of control that can turn the lives of girls and women into a living hell (84).

Yahia encourages Muslim girls to look through old family photos to get a glance at a time when mothers did not scold, shame, and shout at their daughters over matters of so-called "family honor" (24). Some are so stunned at such photographs from the 1950s, 1960s, 1970s, and early 1980s, that they post them on social media (25). They represent a world they have never known. Some celebrate these "good old days" with nostalgia; however most, notes Yahia, would never imitate them as they themselves wear strict *hijab* according to the Salafi vision. They do not belong to traditional, classical, civilizational, spiritual, rationalist, and humanitarian Islam. No. Not at all. As Mimunt Hamido Yahia states: "they are members of a new sect: "European Islam" (25). And they are reconquering their countries of origin. Hence, we have a duty to protect girls and women against this Islamism that is corrupting everything (96).

Although the *hijab* is a choice, warns Yahia, it is not a free choice, and not one without consequences. In Muslim communities, scholars, fathers, brothers, and even mothers feel obliged to guide girls and women (98). Girls born into a Muslim family suffer pressure of all kinds. This pressure increases as they age. If they rebel, they are excluded from their families, communities, and circle of friends. They end upon alone in the world (98). Girls wish to please their parents and families. They do not want to be outcasts. They are willing to go to great lengths to do things out of love and respect for their families, including pretending to believe, praying, fasting, and wearing *hijab*. After all, how will they find good husbands if they do not veil?

The sad fact of the matter, however, is that there is no shortage of secular, agnostic, and even atheist girls and women who "go along with it" to avoid causing any scandals. God forbid they be accused of being apostates who have betrayed their religion and culture (101). To submit or to rebel is a genuinely difficult decision (100). Yahia is well aware that adopting the *hijab* provides some advantages to Muslim women (108). Their families trust them more (92, 100, 147). They allow them to go out more, and even to study and work. They are praised by Muslims and non-Muslims. They are told they are prettier in *hijab* (92). They have succumbed to emotional blackmail (92). However, she warns women who are entertaining the idea of becoming *hijabis* that it is a trap:

> Once you put on the *hijab*, and you do so in such a public fashion, you cannot take it off, at least in public. You will have to live up to the norms that everyone -- Christians and even atheists -- expect from the behavior of a Muslim woman. (62-63)

Adopting the *hijab* now offers plenty of opportunities for some Muslim women. While women are free to adopt the veil in the West, it is not easy for them to stop wearing it. If, at some point, they choose to discard it, out of free choice, they can expect criticism, harassment, and intimidation from all corners (147).

What is more, research suggests that "*hijab* dissociation is a form of compensatory mechanism aimed at minimizing self-discrepancy, restoring self-esteem, gaining personal control, reducing perceived alienation and coping with psychological trauma" (Syahrivar).

Why does Mimunt Hamido Yahia place so much importance on the *hijab*? Are there not more important issues to address? She responds as follows:

> The struggle of North African women has many different fronts, and they are all very important… In this struggle, symbols are extremely important. The *hijab* encompasses all forms of oppression, restrictions, prohibitions, and norms that we are subjected to as Muslim women. The veil symbolizes the acceptance and submission to the patriarchy that imposes these norms upon us. (106)

Islamic fundamentalists tell Yahia that believing Muslim women who do not wear *hijab* are still obliged to do so. Her response is a categorical no. As she explains,

> To be a believer is a vague concept… one can be a believer and more or less practicing or hold personal views regarding which norms really form part of the religion. To wear the *hijab*, however, is to show the world that one has accepted the rules entirely. The women who claim to wear it freely, without coercion, are recognizing that those norms are just. (107)

While it is possible that some women do not wear *hijab* because they have chosen to not be "chaste," others, however, believe in privacy and refuse to wear their chastity on their heads (107). They refuse to bow to the patriarchy (107). The *hijab* is not merely a piece of cloth worn out of "free choice" (107). It is a symbol that defines a woman as "chaste" or "depraved" (107). While she does not ask the question, one should: Why don't Islamists force male sexual harassers, fornicators, and adulterers to wear distinctive attire? Or perhaps they can be forced to wear donkey ears or dress entirely in pink? Better yet, let them wear *niqab,* and allow women to dress as they please. And perhaps members of the LGBTQ community should be required to wear rainbow flags? And Jews should wear yellow stars of David? And French people wear berets? Why should only Muslim women be forced to wear distinctive attire? Would we tolerate such an imposition on any other ethnic, racial, or religious groups?

For Mimunt Hamido Yahia, the *hijab* is a political-religious symbol. If it were merely an article of clothing, it could be prohibited, just like teachers prohibits hats in class (110). That is why Muslims market the obligatory *hijab* as a "free choice" (110). When she states that the *hijab* sexualizes women, so-called feminists claim that so do miniskirts, high heels, make up, and plastic surgery (110). Her response is sharp:

> Nobody kills and nobody imprisons [women] who do not wish to wear

> high-heels or makeup. However, Muslim girls who wish to wear makeup or miniskirts are subjected to violence for doing so. It is ... amazing that they think aesthetic oppression is limited to Western women. Have they not seen veiled girls with fake eyelashes, layers of makeup, and flaming red lipstick? Women who claim to wear the *hijab* by choice do not free themselves from makeup and plastic surgery. Iran and Iraq... rank the highest in the world for nose jobs. They fix their cheeks, tits, and asses. Whether they go around stuffed in a *niqab* that covers their entire bodies is immaterial. Polygyny makes competition very difficult; age is not forgiving, and Arabs have always preferred young, very young, women. Nobody in Spain suffers from such ruthless aesthetic pressure as the girls in countries where the *hijab* reigns. As for the miniskirt... when did we stop seeing it as a symbol of rebellion against patriarchy? (110)

When the Church in Europe used to preach to women from the pulpit how to dress and how to be decent, women revolted: their burned their bras, slipped on miniskirts, marched for equality, and started to show their bodies at the beach (112). They rebelled against centuries of sexualization and stigma (112). Some of these feminists were believers but others were not (112). Religion was never a part of the feminist movement in the Western world (112). As for those who believed, they did not identify themselves as Christians: they identified as women (112). The only thing these new forms of feminism do -- be they, anti-colonial, radical, and Islamic -- is to divide women (113). It divides women into "we" and "you" (113). It sets different standards. It creates distinct classes of women. All that "Islamic feminism" provides is the appearance of equality (117). Not only do they not question Islamic dogmas, but they vindicate them (117). You will never find them denouncing the imposition of *hijab* on millions of women (118). They elevate the *hijab* to a level of importance and centrality that it never had before the twentieth century (118). This "gift" that "Islamist feminists" offer to women is laced with poison (117).

There are those who falsely claim that Islamic feminism originated in Iran (120). In Iran, however, the veil was imposed by law (120). Any criticism of "Islam" was punished with imprisonment or death (120). Under the brutal and blood-soaked Khomeini regime, women had no other option but to "Islamize" their feminism (120). They had to frame their arguments in light of Islam (120). To do otherwise, and to contradict the Qur'an, was illegal (120). And of course Iranian feminists wore *hijab*. They had to: otherwise they would have ended up in prison (120). To take what was a survival strategy under the repressive Khomeini and Khamenei regimes, and treat it as an example of the aspiration of Muslim women, is to play dirty, to ally oneself with the oppressors, to defend their dogmas, and to affirm that this is what their victims desire (120).

For Mimunt Hamido Yahia, these so called "Islamic feminists" are not on the side of women, first and foremost, they are apologists and propagandists for the Islamists and fundamentalists. A real feminist places women above patriarchal religions. A real feminist does not wear *hijab*. "We don't need to be saved," they claim, "because we are already free!" (117). These "Islamic feminists" have no universal feminist aspirations (121). In fact, their only universal aspiration consists in pan-Islamism and globalized Islam. When faced with issues like *hijab*, child marriage, the anti-colonial feminists shrug their shoulders and say: "those are their customs, and we must respect them." Human rights and feminism are supposed to be universal.

For Mimunt Hamido Yahia, "the veil is the white flag of surrender " (98). "Religion," in her view, "is a weapon used by the patriarchy for centuries to keep us in chains" (98). For Yahia, religious scriptures do not need to be changed to create a free and egalitarian society (123). What needs to be changed is society, by setting aside religious scriptures or, better yet, by marginalizing them so they no longer determine the nature of a society (123). What is the message of "Islamic feminists?" Women can study, graduate, work, and choose their spouses, so long as they wear *hijab*, stay virgins until they are married, and avoid getting contaminated by "Western" thought which basically means "critical thinking." Sure, they have some freedoms. However, they are not free to question the patriarchal rules imposed on them for the past fourteen hundred years (124). It is freedom in the confines of a cage.

For Mimunt Hamido Yahia, women, in the eyes of the Islamists, are canon fodder (130). When asked why they wear the veil, some Muslim women claim they do it out of free will (130). Many claim that "there are a thousand reasons to wear the veil, each woman has her own" (130). For Yahia, "this is like saying that each soldier has a different reason for wearing a military uniform" (130). For Yahia, the *hijab* spread from the ghettos of Europe, where Wahhabi preachers radicalized the marginalized, alienated, and disenfranchised, presenting it as a distinguishing feature between "us" and "them" (130). The spread of the *hijab* has gone hand in hand with Wahhabi indoctrination in mosques and madrasas (130). It was then exported to the Maghreb by immigrants from the region who reside in Europe (130). The goal of the Islamists is to control women (130). For them, "it does not matter if a woman wears the *hijab* out of coercion or not or whether she believes in God or not" (130). Their goal is to create a parallel society (131). Far from a symbol of integration, it symbolizes disintegration (131). The Islamists want their ideology to be visible in the public sphere (131).

Many Muslims, both converts, and those of culture, hold romantic ideas about al-Andalus and the Golden Age of Islam (135). They are proud of the past power and glory of Islam. For Yahia, such people have been seduced by fundamentalism and Salafism disguised as love and peace (135). As she makes abundantly clear, it was not Islam that was responsible for the cultural, literary, scholarly, artistic, and scientific accomplishments of the period (135). On the contrary, it was the lack of religion that produced this peak (136).

The philosophical and cultural heritage of al-Andalus was built upon the legacy of Mediterranean culture that stretched from ancient Greece to Persia and which provided the foundation for the European Renaissance (135). Islam did not make the arts and sciences flourish in the Iberian Peninsula (135). It simply did not suppress them (135). Culture and science flourished in al-Andalus and elsewhere when Muslim leaders watered and fertilized them with freedom.

Had the jurists held power in al-Andalus, they would have suffocated all science, art, and culture, except for Islamic jurisprudence. After all, in their view, music is *haram*, art is *haram*, music is *haram*, philosophy is *haram*, logic is *haram*, and every innovation, even if good, is *haram*. Their "Islam" produces a vacuum in which nothing can live. It stifles life, freedom, liberty, and creativity. They are like the Amish on crack. They are like Mennonites on meth.

Mimunt Hamido Yahia also takes issue with Muslim converts, particularly women. She views them as the enemies of secularism in the Islamic world and some of the most virulent defenders of the misogynistic *hijab*, which Muslim women have been trying to get rid of once and for all (138). Rather than help the cause of oppressed Muslim women, they reinforce their oppression by claiming that "the Qur'an is a feminist book" (138). Who cares if the Qur'an addresses "believing men and believing women" when it decrees that a daughter's inheritance is half that of a son? (138). So-called "Islamic feminism" is merely another weapon of the Islamists (138). These "Islamic feminists" are only interested in justifying the unjustifiable, like the verses regarding inheritance and polygyny, without undermining the patriarchy (138). Not only does she describe how women are drawn into Islam and Islamism, but she also exposes the savvy propaganda efforts of Islamist women and *hijabi* influencers (132-148).

> We women have always been exploited by all theocracies, both Christian and Islamist, as the cannon fodder of their ideology... In order to impose any totalitarian regime, it is crucial to rely on the family... In Spain, we had the famous "Women's Section" of the Falangists.... In Germany, the Nazis founded the... League of German Ladies... In Iran ... there are military units composed of women who march with guns, uniforms, and... *hijabs* on their heads... They form part of the infamous "morality police," that impose the veil on girls... In other official Muslim countries, even so-called "moderate" ones, there is no need for a women's league. The population is so "well trained" that everyone feels free to denounce their neighbors... (143-144)

For Mimunt Hamido Yahia, all the racial, multicultural, intersectional, and anti-colonial "feminists" do is justify patriarchal norms when they apply to women who come from a different religious or cultural context (150). In so doing, "they tolerate what for them would be intolerable" (150). In her words,

> That, ladies, is racism… Feminism is a universal ideology… By the very fact that we were born female, we, women … suffer from the violence and control that the patriarchy exerts over our bodies. It matters not whether the patriarchy is western, eastern, North African, or Asiatic… Patriarchy is a universal power structure. (150)

Rather than apply feminism in all places, these "intersectional" feminists insist on not applying it in certain contexts because cultural practices, however sexist they may be, are more important and valuable than feminism itself (151). For Yahia, "invoking 'diversity' is a hidden form of racism" (152).

Secularism needs to draw a line in the sand. Islamists demand that their daughters wear *hijab* to school. It is granted. They demand that their daughters be excused from gym class. It is granted. They demand they be excluded from swimming classes or they must wear *burkinis*. It is granted. They demand that their children be removed from music classes, as it is prohibited in Islam. It is granted (Yahia 153-154). They demand *halal* food in the cafeteria. It is granted. They refuse to allow their children to receive sexual education. It is granted. They refuse to stand for the national anthem or the pledge allegiance. It is granted. They object to activities related to Christmas, Halloween, Easter, or New Year. It is granted. They demand *shari'ah* courts to regulate marriage, divorce, inheritance, and custody of children, according to rules that are disadvantageous to women. And it is granted. It never stops, nor will it ever stop. These are not "reasonable accommodations." The only "reasonable accommodation" is for Muslims to integrate into the secular cultures in which they live or to return to their countries of origin where they will have a rude awakening. After all, most of their governments have even less tolerance for their Islamic extremism.

To oppose the spread of Islamism, and its flag, the *hijab*, is not to oppose Islam. There is nothing racist or bigoted about it. Many Muslims in the Western world, both converts and those of immigrant and refugee stock, are astonished at the spread of radical Islam. In fact, Islamism is spreading more rapidly in the Western world than it is in the Muslim world. Like Yahia, many Muslims have observed, in shock and awe, the fruit of the propaganda of the Wahhabis and the Muslim Brotherhood, among others (160). Muslim females "are convinced that they themselves have chosen to wear a patriarchal symbol" (160). They never question the Muslim patriarchy (160). Years of "anti-Islamophobia" campaigns have empowered them to proudly wear their symbol, the *hijab*, the very symbol of Islamist ideology (160). As Yahia notes, there are now more *burkas* in Girona, Spain, than there are in Morocco (160).

Thanks to misguided "multiculturalism," Westerners are now expected to respect, applaud, and support misogynistic symbols (161). The very notion of prohibiting the *burqa*, for example, is viewed as xenophobic (161). However, the fact that the *burqa* represents a rejection of secular values, human rights, and equality, is lost on them (161). For Yahia, when it comes to prohibiting sexist symbols, Europeans are too cowardly to speak about Islam (162) Why? Because too many petro-dollars are a stake (162). The rights of Muslim women, even those in the West, are sold cheaply (162). However, women fought long and hard to obtain them (163).

Since the veil is a sexist and misogynistic symbol, Yahia believes that it should be prohibited in school. As she argues, "freedom of choice" does not include the freedom to enslave half of humanity (164). Consequently, she stresses that education should be secular and delivered in an egalitarian environment devoid of religious indoctrination (164). When a teacher wears a *hijab* to class, she is sending a signal, namely, that she adheres to Islam, that she does not believe in sex out of wedlock, that homosexuality is a sin that merits a punishment, and that she, herself, is a chaste woman (164).

In a secular society, one teaches children, from an early age, that the fact that a woman wears a short skirt, or shows her bellybutton, does not grant one the right to fondle, harass, or insult her (165). The *hijab*-wearing teacher sends an entirely different message, namely, that her entire body, and even her hair is erotic, that it excites men, and that it can only be shown to her husband and a small circle of male relatives (165). Were she to show her hair, she would excite men (163). As such, if they happened to harass her, she would be responsible for having provoked them (165).

Wearing a veil, be it a *hijab* or a *burqa*, is not the same as wearing a cross around one's neck (166). To commence, the crucifix is worn by both boys and girls (166). What is more, it is not a sexist symbol (166). If a Muslim girl wants to identify her religion, all she has to do is wear a necklace, a bracelet, or a pin with the name of God or with the Islamic profession of faith (166). As much as she opposes *hijab* in public schools, Yahia does not believe that adult women should be prohibited from wearing *hijab*. She is adamant, however, that minors should be prohibited from veiling themselves (166). As most educated *hijabis* are aware, in the past, minors were never veiled (166). Consequently, the State should act (166). As she argues,

> Every day more and more girls between the ages of six and seven wear the *hijab*, and that goes against the human rights of minors. They even put it on babies in the crib. Have you thought that a seven-year-old baby or girl is capable of exciting a man? What do you call that? I call it an apology for pedophilia. (166)

For Mimunt Hamido Yahia, there is no future for women's rights outside secular democracies. What is needed is a strictly secular education (177-178). History of religion can be taught, but not religions *per se* (178). Students should not wear *hijab* (178). They should not be categorized or segregated based on the religion of their parents (178). All subjects, including physical education and swimming, must be mandatory (178). Education should revolve around secular values that focus on equality and feminism and reject racism and sexism (178). Steps should be taken to ensure the secular integration of Muslim immigrants (178). The State should subsidize mosques (178). Foreign funding of Islamic centers, organizations, and associations should be strictly forbidden (179). Safety protocols should be established to provide shelter, support, and counseling for Muslim girls and women who are subject to violence in their homes and communities (179). Finally, a Human Rights Observatory should be created to ensure that the immigrant population respects human rights and they are protected from racism and discrimination (179).

While there is much value in the work of Mimunt Hamido Yahia, her critique of the *hijab* emanates from the old far left and the first waves of feminism. It is a discourse that is fundamentally secular. What is more, it is not one rooted in Islam in any form or fashion. In fact, in recent debates, Yahia has described herself as being "Muslim by birth but non-Muslim by choice." In so doing, she has exercised a right that all Muslims should have: the right to believe or to disbelieve, and the right to remain in Islam or to leave Islam without any negative consequences. People should not be born in the prison of Islam. Like Judaism and Christianity, Muslims should be provided the opportunity to confirm their faith when they become adults and should be free to leave it at any point in the future. Freedom of religion goes both ways. If people should be free to embrace Islam, they should also be free to emancipate themselves from it.

In leaving the religion of her birth, and the faith tradition and culture in which she was raised -- which she has every right to do, and one can empathize with the trauma she has experienced -- Mimunt Hamido Yahia has nonetheless discredited herself in the minds of most Muslims. She could have called for Islamic reform. She could have called for the separation between the State and the Mosque. She could have described herself as a secular Muslim. Call it the fight or flight response. It is easier to escape from Islam than try to reform it. Plainly, she feels Islam is beyond repair and the only viable option is replacing it with secularism. From whence will she flee from the misogyny, patriarchy, gender inequality, and sexism that are equally found in secular systems? She ran from lions into a den of hyenas.

Ideally, for it to be effective, any reform of Islam and Muslim societies should come from within. It should be the product of introspection, self-criticism, and self-improvement. The metamorphosis must come from Muslims. By positioning herself as a non-Muslim, any criticism, however justified, that Mimunt Hamido Yahia makes will be viewed by believers as an attack from the outside. Consequently, she is her own worst enemy. Her critique would have far greater legitimacy if she identified as a Muslim.

8.25 Conclusions

The women surveyed in this chapter come from Morocco, Algeria, Tunisia, Turkey, Iran, France, Canada, and beyond. They represent a broad cross-section of the Muslim world. They include intellectuals, jurists, political scientists, sociologists, psychologists, social workers, activists, and Islamologists. They are educated women who are entitled to express their informed opinions on a topic, such as the *hijab*, which impacts them and their communities directly. The women in question do not belong to a fringe. Their views dominated the educated classes of the Muslim world prior to the so-called "Islamic Revival" which is just a fancy name for the rise of radical, fundamentalist, intolerant, and extremist Islam in the late decades of the twentieth century. They are not minorities.

As a result of the rivalry between Saudi-funded Wahhabi Islamists and Iranian-funded political Shiite Islamists, the views of moderate, traditional, civilizational, spiritual, Qur'anic, liberal, secular, progressive, and reformist Muslims have been basically silenced. Rather than amplify the voices of such women, weak Western nations, who are too cowardly to defend their secular values and human rights, have empowered and emboldened conservative, retrograde, and radical Islam under the banner of "multiculturalism," "diversity," "pluralism," and "inclusion." Terrified of being denounced as "Islamophobes," they act as the allies of radical Islamists rather than stand on the side of moderate and secular Muslims. However, as Mansour Chow warns, in our attempts to defend the oppressed, we should be careful not to end up supporting the oppressors. In fact, he intelligently and systematically dismantles "the ludicrous notion that wearing the *hijab* constitutes a feminist act."

To add insult to injury, rather than support secular universalist Muslim feminists, most Western feminists have sided with so-called "Islamic feminists" who place their misogynistic and patriarchal interpretation of Islam over and above the rights and struggles of women. If the patriarchs of Islam do not make way for the matriarchs of Islam, these women, along with their husbands, brothers, fathers, and sons -- their entire families -- will have no choice but to form their own gender-inclusive Islamic denomination. A separation of the sexes will occur, but not in the submissive sense desired by the patriarchs. These women will break free from the male Muslim hierarchies and create their own sect, with women scholars, and women mosques. Otherwise, they will expel the Islamists from mainstream Islam. This is the reality on the ground. The male supremacist edifice of Islam is starting to crumble apart. The pressure has been building under the tectonic plates of Islam. Nothing can stop the life-altering earthquake that is building underground. The future of Islam belongs to the new religious thinkers.

Chapter 9

A Long, Long Way to Go

9.1 Introduction

Muslim women matter, but Muslim women are not well. Most of them are poor, illiterate, ignorant, and impoverished. They have been conditioned for a millennia and a half to accept that their second-class subservient and submissive status is divinely decreed. They embrace their own oppression. They believe in it. They accept arranged marriages. They accept polygyny. They insist that their husbands have the right to beat them. They march against laws prohibiting marital rape. They march in favor of child marriages. They insist that their daughters be subjected to female genital mutilation. Not all, of course, but far too many. So, it is not a question of counting the heads of women -- or men, for that matter -- but of weighing them. What is in their heads?

One does not pass laws based on the beliefs of the base. If most women in certain communities or countries support the excision of girls, should the practice be legalized out of "respect for religious and cultural diversity?" In the view of some, failing to do so would be "racist" and "imperialistic." We do not govern by the rule of the mob. We rule based on rights. Freedom of religion is not absolute. Any freedom ends when it breaks the law and violates universal human rights. The three monotheistic religions understood this. The rabbis decreed that the law of the land takes precedent over the laws of the Torah. Jesus said render unto Caesar (Matthew 22:21). And the Qur'an said to obey the authorities (4:59). So, secular governments should stand firm by their principles and stop allowing religious and cultural communities to transgress human rights. In the following pages, we examine how Muslim women feel about the *hijab*. However, we should keep another crucial question in the back of our minds: why do Muslim women feel the way they do about the *hijab*? We trace the origin of veiling to ancient pre-Islamic times and ask the crucial question: is the *hijab haram*?

9.2 The *Hijab* in Canada

Since the Muslim community in Canada represents such a rich ethnic and cultural mosaic, a positive or a negative depending on one's political perspective, it can serve to test the pulse of the *ummah*. A study conducted by Reem A. Meshal provides some intriguing results. She found that "52% of Arab women surveyed wear the *hijab*; compared with 40% of Pakistani/Indian women; most of the other groups were evenly split, except for European (converts) Muslim women, where five out of six claim to wear it" (75). As she notes, "these figures are remarkable when contrasted with the incidence of *hijab* in the culture of origin. Arab women's use of *hijab*, depending on the country of origin, more or less coincides with the incident of *hijab* in much of the Arab world" (75). She found that "wearing *hijab* is not... simply a question of 'true' versus 'nominal' faith" (75). The belief that women who do not wear *hijab* are weak of faith, if not hypocrites, or disbelievers, has no basis in reality. Women do not wear their faith on their heads. Their faith is found in their hearts and souls.

Not only was the rate of *hijab* related to ethnicity, but it was also connected to socio-economic and educational background. Meshal found that,

> a) women born in Canada are less likely to wear *hijab* (37%) than immigrant Muslims (54%); and b) women whose families belong to higher socio-economic brackets are also less likely to do so... Class does appear to play a role. Women who do not wear the *hijab* ... come from more educated families in higher income brackets. 59% of those who do not wear the *hijab* had mothers who had completed university or postgraduate work, while among their veiled counterparts only about half that proportion (31%) had educated mothers. Seventy-seven percent of those who do not wear the *hijab* had fathers who had completed university or postgraduate work, as compared to 58% of those wearing it... Better educated families are less likely to raise their daughters to wear the *hijab*. (77)

These findings are not surprising when one considers that religion is the refuge of the poor and ignorant. With rare exceptions, the higher the rate of poverty, the higher the rate of religiosity (Crabtree). Moreover, studies have shown a negative relationship between reasoning and religiosity (Daws and Hampshire). In fact, as Eric W. Dolan notes, "meta-analysis of eighty-three studies produces 'very strong' evidence for a negative relationship between intelligence and religiosity" (Dolan). As Meshal's research found,

> statistics do indicate that the educational level of parents are linked with young women's use of *hijab*... an overwhelming percentage (83%) of fathers of those declining to wear the *hijab* are professionals... Even more significant, twice as many women who do not wear the *hijab* have mothers who are employed outside the home. (78)

While there is a correlation between religiosity and stupidity, I suspect that there is a correlation between spirituality and intelligence. Besides socio-economic and educational factors, the use of *hijab* was correlated with marital status:

> most of the women who wore the *hijab* (63%) were married. Moreover, many of them women who do not presently wear the *hijab* (47%) say that they are open to the possibility of doing so at a future date. Almost a third of them (28%) said they would consider adopting it if urged to do so by a future spouse. (78)

Since many of these marriages are arranged, it goes without saying that fathers who believe in strict *hijab* will insist upon marrying their daughters to men who also believe in strict *hijab*. For conservative Muslims, girls must always be under the guardianship of a man. For many Muslim women, marriage is just a transfer of authority from the father to the husband.

If Meshal's study did not find a correlation between faith and the use of *hijab*, she did find a striking difference regarding religious practice. Women who veil, for example, tended to fast the month of Ramadan more than those who did not. Likewise, more veiled women prayed daily than those who did not (79). "At first glance," notes Meshal, "the claim that women who wear the *hijab* do so 'for purely spiritual and religious motives' ... seems to be substantiated" (80). However, vital questions must be asked: "From whom or where does a woman derive her religious understanding of *hijab*? Whose interpretation of Islam is she availing herself of?" (80).

Not surprisingly, 82% of veiled women had mothers who did so, as well (80). Hence, when a woman adopts the *hijab*, it is not an individual act. It impacts the entire family. It places pressure on their daughters and other female relatives. Meshal, however, cautions that "a high incidence of support for *hijab* within the family is not necessarily an indicator of coercion; rather, it may simply allude to the common shared values of a family unit" (81). At the same time, however, it must not be forgotten that in Muslim families, children often seek to please their parents. They are even willing to make great sacrifices to marry men they do not wish to marry, praying when they do not wish to do so, and wearing *hijab*, despite their dislike and displeasure.

There are *hijab*-wearing "Muslim" women who are agnostics and atheists. They wear *hijab* to placate their families and communities and keep their personal beliefs private. It is their way of buying peace. They do not want to be disowned, harassed, or murdered. The psychological problems that this duality poses are tremendous. In Iran, Islamism has been imposed on a national scale. In the past, religion was a personal matter practiced primarily in the home. After the revolution, Islam had to be displayed in public, while the home became the last bastion of freedom, liberty, and secularism. Political Islam has not made Iranians more religious. It has made them less so.

Returning to Islam in the Canadian context, Meshal found that for many practicing Muslim women, the *hijab* was the symbol of Islam (81). In other words, their use of *hijab* did not represent their integration into a multicultural society but rather their rejection of its values, and the assertion of a separate pan-Islamist identity. It was an act of defiance against secular, liberal, society. As Meshal's study has shown, mosques, and Muslim student associations, play an integral part in propagating the veil. As she notes, "this strongly suggests that the dissemination of a single, hegemonic doctrine on the *hijab* has been successful" (87).

Muslim women have been convinced that the *hijab* is obligatory. In fact, 95% of women who veil in Canada believe that the practice is mandatory, while five percent viewed it as preferable (89). However, only 37% could provide any scriptural support for their beliefs (89). When it comes to women who wear *hijab*, their "acquaintance with the scriptures is minimal" (89). Consequently, "the claim made by the overwhelming majority to having a 'good' to 'very good' knowledge of Islam and to formulating independent views concerning *hijab*, based on primary Islamic scripture, must, therefore, be discounted" (89). Most of them do not act out of knowledge. They act out of ignorance. Finally, as Meshal observed, the issue of *hijab* betrays deep divisions in the Muslim community. As she explains, "Muslim women who did not wear the *hijab* frequently described those who did as "backward," "old fashioned" or "out of touch with reality," while Muslim women who wore it called those who did not "shameful" or "weak in faith" (102). Both sides may speak of the right to choose; however, their choices are not free of value judgments.

9.3 How do Muslim Women Feel about the *Hijab*?

According to the Pew Research Center, most Muslim women believe they should have the right to choose to veil in public. In many nations, the majority of men feel the same way. These are moderate, educated, and often secularized Muslims. They are often professionals who integrate well into Western culture when they migrate to them. However, there are nations where a majority, even a large majority of men, believe that women should have no say in the matter of *hijab*. However, as Bestandji reminds us, "the emancipation of the individual is built upon bodily autonomy" (2021: 344). If they cannot control their bodies, then they are not free.

What is more concerning is that when we separate Muslims who support the establishment of *shari'ah* law from those who oppose it, the overwhelming majority of *shari'ah* supporters do not believe that women have the right to decide whether or not they wear *hijab*. These people are the Muslim fundamentalists and the Islamists who wish to live under "Islamic law" in "Islamic" states, republics, and emirates. They sympathize with jihadist groups and terrorists who wish to overthrow their governments and impose strict *shari'ah* law. In most Muslim-majority nations, these Islamists and jihadists are not tolerated. They are imprisoned and even executed for subversive activities and terrorism. They are threats to the rule of law. They are treated as traitors.

Many immigrate or seek refugee status in the Western world where they have greater freedom to practice their radical religion and, exploiting the inherent weaknesses in secular, liberal, democracies, impose it upon others.

There is a deep divide in the Muslim world between ultra-conservatives, extremists, and Islamists, on the one side, and liberals, moderates, and rationalists on the other. The Western world should be cautious when it comes to selecting sides. Marginalizing Muslims in the Western world can push them defensively into the radical camp. However, giving in to the demands of the radicals provides them inroads into the Western world to further entrench their extreme Islamic ideology.

Moderate, mainstream, tolerant, traditional, and spiritual Islam, even if socially committed, must be fostered; however, the fringe, intolerant, extremist, misogynistic, and violent manifestations of Islam must be curtailed. They have declared war against the West and committed countless acts of terrorism. They do not hide their intentions. They proclaim them loudly and clearly: they wish to conquer the West and impose their perverted interpretation of Islamic *shari'ah* law.

Unless the Western world is suicidal, which it appears to be, it must not empower its avowed enemies. It must curtail them. Freedom of religion is not an absolute right. It cannot infringe upon the rights of others, and it cannot violate the law. Secular societies are not required to capitulate to religious extremists. As the Talmud acknowledges, "the law of the State takes precedence over the law of the Torah" (Meddeb 194). Any Muslim who wishes to live in the Western world must abide by its values and not seek their destruction. They cannot be beholden to a foreign potentate or a hostile ideology.

What Style of Dress is Appropriate for Women in Public?

% who say woman is dressed most appropriately

	Woman 1	2	3	4	5	6
Tunisia	1	2%	3%	57%	23%	15%
Egypt	1%	9	20	52	13	4
Turkey	0	2	2	46	17	32
Iraq	4	8	32	44	10	3
Lebanon	2	1	3	32	12	49
Pakistan	3	32	31	24	8	2
Saudi Arabia	11	63	8	10	5	3
MEDIAN	2	8	8	44	12	4

Source: The Birthplace Of The Arab Spring: Values And Perceptions Of The Tunisian Public In A Comparative Perspective. From the Middle Eastern Values Study, University of Michigan Population Studies Center.

PEW RESEARCH CENTER

Gender and the Right to Choose to Veil in Public

% of Muslims who say it is a woman's right to decide whether to wear a veil

	Women	Men	Diff.
Russia	76	54	***+22***
Pakistan	81	60	***+21***
Uzbekistan	75	56	***+19***
Afghanistan	40	23	***+17***
Palestinian terr.	61	44	***+17***
Tajikistan	65	49	***+16***
Bangladesh	64	49	***+15***
Egypt	54	39	***+15***
Lebanon	69	54	***+15***
Thailand^	84	69	***+15***
Iraq	52	38	***+14***
Kyrgyzstan	69	55	***+14***
Azerbaijan	85	76	*+9*
Jordan	49	41	*+8*
Kazakhstan	82	74	*+8*
Malaysia	81	74	*+7*
Albania	87	82	*+5*
Indonesia	81	77	*+4*
Morocco	87	83	*+4*
Tunisia	91	87	*+4*
Turkey	92	89	*+3*
Bosnia-Herz.	93	91	*+2*
Kosovo	91	91	*0*

Statistically significant differences are shown in bold.

^Interviews conducted with Muslims in five southern provinces only.

PEW RESEARCH CENTER Q58 and Q95.

Support for Sharia and Gender Roles

	Among Muslims who ...		
	Favor sharia	**Oppose sharia**	***Diff.***
% who say wives must always obey husbands			
Albania	78	34	*+44*
Bosnia-Herz.	74	40	*+34*
Kosovo	55	21	*+34*
Russia	86	53	*+33*
Turkey	84	60	*+24*
Kazakhstan	72	49	*+23*
Thailand^	91	72	*+19*
Lebanon	84	70	*+14*
Kyrgyzstan	82	69	*+13*
Bangladesh	89	78	*+11*
% who say a woman should have the right to divorce			
Russia	46	80	*-34*
Albania	71	90	*-19*
Morocco	71	90	*-19*
Kazakhstan	65	83	*-18*
Kyrgyzstan	51	69	*-18*
Tunisia	76	87	*-11*
Jordan	23	11	*+12*
Bangladesh	64	51	*+13*
% who say sons and daughters should have equal inheritance rights			
Kazakhstan	23	67	*-44*
Morocco	13	36	*-23*
Russia	51	74	*-23*
Albania	47	69	*-22*
Lebanon	20	40	*-20*
Bosnia-Herz.	66	82	*-16*
Kyrgyzstan	39	50	*-11*
% who say it is a woman's right to decide if she wears a veil			
Lebanon	39	72	*-33*
Russia	54	80	*-26*
Tajikistan	41	65	*-24*
Kyrgyzstan	51	72	*-21*
Bangladesh	54	68	*-14*

Only countries where differences are statistically significant are shown.
^Interviews conducted with Muslims in five southern provinces only.

PEW RESEARCH CENTER Q58, Q77, Q78, Q79a and Q83.

For French secularists, nationalists, Christians, and moderate, rationalist, Muslims, the *hijab*, the *niqab*, and the *burqa* are not simply religious markers. They are ideological ones The women in question are not wearing the traditional dress from their cultures of origin. They are wearing a pan-Islamist uniform. They are raising the flags of Islamic conquest. These women are the advance troops of the Islamists. Wearing a *burqa* in Paris, London, or elsewhere, is not a fashion choice any more than wearing a Nazi flag. It is a political and ideological statement. Islamist movements wish to occupy the public sphere. The Islamist *hijab* is their banner.

While they invoke "freedom of choice," "religious liberty," "tolerance," "diversity," "equality," "equity" and "inclusion" to promote the *hijab*, Muslims have little tolerance when it comes to women's dress. As Bestandji has shown, the Islamist definitions of "tolerance" and "respect" are not those that are found in the dictionary (2022). In a survey conducted by the University of Michigan's Institute for Social Research, people from seven Muslim-majority nations (Tunisia, Egypt, Iraq, Lebanon, Saudi Arabia, and Turkey) were asked to identify the style of dress that was most appropriate for women in public. They were shown the images of six different women. The first is wearing a complete face veil. The second is wearing a *niqab*, which reveals only her eyes. The third is wearing a *chador*. The fourth wears a tight white *hijab*. The fifth wears a more traditional scarf, which shows some bangs. The sixth wears no head covering, and her hair is loose.

63% of Saudis and 32% of Pakistanis believe that the woman wearing the *niqab* embodies the appropriate dress for women. The *chador* was favored by 31% of Pakistanis, 32% of Iraqis, and 20% of Egyptians. 44% of all respondents from all countries surveyed believed the woman with the tight, white, *hijab*, was the most appropriately attired. Such was the view of 57% of Tunisians, 52% of Egyptians, 46% of Turks, 44% of Iraqis, 32% of Lebanese, 24% of Pakistanis, and 10% of Saudis. This style of *hijab*, however, is a modern Islamist invention. The more relaxed *hijab*, which shows some hair, is much closer to historical Islamic practice, was favored by 23% of Tunisians, 13% of Egyptians, 17% of Turks, 10 % of Iraqis, 12% of Lebanese, 8% of Pakistanis, and 5% of Saudis. While 49% of Lebanese, 32% of Turks, and 15% of Tunisians believe the woman with free hair should represent the norm, the overwhelming majority of respondents did not believe that it was appropriate for a woman to show her hair in public. Such was the view of 85% of Tunisians, 96% of Egyptians, 68% of Turks, 97% of Iraqis, 51% of Lebanese, 98% of Pakistanis, and 97% of Saudis (Poushter).

While one cannot pretend to know the intentions of the pollsters, the results of their survey creates the perception that most Muslims support the *hijab*. Consequently, to support the *hijab* is to support democracy and freedom of choice. The countries surveyed, however, are infamous for their patriarchy, sexism, and misogyny. They are among the worst countries in the world to be a woman (Statistica). The people surveyed do not speak for all Muslims, all Muslim women, and all women. One could argue that the study was designed to produce a desired outcome. One must control surveys for education, class, and culture, among other variables. Even if a majority of Muslims supported the mandatory *hijab*, that would not give it legitimacy, not any more than a majority of Muslims supporting female genital mutilation, wife-beating, sexual segregation, gender apartheid, child marriage, the statutory rape of girls as young as nine, the death penalty for blasphemy and apostasy, suicide bombings, and the stoning of women. In many nations, most Muslim women accept domestic violence, not to mention female genital mutilation (Morrow 2020:210). Does that make them right?

When asked whether women should be able to choose their clothing, 56% of Tunisians agreed, and 52% of Turks. However, 51% of Lebanese, 53% of Saudis, 73 % of Iraqis, 78% of Pakistanis, and 86% of Egyptians insisted that women should not have a choice. The researchers concluded that most people in the region prefer women to cover their hair completely, but not necessarily their faces (Poushter). In reality, it reveals how deeply entrenched patriarchy and misogyny are in the region, and how far Islamic fundamentalism has spread in the region after the 1950s and 1960s. It also reveals that many Muslims who demand the "right" of women to wear *hijab* do not believe that women have the right not to wear *hijab*. It is a duplicitous double discourse. Forget about human rights. It is the rule of the misogynistic mob that determines if a woman can or cannot show her hair.

"In Muslim-majority countries," notes Tarek Fatah, "jihadis do not mince their words or actions" (282). In the West, however, the agenda of the Islamists is to use the mantra of choice to generate support from liberals, leftists, and feminists (282). As he notes, "No one can deny the right of a woman to wear a *hijab*, but the argument of choice espoused by non-Muslim feminist defenders of the *hijab* falls flat. The same Muslim women who demand the right to choose *hijab* refuse to accord the same right of choice to their sisters who refuse to wear it" (297).

"When they invoke human rights," points out Fatah, "they do so to protect the medieval misogyny they have packaged falsely as divine revelations" (299). For Fatah, "the true agenda of Islamists is to promote fear among young Muslim girls about not wearing the *hijab*" (282). Without evidence, they claim that the failure to observe *hijab* contributes to divorce, adultery, rape, illegitimate children, immorality, and murder (283-284). Curiously, all these social evils are prevalent in countries where the *hijab* dominates.

"By removing your *hijab*," they warn girls and women, "you have destroyed your faith" and that "those who refuse submission cannot be called Muslims" (284). They are brainwashed into believing that women are to blame for sexual assault (285). Taj Aldin al-Hilali, the so-called mufti of Australia, echoed the sentiments of many Muslim clerics when he claimed that women were responsible for provoking rape (Fatah 287).

As empirical evidence has long demonstrated, there is no connection between sexual assault and a woman's clothing. Few Muslims are brave enough to denounce the misogynistic attitudes of Islamic clerics who believe in polygyny, slavery, concubinage, the right of husbands to beat their wives, and the right of men to rape captives of war. After all, organized religion is a racket run by hedonistic male supremacists and oppressors. For many reasonable people, Islam is no different, no better, and no worse than other religions when it comes to its treatment of women.

For Islamic fundamentalists, any Muslim who opposes the *hijab* must be silenced (Bestandji 2018: part four). Colossal sums of money are spent promoting Islamic fundamentalism, Islamism, and radicalism. "Faced with the power of the Islamists," notes Bestandji, "the spread of rationalist thought is paltry" (2018: part four). In fact, the works of Qasim Amin, Mohamed Taha Ben Ashour, and Mohamed Talbi, among others, are nowhere to be found thanks to the censorship of the Islamists (Bestandji 2021: 115, 2018: part four). In fact, "the theological weakness of their propaganda is compensated by an ingenious tool: guilt and fear of God" (Part Four). They threaten those who disagree with their religious arguments, invented out of the blue, with accusations of treason against Islam and fear of hell (part four). Anyone who expresses a different opinion or offers a divergent analysis of Qur'anic texts is not only ostracized but puts his or her life in danger (Bestandji 2021: 116). The Islamists dominate all domains: publishing, the internet, and social networks (2018: part four). Those who oppose them are treated as "racists" and "Islamophobes," not only by Muslims, but by Western secularists (2018: part four). They are demonized by the left (2018: part four).

For Bestandji, the *hijab* is a sexist political tool (2018: part four). "Besides being an insult to women," he asserts, "the *hijab*, the symbol of obscurantism, is an insult to Islam" (2018: part four). The future of Islam, reasons Bestandji, is not in the hands of the Islamists. It is in the hands of those who fiercely oppose them (2018: part four). In his words, "this piece of fabric alone carries many stakes, but none of them are spiritual" (2018: part four). For Bestandji, it must never be forgotten that the *hijab* is inherently misogynistic. It is "the legacy of ancient patriarchy, the most sexist and discriminating accessory that man has invented, and the quintessence of gender inequality" (2021: back cover, 335). It is the product of "an exacerbated sexual obsession" and the "political Trojan horse" of the Islamists" (2021: back cover, 335). "Nothing, absolutely nothing can justify sexism," asserts Bestandji, "not even a religion and even less the extremists who pretend to speak in its name" (2021: 352).

The French, among other Westerners, have a difficulty distinguishing between cultural Muslims and radicalized Muslims, between modern, tolerant, well-integrated, Muslim women, who wear modest fashion and retrograde, intolerant, subversive, and seditious women who are Islamists and jihadists. It may be difficult to distinguish a moderate Muslim man from a terrorist. However, in the case of women, the type of clothing they wear, or choose not to wear, provides an exceptionally good indicator of their ideological orientation.

For Islamist women, be they Sunnis or Shiites, the ideal "Islamic" clothing is clear cut: the tight black *hijab*, the black *jilbab*, the black *abayah*, the black *chador*, and the black *burka*. For modern, moderate Muslim women, modesty codes are multiple and fluid. Many young women wish to be modest, but cool, hip, and fashionable. They seek to create a space of their own which is not the culture of their immigrant parents or grandparents nor the negative aspects of Western culture. As part of their attempt to negotiate religion, identity, and ethnicity, they seek to create a subculture of their own. Likewise, in the Middle East, more and more women wish to be "cool, sexy, and devout" (Stratton). However, their dress style is denounced as un-Islamic by radical Islamist men and women. These courageous, fashionable, educated, creative, and ambitious women, who wish to participate in Western society, should be free to do so.

While more liberated than women imprisoned in black *burqas*, liberal Muslims have still succumbed to the brainwashing of the Islamic extremists. How do Islamists convince women to veil themselves? It is essential to understand. As Bestandji explains:

> Islamists use three methods to convince Muslim women to veil themselves. Valuation presents the veil as the packaging of a precious object. The sexual object becomes a jewel, a pearl, whose veil would serve as a case. Guilt is the second method: an unveiled woman would be immodest, disrespectful, and responsible for her fate in the event of sexual assault. Have we ever seen a clothing brand put forward particularly violent and degrading arguments similar to those of the Islamists quoted in this book to promote the mini-skirt or stiletto heels? This is why the veil is classified by Islamists in the category of "modest fashion" (euphemistic marketing to avoid saying "sexist fashion")... The third method, to try to convince the recalcitrant, is the religious argument. The veil would be prescribed by God. Not obeying him would be a one-way ticket to hell... (2021: 277)

Little girls are indoctrinated into wearing *hijab* as early as possible, and long before puberty, to prevent them from rebelling later on (Bestandji 2021: 281-285, 323). For Bestandji, the use of little girls who are covered from head to toe in black as part of publicities for World *Hijab* Day is nothing short than "encouraging child abuse and pedophilia" (2021: 323). After all, these little girls are viewed by Islamic fundamentalists as sexual temptations. That is the very reason for which they are compelled to cover. When one comes to such a realization, the sight of little girls in *hijab* changes from being cute to being creepy. It is as troubling a sight as seeing prepubescent girls in lingerie.

So what if most Muslim women around the world believe that women should have the right to veil themselves? Most of these women believe that husbands have the right to beat their wives. Do we tolerate and legalize wife-beating because most Muslim women defend it? The greater the extent of the veil, the greater the extent of male dominance and control. There is a clear correlation between commitment to *shari'ah* law and domestic violence (Morrow 2020: 41-45). The veil is to a Muslim woman what the black eye is to a battered woman. It is a symbol of subjugation to male domination that the State, the community, the family, or the men of the household can and do impose. Considering the pressure under which girls and women find themselves, the *hijab* can also be self-imposed. The danger of defying this so-called "divine command" is so serious in some cases that females voluntarily adopt it and pressure others to do so it. Some reject it internally, while others rationalize their choice to seek psychological and spiritual stability. "If you cannot beat them," they figure, "might as well join them." Some *hijabis* and *niqabi*s might be convinced of and committed to their ideology. Others, however, suffer from *hijabi* syndrome, a variant of Stockholm syndrome or battered wife syndrome.

The situation of female Muslim converts is not always the same. Those who marry foreign husbands often come under their strict control and that of their families and communities. The situation is all the more severe if they are foolish enough to relocate with them to their repressive countries of origin where women have little to no rights. A female Muslim convert who lives in the West, whether she is single or married, benefits from all the rights and freedoms offered by secular democracies. For many women from troubled pasts, Islam is often an improvement. For them, the *hijab* is not an impediment. They can choose to wear it or decide not to wear it. They can even leave Islam if they find it too constricting and controlling. For moderate, secular, feminists from the Muslim world, the sight of Western women voluntarily adopting the symbol of retrograde fundamentalist Islam is a veritable shock and slap in the face. It is an insult to the struggles they have waged against macho Muslim misogynists for over half a century. Beyond retrograde, it is a return to pre-Islamic and pagan times.

9.4 Pre-Islamic Origins

As far as scholars like Leila Ahmed are concerned, the origin of the *hijab* is pre-Islamic. It was inspired, not by the Qur'an or the true teachings and practices of the Prophet, but by early Muslim contact with the Byzantines, the Assyrians, and the Persians, cultures that used to veil and confine women as a mark of class (1992: 5, 14-15 18, 26, 55-56, Winter 27). The origin of the veil, however, goes back much farther. It traces back to thousands of year before the rise of Islam.

So far, notes Stol, no Sumerian word for veil has been found: "perhaps there were no veiled women in southern Iraq between 3000 and 2000 BC" (26). The same applies to Babylonia, to the south of Assyria, where "we have no proof of veiled women there either" (27). In fact, "only during a wedding did the father of the bride or her brother place a veil on her head, which the bridegroom later ceremonially removed in the bride's room" (27; see also 22).

The first textual evidence of veiling comes from Mesopotamia where the Goddess Innana / Ishtar was associated with sacred prostitution. In a hymn written circa 2300 BCE by the high priestess of the moon god at Ur, the

Goddess is referred to as a hierodule or temple prostitute. Although often depicted in the nude, with wings, a beautiful body, bulging breasts, and a prominent pubic area, her hair is invariably covered with a head covering. By concealing their hair with a veil, married women imitated the Goddess Ishtar, who portrayed herself as a whore (Stol 427). Since Ishtar covered her hair, so did married women, the veil serving as a signal they were under her guardianship and that of their husbands.

The first legal document that mentions sacred prostitutes is the *Code of Hammurabi* which dates from 1730 BCE. By means of the head veil, sacred prostitutes, as well as married women, were distinguished from common prostitutes who were in the commerce of selling profane sex. This contrasted with sacred prostitutes who transmitted the power of fertility through *hieros gamos*, namely, sacred marriage, a ceremonial form of public sexual intercourse. As the *Code of Hammurabi* states, "If anyone "points the finger" (slander) at a sister of a god or the wife of anyone, and cannot prove it, this man shall be taken before the judges and his brow shall be marked (by cutting the skin, or perhaps hair)" (King). In fact, the earliest record of veiling traces back to an Assyrian law from around 1200 BCE which compelled married women to cover their hair in public (Laver 15). The law, which forms part of a clay tablet found in the ancient city of Asur, and which deals entirely with women, provides the following dictates regarding veiling:

> § 40. A wife-of-a-man, or [widows], or [Assyrian] women who go out into the main thorough-fare [shall not have] their heads [bare]. Daughters of a man [... with] either a ...-cloth or garments or [...] shall be veiled, [...] their heads [... (gap) ...] When they go about [...] in the main thoroughfare during the daytime, they shall veil themselves. (Stol 677)

Islamic, as well as Christian and Jewish veiling practices, trace back to this pagan Assyrian law. The same applies to Islamic laws that prohibit slave-girls from wearing *hijab*. As the Assyrian law dictates:

> A concubine who goes about in the main thoroughfare with her mistress is to be veiled. A *qadištu*-priestess whom a husband has taken (in marriage) is to be veiled in the main thoroughfare, but one whom a husband has not taken (in marriage) is to have her head bare in the main thoroughfare, she shall not veil herself. (Stol 677)

The Qur'anic verse that advises Muslim women to cover their bosoms with their scarves to distinguish them from prostitutes also finds its antecedent in Assyrian law. As we read in the Assyrian legal code:

> A prostitute shall not veil herself; her head shall be bare. Whoever sees a veiled prostitute shall seize her, secure witnesses, and bring her to the palace entrance. They shall not take her jewelry; he who has seized her

> shall take her clothing; they shall strike her 50 blows with rods; they shall pour hot pitch over her head. And if a man should see a veiled prostitute and release her and not bring her to the palace entrance: they shall strike that man 50 blows with rods; the one who informs against him shall take his clothing; they shall pierce his ears, thread (them) on a cord, tie (it) at his back; he shall perform the king's service for one full month.
>
> Slave-women shall not veil themselves, and he who should see a veiled slave-woman shall seize her and bring her to the palace entrance: they shall cut off her ears; he who seizes her shall take her clothing. If a man should see a veiled slave-woman but release her, not seize her, not bring her to the palace entrance, and they then prove the charges against him and find him guilty: they shall strike him 50 blows with rods; they shall pierce his ears, thread (them) on a cord, tie (it) at his back. The one who informs against him shall take his garments. He shall perform the king's service for one full month.
>
> If a man would veil his concubine, he shall assemble five or six of his comrades, he shall veil her in their presence, he shall declare, "She is my wife:" she is his wife. A concubine who is not veiled in the presence of the people, whose husband did not declare, "She is my wife:" she is not a wife, she is indeed a concubine. If a man is dead and there are no sons of his veiled wife: the sons of concubines are indeed sons; they shall take the inheritance share. (676-677)

According to the *hadith* literature, both 'Umar and Muhammad al-Baqir struck their concubines for the audacity of wearing a head veil in public, thereby, pretending to be free and honorable women when, in fact, they were sex slaves. By punishing sex-slaves for covering their hair, these figures were following a two-thousand-year-old pagan, pre-Islamic practice, that traced back to the ancient Assyrians. According to these laws, slaves and prostitutes who wore a veil were to be given fifty strokes of a cane and have pitch poured over their heads (Stol 25).

The veil, as a symbol of sacred prostitution, traces back at least five thousand years ago to ancient Mesopotamia. According to scholarly consensus, "every woman ought to have sex with a stranger once in her life in honor of Mylitta, the Assyrian equivalent of Aphrodite" (Anagnostou-Laoutides and Charles). As Heredotus records,

> The foulest Babylonian custom is that which compels every woman of the land to sit in the temple of Aphrodite and have intercourse with some stranger once in her life. Many women who are rich and proud and disdain to mingle with the rest, drive to the temple in covered carriages drawn by teams, and stand there with a great retinue of attendants. But most sit down in the sacred plot of Aphrodite, with crowns of cord on their heads; there is a great multitude of women

> coming and going; passages marked by lines run every way through the crowd, by which the men pass and make their choice. Once a woman has taken her place there, she does not go away to her home before some stranger has cast money into her lap, and had intercourse with her outside the temple; but while he casts the money, he must say, "I invite you in the name of Mylitta" (that is the Assyrian name for Aphrodite). It does not matter what sum the money is; the woman will never refuse, for that would be a sin, the money being by this act made sacred. So she follows the first man who casts it and rejects no one. After their intercourse, having discharged her sacred duty to the Goddess, she goes away to her home.

According to some early Islamic sources, it seems that sacred prostitution was still practiced by some heathen priestesses during the time of the Prophet and his successors. The Twelver Shiite practice of *mut'ah* or temporary pleasure marriage appears to trace back to these ritual sexual transactions. Go to a shrine city. Offer a veiled woman a sum of money. Have sex with her in the name of God. And be on your merry way. The *ahadith* which claim that everyone should do *mut'ah* at least once in their life echoes this ancient pagan practice (Mahajjah).

Muazzez İlmiye Çığ (b. 1914), the Turkish archeologist and Assyriologist, who translated three thousand stone tables from Sumer, noted that headscarves were first worn by women who worked as prostitutes in temples to differentiate them from priests (Aljazeera). In Assyrian society, wearing a head covering was a privilege reserved for wives, widows, concubines accompanying their mistresses, as well as priestesses (Stol 24-25). However, it was specifically prohibited for single women, prostitutes, and slave-girls. "For the former," notes Hannibal Genseric "wearing the veil was a duty, but not an obligation: no sanction is foreseen against them if they go out bare headed."

For J. Assante, married women could decide weather to veil or not (Stol 25, note 118). Sophie Lafont also believes that free Assyrian women could choose to veil or not to veil, and they were not subject to any punishment either way (Stol 25, note 118). Slaves and prostitutes, however, were "subject to humiliating corporal punishment" for veiling (Genseric). Failure to denounce the illicit wearing of veils by women was subject to similar forms of physical punishment. As the *Survey of Historic Costume* relates:

> In Assyrian and late Babylonian times, the veil was considered to be the distinguishing mark of a free, married woman. Slaves and prostitutes were not permitted to wear veils… This custom persists today in some areas of the Middle East… one can see that wearing the veil is a tradition of long duration in the area. (Tortora and Marcketti 31)

This custom has continued in the same geographic region until modern times (Laver 15). Covering the hair of married women with a veil was a marital status marker that had nothing to do with modesty. Many women covered their hair, to signal they were married, while exposing their breasts. What is more, there was nothing to prevent single women from pretending to be married or married women pretending to be single. What is clear is that the "veil police" have been harassing women in the region for thousands of years. This is only one of scores of Babylonian customs and superstitions that persist among such people.

Sumerian, Mesopotamian, and Babylonian veiling practices persisted for thousands of years. They resurfaced, in writing, in the Qur'an, which states that "believing women ... should draw their coverings [*khumur*] over their bosoms [*juyub*]" (24:31) and that "wives and your daughters and the women of the believers" should "draw their cloaks [*jalabib*] close round ... so that they may be recognized and not annoyed" (33:59). This is a clear-cut case of cultural continuity.

If the Qur'an inherited veiling practices from the cradle of civilization, it was also the heir of the ancient Semites, the Canaanites, Phoenicians, Hebrews, and Arabs, who had imposed a symbolic veil on women since they invested the hair on their heads with the same power as the hair in the pubic area. In the second millennium before the Common Era, it was customary for a veil to be placed on the head of a newly married woman. Likewise, when the grand priestess of Baal, the god of life and fertility, was appointed, she would be symbolically wed to the pagan god by having her head covered like a bride with a multi-colored shawl. After paganism was suppressed, and Judaism, Christianity, and Islam prevailed, the association of the veil with pagan sacred prostitution continued, only now it became the accessory of erotic dancers. The veil moved from the sacred to the profane. That being said, the Qur'anic and Islamic laws regarding veiling, not to mention other practices, appear to be derived, directly or indirectly, from Assyrian law. As the *Middle Assyrian Law-Book about Women* states, "a man may [whip] his wife, pluck out her hair, mutilate her ears, or strike her; it bears no offence" (Stol 681). "That a man could punish a woman so harshly according to the last laws," stresses Stol, "shows that women were totally subjugated" (681).

If the veil applied to all married women in late Assyrian times, that was not the case during the late part of the Prophet's mission in Medina. "The Koran does not prescribe the veil for all women," notes Karen Armstrong, "but only for Muhammad's wives, as a mark of their status" (158). "Muslims," she points out, "adopted those customs from the Oikumene which relegated women to second class status" (158). In other words, "they adopted the customs of veiling women and secluding them in harems from Persia and Christian Byzantium, where women had long been marginalized this way" (158). As Minoo Mirshahvalad, the sociologist of Islam, concludes, "the majority of the Islamic ordinances have not been formulated on the basis of the Koran, but through a conciliation of the Koran with the customs of time by means of *hadiths* that sometimes contradict the holy book" (106). As Liyakat Takim, the Twelver Shiite scholar of global

Islam, recognizes, "Legal pronouncements on slavery, child marriage and custody, the testimony and guardianship of women, their capacity to travel without a male guardian, and forms of Islamic punishment were appropriated from customary laws prevalent at the advent of Islam" (2021).

Some Muslim scholars, like Khamis ibn Sa'id Shiqsi al-Rustaqi, admitted that laws varied according to time and place and that it was acceptable, in certain regions, for women to show their hair (Abou El Fadl 259: note 127). He noted that women in Oman covered their hair, not because it was viewed as beautiful, but because it was *qabih* or unattractive not to do so (Abou El Fadl 259: note 127). In fact, in many societies, it was not befitting for men and women to go out in public without some headdress. Once again, we see the connection between social class, culture, fashion, and head-covering. If covering the hair of women is a marker of marriage, a means of conveying a message and not an end in itself, it can be replaced by other symbols. Marital markers in India include sindoor, a red powder or a dot on the forehead, toe rings, bangles, or a mangalasutra, a gold pendant or necklace with black beads or a black string. Married women wear certain hairstyles in parts of Africa. European women also used to plait their hair when they were married. In Tibet, married women wear aprons. In Western societies, a woman indicates she is married by wearing a wedding band on the fourth finger of the left hand. In some parts of the world, marriage is indicated by tattoos or bodily adornments. In certain cultures and religions, a married man must wear a beard while a single man is required to shave. If it is not mandatory for married Muslim men to sport beards it should not be mandatory for married Muslim women to cover their hair.

The concealment of women is not the product of early Islam. It crept into the Muslim faith gradually and steadily. It was canonized during late 'Abbasid times. It was adopted from ancient pagan customs, Jewish law, and Byzantine Christian teachings. Some of the sayings of the Prophet Muhammad, where he describes unveiled women as adulteresses, were copied straight from early Christian literature. Dishonest plagiarists, or honest appropriators, Muslim scholars copied and pasted Jewish and Christian sources and attributed them to the Messenger of God.

Many Muslims submitted to the New Order, with its slavery, concubinage, polygyny, veiling, gender segregation, seclusion of wives, and child marriages. However, some Muslims refused to accept such abominations, namely, the Qarmatians, the followers 'Ali, Hasan, Husayn, Zayn al-'Abidin, Muhammad al-Baqir, Ja'far al-Sadiq, and Muhammad ibn Isma'il, who rebelled against the 'Abbasids, and created a utopian state which aligned with their understanding of Islam. For Fadi A. Fahes,

> The Qarmatian approach to gender appears to have been progressive and emancipatory. Islam "evolved from an initial phase of tolerance to the gradual marginalization of women and their enclosure in the dark

> world of a theologically illegitimate patriarchy" ... This debilitating climate was shattered through a revolutionary interpretation of Islam and the restoration of "early Sufi and Qarmatian thought," long eclipsed by a conservative, male-dominated clerical Islam... Qarmatian society liberated women from their humiliating socio-economic status... Society equated women and men's rights in terms of social rights and their human dignity. This approach also restored their status as respectable mothers, virtuous educators, productive workers, and courageous and progressive activists... Polygamy was not prevalent (if at all existent) in the Qarmatian society... monogamy seems to have been the rule... In the Qarmatian state, women occupied a privileged, or possibly an equal, status. They were partners in the social and political system and received education along with their male counterparts. They worked, took part in military activities, and helped propagate the Qarmatian calling. Historical sources refer to women's active engagement in the propagation of the *da'wah*... supervising ... schools for girls in Bahrain, numerous women engaging in academic debates along with their male counterparts, and women fighting alongside men in battles... Qarmatians did not require women to cover up ... and permitted mingling of men and women in society... (44-45)

The Qarmatian version of Shiite Islam contrasts sharply with that of the Zaydis, other Fatimid Ismailis, and the Ithna Asharis. In fact, all these groups are 'Abbasid-style Shiites. All of them have historically supported slavery, concubinage, polygyny, veiling, gender segregation, the seclusion of wives, and child marriages, and most of their scholars continue to do so down to this day. Rare are those who had the courage, like S.V. Mir Ahmed Ali (1902-1976), to assert that "strictly observing the law, one can have only one [wife]" (1269). What is more, he argued that the Qur'an does not speak about taking slave girls as concubines but as regular wives (365).

The fact that the veil, sexual segregation, and the seclusion of women is not derived from the Qur'an, or the Prophet, was recognized by some Sunni scholars, as well. As Mohammed Alexander Russell Webb (1846- 1916), the American Muslim convert and writer, recognized:

> The *purdah* is not part of the Mohammedan system, but is a custom borrowed from the Hindus and other Eastern people, who practiced it long before Mohammed was born. During the Prophet's life, as well as the reign of the early caliphs, Arabian women were perfectly free to go about as they pleased, and a woman could travel alone in any part of the country by day or night, without being subjected to assault or insult. The idea of seclusion arose from a misconception of the following passage of the Koran: "And speak to the believing women, that they refrain their eyes and observe continence; and that they display not their ornaments... And let them not strike their feet together, so as to

> discover their hidden ornaments." This injunction was intended to induce women to dress modestly and could not have meant that they should be secluded. (45)

As Khaled Abou El Fadl has concluded, the claims that the Qur'an requires women to cover the face or the hair but not the face "are ahistorical in presuming the historical existence of an historical practice that has not been proven" (2016). The only thing that we can say for sure is that the Qur'an called upon women to cover their bosoms (2016). He also objects to the equation of *'awrah* and *zinah*, namely, personal, and private parts, with beauty in general (2016).

As Abou El Fadl explains, what is considered to be *zinah* is a matter of applied ethics: "it differs from one place to another and from one time to another" (2016). In other words, "What is considered to be immodest ornamental displays of beautification in a part of Africa could be entirely different than the same in Mongolia. In essence, the Qur'an is counseling against the immodest flouting of physical appearance" (2016). As far as he is concerned, "there is no evidence that displaying of the hair is by definition a part of a woman's *zinah*." In fact, "depending on the place and context, a woman could be modest while not covering her hair, and the opposite is also true. A woman can cover her hair but still be immodest by displaying her *zinah*." For Abou El Fadl, "it is clear that the Qur'an is repeating and reaffirming a long-established biblical command to lower the gaze, be modest, and avoid displays of flashiness and vain conceit" (2016). It is an ethical order and not a legislative one.

Nasr Hamid Abu Zayd al-Damanhuri (d. 2010), a Qur'an-centered scholar, also argued in his book *Dawa'ir al-khawf* (1999) that the concept of *'awrah* is bound by culture and time. Since it is subject to socio-cultural norms, it is changeable and should not be fixed. As far as he is concerned, the Qur'an does not impose a timeless definition on *'awrah*, nor does the text obligate women to wear *hijab*. For him, it is merely a part of Arabian culture (Jahangir, Zainol 66).

Likewise, Javed Ahmed Ghamidi (b. 1952), the Pakistani philosopher, believes that there are only four injunctions that pertain to Muslim women: lowering the gaze, wearing modest clothing, covering the bosom, and not exhibiting themselves in front of unrelated men (Jahangir). For Farhad Shafti, wearing a *khimar* is not a religious act, nor does it pertain to modesty. In the words of Moiz Amjad (b. 1962), "Islam does not make it mandatory for women to cover their heads" (Jahangir). As far as Mahmoud Mohamed Taha (1909-1985), the Sudanese religious thinker, who was martyred for his beliefs, was concerned, "the veil (*al-hijab*) is not an original precept in Islam" (143). As he explained in *The Second Message of Islam*:

> Islam's original precept is *al-sufur* [unveiling]. The purpose of Islam is chastity, emanating from within men and women, and not imposed through closed doors and long robes. There is no way to achieve inner

> chastity, however, except through education and discipline, and this requires a transitional period when chastity is encouraged through the veil, hence the rule of imposing it. (143)

As Taha shows based on the Qur'an, "the original precept prevailed between Adam and Eve before they committed their first sin" (143). Since they abused their freedom, they were required to cover as a punishment. (144). In the words of Taha, "*Al-hijab*, as practiced at present, is a continuing abrogation of the freedom of *al-sufur* [uncovering], designed by *shari'ah* to be a safeguard for the immature believers (*al-mu'minin*). Only true submitters (*al-muslimin*) can shoulder the responsibility of *al-sufur* [undressing]; hence they are not subject to *al-hijab* [covering/veiling]" (144-145). In other words, unveiling, uncovering, and undressing are not an issue for mature, civilized, human beings, who have self-control.

The Qur'an, however, does not speak of *hijab*: it speaks of *jilbab*. It speaks not of covering the hair but of covering the genitals and bosom. It invites women to cover their bodies when conditions require it and when they decide it is necessary. Men do not have the divinely granted right to dictate to women how they should dress. Women have the right to cover or uncover themselves -- within the stipulated limits -- as they please, and men do not have the right to judge them. If God judges people based on faith and deeds, one can presume that *hijab*-wearing women can and do go to hell and that women who dress more liberally can and do go to heaven. What matters more is moral virtues and righteous deeds, not external appearances. As for conflating *khimar* with *hijab*, it comes as no coincidence. As Asma Lamrabet (b. 1961) rightly asks,

> Since there is a difference between *hijab* and *khimar*, we have the right to ask why we keep using the term *hijab* for what has been named in the Qur'an scarf or *khimar?* This error is currently made unwillingly and … reproduced unconsciously… this semantic shift was not made innocently or casually throughout the history of Islamic intellectual production. The semantic shifts are the result of incorrect translations and interpretations and socio-cultural factors, which aimed at one point in history to create "made-to-measure" concepts to serve the political interests… This is what happened with *hijab* when it was imposed on Muslim women by inserting it willingly in the register of Islamic body ethics.
>
> When we go back to the origin of the term *hijab*, which means to "hide" or "separate," and notice the changing process that it has undergone to bear the name "scarf," we have the right to wonder if this concept was given this double meaning to religiously justify the isolation of Muslim women. The "hijab" was imposed on Muslim women as a way of "separation" in order to show them their place in society, and exclude them, in the name of Islam, from the socio-

political sphere... Replacing the *khimar* with *hijab* means to confuse different and opposing semantic and conceptual fields in order to endorse, in the name of Islam, the exclusion of women from the sociopolitical space behind a curtain!

To substitute the *khimar* with the *hijab* is to confuse two different registers. While *khimar* remains, according to the Qur'anic vision, a sign of women's social visibility, *hijab* undoubtedly symbolizes their relegation to the private space... It is not the *khimar* -- that existed before revelation -- which is important, but rather its new meaning and the context in which it was revealed. The *khimar*, according to its original meaning of women's liberation, and as a symbol of their participation along with men in the socio-political space, was therefore gradually replaced by the other Qur'anic concept of *hijab* to prevent women from participating in the social field.

By considering *hijab* as sacred and disregarding the Islamic vocabulary of *khimar*, a new Islamic social code is invented to endorse the separation of men and women. By "veiling" women, they will lose all the rights acquired at the advent of Islam. And the "veil" or *hijab* will remain the single powerful indicator of the deterioration of Muslim women's legal status, since they will be secluded and excluded from the public space, in the name of this symbol...

Qur'anic ethics seem today to be reduced to women's dress and body, to the way they should be covered, the color, thickness, and uniformity of the dress ... Given that the Qur'an did not insist on a specific clothing or appearance for women, it would be ... simplistic to analyze the few verses on the dress far from the guidance of the spiritual message about the global body ethics for both men and women. The Qur'an invites both men and women to behave with "decency" and "integrity," both physically and morally. The Qur'an does not legislate a ... religious "uniform" as it is shown here, and the first spiritual message did not intend to stipulate rigid or "fixed" dress standards once and for all, but rather to "recommend" an "attitude" or an "ethic" regarding the body and soul...

The first intention of the spiritual message of Islam is often neglected or ... ignored at the expense of a literal reading which keeps no more than "the obligation of wearing the *hijab*" out of all the Qur'anic teachings about women! This contradicts the principles of the spiritual message and its spiritual ethics. The ... *khimar* or scarf is not part of the pillars of Islam, but rather of moral values, behavior, and relational ethics. The religious faith is meaningful only when it is practiced without pressure... Speaking about the obligation of Islam to wear a headscarf or *khimar* is spiritually unacceptable because the Qur'an said: "No compulsion in religion." It is one of the main principles of Islam.

> Reducing the whole global Qur'anic body ethics to the so-called "veil" is to stand against the same message. And this is exactly what happened in the Islamic history by focusing on woman's dress, and the obligation to "hide" and "conceal" her body. As a result, this spiritual symbol has become a sign of oppression in the Muslim world. (2019)

Fadwa El Guindi (b. 1941), the Egyptian American anthropologist, has also forced scholars to reconsider the notion of '*awrah* as unfavorably interpreted to Muslim women. She observes that the term derives from the root '*a-w-r*, which can mean defectiveness, imperfection, blemish, and flaw in the singular form and which can mean pudenda, genitals, or weakness in the plural form (2005: 81). Her analysis of the term as employed in the Qur'an "shows '*awrah* as neither confined to women nor to the body" (2005: 82). The Qur'an speaks of "male slaves or underaged boys not yet sexually mature for contact with women's '*awrat* in intercourse" (24:31). As she notes, the text in question connotes women's genitals (2005: 82). El Guindi cites the following passage of the Qur'an to demonstrate that the term '*awrah* also refers to privacy as well as private space and time: "O believers, male slaves, and underaged boys should not intrude upon your privacy on three occasions: before dawn prayer, when you are resting at noon, and after night prayer. These are three '*awrat*, outside of which interaction is not held against you or them… (24:58)."

As others have done before, El Guindi notes that 33:13 uses the term '*awrah* to connote protection, safety, vulnerability, security, and privacy concerning a home (2005: 82). She also stresses that "there is a context in the Qur'an that is unambiguously about the genitals," namely 7:26-27, which reads: "O ye children of Adam! We have bestowed dress upon you to cover your genitals." A holistic approach to all Qur'anic passages relating to the '*awrah* leads El Guindi to conclude that "a range of contexts are revealed, all of which make sense if the meaning imbued… becomes "inviolate vulnerability" … Several contexts are discerned: women's genitals (sexuality), home, conjugal privacy, women's privacy… '*Awrah*, therefore, does not mean "a blemish on women's bodies" … (2005: 83). As for the so-called "Islamic" dress of the Islamists, El Guindi asserts that "it does not represent a return to any traditional dress form and has no tangible precedent" (2005: 75).

Although "the passage in the Qur'an which tells women to use the head covering (*khimar*) to cover their cleavage has been interpreted as a total covering of the body," Afaf Lutfi al-Sayyid-Marsot (b. 1933), the Egyptian American historian, argues that "it is men from the eighth century onward who interpreted the passage in the Qur'an which enjoins men and women to dress modestly to mean that women should be totally covered and segregated, neither seen nor heard" (11). According to Murad Hoffman (1931-2020), Tedjini Haddam, who was a rector of the Great Mosque in Paris, explained that all that was required is that "a woman be decently dressed" (García). Likewise, Sultan

Abdulmajeed argued that "the idea that all Muslim women are required by Islam to veil themselves (in any form) is false and damaging to women, to Islam, and to people who might otherwise consider accepting Islam as their faith" (García).

For El Guindi, "the reference to drawing the head veil to cover a woman's cleavage may have been in reaction to the way contemporary women in the region… seem to have worn clothes that exposed their bodies" (77). As far as Guindi is concerned, 24:30-31 was tied to cultural notions of respectability, sexuality, eroticism, and privacy (77). In her mind, "Islamic morality prohibits the public flaunting of sexuality… exhibitionist dress and behavior" (78). If Muslim women were encouraged to cover their breasts, argues El Guindi, it was not for sexual reasons. In her words:

> It is most certainly not suggestive of the eroticism of women's breasts (as in American culture) as there is no ethnographic evidence to that effect. While they are considered part of the beauty of a woman's body, in Arabic culture (as in the case of many cultures outside the Euro-American culture) breasts are traditionally more associated with maternity and femininity than with sex. The monothematic sexualization of breasts is a Western influence. (88, note 124)

According to this analysis, breasts were not sexualized in Arab culture. This might explain why some Muslim jurists allowed slave girls to expose their breasts in public. If the Qur'an called upon Muslim women to cover their breasts, it was not because they formed part of their *'awrah* or private parts, which were limited to their vaginas and anuses, but because they formed part of their beauty and were a symbol of maternity. Such allegorical interpretations are not novel. They were forever favored by the Sufis. Commenting on 24:31, Rashid al-Din Maybudi (d. 12th c.) had this to say in *Kashf al-asrar* or *Unveiling the Mysteries*:

> The allusion is that the servant has an adornment that it is not permissible to make manifest, just as women have private parts, and that it is not permissible for them to show their adornment. In the same way, if someone makes manifest to the people the adornment of his secret core, such as the limpidness of his states and the purity of his acts, the adornment turns into a stain, unless he makes manifest something to someone that he did not do on his own or undertake. (545)

As Ziba Mir-Hosseini has noted, the theological validity of *hijab* has even been challenged by Islamist ideologues like Hassan al-Turabi (d. 2016) in Sudan, who stated in 2006 that: "The Qur'an did not refer to this thing as *hijab*. This was called *khimar* and was worn over the chest only… you keep hearing *hijab*, *hijab*, *hijab*… When the words are distorted, they mislead people" (2011: 206). "Scholars like Gamal Al-Banna," she adds:

> have declared that neither the Qur'an nor the authentic *sunnah* demand that women cover their hair; the veil is not an Islamic tradition, but pre-Islamic, from the time when Arabs covered their heads and left the upper part of their chest uncovered. The relevant Qur'anic verses command women to cover their chests, but not necessarily their heads. (2011: 206)

In his capacity as a theologian, al-Banna does not recognize the *hijab* as a religious obligation as it is devoid of Qur'anic foundation (Bestandji 2021: 113). To him, the headscarf is no more sacred than the turban. If the youngest brother of Hassan al-Banna (1906-1949), the founder of the Muslim Brotherhood, can reassess inherited ideas regarding *hijab*, other believers can undoubtedly do so as well. And they most certainly have. The Ismailis, it would appear, abolished the veil and the *hijab* in the twelfth century.

Speaking at the All-Indian Muhammadan Education Conference in New Delhi, India, in 1902, the Sultan Mohamed Shah, Aga Khan III (1877-1957), the forty-eight Imam of the Nizari Ismailis, lamented the status of Muslim women throughout history. As he explained:

> A ... cause of our present apathy is the terrible position of Muslim women... There is absolutely nothing in Islam, or the Qur'an, or the example of the first two centuries, to justify this terrible and cancerous growth that has for nearly a thousand years eaten into the very vitals of Islamic society... The 'Abbasids, borrowing from the practice of the later Persian Sassanian kings, developed the present system ... which means the permanent imprisonment and enslavement of half the nation. How can we expect progress from the children of mothers who have never shared, or even seen, the free social intercourse of modern mankind? This terrible cancer that has grown since the third and fourth century of the *hijra* must either be cut out, or the body of Muslim society will be poisoned to death by the permanent waste of all the women of the nation.
>
> But *purdah*... itself did not exist till long after the Prophet's death and is no part of Islam. The part played by Muslim women at Kardesiah and Yarmuk the two most momentous battles of Islam next to Badr and Honein, and their splendid nursing of the wounded after those battles, is of itself a proof to any reasonable person that *purdah*, as now understood, has never been conceived by the companions of the Prophet. That we Muslims should saddle ourselves with this excretion of Persian custom, borrowed by the 'Abbasids, is due to that ignorance of early Islam which is one of the most extraordinary of modern conditions. (Ismaili Gnosis)

As far as the Aga Khan III was concerned, the Qur'anic verses on the veil were allegorical. In a *firman* he issued in 1905, he asserted that:

> the external *burqa* [veil] is not for you, but [better] for your is a veil of the heart, have modesty in your heart, fill your heart with modesty all the time. You [women] should not cast your eye on other men except your husbands; do not have any thoughts for other men. If in your mind there is desire for other men, you will not gain from your prayers. (qtd. Calderini 56)

In another statement, Sultan Mahomed Shah exhorted his followers in the following fashion, "I appeal to you not to plunge people into whimsical matters, denying women human values.... From now on, do not hide and cover women; educate them, do not pressure them, and do not marry except one wife, the same as I have only one" (Ismaili Gnosis). In 1954, he elaborated upon his views in his memoirs, stating:

> I have always sought to encourage the emancipation and education of women. In my grandfather's and my father's time the Ismailis were far ahead of any other Muslim sect in the matter of the abolition of the strict veil, even in extremely conservative countries. I have absolutely abolished it; nowadays you will never find an Ismaili woman wearing the veil. Everywhere I have always encouraged girls' schools, even in regions where otherwise they were completely unknown. I say with pride that my Ismaili followers are, in this matter of social welfare, far in advance of any other Muslim sect. (Ismaili Gnosis)

In an interview with *Elle Magazine*, on August 20, 1969, the current spiritual leader of the Nizari Ismailis, Shah Karim al-Husayni Aga Khan IV (b. 1936), was asked whether his grandfather's act of abandoning the veil was a revolutionary step. The Aga Khan replied:

> It was a bold step, but more social than religious. Originally, the veil had nothing to do with Islam and the veil was worn in pre-Islamic Arabia. The veil was, initially, what distinguished a free woman from a slave. The slave woman who was not wearing a veil could be bought and exchanged. The woman wearing the evil was not at the disposal of society. The veil has become no longer a symbol but folklore. (Ismaili Gnosis)

If change has come to the East, so has it come to the West. Master W.D. Fard and Elijah Muhammad (1897-1975) encouraged Muslim women to be modest and to wear head coverings during prayer and religious services; however, they never commanded them to do so in the public sphere. Warith Deen Mohammed (1933-2008), who brought the Nation of Islam into a more mainstream Muslim tradition, was also lenient in matters of women's dress. In an article that appears in *World Muslim News* on November 27, 1981, he noted that women's hair is their *hijab*:

> It is believed in the circle of learned scholars in the religion that the

> hair on women should be covered... In our community...we don't make any big to-do about it. If some woman is seen with her hair uncovered, we don't raise the roof, because I understand that where there is some sex appeal in women's hair, there is also religious symbolism attached. This symbolism is good, but I don't think we should enforce these laws too fanatically. If we do, we might cause people of higher intellect to underestimate our intelligence. They might think we are superstitious or fanatical people, and we don't want them to think that.

In an article that appeared in the *Observer-Times* on February 16, 1998, it was mentioned that "covering hair in the mosque for prayer is a need but, in the public, when out shopping it is not a big deal." According to the article, "he noted that a sister can be more seductive with her hair covered than uncovered." For this reason, he was declared an infidel, a heretic, and an apostate by the Salafis who, in reality, are the veritable infidels, heretics, and apostates according to traditional Sunnis, Shiites, and Sufis.

The Babis and the Baha'is have been at the forefront of the struggle against the veil and seclusion since their foundation. 'Ali Muhammad Shirazi (d. 1850), the Bab, and the founder of Babism, supported the symbolic casting off of the veil on the part of Tahirih, Qurrat al-'Ayn (d. 1814/1817-1852), the Persian poet, at a conference in 1848. She was condemned to death for "spreading corruption on earth" for denouncing the veil, polygamy, and restrictions placed on women. Baha'u'llah (1817- 1892), the founder of the Baha'i faith, believed that choice of clothing was a matter of personal discretion that should be informed by principles of modesty. In one talk, 'Abdul-Baha' (1844-1921), his son and successor, noted that:

> The veiling of women is a barrier to teaching and learning. The divines have exaggerated... to the point that they would not allow even the voice of a woman to be heard, even though it is generally admitted that Aisha, the wife of Muhammad, was present when people put questions to him, and he/she gave the answer, and during the circumambulation of the Ka'ba she raised the cry, without a cloth over her mouth or veil on her head... Later they increased [the restrictions] to the point that they made women prisoners and prevented them from teaching or learning, and they sank into deep abasement. This was why Eastern women were excluded from making any progress... Chastity is required, and limits and restraints are ... necessary ... to a degree that does not prevent women from learning and teaching. For the Law of God is the basis for virtues, they should not be hindered from acquiring virtues. An educated woman is better than an ignorant woman...while preserving chastity and virtue. (Bahai Library)

Since the history of oppression is inherently interwoven with the *hijab*, argue contemporary followers of the faith, wearing one is not currently viewed as adhering to Baha'i principles. In fact, it is viewed as unnecessary and even damaging to women's rights.

Opposition to obligatory and enforced *hijab* is particularly strong among progressive, reformist, and Qur'anic Muslims. Commenting on 24:31, Edip Yüksel, the author of *Takanlar ve Takilanlar*, has some strong words to say:

> Righteous men and women should not dress provocatively. A woman should lower her dress (33:59) and cover her chest. God uses flexible language, to allow culture, time, climate, age, and social dynamics and other variables play a role in the decision. The underlying reason for this recommendation is expressed as protection of women from potential male harassment. There is nothing in the Qur'an that instructs the government or the society to force women, in the name of God, to cover themselves. A punishment neither in this world nor in hereafter is issued.
>
> While the male clerics and the followers of their misogynistic teachings are sunk up to their eyebrows in the mud of *shirk,* the only unforgivable sin, somehow, they scrupulously split the hair of women. Does sanctifying the dress code of Christian nuns have anything to do with their psychological and sexual problems? The verses recommending women to cover themselves aim to protect them from the harassment of unrighteous men. Ironically, women are now harassed more by the self-righteous men.
>
> It is up to women, not men, how long they will lower their dress, whether they will cover their breasts or not. It is a different thing to remind a monotheist woman nicely to wear modestly for her protection and perhaps for social order. But using this issue to patronize and subjugate women is not what the Qur'an expects from us. Even worse than this, is to impose this recommendation onto those women who are not Muslims, since that violates many more Qur'anic principles. The male clerics who covered their intelligence by their obsessive interference with women's hair and dress, do not even notice the lesson in verse 7:26. Despite the verse informing us that women were walking in the street with their faces open in front of Muhammad (33:52), they still have the audacity to preach to women to cover their faces with veils. (242)

If women wish, he wrote, "let them walk [around] naked. It is much better than fabricating dress codes in the name of God. The best attire is righteousness (7:26)" (Jilbab).

9.5 Is the *Hijab* Haram?

If many Muslim scholars, past and present, have argued that the headscarf is not mandatory for women, and have offered differing views regarding the extent of the female '*awrah*, which can be as little as their bosoms and private parts, some have issued stern warnings against those who treat is as mandatory. For them, anyone who claims that the head-covering is in the Qur'an is simply not telling the truth. This is dangerous because God condemns those who distort the Qur'an and make the lawful unlawful: "Do not falsely declare with your tongues, "This is lawful, and that is unlawful," only fabricating lies against God. Indeed, those who fabricate lies against God will never succeed" (16:116).

It is a major sin and a grave offense to falsely attribute a command to God and the Qur'an when one is well-aware of the truth. It is true that some jurists ruled that the *hijab* is obligatory. Although some *ahadith* are used to support such rulings, it is not true that there are historically reliable ones in which the Prophet commands it. Most importantly, it is not correct that the Qur'an commands *hijab*, at least, not in the manner that it has been interpreted by hegemonic Islam. Consequently, some critics have adopted an even harsher tone, going as far as asserting that *hijab* is *haram*. For Muhammad Sadiq:

> Accepting orders from others than God is idol-worship. That is how serious the matter of *hijab / khimar* is. Is it possible that women who wear *hijab* in the name of Islam, believing that God has ordered it are committing idol-worship as God did not order it? No, the "Imams" did. These women have found for themselves gods other than the One Who revealed the Qur'an, complete, perfect, and fully detailed.

The al-Azhar educated Ahmed Subhy Mansour takes an equally strong stand on the subject. He insists that "the veil/*hijab* and/or the *niqab*... have nothing to do with Islam" (Fatwas Part Eighty-Six) and that "there is nothing called veil / *hijab* / *niqab* / *burqa* in Islam" (Fatwas Part Seventy-Three). He laments the fact that women have been "erroneously convinced that Islam includes such falsehoods as *niqab* (the full veil covering the face and the whole body), veils (cloth covering hair, ears, neck, and cleavage), and head scarves (cloth covering hair and ears)" (Women's Rights). As a result of this deception and injustice, women have paid a heavy price. Not only does Mansour view the *hijab* as un-Islamic, but he views it as anti-Islamic. In his view:

> It is a crime against God to add to His *shari'ah* laws (about women required to cover chests and legs in public) the invented notion of covering their hair by the so-called veil as an obligation or to force them to wear the so-called *niqab*. There are no dress codes in Islam at all for both genders; those women who wear *niqab* is committing a major sin by thinking that they are doing a "religious" ritual or practice, whereas those wearing bikinis are making a small mistake that may be pardoned by doing good deeds. The worst women of all are those committing fornication; yet they are less sinning in comparison to clergymen of Wahhabism and the rest of earthly, man-made

> creeds/doctrines/religions that ascribe falsehoods to God's religion and *shari'ah* laws. (Fatwas Part Seventeen)

Not only is the *hijab* un-Islamic and anti-Islamic, in the view of Mansour, those who hold it to be obligatory are infidels. As he ruled:

> there is no veil/*hijab* or *niqab* in Islam… Those who assume that the veil/*hijab* and/or the *niqab* are part of Islam are polytheistic disbelievers who ascribe lies to God's Religion; women are to cover their legs and chests; it is ok for them in True Islam (i.e., Qur'anism) to never cover their heads, hair, necks, and hands/arms indoors and outdoors and during prayers and pilgrimage. God will forgive your being forced to wear *niqab* during pilgrimage; make sure that you believe in the fact that *niqab* and *hijab* are never part of Islam. (Fatwas Part Ninety-Seven)

For Naëm Bestandji, the *hijab* does not belong on the heads and bodies of women: it belongs in one place alone, in the museum of patriarchy (2021: 351, 355). The piece of cloth in question is merely a sexist accessory (2021: 351). Far from being a sign of modesty and chastity, it is an immodest and unchaste political and patriarchal exhibition that reflects the sexual insecurity of the men who prescribe it (2021: 351). If Muslim women were so concerned about being modest, and not drawing attention to themselves, they could wear a bonnet, a shawl, or a hoody to conceal themselves, and to be discrete for religious reasons (2021: 265). However, that is not the aim of the Islamist uniform that has spread since its invention in the 1970s: "its purpose is to exhibit, to be recognized, and be identified as a Muslim" (2021: 265). For Bestandji, the *hijab* is the compass that leads the way to the world in which we wish to live. Either we return to a past where the sexism and segregation dictated by Islamism reigns supreme, or we move forward toward greater equality between the sexes without making concessions or accommodations to retrograde ideologies (2021: 351).

As much as it is defended and promoted by Islamist women, Muslim fundamentalists, and "intersectional" feminists, he believes that "the *hijab* is the death shroud of feminism" (2021: 351). By getting rid of it, he argues, by brandishing it at the end of a stick or trampling it under one's feet, it can become a symbol of the struggle against oppression (2021: 352). For the sake of equality between women and men, he stresses that we should never forget what the *hijab* truly signifies (2021: 352). Far from deviants, hypocrites, and disbelievers, Bestandji believes that "Muslim women… who resist the *hijab* are the hope of Islam… their Islam is intimate, spiritual, progressive, not exhibitionist, sexist or political" (2021: 351).

"The future of Islam," argues Bestandji, "is not in the hands of the extremists. It is in the hands of their fierce opponents" (2021: 351). He believes that the next chapter of history will be written by the actions of progressive Muslims as Islam "has no other option but to become secularized" (2021: 351).

In his view, the "religified" veil of the Islamic fundamentalists is a material obstacle (2021: 351). This is why Islamists are so attached to it as can be seen by campaigns to promote the *hijab* in the Maghreb and its imposition as soon as an authoritarian Islamist regime takes power, be it in Iran, Saudi Arabia, Daesh, or Afghanistan (2021: 351). Whether it is a religious obligation or not, Bestandji believes that nothing can justify the *hijab* today (2021: 347). As he explains:

> The Qur'an authorizes polygamy... It authorizes marriage with little girls, the amputation of a hand to punish thieves... Do we accept that today? Do we appeal to secularism to … accommodate these practices? Even if the prescription of the veil had been real, wearing it in the seventh century could be understood. To wear it in the twenty-first century is a sexist anachronism. We know today that it is up to boys to learn to respect girls from an early age. (2021: 347-348)

9.6 Conclusions

Increasingly, scholars from the full spectrum of Islam, including some trained as academics and intellectuals at secular universities and others trained as clerics at religious seminaries, have reconsidered or started to reevaluate the dominant, inherited, rulings regarding matters of women's dress, seeking not to align Islam with Western liberalism, but to realign it with rationality, equality, and universality. They realize, as Ernest Renan (1823-1892), the French Orientalist, did, that "if religions divide men, reason brings them closer" (Meddeb 193).

Although their voices are suppressed and silenced, the new religious thinkers in question have established an evidence-based consensus and represent a valid and legitimate dissenting opinion. Their vision of a compassionate, merciful, just, rational, diverse, pluralistic, peaceful, loving, and tolerant Islam forms the basis of a robust and powerful platform that can contest all competing and conflicting ideologies that are battling for dominance on the third rock from the sun, including leftist liberal secularism, right-wing conservatism, and radical Islamism. While some people might despise the views expressed by these traditional, moderate, progressive, and pragmatic scholars and thinkers, ultimately, it matters not, as millions upon millions of Muslims agree with them and find them enlightening, inspiring, and uplifting. After all, "no one loses hope in God's mercy except those with no faith" (12:87).

General Conclusions

The purpose of this study should be patent to the perspicacious, the sage, and the sagacious: to reclaim the religion of Islam, from the paws and claws of primitive patriarchal misogynists, theological thugs, lascivious lowlifes, and intellectual Lilliputians. To bring tolerance back into a religion that has become intolerant. To oppose the intolerant tolerance of the liberals, leftists, anarchists, and so-called woke feminists of the time. To bring faith into a religion that has become retrograde, ritualistic, and legalistic. To question the man-made, artificial, and manufactured laws of Islam that contradict its divine and rational spirit. To replace blind following with educated and informed critical thinking. To revive a religious jurisprudence that suffers from *rigor mortis* on the one side and sheer lunacy on the other. To replace injustice with justice and inequality with equality. To bring love back into the equation. The jurists have reduced Islam to a black hole: a tiny space whose gravity is so strong that even light cannot escape. Their Islam is a Big Crunch. It is reductionism. Our Islam is a Big Bang. We want to expand Islam to universal size.

Diversity of opinion fosters tolerance. Pluralism is the opposite of reductionism, exclusivism, and absolutism. We seek to share the full spectrum of Islam in its kaleidoscope of colors, display its full tapestry, and examine every thread in its complex quilt. Muslim jurists are like legalistic rabbis. They have reduced Islam to an endless list of arcane and even absurd rules. Their creed is covered in dust. Their *shari'ah* is saturated with sediment. As far as Christians are concerned, Jesus was sent for a reason: to free people from the shackles of a law that had become dry, arid, and devoid of love. For Muslims, Muhammad, the Messenger of God, was meant to reinfuse love into the law and make it a law of love and justice. As Mustafa Akyol notes:

> *Shari'ah* is not specific to Islam; it is the "way" of any Abrahamic religion. In this sense, for any Muslim… the *shari'ah* is God-given. Hence, it is sacred and perfect. However, when Muslims speak of "following" or "implementing" the *shari'ah*, most … go beyond this pristine sense of the term. What they rather refer to is *fiqh* (jurisprudence), which is the human interpretation of the *shari'ah*. (31)

It is, therefore, essential to distinguish between the Qur'an and post-Qur'anic sources (31). After all, "Islamic reformation does not challenge the authority of the divine nor does it challenge the sanctity of the Qur'an" (Takim 2022: 29).

Rather, "the reformation process seeks to revise the judgments and pronouncements of previous jurists exegetically as to apply Islamic law more faithfully in modern times" (29). As Takim notes, "the gender inequalities that are articulated in the texts are not among the essential of Islam" (2022: 27). Rather,

> they are part of its accidentals, which were inserted into juridical manuals either due to the influence of seventh-and eight-century social cultural norms of Arabian society or due to the hermeneutics of later scholars who were influenced by their own horizons and presuppositions concerning the role of women in a society. (2022: 27)

It is not a matter of being anti-*hijab*. A shawl, in an of itself, is innocuous. The *hijab*, however, is saturated with symbolism. Those who oppose it are against extremism, sexism, and gender apartheid. They object to its imposition by force, fines, prison, corporal punishment, acid, beatings, rape, and murder.

No reasonable person objects to traditional Jewish and Christian dress, in which women cover themselves from their collar bones to their knees and their arms to their elbows while partially covering their hair. The same goes for moderate Muslim dress, both traditional and modern, namely, the fashionable *hijab* of ethnicity, individuality, and liberty.

In both East and West, North and South, many modern *hijabis* are pretty and fashionable while remaining modest. The headscarf highlights the beauty of their faces as opposed to their bodies. They look like colorful flowers. They open hearts. In fact, research shows that "while wearing the *hijab* can suppress female facial attractiveness to men… not all *hijab* wearing has this effect, and female facial attractiveness for practicing Muslim men living in their native Muslim country may not be reduced simply by wearing this garment" (Jordan). However, these hip so-called *hijabis* who appears in fashion magazines are not actually following the *hijab* of Islamic jurisprudence. They are free modern professional women who wear colorful headwraps, turbans, and hats, not the strict *hijab* demanded by Islamists and conservative Muslim scholars. They could not dress the way they do under Islamic rule. They could not wear *burkinis* to a pool or beach. Their attire, which they called "hijab," is not considered Islamic according to Muslim fundamentalists. That being said, it still advances the idea that Islam requires women to cover their hair.

When celebrities like Madonna, the Kardashian sisters, Rihanna, Selena Gomez, Katy Perry, Nicole Richie, and others, wear *hijab* and *niqab*, they advance the Islamist agenda and spit on the struggle of women in general, and Muslim women in particular, and influence girls to adopt such attire. As Phyllis Chesler notes,

> They don't understand that they are "slumming;" they can remove their exotic Islamic garb and pose naked whenever they choose to do so.

> This isn't possible for Muslim girls and women who are forced to wear the Islamic veil (headscarf, or face mask or full head, face and body covering) and who risk death when they resist. (2017: 452)

The damage done by Western celebrities and politicians who wear *hijab* when traveling to the Muslim world is immeasurable. It is not an expression of respect for religious and cultural diversity: it is a cowardly act of submission and surrender. It is "veiled betrayal" (452).

"The *hijab* should not be feared," we are reassured by liberals, leftists, and the woke mob. That might apply to the *hijab* of fashion; however, it certainly does not apply to the *hijab* of the Islamists, extremists, and terrorists. "The *hijab* should not be feared?" Tell that to Iranian women, Afghan women, Nigerian women, and Algerian women. Tell that to the women who have been fined, imprisoned, beaten, raped, sprayed with acid, condemned to death, and murdered for objecting to it. "As long as women are forced to wear face masks and *burqas*, or even to wear the heavy *hijab*," notes Phyllis Chesler, it renders naked-faced women vulnerable both in Muslim lands and in the West" (2017: 454). As she notes,

> Not wearing the Islamic veil (*burqa*, *chador*, *niqab*, *hijab*) is often interpreted as: "The woman is fair game, she's an infidel and a prostitute." Thus, wearing Islamic head, face, and body-gear targets those women who are not "covered." And, by the way, many "covered" women have, nevertheless, been assaulted any way. (2017: 460)

Simply because the spread of *hijab* is an ominous sign for some Muslims and non-Muslims, and an auspicious one for Islamists, does not suggest that little girls, teens, or women in headscarves should suffer from any harassment or harm. Most of them have no idea why they wear *hijab* in the first place. Many are illiterate or uneducated. Many are convinced or coerced into wearing it. Some are completely confused, wearing high heels, black miniskirts, and a black headscarf. Some squeeze into yoga pants but wear a tight *hijab* on their head. Some wear "proper" *hijab* but cover themselves with more makeup than a clown. There are girls who wear *niqab* with a tight, short-sleeve top, and skin-tight jeans. If they wanted to be modest, they would be better off showing their hair and wearing a shirt that covers their rear end. A teenage boy or man will not look twice at a girl's hair; however, they will check out their derrières and legs in form fitting jeans. Many Muslim girls and women genuinely and sincerely believe that *hijab* is a religious prescription. Some are even highly educated and deeply committed Muslims or radical Islamists.

The black *chadors*, *burqas*, *niqabs*, and *abayahs* of the ultra-conservatives, Islamists, and extremists are foreboding. They deny individuality. They seek to erase women from existence. They close human hearts like a clenched fist. For Phyllis Chesler,

> The *burqa* and *niqab* are sensory deprivation isolation chambers and, as such, violate the wearer's human rights. In addition, the increasing appearance of heavy *hijab*, *niqab* (face veils), and *burqas* on Western streets, psychologically rattles infidel and secular women. First, they cannot free these women -- who also serve as a warning: If radical Islam succeeds, this can happen to them. (2017: 442)

"Whenever *burqas*, heavy face veils, and dark, Iranian-style head, shoulder and shapeless body coverings appear in the West," warns Chesler, "we must consider this as a symbol of radical Islam -- or of Islamic *jihad*" (2017: 442).

Such clothing, however, is not in the least bit traditional, much less Islamic. It is religiously and historically misleading to claim that the black crows of Qum, Najaf, Karbala, or elsewhere are "following the *sunnah*." They most certainly are not. They are women who have lost their sense of beauty, follow a false *shari'ah* fashion, and condemned the gorgeous traditional dress of their cultures -- so elegant, colorful, beautiful, and feminine -- to perdition. Writing in the 1980s, Heather Colyer Ross (b. 1936), the fashion historian, complained that "the last vestiges of Arabian traditional costume" were disappearing and that we were "witnessing the end of the old Arabian way of life and its costumes as a functional aspect of life" (9). They have cast aside their love for color, embellishment, and glitter in favor of plain black cloaks. As Walter Ashlin Fairservis (1921-1994), the American archeologist, attested, "The aesthetic loss to the world... is incalculable" (Ross 9). If this modern Islamist clothing is out of place in the East, it is all the more so in the West. As Bahram Eftekhari, the Iranian philosopher, admits, "ninja type *hijab* is not suitable in the West ... the *chador*, *burka*, and full facial veils... reflect patriarchal rather than Islamic culture" (224).

As Richard Thompson Ford (b. 1966), the American jurist and fashion historian, recognizes, "the traditional *hijab* is a barrier. By contrast, the fashionable *hijab* is not a partition that conceals; like all fashion, it reveals a distinctive, individual personality" (291; see also Lewis 2015). That would be the middle of the road for the proponents of balance and the opponents of extremes. However, that is the norm, and it is not a rigid one that applies at all times and places. We need to replace rigidity with flexibility.

After all, even some Amish women, who are very modest, wear bathing suits when swimming in pools and public beaches. Some older women may wear dresses when they dip themselves in the water. Others opt for full-body bathing suits. Others wear regular bathing suits with long shorts. Yet others wear one-piece bathing suits. And others opt for two-piece ones. As for the Mennonites, it should be recalled that only Old Order and Conservative Mennonites maintain plain dress. Mainline Mennonites, who represent the majority, are indistinguishable from the general population. Some of their women are very fashion conscious, wearing high heels and miniskirts. For them, modesty and simplicity are not just about clothing but about personal qualities and character traits. The distinction between conservatives and liberals is found in all faith traditions.

There are times when women can wear less, and there are times when women can wear more. Lack of coercion is the key. There should be no compulsion in religion. Men should not pressure them to cover themselves, nor should they be pressured by men to uncover themselves. What is more, women need wiggle room. They need room to breathe, move, and express themselves without being treated like trollops, harassed, assaulted, murdered, or forced out of Islam. To put it plainly: a woman who does not wear *hijab* is not a *de facto* harlot. Since "there is no compulsion in religion," argues Mohamed Talbi, "Islam was born secular" (Zouari). As he explains:

> The Qur'an is the only holy book that contains this phrase, so clear, and so secular. Everyone has the right to follow the religion he wishes. The State cannot interfere in religious affairs. Its only function is to create an atmosphere of peace for all. In contrast, what do Islamist states do? They engage in religious coercion. And the Qur'an says no to Islamic states…
>
> Islam came to bring modernity and rationality. The Qur'an calls to reason and hence to secularism. We have the Qur'an. The Islamists have a man-made *shari'ah.* We have the founding text of Islam. They have commentaries composed in the second century of the *hijrah* (the eighth century AD). Until then, Muslims lived without *shari'ah* law and managed very well. Their misfortune started when they developed an Islamic law at the service of despots who wanted to rule and the power to kill legally. The *shari'ah* is nothing but that. (Zouari).

Although the Qur'an does not command women to cover their hair, if a woman embraces Islam, she is immediately expected to wear the *hijab*. If she fails to do so, she is viewed as insincere and shunned. And yet, if we believe the traditional account, the authenticity of which is not established, the so-called *hijab* verse was revealed no earlier than the fifth year of the *hijrah* and, according to some accounts, in the year before the Prophet's death. In other words, according to the traditional account, Muslim women were not religiously required to cover their hair and bodies for sixteen years to twenty-two years of the Prophet's twenty-three-year mission. Khaled Abou El Fadl, for example, warned Muslim converts against immediately adopting the *hijab* upon embracing Islam. As he explained in his "Original Fatwa on *Hijab*:"

> At the time of the Prophet … that *hijab* was not an issue and was not raised as a topic until a year before the Prophet's death, meaning that many Muslim women worked on their *iman* and their belief for ten and in some cases fifteen years before they had to even think about the matter of *hijab*… When it comes to converts or people who have not

> been practicing Muslims for most of their lives and then decide to become religious, first, work on *'aqidah*, your *iman*, your understanding of the wisdom and the purpose of Islam before you start delving into the legalities of *hijab* or no *hijab*... Every convert or practicing Muslim is a living, breathing, ambassador of Islam in the West... There are priorities ... that pertain to the sincerity and substance of our agency on behalf of Allah's message... The matter of *hijab* of a *Muslima* in this day and age has become of a highly exaggerated importance.

As much as some Muslims have turned *hijab* into the sixth pillar of Islam, there is no *hijab* verse in the Qur'an. The verb *hajaba* means to screen, separate, hide from sight, and make invisible. The *hijab* refers to a curtain. It symbolizes sexual segregation. There is no incontrovertible evidence that the Qur'an, the Prophet, or the Imams wanted to institute such a practice. However, it appears to have been fraudulently attributed to them in the centuries that followed.

Although there is no *hijab* verse, there is, however, an *'awrah* verse, a *khimar* verse, and a *jilbab* verse, namely, a verse calling for men and women to cover their genitals, a verse calling for women to cover their cleavage, breasts or bosoms, and a verse calling for women to wear outer garments, such as shawls, dresses, or cloaks, particularly at night in precarious situations where there was lack of safety and security. As we have seen, *'awrah* signifies a weak point along a border, namely, something that is dangerous to expose. When applied to homes, it can refer to privacy. When it comes to people, it refers to their shameful or private parts. The word *khimar* is derived from *kh-m-r*, which means "to cover," and *jilbab* derives from *ja-la-ba* , which means "to clothe." As Edip Yüksel has noted, "*jilbab* is [an] outer garment... any type of cloth that people normally wear outside, which is not their underwear or night clothes" (Jilbab).

Although "the link between female head covering and Islamic tradition or prescriptions is tenuous" (Winter 27), misogynistic Muslim men have given Muslim women a guilt trip for over a thousand years. They brainwash them into believing that Islam is *hijab* and *hijab* is Islam. They coerce them into covering through threat of punishment in this life and fear of punishment in the next life. They claim that women who uncover their heads in public will hang from their hair in hell, where they will burn for eons or eternity. These traditions, which were falsely ascribed to the Prophet Muhammad and the twelve Imams by women-hating men, are blasphemous, contemptuous, and scandalous. Using them to terrify and control women is the worst case of religious and spiritual abuse.

As many Muslims have come to realize, *hijab* means nothing in and of itself. As pretty as some Muslim women look in their headscarves, you cannot judge a woman by her *hijab*, particularly when it is imposed by law, culture, or family pressure. At the same time, and as difficult as it may seem for some men to understand, you cannot judge a woman by her short dress, shorts, or bathing suit. You can only judge a woman by her character. It is the inside that counts. You can, however, judge a man by how he views and treats women.

Clothing conveys meaning. As Sposito states, "fashion… reaffirms specific moral values: opulence, ostentation, dissipation, modesty, reserve, austerity, power, conformity, and provocation, to name just a few" (Sposito 5). It expresses power and gender (Silverman 18). As art historians Ludmila Kybalova (1929-2012), Olga Herbenova, and Milena Lamarova note, "Ideas of modesty vary according to habit and tradition in different parts of the world" (15). In most cultures, "the criterion of modesty is usually the extent of the *décolleté*" (15). Speaking of the Muslim world, Stillman notes that:

> Fashions, or modes of dress… reflect … social mores and values (the "modesty/immodesty factor," or "reveal/conceal factor")… Dress is often a clear economic indicator… More subtly and often symbolically, clothing reflects religious and political norms. In Islamic society, clothing has historically been intimately connected with notions of purity and impurity… ritual behavior… and the differentiation of the believer from the unbeliever… as well as the separation of the genders. (1)

While modesty is a virtue, sexism and classism are not. While purity is positive, treating non-Muslims as impure is negative. While believing in Islam can be good, social isolation of Muslims is not, nor is discrimination against other religious communities. While chastity is to be cherished, it can be achieved without gender segregation, forced marriages, female genital mutilation, violence, and *de facto* domestic and reproductive slavery. In short, the values that the *hijab* of the Islamists and misogynists represents are not values that are compatible with equality, equity, and human dignity. Submissiveness only serves as a perverse form of patriarchy.

The arguments presented in this study are not extreme or unreasonable. They set limits. Moderation is where both sides meet in the middle. One extreme is exposing one's genitals in public. The other extreme is covering oneself completely in public, including one's face, hands, and feet. The scholars cited do not espouse radical views. They do not promote complete covering or complete uncovering. They merely expand the limits of what should be religiously and legally allowable in a free, law-abiding society that respects human and civil rights. That being said, Nimat Hafez Barazangi is correct when she warns that wearing or not wearing the *hijab* and the *jilbab* will not emancipate women one way or another (85). It is mere window dressing. The status of women will only improve in Muslim societies and communities when their understanding of Islam changes along with their attitudes, perceptions, and actions. What is required is a complete and total metamorphosis. It can be the product of incremental change or a paradigm shift. It can occur precipitously.

As much as Rameez Abid, the Pakistani American blogger and student of the Hanbali school of thought, may claim that the arguments of "neo-liberal progressive Muslims" on the non-obligatory nature of the *khimar* and the *jilbab* are "unfounded" and that "no reputable scholar" in the history of Islam "ever questioned the requirement for a Muslim woman's covering," this jurisprudential survey confirms that this is not the case. Consequently, Muslim women, as sentient human beings endowed with intelligence and reason, are entitled to be presented with the full spectrum of scholarly opinions regarding what constitutes the *'awrah* they are expected to cover in public, and they should feel free to accept the position that they find most convincing without being coerced or unduly pressured in any form or fashion. The same applies to men, husbands, and fathers. We must answer the call of our conscience.

Despite the claims of the Islamists, there is no basis for the *hijab* in any of its manifestations in the Qur'an. What is more, there has been no consensus on this subject throughout Islamic history. There has only been the consensus of like-minded misogynists, not a universal and infallible agreement of Muslim scholars, much less the Muslim community. We are presented with an illusion of consensus which has been imposed by the silencing of differing views by the powerful, past, and present. The meaning of arguably vague and ambiguous terms like *khimar*, *jilbab*, *zinah*, *tabarruj*, and *'awrah* have been the subject of unabated discussions and debates from the dawn of Islam to the present. The problem is that most Muslims are only presented with one side of the story, the one forced upon them by those who wish to control their minds and behavior, turning them into robots, clones, or soldiers at the service of their sexist and subversive ideology.

To summarize, the rulings on the subject of Muslim women's dress in public are as follows: 1) Women must cover their genitals; 2) Women must cover their genitals and their breasts; 3) Women must cover all cleavage: genitals, buttocks, breasts, and armpits; 4) Women must cover their genitals, their breasts, and their bodies from the navel to the knee; 5) Women must cover from the shoulders to the knees; their arms and calves need not be covered; 6) Women must cover their bodies from the shoulder to the knees, as well as their arms down to the elbow; 7) Women must cover their bodies, arms to the wrists, and legs to ankle; leaving the head covering as recommended as opposed to required; 8) Women must cover everything but what is washed during ritual ablutions; in other words, they can show their faces, hair, necks, arms up to the elbow, and feet up to the ankles; 9) Women must cover their entire bodies and their hair with the exception of their hands and feet; 10) Women must cover their entire bodies and their hair with the exception of their hands; 11) Women must cover their entire bodies, their hair, and their faces with the exception of the eyes; 12) Women must cover their entire bodies, their hair, and their faces, with the exception of a single eye; 13) Women must cover their entire bodies, their hair, their faces, and even their eyes; 14) The only way to ensure that women observe *hijab* is to keep them confined in their homes; and finally; 15) Women are only adequately and correctly covered when they are dead and buried.

Honest and transparent scholars of religion do not impose views on women. They present them with all the positions. They engage in comparative jurisprudence and stress higher ethical objectives. They educate women. They foster critical thinking. They respect freedom of thought, conscience, and choice. They might point out that the Qur'an opposes extremism, that Muslims are encouraged to follow the middle ground, and that the Messenger of God believed in making religion easy for people as opposed to difficult, oppressive, and overbearing.

Boundaries vary due to time and place, and what is moderate may fluctuate. Wearing a bikini in a bank might be inappropriate; however, wearing one on a beach is acceptable. In some places, swimwear is appropriate on the beach, around the pool, in resorts, but not on public streets and business districts in towns and cities. Wearing an *abayah* in a mosque may seem normal; however, diving into a pool with an *abayah*, a headscarf, socks, and shoes, is abnormal. Swimming fully clothed in a *burka* is absurd, unreasonable, unhygienic, and dangerous. While women have the right to choose to be more conservative or more liberal in matters of clothing, they should respect the views and rights of other women. Gossip, slander, libel, and defamation of character are not godly actions. People should focus on positives as opposed to perceived faults. They should judge themselves rather than judge others.

Although she believes that the headscarf is a religious requirement, albeit one which cannot be compelled or coerced, Abla Hasan admits that "the generality and the flexibility of the Qur'anic description of *zinah*, translated here as 'charms,' shows tolerance; the verse can be interpreted broadly to meet the changing spatiotemporal, cultural, and ethnic needs" (106). Fashion should not be fossilized. As Bronwyn Winter points out, "the claim that the *hijab* has greater 'traditional authenticity' where it is worn than, for example, Western forms of dress" is feeble (27). "In most places where the *hijab* (and *jilbab*) are worn today," notes the author, "they are introduced garments" (27). In other words, "they are not more 'traditional' or 'authentic' than the Western high heels that are often worn under the long skirts, coats, or tunics" (27). As Valentine Moghadam (b. 1952), the Iranian American feminist scholar, sociologist, and activist comprehends, the *hijab* is a "novel contemporary ensemble, deployed as a uniform" (Winter 27). For far too many Muslims, the more religious you are, the more you require women to cover in black Arab-style *abayahs* or Persian *chadors*, and the stricter you are regarding gender segregation. They associate increased sexism, gender discrimination, and misogyny with increased religiosity. As conceived by ultra-conservative misogynists, Islamic dress denies women their essential femininity.

An Inuit woman should not be expected to wear a *chador* any more than a Brazilian woman should be required to wear a *burqa*, and no Polynesian woman should suffer the indignity of *purdah*. Muslim women should not be forced to wear bikinis at beaches, pools, or waterparks. They should have the right to wear one-piece bathing suits. So long as they cover their private parts, women should be free to dress as they please. The more they cover, the more they might be modest; however, not necessarily so since there is no direct correlation between clothing and chastity. In many parts of the Muslim world, including Mamluk Egypt, the anonymity of the veil facilitated debauchery (Mansour). As Toby Fischer-Mirkin points out, "veils add to a woman's allure, sending a signal of flirtation and mystery. They conceal your identity and relieve you of the obligation to be yourself" (242). In fact, showing more does not attract more. As studies have shown, "men… respond more favorably to those looks that send some degree of moderation" (69-70).

The rate of fornication in Iran, Saudi Arabia, and other nations where obligatory *hijab* is imposed, shows this to be true. When 80% of Iranian women living under strict *shari'ah* law engage in pre-marital sex, what purpose does mandatory *hijab* serve? (Barker, The Economist, Fox News). What is more, what right does any government have to force religion upon a people? As of 2018, fewer than 35% of Iranians viewed the *hijab* as a "valued principle," 50% fewer than during the years following the creation of the Islamic Republic in 1979. By 2020, "58% said they do not believe in the *hijab* … altogether. Around 72% opposed the compulsory *hijab*, while 15% insist on the legal obligation to wear the *hijab* in public" (Maleki and Arab 2). After four decades under the dictatorship of the mullahs, most Iranians no longer identify as Shiite Muslims. In fact, only 32.2% do. 22.2% do not identify with any religion. 8.8% consider themselves to be atheists. 7.1% describe themselves as "spiritual." 5.8% are agnostic. 3.2% are Sufis. And 2.7% are humanists. Not surprisingly, "approximately half of the population reported losing their religion" (Maleki and Arab 1). Overall,

> 78% of Iranians believe in God, 37% believe in life after death, 30% believe in heaven and hell, 26% believe jinns exist, and 26% believe in the coming of a savior. Around 20% of the target population does not believe in any of the abovementioned. (1)

60% of Iranians do not pray at all. 40% do so sporadically. Only 27% do their five daily prayers. 68% of Iranians believe that religious prescriptions should be excluded from laws. Only 14% believe that they should accord with religious prescriptions. 71% oppose state funding for religious institutions. 41% believe that all religions should be free to proselytize. However, 43% are opposed to proselytization on the part of any religion, including Islam. 56% of Iranians are opposed to religious education in schools. However, they support teaching them about world religions in general. Approximately 35% of Iranians drink alcohol regularly or occasionally (Maleki and Arab 1).

Why does the Iranian regime insist on imposing *hijab* on women when 60% of the population never prays at all? The "Islamic" Revolution of Iran, and its attempted "Islamization" of Iranian society, has been a complete and total failure and fiasco. Only a small minority supports radical political Shiism. The Islamists are deeply fragmented and divided into opposing factions. Their regime lacks legitimacy and popular support, resulting in pathological levels of paranoia among its partisans. For a majority of Iranians, their government is a misogynistic, murderous, and oppressive dictatorship that violates the very foundations of the Islamic faith.

81% of Iranians do not want to live in an "Islamic" Republic and would vote against it in a free national referendum. Only 15% would vote for it. 80% of Iranians support the protests against mandatory *hijab*. Approximately 15% oppose them. 60% of Iranians want regime change as a precondition for change. 16.2% prefer structural changes and a transition to another form of government. 6.5% support gradual reform within the framework of the "Islamic" Republic. A mere 11.5% are proponents of the principles of the "Islamic" Revolution and the Supreme Leader (Maleki and Arab 23). 66% of Iranians view 'Ali Khamenei negatively; only 26% view him favorably (Sinaee). Likewise, 64% of Iranians now view Khomeini poorly; only 28% hold him in a positive light (Sinaee). President Ebrahim Raisi only has the support of 17% of the population. In contrast, 65% view Reza Shah Pahlavi (1878-1944) favorably while 64% view Mohammad Reza Pahlavi (1919-1980) positively.

After the collapse of the Iranian Islamist regime, 40% of Iranians favor the creation of a secular republic, 28% support a presidential republic, and 12% favor a parliamentary republic. 22% would opt for a constitutional monarchy. 21% were uncertain which type of government would be best. And only 22% favored some sort of "Islamic" republic. In total, 88% of Iranians preferred a "democratic political system" while 67% opposed "a system governed by religious law." Only 28% believed that religion had a place in government (Maleki and Arab 7). 70% of Iranians agreed that the Revolutionary Guard Corps should be treated as a terrorist organization (2).

If the "Islamic" Republic of Iran is overthrown, 16.3% of Iranians support revolutionary executions of its former officials while 28.9% believe that they should only receive the death penalty after a fair trial. 24.4% believe they should receive life in prison or long sentences. In other words 45.2% of Iranians believe that those who served a regime that oppressed and murdered thousands should be put to death and nearly 70% believe they should be held accountable for their actions. Only 3.2% of Iranians felt they should be forgiven or given a general amnesty (Maleki and Arab 3, 20-22).

Far from winning the *hijab* wars, the Iranian regime continues to lose support and legitimacy. According to one of the latest surveys conducted in Iran,

78% of Iranian women oppose compulsory *hijab* (Asgari 10). Only 22% of women agree with it. 100% of the interviewees stated that most of the people they know disagree with obligatory *hijab* (12). 70% wear a looser *hijab* than what officials demand (12). They explain that they only do so to avoid harassment and repression (13).

Only 30% of the Iranian women surveyed wear the full *hijab* (12). 30% would continue to wear *hijab* even if it were not mandatory (12). 60% stated that they would not wear it at all (12). Another 10% said they would decide when the time would come (12). 80% of the Iranian women who were interviewed insisted that compulsory *hijab* violates freedom of choice/opinion and that it was a human rights violation (12). The 30% who wear *hijab* say they do so because of their beliefs (12). The 70% say they have no choice in the matter as it is imposed upon them by law (12).

Only 5% of the Iranian women who were interviewed were familiar with the legal sources of mandatory *hijab* (12). A minority of women believe that the *hijab* is related to the *shari'ah* and Islam (12). Ironically, they could not quote a Qur'anic verse or *hadith* to support this claim if their lives depended on it. However, 50% of them believe that "the government relates *hijab* to *shari'ah*, Qur'an, and Islam," when, in reality, Islam does not mandate it (12). 90% of Iranian women who were surveyed asserted that there would be no mandatory *hijab* in the future (13). 100% of them assert that the full *hijab* has almost completely disappeared (13).

The hypocrisy of the *hijab* is not only exposed in Iran. It is found throughout the Muslim world. As Ahmed Subhy Mansour points out:

> With *niqab* and *hijab* dominating over most countries of the Muhammadans, as supposedly religious duties forced on Islam for no reason, we see how fornication, rape, and sexual harassment thrive among the gravest sins in such countries of Shiites and Sunnites: the former allow fornication by allowing Shiite women to remarry many times (for pleasure of both sexes) without the required three-month waiting period, and the latter allow "sex *jihad*" like ISIS terrorists as well as Salafist and MB terrorists in their times of armed aggressions. Let us not forget that the Sunnite Wahabi ISIS terrorists allow in their religion rape of captured women! Yet, those fanatics of Shiites and Sunnites prohibit lawful items such as arts, singing, and music and allow the prohibited sins of murder, rape, fornication, looting, and massacring of innocent peaceful ones. Hence, the overemphasis on growing beards, wearing male and female *djellaba*, and wearing *hijabs* and *niqabs* are over signs of covering up vices, corruptions, immorality, fornication, eating from ill-gotten money, etc. and are signs of earthly, man-made, fabricated creeds that have clergymen; hence ISIS terrorists commit rape and massacres while imposing *niqab* on women. (Women's Clothing)

Ultimately, it is up to men to respect women, restrain their tongues, lower their gaze, and control their lust. The bearer of a burden should not bear the burden of another (35:18). Women are not responsible for the sins of men, and their freedom should not suffer as a result. Men who cannot tolerate the presence, sight, smell, sound, or warmth of a woman left on a chair, should be confined to their homes, prison cells, or religious asylums for the morally and spiritually deranged.

As Nimat Hafez Baranzangi has pointed out, the Qur'anic principles of morality, modesty, and justice have been reversed in actual Muslim practice. Placing perverts on a pedestal and taking corrupt young men as models and examples, Muslim jurists devised laws to protect their interests and accommodate for their insecurity, inadequacy, and immorality. As Khaled Abou El Fadl notes, "arguing that women … are a walking, talking, bundle of seduction… strikes me as morally offensive" (213: 270). If we cannot say the same for men, we cannot say the same for women. Otherwise, it is a case of *reductio ad absurdum*.

Questions must be asked. Answers must be sought. Issues need to be addressed. Problems must be solved. Who holds power? Who makes the laws? Why are they made? And whose interests should they serve? As Bestandji asks:

> Who decided that the veil would be a sign of modesty? Who decided that hiding your hair, ears, neck, and everything else would be an act of sartorial modesty (and only for women. Men don't have to make this "free choice"). Who decided all this, if not men? (2021: 336)

When addressing modesty issues, Khaled Abou El Fadl notes that the Qur'an was careful to blame the hypocrites who harassed and molested innocent women (2013: 234). The jurists, however, wish to put all men in the same category. As Khaled Abou El Fadl expresses:

> Whether a person covers his or her '*awrah* or not, he or she should not be made to suffer from the indiscretions or impiety of others. Put bluntly, whether a person is sexually aroused or not is entirely irrelevant as to what the object of arousal must or must not do. The laws and imperatives of modesty ought to be set by God and not by immoral individuals who are violating the law of God. (2013: 235)

For Bestandji, "the Islamists are the hypocrites of the age;" "the hypocrites are … the extremists;" and "the hypocrites are those who prescribe the veil" (2022).

Islamic laws of *hijab* and sexual segregation do not serve the interests of women. What is more, they do not serve the interests of men either. They serve the interests of sexual degenerates -- making women suffer for their iniquities -- and they place all men into the category of perverts devoid of any self-control. This becomes a self-fulfilling prophecy. If you believe men are naturally pigs, you can expect them to act like swine. The strict "Islamic *hijab*" of the jurists and Islamists is an innovation of spiritually and morally weak men that signals that males cannot trust females and that these self-righteous men with piety complexes cannot control themselves. Were they as moral and righteous as they claim to be, they would run no risk of succumbing to sin and temptation.

So sick and extreme were some jurists and traditionists that women were even required to veil themselves in the presence of blind men. They even prohibited men from looking at prepubescent boys lest they be overtaken by pederastic lust. As we have seen, some also forbade brothers from looking at their sisters' hair, or sons from looking at the limbs of their mothers, lest they succumb to incestuous sin. Ibn Taymiyyah even ruled that women should be segregated from male monkeys since they may become sexually attracted to them (Asharis Assemble). To top it all off, there is no shortage of *fatwas* prohibiting women from purchasing bananas, cucumbers, or anything else that resembles a phallus or could be used for masturbation (Nomani). These laws are the product of perverse minds and sick societies. The exception does not make the rule.

Rather than deprive women of their rights and freedoms, and allow men to harass women with impunity, why didn't the jurists place restrictions on immoral men? Why didn't they make it mandatory for men to lower their gaze and punish them for ogling women? Sure, they ruled that men were prohibited from looking at women with lust; however, it never went beyond that. Why didn't they prohibit sexual harassment and call for the punishment of the perpetrators? Why did they make the outside world a male dominion while confining women to their homes? Why didn't they provide women with a safe public sphere? If they believed that men and women should live in parallel societies, why did they fail to create a female one. As the Supreme Court of the United States unanimously ruled on May 17, 1954, separate is not equal. This principle applies to gender as much as to race.

Comically, the one verse of the Qur'an that seems to hold men accountable, telling them to lower their gaze (24:30), has been interpreted away. In fact, according to a tradition attributed to Muhammad al-Baqir (679-743) it was revealed about a young man from the Ansar or Helpers, who was ogling and following a woman who wore her scarf behind the neck, as the women supposedly did at that time. He kept following her, stalking her, and even following her down an alley. So focused was he on checking her out that he failed to notice a bone or a piece of glass protruding from a wall, slicing his cheek in the process. As he lost sight of the woman, he realized his face was dripping blood onto his chest and clothing. He decided to see the Messenger of God and tell him what happened. At that point, Gabriel revealed the verse in question (19). What, then, is the meaning of the verse? Do not ogle women? Do not stare at them? Do not check them out? Do not follow them and stalk them? Do not harass them? No, basically, it means "watch where you are going;

otherwise, you might hurt yourself" (Hubeali *Hijab*: 4). This is a lame "reason for revelation" if there ever was one.

The real reason early Arab Muslim women were asked to cover themselves with a *jilbab* was because they had a relaxed attitude toward nudity. The real reason early Muslim women were asked to cover their *juyub* or breasts was because it was common for them to go bare breasted. In fact, as Ibrahim B. Syed pointed out, they used to flash their breasts before and during battles to incite their warriors to fight and to tease and provoke enemy combatants (Fatah 291). Muslim scholars attempted to interpret the Qur'an centuries after the facts they describe. These exegetes, often based in sophisticated cities like Baghdad, Damascus, and elsewhere, seem to have had little to no knowledge of the pre-Islamic past. It is also conceivable that certain shameful elements were suppressed. According to the transmitted accounts, Muslim women used to let their scarves hang down the back of their heads. Was it really such a big deal for Muslim women to show their throats and necklines? Was this such a major issue that it required a divine revelation to redress?

If one understands how Arab women used to dress or undress in the seventh-century, circumambulating the Ka'bah and the other shrines of their idols naked -- shaking, shimmying, and quivering their buttocks, as part of fertility cults -- lounging in the nude in their homes in front of relatives and non-relatives, wearing bodices that pushed up their exposed breasts, walking around topless in public, and flashing their bouncing breasts in battle, to the beating of the drums, while they cheered on their warriors like a mutant combination of Dallas Cowboy cheerleaders and drunken Mardi Gras girls, then the real reason the so-called *hijab* verses were revealed takes on an entirely different meaning and dimension. The revelations in question were meant to curb the type of misbehavior that takes place during Spring Break and the Carnival in Rio.

On a darker note, this was a culture in which women cheered on their men as they raped the women, and even the men, of the enemy, to humiliate them. It was a culture in which the women would run onto the battlefield to mutilate the dead, cannibalize their corpses, and make jewelry out of their ears and noses. The battles of the pagan Arabs were a mutant combination of exhibitionism, sexual violence, murder, and mutilation. Some of these practices were seen in the early battles between the pagan and Muslim Arabs, with Hind, the wife of Abu Sufyan, chewing the liver of Hamza, the uncle of the Prophet. Even after she became a Muslim, she would cheer on the Islamic warriors, in pagan fashion, while promising to circumcise the penises of the infidels. These heathen practices continued throughout much of Islamic history. If they were not killed in battle, the surviving men would be castrated while their women and girls would be circumcised and forced into sexual slavery.

It makes perfect sense that Islam would call Arab men and women to modesty. After all, they had been equally shameless. However, when the "Islamic" dress code was imposed, it was not uniform. The heavy burden of modesty and honor fell upon women while the men granted themselves every leeway possible. They filled hell with women who showed their hair. Where are the depictions of immodest men burning in hell? In more recent times, the Saudis and the Iranians have introduced physical punishments for women who violate Islamic codes of modesty. Thousands have been punished. But what of the men who have no regard for modesty at all? Those hideous, hairy beasts, who walk around in speedos? Why not whip them for showing their thighs? After all, there are traditions that require Muslim men to cover their heads during prayer. Rather than treat the commands as obligatory, jurists treated them as encouraged. Some traditions call for men to cover their arms, thighs, and torsos. Once again, they were viewed as recommendations and not obligations. Most jurists declared that men only had to cover between the navel and the knee. Others, however, ruled they only had to cover their genitals. When it came to men, moderation was the norm. When it came to women, the rulings were ridiculously and oppressively restrictive.

Why do Muslim women have to cover virtually everything while men can walk around in shorts and t-shirts or even show their torsos and legs in public? In some Muslim societies, men only wear loincloths. If women are so morally weak, why allow men to tempt them? And why is it that in places like Afghanistan, Pakistan, India, and Africa, Muslim men will not hesitate to pull out their penises and urinate in public, not to mention defecate. If a woman were to crouch down, even entirely covered, and relieve herself by a tree, she would risk being raped and stoned to death. And what of all the millionaire and billionaire Arabs who gamble, drink alcohol, do drugs, gamble, and frequent prostitutes, women, and children, in Las Vegas, Phuket, and other destinations of depravity? Why are they never held accountable by the "morality police?" If they expect their womenfolk to wear the *hijab* and the *jilbab*, why don't they wear turbans and long robes at all times and places, even while swimming?

In the world of Islam, the sexist double standards have no end. In fact, as the Persian poet Nizami Gencevi (1140-1209) wrote, "If it is a sin to look at a woman, cover your eyes, and not the woman" (Bestandji 2021: 77). As Qasim Amin (1863-1908) asked in *The Liberation of Women* (1899), "If men feared that women would be tempted, why were not men ordered to wear the veil?" (42). He noted that "veiling is the symbol of an ancient ownership" (134), that the veil and the cloistering of women was "the most abominable kind of slavery" (133), and that "the first step for women's liberation is to tear off the veil and totally wipe out its influence" (134).

Relying upon fabricated *hadiths*, the fanatics and fundamentalists insisted upon the need to cover up and cloister women. This violation of freedom was justified on the grounds that women could arouse men. The fact of the matter is that the male body can be as attractive to women as the female body can be to men. The Qur'an, however, makes no distinction between the moral responsibility of men and women. If the problem is male arousal, rather than confine women indoors and cover them up in public, it would be more logical for men to remain indoors and wear a covering that obstructs their view of women if they have to go outside. Why not eliminate the risk instead of requiring women to cover up? Because men have to work? Why not allow women to work freely and unfettered in the attire of their choice while the men devoid of self-control are kept safely out of the public sphere? They could be house husbands.

As Khaled About El Fadl pertinently points out, 33:60 is always ignored when addressing matters of modest dress. As Almighty God warns in the Qur'an:

> If the hypocrites do not desist, and likewise those in whose heart is a disease, as well as those who spread false rumors in the city. We shall surely spur thee against them; then they will not be their neighbors therein, save for a short while. Accursed! They will be seized wheresoever they are found and utterly slain. (33:60)

As Abou El Fadl notes:

> Verse 33:60 threatens the men causing the problem (i.e. the harassers or molesters) by saying that if the hypocrites, perverts, and rumor mongers in Medina do not desist from causing harm, they might be expelled from the city all together. Various sources report that at the time of the Prophet, scoundrels would hang out in the streets, and harass or molest slave girls. If a woman would turn out to be free, these men would leave her alone. (2016)

So, rather than control, repress, and punish women for wearing "bad *hijab*," which, according to Article 638 of the Iranian penal code, can result in seventy-four lashes, jail sentences up to two months, and fines up to half a million riyals, why don't conservative clerics and Islamists implement 33:60? In this Qur'anic passage, God Himself warns that hypocrites who sexually harass women, perverts who make catcalls, and men who offend the honor of women should not be treated as neighbors. They are cursed men who should be expelled from the community or put to the sword. How is that for Qur'anic gender justice?

Men should not tell women how to dress. Women have authority over themselves. If a woman wishes to wear a headscarf, without coercion or compulsion, so let it be. Nobody has the right to judge her. If a woman wishes to wear lower-cut clothing, so let it be. Nobody has the right to judge her or claim that she is hell-bound. God is the best of judges and God does not judge a book based on its cover. He considers its content. He judges women based on the content of their character, not the length of their dresses or their hairstyle.

As for why conservative clerics and Islamists do not apply 33:60, the answer is evident: they would have to condemn themselves for the crime of misogyny. So, as Jesus would say: "Thou hypocrite, first cast out the beam out of thine own eye; and then shalt thou see clearly to cast out the mote out of thy sister's eye" (Matthew 7:5). Shame on those turban-wearing terrorists and oppressors who condemn women to twenty-four, forty-two, and even fifty-five years in prison -- on charges of "disrespecting compulsory *hijab*," "spreading corruption and prostitution," "spreading propaganda against the state," and "assembly and collusion" -- for objecting to the imposition of the veil.

"I will make you suffer!" promised Mohammad Moqisseh (b. 1956), the notorious judge who presides over Branch 28 of Tehran's "Revolutionary" Kangaroo Court, when condemning women to half a century in prison for showing their hair and charging them with "disrespecting compulsory *hijab*," "acting against national security," "spreading corruption on earth," and "promoting prostitution."

Even those who believe that *hijab* is an Islamic obligation, like Mehdi Karroubi (b. 1937), a reformist cleric and former presidential candidate, question whether it can be implemented by force. As he stated, "I am personally against the mandatory *hijab*. When the *hijab* became mandatory after the revolution, it was the wrong thing to do. It was a political decision and a bad one" (Mithiborwala). "One day the *hijab* will no longer be compulsory in Iran, this is part of progress and development," affirmed Parvaneh Salashouri (b. 1964), a sociologist and reformist lawmaker in the women's faction of the Iranian Parliament (Mithiborwala).

"The *hijab* in the Qur'an is for women's protection but what we've done is holding the *hijab* over women like a club," complained former President Hassan Rouhani (Mithiborwala). "I said during the 2005 elections that I oppose the forced *hijab* and I repeated it 50 times," asserted former President Mahmoud Ahmadinejad (b. 1956) (Mithiborwala). He found the overemphasis on *hijab* and the aversion to female hair absurd. As he stated in a televised debate in 2005: "Is the appearance of our children's hair really a problem facing our people today? Let them make their hair however they want, what business is it to me and you? We have to take care of the country's fundamental problems" (Mithiborwala). In a televised interview conducted in 2010, he remarked that the government should not fight against bad *hijab* (Ridgeon 212). He found it insulting that men and women could be interrogated on the streets about their relationship (Ridgeon 2012). It was Ahmadinejad's views on *hijab* that placed him in the bad graces of Khamenei (Ridgeon 211-213). In fact,

> The conflict between Ahmadinejad and Khamenei spilled out into the public in 2011, when the controversy intensified over a 256-page supplement on the *hijab*, published by a newspaper... Although the supplement endorsed the *hijab*, the problem lay in the attempt to place the *hijab* in a historical context, which ... opened the door to divorcing rulings on the *hijab* from connections with sacred scripture. (213)

On August 22, 2022, twenty-one leading Iranian political and civil rights activists issued a statement asserting that the policy of mandatory *hijab* was "a mistake." Its signatories included Zahra Rahnavard (b. 1945), Faezeh Hashemi Rafsanjani (b. 1963), Mostafa Tajzadeh (b. 1956), Ahmad Montazeri (b. 1955), all leading and powerful ruling class figures. In their words:

> Mandatory *hijab* was a wrong decision from the beginning and the passage of time has made it obvious. Although there are serious theological differences as to whether the *hijab* is necessary or not, and to what extent women should cover their hair, there's no dispute about the fact that imposing the *hijab* does not have a defensible legal basis in *shari'ah* law. (Mithiborwala)

The Persians, Afghans, Arabs, and other Muslims are not the only people to have imposed dress codes upon women. Christian fundamentalists have a long history of restricting the freedom of women. As Ali Basye points out, it was once forbidden for women in Elizabeth, New Jersey, to walk down Broad Street without wearing petticoats (55). In Charlotte, North Carolina, "women had to have their bodies covered by at least sixteen yards of cloth at all times" (55). In Michigan, "it was against the law for a lady to lift her skirt more than six inches when walking through a mud puddle" (55). In Minnesota, "a bill went to the state legislature in 1893 to prohibit the wearing of hoopskirts" (55). In 1921, a proposed ordinance "set a fine and imprisonment to any women who wore on the streets skirts higher than three inches above the ankle" (Rabinovich-Smith 105). In Virginia, "another bill... proposed banning skirts higher than four inches from the ground and prohibited dress cleavages that displayed more than three inches of a woman's throat" (105). Unlike the Muslim world, these bills never became law. However, in places like Chicago, Cleveland, and even Atlantic City, regulating women's swimming attire proved more successful (104).

Prior to the introduction of the modern bathing suit, Western women were required to use "bathing machines," a beach buggy, swimming platform, and modesty screen (Lenčet and Bosker 22-23). It completely covered the patch of water where the woman could bathe "shielded from the eyes of the public and the rays of the sun" (22). Early swimwear for women was cumbersome, prevented women from learning to swim, and was downright dangerous (22-30). Even girls were forced to wear hats, shoes, stockings, and shoes to go swimming (24). Women wore swimming tents to enter the water, posing a grave drowning risk. So, there was a time, not long ago, when Western women, particularly in the United States, with its puritanical Christianity, had to cover their entire bodies in public, including their legs, arms, feet, and even hands.

In 1907, Anette Kellerman (1887-1975), a polio victim, "who had taken up swimming to strengthen her legs... offered the first practical alternative to aquatic nudity in the form of an improvised, tight-fitting, black wool one-piece that nearly overnight made her a household word" (36). "I want to swim," she announced to an incredulous public, "And I can't swim wearing more stuff than you hang on a clothesline" (36). Since her suit was tight-fitting, devoid of sleeves, and cut two inches above the knees, "she was arrested for indecent exposure and was denounced as a wanton" after "she appeared in Boston's Revere Beach dressed only in this body stocking" (36). Although she sometimes wore leggings that covered her feet and legs under her suit, it was still deemed indecent. This account is disputed by some who claim that no records of any such arrest survives. However, it is possible that no charges were pressed or that the records are no longer extant. Either way, such arrests were commonplace during the early days of modern women's swimwear. The fact remains that the sight of bare-armed women was too much for some men to handle. In fact, in 1913, a woman was assaulted by an angry crowd for wearing a short bathing suit at Atlantic City (38). In 1917, the American Association of Park Superintendents stipulated that ladies could not wear bloomers, skirts, or trunks that were shorter than four inches above the knee "(41).

"As late as the 1920s," note fashion historians Richard Martin (1947-1999) and Harold Koda (b. 1950), "some local ordinances in America called for women to be fined and removed from the beach for indecent exposure, including, legs without stockings, despite beach shoes and long skirts" (58-60). In 1921, "the Board of Alderman in Zion, City, Illinois, was split over a new ruling that required … a skirt to be worn over the thighs" (43). In Cleveland, Chicago, and Miami, the sleeves of bathing suits had to be one-quarter long at minimum, while white- and flesh-colored suits were prohibited (43). Private resorts and country clubs imposed dress codes on women (40). So threatening were women in one-piece bathing suits that "authorities deployed measuring tapes and dispatched paddy wagons to public beaches" to impose so-called standards of modesty (44). "Throughout the twenties," note Lena Lenčet and Gideon Bosker, "newspaper were filled with accounts of pitched battles between the proponents of the new one-piece suits and the guardians of public morality" (45). Women were brutally arrested and imprisoned for showing their arms and legs. "Although these regulations varied greatly from one place to another," relates Rabinovich-Smith, "almost all of them banned the one-piece bathing suit that revealed women's arms as well as hips" (105). At beaches and pools throughout the United States, police officers used to measure how much leg women were showing in their bathing suits, fining, and imprisoning them for any violations (Rabinovitch-Fox: front cover). They were the American Christian Taliban.

When the *atome* and the *bikini*, two-piece bathing suits, resurfaced in 1946, separately but nearly simultaneously launched by designers Jacques Heim (1899-1967) and Louis Réard (1896-1984), the backlash was tremendous, and the swimwear was banned from many beaches and public places. The bikini was banned on French coastlines in 1949. For decades it was also prohibited in

Belgium, Spain, Italy, Portugal, and Australia. In Germany, it was prohibited in public pools until the 1970s. Many communist countries banned it as a form of "capitalist decadence." In the 1960s, "entire nations, including Madagascar, Swaziland, and Malawi, outlawed the miniskirt" (Basye 150). Schools and businesses in the Western world continue to impose dress codes that specifically target girls.

Since the 1990s, law enforcement in cities like Myrtle Beach, South Carolina, among other seaside locations, have been arresting, charging, and fining women who violate ordinances prohibiting thong bikinis. Although legal in most of the United States, thong bikinis and G-strings are currently illegal in several states, cities, municipalities, and jurisdictions. As much as we may condemn the "morality police" in Iran, Afghanistan, and other Muslim-majority nations, where showing a strand of hair is a sin, the United States also has its own "swimsuit" and "bikini police" who arrest women for "turning the other cheek."

Muslims may have a long way to go when it comes to the emancipation of women. However, we Westerners were in a similar place a mere century ago, albeit considerably less violent, and we still have much work to be done on women's rights. So let us show our solidarity to Muslim women without any air of superiority. The struggle remains the same, and the disease has a name: misogyny, patriarchy, and male supremacy. Its only cure is equality. Changing laws, however, does not necessarily change misogynistic religious madmen. There are no mandatory modesty codes in most of the world, even in Muslim majority nations. Crimes against women, however, are terrifyingly common. Laws, of course, must be changed, and enforced. Ultimately, however, it is men who must be made to change.

Far from a measure of piety, the *hijab* symbolizes the submission of women to male authority and superiority (Bestandji 2021: 335). Far from a simple piece of cloth, the *hijab* disrupts male-female relations and imposes a symbolic and concrete separation between them (2021: 350). As for the *hijab*, this formidable political weapon of the Islamic fundamentalists, created and commanded by ultra-misogynistic men, it is non-existent in the Qur'an (2021: 348). "By bringing it back to its real terrain," notes Bestandji, "it becomes its Achilles heel" (2021: 348). Is the *hijab* the Word of God or the Word of Man? For many men and women cited in this work, the writing is one the wall, and the truth has been made manifest. In the final analysis, the onus is on women and men to examine all the arguments presented in this work, and ideally in the most important ones cited, and follow their minds, hearts, consciences, and souls.

Islamic fundamentalism and woke secularism pose an existential threat to women. The former wish to deny women their rights and make them disappear under layers of clothing while the latter seek to deny their very existence. At such a time, and more than ever, it behooves women to be fiercely feminine for the sake of their own survival. Let them be empowered female presences. Let them channel the Sacred Feminine, the One and Only Mother Goddess, Allah, and Her Most Beautiful Attributes. And let them channel the Sacred Masculine, the One and Only Father God, Allah, and His Attributes of Might and Majesty so that harmony can return to the whole. And let men do the same so they can live in spiritual symbiosis.

Appendix 1

Timeline

The Qur'an, the revelation of which ended in 632, suggests that women cover their *saw'at*, their shame or pudendum (7:26-27), namely, their genitalia.

The Qur'an states that women should guard their *furuj* or genitals (24:31), and not display their *zinah* or beauty (24:31), namely, their private parts.

The Qur'an counsels women to cover their *juyub* or breasts with their *khumur* or coverings (24:31) in dangerous times and places.

The Qur'an tells women they can show *ma zahara minha*, or "what may be apparent" (24:31), namely, everything but their private parts and perhaps their bosom.

The Qur'an cautions the wives of the Prophet against *tabarruj* which has been interpreted as "making a dazzling display of themselves" as women did during the Days of Ignorance (33:33). As Cyrille Moreno al-'Ajami has shown, however, the verb *tabarraja* originally signified "to show off with pride" (2020: 238). It was later exegetes who gave it the sense of ostensibly exhibiting beauty, thereby modifying the sense of the Qur'an (2020: 238-239). This verse has nothing do with the eternal obligation of gender segregation (2020: 238). What is more, it only applied to the wives of the Prophet (2020: 238). The exegetes and jurists twisted and distorted this verse, and applied it to all Muslim women, when the Qur'an stated clearly that it referred only to the wives of the Prophet as they were not like other women (33:32).

According to Tabari, this verse was revealed in response to their desire for material acquisitions and their wish to lead a leisurely and luxurious lifestyle (El Guindi 200: 156). Such materialism so infuriated the Prophet, who was a proponent of humility, that he secluded himself from his wives in protest (El Guindi 200: 156).

The Qur'an instructs women to wear a *jilbab* or garment when going out so they may be recognized and not annoyed (33:59).

The Qur'an explains that the dress code can be relaxed among family members (33:55) and need not be adhered to by older women (24:60).

The Qur'an asks women to wear beautiful clothing (7:31).

The Qur'an describes the attire of the women of Paradise as if they were straight out of a Vogue magazine (7:26, 7:31, 18:31, 22:23, 76:21).

Qatadah (d. c. 644) stated that women could show their bracelets, implying that women can show part of their arms.

'A'ishah (d. 678) stated that women could show their bracelets, implying that women can show part of their arms.

Sa'id ibn Jubayr (d. 714), a follower of the companions, and a leading early jurist, ruled that there was no Qur'anic requirement for women to cover their hair. According to some accounts, he was a companion of 'Ali. According to others, he was a companion of Zayn al-'Abidin, which seems more sensible. As al-Jassas (d. 981), the Hanafi jurist noted in *Ahkam al-Qur'an*, Sa'id ibn Jubayr was asked whether it was prohibited for men to look at the hair of non-*mahram* women. He responded: "It is not in the verse."

The 'Ibadis, the earliest sect of Islam, required women to cover everything but their face, hands, and feet. They did not believe in the *niqab*.

The school of Zayd ibn 'Ali (d. 740) ruled that women must cover their entire bodies, except for the face and the hands. The feet are considered part of their *'awrah.*

Abu Hanifah (d. 767) ruled that women must cover their entire bodies, except the face, hands, and feet, in public. According to another account, however, he included the feet in the *'awrah.* Veiling the face, while not mandatory, was recommended.

Malik (d. 795) ruled that women must cover their entire bodies, except for their faces and hands, in public. He considered the feet to form part of women's "lesser *'awrah.*" Veiling the face, while not mandatory, was recommended.

Shafi'i (d. 820) ruled that women must cover everything in public, including their faces, hands, and feet.

Ahmad ibn Hanbal (d. 855) ruled that women must cover everything in public, including their faces, hands, and feet.

Virtually all Sunni and Shiite jurists concluded that enslaved Muslim women were not permitted to cover their hair in public or while performing their ritual prayers. Others viewed it as detestable. Only a minority of jurists, like Ibn Hazm (994-1064), the Andalusian polymath, believed that the dress code for enslaved women was the same as that of free women. The vast majority held that slave girls only had to cover their genitals, or between the navel and the knees, and could appear in public with their breasts bare. Ironically, they gave more freedom to their female slaves than to their "free" wives.

The 'Alawites do not require women to wear *hijab.* This theologically extreme Twelver Shiite sect was founded by Muhammad ibn Nusayr (d. after 868). He was considered the representative of 'Ali al-Naqi and Hasan al-'Askari, the tenth and eleventh Imams of the Twelver Shiites. He claimed to be the *bab* or gate to the Hidden Imam, Muhammad al-Mahdi.

In 963, Mu'izz al-Dawla, the Buyid sultan, "ordered that... women should... go into the markets with their faces and their hair disheveled, beating their faces and wailing over Hussein" (Aghaie 2007: 118). If the *hijab* were *wajib*, why would he have commanded them to do so?

The Shafi'i jurist, traditionist, and Qur'anic commentator, Muhammad al-Shashi (904-976), known as al-Qaffal al-Kabir, argued that the extent of bodily exposure was a matter of prevailing of prevailing custom: *al-'adah al-jariyyah*.

Muhammad al-Tabari (d. 923), the Muslim historian, scholar, and exegete of the Qur'an, acknowledged that some early authorities believed that the '*awrah* of women consisted only of their genitalia. He confirmed that the *khimar* extended to everything that covered the body with the exception of the head ('Ajami 2020: 132). He noted, however, that contemporary scholars wanted to extend its meaning to cover women's hair (132).

Tabari (d. 923), Abu Yusuf (d. 798), and Sarakhsi (d. 1090) noted that some early jurists did not include the arms or forearms in the '*awrah* of women.

Ibn Junayd al-Iskafi (d. 991), one of the earliest Twelver Shiite jurists, part of the *qadimayn*, or "ancient ones," believed that the '*awrah* of women consisted of their genitals, the front, and the back, namely, the vagina and the anus, and that men and women were equal in this regard. He acted as an agent for the Twelfth Imam, corresponded with him, and collected money on his behalf (Rasekh 25, note 3). If he were wrong regarding the '*awrah* of women, would not the Mahdi have corrected him?

The Zahiri school of jurisprudence, the leading exponent of which was Ibn Hazm (d. 1064), ruled that women must cover everything but their faces and hands.

In his dictionary of rare words found in the Qur'an, al-Raghib al-Isfahani (d. 1108/1109) noted that the term *khimar* derived from the root *khamara* which means: to cover, to envelop, and to hide, and that etymologically, it designated anything that blocks the gaze ('Ajami 2020: 132). He noted, however, that its meaning had been stretched to include the sense of something that covers the heads of women ('Ajami 2020: 132). This meaning, however, was posterior to the Qur'an ('Ajami 2020: 132).

Ibn al-Barraj al-Tarabulusi (b. c. 1009/1010-d. c. 1088), a Twelver Shiite jurist and judge, who was a student of al-Sharif al-Murtada (b. 956/959-1044), a Twelver Shiite jurist and theologian, and al-Tusi (995-1067), a Twelver Shiite jurist and traditionist, noted that some Shiite scholars did not believe that women were required to cover their heads and necks (Ridgeon 182). He acknowledged that "a group of jurists have differences of opinion about whether it is necessary to cover all the hair" (Ridgeon 188). He also noted that "a group of jurists believe it is not necessary to cover hair which is longer than the head and neck" (Ridgeon 188). This is precisely the style that prevailed during much of Islamic history. Women covered part of the hair on their head -- the crown -- but did not cover anything that extended beyond the neck. Rather than follow the "*hijab* of ethnicity," they were clearly in conformity with Islamic law, as understood by many jurists of the time.

Zamakhshari (d. 1074), the Mutazilite theologian, linguist, and commentator of the Qur'an, argued that what women cover or uncover is determined by custom and nature.

'Ali ibn Ahmad al-Wahidi (d. 1075), the Qur'anic commentator, argued that women could uncover half of their arms.

Ibn Hayyan (987-1075), the Andalusian Berber historian, believed that clothing was determined by custom, nature, and practicality. In his mind, working class women should not be required to cover like upper class women.

Ibn 'Atiyya (d. 1147), the Qur'anic exegete, allowed women to uncover half of their arms.

The Qarmatians, an Ismaili movement, active between 899-1077, were known for their egalitarianism. They were monogamous and prohibited polygyny. They did not practice gender segregation. And their women went unveiled. They were followers of seven Imams from *ahl al-bayt*. They were Shiite abolitionists. They did not believe that the Prophet and the Imams were slave masters who owned concubines. For them, this was just another one of countless innovations introduced by the Umayyads, the 'Abbasids, and even other Shiite sects.

Nizam al-Din al-Nisaburi (d. 1328/1329), the exegete of the Qur'an, allowed women to uncover their arms to the elbow.

According to Ibn 'Abidin (d. 1836) some early jurists ruled that women were permitted to show their arms.

Yusuf al-Qaradawi (d. 2022) noted that some early jurists ruled that women could show four inches to half of their arms.

Ibn 'Ashur (d. 1973) noted that some early jurists ruled that women could expose their heads and hair in public.

Among the Almoravids (r. 1050-1147), men, not women, wore the *litham* or face veil at all times, including during communal prayers. Ibn Rushd (d. 1126) even passed an edict in favor of this unorthodox practice. After all, veiling the face of men was the practice of the Touareg since time immemorial. Their men veil their faces while their women show their hair freely.

The Almohads (r. 1121-1269) mocked Almoravid men for covering their faces while the faces of their women went uncovered in an inversion of their understanding of Islam. Among the Almoravids, gender norms differed from those of other groups. Their women had a relatively high status and were not required to veil themselves.

Increasingly, many Amazigh women in North Africa reject the *hijab* and choose to show their hair to signify their rejection of Arabic-Islamic imperial imposition. They stress the matriarchal nature of Berber culture, reject strict female dress standards and gender segregation. They are undergoing an evolution of identity (Almasude).

Fakhr al-Din al-Razi (d. 1209), the polymath and Qur'anic commentator, believed that women could uncover their faces, hands, and feet; however, he noted that the extent of bodily exposure was a matter of prevailing custom (*al-'adah al-jariyyah*). In other words, it was subject to variation based on various factors.

Most jurists from the Twelver Shiite school of jurisprudence ruled that women must cover everything in public, except their face and hands. Their feet are part of their *'awrah* in public, but not in private prayer.

Many Sufi exegetes of the Qur'an did not comment upon the so-called *hijab* verses. Their silence screams. Those who did gave them a mystical significance. For Rashid al-Din Maybudi (d. 12th century), 24:31 did not speak about literally covering one's bosom, but rather, covering one's heart and secret core. It referred to spiritual modesty.

In 1019, the Druze asked the chief judge of the Fatimid state to adjudicate their cases according to the standards of the spiritual law. This would have included the right of women to be relieved of the *hijab*.

The Fatimid Ismailis abolished the veil and *hijab* at some point in the twelfth century, along with other aspects of the external law.

Ibn 'Arabi (d. 1240), the scholar, mystic, poet, and philosopher, ruled that the *'awrah* of women was limited to their genitals.

The Bektashi *tariqah*, a Twelver Shiite/Sufi sect founded by Haji Bektash Veli (d. 1271), does not practice gender segregation, nor does it require women to veil themselves. It is not customary for Bektashi women to wear headscarves.

The Alevis, another Twelver Shiite/Sufi sect, who follow the teachings of Haji Bektash Veli (d. 1271), do not practice gender segregation, nor do they require women to wear headscarves.

Ahmad ibn Muhammad al-Ardabili, also known as al-Muhaqqiq al-Ardabili (d. 1585), the Twelver Shiite jurist and expert in intellectual and narrative sciences, believed that the interpretation of the verse "except what [ordinarily] appears thereof" (24:31) depended on the norms and customs of the time. He did not view the veil or *hijab* as an essential and immutable part of Islam. As Ahmad Ghabal notes,

> Muqaddas Ardabili gave his opinions about the … [bodily] parts that were not usually covered: "If one looks at the apparent custom and tradition of the time [when] the verse was revealed, in particular, [the custom of] poor women, usually the neck, the upper chest, the forearms, the shins, and some other places too were uncovered, and … the command on the issue is problematic." So, there are no clear words on the subject of "the need to cover the head and neck" in the verse of sura 24… It confirms the permissibility of not covering parts of the body (that according to the custom of the time when the revelation came), as it was fashionable not to cover them. Historical research … confirms the unfashionable [nature] of covering the head and shoulders (in all circumstances and in all public places). (Ridgeon 195)

Muhammad ibn ‘Ali al-Musawi al-‘Amili (d. 1600), known as *Sahib al-Madarik*, ruled that it was not obligatory for women to cover their heads and necks (Ridgeon 182). He was a maternal grandson of al-Shahid al-Thani (d. 1557), the Twelver Shiite jurist, and a descendant of ‘Allamah al-Hilli (d. 1325), a scholar of such erudition that he was the first to be called *ayatullah* or sign of God. As ‘Amili wrote in *Madarik al-ahkam*,

> Know that in this passage, just as [in the] declarations of other Shi‘i jurists, there has been no engagement with “the need to cover the hair.” Rather, from this passage it is clear that “covering the hair is not necessary”… and Shahid-i Avval has considered it closer [to the truth] (*nazdiktar bi vaqi‘a*) and his support is a report of “Ibn Babuya from Fuzayl” which has been reported by Imam Baqir … and this narration, if its chain of transmission (*sanad*) is trustworthy, does not include any proof for the need to cover the hair. Yes, one can reason the lack of need to cover the hair from this narration, and the narration of “Zarara” … too points to the lack of necessity for covering. (Ridgeon 189)

As far as Muhammad ‘Amili was concerned, the traditions address covering during prayers, not covering the hair in general situations (Ridgeon 189-190).

Muhammad Baqir Sabzavari (1608-1679), the author of *Kifayat al-ahkam* [*Sufficiency of the Commands*], and the grand mufti of Isfahan, admitted that,

> There are problems on the topic of proving the command for “the need to cover a woman’s neck” and in most declarations and expressions of the jurists there has been no mention of “the need to cover the hair.” Although Shahid-i Avval considered it necessary, one should hesitate in agreeing with his perspective on this topic. (Ridgeon 189)

Majlisi (d. 1627-1699), the influential Twelver Shiite scholar from Safavid times, noted that there was no consensus among jurists that women were required to cover their hair. He noted that most Shia jurists up to his time had never decreed that women were required to cover their hair with a *hijab*. He recognized that men and women were mandated to conceal their private parts. He defined the private parts of men as the penis, testicles, and anus, and that of women as the vagina till the anus. He pointed out that for some jurists, the private parts of men and women extended from the navel to the knee, and for others, from the navel till half the thigh (*Haqqul Yaqeen* 849). As he wrote in *Bihar al-anwar*,

> Know that in the discussions of many Shi‘i jurists there is no talk of “the need to cover the hair.” Shahid-i Avval considered the need to cover the hair as closer [to the truth)… and this approach of his corresponds more with [the principle of] caution. (Ridgeon 190)

As Ahmad Ghalab emphasized, the question begs to be asked,

> How has it come to pass that one of the most famous Akhbari Shi'i jurists, who has assembled the most comprehensive collection of Shi'i *hadith* (*Bihar al-anwar*, 110 volumes) -- and there is no other more famous among Shi'i Akhbaris -- ultimately resorted to [the principle of] caution and could not find support for a "fatwa" and "clear command" specific to covering hair? (Ridgeon 191)

Two things become immediately clear: 1) there is no basis for the *hijab* in the *hadith* literature and 2) many jurists up the early eighteenth century believed that the '*awrah* or *saw'at* of men and women were the same and consisted only of their genitals.

Khamis ibn Sa'id Shiqsi al-Rustaqi (17th c), the 'Ibadi scholar, noted that laws vary according to time and place and that it was acceptable, in some regions, for women to show their hair. He noted that if women covered their hair in Oman, it was not because it was viewed as beautiful but because showing hair was considered ugly. So, the *hijab*, in their social context, was for beautification.

In *Mustanad al-Shi'ah*, Muhaqqiq Naraqi (1772-1829), an influential *mujtahid*, also conceded that,

> The command [of the *shari'ah*] related to "hair" is clear, and "covering the hair is not necessary," just as some Shi'i jurists have argued. But the [*shari'ah*] command also makes clear "the lack of a need to cover the neck," just as some jurists have related. And the command for "the lack of a need to cover the ears" is also clear. (Ridgeon 191)

Like many other jurists, Naraqi recognized that there was no explicit basis for the *hijab* in primary and even secondary Islamic sources. At best, it was a matter of *ihtiyat* or precaution. Shiite scholars, like their Sunni counterparts, eventually caved and capitulated under cultural or political pressure. Consequently, a non-obligation became a precaution, a precaution became a recommendation, and a recommendation became an obligation. The Islamic ruling on the covering required of women experienced a *volte-face*. It was turned upside down.

In 1848, Tahirih, also known as Qurrat al-Ayn (d. 1842), the courageous Persian poet and follower of the Bab (d. 1850), cast off her veil at a conference in a revolutionary act of defiance. She was the first Iranian executed for "waging war against God."

Baha'u'llah (d. 1892), the founder of the Baha'i faith, believed that the choice of clothing was a matter of personal discretion that principles of modesty should inform.

Aqa Rida Hamadani al-Najafi (d. 1904), the Twelver Shiite jurist who became the leading religious authority after the death of his teacher, Mirza Shirazi (d. 1895), another source of emulation, did not believe that *hijab* was a religious requirement. In fact, as Ahmad Ghabal noted, "Hamadani … said on the reliable narration of Ibn Bakir from Imam Sadiq that 'the free Muslim woman can pray without covering the body'" (Ridgeon 197).

'Ali Tabataba'i (1748-1815/1816), a Twelver Shiite jurist who studied under Wahid Bihbihani (1706-1791), ruled that women were not required to cover their heads and necks (Ridgeon 182).

Muhammad Hasan al-Najafi (1785-1850), the Twelver Shiite source of emulation, ruled that there was consensus among jurists that the *'awrah* of women had to be covered but that there was no consensus that this extended to their hair (Ridgeon 182). Najafi noted that "covering head hair is based upon [observing] caution" (Ridgeon 182, 188). He also spoke of the "probability for the exemption of long hair" (Ridgeon 188).

When a jurist defers to *ihtiyat* or precaution, he is not issuing an edict of *halal* or *haram*. His opinion on the subject is not binding and his followers or *muqallidin* are therefore free to follow the edict of another *mujtahid* on the issue. So, if Najafi said that wearing *hijab* was a matter of *ihtiyat*, however strong, his followers could ascribe to the view of scholars who hold that it is mandatory or adhere to the opinion that it is not obligatory. For Najafi, it was merely *mustahab* (Ridgeon 188). He admitted that "reliable, related proofs" for definitive commands on the "necessity of absolute covering of the head hair of free Muslim women do not exist in primary *shari'ah* texts" (Ridgeon 188).

Muhammad 'Abduh (d. 1905), the Egyptian scholar, "lashed out at the triple stigmatization of the Muslim female: a shameful nakedness, a dangerous temptation to immorality, and an uncontrollable lust" (Hajjaji-Jarrah 210). He argued that men who viewed women as a source of *fitnah* or temptation to immorality were women-phobic and that "women are not required to assess it or to recognize it" (211). It was up to those men to lower their gaze (211). If men were so concerned about being tempted by women, he suggested they should be the ones to veil and conceal themselves (211).

On January 8, 1936, Reza Pahlavi (d. 1944), the Shah of Iran, banned the veil in all its forms. In so doing, he was aware that there were different views on the subject in Islamic jurisprudence and counted on the support of the clerics that he had consulted. The edict, known as *Kashf-e hijab*, prohibited the *hijab* and the *chador*. Its swift and brutal implementation would prove to be a catastrophe that backfired and added fuel to the fundamentalist opposition.

Mustafa Ghalaynini (d. 1944), a Lebanese theologian, noted that veiling was a pre-Islamic custom that had been adopted by Muslims from other cultures.

In 1947, the General Assembly of the Islamic Community in Bosnia and Herzegovina supported banning the *niqab* and *jilbab*. The Islamic leadership concluded that veiling was a cultural practice and that it was wrong and damaging to mistake such customs as forming part of the principles of Islam (Mekić 144).

In the 1950s, President Gamal Abdel Nasser (d. 1970) mocked the request made by Muslim Brotherhood leaders to veil all women.

'Abd al-Qadir al-Maghribi (d. 1956) viewed *hijab* as an aristocratic custom that distinguished wealthy and prestigious women from others.

In 1957, President Habib Bourguiba (d. 2000) of Tunisia prohibited wearing the veil in schools.

Sultan Mohamed Shah (d. 1957), Aga Khan III, expressed opposition to *purdah*, the *burqa*, and *hijab*, insisting that Islam did not mandate them.

Tahar Haddad (d. 1935), the Tunisian scholar and reformer, concluded that the *hijab* was not rooted in the Qur'an. He viewed it as the manifestation of male immorality. He was declared a heretic and an apostate. Since he was declared an unbeliever, the establishment decreed he was prohibited from marrying any Muslim woman.

Regarding 33:59, the so-called *hijab* verse, Muhammad Muhaqqiq Damad (1907-1968), the Twelver Shiite jurist, provided some needed clarity. As he explained,

> Discovering the secret of this verse and the confusion of its beginning and the end renders a conclusion contrary to proving the need to cover. It convinces the jurist that the command in this verse explains non-obligatory [but] preferential customs… and it is clear that these words and the language that is used is not in principle an expression of requirement or necessity… So, the glorious verse, in relation to conveying necessity is incomplete. (Ridgeon 195-196)

Shah Karim al-Husayni (b. 1936), Aga Khan III, has reiterated his refusal to recognize the *hijab* as an Islamic obligation, viewing it as an antiquated social custom.

Abdullah Yusuf Ali, the Muslim scholar and translator the Qur'an, noted in his commentary to verse 53 that "for Muslim women generally, no screen or *hijab* (*purdah*) is mentioned, but only a veil to cover the bosom and modesty in dress."

Muhammad Mehdi Shams al-Din (d. 2001), the Twelver Shiite jurist, declared that the *hijab* was not obligatory, only recommended, and it could not be coerced. "The language of this verse," he notes, "does not [indicate] compulsion or necessity; perhaps it expresses desirability and dictate more than anything" (Ridgeon 196). He viewed the *hijab* as divisive to social cohesion and national unity. He did not believe that Muslim women should be visibly distinguished from Christian ones.

Mohamed al-Talbi (d. 2017), the Tunisian historian and Islamologist, asserted that the Qur'an said absolutely nothing about the *hijab*. In fact, he argued that "all the problems of the *shari'ah* are connected to the problem of the *hijab*." He believed that "If Muslim women abandoned the *hijab*, out of faithfulness to the Qur'an, men would follow, and Muslim thought would be renewed" (Bestandji 2021: 112). Talbi was condemned to death by three Islamist movements, and the police refused to provide him protection. He remained defiant until his death, insisting that true Islam was freedom.

On March 6, 1979, Khomeini declared that "naked women must not enter Islamic ministries. Women must wear the *hijab* in all ministries" (Ridgeon 132). In response, over one hundred thousand Iranian women marched on March 8, 1979, to celebrate International Women's Day (Ridgeon 132). The women, who came "from all sectors of society," including the young and the old, demonstrated for six days (Ridgeon 132).

Mahmoud Taleghani (d. 1979), the Twelver Shiite source of emulation, ruled that "*hijab* is not compulsory." He assured women it would not be enforced and would only be voluntary (Ridgeon 133).

In 1983, after consolidating their power, Khomeini and his Islamist supporters felt secure enough to impose the *hijab* by law and force (Ridgeon 133). Moral law enforcers, both male and female, were deployed to chastise and punish women who showed a single strand of hair (Ridgeon 133). They harassed women for wearing tight clothing, makeup, lipstick, nail polish or perfume (Ridgeon 133). As Kaveh Basmenji describes,

> "Moral police" … aided and abetted by Ansar-e-Hezbollah thugs… under the watchful gaze of officers in olive-colored uniforms, [and] female police agents clad in black chadors stopped young women, barking at them, questioning them, and dragging the more defiant ones towards buses waiting in line. Members of Ansar-e-Hezbollah were chanting "Marg bar Badhejab" (death to those with improper *hijab*), breaking with stones the windows of shops displaying lingerie or short robes, and beating up whoever happened to be in their way. (Ridgeon 133-134)

Warith Deen Mohammed (d. 2008), who brought the Nation of Islam into a more mainstream Muslim tradition, only believed that women should wear *hijab* in the mosque and while performing their prayers. He did not view the *hijab* as a religious obligation. He was denounced as a heretic and an infidel by Salafi terrorists.

In the early twentieth century, Farzana Hassan (b. 1957), the former president of the Muslim Canadian Congress, asserted that "the modesty recommended in the Qur'an has more to do with modesty in conduct and demeanor" (Fatah 292). She noted that "the Qur'an remained silent as to the specific apparel worn [by women]… except for the occasion where it specifically suggested covering the bosom with a *khimar*," something that was "specifically designed to discourage the practice of earlier times when women dressed scantily with their bosoms remaining exposed" (Fatah 292). As a result, Islamist terrorists threatened to assassinate her on grounds of apostasy.

For Tarek Fatah (1949-2023), an author and journalist, "the commandment in the verse is clear: cover your chest or bosom" (293). However, due to the "fabrication of medieval scholars and the cowardice of contemporary translators… Muslims are being told that the Qur'an prescribes the covering of one's head or hair" (293). He made the following "Plea to My Sisters:"

> Originally a reflection of modesty, the *hijab* has now become a political tool. All women have, at some time in their lives, chosen to wear a head cover, whether in a snowstorm or freezing rain. At times, the covering of the head, irrespective of what religion one practices, is crucial to one's survival. In the deserts of Arabia, whether one is a Muslim or a pagan, the covering of one's head and face is an absolute necessity -- not just when facing a blistering sandstorm, but any time one steps out of the home into the searing sunshine. But what is essentially attire for a particular climate and weather has been turned into a modern symbol of defiance and, at best, a show of false piety by Islamists and orthodox Muslims…
>
> There is not a single reference in the Qur'an that obliges Muslim women to cover their hair or their face, or to lower the voice. The only verse that comes close to such a dress code, Sura 24:31, directs believing women to cover their bosoms. Yet, in the past few decades, Islamists and orthodox Muslims have made the covering of a woman's head the cornerstone of Muslim identity. It is true that through history some Muslim women have chosen to wear the *hijab* for reasons of modesty. Today, however, some wear it for the opposite reason. "Young women put on a *hijab* and go dancing, wearing high heels and lipstick. They wear tight jeans that show their bellies," seventy-five-year-old Nawal Al-Saadawi, Egypt's leading feminist, noted recently, adding that "The *hijab* has nothing to do with moral values."
>
> Beyond fashion, however, this supposed symbol of modesty has assumed a decidedly political and religious tenor, dominating the debate on civil liberties and religious freedoms in the West. Any opposition to the *hijab* is viewed as a manifestation of Islamophobia. It should be noted that the head scarf that pre-dated the *hijab*, was worn by Arab women before the Qur'an's stipulations on modesty of dress and demeanor… 24:31 did not introduce the garment but modified its use when it said that Muslim women should "wear their *khimar* over their bosoms" -- previously, breasts were left bare, although bedecked with jewelry and ornaments.
>
> Therefore, to turn the *hijab* or *khimar* into a religious and political issue belies its original intent. Muslim women who so vociferously defend its use should consider its history before deciding whether they must wear it. Islamists have turned the *hijab* into the central pillar of Islam… Islamists consider Muslim women who do not cover their heads -- the majority -- as sinners or lesser Muslims. They ban the books of women who stand up to spousal abuse and depict Muslim feminists as women of questionable character. As despicable as this blackmailing is, it pales in comparison to the fact that these men in

> robes are using young Muslim girls as shields behind which they pursue a political agenda. Can God be fooled? (301-302)

Based on his theory of limits, Muhammad Shahrur (d. 2019), the Syrian intellectual and philosopher, concluded that the minimum Muslim women had to cover in the public sphere were their genitals and breasts. In other words, a Muslim woman who wore a bikini by a pool or a beach was abiding by the minimum limit of the law. In his view, covering cleavage, which includes the breasts, armpits, and buttocks, was generally required, and could be fulfilled by wearing a t-shirt and a pair of shorts. However, he had no qualms about women showing more in specific social settings, such as concerts, celebrations, the theatre, and the opera. In contrast, the maximum that a woman could cover would be everything but her face and hands.

Afaf Lutfi al-Sayyid-Marsot (b. 1933), Leila Ahmed (b. 1940), Fadwa El Guindi (b. 1941), Nimat Hafez Barazangi (b. 1943), Riffat Hasan (b. 1943), Amina Wadud (d. 1952), Asma Barlas (1950), Ziba Mir-Hosseini (b. 1954), Asma Lamrabet (b. 1961) Ayesha S. Chaudhry, Nevin Reda, Aysha A. Hidayatullah, and Zahra Jalaeipour, among many other Muslim women scholars, have provided evidence that the *hijab* is not obligatory in Islam.

Abla Hasan, the Syrian American professor, does not believe that *hijab* can be forced upon women in any shape or form.

Tedjini Haddam, who was a rector of the Great Mosque in Paris, explained that all that was required was that "a woman be decently dressed."

Sultan Abdulmajeed argued that "the idea that all Muslim women are required by Islam to veil themselves (in any form) is false and damaging to women, to Islam, and to people who might otherwise consider accepting Islam as their faith."

According to Gamal Al-Banna (1920-2013), the Egyptian author and critical thinker, nothing in the Qur'an or authentic *sunnah* requires women to cover their hair. The relevant Qur'anic verses command women to cover their chests. In his words, "nothing in the Qur'an, nor the *hadith* require women to wear a headscarf" (Guitta).

Fatima Mernissi (d. 2015), the Moroccan sociologist and feminist, argued that the veil was a symbol of unjust male authority over women that was "a construction of the '*ulama,*' the male jurist-theologians who manipulated and distorted the religious texts in order to preserve the patriarchal system." It should be noted, however, that Mernissi wrote her famous book, *The Veil and the Male Elite*, at a time when nobody in Morocco even knew what a *hijab* was (Yahia 121).

In her book, *Hijab: A Modern Vision*, Iqbal Baraka (b. 1944), an influential feminist in the Arab world, argued that veiling is a demeaning pre-Islamic practice not stipulated in the Qur'an or the *hadith* (Lichter 100). Far than having anything to do with Islam, the *hijab*, in her view, is a relic of the Dark Ages. Not only is she opposed to the *hijab*, but she advocates abolishing the *niqab* (MEMRI).

Ziauddin Sardar (b. 1951), the British-Pakistani intellectual, has concluded that there is no Qur'anic warrant for *burqas*, *chadors*, *abayahs*, and *niqab*.

Azar Nafisi (b. 1955), the Iranian American academic, argues that the veil is a political tool of the totalitarian Islamists to control people (Lichter 182). She views the imposition of mandatory veiling as a usurpation of Islam, namely, "changing what had been a freely chosen expression of religious faith into a rote act imposed on them by the state" (Lichter 182).

Cyrille Moreno al-'Ajami, a French theologian who specializes in Arabic language, literature, and Qur'anic exegesis, believes that the Islamic obligation to wear the *hijab* has no basis in the Qur'an and that "nothing obliges Muslim women to wear *hijab*." The text calls upon women to be chaste, decent, and reserved, a standard that applies equally to men.

Al-'Ajami stresses that the term *khimar* simply signified a covering in Qur'anic usage and that women were only required to cover their cleavage and private parts (2020: 133). To claim that the Qur'an asks women to cover their cleavage in order to cover their hair is, in his view, "farfetched" and an act of "exegetical trickery" (2020: 133). As he insists, "any command must necessarily be explicit and unambiguous" (2020: 133). "Since the Qur'an did not visibly say what Islam wanted it to say, some *hadith* were produced to obtain the result was expected by legal exegesis" (2020: 134-135).

Khaled Abou El Fadl (b. 1963), an Islamic jurist, has ruled that it is permissible to not wear *hijab*.

Numerous Twelver Shiite scholars, both traditionalists, and reformists, have expressed their opposition to obligatory *hijab*, including Muhammad Ishaq al-Fayyad (b. 1930), a senior source of emulation, Muhammad Kazem Mousavi Bojnourdi (b. 1942), and Hasan Khomeini (b. 1972)

Wassyla Tamzali (b. 1941), the Algerian writer, lawyer, Muslim, freethinker, and secular feminist, strongly opposes the veil.

Twelver Shiite jurist, Hassan Yousefi Eshkevari (b. 1950), argues that the *hijab*, as understood and practiced, is not based on the Qur'an, and cannot be imposed on women. He does not believe that women are required to cover their hair. What is more, he argues that the concept of modesty is social, contextual, and changeable. The Islamist regime in Iran condemned him to prison and defrocked him.

In his study on the history of the *hijab*, Twelver Shiite scholar, Amir Hussein Torkashvand (b. 1964), drew attention to the divergent rulings on the subject. He noted that the main position, which has been shared by contemporary scholars, and those from the recent past, is that the '*awrah* applied to all parts of a woman, except her face and hands, with a minority including the feet as well. Although known to few, he notes that the earliest view was that the '*awrah* of women referred only to their genitals. He concluded that the original view was between both positions and that the *'awrah* women, like men, extends from the shoulders to the knees. In other words, women, like men, are free to show their hair, arms, and lower legs.

In "A Religious Revision of *Hijab*," published in 2007, Moslem Khalafi (b. 1969) reminded Muslims of the various rulings regarding women's dress and asked why it was that only the strictest views that mandate the veil are known while moderate ones are entirely unknown.

Elham Man'ea (b. 1966), the Yemeni-Swiss political scientist, issued the following plea to Muslim women:

> I call on you, my Muslim sister, to take off the veil. This is an honest call… Its intention is not to defile you, nor to encourage you to [moral] lassitude. I call on you to exercise [free] thought and to use your own mind. I am not calling on you to stop praying, fasting, or believing in Allah. I call on you to take off the veil… Be yourself -- a woman -- and not [a collection of] private parts. (Lichter 369)

Zaki Badawi, the Imam and founder of the Muslim College in the United Kingdom, who passed away in 2006, asserted that the *hijab* was not obligatory and that the face-veil was an innovation devoid of any Islamic foundation (Goodwin 30).

In 2004, Ahmad Ghabal (d. 2012), the Twelver Shiite jurist, ruled that women did not need to cover their hair and necks according to Islamic law and that it was only recommended. He still insisted they should cover their bodies. In 2016, he warned,

> A red line has been drawn for the controversy of covering the head and neck and a sanctuary has been made for it. It is as if no duty existed but regurgitating repetitions and confirming populist understandings for researchers and jurists of the current age. Establishing the limits for [the *hijab*] has reached the extent that it has been called "the Islamic flag," an invented name, and all efforts of our great [scholars] in *fiqh* have been and are spent to protect it. (Ridgeon 199)

The Islamist regime in Iran arrested him numerous times and convicted him of waging war against the ruling system and insulting the "Supreme" Leader. He died while under hospital arrest.

Kassim Ahmad (d. 2017), the Malaysian philosopher, has declared that the Qur'an does not ordain the *hijab* and that women's hair is not a part of their *'awrah* or private parts.

Mohammed Arkoun (d. 2010), an original and influential scholar of Islam, affirmed that "The *hijab* has never been a canonical obligation." He denounced Islamist movements for turning it into an imaginary obligation.

Abul-Ghasem Fanaei (b. 1959), the Twelver Shiite scholar, concluded that there was no basis in the Qur'an for the laws of *hijab* and that two vague verses cannot be used to make laws and limit the freedom of women. He noted that modesty is contextual and varies according to time and place. He believes women should not flaunt their bodies to sexually arouse men deliberately. He recognizes that, in some countries, wearing a bikini at a beach is not viewed as provocative, does not endanger women, and does not result in sexual harassment. In short, he believes that modesty rules are mutable, flexible, and changeable.

Mahmoud Mohamed Taha (d. 1985), the seminal Sudanese scholar, declared that "the veil (*al-hijab*) is not an original precept of Islam."

In 1994, Muhammad Sa'id al-Ashmawi (d. 2013), an Egyptian judge, ruled that the *hijab* was not part of the *shari'ah* and was not a religious obligation (*fard*). He insisted that the *fatwa* on the veil was religiously illegitimate. It was a pre-Islamic practice that early Muslim jurists wrongly and mistakenly adopted. Since there has never been any proof that *hijab* was an absolute religious requirement, and considering changes in social conditions, he believed there was no convincing ground for maintaining it (Bloesch and Minister 60). He argued that "the real meaning of *hijab* lies in thwarting the self from straying toward lust or illicit desires and keeping away from sinful behavior, without having to conjoin this [understanding] with particular forms of clothing and attire" (Bucar). For daring to opine that Muslim women did not have to cover their hair, he received death threats from Islamists and was placed under protection (Stratton 167).

In 1999, 'Abdollah Nuri (b. 1950), a cleric who served as Khatami's Minister of the Interior, was taken to court for advocating greater tolerance and pluralism (Ridgeon 143). The court argued that granting people greater freedom of choice endangered Islamic principles and promoted corruption and immorality (Ridgeon 143). "By pointing to the non-compulsion for the *hijab* on non-believing women and non-Muslims," writes Ridgeon, "Nuri suggested that the requirement to cover the head was not as straightforward as some have asserted" (144). Although Nuri neither supported nor opposed the *hijab*, "his defense of the general principle to allow different lifestyles indicated where his sympathies lay" (144). Despite his long years of service to the Islamic Republic, and his commitment to Khomeini's doctrines, he was condemned to five years of prison.

Twelver Shiite scholar, Mohsen Kadivar, previously believed that the minimum boundaries of *hijab* remain the same: namely, they should cover from the neck to the knees. Depending on the context, he conceded that covering the hair might not always be necessary. While his views have evolved, and he once held the dominant restrictive interpretation of *hijab*, he now believes that the *hijab* is neither necessary nor desirable, that clothing should accord with custom, and that it should not violate the ethical basis of the Qur'an (Ridgeon 8, 234). In fact, "he goes as far as saying that there is no Qur'anic imperative for women to wear the *hijab*" (Ridgeon 8).

Twelver Shiite scholar, Moslem Khalafi, has pointed out that Islamic sources include extremely permissive and restrictive narrations regarding women's dress. Some, for example, allowed women to pray without head coverings and allowed men to look at the faces of women, even with attraction. Why, he asks, have only the most restrictive positions regarding women's dress been favored over the more permissive ones?

Most of the children, grandchildren, and great-grandchildren of the leaders of the Islamic Revolution of Iran belong to the reformist camp, including Hasan Khomeini, the grandson of Ruhollah Khomeini, and are proponents of voluntary as opposed to compulsory *hijab*.

Javed Ahmed Ghamidi (b. 1952), the Pakistani philosopher, believes that Muslim women are required to lower their gaze, wear modest clothing, cover their bosom, and not expose themselves in public.

Farhad Shafti, a professor who holds a PhD in Islamic Studies, has asserted that wearing a headscarf is not a religious act and has nothing to do with modesty.

Moiz Amjad (b. 1962) concluded that "Islam does not make it mandatory for women to cover their heads."

In 2001, the *Arab Times* published a "Letter from Queen Rania" that was sent to them directly from the email of Her Majesty on December 11 of that year. It provided a synthesis of Qur'anic teachings on the *hijab*. It allowed the newspaper to publish the piece so long as it withheld the email of the Queen and did not sell or exploit it without the permission of the Royal Hashemite Court.

On January 14, 2002, New York attorney John S. Willems sent a letter to the editor of the *Arab Times* claiming that the article should not be attributed to Queen Rania. The editor, Osama Fawzi, responded by noting that the attorney failed to identify the party he represented. Was he retained by Queen Rania personally, Her Majesty's husband the King of Jordan, the Royal Hashemite Court, the Jordanian Embassy in Washington, or the Jordanian Intelligence Agency? To all appearances, no further communications came from the attorney and the "Letter from Queen Rania" has been available online, on numerous sites, since 2001. Although more detailed than the sound bites she provides in interviews, the views shared in the letter, and the language and style in which they are expressed, sound very much like those of Queen Rania. In fact, she has been repeating the talking points found in that disputed article for over two decades. Apparently, her interview with Oprah Winfrey in 2001, which touched upon the sensitive religious issue of *hijab*, had struck some nerves, and Jordanian intelligence was attempting to put out some fires to placate the Islamists. The entirety of the letter is found online.

In 2002, the Iranian regime banned the Persian translation of Fatima Mernessi's *The Veil and the Male Elite*, a timid work on the topic.

When Oprah Winfrey contrasted Queen Rania's westernized look to that of women who wear hoods, *burqas*, and *hijabs,* during the course of an interview in 2001, Her Majesty answered as follows:

> [Just] like in Christianity, there are different interpretations of Islam, and there are different degrees of conservatism. It's a personal choice. Some people are more conservative than others. The important thing is the spirit of Islam. That is all about tolerance, about doing good, diversity, equality, and human dignity. The fact that Islam is very tolerant means that it doesn't impose anything on other people. You are supposed to behave in a certain way, or dress in a certain way out of conviction, not because somebody imposes their own ideology on you. I believe one's relationship with God, and how one chooses to practice religion, is an intensely personal choice.

"So you as an individual choose whether or not you want to be robed or not robed, or wear your head covered or not?," asked Oprah, "That's not imposed upon you by your religion?" "In our country," responded the Queen, "that is what we believe. We give women the choice to wear the headscarf or not. It's a personal choice. As I said, it is not the state that is supposed to impose on individuals what they believe in. That is their own personal choice" (Come and See).

In 2003, Queen Rania of Jordan denounced the fact that the identity of Arab women was being reduced to a single article of clothing, the *hijab* (Queen Rania).

In 2006, Hossein Khomeini, the oldest grandson of Ruhollah Khomeini, stated that "the *hijab* is a personal issue. If a woman wants it, she may [wear it], and if she doesn't, she may [refuse it]" (Ighani).

In a 2007 interview with the Italian daily *Corriere della Serra*, Queen Rania of Jordan insisted, "Islam neither requires one to be practicing, nor to dress in one way or another… Imposing the veil on a woman is contrary to the principles of Islam… Wearing the veil is a free personal choice." She urged "all moderates to stand up and let their voices be heard." As she explained,

> Many people are frustrated in the Arab world. Many give in to anger because they are accused of violence. But instead we should get up, explain who we are and what we believe in. Over the last three years, most victims of terrorism have been Muslim. So there's not a war between Muslims and non-Muslims, but between extremists and moderates of all the religions. What is important is not to live in fear. The most dangerous [thing to do] is to give up and lose hope. The main enemy is not terrorism or extremism, but ignorance. (ABC)

In 2007, Ramzan Kadyrov (b.1976), the Chechen despot, commenced a so-called "virtue campaign" to impose the headscarf and the rules of *hijab*. He proclaimed that he wanted Chechnya to be "more Islamic than the Islamists." Kadyrov "openly asserted that women were inferior and should be subjugated to men, equating women with male property." He decreed that "all women working for state institutions had to wear headscarves and expected to see his wishes carried out immediately." He did the same for schools, introducing an Islamist uniform that included headscarves. By 2009 and 2010, the "headscarf rule" started to spread throughout the rest of society. Men and women viewed the imposition of the headscarf policy as deeply offensive and humiliating; however, they were coerced to comply out of fear for themselves and their families (Human Rights Watch).

Natalya Estemirova (1958-2009), a human rights activist, expressed her opposition to the compulsory Islamic dress code. In a 2008 interview, she insisted that forcing Chechen women to wear headscarves was "wrong, unlawful, and constituted a blatant violation of the right to privacy." Kadyrov "personally dismissed Estemirova from the Grozny City Human Rights Council, raising his voice to her, making derisive remarks to try to shame her for not adhering to modesty laws, and threatening her with repercussions for her unyielding criticism."

On July 15, 2009, Natalya Estemirova was abducted and executed by an Islamist death squad. Since then, women who do not wear *hijab* have been shamed, threatened, and assaulted by Islamists, some even suffering from paintball attacks committed by former Chechen fighters. The Islamist vigilantes, all Kadyrov enforcers, left behind leaflets warning women that if they failed to wear a headscarf, they would resort "to more persuasive measures." Kadyrov stated that the men involved in such actions deserved to receive awards and that the women who were targeted deserved to "disappear from the face of the earth." Not surprisingly, there was a direct correlation between the virtue campaign and the rise in so-called "honor killings" (Human Rights Watch).

In 2005, Seyran Ateş (b. 1963), a German-Turkish attorney, feminist, and author, was named "woman of the year" for her work in "defense of Muslim women in immigrant communities" (Bridge). In her 2017 book, *The Multicultural Mistake: How We Can Live Together Better in Germany*, she argued that Muslim women are pressured into wearing the *hijab* by their religious communities (Bridge). In a 2009 interview, she asserted that "this headscarf is nothing but an expression of oppression and inhibition, and the fact that men would prefer to hide women" (Bridge). In 2018, she warned that "just by wearing the headscarf," a woman "signals the strict interpretation of Islam, that the woman must be hidden from the eyes of men" (Bridge). In a 2021 article, she is said that "[The headscarf] is not for God, it is for men" (Arafat).

Seyran Ateş founded the Ibn Ruschd-Goethe Mosque in 2017, where she leads prayers as the first female Imam in Germany. The mosque welcomes all women, with or without *hijab*, but refuses to admit women who wear the *burqa* or the *niqab* (Bridge). Obviously, this signals that such women are committed to the most extreme and misogynistic interpretation of Islam. Admitting them would be like accepting men in Ku Klux Klan robes into an African American church. They may all be Christians; however, they do not share the same interpretation of the faith. Why, one wonders, would a Klansman want to enter a black church? Likewise, why would a radical Islamist wish to enter the premises of a liberal, women-led, mosque, particularly when the women who operate and attend it receive regular death threats. For Ateş, the full veil has nothing to do Islam. It is the symbol of a political ideology (Dege).

Seyran Ateş is also opposed to mandatory *hijab*, as well as the *hijab* worn by teachers and public servants, as it is contrary to secular values, contributes to the creation of parallel societies, and prevents proper socio-cultural integration (Bridge). In 2019, she was awarded the prestigious Urania Medal for her inclusive vision. She is required to live under constant police protection in Germany (Dege). Even the Turkish government has accused Ateş and her mosque of being a "terrorist organization."

In a 2006 interview with Oprah Winfrey, Queen Rania of Jordan was asked why some women wore the veil while others did not. She responded that "it's a personal choice… as long as a woman does it because she wants to and she's not coerced into it then that is her right" (Queen Rania). As a result, many Muslim women accused her of being a *kafirah* or infidel for supposedly flouting a divine command. Little did they know that no such order was to be found in the Qur'an. Is it not a mortal sin and crime in Islam to slander and defame women and to issue death threats?

When asked about the *hijab* during an interview with *Time Magazine* in 2007, Queen Rania of Jordan had this to say:

> For many, the *hijab* represents modesty, piety, and devotion to God, and I truly respect that. Unfortunately, too many people in the Western world mistakenly perceive it as an expression of powerlessness and oppression. And increasingly it is being turned into a political tool. Modernity is not about dress codes. Religion and modernity are not necessarily mutually exclusive. In Jordan, a woman cannot be forced to wear a veil against her will. (Time)

When Fareed Zakaria (b. 1964) asked her why more women were wearing *hijab* now than thirty or forty years ago, Queen Rania of Jordan provided an intelligent assessment of the factors at play:

> All over the world a lot of societies are feeling challenged by globalization. They are feeling that … Western values are being imposed upon them. They fear that … they are losing their sense of identity so there is a whole movement to feel indigenous now… Sometimes… going back to your traditions gives you that sense of maintaining your identity. What we're trying to do in Jordan is to demonstrate that you can be an Arab, you can be a Muslim… you can

> be a world player. You can be progressive. You can have political, economic, and social reform but these things are not mutually exclusive so setting that model of moderation is extremely important..
>
> I am not trying to paint a rosy picture. There are still a lot of challenges for women in the Arab world, not least of which is literacy rates, unemployment rates, cultural constraints that limit their civil, their personal liberties, so we still have a long way to go but there is progress being made and mindsets are slowly… changing. You will always have though elements of society who have political agendas and who will justify those political agendas through Islam and sometimes that will reflect on how they feel women should behave and should dress. But again… it's all about education, it's about reform and hopefully, as long as we keep the balance and it doesn't tip to one side then we can hopefully … help those societies. (Queen Rania)

During an interview conducted in 2008, Muhammad Mujtahid-Shabistari (b. 1936), the professor, philosopher, theologian, and specialist in hermeneutics, admitted,

> There is no mention of wearing of veils in the Qur'an. There is an expression in the Qur'an that says that one should keep a dignified appearance. That refers to a way of life for a particular society and the Prophet's precepts were intended to be appropriate for that society at that time. But that does not mean that these precepts with regard to ritual or other points mentioned belong to the core of the faith. (Ridgeon 47-48)

He also pointed out that the Prophet never criticized unveiled women (Ridgeon 213). In fact, he argued that such "distortion" took place during 'Abbasid times (Ridgeon 213).

In 2010, Hassen Chalgoumy (b. 1972), a French Imam of Tunisian birth, who leads the Drancy mosque, near Paris, expressed support for banning the *burqa*. Since then, he is forced to wear a bullet-proof vest and requires the protection of two bodyguards, even when he leads congregational prayers at the mosque, which is itself surrounded by high security fences. As one can imagine, he longs for the enlightened, Sufi-inspired, Islam that he experienced as a child in Tunisia.

In an interview with the BBC, conducted in 2010, Queen Rania of Jordan stated, "I am a staunch supporter of every woman's right to wear the *hijab*, just as I am a staunch supporter of every woman's right not to wear it" (Queen Rania).

In 2011, Raj Bhala (b. 1962), an Indian American jurist and distinguished professor who focuses on Islamic law, asked a crucial question:

> To what does the phrase "privates parts" refer? The common understanding in the non-Muslim world is that it means, for men, the

> genitalia, and buttocks. For women, it means genitalia, buttocks, and breasts. If this interpretation were the one held in the Muslim world… it would imply neither men nor women should appear in public, in front of … non-close family relatives with these parts of their bodies exposed. It would be forbidden… for a Muslim man or woman to go nude to a nude beach, or topless at a topless beach -- though being in such a beach, in suitable bathing clothes, would be a different matter. Conversely, hands and feet, arms and legs, head and neck, face, and portions of the mid-section and back, are not normally understood to be "private parts" -- at least not throughout the non-Muslim world.

After providing an informed overview of the history of the veil in a 2014 article, Hannibal Genseric, an engineer, journalist, and Amazigh activist, concluded that "the veil is neither Arabic nor Islamic."

In a study published in 2011, Mohammad Hashim Kamali (1944), a Muslim jurist, academic, and professor, concluded that "there is no mandate on veiling (*hijab*) and face cover (*niqab*) in the Qur'an and *Sunnah*" (49).

Zahra Eshraghi (b. 1964), the granddaughter of Ruhollah Khomeini, opposes Iran's mandatory *hijab* laws. She insists that the *chador* was forced upon women and that a traditional garment was turned into a revolutionary symbol. "People have lost respect for it," she stressed, "I only wear it because of my family status" (Ighani).

Naeimeh Eshraghi (b. 1965), the granddaughter of Ruhollah Khomeini, insists that her grandfather opposed the imposition of the *hijab* by force. She claims that he wrote a manifesto in which he only supported the use of gentle enforcement methods and prohibited offending women in the process. While she admits that she is not a jurist, she cites legal authorities who state that it is forbidden to mandate *hijab* since there is no "legal limit defined for *hijab*" in Islamic law (Habibi).

Naeimeh Eshraghi's daughter, who bears the same name, has made her position on the *hijab* perfectly clear by baring her legs, thighs, and arms in mini dresses while studying in Canada, the "infidel country" denounced by her great grandfather, Khomeini. Likewise, the granddaughters of other Iranian ayatollahs are notorious party girls who are famous for wearing micro miniskirts, high heels, and denim booty shorts. They rebel against the restrictions of the regime via their clothing. Just like the *chador* and the *hijab* became symbols of rebellion against the rule of the Shah, Western club wear has become an act of revolt against Islamic fundamentalism and political Shiism.

"By reducing Muslim women to their bodies, and pretending that modesty is their primary duty," argued Moin Qazi in 2017, "we strip them of their personhood."

Azam Taleghani (d. 2019), a progressive Islamist, and daughter of Mahmoud Taleghani, was strongly opposed to mandatory *hijab*.

Like Azam Taleghani, Zahra Rahnavard (b. 1945), the former Chancellor of al-Zahra University, was a staunch supporter of the *hijab*, even authoring a book on the topic. However, like many former hardliners, she had a change of heart and opposes mandatory *hijab*. She believes that women should have the right to wear or not to wear the *hijab* based on their level of religiosity. A leader of Iran's 2009 Green Movement, and a former advisor to President Khatami, she has been under house arrest since 2011. In response to repression on the part of the state apparatus, she stated defiantly: "Either kill me as well or give in to the demands of the Iranian people."

In a 2014 interview, Asma Lamrabet, a Moroccan medical doctor and intellectual, asserted that "*khimar* is not important… The debate over *hijab* and *khimar* is outdated… it is not an obligation at all" (Mir-Hosseini 2022: 135). She described the *hijab* as absurd and noted that "God is not waiting for me to wear *khimar*" (Mir-Hosseini 2022: 135). In a 2014 interview, Ziba Mira-Hosseini, an Iranian anthropologist, asked the crucial question: "Why should God care about us covering our hair?" (2022: 135). In a conference in the same year, she lambasted the '*ulama*' in the following terms:

> I recognize your work but you do not want to recognize mine. I will tell you why: because I know the reality of my context, but you are blind to it; you may know the text, but you do not know the context. You are not real ulema as the ulema were in the past; those ulema who knew the text and the context and delt with both. You may know all the verses of the Qur'an; but you do not want to recognize that our society has changed, evolved. (Mir-Hosseini 2022: 14)

In 2014, Masih Alinejad launched *My Stealthy Freedom*, a Facebook page which encourages Iranian women to defy *hijab* laws by posting photographs of themselves with their hair uncovered. Alinejad is not opposed to *hijab*, *per se*. She simply believes that women should not be arrested, fined, and imprisoned for not doing so. She was eventually forced into exile and now lives in the United States. Despite having reasonable and rational views, the Iranian regime views her a serious threat that must be eliminated by any and all means. Apparently, mandatory *hijab* is the hill upon which the "Islamic" Republic of Iran has chosen to die.

In 2014, President Hasan Rouhani of Iran released a survey, conducted by a government research group, that found that 49.8% of Iranians viewed *hijab* as a personal matter in which the government should have no say (Ridgeon 13). "You can't send people to heaven by the whip," he stated in the same year, apparently alluding to the *bad-hijab* vigilante squads (Ridgeon 214). In his memoirs, he admitted that he was involved in making *hijab* mandatory in Iran; however, his views on the subject seem to have mellowed over the years (Ridgeon 214).

In 2015, Muhammad Riza Za'iri asserted that "I strongly believe the policy of mandatory *hijab* has been totally wrong" (Ridgeon 14). Since then, however, he seems to have bowed to the authority of Khamenei (Ridgeon 14).

In 2016, Hassan Khomeini (b. 1972), the grandson of Ruhollah Khomeini, asserted that there was more to Islam than *hijab* (Karami).

In 2016, Saliha Marie Fetteh (b. 1962) and Sherin Khankan opened the first women's mosque in Denmark (b. 1974). "When people wonder why I am not wearing *hijab*, I tell them I do," explains Khankan, "I just have a different interpretation of the meaning of *hijab*. To me, the *hijab* is about sincerity. It is about being close to Allah" (Shibeeb). "To me," she says, "the *hijab* is a metaphor for sincerity" (Turner). Hence, she stresses "the inner *hijab*, which is your sincerity and kindness" (Turner). She believes that women should have the freedom to dress as they please. In her words, "I'm fighting for any woman's right to wear the *hijab* and not to wear the *hijab*" (Buys). Unlike other Islamic feminists, Khankan even backs the *burqa*. In her words, "If a woman is isolated and forced to wear a *burqa* or the *niqab*, by criminalizing it, you will isolate her even more, because she might not be able to go out… It is important to fight for any women's right to wear the *hijab* or not, to wear the *niqab* or not -- if it is her own choice and her own free will" (Reuters).

These comments, however, are oxymoronic. She admits that women who wear the *burqa* or the *niqab* are isolated and forced into wearing it. She recognizes that they are convinced or coerced into doing so by paleoconservative Muslims. However, she opposes its prohibition on grounds that it further isolates isolated women. She then stresses that women should be free to wear the *niqab* out of their own free will. However, she previously admitted they did not do so freely. According to this logic, we should not criminalize domestic abuse because battered women are isolated and criminalizing it would further isolate them. God forbid they would go outside with a black eye. If there is a problem, one must face it and address it. What is more, one does not defend the freedom of dress of women who do not believe that women should have freedom of dress.

In 2016, Maya Ksouri, the Tunisian attorney, author, and activist, asserted that "the veil represents regression and the enslavement of women."

In 2016, the otherwise hardline Naser Makarem-Shirazi allowed women in the West to discard the *hijab* due to the "onslaught" of Islamophobic sentiment. In his words, "If committed Muslim females are deprived of higher education… pious believers will be authorized under such special circumstances to unveil, but in other cases they are to abide by and maintain the *hijab*" (Ridgeon 201). In so doing, he acknowledged that the *hijab* was not the end all and be all and that education was more important. One could also argue that employment overrides the importance of the *hijab*. Such a ruling provides women who live and study outside the Muslim world a degree of flexibility.

Mohsen Kadivar, however, was quick to point out the edict's logical flaws. He noted that "the respected *marja* has said that covering a woman's hair, head, and neck, is not as important as covering the rest of the body, because it is possible to ignore [the command] in necessary circumstances" (Ridgeon 231-232).

Although a woman's face is more beautiful than her hair, Kadivar found it strange that it is not considered part of her *zinah* or beauty that must be concealed (Ridgeon 252). The requirement for women to cover their private parts, he notes, derives from the Qur'an, a primary source, whereas "covering a woman's head hair is based on local culture, regional conditions and time and place more than legal requirements" (232).

In 2016, Yousef Saanei, a Twelver Shiite source of emulation, ruled that "if a commonly acceptable *hijab* causes such hardship and problems for Muslim women, they may wear coverings such as wigs so they can get rid of the problems and, at the same time, they will be observing the laws of *shari'ah.* They may have some difficulties wearing wigs, but they should bear them for God's satisfaction and for their salvation and beatitude" (111). Sa'id al-Hakim (d. 2021) had passed a similar edict a few years earlier, allowing Muslim women to wear wigs while remaining technically veiled (369). Mind you, this was a man who prohibited colored eye contacts or bright *hijabs* if they turned men on. However, he found human cloning to be perfectly legal and ethical. Rather than require Muslim women in the West to wear wigs, like Orthodox Jewish women, why not opt for a simpler solution? Let them show their hair freely.

Asked about her decision not to wear *hijab* in 2017, Queen Rania of Jordan responded,

> I really do think that religion is a very personal thing. I feel that it's wrong to try to deal with our differences by trying to impose homogeneity. Many women in my country wear the *hijab*, and you'll also find many women dressed like me. It just baffles me sometimes that there's a huge debate about an issue that should really be a non-issue. (Sunday Times).

"Everywhere she goes," notes the *Los Angeles Times*, "she talks about her decision not to wear the *hijab*" (Hall). As she often responds, "It's more important to judge a woman by what's in her head, not on her head." When pressed why she chooses not to wear it, she answers, "for the same reason that any woman decides how she wants to wear her hair or how she wants to dress. It's a personal choice. The funny thing is I get asked more about not wearing the veil when I'm abroad than when I'm in Jordan" (Hall).

In 2017, Masih Alinejad launched White Wednesdays to protest Iran's mandatory *hijab* policy. It encourages women to wear white and to cast off their *hijabs* in public as an act of protest.

Faezeh Hashemi Rafsanjani (b. 1963), the daughter of former president, 'Ali Akbar Hashemi Rafsanjani, believes that imposing *hijab* leads to opposing Islam. She was imprisoned on two occasions for supporting the 2009 Green Movement. She was also arrested in 2022 for supporting the anti-*hijab* protests. A mob of Islamist hardliners called her a whore and demanded that she be put to death.

In a 2018 television interview, Taj Hargey, a specialist in Islamic history, Muslim theology, and Qur'anic hermeneutics, noted: "Nowhere in the Qur'an does it actually say that women should cover their face, let alone their hair."

In 2018, Mohsen Kadivar, an exiled Iranian *mujtahid*, declared that "the mandatory veil was born with the Islamic Republic and it will die with the Islamic Republic" (Ridgeon 233).

In 2018, Mufti Abu Layth, a British-Pakistani Muslim cleric, argued that *hijab* was not mandatory as the head of a woman was not part of her *'awrah.*

In 2018, Abdullah bin Bayyah and Hamza Yusuf argued that Muslim women could discard the headscarf and perhaps wear hats to avoid harm or harassment.

In 2018, Mohammad Taqi Fazel Meybodi (b. 1953), an Iranian "ayatollah," asserted that "forced *hijab* by the way of threats, fear, and imprisonment is not pragmatic at all. This approach is not backed by strong logic and will ultimately have [bad] consequences for the society."

In 2019, Adnan Ibrahim, a Palestinian Islamic scholar with a PhD in Arabic Studies from the University of Vienna, argued that the *hijab* was not a religious obligation.

In 2019, Khalid Zaheer, an Islamic scholar with a PhD from the University of Wales, explained that the *hijab* was recommended at most, but not obligatory based on Qur'anic evidence.

Hassan Farhan al-Maliki (b. 1970), a Saudi scholar of Islam, does not believe that the *hijab* is obligatory. Imprisoned since 2017, prosecutors sought the death penalty against him in 2019 on grounds of heresy and apostasy.

In 2019, over half a dozen Belgian scholars, intellectuals, professionals, and activists of Muslim culture and background issued a position paper titled "The *Hijab* is a Sexist, Deadly, Alienating Prison." In their words:

> **It is no coincidence that the veil spreads at the same rate as Islamism. To remain silent on the subject of the veil or to surrender is not a matter of defending Muslims. It is to refuse to treat others as equals.** In recent years, each season is the occasion of a new episode in the saga of the veil... A poster from the Walloon Youth Parliament featured the image of a veiled young girl, while Décathlon offered a jogging *hijab* for sale.... As summer approaches, it is the *burkini* that will resurface. Each season, the issue of the veil resurfaces: the veil at school, the veil at work, the veil at the beach, and the veil in politics. It is now commonplace to see veiled women and girls in the

street, advertisements, or magazines, when it is not on electoral lists or within institutions themselves… White supremacists and assassins sow death in New Zealand and …the Prime Minister of New Zealand wears the veil… As soon as someone dares to question its deep meaning, that person is ordered to remain silent, sometimes with extreme violence. The words "racist!" and "Islamophobe!" are cast and it is no longer possible to speak to each other. Under cover of tolerance, some impose a real *omerta*.… It is no coincidence that the veil spreads at the same rate as Islamism.

What is the Meaning of *Hijab*?

The *hijab* is a cloth that covers the hair, neck, and ears. It treats the entire female body as impure and cannot be removed [in public], no matter the occasion. The *hijab* helps protect men who otherwise would be unable to control themselves. Let us call a spade a spade: according to this logic, women are temptresses, sluts, men are weak and libidinous. The veiling of little girls, sometimes babies, accustoms them to being ashamed of their bodies and prepares them to maintain their status as sexual objects. The *hijab* is a sexist, deadly, alienating prison, and its development is directly linked to the Islamization of societies. Before the Islamist wave, Muslim women, for the most part, did not wear the veil. Let us remember the famous video of the Egyptian Head of State Nasser who, in 1953, aroused the hilarity of the assembly by narrating his response to the Muslim Brotherhood who wanted him to impose the veil on women: "I answered him that it was a throwback to the days when religion ruled, and women were only let out after dark." The veil imposed itself alongside Islamism, first in Iran, then in Algeria, Tunisia... Have you wondered why the first act of Islamists is to impose the veil, while that of women liberated from Daesh, from sexual slavery, is to burn *hijabs*?

Resisters at the Risk of their Lives

Women *and* men resist and place their lives at risk. They are whipped, locked up, murdered for refusing the veiling of women! Men, also, because the veil is not just a matter related to women: it is a political issue… Lawyer Nasrin Sotoudeh, who defends Iranian women who dared to remove their veils, was sentenced to lashes and imprisonment for conspiracy and propaganda against the system. Her original sentence was increased for indecency because she appeared bareheaded at her trial. Why would a woman be willing to be whipped and locked up, if this [struggle] was only about hair? Why did Décathlon call its running accessory "hijab" and not a "running balaclava?" Let us be realistic, it is a product intended for countries where the veil is not imposed. In Islamist countries, women do not need it since they are not allowed to run, swim, or ride a bike. The introduction of the *hijab* in our societies is a political act of political Islam. To remain silent, or give in on the question of the veil is not to defend Muslims. It is to not treat others as equals. Around the world, Muslims are the first victims of Islamists!

Listen to the Voices

From Morocco to Algeria, via Canada, Iran, France, Belgium, or Sudan, many voices are raised to denounce the political extremism of which the *hijab* is the symbol. It is time to hear them! We, women and men of Muslim culture or background, having lived or undergone the Islamization of our societies, are concerned to see the development of an identity argument as rampant Islamism develops in parallel, like what we have seen and experienced in our countries of origin. We ask that our voices and our experiences on the issue of the veil and what it prefigures as a political project be heard, and recognized. We ask everyone -- journalists, politicians, citizens, whatever your origins or commitments -- to join in this debate. It belongs to you, as much as to us, by ideal and convictions, but also because contradiction is what extremists of all persuasions fear the most.

Signatories: Bahareh Dibadj; Fadila Maaroufi; Djemila Benhabib; Daoud Azam Daimoussi; Mouna Messaoudi; Latifa Drissi; Amir Dibadj; Yeter Celili; Waleed Al-Husseini; Chemsi Cheref-khan; Hamid Zanaz; Salwa Tazi; Hamid Benichou; Fathi Nouhad; Jamila Si M'Hammed; Mahyne Nasseri Manzar Banal; Youcef Hadbi; Mohammed Guerroumi; Sémira Tlili; Omar Gousmi; Fatiha Boudjahlat; Mohammed Louizi; Khaled Slougui; Kamel Bencheikh; Abdel Serghini; Sam Touzani. (La Libre)

In 2019, sick of being patronized by the arrogant, self-appointed guardians of Islam, who harassed, intimidated, and derided her for being a woman, Asma Lamrabet finally abandoned the *hijab* that she had worn in the past in solidarity with Muslim women. She explained her decision as follows:

> I arrived at a point where I ... felt like a hypocrite with myself ... and the creator... One day, I just said, "it's over, I can't handle this anymore"... In a certain way... it was like agreeing to play the game of the Islamists... [The Islamists] have ... instrumentalized the veil for political purposes. I felt like I was manipulated by political Islam and their slogans; they want us to be visible. For them this visibility is important, to have women with the veil, it comforts them and confirms ... they are politically ... strong. One day last year [2019]... I went to my car without my scarf; and I felt so free, so relieved... it had been like a responsibility, a lie, something on my shoulder. I said, "Oh my God, I am now Asma, I am what I am." Spiritually, I was free... I have

> the right to choose; in the past I chose *khimar* and now I choose not to wear it. (Mir-Hosseini 2022: 147-148)

As a result of their actions against her and her family, Masih Alinejad sued the Iranian government for harassment in 2019. In 2021, four Iranian intelligence officials were charged with plotting to kidnap her and take her by speedboat to Venezuela. In 2022, the Federal Bureau of Investigations thwarted an assassination attempt against her. Alinejad quoted an FBI agent as saying, "This time their objective was to kill you."

In 2022, Twelver Shiite scholar, Mohamad Ali Ayazi, decreed that forcing women to wear *hijab* has no basis in Islamic law and that it was opposed by scholars like Morteza Motahhari, Mohammed Beheshti, and Mahmoud Taleghani, some of the founders of the Islamic Republic of Iran (Ridgeon 13, 216). Although he believes the *hijab* is mandatory, Ayazi noted the following on his website: "My belief is that the *hijab*, like prayer, fasting, [and paying religious] taxes, is a personal legal matter. The *hijab* is like the use of people's property; it is not a social issue that entails punishments… The Islamic government can give teachings about the *hijab* and encourage people to follow it, but there has never been any command for retributive clashes" (Ridgeon 13-14, note 40).

In 2022, Mohammad Taqi Fazel Meybodi, the Iranian theologian and jurists, mocked the claims of the regime that "bad *hijab*" was the cause for the woes of the country. "If not observing the *hijab* is the cause of high prices," he responded, then the world must be starving." "Think a little," he urged officials (Stone).

In the twenty-first century, several scholars, like Edip Yüksel, who place the Qur'an first and foremost, have warned that it is disingenuous to claim that it requires women to wear the *hijab*. For Muhammad Sadiq, accepting religious orders from anyone but God is idolatry.

On 16 September 2022, Mahsa Amini died in a hospital in Tehran after being arrested by Iran's "morality" police. According to eyewitnesses, she was brutally beaten, a claim supported by leaked medical scans. She appears to have died of cerebral hemorrhage or stroke due to head injuries inflicted upon her. She was only one of many victims of the "*Hijab*-Military-Industrial-Complex."

In a Facebook post, dated September 19, 2022, Masih Alinejad described the mandatory *hijab* as the Berlin Wall of the Iranian regime. "If we tear this wall down," she claimed, "the Islamic republic won't exist." When it comes to the "Islamic" Republic, the mandatory *hijab* is a Berlin Wall of their own making. Presenting the matter in such terms, and linking it to regime change, is perilous. If abolishing obligatory *hijab* is an existential threat to the regime, it will respond with even greater brutality during its death throes. Countering Islamism with secularism is counterproductive. Delegitimizing compulsory *hijab* from an Islamic perspective is more propitious. Rejecting *hijab* is not a rejection of Islam. It is a rejection of the Islam of Darkness and an affirmation of the Islam of Enlightenment.

Ahmed Subhy Mansour (b. 1949), an Egyptian jurist, has ruled that the veil, *hijab*, *niqab*, and *burqa* have nothing to do with Islam, viewing them as a prohibited innovation and a major sin. He holds that anyone who holds the *hijab* to be commanded by God is a polytheist, infidel, and an unbeliever.

Edip Yüksel (b. 1957), the Qur'an translator and commentator, has also adopted the same staunch stance, denouncing those who attribute lies to God. In his view, righteous women should dress modestly and not provocatively; however, it was entirely up to women to decide how they dressed, how much they covered, and how much they uncovered, including whether or not they covered their breasts. The bare minimum they have to cover is their external genitals. While exposing the pudendum would represent a major sin, exposing other parts was a minor sin. As far as he is concerned, even exposing their vaginas would be a lesser sin than fabricating dress codes in the name of God.

Numerous scholars, including Youssef Seddik, Hichem Djaït, Hamadi Redissi, Raja Ben Slama, Olfa Youssef, and Abdelwahab Meddeb affirm that the *hijab* is not a religious prescription but rather an inherited patriarchal custom (Bestandji 2021: 112).

According to Latifa Lakhdar, the Tunisian historian, professor of Islamic Thought, and former Minister of Culture, "the *hijab* is not a simple practice; it is the visible symbol of a vision of the world based on the rupture of the universal into two parts, men, and women." For her, "the *hijab* is the symbol of the theological confinement of women" (Bestandji 2021: 113)

For Razika Adnani, the Franco-Algerian philosopher and Islamologist, "[The *hijab*] cannot be justified morally, socially, historically, or even religiously" (Bestandji 2021: 347).

Naëm Bestandji, a French author and activist, who represents the views of many feminist, universalist, and secular Muslims, views the *hijab* as a "sexist heresy" and a "sexist innovation" devoid of any Qur'anic foundation whatsoever (Bestandji 2021: 82, 102). Not only is the *hijab* a fetish, but it is also idolatrous, masochistic, and blasphemous (Bestandji 2021: 89). Since it is not found in the Qur'an, and is apocryphal and unorthodox, adopting this theological aberration is an act of opposition against it (Bestandji 2021: 89, 104).

As Bestandji explains, the Qur'an intended to protect women from being offended by asking them to cover their cleavage (33:59) (2016). Its goal was to help humanity to advance (2016). By deforming the meaning of the Qur'anic verses in question, in a desire to return to a so-called "authentic Islam," many Muslims do the opposite of what God and the Prophet desired (2016). "By trying to bring Islam back to the Middle Ages," explains Bestandji, "by alienating and veiling women, the partisans of veiling are committing a 'sin'" (2016). For him, "the veil, with all the values it conveys, is an insult to God and his Prophet" (2016). Since they pressure, intimidate, and coerce women into wearing *hijab*, and insult and threaten women who do not wear it, Bestandji believes that the radicals and extremists are the hypocrites condemned in the Qur'an, those in whose heart is a disease, who slander women, who are cursed by God, and who are threatened with arrest and execution: "If the hypocrites do not desist, and likewise those in whose heart is a disease, as well as those who spread false rumors in the city, we shall surely spur thee against them; then they will not be their neighbors therein, save for a short while. Accursed! They will be seized wheresoever they are found and utterly slain. (33:60)

"The veil," in the view of Bestandji, "is the yoke of women" (2021: 264). It is a personal prison (2021: 244). Since Islam resides in the heart and not on the head, to cast off the veil is a rejection of the Islam of appearance in favor of the Islam of being (2016). To reject the *hijab* is to reject Salafism, Islamism, extremism, and fanaticism (2016). The courageous women who cast off their veils reject voluntary servitude (2016). They refuse to allow radical Muslim men to control their lives and their bodies (2016). They understand that by removing their *hijab* they do not become two-dollar hookers, to be passed around from penis to penis, as Hani Ramadan poetically described unveiled women (2016). On the contrary, they become free women and more mature Muslims (2016). Nothing prevents them from being fully secular and fully Muslim (2016). After all, it is up to the secular state, and not Islam, to protect women (2016). Islamic organizations are concerned with defending the rights of women to veil themselves: not the rights of Muslim women to unveil themselves and to free themselves from the shackles placed upon them by extremists and terrorists.

In her 2022 study, *No Truth without Beauty: God, the Qur'an, and Women's Rights*, Leena El-Ali asserted that:

> The only three verses in the Qur'an that say something specific about women and clothing (24:31, 24:60, 33:59) simply tell us that women's groin area and, ideally, breasts also must be covered, and indicate a way for Muslim women at the time to identify themselves upfront when alone in the wild to ward off hypocritical sexual assailants. (213)

In fact, "apart from covering our private parts (ideally including a woman's breasts), and urging us to wear beautiful outfits in general, the Qur'an is neutral on clothing for women and men alike" (221).

On March 15, 2022, the High Court of Karnataka in India ruled that wearing the *hijab* was not an essential religious practice of the Islamic faith. As such, it was not protected by the Constitution of India's article on religious freedom. Schools were within their right to institute dress codes as these did not violate freedom of speech or expression. According to the ruling, restricting *hijab* in educational institutions is both reasonable and constitutionally permissible in the secular nation of India.

In 2022, Kahina Bahloul (b. 1979), France's first female Imam, insisted that "We must stop making the veil a symbol of Islam."

In 2022, Mimunt Hamido Yahia published her poignant book, *No nos taparán* [*They Will Not Cover Us Up*], which launched a movement of Muslim women, and women from Muslim cultures, against the veil. Their campaign revolves around four points: hair, mouths, minds, and cunts:

> They will not cover our hair... : We do not wear a veil, nor will we let them tell us that every Muslim woman must wear it by divine commandment. Our mothers did not wear it. They will not cover our mouths... We will not allow them to silence us or … call us Islamophobes for criticizing those who limit our freedom. They will not cover our... minds: We will not allow anyone to tell us what our religion should be and what we can and cannot discuss. They won't cover our... cunts. We will not give up our sexuality, our bodies, and our freedom to share it with who we want and how we want. (175-176)

In 2022, Reza Hosseini Nasab, an Iranian "grand ayatollah" based in the Greater Toronto Area in Canada, ruled that "it is not permissible to force women to cover their hair" and that "it is necessary to respect the gender equality of men and women in law and rights." When asked whether covering a Muslim woman's hair was obligatory in Islam, he issued the following edict:

> Covering the body of a Muslim woman is obligatory in Islamic law. However, the ruling on covering the hair of a Muslim woman based on the Qur'anic verses and Islamic narrations … was one of the Islamic governmental rulings to differentiate the free Muslim woman from the non-free maid in a certain period of time when the system of slavery was still in place.

In 2022, Khalil Andani, an Assistant Professor of Religion at Augustana College, who holds a doctorate in Islamic Studies from Harvard University, recognized that, "There's no Muslim consensus on *hijab* being mandatory."

In 2023, Paola García, the jurist and scholar of Islam, reiterated her position on the *hijab*:

> If we accept that Islam is universal across time and space, how can we expect the vast diversity of human cultures to adopt a dress code rooted within the context and realities of seventh century Arabia? It seems absurd to me to claim that a Muslim woman living in the twenty-first century in let's say the Dominican Republic should wear the same clothing as a woman who lived in seventh century Arabia, especially if we simultaneously claim that Islam is universal. I believe this fixation with the *hijab* reduces Islam to its most superficial layer, mutes the uniqueness of each culture, and, most problematically, imposes unwarranted burdens on women that contradict the Qur'anic principle that Allah intends for us ease…

In 2023, the US Department of Justice charged Rafat Amirov, Khalid Mehdiyev, and Polad Omarov with conspiring to assassinate Masih Alinejad on behalf of the Iranian regime.

In 2023, the Iranian regime started to install closed circuit cameras and facial recognition software to identify women who violate *hijab* laws. They would receive text warnings and be subjected to fines, arrest, imprisonment, and potential corporal punishment.

In 2023, Muhammad Javad Alavi Borujerdi, a Twelver Shiite jurist bemoaned the Iranian regime's obsession with the veil and the anti-clerical sentiment that dominates the nation,

> The Imam of the mosque used to be the community's pillar! People would die for him! Even girls who did not wear a full *hijab* would come to the Imam and ask their religious questions. We are now only insisting that this girl fix her *hijab*, while her original beliefs are gone! Belief is one story; action is another. Belief precedes action, but belief has been damaged. We have a problem in passing this heritage to the next generation. (Article Eighteen)

In 2023, the Iranian Islamist regime decreed that opposition to obligatory *hijab* was a crime and that anyone who encouraged women to remove their veils would be prosecuted in criminal court, without the right to appeal. Pro-Iranian Islamist clerics abroad describe the women protesting against mandatory *hijab* as "soldiers of Satan." Iranian women asked for little: no more than the right to feel the wind and sun in their hair. If this is deprived of them, and they are repressed, and have their skulls cracked for peacefully protesting, they will not be satisfied with this simple concession. Some will burn their bras and toss off their panties.

Spanish women lived under Catholic fundamentalism and fascism from 1936 to 1975. As the bishop of Malaga decreed in 1943,

> 1. Dresses must not be so tight that they provocatively show off the shape of the body.
> 2. Dresses must not be so short that they do not cover the best part of the legs; it is not acceptable for them to stop at the knee.
> 3. A low neckline goes against modesty and there are some that are so daring that they could be gravely sinful because of the dishonest intention they reveal or the scandal they provoke.
> 4. It is against modesty not to cover the arm at least to the elbow. Those who always wear long sleeves which go below the elbow and cover the whole arm are very worthy of praise.
> 5. It is against modesty not to wear stockings.
> 6. It is also against modesty to wear transparent dresses, or dresses with lace, in places that should be covered.
> 7. Girls' skirts must go to the knee and those twelve years and older must

wear stockings.

8. Boys must not show their bare thighs.

9. For going to church one must wear long sleeves that cover the arm and forearm, with stockings and dresses that cover most of the legs, without low necklines or transparent fabric or lace.

10. Girls' teachers -- especially the religious ones -- should know that the Sacred Congregation of the Council … orders that they do not accept in their schools and convents those who wear less honest dresses and that, even when those already admitted, if they do not make amends, expel them. …

11. It is a sin against Christian modesty and honesty for men and women to swim together; to mingle together -- in bathing suits -- during games or pastimes, or to wear indecent and revealing bathing suits, hiding from view the most elemental rules of modesty.

NOTE: To be widely distributed among women, especially young women. (Otero-González)

This dress code was posted on church doorways. It was published in the press. Unrelated men and women could not even shake hands unless they wore gloves. In fascist Spain, women's dress was determined by the Church and Franco. They determined what it meant "to be a woman." "In the end," notes Uxía Otero-González, "they transformed the social fabric and led to the collapse of the predominance of Catholic values and, by extension, Francoism." After the death of Franco, and the fall of fascism, Spanish women revolted against the Roman Catholic Church, fervently embracing secularism and liberalism. They went from the most ultra-conservative women to the most sexually liberated overnight.

The secular revolution that took place in Spain is set to happen in Iran and elsewhere. Iranians, including believing, pious, and devout Muslims, overwhelmingly loathe the radical Islamist mullahs and those who support them. Throughout the Muslim world, the Islamists are widely despised by secularists. Just like the fall of Franco brought down the Church, so will the fall of the Supreme Oppressor, the Seminary, and the Mosque bring about collapse of socio-political and ideological Islamism. As much as Islamist leaders may claim that there is a war against Muslim women, the fact of the matter is that "Islam" is at war with women.

Islamists, along with their apologists and accomplices, may call for choice; however, how many are willing to give Muslim women the choice not to wear *hijab*, the choice to express themselves freely, the choice to criticize Islam, and the choice to give their bodies to whom they please? Few Muslims would be willing to go so far. Some might concede that women should not be forced to cover their hair; however, many would insist that such freedom should only exist outside of a Muslim state. Under Islamic rule, many would argue that *hijab* can or should be imposed by force of law.

While Islamists, along with their apologists and accomplices might demand the freedom to spread their violent, hateful, sexist, misogynistic, and totalitarian ideology, none of them would support the rights of Muslims and non-Muslims to criticize Islam, the Qur'an, the Prophet, or other religious personalities. Their propagandists can mock, deride, offend, and insult the tenets of Judaism and Christianity but God forbid anyone express the slightest criticism of Islam and Muslims. In this Woke New World, one cannot even study portraits of the Prophet Muhammad, paintings that were produced out of love by Muslim artists, without getting "cancelled" by intolerant quacks and fired from positions in academia. A monolithic Islamist Islam has been imposed as the sole expression of the Muslim faith. A choir of angelic voices has been silenced, leaving only a single cacophonous soloist to spoil the sound and image of Islam. Apparently, diversity, equity, and inclusion do not include the broad spectrum of opinion that is found in the Islamic tradition. Billionaire Islamo-fascists and capitalists have hijacked Islam. The New Game of the globalists is Grand Theft Islam. True Islamic values lie in ruins. No more!

As for sexual freedom, this is not something that any Islamist or religious Muslim would support when it comes to women. Men, of course, have free reign to fornicate and commit adultery without consequence. Women, however, who commit the slightest indiscretion are forced into arranged marriages, disowned, expelled from their homes, beaten, raped, turned over to brothels, or murdered for offending family honor. The women of We Will Not Be Covered Up reject the sexist double standards of so-called Islamic and Muslim societies and cultures. They are informed by the universal values of secularism, feminism, and human rights. Men and women must be held to the same standards. If Muslim men are not coerced into covering up, then neither should Muslim women. If Muslim men are not required to be chaste, then neither should Muslim women. They refuse to allow men, and the women who serve as their police dogs, to control their minds and bodies.

As can be appreciated from this comprehensive overview of all opinions on the subject, there is no conclusive Qur'anic proof that the veil, in any of its forms, is mandatory in original Islam. There are no trustworthy traditions from the Prophet and the Imams that it is so. Except for like-minded men, scholars who lived in echo-chambers of misogyny, there has never been consensus on the subject. Consequently, Mir Jalili and Mohammad's claim that "the necessity of *hijab*... is definitely unquestionable" according to the Qur'an and traditions is dishonest and disingenuous, particularly when they demonstrated that the companions of the Prophet Muhammad did not share common views on the subject and that their views were the product of independent reasoning or cultural and political influence.

The opinions surveyed in this study, which span the past millennium and a half, were emitted by scholars from all walks of life and schools of thought and jurisprudence. They include Sunnis, Sufis, 'Ibadis, Mutazilites, Qur'anists, and

Shiites of all sects. They include so-called orthodox and so-called heterodox groups as well as off-shoots of Islam like the Druze and the Baha'i. The authors cited in this study include jurists, attorneys, theologians, traditionists, exegetes, academics, and intellectuals with expertise in a wide array of fields. Some were traditionally trained in Islamic religious seminaries. Others are the product of universities. They are all perfectly competent authorities. Their views are neither new nor on the fringe.

The opinions highlighted in this work have been expressed down the centuries from the dawn of Islam to the present. They belong to more moderate, tolerant, and women-friendly currents of Islam that have always flowed below the surface of the patriarchal sea. God, the Father, must not be replaced by God, the Mother. The dictatorship of the Matriarch should not supplant the dictatorship of the Patriarch who was placed in power thanks to the *coup d'état* orchestrated by misogynistic males. On the contrary, the democracy of the divine must be restored, namely, the universal harmony of the Sacred Masculine and the Sacred Feminine. Only then will the rights of men and women be respected.

Muslim women, as free women, have the right to know the full spectrum of opinions on the subject of so-called Islamic dress and should have the freedom to select the one that convinces them the most or to come up with their own interpretation. The onus is on them, after study and soul-searching, to decide whether *hijab* is *fard*, a religious duty, or a fraud. Muslim women can choose which opinion to follow.

Either way, women have the right to wear want they want without being given guilt trips, spiritually threatened, forced, punished, assaulted, tortured, raped, imprisoned, and murdered. If Islam is freedom, and there is no coercion in Islam, then women have the right to dress as they seem fit based on a variety of factors. If men continue to deprive women of liberty, in the name of God, Islam, the Prophet, and the Imams, women from Muslim backgrounds may seek it elsewhere. Some have created mosques for women as safe spaces. Others have embraced secularism or left Islam entirely. If you cannot beat them, leave them. After all, why be a slave when you can be free? A slave to God is not a problem. A slave to men and their enforcers, male and female, most certainly is.

Rather than continue disputing the succession of the Prophet Muhammad, which is the root of all divisions between Islamic sects, Muslims should realize that they, as human beings, both men and women, are divinely appointed guardians and custodians, the successors of the Prophet Muhammad, the heirs of the prophets, and the viceregents of God on earth. It is high time they started acting like it. As the caliphs of God, we are our rulers. The divine spark or spirit resides in all of us. Consequently, we have the right to confirm or nullify previous religious laws and enact new ones. Although there were a dozen different views on the appropriate attire for Muslim women, a handful of male, medieval, imams decreed that the veil was mandatory for women. Their jurisprudence was adopted by empires and imposed with the force of law. We have the right, in fact, we have to duty, to reconsider those rulings, reject them, and replace them with others that are more closely aligned with the Qur'an and the dignity of humanity. Nothing is sacred. And nothing is written in stone. The guidance of God is withing us. As for the mandatory *hijab*. Lo and behold! It is the greatest lie ever told.

Appendix 2

Veiled Versus Unveiled

A survey of pro-*hijab* sources showcases how the partisans of the *hijab* view women who are veiled and those who are unveiled.

The *Hijabi* is... / The Non-*Hijabi* is...

A Believer / An Unbeliever
Sincere / A Hypocrite
Modest / Immodest
Chaste / Unchaste
Moral / Immoral
Sincere / Insincere
Obedient / Disobedient
Faithful / Unfaithful
A Private Woman / A Public Woman
Innocent / Corrupt
Dignified / Undignified
Protected / Unprotected
Noble / Degraded
Equal / Unequal
Serious / Idle
Kind / Unkind
Independent / Dependent
Pure / Impure
Successful / Unsuccessful
Dignified / Dishonored
Respected / Disrespected
Liberated / Subjugated
Respected / Exposed
Purified / Sullied
Confident / Insecure
Obedient / Sinful
Covered / Naked
Belonging to One Man / Belonging to all Men
Guarded Pearls / Prostitutes
Heaven-bound / Hell-bound

Appendix 3

Rulings Regarding *Hijab*

From the dawn of Islam until the twenty-first century, Muslim scholars have issued the following rulings regarding *hijab*.

1) The *hijab* is *wajib* / *fard;* namely, it is obligatory.

2) The *hijab* is *mustahab*; namely, it is recommended but not required.

3) The *hijab* is optional and depends on time and place.

4) The *hijab* is *ja'iz* or *mubah*, namely, allowable. It is neither mandatory nor prohibited.

5) The *hijab* is neither necessary nor desirable. It is neither *wajib* nor *mustahab*.

6) The *hijab* is *haram* and *bid'ah*; namely, it is a prohibited innovation.

7) The *hijab* is *shirk* or idolatrous, an idol placed on the heads of women.

8) To claim that the *hijab* is a divine command, when it is not, is *kufr* and *riddah*, namely, disbelief and apostasy.

9) It is better for women to go around nude than for people to fabricate dress codes in the name of God.

Appendix 4

Fifteen Islamic Options for Muslim Women

Islamic authorities have expressed over a dozen different opinions regarding the minimum extent of clothing required of Muslim women to cover their *'awrah*, the definitions of which vary tremendously, namely, from the genitals to the entirety of the female form, face, and eyes. The rulings are as follows:

1) Women must cover their genitals. In other words, the thong or G-string is the *hijab* of Islam.

2) Women must cover from the navel to the knees. In other words, the short sarong or miniskirt, while topless, is the *hijab* of Islam.

3) Women must cover their genitals and their breasts. In other words, the bikini is the *hijab* of Islam.

4) Women must cover all cleavage: genitals, buttocks, and breasts. In other words, a pair of shorts and a tank-top is the *hijab* of Islam.

5) Women must cover their genitals, their breasts, and their bodies from the navel to the knee.

6) Women must cover their bodies from the shoulder to the knees, as well as their arms down to the elbow.

7) Women must cover their bodies, arms to the wrists, and legs to the ankles; leaving the head covering as recommended, as opposed to required.

8) Women must cover everything but what is washed during ritual ablutions; in other words, they can show their faces, hair, necks, arms up to the elbow, and feet up to the ankles.

9) Women must cover their entire bodies and their hair, except for their faces, hands, and feet.

10) Women must cover their entire bodies and their hair, except for their hands.

11) Women must cover their entire bodies, their hair, and their faces except for the eyes.

12) Women must cover their entire bodies, their hair, and their faces, with the exception of a single eye.

13) Women must cover their entire bodies, their hair, their faces, and even their eyes.

14) The only way that women can observe *hijab* is by never leaving their homes.

15) Women are only properly covered when they are dead and buried.

If Muslims truly believe in choice, Muslim females should be free to follow options one through nine. For paleoconservative Muslims, however, women should only be free to follow options nine through fourteen. As for myself, I do not view these options as absolute laws but as a spectrum of general guidelines that set reasonable limits as to what should be legally, socially, and religiously permissible.

Except for covering the hair, the Jewish dress code which distinguishes between unacceptable, acceptable, and ideal, exemplifies a reasonable dress code for everyday life. Depending on one's occupation, however, and considering climate, the clothing could be longer or shorter. What is appropriate in an office, a court of law, and a place of worship differs from what is appropriate at the gym, the pool, the beach, or at a wedding. The middle of this spectrum is the norm. Wearing more or wearing less would depend on the context. Most Muslim women who are educated and cultured are moderate in their appearance. They do not bury themselves in black *burkas* nor walk around in black cocktail dresses and stiletto heels as both extremes hyper-sexualize women. They follow the philosophy of *wasatiyyah* or moderation, namely, the middle path. They adjust their dress style based on what they deem appropriate according to the setting. They strive to avoid extremes and to stay within limits of decency determined by revelation and reason. Their dress code is not rigid and brittle but flexible, malleable, and accommodating. Most importantly, they are beautiful as God intended them to be.

Appendix 5

The Judeo-Christian Dress Code

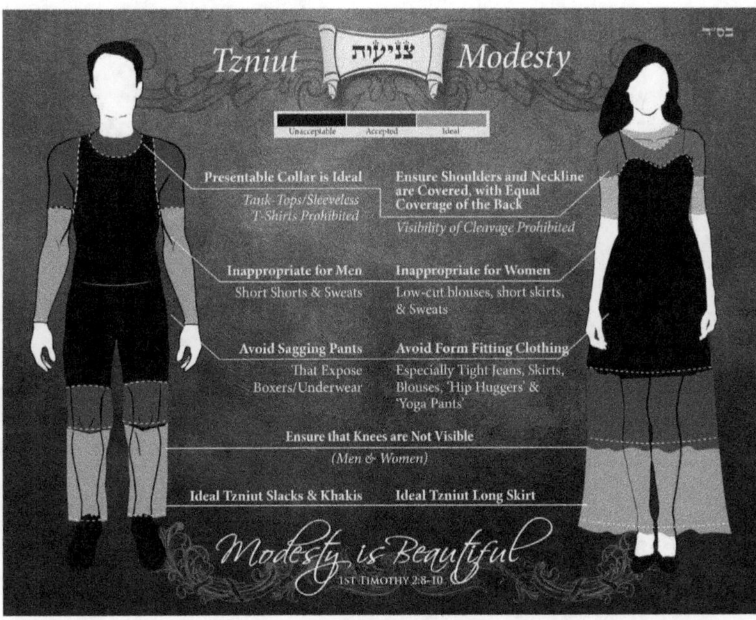

(Public Domain)

Appendix 6

Islamic Rulings Regarding the Minimum Dress for Muslim Women

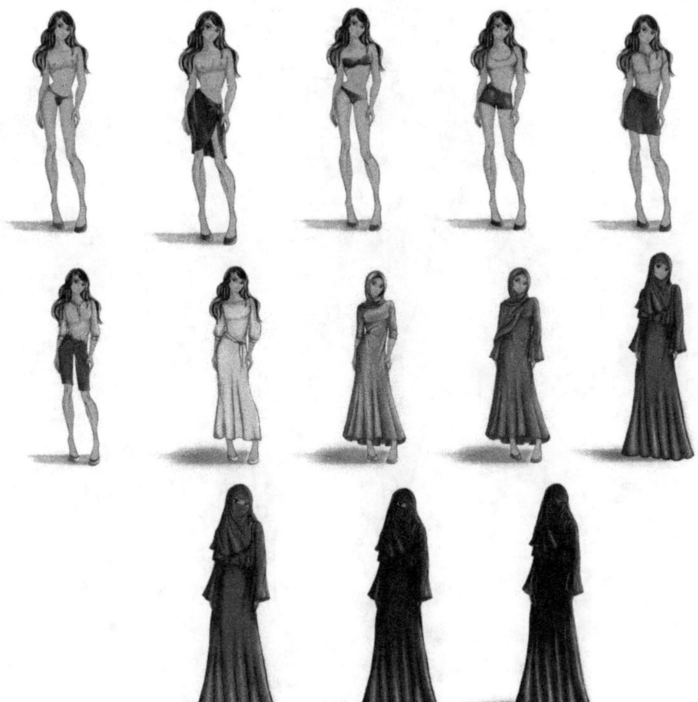

OPTION 1

OPTION 2

(© Kristin Morse 2023)

OPTION 3

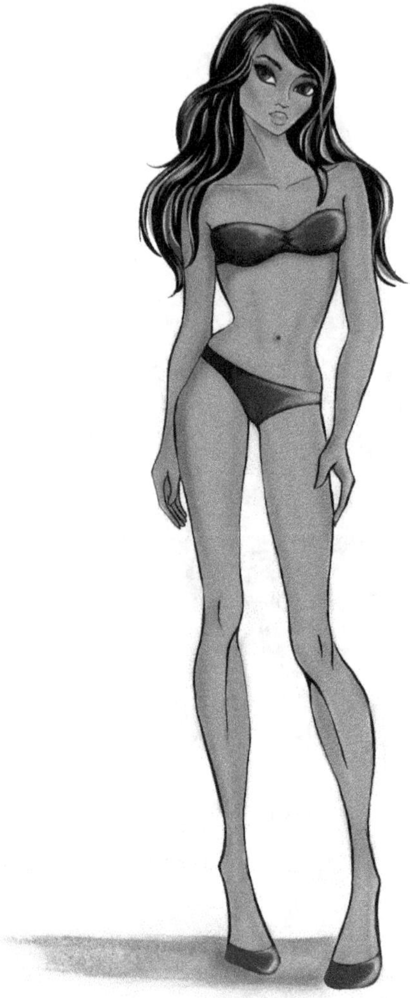

OPTION 4

(© Kristin Morse 2023)

OPTION 5

(© Kristin Morse 2023)

OPTION 6

(© Kristin Morse 2023)

OPTION 7

(© Kristin Morse 2023)

OPTION 8

(© Kristin Morse 2023)

OPTION 9

(© Kristin Morse 2023)

OPTION 10

(© Kristin Morse 2023)

OPTION 11

(© Kristin Morse 2023)

OPTION 12

(© Kristin Morse 2023)

OPTION 13

(© Kristin Morse 2023)

OPTION 14

(Public Domain)

OPTION 15

(Public Domain)

Appendix 7

"Islamic" Depiction of the Destiny of Unveiled Women

("Women in Hell," Wikipedia,
Creative Commons Attribution License, Public Domain)

These fifteenth-century Persian paintings depict the destiny of "wicked women." Evoking the mythological *Isra* and *Miraj* or Night Journey, it features the Angel Gabriel, the Prophet Muhammad riding on Buraq, and a demon who is torturing women in hell. It is a visual depiction of a dubious *hadith* which describes women being burned and boiled, hung by their breasts, tongues, and feet; women cannibalizing themselves; women with their brains oozing out of their skulls; women being bitten by snakes and scorpions; women confined in cages of fire; women whose limbs are falling off from leprosy; women being shred to pieces by scissors of fire; women with heads of pigs and dogs and bodies of donkeys; and women being beaten by iron rods.

("Women in Hell,"
Wikipedia, Creative Commons Attribution License, Public Domain)

What sins did these women commit? Declining to have sex with their husbands. Going out of their homes without asking for permission from their husbands. Failing to bathe after sexual relations. Backbiting, gossiping, and lying. Being jealous. And, most relevant to this study, showing their beauty to men other than their husbands. In other words, failing to observe *hijab* in front of non-*mahram* men. These women are hung by hooks through their breasts and are burning in hell for eternity. Another painting, included below, specifically describes the "shameless" women of hell, namely, those who did not wear *hijab*. As a punishment, they hang from their hair while they burn in hell.

("Women in Hell," Wikipedia,
Creative Commons Attribution License, Public Domain)

Blame God, Muhammad, and Islam? That would hardly be fair. These descriptions are drawn directly from apocryphal Christian sources that were absorbed into Islam after the passing of the Prophet. Consider these passages from the *Apocalypse of Peter*:

> 20. And over against that place I saw another, squalid, and it was the place of punishment; and those who were punished there and the punishing angels had their raiment dark like the air of the place.
>
> 21. And there were certain there hanging by the tongue: and these were the blasphemers of the way of righteousness; and under them lay fire, burning and punishing them. 22. And there was a great lake, full of flaming mire, in which were certain men that pervert righteousness, and tormenting angels afflicted them.
>
> **23. And there were also others, women, hanged by their hair over that mire that bubbled up: and these were they who adorned themselves for adultery; and the men who mingled with them in the defilement of adultery, were hanging by the feet and their heads in that mire.** And I said: I did not believe that I should come into this place.
>
> 24. And I saw the murderers and those who conspired with them, cast into a certain strait place, full of evil snakes, and smitten by those beasts, and thus turning to and fro in that punishment; and worms, as it were clouds of darkness, afflicted them. And the souls of the murdered stood and looked

upon the punishment of those murderers and said: O God, thy judgment is just.

25. And near that place I saw another strait place into which the gore and the filth of those who were being punished ran down and became there as it were a lake: and there sat women having the gore up to their necks, and over against them sat many children who were born to them out of due time, crying; and there came forth from them sparks of fire and smote the women in the eyes: and these were the accursed who conceived and caused abortion.

26. And other men and women were burning up to the middle and were cast into a dark place and were beaten by evil spirits, and their inwards were eaten by restless worms: and these were they who persecuted the righteous and delivered them up.

27. And near those there were again women and men gnawing their own lips, and being punished and receiving a red-hot iron in their eyes: and these were they who blasphemed and slandered the way of righteousness.

28. And over against these again other men and women gnawing their tongues and having flaming fire in their mouths: and these were the false witnesses.

29. And in a certain other place there were pebbles sharper than swords or any spit, red-hot, and women and men in tattered and filthy raiment rolled about on them in punishment: and these were the rich who trusted in their riches and had no pity for orphans and widows, and despised the commandment of God.

30. And in another great lake, full of pitch and blood and mire bubbling up, there stood men and women up to their knees: and these were the usurers and those who take interest on interest.

31. And other men and women were being hurled down from a great cliff and reached the bottom, and again were driven by those who were set over them to climb up upon the cliff, and thence were hurled down again, and had no rest from this punishment: and these were they who defiled their bodies acting as women; and the women who were with them were those who lay with one another as a man with a woman.

32. And alongside of that cliff there was a place full of much fire, and there stood men who with their own hands had made for themselves carven images instead of God. And alongside of these were other men and women, having rods and striking each other and never ceasing from such punishment.

33. And others again near them, women and men, burning and turning themselves and roasting: and these were they that leaving the way of God

And consider these passages from the *Apocalypse of Paul*:

37 And I saw another multitude of pits in the same place, and in the midst thereof a river filled with a multitude of men and women, and worms devoured them. But I wept and sighed and asked the angel: Lord, who are

these? And he said unto me: These are they that extorted usury on usury and trusted in their riches, not having hope in God, that he was their helper.

And after that I looked and saw a very strait place, and there was as it were a wall, and round about it fire. And I saw within it men and women gnawing their tongues, and asked: Who are these, Lord? And he said unto me: These are they that mocked at the word of God in the church, not attending thereto, but as it were making nought of God and of his angels: therefore now likewise do they pay the due penalty.

38 And I looked in and saw another pool (Lat. old man!) beneath in the pit, and the appearance of it was like blood: and I asked and said: Lord, what is this place? And he said unto me: Into this pit do all the torments flow. And I saw men and women sunk up to the lips, and asked: Who are these, Lord? And he said unto me: These are the sorcerers which gave unto men and women magical enchantments, and they found no rest (i. e. did not cease ?) until they died.

And again I saw men and women of a very black countenance in a pit of fire, and I sighed and wept and asked: Who are these, Lord? And he said unto me: These are whoremongers and adulterers who, having wives of their own, committed adultery, and likewise the women after the same sort committed adultery, having their own husbands: therefore do they pay the penalty without ceasing.

39 And I saw there girls clad in black raiment, and four fearful angels holding in their hands red-hot chains, and they put them upon their necks (heads) and led them away into darkness. And again I wept and asked the angel: Who are these, Lord? And he said unto me: These are they which being virgins defiled their virginity, and their parents knew it not: wherefore without ceasing they pay the due penalty.

And again I beheld there men and women with their hands and feet cut off and naked, in a place of ice and snow, and worms devoured them. And when I saw it I wept and asked: Who are these, Lord? and he said unto me: These are they that injured the fatherless and widows and the poor, and trusted not in the Lord: wherefore without ceasing they pay the due penalty.

And I looked and saw others hanging over a channel of water, and their tongues were exceeding dry, and many fruits were set in their sight, and they were not suffered to take of them. And I asked: Who are these, Lord? And he said unto me: These are they that brake the fast before the time appointed: therefore without ceasing do they pay this penalty.

And I saw other men and women hanged by their eyebrows and their hair, and a river of fire drew them, and I said: Who are these, Lord? And he said unto me: These are they that gave themselves not unto their own husbands and wives, but unto adulterers, and therefore without ceasing they pay the due penalty. (For this Copt. has: men and women hung head downwards, torches burning before their faces, serpents girt about them devouring them. These are the women that

beautified themselves with paints and unguents and went to church to ensnare men. Syr. and Gr. omit.)

And I saw other men and women covered with dust, and their appearance was as blood, and they were in a pit of pitch and brimstone and borne down in a river of fire. And I asked: Who are these, Lord? And he said unto me: These are they that committed the wickedness of Sodom and Gomorrah, men with men, wherefore they pay the penalty without ceasing. (Copt., Syr., Gr. omit this paragraph.)

40 And I looked and saw men and women clad in white (bright) apparel, and their eyes were blind, and they were set in a pit, and I asked: Who are these, Lord? And he said unto me: These are they of the heathen that gave alms and knew not the Lord God; wherefore without ceasing they pay the due penalty.

And I looked and saw other men and women upon a spit of fire, and beasts tearing them, and they were not suffered to say: Lord, have mercy on us. And I saw the angel of the torments (Aftemeloukhos, Copt.) laying most fierce torments upon them and saying: Acknowledge the Son of God. For it was told you before, but when the scriptures of God were read unto you, ye paid no heed: wherefore the judgement of God is just, for your evil doings have taken hold upon you, and brought you into these torments. But I sighed and wept; and I inquired and said: Who are these men and women that are strangled in the fire and pay the penalty? And he answered me: These are the women which defiled the creation of God when they brought forth children from the womb, and these are the men that lay with them. But their children appealed unto the Lord God and unto the angels that are over the torments, saying: Avenge us of our parents: for they have defiled the creation of God. Having the name of God, but not observing his commandments, they gave us for food unto dogs and to be trampled on by swine, and others they cast into the river (Copt. adds: and did not permit us to grow up into righteous men and to serve God). But those children were delivered unto the angels of Tartarus (Gr. unto an angel) that they should bring them into a spacious place of mercy: but their fathers and mothers were haled (strangled) into everlasting torment.

Works Cited

(URLs are truncated)

Abdulhameed, Sultan, and Syed Asad. "What is Sharia?" *Muslim Reform Movement* (October 5, 2022). Internet: https://mrmo.org

'Abdul Hakim, Mansoor. *Women Who Deserve to Go to Hell*. Trans. Rafique Abdur Rahman. Karachi: Darul Ishaat, 2004. Internet: https://ia600608.us.archive.org

Abid, Rameez. "Evidences for the Obligation of a Muslim Woman's Headscarf (*Khimar*) & Outer Garment (*Jilbab*)." *The Thinking Muslim* (December 30, 2015). Internet: https://thethinkingmuslim.com

Abou El Fadl, Khaled. 2016. "Fatwa: On *Hijab* (The Hair Covering of Women)." *The Search for Beauty*. Internet: https://www.searchforbeauty.org

---. *The Search for Beauty in Islam: A Conference of the Books*. Lanham, MA: Rowman & Littlefield, 2006.

---. *Speaking in God's Name: Islamic Law, Authority and Women*. London: One World, 2013.

Abou-Taleb, Amira. "Constructing the Image of the Model Muslim Woman: Gender Discourse in Ibn Sa'd's *Kitab al-Tabaqat al-kubra*." *Islamic Interpretive Tradition and Gender Justice: Processes of Canonization, Subversion, and Change*. Ed. Nevin Reda and Yasmin Amin. Montreal and Kingston: McGill-Queen's University Press, 2020. 179-208.

Abu Rayyah, Mahmud. *Lights on the Muhammadan Sunnah or Defense of Hadith*. Internet: https://www.al-islam.org

Abu Zayd, Nasr Hamid. *Dawa'ir al-khawf*. Beirut: Markaz al-Thaqafi al-'Arabi, 2007.

Abyad, Amr El-. "Figurative and Nude Islamic Art." *Amr El-Abyad* (September 21, 2021). Internet: https://elabyad.wordpress.com

Adnani, Razika. *Maghreb: The Impact of Islam on Social and Political Evolution*. Paris: Fondation pour l'innovation politique, 2022. Internet: https://www.fondapol.org

---. "Razika Adnani "Voile: l'État doit avoir une parole ferme." *Razika Adnani* (November 6, 2019). Internet: https://www.razika-adnani.com

---. "Le voile, c'est la discrimination qui s'installe dans l'espace public." *Razika Adnani* (June 16, 2022). Internet: https://www.razika-adnani.com

Aghaie, Kamran Scot. “The Passion of Ashura in Shiite Islam.” *Voices of Islam*. Ed. Vincent J. Cornell. Vol. 2. London: Praeger Perspectives, 2007: 11-124.

Anagnostou-Laoutides, Eva, and Michael B. Charles. “Heredotus on Sacred Marriage and Sacred Prostitution at Babylon.” *Kernos: Revue international et pluridiscipline de religion grecque antique* (2018). Internet: https://journals.openedition.org

Ahmad, Kassim. “Muslim Women Headscarf.” *Kassim Ahmad* (July 13, 2017). Internet: http://kassimahmad.blogspot.com

Ahmed, Leila. *A Quiet Revolution: The Veil's Resurgence, from the Middle East to America*. New Haven and London: Yale University Press, 2011.

---. *Women and Gender in Islam*. New Haven & London: Yale University Press, 1992.

‘Ajami, Cyrille Moreno al-. *Que dit vraiment le Coran?* Paris: Erick Bonnier, 2020.

---. “Le voile selon le Coran et en Islam.” *Que dit vraiment le Coran ?* (January 20, 2018). Internet: https://www.alajami.fr

---. “Le voile comme signe distinctif des musulmanes.” *Que dit vraiment le Coran?* Intenet: https://www.alajami.fr

Akyol, Mustafa. *Why, as a Muslim, I Defend Liberty*. Washington DC: Cato Institute, 2021.

Ali, Ayaan Hirsi. *Prey: Immigration, Islam, and the Erosion of Women's Rights*. New York: Harper Collins, 2021.

---. *The Caged Virgin: An Emancipation Proclamation for Women and Islam*. New York: Free Press, 2006.

Ali, Leena El-. *No Truth without Beauty: God, the Qur'an, and Women's Rights*. Cham: Switzerland, 2022.

Ali, S.V. Mir Ahmed, trans. *The Holy Qur'an*. Elmhurst, NY: Tahrike Tarsile Qur'an, 1988.

Ali-Karamali, Sumbul. *Demystifying Shariah: What it Is, How it Works, and Why it Is Not Taking Over Our Country*. Boston: Beacon Press, 2020.

Alibhai-Brown, Yasmin. “As a Muslim Woman, I see the Veil as a Rejection of Progressive Values.” *The Guardian* (March 20, 2015). Internet: https://www.theguardian.com

Aljazeera. “Turkish Court Clears Historian.” *Aljazeera* (November 1, 2006). Internet: https://www.aljazeera.com

Almasude, Eden. “Amazighité and Secularism: Rethinking Religious-Secular Divisions in Amazigh Political Imagination.” *Decolonization: Indigeneity, Education & Society* 3.2 (2014): 131-151. Internet: https://jps.library.utoronto.ca

Alukah. “Why Should I Wear the *Hijab*?” *Alukah* (August 16, 2014). Internet: https://en.alukah.net

Amer, Sahar. *What is Veiling?* Chapel Hill: University of North Carolina Press, 2014.

Amin, Qasim. *The Liberation of Women and The New Woman: Two Documents in the History of Egyptian Feminism*. Trans. Samiha Sidhom Peterson. Cairo: The American University in Cairo Press, 2000.

Andani, Khalil. "No Muslim Consensus on *Hijab* Being Mandatory." *Twitter* (September 25, 2022). Internet: https://twitter.com

Andrés Serrano, Gonzalo. "La guerra del bikini, un giro en medio siglo: Es interesante cómo va evolucionando la sociedad." *Noticias UAI* (29 de enero de 2018). Internet: https://noticias.uai.cl

Angel, Marc. D. "A Modesty Proposal: Rethinking *Tseniut*." *Ideas: Institute for Jewish Ideas and Ideals*. Internet: https://www.israelnationalnews.com

Apocalypse of Paul. Trans. M.R. James. *Wikisource.* Internet: https://en.wikisource.org

Apocalypse of Peter. Trans. Alexander Roberts and James Donaldson. *Early Christian Writings*. Internet: https://www.earlychristianwritings.com

Arafat, Zalna. "How a Revolutionary Turned Berlin Mosque into a Declaration of Love." *Xtra* (May 28, 2021). Internet: https://xtramagazine.com

Article Eighteen. "I Have to Bring Back the Child Who Became a Christian, Says Shia Cleric." *Article Eighteen* (March 10, 2023). Internet: https://article eighteen.com

Asad, Muhammad. *The Message of the Qur'an*. Internet: http://www.archive.org

Asgari, Alireza. *Compulsory Hijab in Iran: Women's Choice or a State's Demand?* (March 2022). Internet: https://ehs.se

Asharis Assemble. "Many Muslim Leaders Denounce ISIS Out of Convenience, Not Conviction." *Asharis Assemble* (July 5, 2015). Internet: https://asharisassemble.com

Ashley, Robert. "How Much Sunshine do I Need for Enough Vitamin D?" *UCLA Health* (March 23, 2018). Internet: https://www.uclahealth.org

Ashmawi, Muhammad. "*Fatwa al-hijab ghayr shari'iyyah*." *Ruz al-yusuf* (8 August 1994): 28.

---. "*Al-hijab laysa farida*." *Ruz al-yusuf* (June 13, 1994): 22.

Attalah, Lina. "This Movement Wants to Reclaim Life: A Conversation with Fatemeh Sadegui on Iran's Protests." *Madamasr* (October 25, 2022). Internet: https://www.madamasr.com

Austin, R.W.J. trans. *The Bezels of Wisdom*. Ibn 'Arabi. Mahwah, NJ: The Paulist Press, 1980.

Azaiez, Mehdi. "Sourate 24." *Le Coran des Historiens*. Ed. Mohammad Ali Amir-Moezzi et Guillaume Dye. Vol. 2a. Paris: Les Éditions du Cerf, 2019: 869-889.

Azal, Wahid. "Fatima *Fatir*: The Divine Feminine in Islam." *The Way of the Sufi* (September 29, 2017). Internet: http://zoya-thewayofasufi.blogspot.com

Azami, M.M. *Studies in Hadith Methodology and Literature*. Indianapolis: American Trust Publications, 1977.

Azmat, Tanveer. "*Asbab al-Nuzul* and Irfan A. Khan." *Islamic Perspective* 22 (2019): 61-82.

Azmeh, Aziz al-. *Secularism in the Arab World.* Edinburgh: Edinburgh University Press, 2019.

Badran, Margot. *Feminism in Islam: Secular and Religious Convergences.* Oxford: One World, 2009.

Bahai Library. "Can a Baha'i Woman Wear a Headscarf." *Bahai Library* (2009). Internet: http://bahai-library.com

Bahla, Raj. *Understanding Islamic Law (Shari'a).* New York: LexixNexis, 2011.

Bailey, David A. and Gilane Tawadros, eds. *Veil: Veiling, Representation, and Contemporary Art.* Cambridge, MA: The MIT Press, 2003.

Barazangi, Nimat Hafez. *Women's Identity in the Qur'an: A New Reading.* Gainesville, Florida: University Press of Florida, 2006.

Barlas, Asma. *Believing Women in Islam: Unreading Patriarchal Interpretations of the Qur'an.* Austin: University of Texas Press, 2019.

Barnes, Ruth, and Joanne B. Eicher. *Dress and Gender: Making and Meaning.* New York: Berg, 1992.

Basye, Ali. *The Long [and Short] of It: The Madcap History of the Skirt.* New York: Harper Entertainment, 2007.

Batieha, A. et al. "Vitamin D Status in Jordan: Dress Style and Gender Discrepancies." *Nutrition & Metabolism* 2011; 58: 10-18. Internet: https://www.jstor.org

Bayhaqi. *Sunan al-Kubra.* Beirut: Dar al-Kutub al-'Ilmiyyah, 2003.

Bayindir, Abdulaziz. "Women Swimming in Public Beaches." *Islam and Qur'an* (April 12, 2013). Internet: https://www.islamandquran.org

---. "Why do Muslim Women Cover their Hair and Body." *Islam and Qur'an* (October 13, 2020) Internet: https://www.islamandquran.org

Barker, Emma. "Report Finds that Young Iranians -- Gasp! -- Have Sex." *Cosmopolitan* (August 10, 2014). Internet: https://www.cosmopolitan.com

BBC News. "Rickets Cases Rise Among Asians." *BBC News* (October 30, 2007). Internet: http://news.bbc.co.uk

Bell, Richard. *A Commentary on the Qur'an.* Ed. Edmund Bosworth and Mervyn E.J. Richardson. 2 vols. Manchester: University of Manchester, 1991.

Ben Rhouma, Hanan. "Ghaleb Bencheikh s'explique après la polémique née autour de ses propos sur le voile." *Saphir News* (February 1, 2019). Internet: https://www.saphir news.com

Benhabib, Djemila. "I am Not Ashamed to Have Been Born a Woman. I Don't Have to Apologize for that. I Don't Have to Hide from it." *Feminist Resources* (March 21, 2020). Internet: https://ressourcesfeministes.fr

Bestandji, Naëm. "Avec Naëm BESTANDJI, LE LINCEUL DU FÉMINISME. Caresser l'islamisme dans le sens du voile." *Deviens ce que tu es, par Pascal Hubert / YouTube* (February 5, 2022). Internet: https://www.youtube.com

---. *Le linceul du féminisme: caresser l'islamisme dans le sens du voile.* Paris: Editions Séramis, 2021. Internet: https://www.naembestandji.fr

---. "La diabolisation du corps féminin par la promotion du voilement se poursuit." *Naëm Bestandji* (May 1 2019). Internet: https://www.naembestandji.fr

---. "L'islamisme progresse grâce à l'occultation du corps des femmes." *Naëm Bestandji* (March 18, 2019). Internet: https://www.naembestandji.fr

---. "L'obligation religieuse du voile crée par les intégristes: une hérésie sexiste combattue par les musulmans rationalistes, Coran à l'appuis (4ième partie)." *Naëm Bestandji* (September 16, 2018). Internet: https://www.naembestandji.fr

---. "L'obligation religieuse du voile crée par les intégristes: une hérésie sexiste combattue par les musulmans rationalistes, Coran à l'appuis (3ième partie)." *Naëm Bestandji* (September 16, 2018). Internet: https://www.naembestandji.fr

---. "L'obligation religieuse du voile crée par les intégristes: une hérésie sexiste combattue par les musulmans rationalistes, Coran à l'appuis (2ième partie)." *Naëm Bestandji* (September 14, 2018). Internet: https://www.naembestandji.fr

---. "L'obligation religieuse du voile crée par les intégristes: une hérésie sexiste combattue par les musulmans rationalistes, Coran à l'appuis (1ière partie)." *Naëm Bestandji* (September 12, 2018). Internet: https://www.naembestandji.fr

---. "Le voile, un 'marqueur de féminité' comme la mini-jupe ou les talons aiguilles?" *Naëm Bestandji* (September 12, 2017). Internet: https://www.naembestandji.fr

---. "Henda Ayari, du salafisme à l'Islam: une citoyenne libre, une musulmane épanouie." *Naëm Bestandji* (November 11, 2016). Internet: https://www.naem bestandji.fr

---. "Burqini." *Naëm Bestandji.* Internet: https://www.naembestandji.fr

Bible. Internet: https://www.biblegateway.com

Bin Bayyad, Abdallah. "The Question of *Hijab* These Days." *Bin Bayyah* (April 3, 2018). Internet: https://binbayyah.net

Blachère, Régis. *Le Coran.* Paris: Maisonneuve, 1949

Bliss, Robert. "10 Hours of Walking in NYC." *YouTube* (2015). Internet: https://www.youtube.com

Bloesch, Sarah J. and Meredith Minister. *The Bloomsbury Reader in Cultural Approaches to the Study of Religion.* London: Bloomsbury Academic, 2018.

Booth, David, Ashira Konigsburg, and Baruch Frydman-Kohl. *Modesty Inside Out: A Contemporary Guide to Tzniut*. Rabbinical Assembly (February 2, 2017). Internet: https://www.rabbinicalassembly.org

Bouchard, François. *20,000 Years of Fashion: The History of Costume and Personal Adornment*. New York: Harry N. Abrams, 1959.

Boussouf, Malika. "What is a Veil but the Physical Illustration of this Subjugation Ordered by all the Fundamentalists of the World?" *Feminist Resources* (July 13, 2020). Internet: https://ressourcesfeministes.fr

Braun, Louis, Wilhelm von Diez, Ernst Frölich, Johannes Gehrts, Carl von Haeberlin, Friedrich Michael Heil, Andreas Müller, and Ferdinand Rothbart. *Zur Geschichte der Kostüme: 125 Bogen, enthaltend 500 Kostümbilder aus verschiedenen Jahrhunderten*. München: Braun & Schneider, 1890. Internet: https://babel.hathitrust.org

Bridge Initiative Team. "Factsheet: Seyran Ateş." *Bridge* (October 10, 2019). Internet: https://bridge.georgetown.edu

Brown, Daniel. *Rethinking Tradition in Modern Islamic Thought*. Cambridge: Cambridge University Press, 1996.

Bruhn, Wolfgang and Max Tilke. *A Pictorial History of Costume*. New York: Praeger, 1955.

Buechner, Vanessa L., and Markus A. Maier. "Not Always a Matter of Context: Direct Effects of Red on Arousal but Context-Dependent Moderations on Valence." *PeerJ*. 2016; 4: e2515. Published online 2016 Sep 27. Internet: https://www.ncbi.nlm.nih.gov

Bucar, Elizabeth M. *The Islamic Veil: A Beginners' Guide*. Oxford: One World Publications, 2012.

Bukhari. *Sahih al-Bukhari*. Internet: https://sunnah.com

---. *Sahih al-Bukhari*. Beirut: Dar Ibn Kathir, 2002.

Burgos, Antonio. "Rodrigo Bocanegra, el arcipreste del bikini." *Antonio Burgos* (11 de agosto de 1993). Internet: http://www.antonioburgos.com

Buys, Erik. "Sherin Khankan on Islam." *Mimetic Margins* (May 31, 2017). Internet: https://mimeticmargins.com

Calderini, Simonetta. "Female Seclusion and the Veil. Two Issues in Political and Social Discourse." *Islam and the Veil: Theoretical and Regional Contexts. Ed. Theodore Gabriel and Rabiha Hannan*. London: Continuum International Publishing Group, 2011. 48-62.

Catechism of the Catholic Church. St. Charles Borromeo Catholic Church. Internet: http://www.scborromeo.org

Chafik, Sérénade. "Islamophobia has Become the New Preferred Verdict of the New Inquisitionists." *Feminist Resources* (2020). Internet: https://ressources feministes.fr

Chafiq, Chahla. "Choosing the Veil is not Equivalent to Choosing a Lipstick." *Feminist Resources* (August 13, 2020). Internet:

https://ressourcesfeministes.fr

Chebel, Malek. *L'esclavage en terre d'Islam*. Domont: Pluriel, 2010.

Chesler, Phyllis. *Islamic Gender Apartheid: Exposing a Veiled War against Women*. Nashville: New English Review Press, 2017.

---. *An American Bride in Kabul*. New York: St. Martins's Griffin, 2013.

---. *The Death of Feminism: What's Next in the Struggle for Women's Freedom*. New York: Palgrave McMillan, 2005.

Chow, Mansour. "The Myth of the Feminist *Hijab*." *Medium* (September 23, 2016). Internet: https://megapad.medium.com

Clark, Lynda. "*Hijab* According to the *Hadith*: Text and Interpretation." *The Muslim Veil in North America*. Ed. Sajida Sultana Alvi, Homa Hoodfar, and Sheila McDonough. Toronto: Women's Press, 2003. 214-286.

CNN. "Iranian Reformists Condemn Hardline Clerical Court." *CNN* (October 19, 2000). Internet: http://www.cnn.com

Cole, Juan. *Muhammad: Prophet of Peace Amid the Clash of Empires*. New York: Nation Books, 2018.

Coomaraswamy, Rama P. "Feminism and the Veiling of Women." *Projet René Guénon* (June 3, 2006). Internet: http://elkorg-projects.blogspot.com

Cosgrave, Bronwyn. *The Complete History of Costume & Fashion from Ancient Egypt to the Present Day*. New York: Checkmark Books, 2000.

Courtais, Georgine de. *Women's Hats, Headdresses, and Hairstyles: With 453 Illustrations, Medieval to Modern*. Mineola, NY: Dover, 1986.

Crabtree, Steve. "Religiosity Highest in World's Poorest Nations." *Gallup* (August 31, 2010). Internet: https://news.gallup.com

Daws, Richard E. and Adam Hampshire. "The Negative Relationship between Reasoning and Religiosity is Underpinned by a Bias for Intuitive Responses Specifically when Intuition and Logic are in Conflict." *Frontiers in Psychology* 8 (December 19, 2017). Internet: https://www.frontiersin.org

Daylami. *Irshad al-qulub*. Beirut: Muassasat al-A'lamii li al-Matbu'at, 1993.

Dege, Stefan. "Founder of Berlin's Liberal Mosque Wins Urania Medal." *DW* (November 26, 2019). Internet: https://www.dw.com

Djavann, Chahdortt. "The Veil is a Physical and Psycho-Sexual Violence Inflicted on Girls." *Feminist Resources* (2020). Internet: https://ressourcesfeministes.fr

Diamond, Terrence H. et al. "High Bone Turnover in Muslim Women with Vitamin D Deficiency." *The Medical Journal of Australia* 2020; 177 (3): 139-141. Internet: https://www.mja.com.au

Didascalia Apostolorum in Syriac, The. London: Trans. Margaret Dunlop Gibson. Cambridge University Press, 1903.

Didascalia Apostolorum. Trans. R. Hugh Connolly. Oxford: Clarendon Press, 1929.

DK. *Fashion: The Definitive History of Costume and Style*. New York: DK, 2012.

Dolan, Eric W. "Meta-Analysis of 83 Studies Produces 'Very Strong' Evidence for a Negative Relationship between Intelligence and Religiosity." *PsyPost* (November 14, 2019). Internet: https://www.psypost.org

Droge, A.J. *The Qur'an: A New Annotated Translation*. Bristol, CT: Equinox, 2013.

Dubitsky, Stephanie. "The Health Care Crisis Facing Women Under Taliban Rule in Afghanistan." *Human Rights Brief* 6.2 (1999): 10-11.

Economist, The. "Throwing Off the Covers: An Official Report Blows the Lid Off the Secret World of Sex." *The Economist* (August 9, 2014). Internet: https://www.economist.com

---. "Economist Rankings Obesity Women." Internet: https://wikiislam.net

Edwards, Jennifer C. *Daily Life of Women in Chaucer's England*. Santa Barbara: Greenwood, 2022.

Efthekhari, Bahram. *The Meaning of Life: A Final Solution*. Qum: Ansariyan, 2010.

Elliot, Andrew J. et al. "Red, Rank, and Romance in Women Viewing Men." *Journal of Experimental Psychology* 139.3 (2010): https://www.apa.org

Eltahawy, Mona. *Headscarves and Hymens: Why the Middle East Needs a Sexual Revolution*. New York: Farrar, Straus, and Giroux, 2015.

Emirates 24/7. "Gulf Women Hide Weight Under Gowns." *Emirates 24/7* (January 12, 2011). Internet: http://www.webcitation.org

Encyclopedia Iranica. "Clothing." *Encyclopedia Iranica* (2011). Internet: https://www.iranicaonline.org

Escalante, Ana. "Wearing a Sheer Dress May Just be this Year's Defining Fashion Trend." *Glamour* (August 22, 2022). Internet: https://www.glamour.com

Ettinghausen, Richard. *Islamic Art and Archaeology: Collected Papers*. Berlin: Gebr. Mann Verlag, 1984.

Evangelical Wesleyan Church. *The Discipline of the Evangelical Wesleyan Church*. The General Conference, 2015.

Evans, Malcolm. "Bikini vs. Burka." *The Society Pages*. Internet: https://the societypages.org

Fahes, Fadi A. *Social Utopia in Tenth Century Islam: The Qarmatian Experiment*. Master of Arts thesis. Dominguez Hills, CA: California State University, 2018. Internet: https://scholarworks.calstate.edu

Faith Freedom. "*Hijab* and Women in Islam." *Faith Freedom*. Internet: https://www.faithfreedom.org

Fanack. "Homosexuality in Saudi Arabia: A Story of Persecution, Guilt, and Secrecy." *Fanack* (April 26, 2018). Internet: https://fanack.com

Fatah, Tarek. *Chasing a Mirage: The Tragic Illusion of an Islamic State*. Mississauga, Ontario: John Wiley & Sons, 2008.

Ford, Richard Thompson. *Dress Codes: How the Laws of Fashion Made History*. New York: Simon & Schuster, 2021.

Fowden, Garth. *Qusayr Amra: Art and the Umayyad Elite in Late Antique Syria*. Berkeley: University of California Press, 2004.

Fox News. "Iranian Study Finds Singles Having Sex." *Fox News* (August 20, 2014). Internet: https://www.foxnews.com

France Fraternités. "Ghaleb Bencheikh dénonce l'obsession du voile et prend la défense d'un islam réformé." *France Fraternités* (September 21, 2019). Internet: https://france-fraternites.org

Frayne, Douglas R. and Johanna H. Stuckey. *A Handbook of Gods and Goddesses of the Ancient Near East*. University Park, PA: Eisenbrauns, 2021.

Gabriel, Theodore, and Rabiha Hannan, eds. *The Veil: Theoretical and Regional Contexts*. London and New York: Continuum International Publishing Group, 2011.

Ganon, Megan. "Muslims Have Least Sex Outside Marriage, Study Suggests." *NBC News* (October 18, 2012). Internet: https://www.nbcnews.com

García, Paola. "Hijab." Personal correspondence (May 19, 2023).

--. "Why Wearing the Veil is not Required in Islam." *Morocco World News* (December 11, 2014). Internet: https://www.moroccoworldnews.com

Garland, Madge. *The Changing Face of Beauty*. New York: M. Barrows and Company, 1957.

Giafferri, Paul Louis de. *Women's Costume of the Ancient World*. Mineola, NY: Dover Publications, 2005.

Genseric, Hannibal. "Le voile n'est ni arabe ni islamique." *Agora Vox* (January 6, 2014). Internet: https://www.agoravox.fr

Goodwin, Jan. *Price of Honor: Muslim Women Lift the Veil of Silence on the Islamic World*. New York: Plume Books, 2003.

Gorsline, Douglas. *What People Wore: 1,800 Illustrations from Ancient Times to the Early Twentieth Century*. New York: Dover Publications, 1980.

Grabar, Oleg. "The Story of Portraits of the Prophet Muhammad." *Studia Islamica* 96 (2003): 19-38. Internet: https://www.jstor.org

Gray, John Gray. *The Legacy of Canaan: The Ras Shamra Texts and their Relevance to the Old Testament*. Leiden: Brill, 1965.

Gruber, Christiane. *The Praiseworthy One: The Prophet Muhammad in Islamic Texts and Images*. Bloomington: Indiana University Press, 2019.

---. "The Koran Does Not Forbid Images of the Prophet." *Newsweek* (January 8, 2015). Internet: https://www.newsweek.com

Guardian, The. "How the *Hijab* has Made Sexual Harassment Worse in Iran."

The Guardian (September 15, 2015). Internet: https://www.theguardian.com

Gueguen, N. and C. Jacob. "Clothing Color and Tipping: Gentleman Patrons Give More Tips to Waitresses with Red Clothes." *Journal of Hospitality & Tourism Research* 2021. Internet: https://journals.sagepub.com

Guindi, Fadwa El. "The Veil Becomes a Movement." *Women and Islam: Critical Concepts in Sociology*. Vol. 2. Ed. Haideh Moghissi. New York: Routledge, 2005. 70-91.

---. *Veil: Modesty, Privacy, and Resistance*. Oxford: Berg, 1999.

Guitta, Olivier. "The Veil Controversy." *The Weekly Standard* (December 4, 2006). Internet: https://www.washingtonexaminer.com

Habibi, Alborz. "Exclusive: Interview with Ayatollah Khomeini's Granddaughter." *Your Middle East* (December 26, 2012). Internet: https://yourmiddleeast.com

Haddad, G.F. "Al-Awza'i." *Damas*. Intenet: https://damas-original.nur.nu

Hajjaji-Jarrah, Soraya. "Women's Modesty in Qur'anic Commentaries: The Founding Discourse." *The Muslim Veil in North America*. Ed. Sajida Sultana Alvi, Homa Hoodfar, and Sheila McDonough. Toronto: Women's Press, 2003. 181-213.

Hakeem, Mohammad Saeed al-. *Muslims' Guide: Guidance and Edicts*. Trans. Yasin Jibouri. Najaf: Dar al-Hilal, 2013.

Hakim, Muhammad ibn 'Abd Allah al-. *al-Mustradrak*. Beirut: Dar al-Kutub al-'Ilmiyyah, 2009.

Hall, Carla. "Jordan's Queen Aims to Defuse Stereotypes." *Los Angeles Times* (October 25, 2007). Internet: https://www.latimes.com

Hamid, Shadi. "The Right to Choose to Wear (or Not) *Hijab*." *Brookings* (January 19, 2016). Internet: https://www.brookings.edu

Hasan, Abla. *Decoding the Egalitarianism of the Qur'an: Retrieving Lost Voices on Gender*. Lanham: Lexington Books, 2020.

Hasan, Usama. "The Veil: Between Tradition and Reason, Culture and Context." (2011). *Academia.edu*. Internet: https://www.academia.edu

Hassan, Riffat. "Why Educating Women Does Not Go Against Islamic Rules, Here's What the Qur'an Says." *Courier Journal* (October 14, 2021). Internet: https://courier-journal.com

---. "The Qur'an on Women's Public Conduct." *The Express Tribune* (August 4, 2010). Internet: https://tribune.com.pk

---. "Feminism in Islam." Ed. Arvind Sharma and Katherine K. Young. *Feminism and World Religions*. Albany: State University of New York Press, 1999. 248-277.

Higgs, Johanna. "Unveiling Sexual Harassment against Women in Iran." *Independent Australia* (May 19, 2018). Internet: https://independentaustralia.net

Hilli, 'Allamah al-. *Mukhtalif al-shi'ah fi ahkam al-shari'ah. Lib.Eshia.Ir.*

Internet: https://lib.eshia.ir

Hirsch, Hadas. "Clothing and Colours in Early Islam: Adornment (Aesthetics), Symbolism, and Differentiation." *Anthropology of the Middle East* (March 1, 2020). Internet: https://www.berghahnjournals.com

Hobbs, Raymond D. "Severe Vitamin D Deficiency in Arab American Women Living in Dearborn, Michigan." *Endocrine Practice* 15(1): 35-40. Internet: https://www.endocrinepractice.org

Horchani, Salah. "À propos du droit/de l'obligation de port du foulard, du voile, du burkini, du *niqab*." *Le Club de Mediapart* (September 7, 2016). Internet : https://blogs.media part.fr

Hopwood-Phillips, Henry. "Cover Yo Woman: The Byzantine Stance on Veiling Women." *The Byzantine Ambassador* (April 16, 2020). Internet: https://www.byzantineambassador.com

Hosseini Nasab, Reza. "Covering a Muslim Woman's Hair." *Hoseini.org* (2022). Internet: http://www.hoseini.org

Houda-Pepin, Fatima. "At the Origins of the So-Called Islamic Veil, there is Rape and Prostitution." *Feminist Resources* (March 5, 2020). Internet: https://ressourcesfeministes.fr

Houston, Mary G. *Ancient Egyptian, Mesopotamian & Persian Costume and Decoration.* 2nd ed. New York: Barnes & Noble, 1954.

Howell, Sally. *Old Islam in Detroit: Rediscovering the Muslim American Past.* Oxford: Oxford University Press, 2014.

Hubeali. *Hijab.* Internet: https://hubeali.com

Human Rights Watch. "Virtue Campaign on Women in Chechnya under Ramzan Kadyrov." *Human Rights Watch* (October 29, 2012). Internet: https://www.hrw.org

Huraibi, Nahla Abdullah. *Islam, Gender, and Integration in Transnational / Heterolocalist Contexts: A Case Study of Somali Immigrant Families in Columbus, Ohio*. 2009. Doctoral dissertation. Ohio State University. Internet: https://etd.ohiolink.edu

Husain, Nazik Elmalaika, et al. Vitamin D Level and its Determinants among Sudanese Women." *Journal of Family Medicine and Primary Care* 8.7 (July 2019): 2389-2394. https://journals.lww.com

Ibn 'Arabi. *The Meccan Illuminations: Selected Texts.* William C. Chittick et al. Paris: Sindbad, 1989.

---. *The Bezels of Wisdom*. Trans. R.W.J. Austin. Mahwah, NJ, 1980.

---. *al-Futuhat al-Makkiyyah*. Cairo: n.p., 1911.

Ibn 'Ashur, Muhammad al-Tahir. *Treatise On Maqasid al-Shar'iah*. Trans. Mohamed El-Tahir El-Mesawi. London: The International Institute of Islamic Thought, 2006.

Ibn Battutah. *The Travels of Ibn Battutah*. Ed. Tim Mackintosh-Smith. London: Picador, 2002.

Ibn Hibban. *Sahih Ibn Hibban*. Beirut: Mu'assasat al-Risalah, 2011.

Ibn Ishaq. *The Life of Muhammad*. Trans. A. Guillaume. Oxford: Oxford University Press, 1987.

Ibn Kathir. *Tafsir al-Qur'an al-Karim*. Internet: http://ar.lib.eshia.ir

---. *al-Bidayah wa al-nihayah*. Beirut: Dar al-Kitab, 1985.

Ibn Manzur. *Lisan al-'Arab*. Internet: http://arabiclexicon.hawramani.com

Ibn Abi Shaybah, Abu Bakr. *al-Musannaf*. N.p.: n.p., 1999.

Ingram, Aleah. "From Grubbies to Spiritual Guidance: Dress Standards in the *For the Strength of Youth* Over the Years." *LDS Daily* (October 5, 2022). Internet. https://www.ldsdaily.com

Iran International. "Death of *Hijab* Victim Deepens Rejection of Islamic Republic." *Iran International* (September 19, 2022). Internet: https://www.iranintl.com

---. "Ali Motahari: Voluntary *Hijab* Leads to Nudity." *Iran International* (February 3, 2019). Internet: https://old.iranintl.com

Ighani, Hella, and Garrett Nada. "Khomeini's Rebel Grandchildren." *The Iran Primer* (May 29, 2013). Internet: https://iranprimer.usip.org

Iran Wire. "Presidential Hopeful's Sexist and Racist Comments Shock Even His Most Ardent Followers." *Iran Wire* (April 7, 2021). Internet: https://iranwire.com

Iraqi, Fakhruddin. *Divine Flashes*. Trans. William C. Chittick and Peter Lamborn Wilson. New York: Paulist Press, 1982.

Islam, Joseph A. "Hijaab." *The Qur'an and its Message* (July 25, 2012). Internet: http://quransmessage.com

---. "Aggressive (Mis)translations of the Qur'an to Enslave Women." *The Qur'an and its Message* (November 16, 2011). Internet: http://quransmessage.com

Ismaili Gnosis. "Why Don't Ismaili Women Wear *Hijabs* (Veils)?" *IsmailiGnosis.Com* (2017). Internet: https://ask.ismailignosis.com

Jahangir, Junaid. "5 Muslim Scholars on the Permissibility of Not Wearing the Headscarf." *Huffington Post* (January 1, 2017). Internet: https://www.huffingtonpost.ca

Jalaeipour, Zahra. *Hijab in Transition: Dress Code Changes amongst Iranian Diaspora in London*. M.Phil. thesis. Sussex: University of Sussex, 2016. Internet: http://sro.sussex.ac.uk

Jebara, Mohamad. *Muhammad, The World-Changer: An Intimate Portrait*. New York: St. Martin's Essentials, 2021.

Jeffery, Arthur. *The Foreign Vocabulary of the Qur'an*. Baroda: Oriental Institute, 1938. Internet: https://archive.org

Jenkins, Russell. "Rickets among Asians." *The Times* (October 30, 2007).

Jordan, Timothy R. et al. "Further Investigation of the Effects of Wearing the

Hijab: Perception of Female Facial Attractiveness by Emirati Muslim Men Living in their Native Muslim Country." *PLoS One* 2020; 15(10): e0239419. Internet: https://www.ncbi.nlm.nih.gov

Joselit, Jenna Weissman. *A Perfect Fit: Clothes, Character, and the Promise of America*. New York: Henry Holt and Company, 2014.

Juan, Stephen. "What Color is the Most Sexually Attractive?" *The Register* (July 7, 2006). Internet: https://www.theregister.com

Kacem, Abelaziz. *Le voile est-il islamique ?* Montpellier: Chèvre-feuille étoilée, 2004.

Kadivar, Mohsen. "Rethinking Muslim Marriage Rulings through Structural *Ijtihad*." *Kadivar* (January 7, 2023a). Internet: https://english.kadivar.com

---. "Human Dignity / *Karamah*." *Kadivar* (January 6, 2023). Internet: https://english. kadivar.com

---. "The Rights of Mankind: Human Rights and Reformist Islam." *Kadivar* (January 6, 2023). Internet: https://english.kadivar.com

---. *Kalam ajmal fi sitr al-mara'h. Kadivar.com*. Internet: https://kadivar.com

Kamali, Mohammad Hashim. "Islamic Family Law Reform: Problems and Prospects." *Islam and Civilization Renewal: A Journal Devoted to Contemporary Issues and Policy Research* 3.1 (2011): 37-52.

Kamrava, Mehran. *Iran's Intellectual Revolution*. Cambridge: Cambridge University Press, 2008.

Karami, Arash. "Khomeini's Grandson Says there is More to Islam than *Hijab*." *Al-Monitor* (June 2, 2016). Internet: https://www.al-monitor.com

Kashani, 'Abd al-Razzaq al-. *Tafsir al-Kashani. Part 1: Surahs 1-18*. Trans. Feras Hamza. Louisville, KY: Fons Vitae, n.d.

Kayhan. "Ayatollah Taleghani: No One Forces Women to Wear *Hijab*." *Kayhan* (March 11, 1979). Internet: https://iranbahaipersecution.bic.org

Keddie, Nikki. *Women in the Middle East: Past and Present*. Princeton: Princeton University Press, 2007.

Khamenei, 'Ali. "*Hijab* Have [Sic] Roots in all Cultures." *Khamenei* (April 21, 2010). Internet: https://english.khamenei.ir

Khan, Bashir. "Vitamin D Status and its Correlation to Depression." *Annals of General Psychiatry* 21: 32 (2022). Internet: https://annals-general-psychiatry.biomedcentral.com

Khan, Irfan Ahmad. "Authenticity and Development of Islamic Thought." *International Journal of Islamic and Arabic Studies* 4.2 (1987): 31-47.

King, L.W., trans. *The Code of Hammurabi. The Avalon Project*. Internet: https://avalon.law.yale.edu

Kramer, Jane. "Taking the Veil: How France's Public Schools Became the Battleground in a Culture War." *The New Yorker* (November 14, 2004). Internet: https://www.newyorker.com

Ksouri, Maya. "Vu de Tunisie: le burkini, insulte au combat mené chaque jour par les femmes arabes." *Marianne* (September 9, 2016). Internet: https://www.marianne.net

Kulayni. *al-Kafi*. Trans. Muhammad Sarwar. 8 vols. New York: The Islamic Seminary, 2015.

---. *al-Kafi*. Tehran: Dar al-Kutub al-'Ilmiyyah, 2000.

---. *al-Kafi*. Internet: http://shiaonlinelibrary.com

Kybalova, Ludmila, Olga Herbenova, and Milena Lamarova. *The Pictorial Encyclopedia of Fashion*. New York: Crown Publishers, 1970.

La Libre. "Le *hijab* est une prison sexiste, mortifère, aliénante." *La Libre* (April 25, 2019). Internet: https://www.lalibre.be

Lamb, Kate. "Indonesian Girls Traumatized by Push to Wear *Hijab*." *Reuters* (March 18, 2021). Internet: https://www.reuters.com

Lamrabet, Asma. "How Does the Qur'an Address the Issue of Muslim Woman's Veil or *Hijab*?" *Asma Lamrabet* (July 2019). Internet: http://www.asma-lamrabet.com

---. *Women in the Qur'an: An Emancipatory Reading*. Leicestershire: Square View, 2018.

Lachgar, Ibtissam. "Feminism Based on Islam is a Sham. No More and No Less." *Feminist Resources* (February 21, 2021). Internet: https://ressourcesfeministes

Laver, James. *Costume and History: A Concise History*. New York: Thames & Hudson, 2012.

Lenčet, Lena, and Gideon Bosker. *Making Waves: Swimsuits and the Undressing of America*. San Francisco: Chronicle Books, 1989.

Leventon, Melissa, ed. *What People Wore When: A Complete Illustrated History of Costume from Ancient Times to the Nineteenth Century for Every Level of Society*. East Sussex: Ivy Press, 2008.

Lewis, Reina. *Muslim Fashion: Contemporary Style Cultures*. Durham and London: Duke University Press, 2015.

Lichter, Ida. *Muslim Women Reformers: Inspiring Voices against Oppression*. New York: Prometheus Books, 2009.

Lite, Jordan. "Does Modest Dress among Arab-American Women Promote Vitamin D Deficiency?" *Scientific American* (February 16, 2009). Internet: https://blogs.scientific american.com

Luxenberg, Christoph. *The Syro-Aramaic Reading of the Koran: A Contribution to the Decoding of the Language of the Koran*. Berlin: Schiller, 2007.

Mabrouk, Nadia El. "Secularism is a Great Step Forward towards Freedom and Emancipation." *Feminist Resources* (March 15, 2020). Internet: https://ressourcesfeministes.fr

Magister, Sandro. "The Virgins and the Grapes: The Christian Context of the Koran: An Interview with 'Christoph Luxenberg.'" *Dabran* (2018).

Internet: https://www.dabran. org

Mahajjah. “Virtues of Mut‘ah.” *Mahajjah*. Internet: https://mahajjah.com

Mahmoud, M.A. “Mansour Fahmy: Pioneer of Islamic Feminism in Modern Egyptian Thought.” *RUDN Journal of Philosophy* (25.2 (2021). Internet: https://journals.rudn.ru

Majlisi, Muhammad Baqir. *Bihar al-anwar*. Beirut: Mu’assasat al-A‘lami, 2008.

---. *Hayat al-Qulub. Vol. 1. Stories of the Prophet*. Internet: https://www.al-islam.org

---. *Haqqul Yaqeen: A Compendium of Twelver Shia Religious Beliefs*. Qum: Ansariyan, n.d.

Maleki, Ammar, and Pooyan Tamimi Arab. *Iranians’ Attitudes Toward the 2022 Nationwide Protests. GAMAAN* (February 2023). Internet: https://gamaan.org

---. *Iranians’ Attitudes Toward Religion: A 2020 Survey Report. GAMAAN* (August 2020). Internet: https://gamaan.org

Mansour, Ahmed Subhy. “They Ask You About the Veil.” *Ahl al-Qur’an* (October 25, 2009). Internet: https://www.ahl-alquran.com

---. “Women’s Right to Aspire to the Presidency of any Islamic State.” *Ahl al-Qur’an* (January 30, 2016). Internet: https://www.ahl-alquran.com

---. “Fatwas: Part Seventeen.” *Ahl al-Qur’an* (January 18, 2017). Internet: https://www.ahl-alquran.com

---. “Awra.” *Ahl al-Qur’an* (March 23, 2017). Internet: https://www.ahl-alquran.com

---. “Fatwas: Part Seventy-Three.” *Ahl al-Qur’an* (February 8, 2018). Internet: https:// www.ahl-alquran.com

---. “Fatwas Part Eighty-Six.” *Ahl al-Qur’an* (June 19, 2018). Internet: https://www.ahl-alquran.com

---. “Fatwas Part Ninety-Seven.” *Ahl al-Qur’an* (October 23, 2018). Internet: https://www.ahl-alquran.com

Maranlou, Sahar. “*Hijab* Law in Iran over the Decades: The Continuing Battle for Reform.” *The Conversation* (October 7, 2022). Internet: https://theconversation.com

Martin, Richard, and Harold Koda. *Splash! A History of Swimwear*. New York: Rizzoli, 1990.

Martineau, Richard. “Le racisme est-il plus grave que le sexisme?” *Le Journal de Montréal* (March 13, 2023). Internet: https://www.journaldemontreal.com

---. “Burkini: le monde à l’envers.” *Le Journal de Montréal* (August 22, 2016). Internet: https://www.journaldemontreal.com

Masjid Tucson. “The Woman’s Hair: Up to their Eyebrows in Idolatry but Worried about the Woman’s Hair.” *Masjid Tucson*. Internet:

https://www.masjidtucson.org

---. "Dress Code for Women Based on Qur'an." *Masjid Tuscon*. Internet: https://www.masjidtucson.org

Maybudi, Rashid al-Din. *Kashf al-asrar: Unveiling the Mysteries*. Trans. William C. Chittick. Louisville, KY: Fons Vitae, 2014. Internet: https://rissc.jo

Meddeb, Abdelwahhab. *The Malady of Islam*. Trans. Pierre Joris and Anne Reid. New York: Basic Books, 2003.

Mekić, Sejad. *A Muslim Reformist in Communist Yugoslavia: The Life and Thought of Husein Đozo*. London and New York: Routledge, 2017.

MEMRI. "Egyptian Women's Rights Activist Iqbal Baraka Slams the Muslim Brotherhood for Hypocrisy: They Have Learned from Turkish PM Erdogan, an 'Extremely Despicable' and 'Dangerous' Man." *MEMRI* (May 29, 2011). Internet: https://www.memri.org

Mernissi, Fatima. *Beyond the Veil: Male-Female Dynamics in Modern Muslim Society*. Bloomington: Indiana University Press, 1987.

---. *The Veil and the Male Elite: A Feminist Interpretation of Women's Rights in Islam*. Trans. Mary Jo Lakeland. New York: Basic Books, 1992.

Meshal, Reem A. "Banners of Faith and Identities in Construct: The *Hijab* in Canada." *The Muslim Veil in North America: Issues and Debates*. E. Sajiad Sultana Alvi, Homa Hoodfar, and Sheila McDonough. Toronto: Women's Press, 2003. 72-104.

Meyer, Nick. "Do Women in *Hijabs* have a Greater Risk of Vitamin D Deficiency?" *The Arab American News* (December 24, 2018). Internet: https://arab americannews.com

Middle East Online. "Up to 70% of Gulf Women are Obese." *Middle East Online* (September 29, 2005). Internet: https://webcitation.org

Mill, John Stuart. *On Liberty*. 1859. Internet: https://www.utilitarianism.com

Mir-Hosseini, Ziba. *Journeys Toward Gender Equality in Islam*. London: Oneworld Academic, 2022.

---. "*Hijab* and Choice: Between Politics and Theology." *Innovation in Islam: Traditions and Contributions*. Ed. Mehran Kamrava. Los Angeles: University of California Press, 2011. 190-212. Internet: http://www.zibamirhosseini.com

Mir Jalili, Kazem, and Mohammad Taqi Gol Mohammad. "Critical Analysis and Exegesis on *Hijab* from the Viewpoint of Companions of the Prophet." *Comparative Interpretation Research* (2019). Internet: http://www.ptt.qom.ac.ir

Mirshavalad, Minoo. "Can Iranian Women Compensate for their Absence from the World of *Fiqh*?" *Jura Gentium* 14.2 (2017): 86-107. Internet: https://www.juragentium.org

Mithiborwala, Feroze. "The Only Option for Iran is to End the *Hijab* Mandate."

Countercurrents (September 9, 2022). Internet: https://countercurrents.org

Mohammed, Syed. "*Burqa*-Clad Women Prone to Vitamin D Deficiency." *The Times of India* (June 7, 2013). Internet: https://timesofindia.indiatimes.com

Monaghan, Patricia. *Encyclopedia of Goddesses and Heroines*. Vol. 1. Santa Barbara: ABC-CLIO, 2010.

Morrow, John Andrew. *Controversies in Islam: Religious Law, Qur'anic Ethical Imperatives, and Higher Moral Objectives*. Newcastle upon Tyne: Cambridge Scholars Publishing, 2023.

---. *The Most Controversial Qur'anic Verse: Why 4:34 Does Not Promote Violence Against Women*. Lanham: Hamilton Books, 2020.

---. *Amerindian Elements in the Poetry of Ernesto Cardenal: Mythic Foundations of the Colloquial Narrative*. Lewiston: Edwin Mellen Press, 2010.

Murata, Sachiko. *The Tao of Islam: A Sourcebook on Gender Relationships in Islamic Thought*. Albany: SUNY, 1992.

Musa, Aisha Y. *Hadith as Scripture: Discussions on the Authority of Prophetic Traditions in Islam*. London: Palgrave-MacMillan, 2008. Lanham: Hamilton Books, 2020.

Muslim. *Sahih Muslim*. Internet: https://sunnah.com

---. *Sahih*. Riyadh: Dar Tayyiba lil-Nashr wa al-Tawzi,' 2006.

Muslim, Ammaar. "Muhammad b. Sinan: A Controversial Narrator." *Iqra Online* (January 23, 2019). Internet: https://iqraonline.net

Mustaqim, Abdul. "Shahrur and the Theory of Limits." *Sabyl* (September 23, 2004). Internet: https://sabyl.forumactif.com

My Stealthy Freedom. "Presidential Candidate: Not Wearing *Hijab* is an Animal Instinct." *My Stealthy Freedom* (April 12, 2021). Internet: https://www.mystealthyfreedom.org

Na'im, Abdullahi Ahmed An-. *Islam and the Secular State: Negotiating the Future of Shari'a*. Cambridge: Harvard University Press, 2008.

---, trans. *The Second Message of Islam*. Mahmoud Mohamed Taha. Syracuse: Syracuse University Press, 1987.

Nasr, Seyyed Hossein, ed. *The Study Qur'an*. New York: HarperOne, 2015.

---. "Preface." *Divine Flashes*. Fakhruddin 'Iraqi. Trans. William C. Chittick and Peter Lamborn Wilson. New York: Paulist Press, 1982.

Nomani, Asra. "The *Fatwa* against Women Touching Bananas and Other Stupid Islamic Orders." *New Age Islam* (December 10, 2011). Internet: http://www.newageislam.com

National Post. "Children Wearing Sunscreen, Religious Garments, at the Root of Vitamin D Deficiency, Rise in Rickets: UK Doctor." *National Post* (October 29, 2013). Internet: https://nationalpost.com

Nu'man, Qadi al-. *The Pillars of Islam*. Vol. 1. Trans. Asaf A.A. Fyzee. Ed.

Ismail Kurban Husein Poonawala. Oxford: Oxford University Press, 2006.

---. *The Pillars of Islam*. Vol. 2. Trans. Asaf A.A. Fyzee. Oxford: Oxford University Press, 2007.

---. *Da'a'im al-Islam*. Cairo: Dar al-Ma'arif, 1963.

O'Connell, Mark, and Raje Airey, eds. *Signs & Symbols*. London: Lorenz Books, 2005.

Ojah, Rani C.I., and Jo. M. Welch. "Vitamin D and Musculoskeletal Status in Nova Scotian Women Who Wear Concealing Clothing." *Nutrients* 2021 May; 4(5): 399-412). Internet: https://arabamericannews.com

Otero-González, Uxia. "Catholic Dressing in the Spanish Franco Dictatorship (1939-1975): Normative Femininity and its Sartorial Embodiment." *Journal of Religious History* (November 17, 2021). Internet: https://onlinelibrary.wiley.com

Pars Times. "Historical and Period Costumes in Iran." *Pars Times*. Internet: https://www. parstimes.com

---. "Iranian Traditional Costume." *Pars Times*. Internet: https://www.pars times.com

---. "Fashion in Pre-Revolutionary Iran." *Pars Times*. Internet: https://www. parstimes.com

---. "*Hijab* in Post-Revolutionary Iran." *Pars Times*. Internet: https://www.pars times.com

Payne, Blanche, Geitel Winakor and Jane Farrell-Beck. *The History of Costume*. 2nd ed. New York: HarperCollins, 1992.

Peacock, John. *The Chronicle of Western Fashion from Ancient Times to the Present Day*. New York: Harry N. Abrams, 1991.

Pérez Rivera, José Manuel, Virgilio Martínez Enamorado, Silvia Nogueras Vega. *Magia talismánica en la Ceuta del siglo XIII*. Ceuta: Museo de Ceuta, 2021. Internet: http://www.academia.edu

Pérez Rivera, José Manuel, and Virgilio Martínez Enamorado. "Talismán antropomórfico andalusí y la 'ciencia de la balanza." *Revista Atlántica-mediterránea* (2019) 21: 111-124. Internet: https://revistas.uca.es

Pew Research Center. "How People in Muslim Countries Prefer Women to Dress in Public." *Pew Research Center* (January 8. 2014). Internet: https://www.pew research.org

Phang, Sara Elise. *Daily Life of Women in Ancient Rome*. Santa Barbara: Greenwood, 2022.

Plackett, Benjamin. "Researchers Find Vitamin D Deficiency High in Arab Women." *Al Fanar Media* (October 4, 2017). Internet: https://www.al-fanarmedia.org

Pogontseva, D.V. "Female Attitudes Towards Women in *Hijabs* in South Russia." *Psychology in Russia* (2017) 10.2. Internet: http://psychologyinrussia.com

Powers, David S. "Le Coran et son environnement légal." *Le Coran des historiens*. Vol. 1. Ed. Mohammad Ali Amir-Moezzi and Guillaume Dye. Paris: Les Éditions du Cerf, 2019. 615-649.

Pradza, Adam D., and Andrew J. Elliot. "Sexy Red: Perceived Sexual Receptivity Mediates the Red-Attraction Relation in Men Viewing Woman." *Journal of Experimental Social Psychology* 48.3 (May 2012: 787-790. Internet: https://www.sciencedirect.com

Prenner, Karl. "The Practice of Veiling as an Expression of the Moral Behavior of Women and their Social Status in the Qur'an." *Headscarf and Veiling: Glimpses from Sumer to Islam*. Ed. Roswitha Del Fabbro, Frederick Mario Fales, and Hannes D. Galter. Venezia: Edizioni Ca'Foscari, 2021. 119-134.

Qaradawi, Yusuf al-. *The Lawful and the Prohibited in Islam*. *Islamic Studies*. Internet: http://www.islamicstudies.info

Qazi, Moin. Islam Enjoins Modesty for Both Men and Women." *Khutba Bank* (October 8, 2017). Internet: https://khutbahbank.org.uk

Quillen, Stephen. "Twenty Years On, Viagra Sheds Light on Male Attitudes in the Arab World." *The Arab Weekly* (July 4, 2018). Internet: https://thearabweekly.com

Qur'an. Internet: https://al-quran.info

Qur'an. Internet: https://islamawakened.org/quran

Racinet, Auguste. *The Costume History*: *From Ancient Times to the 19th Century*. Köln: Taschen, 2015.

Raasi, Tala. "Bikinis and Burkinis are about Freedom." *Tala Raasi* (August 30, 2016). Internet: https://talaraassi.com

Rabinovitch-Fox, Einav. *Dressed for Freedom: The Fashionable Politics of American Feminism*. Chicago: University of Illinois Press, 2021.

Radio Farda. "Support for Compulsory *Hijab* Waning, Report Says." *Radio Farda* (July 29, 2018). Internet: https://en.radiofarda.com

---. "Conservative Cleric Advises Police to be Tough on Anti-*Hijab* Protesters." *Radio Farda* (March 25, 2022). Internet: https://en.radiofarda.com

Rahim, Sameer. "Eye of the Beholder: How the Prophet Muhammad has been Depicted through the Centuries." *Apollo Magazine* (December 18, 2019). Internet: https://www.apollo-magazine.com

Rania, Queen. "Queen Rania Explains." *Come and See* (October 11, 2001). Internet: http://www.comeandsee.com

---. "Queen Rania's Live Q&A at the World Economic Forum Meeting 2003, Davos, Switzerland." *Queen Rania* (January 27, 2003). Internet: https://www.queenrania.jo

---. "Jordan's Queen Says Islam Does Not Command Veil." *ABC News* (February 9, 2007). Internet: https://www.abc.net.au

---. "Queen Rania to Oprah." *Queen Rania* (May 17, 2006). Internet: https://www.queenrania.jo

---. "Queen Rania to Fareed Zakaria." *Queen Rania* (October 19, 2008). Internet: https://www.queenrania.jo

---. "Queen Rania's Interview with BBC -- 2010." *Queen Rania* (January 31, 2010). Internet: https://www.queenrania.jo

Rasekh, Ali-Ahmad. *Agents of the Hidden Imam: Shiite Juristic Authority in Light of the Doctrine of Deputyship*. PhD thesis. Montreal: Concordia University, 2015.

Reuters. "Islam Shows its Female Face with Rise of Women's Mosques." *Hindustan Times* (September 6, 2018). Internet: https://www.hindustan times.com

Reynolds, Gabriel Said. *The Qur'an and the Bible: Text and Commentary*. New Haven and London: Yale University Press, 2018.

Reynolds, Helen. *A Fashionable History of Makeup & Body Decoration*. Chicago: David West Books, 2003.

Rhazoui, Zineb El. "The Veil is a Visual Marking Technique, Not of Those Who Wear it, but of Those Who Do Not." *Feminist Resources* (2020). Internet: https://ressources feministes.fr

Ridgeon, Lloyd. *Hijab: Three Modern Iranian Seminarian Perspectives*. London: Gingko, 2021.

Riedemann, Bárbara. "Cuando nos atrevimos a mostrar el cuerpo." *La Tercera* (5 de septiembre de 2017). Internet: https://www.latercera.com

Rizvi, Muhammad. *Hijab, the Muslim Women's Dress, Islamic or Cultural?* Internet: https://www.al-islam.org

Rosenblum, Amalia. "Visiting Dubai is like Standing on the Sidelines of a Gang Rape." *Haaretz* (November 30, 2020). Internet: https://www.haaretz.com

Ross, Heather Colyer. *The Art of the Arabian Costume: A Saudi Arabian Profile*. Studio City, CA: EPS / Players Press, 1994.

Roth, Norman, ed. *Medieval Jewish Civilization: An Encyclopedia.* New York and London: Routledge, 2003.

---. "Some Customs of Jews in Medieval Spain." *From Catalonia to the Caribbean: The Sephardic Orbit from Medieval to Modern Times*. Ed. Joshua Holo. Leiden: Brill, 2018. 27-42.

Rubens, Alfred. *A History of Jewish Costume*. New York: Crown Publishers, 1973.

Rubinstein, Ruth P. *Dress Codes: Meanings and Messages in American Culture*. Boulder: Westview Press, 1995.

Rumi, Jalal al-Din al-. *Signs of the Unseen*. Trans. W.M. Thackston, Jr. Putney, VT: Threshold Books, 1994.

Sabbahy, Lisa K. *Women in Ancient Egypt*. Santa Barbara: Greenwood, 2022.

Sadiq, Ja'far al-. *Lantern of the Path*. Trans. Fadlallah Haeri. Qum: Ansariyan Publications, 2007.

Sadiq, Muhammad. "Three Rules for Women's Dress Code." *Ahl al-Qur'an* (November 25, 2009). Internet: https://www.ahl-alquran.com

Saduq, Shaykh al-. *'Illal al-shara'i*. Vol. 2. Part 9. *Hubeali*. Internet: https://hubeali.com

Saanei, Yousef. *Istiftas: Fatwas for those Living Out of Iran*. Trans. Mohammad Yaser Kimyaee Far. Qom: Fiqh al-Thaqalayn Publications, 2016. Internet: https://saanei.org

Sadegui, Fatemeh. "Why We Say No to the Compulsory *Hijab*." *Iranian Progressives* (May 2008). Internet: http://www.iranianprogressives.org

SAMINT. "Voilement islamique par 'burkini' interposé: Sea, Salafism and Sun." *Révolution Féministe* (September 3, 2016). Internet : https://revolutionfeministe.wordpress.com

Sanchez, Hazel. "Egyptian Bead-Net Dress." *Hazel Sanchez* (May 23, 2016). Internet: https://hazelsanchez.wordpress.com

Sardar, Ziauddin. *Reading the Qur'an: The Contemporary Relevance of the Sacred Text of Islam*. Oxford: Oxford University Press, 2011.

Sawma, Gabriel. *The Qur'an Misinterpreted, Mistranslated, and Misread: The Aramaic Language of the Qur'an*. Plainsboro, NJ: 2000.

Sayyid-Marsot, Afaf Lutfi al-. *Society and the Sexes in Medieval Islam*. Malibu: Undena Publications, 1979.

Scarce. Jennifer. *Women's Costume of the Near and Middle East*. London: Unwin Hyman, 1987.

Scott, Georgia. *Headwraps: A Global Journey*. New York: Public Affairs, 2003.

Shahrur, Muhammad. *The Qur'an, Morality, and Critical Reason: The Essential Muhammad Shahrur*. Trans. Andreas Christmann. Leiden & Boston: Brill, 2009.

Shawi, Muna al-. "Significance of Colors in the Noble Qur'an and Ethics of Translating Them into English: An Empirical Study on Some Verses." *Arab World English Journal* 5.3 (2014). Internet: https://portal.arid.my

Shaykh, Sa'diyyah. "Islamic Law, Sufism, and Gender." *Men in Charge? Rethinking Authority in Muslim Legal Tradition*. Ed. Ziba Mir-Hosseini, Mulki Al-Sharmani, and Jana Rumminger. London: One World, 2018. 106-131.

Sherrow, Victoria. *Encyclopedia of Hair: A Cultural History*. Westport, CT: Greenwood Press, 2006.

Shibeeb, Dina al-. "Female-Run Mosque in Denmark 'Part of Global Trend,' Says Founder." *Al Arabiya* (May 20, 2020). Internet: https://english.alarabiya.net

Shirazi, Faegheh. *The Veil Unveiled: The Hijab in Modern Culture*. Gainesville: University Press of Florida, 2001.

Sichon, Marion. *History of Women's Clothing*. New York: Chelsea House Publishers, 1985.

Siddiqui, Zeba. "'This is How We Dress:' Afghan Women Overseas Pose in Colorful Attire." *Reuters* (September 15, 2021). Internet: https://www.reuters.com

Silverman, Eric. *A Cultural History of Jewish Dress*. London: Bloomsbury, 2013.

Sinaee, Maryam. "Over 60% of Iranians Want Transition from Islamic Republic." *Iran International* (April 1, 2022). Internet: https://www.iranintl.com

Siri, Giuseppe. *Notification Concerning Men's Dress Worn by Women*. Genoa, 1960. Internet: https://web.archive.org

Soroush, Abdolkarim. "Contraction and Expansion of Women's Rights." *Abdol Karim Soroush* (February 1, 2000). Internet: http://drsoroush.com

Sposito, Stefanella. Fashion: *The Ultimate History of Costume: From Prehistory to the Present*. Barcelona: Promopress, 2016.

Statistica. "The Global Gender Gap Index 2022." *Statistica*. Internet: https://www.statista.com

Steele, Valerie. *The Red Dress*. New York: Rizzoli, 2001.

Stillman, Yedida Kalfon. *Arab Dress: From the Dawn of Islam to Modern Times: A Short History*. Leiden: Brill, 2000.

Stol, Marten. *Women in the Ancient Near East. 662-682*. Berlin: De Gruyter, 2016. Internet: https://www.degruyter.com

Stone, Pooya. "Iran's Regime and its Expertise in Reversing the Truth." *Iran Focus* (May 9, 2022). Internet: https://iranfocus.com

Stratton, Allegra. *Muhajababes*. Victoria: Melbourne University Press, 2006.

Submission. "Women's Dress Code According to Qur'an." *Submission* (2013). Internet: https://submission.org

Sunday Times. "The Interview: Queen Rania of Jordan on the Refugee Crisis, ISIS, and Being a Muslim Woman." *The Sunday Times* (April 30, 2017). Internet: https://jordanian royals.tumblr.com / https://officialbespoke.com

Suyuti, Jalal al-Din al-. *al-Dur al-manthur*. Beirut: Dar al-Kutub al-'Ilmiyyah, 2010.

---. *al-Dur al-manthur*. Internet: http://ar.lib.eshia.ir

Syahrivar, Jhanghiz. "*Hijab* No More: A Phenomenological Study." *J Relig Health* 2021; 60(3): 1969-1991. Internet: https://www.ncbi.nlm.nih.gov

Syal, Rajeev, and Julie Henry. "For Her to be Absolved of Guilt, a Raped Woman Must Have Shown Good Conduct." *The Telegraph* (July 11, 2004). Internet: http://telegraph.co.uk

Syed, Ibrahim B. "Misinterpretation of Qur'anic Verse on *Hijab*." *Islamic Research Foundation International*. Internet: https://www.irfi.org

Tabarani, al-. *al-Mu'jam*. Beirut: Dar Ihya al-Turath, 1985.

Taha, Mahmoud Mohamed. *The Second Message of Islam*. Trans. Abdullahi

Ahmed An-Na'im. Syracuse: Syracuse University Press, 1987.

Taheri, Amir. *The Persian Night: Iran under the Khomeinist Revolution.* New York: Encounter Books, 2008.

Takim, Liyakat Ali. "Islamic Law and the Neo*ijtihadist* Phenomenon." *Religions* 12.6 (2021). Internet: https://doi.org

Talbi, Mohamed. "Le port du voile est-il exigé par le Coran?" *Coraniste Français* (September 20, 2019). Internet: http://garbi.unblog.fr

---. *L'islam n'est pas voile, il est culte.* Tunis: Cartaginoiserie, 2011.

Tamzali, Wassyla. "Feminist Translations." *Resources Féministes* (2020). Internet: https://ressourcesfeministes.fr

---. "Wassyla Tamzali à eMarrakech: 'Le droit des femmes, c'est mon butin de guerre.'" *CCME.* Internet: https://www.ccme.org.ma

Time Magazine. "More Questions with Queen Rania." *Time Magazine* (Friday, May 11, 2007). Internet: https://content.time.com

Timsit, Annabelle. "How Oriana Fallaci's Writings on Islamism are Remembered -- and Reviled." *The Atlantic* (December 15, 2017). Internet: https://www.theatlantic.com

Tirmidhi. *al-Jami' al-Sahih.* Internet: https://sunnah.com

---. *Jami'*. Beirut: Dar al-Gharb al-Islami, 1996.

TNI News. "*Aurat*: Don't Use that Dirty Islamic Word for Woman." *TNI News* (November 22, 2021). Internet: https://truenewsindia.com

Torkashvand, Amir. *Hijabe shari'e dar asre payambar* [*Hijab in the Time of Prophet Muhammad*]. Tehran: n.p., n.d. Internet: https://archive.org

Torres Garcías, Francisco. "Y Franco, con una sonrisa, legalizó el bikini en 1953." *Francisco Torres García* (8 de mayo de 2018). Internet: https://franciscotorres garcia.com

Tortora, Phyllis G. and Sara B. Marcketti, ed. *Survey of Historic Costume.* 6th ed. London: Bloomsbury, 2015.

True Islam. "The Dress Code in the Qur'an for Women." *True Islam.* Internet: https://www.quran-islam.org

---. "Is the Hair of the Woman a '*Awrah*?" *True Islam.* Internet: https://www.quran-islam.org

Turner, Janice. "Is Sherin Khankan the Future of Islam?" *The Times* (June 2, 2018). Internet: https://www.thetimes.co.uk

Tutten, Belle S. *Women in Medieval Europe.* Santa Barbara: Greenwood, 2022.

Twitter. "Faire porter le voile à des filletes." @BencheikhGhaleb. Internet: https://twitter.com/bencheikhghaleb

Uygarkızım Yağmur. "Postfeminism and Veiling, Story of an Unhappy Marriage: Conceptualising Veiling through Postfeminism." *Borazan Sesli* (January 11, 2021). Internet: https://borazansesli.com

---."Blinded by the Veil." *Feminist Resources* (2020) Internet:

https://ressourcesfeministes.fr

Universes. *Qusayr Amra Tour*. Internet: https://universes.art

Van Reeth, Jan M.F. "Sourate 33." *Le Coran des Historiens*. Ed. Mohammad Ali Amir-Moezzi et Guillaume Dye. Vol. 2b. Paris: Les Éditions du Cerf, 2019: 1119-1147.

Valdez, P. and A. Mehrabian. "Effects of Colors on Emotions." *J Exp Psychol Gen* 1994 Dec;123(4):394-409. Internet: https://pubmed.ncbi.nlm.nih.gov

Vecellio, Cesare. *Vecellio's Renaissance Costume Book: All 500 Woodcut Illustrations of the Famous Seventh-Century Compendium of World Costume*. New York: Dover Publications, 1977.

Wadud, Amina. *Inside the Gender Jihad: Women's Reform in Islam*. London: One World, 2018.

Wahi, Sukriti. "28 of the Best 'Naked' Red Carpet Dresses of all Time." *Elle* (December 11, 2019). Internet: https://www.elle.com.au

Walia, Mark. *A Tale of Two Cultures: Islam and the West*. Kingsville MO: Father's Press, 2011.

Walker, John. "Asiya: The Wife of Pharoah." *The Muslim World* 18 (1928): 45-48. Internet: https://www.answering-islam.org

Watson, Philip J. *Costume of Ancient Egypt*. New York: Chelsea House Publishers, 1987.

Webb, Mohammed Alexander Russell. *Islam in America: A Brief Statement of Mohammedanism and an Outline of the American Islamic Propaganda*. New York: The Oriental Publishing Co., 1893.

Weir, Shelagh. *Palestinian Costume*. Northampton, MS: 2009.

Williams, Betsy. "Walid II." *Met Museum* (June 12, 2012). Internet: https://www.met museum.org

---. "Khirbat al-Mafjar." *Met Museum* (April 26, 2012). Internet: https://www.met museum.org

Winter, Bronwyn. *Hijab & The Republic: Uncovering the French Headscarf Debate*. Syracuse: Syracuse University Press, 2008.

Woodlock, Rachel. "Veiling and *Hijab* as Understood by Muslim Feminists." *Islamic Research Foundation International*. Internet: https://www.irfi.org

Yahia, Mimunt Hamido. *No nos taparán: Islam, velo, patriarcado*. Madrid: Akal, 2021.

---. "Sin bikini no hay democracia." *No Nos Taparán* (2021). Internet: http://www.nonostaparan.org/

---. "Velo." *No Nos Taparán* (2021). Internet: http://www.nonostaparan.org

---. "Mente." *No Nos Taparán* (2021). Internet: http://www.nonostaparan.org

---. "Boca." *No Nos Taparán* (2021). Internet: http://www.nonostaparan.org

---. "Coño." *No Nos Taparán* (2021). Internet: http://www.nonostaparan.org

---. "Inicio." *No Nos Taparán* (2021). Internet: http://www.nonostaparan.org

Yahya, Abdullah. "Proof Muslim Women Don't Have to Cover their Hair." *Abdullah Yahya* (September 21, 2019). Internet: http://www.abdullahyahya.com

Yarwood, Doreen. *Illustrated Encyclopedia of World Costume*. Mineola, NY: Dover Publications, 2011.

Yüksel, Edip. *Takanlar ve takilanlar*. Istanbul: Ozan Yayıncılık Ltd., 2008.

Yüksel, Edip, Layth Saleh al-Shaiban, and Martha Shulte-Nafeh. *Qur'an: A Reformist Translation*. USA: Brainbow Press, 2007.

---. "Girl Praying in Bikini." *YouTube* (August 12, 2017). Internet: https://www.youtube.com

---. "Jilbab." *19.org* (August 20, 2013). Internet: https://19.org

Zaman. "Tareq Oubrou: 'Le foulard est devenu un objet obsessionnel.'" *Saphir News* (October 28, 2013). Internet: https://www.saphirnews.com

Zaniel, Nur Zainatul Nadra, Latifah Abd Majid, and Muhd Najib Abdul Kadir. "Nasr Hamid Abu Zayd as a Modern Muslim Thinker." *International Journal of Islamic Thought* 5 (June 2014). Internet: http://www.ukm.my

Zellentin, Holger Michael. *The Qur'an's Legal Culture: The* Didascalia Apostolorum *as a Point of Departure*. Tübingen: Mohr Siebeck, 2013.

Zin al-Din, Nazira. *al-Sufur wa al-hijab*. Beirut: Quzma Publications, 1928.

Zouari, Fawzia. "There can be no Eastern or Western Feminism." *Feminist Resources* (2020). Internet: https://ressourcesfeministes.fr

Index

C

D

O

P

Q

R

Y

Z

www.ingramcontent.com/pod-product-compliance
Lightning Source LLC
LaVergne TN
LVHW010718210926
848485LV00008B/1437/J